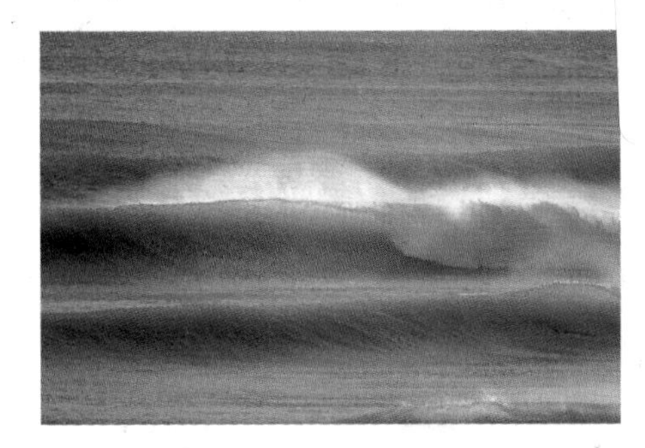

stormrider GUIDE europe

LOW PRESSURE publishing©

First Published in 1992 by
Low Pressure Publishing Ltd©
Unit 33, Pall Mall deposit
124 Barlby Rd
London W10 6BL
Tel/Fax: 0181 960 1916
e-Mail: lowpressure@mail.bogo.co.uk

Low Pressure Europe©
Tel/Fax: (33) 58 77 76 85

Second edition 1995
First impression 1995

The representation in this guide of a road is no proof of the exisrtence of a right of way, likewise the frontiers shown do not imply any recognition or official acceptance on the part of the Publishers. Surfing is a dangerous and addictive sport. The Authors and publishers take no responsibility for either loss of job and wife, or accident and injury as a result of using information contained within it.

A catalogue record for this book can be obtained from the British Library

ISBN Softback 0 9519275 2 3

Photo: Alex Williams

Publishing Editors
Ollie Fitzjones and Tim Rainger

Art Director
Dan Haylock

Print/Repro Production
Paul Bradley/Avanti Graphics

Co-ordination
Antony Colas - France
Ricardo Villas Boas - Portugal
Martijn Drenth/HSA - Netherlands
Hamid Jaafari/ACS - Morocco
Niklas Langstrom - Sweden
Norbert Hoischen/DWV - Germany
Andrea Tazzari/FISO - Italy

Translation
Antony Colas, Laurant Masurel, Luïc Granget, Ricardo Villas Boas
Jose Lekanda, Alvero Gonzalez, Roberto Nuño, Martijn Drenth,
Deidre Gaspari, Andrea Loerzer

Editorial Contributors
Jamie Blair, The Brothers Macwatt, Gordon Forbes,
Rachel Sutherland, Gabriel Davies, Roger Povey, Trevor Sergeant,
Grant Winter, Shaun Thomas, Andrew Hanson, Guy Penwarden,
Pauly Gabriel, Simon Crawford, Duncan Bartlett, Peter Cade, Alex Williams,
Nigel Moyce, Rick Abbott, Steve Wilkinson, Andy at Freedom,
Chris Mason, Pete Jones, Carwyn Williams, Phil Holden, Alex Badley,
Ian & Andy Hill, Brian Britton, Roci Allan, Thomas Buckley, Jamie Knox,
Henry Moore, Fred Jump, Martijn Drenth, Norbert Hoinschen,
Windsurf Borkum, Jan Erik Jensen, Niklas Langstrom, Guy Fierens,
Vincent Chasselon, Nicolas Dejean, Fabrice Allain, Jean-Pierre Verhnes,
Thierry Fernandez, Christophe Reinhardt, Joel H, Luc Petit, Javier Amezaga,
Roberto Nuño, Diego Méndez, Carlos Bremón, Nick Uricchio,
Eduardo & Alvaro Costa, João Valente, Pedro Urrestarazu, Miguel Ortega,
A.D.E.S, Hamid Jaafari, Brian Wood, Hervé Pignoges, Association Cap Surf,
Matt Moon, Andrea Tazzari, Paolo Perucci, Monica Proietti,
Carlo Marrazzi, Gilberto Bonasegale, King Surfer and Surf News Mags.

Photographers
Tim Rainger, Alex Williams, Phil Holden, Peter Cade, The Gill,
Chris Power, Mike Searle, Andy Bennetts, Simon McComb, Malcom Macwatt,
Granite Reef, Roy Major, Rick Abbott, EstPix, Turtle Photography,
Rod& John Sumpter, T. Sinclair, Mark Stevenson, Gabriel Davies,
Miles Masterton, Dan Hutton, Andy Jackson, Al Green,
Irish Surfing Association, Nick & Wilmer Gammon, Margaret O'Brien Moran,
Eric Chauché, Thierry Organoff, Marc Féniès,
Serge Morin, Tim McKenna, Phillipe Chevodian,
J.M.Herbert,Phillipe Mombet,
Jakue Andikoetxea, Javier Amezaga, Xavier Gonzales, Rudolf Wild,
João Valente, Zé Pirrayt, Luis Qunita, L.M. Franzão,
João Barbosa, Mario Pires, Miguel Losia,
Luca Garibaldi, Carlo Azzarone, Federazione Italiana Surf da Onda

Special Thanks
Andrea & the unborn child, Sheila & Jake
Sarah & Finnbarr, Julie & William
John, Sue, Mathew & Adam
Marc, Kore, Stephen, Danny, Deidre, Neil, Anton,
All at Trip Surf, All at Tres 60, All at Surf Portugal
Pilar Pereira at ICEP - London, Air Açores, Air Portugal
All our advertisers for their patience
everyone else... you know who you are.
Thanks.

patagonia

LOW PRESSURE publishing

contents

EUROPE

GREAT BRITAIN

WALES

SCOTLAND

EIRE & NORTHERN IRELAND

ENGLAND

NORTH SEA NATIONS

FRANCE

ITALIA

ESPAÑA

PORTUGAL

MAROC

ISLAS CANARIAS

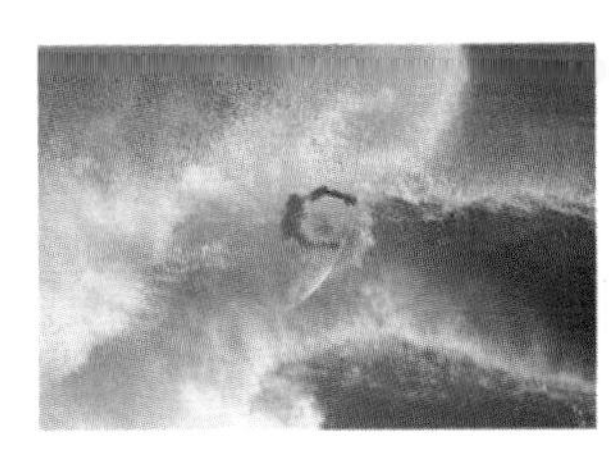

AÇORES

IF YOU
DON'T LIVE
HERE
ON'T SURF
HERE

Photo: Tim Rainger, LP

Photo: Eric Chauché

Photo: Alex Williams

Photo: Tim Rainger, LP

introduction

Since we published the first edition of The Stormrider Guide Europe, in1992, we have been flooded with enquiries, requests for more info, and advice on how we could have done it better. In response, the format of the 2nd book has changed dramatically and we hope it works better for you. Tens of thousands of people have enjoyed the information and had great surf trips as a result. At the same time, there have been elements of opposition to it, and the idea of travellers coming to their spots, by people who travel themselves. This complex situation naturally raises one of the biggest problems facing the global surf community now...localism.

Too many incidents of aggression and violence get relayed every day for anyone to feel complacent about the current situation, and if we ignore it, our actions will make us no better than those of the pigs who profit from knowingly polluting the oceans. We are shitting in our own nests if we allow Europe's line-ups to fill-up with egotistical, aggressive and narrow minded ideas.

Respect and preservatory attitudes should flow both ways in the surf world. The choice remains with the individual whether to be calm, and foster good relations in the water, but might we state what should be obvious to aware people, that only by adopting a relaxed attitude to wave selection can surfing remain an enjoyable sport. Especially when at foreign breaks, you should be prepared to sacrifice a percentage of waves in order to show respect to a hierarchy which already exists and which will continue to do so after you leave.

We hope the new format assists communication and friendship among surfers of all nationalities. We also hope our spelling and grammar aren't so bad as to be a distraction, but we thought it better to attempt and possibly fail than not attempt it at all. It is the same with the individual when travelling in Europe, with issues of language and culture being so important; better to attempt communication and fail, than not to attempt it at all. The world loves a trier!

Depuis que nous avons publié en 1992 la première édition du Guide Stormrider en Europe, nous avons été submergés de demandes pour plus d'informations et de conseils sur la façon de mieux le réaliser. En réponse, le concept de la deuxième édition a changé radicalement. Nous espérons donc qu'il vous conviendra mieux. Plus de dix mille lecteurs ont déjà apprécié nos informations et ont pu donc faire de super trips. En même temps, il y a eu des signes d'opposition, de la part des gens qui eux-mêmes voyagent, à l'idée de partager leurs spots. Cette situation complexe nous amènent naturellement à un des plus problèmes les plus épineux de la communauté des surfers: le localisme.

Trop d'incidents d'agression et de violence sont relatés chaque jour pour qu'on puisse se sentir satisfait de la situation actuelle et si on y ferme les yeux, on ne sera pas mieux que les sauvages qui profitent sciemment de cette "pollution" des océans. On crache dans la soupe si on laisse les line-ups européens se remplir de locaux égoïstes, agressifs et à l'esprit souvent étroit.

On devrait plutôt voir couler dans les deux sens, dans le monde du surf, des attitudes de respect et de préservation. il reste à chacun de déterminer s'il faut être calme et entretenir de bonnes relations dans l'eau mais quand bien même on constaterait ce qui devrait être évident aux yeux de tous, c'est seulement en adoptant un comportement responsable par rapport à la sélection des vagues qu'on pourra continuer de se faire plaisir en surfant. Il faut donc être prêt à sacrifier quelques vagues, surtout sur des spots étrangers, pour montrer un certain respect pour la pseudo-hiérarchie qui existe déjà et qui se perpétuera bien après vous.

Nous espérons que cette nouvelle édition aidera à la communication entre les surfers de toutes les nationalités. Nous espérons aussi que le vocabulaire et la grammaire ne seront pas trop bafoués à tel point que la lecture en devienne pénible, mais nous pensons qu'il valait mieux essayer malgré les erreurs possibles que de ne pas essayer du tout. C'est la même chose pour celui qui voyage à travers l'Europe, concernant ces différences de langages et de cultures qui sont cruciales. Mieux vaut essayer de communiquer et se tromper que de ne pas essayer. Le monde adore ceux qui osent se jeter à l'eau !

Desde la publicación en 1992 de la primera edición de "The Stormrider Guide", hemos recibido multitud de preguntas, peticiones de información, y consejos sobre como podíamos hacerlo mejor. A consecuencia de esto, el formato de esta segunda entrega ha cambiado sustancialmente y confiamos que sea para mejor. Decenas de miles de surfers han aprovechado la información de la guía disfrutando de magníficos surfaris. Sin embargo y de un modo simultáneo, han surgido elementos de oposición protagonizados por gente que no quería visitantes en sus picos. Esta compleja situación ha derivado en uno de los mayores problemas que tiene que afrontar la comunidad surfera internacional....el localismo.

Hay demasiados incidentes cotidianos de carácter violento, que nos hacen sentirnos a disgusto con la situación, y si caemos en la tentación de ignorarlos, nos vamos a parecer a los irresponsables que de un modo consciente están obteniendo beneficios contaminando los océanos. Estamos tirando piedras contra nuestro propio tejado, si permitimos que los picos de toda Europa se llenen de locales agresivos, egoístas y de pocas luces.

Esto no implica que el respeto no pueda coexistir con las actitudes locales de salvaguarda de los spots. Es una elección individual estar tranquilo y amistoso en la agua, pero nosotros queremos advertir que, aunque parezca obvio, no hay mejor modo de disfrutar del surf que estando relajado, lo que supone que en muchos spots, hay que estar dispuesto a sacrificar un cierto porcentaje de olas con el fin de demostrar respeto hacia una jerarquía que esté presente y va a seguir ahi después de que nos marchemos.

Esperemos que el nuevo formato trilingüe ayude a comunicarse a los surfers de los diferentes paises. Asimismo esperamos que la gramática y la ortografía no sufran demasiado. Pensamos que era mejor intentario, corriendo el riesgo de fallar, que no hacerlo. Al igual que cuando viajas por Europa en donde existen tantas lenguas y culturas distintas, es mejor intentar comunicarse aún fracasando, que no intentario. !El mundo es para los que se arriesgan!

Physical & Political Detail
Carte Physique et Politique
Mapa Físico y Político

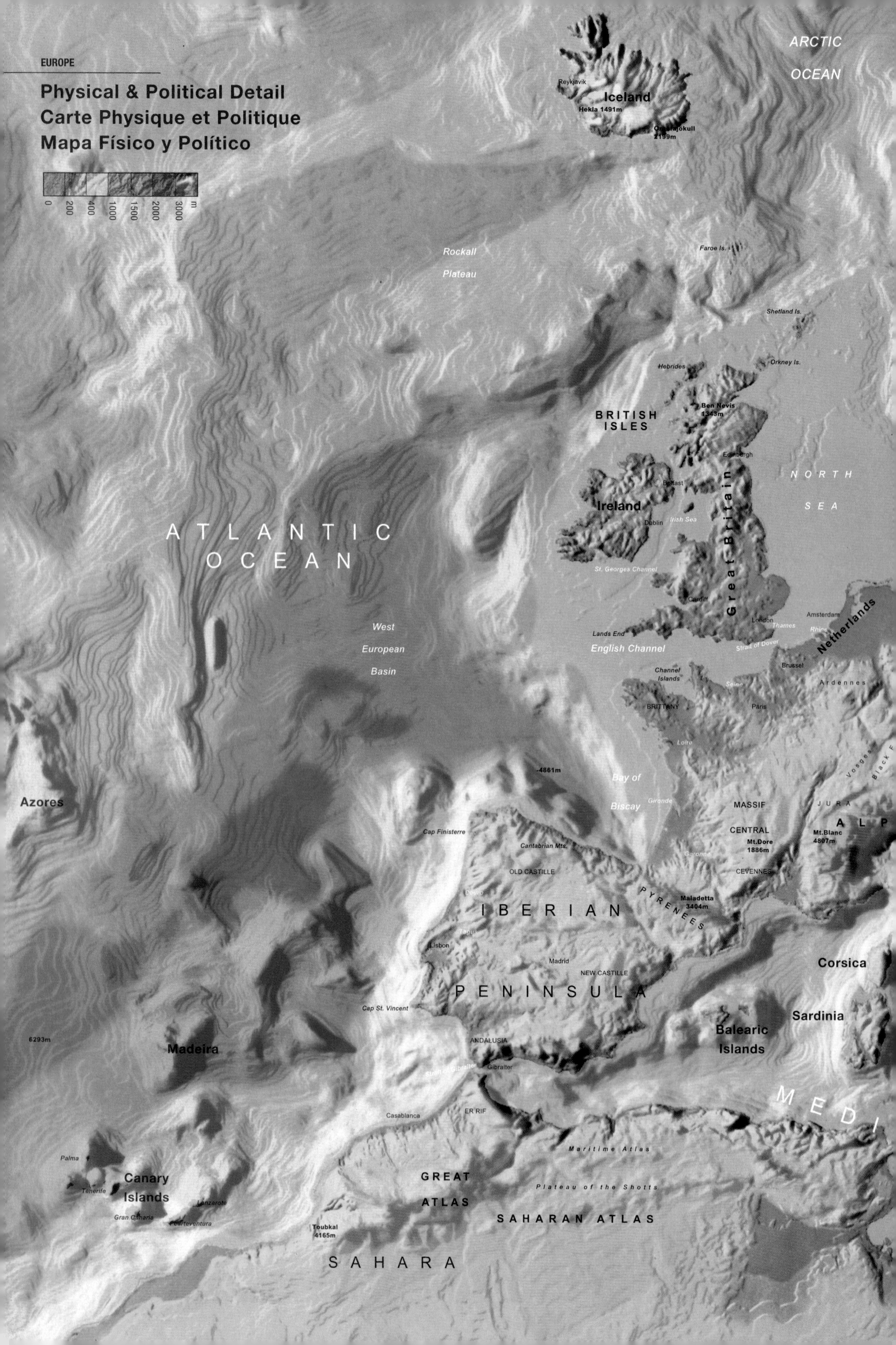
0
200
400
1000
1500
2000
3000
m
ARCTIC OCEAN
Reykjavik
Iceland
Hekla 1491m
2119m
Rockall Plateau
Faroe Is.
Shetland Is.
Orkney Is.
Hebrides
Ben Nevis 1343m
BRITISH ISLES
Edinburgh
NORTH SEA
Belfast
Ireland
Dublin
Irish Sea
Great Britain
ATLANTIC OCEAN
St. Georges Channel
Cardiff
London
Thames
Amsterdam
Rhine
Netherlands
West European Basin
Lands End
English Channel
Strait of Dover
Brussel
Channel Islands
Seine
Ardennes
BRITTANY
Paris
Loire
Vosges
Black F
-4861m
Bay of Biscay
Gironde
Azores
MASSIF CENTRAL
Mt.Dore 1886m
JURA
ALP
Mt.Blanc 4807m
Cap Finisterre
Cantabrian Mts.
Garonne
OLD CASTILLE
CEVENNES
Douro
IBERIAN PENINSULA
PYRENEES
Maladetta 3404m
Tagus
Lisbon
Madrid
NEW CASTILLE
Corsica
Cap St. Vincent
Sardinia
6293m
Madeira
ANDALUSIA
Balearic Islands
Gibralter
MEDI
Casablanca
ER RIF
Maritime Atlas
Palma
Canary Islands
Tenerife
Lanzarote
Gran Canaria
Fuerteventura
GREAT ATLAS
Plateau of the Shotts
SAHARAN ATLAS
Toubkal 4165m
SAHARA

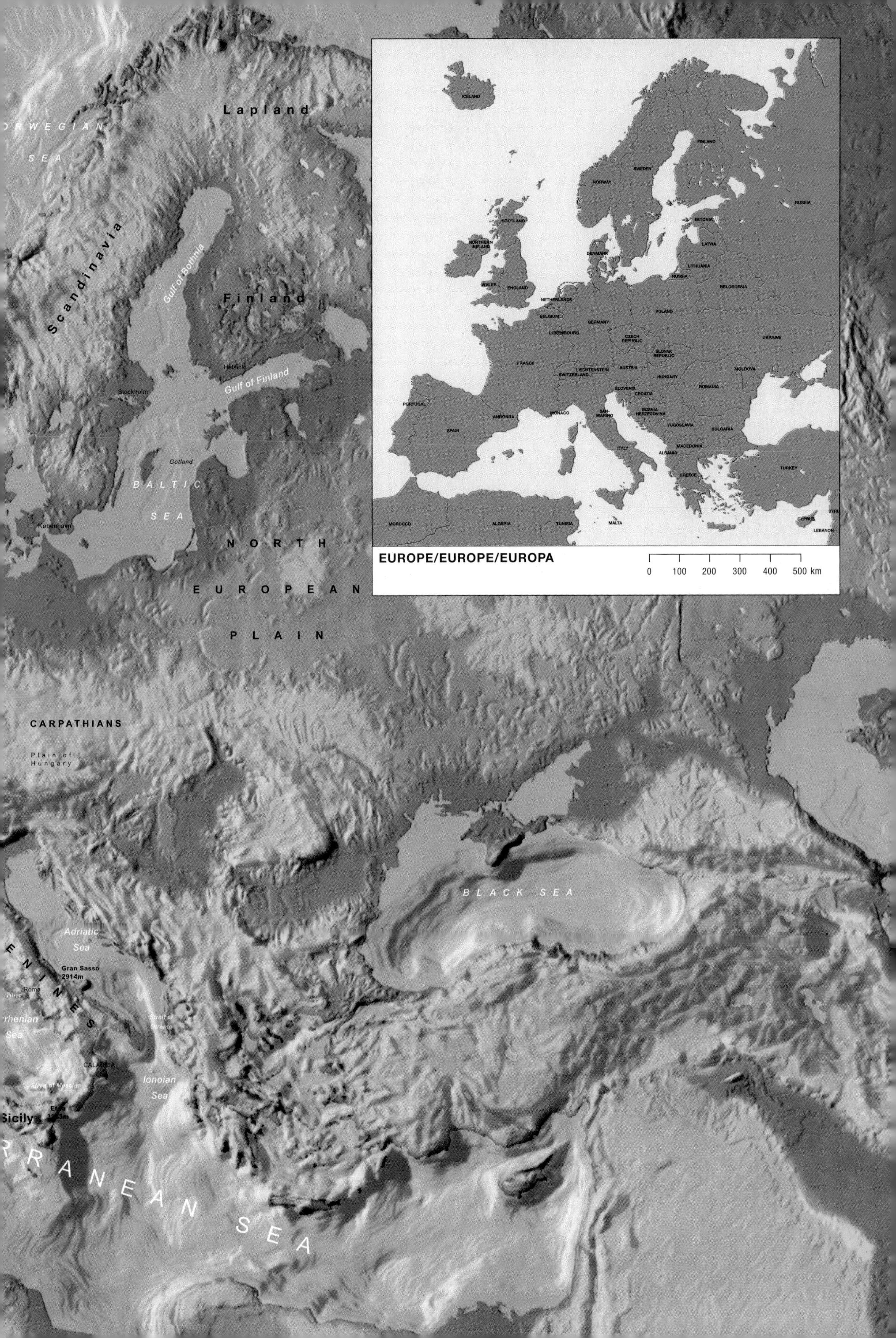
Lapland
Scandinavia
Gulf of Bothnia
Finland
Helsinki
Gulf of Finland
Stockholm
Gotland
BALTIC SEA
København
NORTH EUROPEAN PLAIN
CARPATHIANS
Plain of Hungary
BLACK SEA
Adriatic Sea
Gran Sasso 2914m
Roma
Tiber
Strait of Otranto
CALABRIA
Strait of Messina
Ionoian Sea
Sicily
EUROPE/EUROPE/EUROPA
0
100
200
300
400
500 km
ICELAND
FINLAND
SWEDEN
NORWAY
RUSSIA
ESTONIA
SCOTLAND
NORTHERN IRELAND
LATVIA
DENMARK
LITHUANIA
WALES
ENGLAND
BELORUSSIA
NETHERLANDS
POLAND
BELGIUM
GERMANY
LUXEMBOURG
CZECH REPUBLIC
UKRAINE
SLOVAK REPUBLIC
FRANCE
AUSTRIA
LIECHTENSTEIN
SWITZERLAND
MOLDOVA
HUNGARY
ROMANIA
SLOVENIA
CROATIA
PORTUGAL
ANDORRA
MONACO
SAN MARINO
BOSNIA HERZEGOVINA
SPAIN
YUGOSLAVIA
BULGARIA
MACEDONIA
ITALY
ALBANIA
TURKEY
GREECE
MOROCCO
ALGERIA
TUNISIA
MALTA
CYPRUS
LEBANON

The Birth of Swell
Les Previsions de Houle
Prediccion de Marejadas

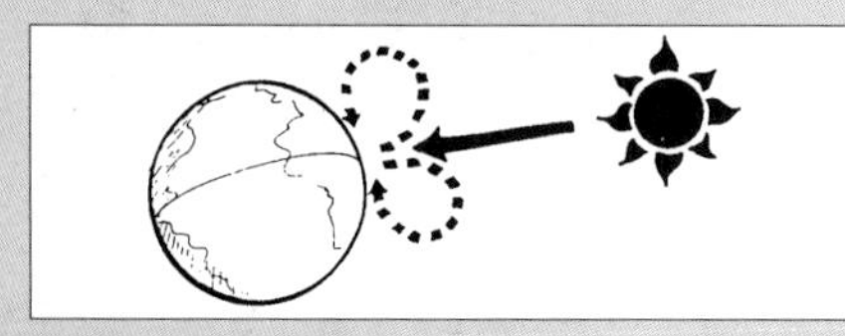

When the sun heats the earth, hot air rises and is replaced by cool air.The rotation of the earth disturbs this air movement and forms wind.This uneven heating of the planet causes bands of different pressures and winds.

Quand le soleil réchauffe la Terre, l'air chaud s'élève en étant remplacé par de l'air plus frais. La rotation de la Terre perturbe ce mouvement d'ascendance et forme les vents. Le réchauffement inégal de la planète entraîne la fornation de bandes de différentes pressions et de vents.

El sol calienta el planeta y con ello provoca un flujo de aire que se produce al ascender el aire caliente siendo reemplazado por aire frío. Este movimiento es entorpecido por la rotación de la tierra dando lugar a corrientes de aire. El calentamiento desigual del globo se traduce en zonas de distinta presión y vientos asociados. El elevado número de factores intervinientes en estos procesos es el motivo de la difícil previsión meteorológica.

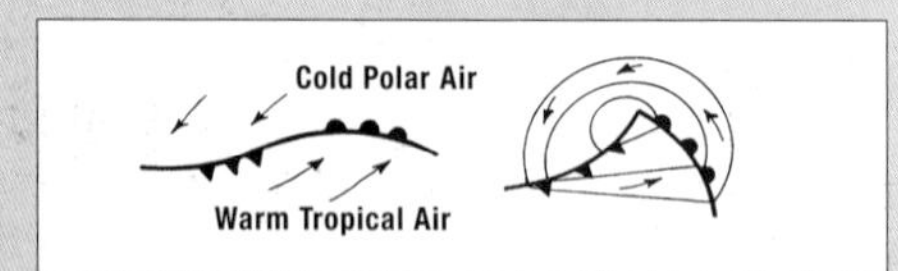

When warm and cold air systems collide, they form an eddy which spirals anticlockwise (in the Nth hemisphere) becoming a Low Pressure system (also known as a cyclone or depression). The warm air rises over the cool air and the cold air tries to undercut the warm air.

Quand les systèmes d'air chaud et d'air froid se rencontrent, ils forment un tourbillon qui tourne dans les sens contraire des aiguilles d'une montre dans l'hémisphère nord (et vice-versa) pour devenir un système de basses pressions (ou cyclone ou dépression). L'air chaud s'élève au-dessus de l'air froid qui essaye de lui barrer la route.

Esta colisión de corrientes de aire a diferentes temperaturas converge en los centros de baja presión (borrascas o depresiones) rotando espiralmente en sentido antihorario en el hemisferio norte (al contrario en el hemisferio sur).

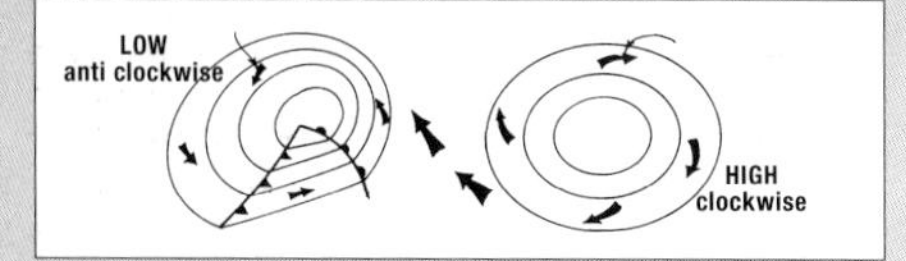

A weather map uses isobar lines to measure the areas of equal pressure. High areas are called Highs and low areas, Lows. Wind always blows from regions of high pressure to areas of Low Pressure. The steeper the pressure gradient, the closer together the isobar lines and the stronger the wind speed. The Low itself can move at speeds approaching 70 knots directed by the winds above them, though the cold front usually catches up with the warm one, and they become an occluded front.

Une carte météorologique utilise des lignes isobariques pour mesurer les zones de pressions égales. Les hautes pressions sont appelées des anticyclones. Les vents soufflent toujours des zones de hautes pressions vers les basses. Plus le gradient de pression est élevé, plus les lignes isobariques sont rapprochées et plus le vent est fort. La dépression en soi peut se déplacer à une vitesse qui peut atteindre 70 noeuds suivant la direction des vents eux-mêmes, bien que les front froids finissent souvent par rattraper le front chaud, ce qui devient unfront occlus.

En los mapas del tiempo aparecen isobaras delimitando las zonas de igual presión. Los centros de altas presiones se denominan anticiclones en contraposición a los circlones o barrascas. El viento converge en las borrascas y diverge de los anticiclones. Cuanto mayor es el gradiente o diferencia de presión más fuerte es el viento y esta situación se representa con isobaras muy juntas. Una borrasca puede moverse a velocidades de 120 kms/h, sin embargo habitualmente el frente frío se asocia al cálido ocluyéndose el frente.

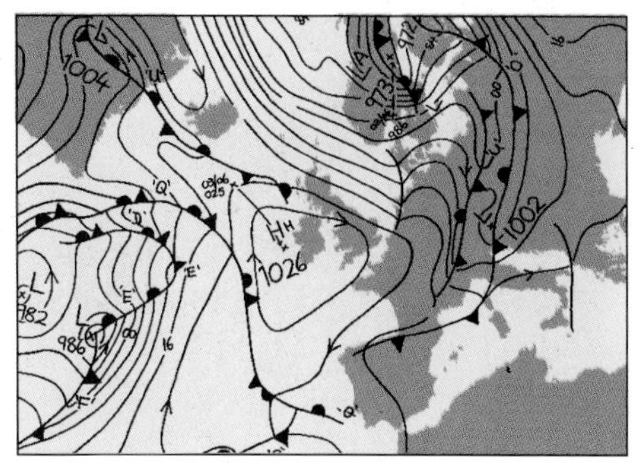

North Sea

Sometimes Lows which grew in the Atlantic pass over, or North of Britain into the Nth Sea and die out over Scandinavia. Other times they develop over the continent or in the channel, but either way, they make swell in the Nth Sea. The best situation is when a high pressure system follows behind the Low, and sits over the U.K., forcing the isobars of the low to align heavily north to south (strong N winds).

La Mer du Nord

Parfois, les dépressions qui se sont développées dans l'Atlantique passent au nord de la Grande-Bretagne pour aller en Mer du Nord et mourir en Scandinavie. D'autres fois, elles se développent sur le continent ou en Manche mais quoiqu'il arrive, elles fabriquent des houles en Mer du Nord. La meilleure situation est quand un anticyclone suit une dépression et s'installe sur la Grande-Bretagne, forçant les isobares de la dépression de s'aligner radicalement du nord au sud (vents de nord forts).

Mar del Norte

Cuando las borrascas atlánticas pasan al norte de Gran Bretaña o por encima de la isla hacia el Mar del Norte para perder fuerza sobre Escandinavia o cuando la depresión procede del continente o del Canal, se generan marejadas en el Mar del Norte. La mejor situación es cuando la borrasca va seguida de un anticilón que se situa sobre el Reino Unido, forzando a las isobaras de la borrasca a alinearse de norte a sur generando fuertes vientos de componente norte.

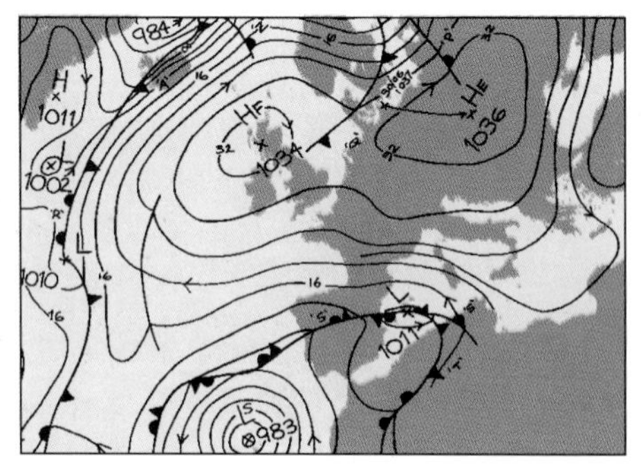

The Med

The low pressure activity in the Med is tightly linked with those roaring up in the North Atlantic. Due to its small size, the Med does not develop deep lows with strong pressure gradients but occasionnal gusty winds sometimes have enough fetch to produce a so-called wind swell, in the 2-6' range. These waves have a short duration, have a short period and sometimes lack power. Great depths means these swells travel fast. Last, be aware of the lack of tides.

La Méditerranée

L'activité dépressionnaire en Mediterranée est également liée' aux systèmes de pertubations dans l'Atlantique nord. Compte tenu de son exiguité, la Mediterranée n'a pas le temps de développer de profondes dépressions avec de forts gradients de pressions mais les coups de vents violents occasionnels ont parfois un fetch suffisant pour produire une houle dite de vents, comprise entre 50 cms et 2m. Les vagues produites sont de courte durée, de courte période et manquent parfois de puissance. Les profondeurs importantes contribuent à une propagation rapide de ces houles. Signalons enfin l'absence de marées.

Mediterráneo

La actividad de las depresiones que afectan al Mediterráneo está estrechamente ligada a la de las borrascas del Atlántico Norte. Debido a sus reducidas dimensiones en este mar no se desarrollan borrascas profundas, pero en ocasiones la fuerza del viento puede producir "olas de viento" desde medio metro hasta dos metros. Estás olas no suelen tener mucha fuerza, rompen con un intervalo de tiempo reducido entre unas y otras, y en general el período de olas es de corta duración. Otros factores a considerar son la falta de mareas y la gran profundidad submarina que hace que estas marejadas se muevan a gran velocidad.

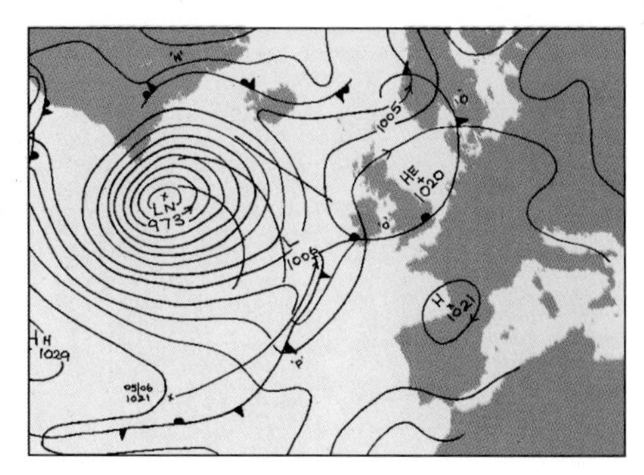

Atlantic Ocean

The Atlantic ocean experiences a phenomena known as residual swell i.e. it's almost never flat. Waves are created by the wind off the passage of Lows, which most frequently begin life further south and deepen as they move N.E. They can appear and recede at any point in the North Atlantic and Bay of Biscay, or alternatively they can develop over the land, but they always spiral anti-clockwise in the northern hemisphere, the reverse of southern hemisphere lows. Their trajectory normally keeps them well out to sea in summer, though G.B. can still be lashed by the fronts which spin off the leading edge. In winter they deepen considerably and pass through continually, often right over the top of G.B. and Ireland, before roaring into the Nth sea. The variations are endless, but the ideal situation is for high pressure to keep the Low at bay without filling it in, leaving offshore winds and swell, which arrives a few days after the low forms.

L'océan Atlantique

L'océan Atlantique subit un phénomène connu sous le nom de houle résiduelle, à savoir qu'il n'est jamais plat. Les vagues sont créées par les vents au passage des dépressions, qui se forment fréquemment plus au sud et ont tendance à se creuser alors qu'elles se déplacent vers le nord-est. Elles peuvent apparaître ou disparaître n'importe où dans l'Atlantique nord et la baie de Biscay, ou alors elles peuvent se développer au-dessus des terres mais elles tournent toujours dans le sens contraire des aiguilles d'une montre. Leur trajectoire évite en général les terres en été, bien que le Royaume-uni puisse être balayée par les fronts qui s'enroule autour du centre directeur. En hiver, elles se creusent considérablement et passent sans arrêt, en général juste au-deÅssus de la Grande-Bretagne, avant d'aller sévir en Mer du Nord. Les variations sont infinies mais la situation idéale est une haute pression qui garde une dépression au large sans la combler, provoquant vents off-shore et houle, qui arrive quelques jours après après que la dépression se soit formée.

Océano Atlántico

Este océano experimenta un fenómeno conocido como marejada residual que hace que rara vez este el mar plato. El viento asociado a las depresiones genera las marejades. Estas borrascas se suelen mover hacia el nordeste desde su origen más meridional, en esta trayectoria se van haciendo más profundas. Las borrascas, ya se hayan generado en pleno Atlántico o en el Golfo de Vizcaya o sobre tierra, giran siempre en sentido antihorario (salvo en el hemisferio sur). Durante el verano suelen estar muy al norte, afectando los frentes asociados sólo en ocasiones a las islas británicas. En invierno son mucho más profundas y siguen multitud de trayectorias diferentes, barriendo los frentes asociados todo el continente, con especial intensidad las zonas más septentrionales. La situación ideal es que un anticiclón se estabilice sobre tierra dejando que la borrasca envíe olas de un modo continuo, el viento sople terral y los frentes sigan una ruta alejada de nosotros. La marejada suele tardar dos o tres días en llegar a la costa desde el nacimiento de la borrasca.

Climate
Climat
Clima

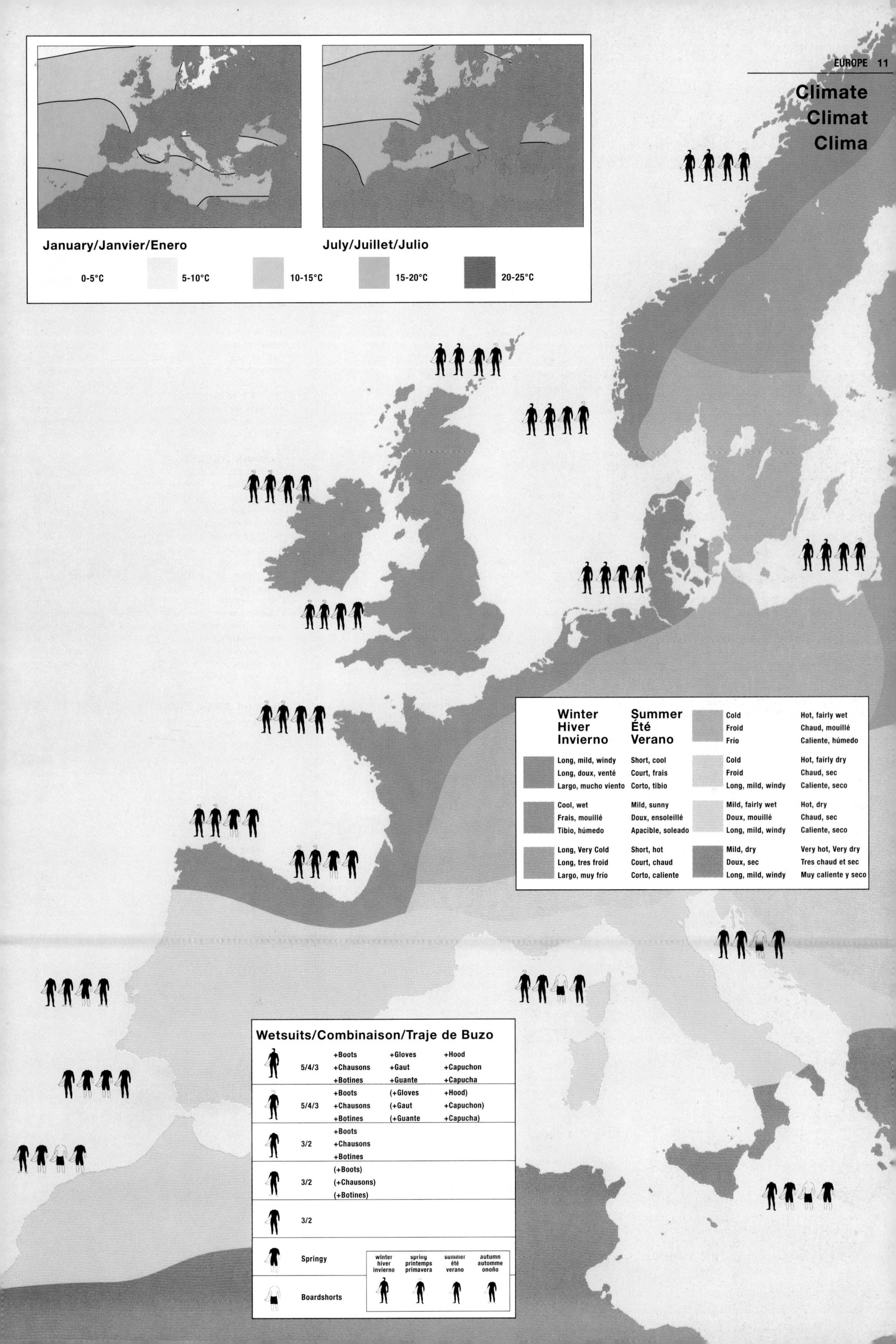
January/Janvier/Enero
July/Juillet/Julio
0-5°C
5-10°C
10-15°C
15-20°C
20-25°C
Winter Hiver Invierno
Summer Été Verano
Long, mild, windy / Long, doux, venté / Largo, mucho viento — Short, cool / Court, frais / Corto, tibio
Cool, wet / Frais, mouillé / Tibio, húmedo — Mild, sunny / Doux, ensoleillé / Apacible, soleado
Long, Very Cold / Long, tres froid / Largo, muy frío — Short, hot / Court, chaud / Corto, caliente
Cold / Froid / Frío — Hot, fairly wet / Chaud, mouillé / Caliente, húmedo
Cold / Froid / Long, mild, windy — Hot, fairly dry / Chaud, sec / Caliente, seco
Mild, fairly wet / Doux, mouillé / Long, mild, windy — Hot, dry / Chaud, sec / Caliente, seco
Mild, dry / Doux, sec / Long, mild, windy — Very hot, Very dry / Tres chaud et sec / Muy caliente y seco
Wetsuits/Combinaison/Traje de Buzo
5/4/3 +Boots +Chausons +Botines +Gloves +Gaut +Guante +Hood +Capuchon +Capucha
5/4/3 +Boots +Chausons +Botines (+Gloves (+Gaut (+Guante +Hood) +Capuchon) +Capucha)
3/2 +Boots +Chausons +Botines
3/2 (+Boots) (+Chausons) (+Botines)
3/2
Springy
Boardshorts
winter hiver invierno
spring printemps primavera
summer été verano
autumn automme onoño

Photo John Callahan -Portrait Rick Werneck Design 2021

Shane
Living in the pit
Dorian
European Headquarters • Fax: 351·1·486 2131

REDLEY
Ocean Soul™

Route Planner
Carte Routiére
Mapa de Carreteras

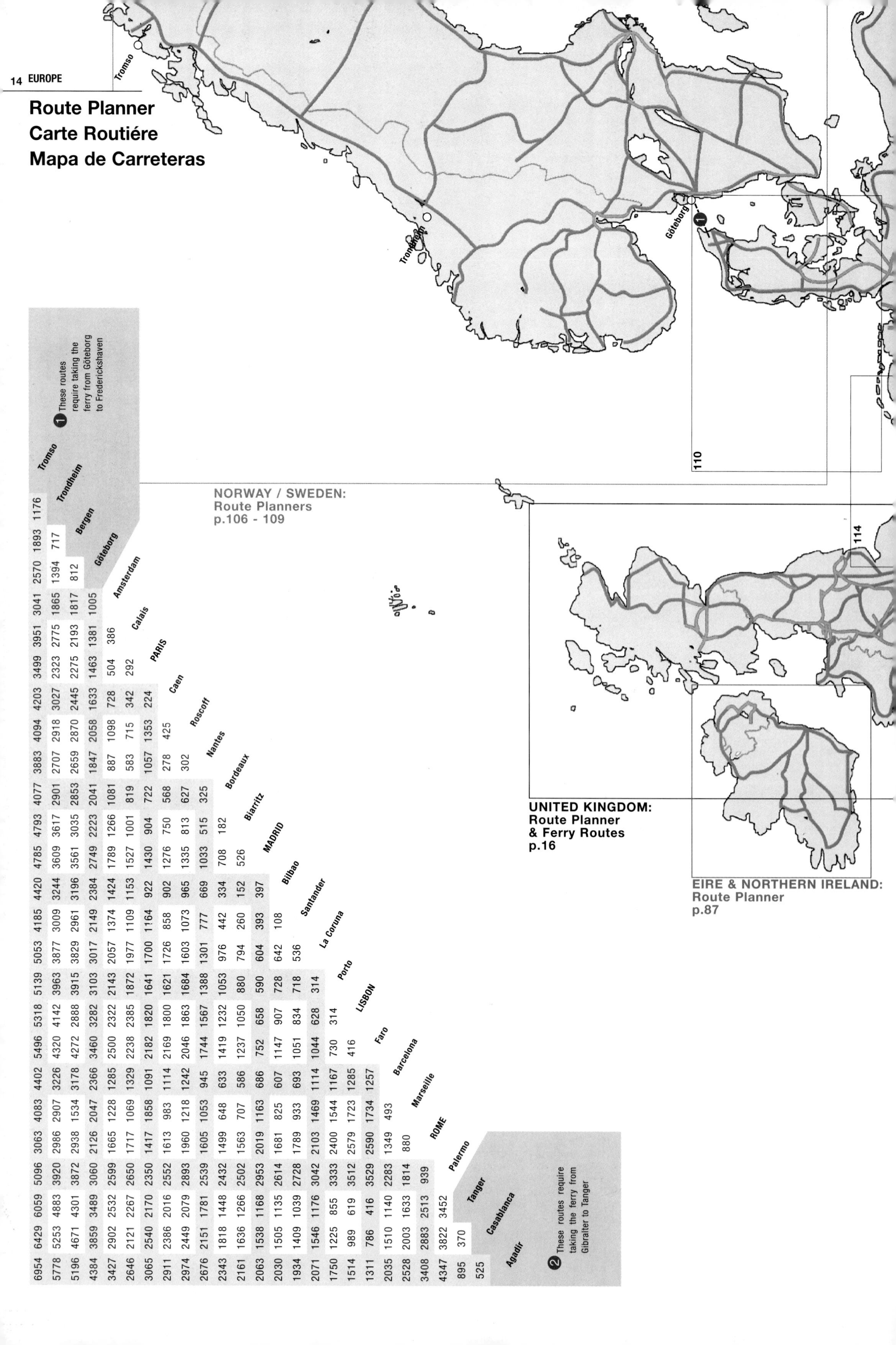

	Trondheim	Bergen	Göteborg	Amsterdam	Calais	PARIS	Caen	Roscoff	Nantes	Bordeaux	Biarritz	MADRID	Bilbao	Santander	La Coruna	Porto	LISBON	Faro	Barcelona	Marseille	ROME	Palermo	Tanger	Casablanca	Agadir
Tromso	1176	1893	2570	3041	3951	3499	4203	4094	3883	4077	4793	4785	4420	4185	5053	5139	5318	5496	4402	4083	3063	5096	6059	6429	6954
Trondheim		717	1394	1865	2775	2323	3027	2918	2707	2901	3617	3609	3244	3009	3877	3963	4142	4320	3226	2907	2986	3920	4883	5253	5778
Bergen			812	1817	2193	2275	2445	2870	2659	2853	3035	3561	3196	2961	3829	3915	2888	4272	3178	1534	2938	3872	4301	4671	5196
Göteborg				1005	1381	1463	1633	2058	1847	2041	2223	2749	2384	2149	3017	3103	3282	3460	2366	2047	2126	3060	3489	3859	4384
Amsterdam					386	504	728	1098	887	1081	1266	1789	1424	1374	2057	2143	2322	2500	1285	1228	1665	2599	2532	2902	3427
Calais						292	342	715	583	819	1001	1527	1153	1109	1977	1872	2385	2238	1329	1069	1717	2650	2267	2121	2646
PARIS							224	1353	1057	722	904	1430	922	1164	1700	1641	1820	2182	1091	1858	1417	2350	2170	2540	3065
Caen								425	278	568	750	1276	902	858	1726	1621	1800	2169	1114	983	1613	2552	2016	2386	2911
Roscoff									302	627	813	1335	965	1073	1603	1684	1863	2046	1242	1218	1960	2893	2079	2449	2974
Nantes										325	515	1033	669	777	1301	1388	1567	1744	945	1053	1605	2539	1781	2151	2676
Bordeaux											182	708	334	442	976	1053	1232	1419	633	648	1499	2432	1448	1818	2343
Biarritz												526	152	260	794	880	1050	1237	586	707	1563	2502	1266	1636	2161
MADRID													397	393	604	590	658	752	686	1163	2019	2953	1168	1538	2063
Bilbao														108	642	728	907	1147	607	825	1681	2614	1135	1505	2030
Santander															536	718	834	1051	693	933	1789	2728	1039	1409	1934
La Coruna																314	628	1044	1114	1469	2103	3042	1176	1546	2071
Porto																	314	730	1167	1544	2400	3333	855	1225	1750
LISBON																		416	1285	1723	2579	3512	619	989	1514
Faro																			1257	1734	2590	3529	416	786	1311
Barcelona																				493	1349	2283	1140	1510	2035
Marseille																					880	1814	1633	2003	2528
ROME																						939	2513	2883	3408
Palermo																							3452	3822	4347
Tanger																								370	895
Casablanca																									525

1 These routes require taking the ferry from Göteborg to Frederickshaven

2 These routes require taking the ferry from Gibralter to Tanger

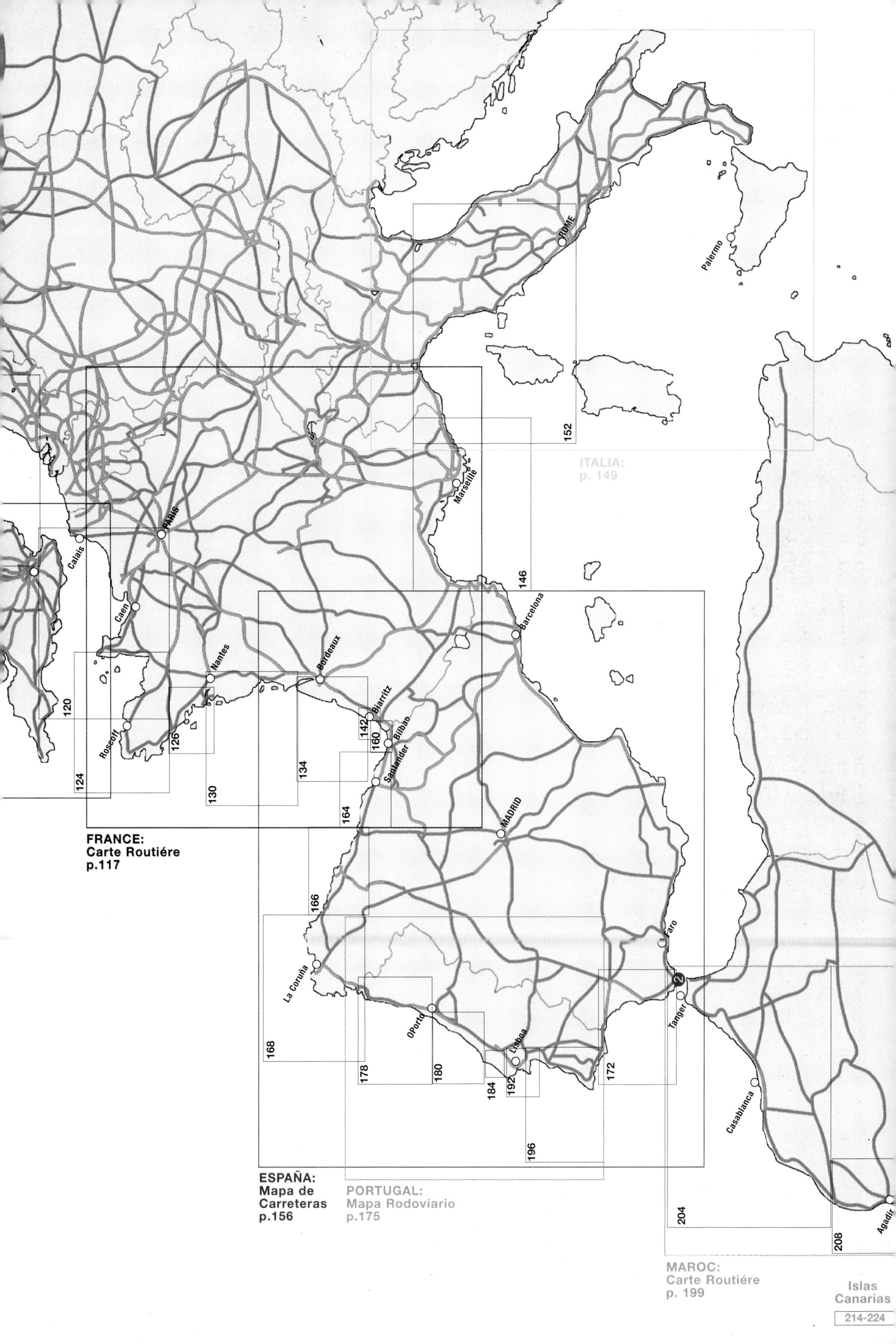

Palermo
ROME
152
ITALIA:
p. 149
Marseille
PARIS
Calais
Caen
146
Barcelona
Nantes
Bordeaux
Biarritz
Bilbao
Santander
120
Roscoff
126
124
130
134
142
160
164
MADRID
FRANCE:
Carte Routiére
p.117
166
Faro
2
La Coruña
Tanger
OPorto
Lisboa
168
178
180
184
192
172
Casablanca
196
ESPAÑA:
Mapa de
Carreteras
p.156
PORTUGAL:
Mapa Rodovíario
p.175
204
Agadir
208
MAROC:
Carte Routiére
p. 199
Islas
Canarias
214-224

GREAT BRITAIN

	Capital:	London
	Population:	55,514,000
	Area:	244,755 km²
	Time:	GMT (verão GMT+1)
	Language:	English, Welsh, Gaelic
	Currency:	Pound Sterling £ (GBP)
		£1 = 100 pence

UK - Route Planner

0 50 100 150 200 km

	Aberdeen	Edinburgh	Hull	LONDON	Dover	Southampton	Plymouth	Newquay	Swansea	Belfast	Galway	Cork
Thurso	373	455	806	1067	1181	1136	1069	1333	1271	577	900	998
Aberdeen		201	795	810	927	880	586	1052	990	374	697	795
Edinburgh			631	608	723	678	348	860	798	173	496	594
Hull				332	446	412	417	828	571	417	740	838
LONDON					114	124	612	413	351	572	625	312
Dover						230	441	543	465	711	764	441
Southampton							259	321	243	604	657	259
Plymouth								395	332	693	851	332
Newquay									78	755	808	1011
Swansea										461	514	
Belfast											323	421
Galway												208
Cork												

On the Road

KMH	112	112	96	48
If towing	96	96	80	48

4 Star	£0.59p l
Unleaded	£0.57p l
Diesel	£0.50p l

Alcohol Levels

1 Pint

2 Glasses of Wine

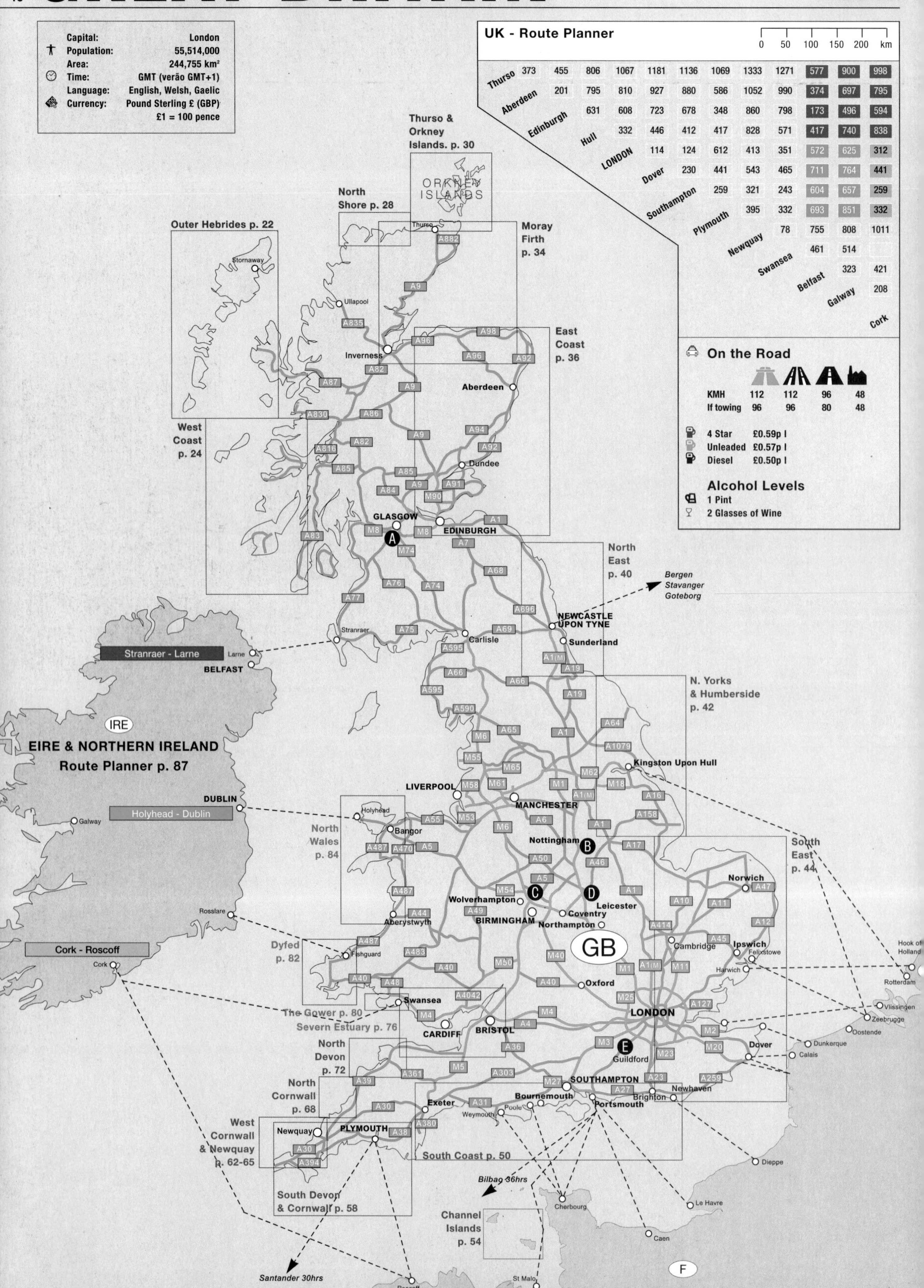

Shops

A **CLAN**
45 Hyndland Street
Partick, Glasgow
G11 8QF
Tel: 041 339 6523
Surf, Skate, Snow boards.
Clothing footwear & essential equipment for all your riding needs at the home of Poizone.
Advice and hire for all scottish conditions.

B **NON STOP SURF**
14 James Street
Nottingham
NG1 6FG
Tel:0155 9531002
Fax:0155 9475886
Surfboards - Bodyboards - Snowboards - Skateboards
All the major brands.
New & Second-hand.
Wetsuits, clothing, swimwear, footwear, eyewear and all the accessories. Full hire facilities.
Fast & efficient mail order service.

C **Grand Prix**
20 Cross Street
Bridgtown, Cannock
Staffs WS11 3BZ
Cannock 01543 570813
Tamworth 01827 251045
Congleton 01260 299771
Established for over 10 years.
Stockists of the biggest names in surfing, windsurfing, snowboarding & skate.
Plus the lagest stock of wetsuits under one roof.

D **M.D.E Ltd**
57 Sparkenhoe St
Leicester LE2 0TD
Tel:01162 624262
Fax:01662 512227
SURF - SNOW - DIVE

Clothing

Accessories

Hardwear

E **BIG BLUE**
Showing attire from:-
Stüssy - 24•7 - Fresh Jive - X-Large - Low Pressure - Quiksilver - Raggy - Fuct - Duffs - Simple
55 Lower Mall
The Friary Centre
Guildford, Surrey
Tel:01483 302686
&
16 St Leonards Road
Windsor, Berkshire
Tel:01753 830857

UK Travelling Around

Telephoning

UK	44 +
UK	00 +
Directory Enquiries	192
INT. directory	153
INT. operator	155
Emergência	999

Airports

London - Heathrow:	0181 759 4321
London - Gatwick:	01293 535353
Stanstead	01279 680500
Manchester:	0161 4893000
Bristol	01275 474444
Cardiff	01446 711111
Swansea	01792 204063
Edinburgh:	0131 333 1000
Glasgow:	0141 8871111

Ferries

P&O :	01304 223000
Stena Sealink	01233 647047
Sally Line:	0171 4092240
Hoverspeed:	01304 240241
Brittany Ferries - Portsmouth:	01705 827701
Brittany Ferries- Plymouth:	01752 221321
North Sea Ferries - Hull:	01482 77177
Color Line - Newcastle :	0191 296 1313
Scandinavian Seaways - Newcastle :	0171 409 6060
P&O - Cairnryan:	01581 200276

Trains

BR Euro Travel Centre (Victoria):	0171 834 2345
Enquiries-	
The West and Sth Wales:	0171 262 6767
The NE & East Scotland:	0171 287 2477
Victoria:	0171 928 5100
London Transport Info Line:	0171 222 1234
Plymouth :	01752 221300
Swansea :	01792 4667777
Edinburgh:	0131 556 8464
Glasgow:	0345 212282

Buses & Coaches

UK- National Express (Victoria):	0171 730 0202
Europe- Eurolines (Victoria):	0171 730 8235

Embassies

Australian High Commission — 0171 3794334
Australia House, The Strand
London WC2B 4LA
0171 3794334

New Zealand High Commission
New Zealand House
The Haymarket, Pall Mall
London SW1Y 4TQ

The United States Embassy — 0171 4999000
31 Grosvenor Sq
London W1A 1AE

South African Embassy — 0171 9304488
Trafalgar Sq
London WC2N 5DO

Tourism

Trafalgar Square — 0171 930 8661
London
09.00 - 18.00 Hrs

Cost of Living

Restaurant *	£12
Bed & Breakfast (1 Night) *	£14
Camping	£ 2
1 Pint Beer	£ 2

UK Manufacturers & Distributors

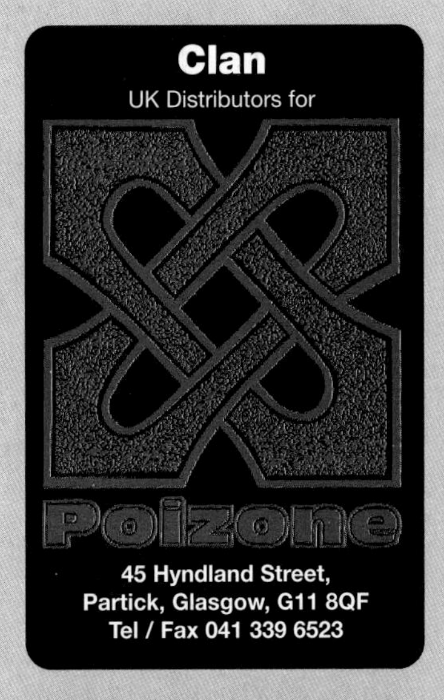

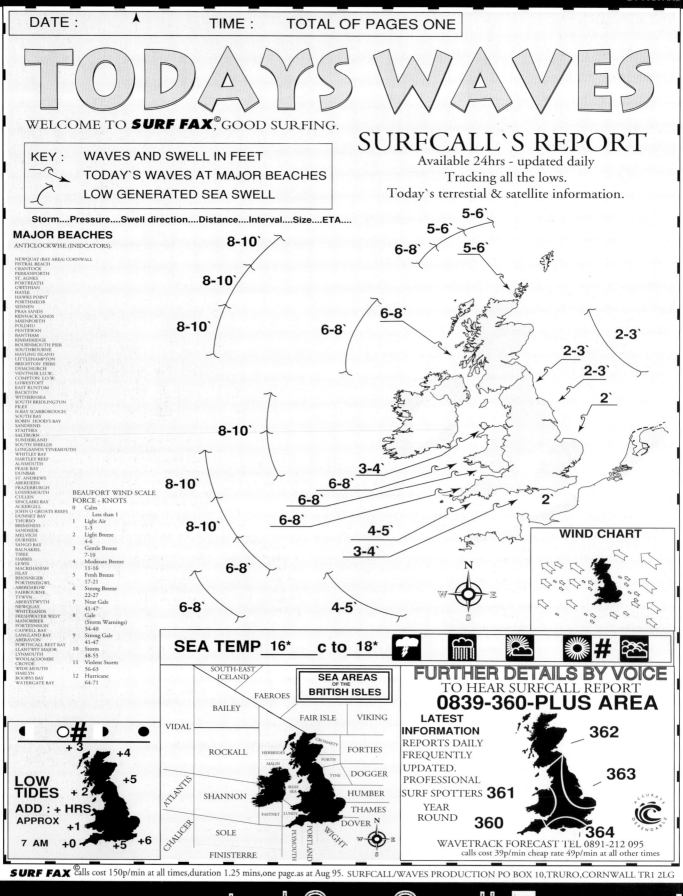

BBC Weather Forecast - Photo: Chris Power

forecasting swell

by Rod Sumpter

Reports are coming in of ace surfing conditions. It's 4 ft and lined up. Big waves are expected. When you first experience it, you're sure you'll never forget it....flat at dawn, small waves start arriving mid morning... good lines...consistent, powerful ankle snappers...this is good. Paddle out and start riding 3-4 ft perfect glassy walls. Its crystal clear and you make your first tube of the day. The sets get bigger while you're out there. Suddenly its 6ft with double-up faces. The tide is pushing and its over 8ft by the evening. It happens all the time. Why? The weather forecast shows a 960mb Low Pressure system situated900miles due west of Lands End. Twisting out from the centre radiate comet like trails, the cold and warm fronts chasing their own tails around an onion ring core, isobar lines tightly packed. This is a good looking chart! Its going to get bigger, a lot bigger, and where you are right now its going to be all time for a couple of days.

For most surfers, finding the best waves is the key objective of a forecast. Forecasting is not an exact science, and swell forecasting even less so, but you need to see a daily weather report or forecast to know what is happening. They show the approaching Lows. T.V. has a lot of advantages, and in Britain B.B.C.1 is the best. The scenario goes like this. Michael Fish stands in front of the Lows, looking left at the map of G.B. He's got two minutes for the whole nation and has prepared the forecast before reading it live. Behind him are the depressions, the first after weeks of high pressure flatness. We're all shouting at him, " GET OUT OF THE WAY OF THE PICTURE!!!" He does and we see it in all its glory...the house is brought down...a 960 Millibar Low. Everything in a forecast is helpful, but it won't necessarily tell you swell size today, only a hint of what its going to be like in a few days (on shore or off shore, strong or light wind, air temps, etc..). Surf travels at rates of up to 600 miles in a day, even still from the time you see a low way west in the Atlantic, it'll probably be at least a couple of days for the swell to hit the beaches and reefs.

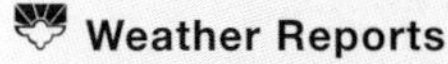

Weather Reports

BBC 1 - Daily at 13.25, 18.25, 21.25
BBC 1 - Weekly Forecast at Sunday Lunchtime

Newspapers: Independent, The Times & Sunday Times have good meteorological maps.

The Met Office - METFAX	**0336 400 444**
Met Office Helpline	**Tel-01344 854435**
	Fax-01344 854018

Calls are charged at 39p/min cheap rate, 49p/min at all other times

On prévoit des conditions de surf exceptionnelles. Ca fait 1,5m, bien rangé et on attend de grosses vagues. La première fois, on ne l'oublie jamais. C'est flat le matin puis de petites vagues arrivent dans la matinée, de belles lignes bien consistantes, à hauteur de chevilles mais bien puissant...C'est bon. Ramez et commencez à surfer des murs glassy et parfaits de 1m-1,5m. L'eau est transparente et vous prenez le premier tube de la journée. Les séries grossissent pendant que vous êtes dans l'eau. Soudain, ça fait deux mètres avec des vagues qui se lèvent trés haut. La marée monte et ça fait plus de 2,5m le soir. Cela arrive tout le temps. Pourquoi? Le bulletin météo montre une dépression à 960 milibars à envrion 1500 kms à l'ouest de Lands End. Partant du centre, les isobares se propagent comme des cercles dans une mare, les fronts froid et chaud chassent leurs extrémités autour d'un coeur en forme d'oignons, les lignes isobariques bien serrées. C'est une carte qui a belle allure. Ca va grossir encore et encore et là où vous êtes, ça va être épique pour quelques jours.

Préparer les prévisions: pour la plupart des surfers, trouver les bonnes vagues signifie obligatoirement de prévoir la météo. Cela n'est pas une science exacte et la prévision de houle encore moins, mais il faut voir un bulletin météo quotidien pour savoir ce qui se passe. Ils montrent les dépressions qui approchent. La télé a un gros avantage, la BBC 1 étant la meilleure. Le scénario se déroule de la façon suivante. Michael Fish se trouve devant les perturbations, regardant à gauche vers la Grande-Bretagne. Il a deux minutes pour le tout et à préparé son discours avant de débiter son texte. Derrière lui apparaissent les dépressions, la première aprés des semaines sans vagues à cause des hautes pressions. On lui crie·" Barre-toi de là, tu caches l'image" Il le fait et on la voit dans toute sa splendeur. La maison est en branle-bas de combat: 960 milibars! Tout est utile dans la prévision mais ça ne vous dira pas forcément la taille le jour-même, seulement un indice de ce que ça va être dans les prochains jours (vent de mer ou de terre, fort ou léger, températures, etc) La houle voyage environ 1000 kms par jour, bien qu'à partir du moment où vous voyez une dépression bien à l'ouest de l'Atlantique, il faudra probablement au moins deux jours pour que la houle atteigne les plages et les reefs.

Está llegando el momento de los partes de olas...Un metro ordenado y se espera que aumente el tamaño. La primera experiencia es inolvidable...Ha amanecido plato... a media mañana aparecen unas olitas...líneas consistentes...entras al agua con paredes glassy de un metro...te entubas como si fueras en cristal liquido. Cada vez las series son mayores, metro y medio con la marea bajando se transforma en más de dos metros durante la tarde. Este es el comienzo cuando una borrasca de 960 mb, se sitúa 900 millas al oeste de Lands End. Como si fuera una rodaja de cebolla con los frentes frios y cálidos colgando y las isobaras apiñadas...este es un mapa excelente y se va a poner mucho más grande y tu spot va funcionar clásico durante un par de días.

Una buena predicción es pare la mayoria de los surfers un requisito previo para ponerse en marcha hacia las olas. La predicción no es siempre exacta, especialmente cuando se trata de algo tan influenciable como el oleaje, pero es necesaria para saber que está sucediendo. La BBC 1 da el mejor parte en Inglaterra, suele ocurrir lo siguiente. Aparece el presentador Micheal Fish con sólo dos minutos para dar el parte de todo el pais y se planta frente a la cámara ocultando la zona del mapa donde deberia verse la borrasca, después de semanas de mar plato. ¡ No tapes el mapa! Al fin se mueve, y lo que vemos es gloria bendita, un borrascón de 960 mb. Esta información es útil, pero es una mera aproximación de todas las variables que interactuan para que haya buenas olas: dirección y fuerza del viento, mareas... La marejada recorre 600 millas al día desde que se forma, por lo que necesita al menos un par de días para presentarse en nuestras costas.

SCOTLAND

Capital:	Edinburgh
Population:	5,090,000
Area:	32,714km²
Time:	GMT (summer GMT+1)
Language:	English, Gaelic

Photo: Alex Williams

SCOTLAND

Historically the nation is a melting pot of Gaelic tribes from the North, Picts from the East, Viking / Norse raiders and Anglo-Saxon conquerors from England. There remains a strong feeling of separation and animosity between the Scots and English, particularly since the Stuart Kings acceded the English throne in 1603. 150 years later the English regained a firm grip on the throne, outlawed clans, declared bagpipes and kilts illegal and ruthlessly suppressed other aspects of highland culture. The Scots still maintain a certain separation marked by distinctive accents, schools, judicial system and currency. The predominant language is English, though Gaelic is widely spoken. Scottish accents differ widely, though all are a joy to uninitiated ears. Don't be afraid to make non-comprehension clear...they know many people have problems with the tongue and are far from ashamed of it.

ECOSSE

La nation est un mélange de tribus gaéliques du nord, de Picts de l'est, d'aventuriers Viking ou Norse et de conquérants anglo-saxons. Il en reste un vif sentiment de séparation et d'animosité entre les écossais et les anglais, surtout depuis que la dynastie des Stuart accéda au trône en 1603. 150 ans plus tard, les anglais reprirent fermement le trône, déclarèrent les clans hors-la-loi, les cornemuses et les kilts illégaux et réprimèrent sévèrement les autres aspects de la culture écossaise. Les écossais en gardèrent quand même certaines différences comme l'accent, les écoles, le système juridique et la monnaie. La langue dominante est l'anglais, bien que le Gaëlique soit souvent parlé. Les accents écossais varient drôlement, bien que tous soient un délice à attendre pour l'oreille inexpérimentée. N'hésitez pas à vous faire répéter si vous n'y comprenez rien, ils savent que plein de gens ont des problèmes à les comprendre mais ça ne les dérange pas pour autant.

ESCOCIA

Históricamente esta nación surge de la mezcla de las tribus gaélicas del Norte, los Pictos del Este, los aventureros Vikingos y Nórdicos y los conquistadores anglosajones procedentes de Inglaterra. Pervive un fuerte sentimiento separatista y una apreciable animosidad entre Escoceses e Ingleses, especialmente a raiz de la subida al trono inglés en 1603 de la dinastía de los Estuardo, 150 años después los ingleses recuperaron el trono, pusieron los clanes al margen de la ley, prohibieron el uso de las gaitas y de la falda tradicional escocesa (kilt) y suprimieron rudamente otros aspectos de la cultura de las Tierras Altas. Los Escoceses mantienen un cierto grado de separación apreciable en los distintos acentos, escuelas, sistema judicial y moneda. El idioma predominante es el inglés, aunque el gaélico es ampliamente utilizado. Los acentos escoceses son muy variados, constituyendo un placer para los oìdos no acstumbrados. No te importe dejar claro que no les entiendes, están habituados a eso y no se averguenzan de ello.

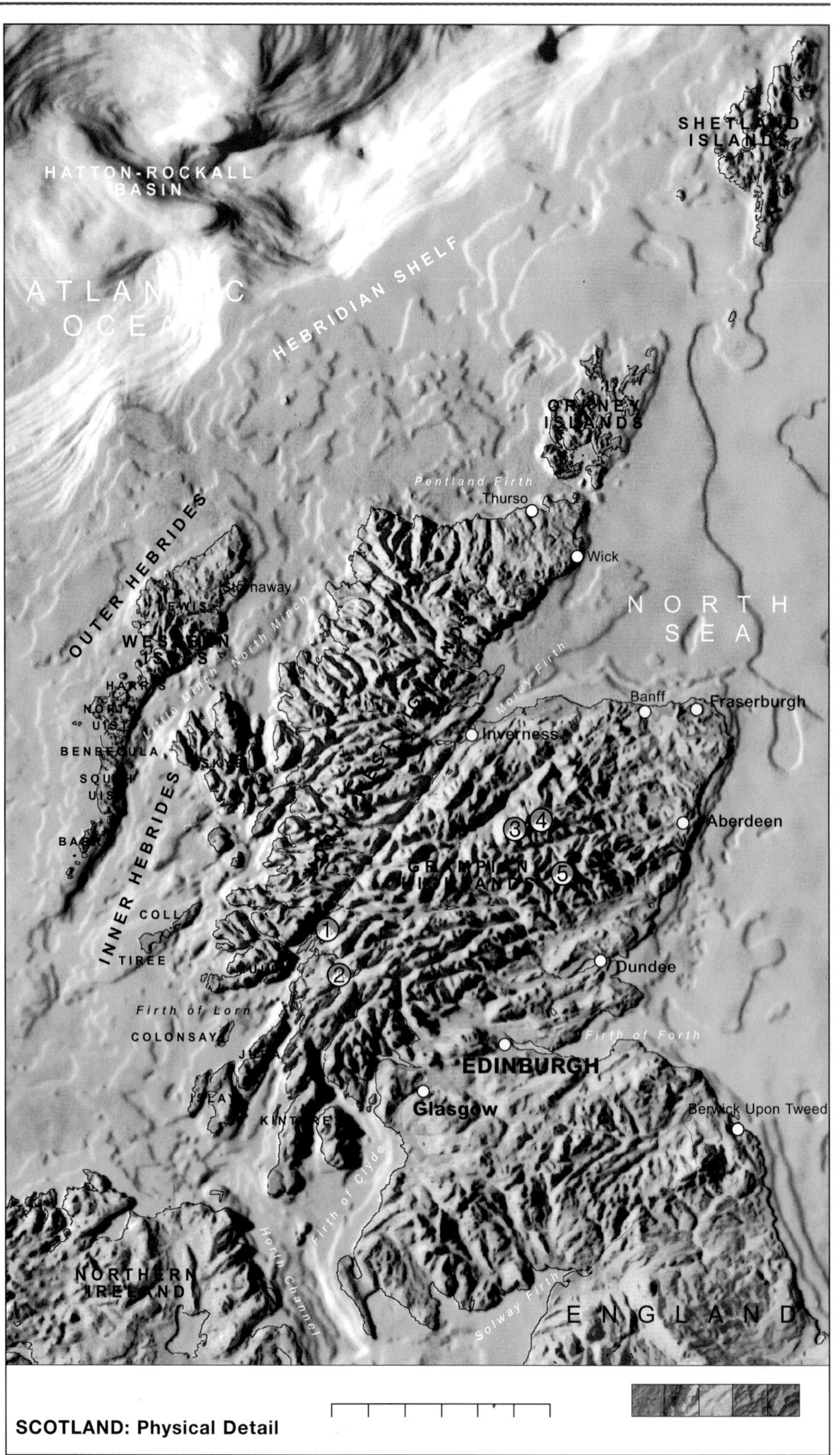

SCOTLAND: Physical Detail

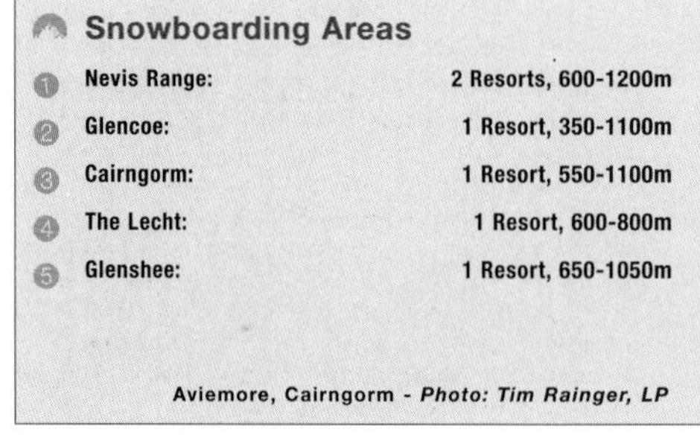

Snowboarding Areas

1	Nevis Range:	2 Resorts, 600-1200m
2	Glencoe:	1 Resort, 350-1100m
3	Cairngorm:	1 Resort, 550-1100m
4	The Lecht:	1 Resort, 600-800m
5	Glenshee:	1 Resort, 650-1050m

Aviemore, Cairngorm - *Photo: Tim Rainger, LP*

Sinclair's Bay (North Sea) - *Photo: Alex Williams*

Photo: Tim Rainger, LP

Scottish Surfing Federation
Gordon Wheeler
35 Provost Noble Ave, Fraserburgh, Aberdeenshire, Scotland
Tel: (44) 01346 51 64 51 Fax: (44) 01346 51 59 02

The Surf & the Weather

The surf breaks fall into five groups, with surf coming in from three directions, depending on the location of the lows. **The Outer Hebrides** present the largest undiscovered coasts in Europe and their isolation makes them an explorer's dream. The inner islands of **Coll, Tiree** and **Islay** are also surfed regularly, offering a vast array of wind and swell direction and protection. The **Mull'O'Kintyre's** beauty is legendary and it picks up W swell from the Atlantic and S swell from the Irish Sea.

N and NW swells hit the **North Shore**, where some of Europe's most powerful waves break on a stretch of coastline as beautiful as it is varied. Locals of Orkney even surf these exposed northern latitudes.

The **Moray Firth** receives the lion's share of N.Sea swells, occurring frequently in deepest winter. Despite cooler conditions, an abundance of reefs and points break swell and predominant winds blow offshore.

The **East Coast** is more heavily populated, and less spectacular than other parts, but conditions are similar to those on the Moray Firth and there is good surf to be found.

The surf population numbers a few thousand, concentrated mainly in Thurso, Fraserburgh, Edinburgh, Aberdeen and Glasgow. For many, the idea is inconceivable, but humans being what they are, cold climates can be adapted to. For the young folk presently taking up surfing, there has been little precedent for their new sport and we urge respect and encouragement, both in and out of the water. With a good wetsuit and a big heart, you'll find Scotland a superb surf destination.

Scotland, like Ireland sits very close to the Lows that storm through the Atlantic all year round, often passing over her with accompanying strong winds and rain which are predominant features of the climate. Combine this with lower sunshine hours and general temperatures than the remainder of the UK and you'll understand the term 'Land of the Brave' better.

Le Surf et le Temp

Les spots de surf en Ecosse se répartissement grosso modo en 5 groupes, avec des vagues venant principalement de 3 directions, selon la position des dépressions.

La beauté de Mull 'O Kintyre est légendaire avec des vagues qui valent le coup. Ca lève avec des houles d'ouest de l'Atlantique et des houles de sud de la Mer d'Irlande. Les iles intérieures de **Coll, Tiree** et **Islay** sont aussi régulièrement surfées avec une bonne palette d'exposition et de protection aux vents et aux houles. **Les Outer Hebrides** offrent le plus fort potentiel de côtes inexplorées en Europe, leurs isolement en faisant un rêve pour chercheur de vagues. On entend des histoires de locaux d'Orkney ayant surfé dans ces latitudes extrêmes mais jusqu'à maintenant trés peu de voyageurs ont pu les confirmer. Les houles de nord générées haut dans l'Atlantique ont une influence particulière sur **la côte nord** par rapport aux autres plages. Entre John O' Groats et Sandwood Bay, sur une côte aussi belle que variée, cassent certaines des plus puissantes vagues d'Europe. Alors que les environs de Thurso sont souvent surfés (tout est relatif), la plupart des autres zones offre des conditions de surf idéales sans la foule avec des plages et des reefs qui renferment des vagues de qualité exceptionnelle.

La côte de **Moray Firth** de Skirza à Fraserburgh reçoit la part du lion des houles de la Mer du Nord, générées par des dépressions plus fréquentes dans les mois d'hiver. Malgré des températures plus froides, bon nombre de reefs et de point breaks avec des vents dominants étant off-shore permettent un surf fréquent en hiver.

La côte est de Peterhead à Berwick est plus urbanisée et polluée et certainement moins pittoresque que le reste du pays, mais les conditions sont semblables à celles de Moray Firth avec des bonnes vagues à choper.

La population des mordus se réduit à quelques centaines. Ils sont surtout concentrés sur Thurso, Fraserburgh, Edinburgh, Aberdeen et Glasgow, même si l'on trouve dans tout le pays des types avec une planche chez lui pour la session du dimanche. Le surf est encore en plein développement. Pour beaucoup, l'idée semble encore inconcevable mais il faut savoir que les êtres humains s'adaptent aux climats les plus froids. Pour les gamins écossais (ou irlandais) qui se mettent maintenant au surf, il y a peu ou pas de précédent ^pour ce nouveau sport. L'attitude des communautés par rapport au surf prouvent qu'elles sont encore mal informées.

El Surf y El Tiempo

Podemos distinguir cinco zonas. Las marejadas pueden proceder de tres direcciones en función de la ubicación de las borrascas. **Las Outer Hebrides** presentan la mayor costa sin explorar de toda Europa, y su aislamiento hace que sean el sueño del surfer aventurero. Las islas interiores de **Coll, Tiree** e **Islay** son surfeadas regularmente, ofreciendo una vasta gama de lugares adecuados a las distintas direcciones del viento y de las marejadas. La belleza de **Mull'o'kintyre** es legendaria y recibe los mares del Oeste provinientes del Atlántico, asi como los del Sur procedentes del Mar de Irlanda.

Las marejadas del Norte y del Noroeste golpean la bella y variada **Costa Norte**, en la que rompen algunas de las olas más potentes de toda Europa. En las islas Orkney hay locales que surfean incluso en esas latitudes extremas.

Moray Firth recibe la parte del león de las marejadas del Mar del Norte, frecuentes bien entrado el invierno. Pese a las frías condiciones, la abundancia de arrecifes y points proporciona olas surfeables con vientos terrales predominantes.

La **Costa Este** es la más poblada y la menos espectacular, sin embargo las condiciones no difieren de las de Moray Firth y se puede encontrar buenas olas.

El número de practicantes alcanza unos pocos miles, concentrados en Thurso, Fraserburgh, Edinburgh, Aberdeen y Glasgow. Para muchos, la simple idea de meterse al agua es inconcebible, pero el organismo humano permite la adaptación a esta climatología. Para aquellos jóvenes que comienzan a surfear en esta región con poca tradición surfera, es necesario recordarles la importancia del coraje y del respeto, tanto en el agua como fuera de ella.

Con un buen traje de invierno y un corazón fuerte, encontrarás que Escocia es un magnífico destino surfero. Te llevará al pico. Hay aparcamiento junto al embarcadero.

Escocia al igual que Irlanda están muy cercanas a las grandes depresiones atlánticas que embravecen el Océano a lo largo del año, y a menudo estas borrascas se desplazan por encima de ellas dejando a su paso la climatología habitual caracterizada por los fuertes vientos acompañados de precipitaciones. Todo esto combinado con pocas horas de insolación y una media de temperaturas inferior a la del resto del Reino Unido te permitirán comprender lo apropiado de la expresión "Tierra de Valientes".

Outer Hebrides

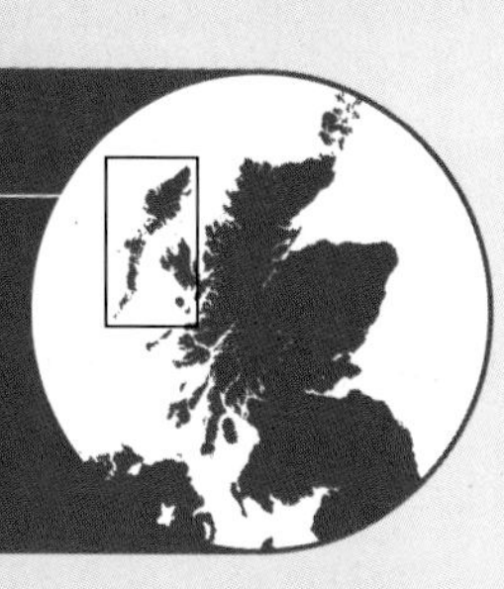

Russell Henderson

Without any doubt, the Outer Hebrides eat some of the biggest swells in Europe. 150 miles of exposed coast angles north-west into the wrath of all Atlantic depressions, presenting an almost limitless variety of wave breaking surfaces, with fantastic undiscovered surf possibilities. Clean clear waters. White sands. Desolate rocky points. Little chance of a drop in. However you have to travel to get it.
The main Islands are : Harris / Lewis, North Uist, Benbecula, South Uist and Barra. Together they form a huge stormbreak for the Western Highlands and the the northern islands of the Inner Hebrides. Lewis-Harris is a single island with a population of 25,000, hosting the main town of Stornoway, port and airport. Nth Uist, Benbecula and Sth Uist have been joined by causeways to form a single long island and whilst they sport many local differences, they share a particularly beautiful western facing coastline of sparkling shell-sand backed by grassland bright with flowers.
Travel options involve either ferry crossingor flights but public transport on the islands is skeletal e.g. two buses a week to Cliff from Stornoway, and hitching with surfboards amuses the locals no end. Bring your own transport or allow yourself lots of time. The roads are idiosyncratic, but you soon get into island mode. B&B's are scattered throughout the islands, and cottages can be rented easily. I'd definitely recommend bringing a tent as well for in the winter months, light is limited and best spent in the water, not driving.

The Culture: Gaelic is widely spoken, but if you start a conversation in English you'll get on fine. Tell them you are there to surf, these are islanders with a deep regard for and understanding of the sea, who like people with a similar appreciation. Sundays are however a day of strict rest, which means no surfing. Of course, no one will stop you, but your ignorance and lack of understanding will cut you no favours.

The Coastguard: Contact the coastguard in Stornoway on arrival. If possible, go and visit them at their new headquarters. Many of the members surf, and will happily recommend breaks and provide weather charts and forecasts. They will want an itinerary of where you are going to surf, to stop false alarms if someone calls, describing a person flapping about in the waves. If there are only a couple of you, it is a good idea to phone the coastguard each day before going out, giving a call back time, after which they will go looking for you. It may sound like hassle but it makes exploratory surfing safer.

Sans aucun doute, les Outer Hebrides récupèrent certains des plus grosses houles d'Europe. 220 kms de côtes exposées orientées vers la fureur des dépressions de l'Atlantique, offrant une variété presque sans limite de surfaces où cassent des vagues, avec un potentiel de surf fantastique. Une eau limpide, du sable blanc, des reefs solitaires, personne pour vous dropper dessus. Cependant, il va falloir y arriver.

Les iles principales sont: Harris/Lewis, North Uist, Benbecula, South Uist et Barra. Ensemble, elles constituent un méga-bouclier contre les tempêtes sur les Western highlands et les iles septentrionnales des Inner Hebrides. L'ile de Lewis-Harris elle-seule compte 25,000 habitants, la plupart à Stornoway, port et aéroport. North Uist, Benbecula et South Uist ont été joints par des chaussées pour former une seule ile. Même si elles ont des différences locales, elles partagent une côte orientale splendide avec des sables étincelants et des prairies florissantes.

Pour y aller, on a le choix entre le ferry et l'avion. Les transports publics sur l'île sont ridicules: par exemple, deux bus par jour de Cliff à Stornoway et le stop avec les planches n''amuse plus les locaux. Venez donc avec votre voiture ou restez longtemps. les routes sont capricieuses mais vous vous ferez vite à l'ambiance de l'île. On trouve des Bed & Breakfast un peu partout et on peut facilemnt louer des cottages. Mieux vaut porter une tente aussi pour les mois d'hiver (!) parce que les jours sont trés courts et qu'il vaut mieux passer ce temps dans l'eau que sur la route.

La Culture: Beaucoup de gens parlent gaélique mais si vous commencez à parler anglais, ça ira. Dites-leur que vous êtes là pour surfer car ces insulaires éprouvent un profond respect pour la mer et les gens qui ont les mêmes considérations. Dimanche est un jour de repos complet, ce qui veut dire pas de surf. Bien sûr, personne ne vous en empêchera mais ectte ignorance ou ce non-respect peut vous jouer des mauvais tours.

Les garde-côtes: Rentrez en contact avec le garde-côte de Stornoway à votre arrivée. Si possible, allez les voir dans leurs nouveaux locaux. Beaucoup d'entre eux surfent et seront contents de vous donner quelques instructions sur les spots, quelques prévisions avec des cartes marines. Ils voudront un itinéraire de là où vous allez surfer pour être au courant si quelqu'un donne l'alerte parcequ'il a vu quelqu'un s'agiter dans les vagues. Si vous êtes deux, n'hésitez pas à appeler les garde-côtes avant de partir, de convenir d'une heure pour rappeler pour qu'il parte à votre recherche au-delà. Ca peut sembler contraignant mais ça rend l'exploration des spots plus rassurante.

Sin duda alguna, las Hebrides exteriores se llevan algunas de las marejadas más fuertes de Europa.150 millas de costa que asoman al noroeste en el furor de las depresiones del Atlántico, se dan todo tipo de olas, con posibilidades surfísticas todavía por descubrir. El agua es limpia y clara. La arena es blanca. Hay muchas zonas rocosas y desoladas. Pocas posibilidades para un baño. Pero tienes que moverte para conseguirlo.

Las principales islas son: Harris / Lewis, North Uist, Benbecula, South Uist y Barra. Todas juntas forman una barrera protectora de las tormentas para las Tierras Altas del oeste así como para las islas al norte de las Hebrides Interiores. Lewis/Harris es una isla solitaria con una población de 25000 habitantes, aquí se encuentra el mayor pueblo de Stornoway, también hay un puerto y aeropuerto. North Uist, Benbecula y South Uist están unidos por arrecifes formando una única isla alargada a pesar de sus diferencias, comparten una costa particularmente hermosa orientada al oeste, con brillantes arenas de concha y arropada por una campiña rebosante por el colorido de sus flores.

Las opciones de viajar pasan o por tomar el ferry de dos horas y media desde Ullapool, o sino se amplía con viajes desde Uig o Oban hasta Lochboisdale, Lochmaddy o Tarbert. El transporte público de las islas es paupérrimo, por ejemplo hay dos autobuses semanales desde Stornoway hasta Cliff, aunque coger a dedo a los surfistas entretiene a los locales. Llevate tu medio de transporte o sino ya sabes el tiempo que vas a perder. Las islas son un tanto precarias aunque enseguida te acostuumbras. Hay un servicio telefónico B&B esparcido por toda la isla, y se pueden alquilar casas de campo sin problema. Se recomienda llevar una tienda para los meses de invierno, el sol no dura mucho y es mejor estar en agua que no recorriendo las carreteras.

La Cultura: El gaélico está muy extendido, pero siempre te podrás comunicar en inglés. Haz saber que has ido a surfear ya que a los isleños, con sus vidas dependientes del mar, les gusta que la gente lo aprecie. Los domingos son estrictamente para descansar, lo que significa que no se surfea. Nadie te va a obligar, pero tu ignorancia y falta de entendimiento te puede negar cualquier favor.

Los guardacostas: Ponte en contacto con los guardacostas en Stornoway nada más llegar. Y si es posible vete a visitarles al puesto de mando. Muchos de ellos surfean, y a gusto te recomendarán algún pico y te proveerán con cartas y mapas del tiempo. Querrán conocer tu itinerario para surfear, y así no alarmarse si alguien llama avisando que hay gente ahogandose en las olas. Si solo está es una pareja será buena idea que llameis a los guardacostas antes de que salgais cada dia, quedando para una llamada posterior tras la cual, de no haberse producido, os irían a buscar. Esto puede parecer estúpido pero hace que el surf de aventura sea más seguro.

Photo: Alex William

1. Eoropie

Steep and barreling beach and reef waves. The locals at Barvas speak of this area in hushed tones and with a degree of awe.

Plage en pente avec des tubes et des vagues de reef. Les locaux de Barvas parlent de cette zone à demi-mot avec une certaine frayeur.

Es una playa escarpada y con escollos donde salen olas de arrecife. Los locales de Barvas hablan de forma sosegada y con un cierto respeto.

2. Rubh' a' Bhiogair

Sand covered rock point that holds big swell, reputedly the best wave on the island, but very exposed to the wind. A fast take off soon subsides into a long wall. Much potential.

Une langue rocheuse couverte de sable qui tient bien la houle, réputée comme la meilleure vague de l'île mais trés exposée aux vents. Un take-off rapide s'aplatit rapidement pour donner un long mur, bon potentiel.

Es un pico de roca cubierto de arena que aguanta una gran marejada, tiene la reputación de ser la mejor ola de toda la isla, aunque está muy expuesta al viento. Tras un rápido take off te encontrarás con una pared muy larga. Es muy potente.

3. Carloway to Bragar

Dalmore, Dalbeg, Loch Shawbost, Port Mhor Bragar are all protected coves with small sand beaches and waves of unconfirmed quality. Located off the A858 North of Carloway.

Toutes ces sorties depuis l'A858 au nord de Carloway. Ce sont toutes des petites anses avec un peu de sable et des vagues de qualité variable.

A todas éstas se llega por la A858 al norte de Carloway. Todas son pequeñas cuevas protegidas con playas de arena y olas de calidad por confirmar.

4. Cliff

Works with any swell to produce long walls. A rip to the right, can sometimes be the only way out and while it can be a handy conveyer belt, respect its knottage. Park near some sheep pens. If it looks small from here, suit up...chances are it's overhead.

Marche avec n'importe quel swell, de longs murs en perspective. Un courant, sur la droite peut être la seule façon de sortir mais si ça peut être un tapis roulant pratique, attention au timing. On trouve un parking prés d'un enclos à moutons. Si; ça paraît petit de là, y'a des chances que ça fasse un bon mètre.

Aparecen paredes largas con cualquier marejada. A veces la única forma de salir es por la corriente a mano derecha y aunque puede resultar un transporte comodo y seguro, ten cuidado. Hay un aparcamiento de coches cerca de unas cuadras. Y aunque desde aquí parezca pequeño, ten en cuenta que este sitio se encuentra muy elevado.

Photo: Andy Bennetts

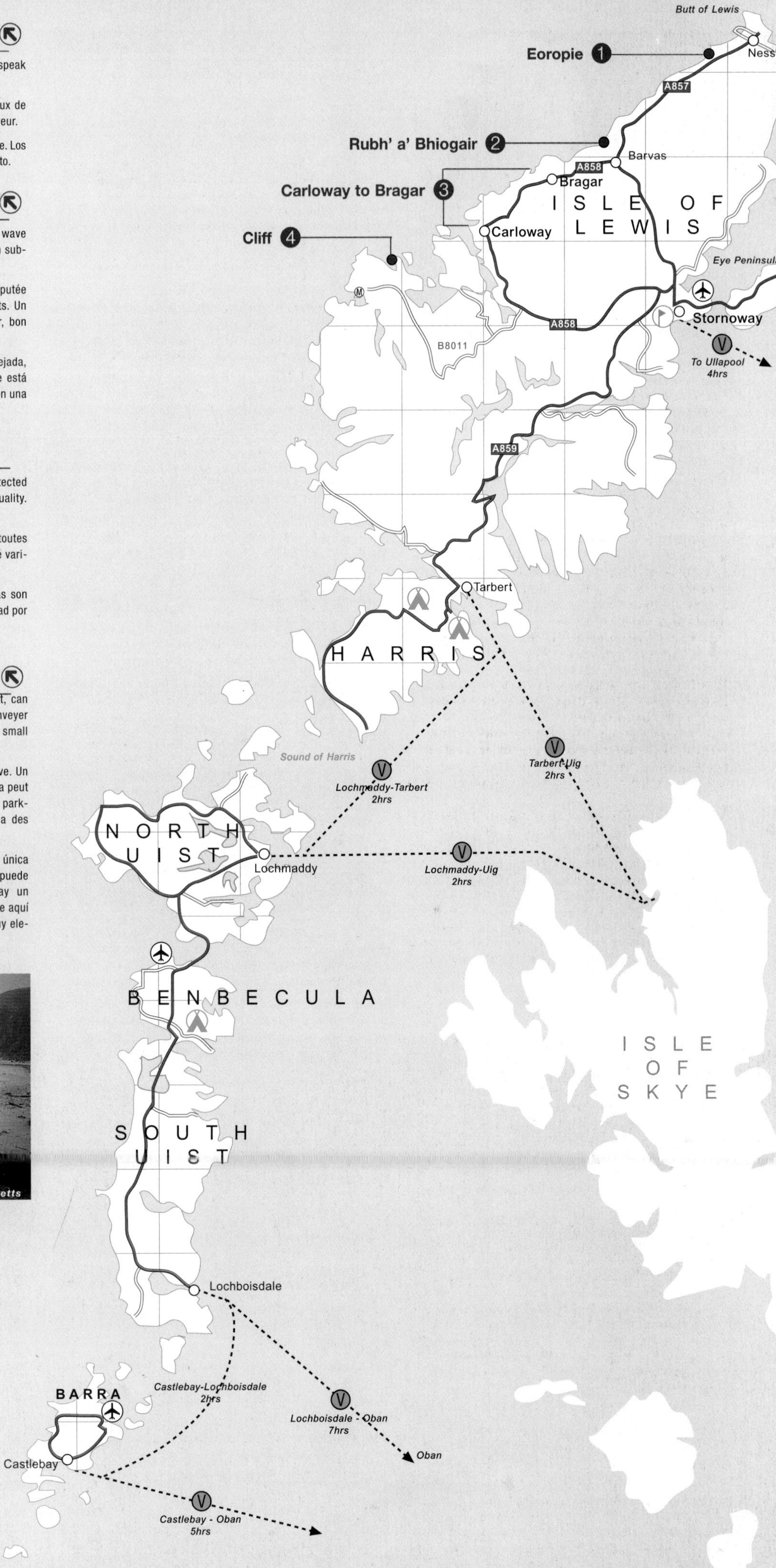

West Coast

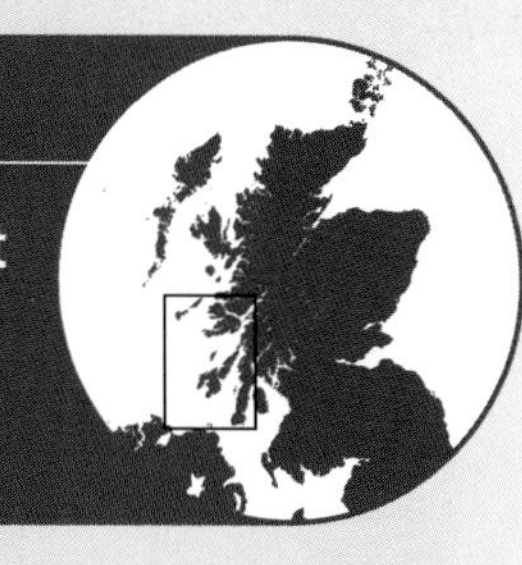

Jamie Blair - *Clan*
Rachel Sutherland

Coll: A strange and barren, swell-drenched island, much of the western seabord is bright shell sand heaped into huge dunes, some up to 100ft. There is one small town, Arringour. Less exposed to swell than nearby Tiree, but a great island for the remotest-of-all surf experiences.

Tiree: The most popular of all the Hebrides due to its high wave quota and ease of access from Oban. The shape and size of the island combined with a wide variety of reefs and beaches make it a great place to surf. Tiree recieves so much swell, but it is a flat and exposed island, this is often a disadvantage for surfers, but helped to put it on the map as a world class wave-jumping spot. Winter would be a tough time to visit, but empty waves and some of the U.K.'s highest sunshine levels make it a spring gem.

Islay: The closest and most varied of the surfable inner Hebrides lies just 16 miles west of Kintyre. It is relatively lush and hilly with a variety of beaches and reefs, some very good.

Macrihanish: Due to the sheltering presence of Scotlands' Isles, the Western mainland recieves little surf. This is found only at the extreme north of the country, or in a small swell window south of the islands of Islay and Jura. When depressions move off northern Ireland, a few waves get in here.

Coll: Une île des Hebrides étrange et dénudée, pétrie de houles. La plupart de la côte ouest est comme un coquillage brillant sur le sable jonché de méga-dunes dont certaines atteignent plus de 30 mètres, reliées ensemble par l'herbe Machir. Quelques fermes élèvent du bétail et il y a une petite ville, Arringour. Coll est moins exposée à la houle que Tiree à côté, mais reste une super île pour une expérience de surf des plus reculées.

Tiree: La destination la plus en vogue des Hebrides grâce à un bon quota de vagues et son accessibilité facile depuis Oban. La forme et la taille des trois îles combinées avec une variété assez large de reefs et de plages en fait un bon endroit pour surfer. Tiree reçoit énormément de houle mais c'est une île plate et exposée avec des vents qui la traversent quaisment sans arrêt. C'est souvent un désavantage pour les surfers, mais aide à considérer l'endroit comme un spot de windsurf de qualité mondiale. Tandis que l'hiver s'avère une période trop austère, il faut considérer que des vagues vierges et un des meilleurs ensoleillements du Royaume-Uni en font une perle au printemps comme à l'été.

Islay: Le plus proche et le plus varié des spots surfables des Hebrides intérieures se trouve juste à 25 kms de Kintyre. C'est relativement vert et vallonné avec une variété de plages et de reefs, dont les cinq spots de Tiree.

Macrihanish: A cause de la protection des îles orientales de L'Ecosse, le pays à l'Ouest reçoit trés peu de surf. On peut seulement en trouver à l'extrême nord du pays, ou dans une petite fenêtre au sud des îles Islay et Jura. Quand les dépressions passent au nord, au large de l'Irlande, quelques vagues filtrent ici.

Coll: Es una isla un tanto extraña, donde parte de su costa oeste está tomada por una serie de dunas de arena de concha, algunas llegan a alcanzar los 30m de altura. No está tan expuesta a la marejada como la cercana Tiree. Pero aun queda isla para las experiencias surfísticas más remotas.

Tiree: Es el lugar más conocido de todas las Hebrides debido a sus olas grandes y al fácil acceso desde Oban. El contorno y el tamaño de la isla se combinan con una gran variedad de escollos y de playas convirtiendo a la isla en un sitio ideal para surfear. En Tiree entra mucha marejada pero es una isla lisa y desolada. Y esto es una desventaja aunque luego figure en los mapas como un sitio de olas de categoría mundial. Visitarlo en invierno es más crudo, pero al estar las olas vacías y al disponer en primavera y verano de los niveles de sol más favorables del Reino Unido, hacen de esta una joya de buen tiempo.

Islay: Es la isla más cercana al continente de todas las surfeables de las Hebrides Interiores, está solo a 16 millas al oeste de Kintyre. Es realmente lozano y jugoso con una gran cantidad de playas y picos, algunos muy buenos.

Macrihanish: Por la protección que le proporcionan las islas del oeste de Escocia, hay poco surfing para practicar. Solo se puede practicar en el extremo más al norte del pais o en pequeñas zonas orientadas hacia el sur de las islas de Islay y Jura, pero con depresiones situadas al norte y viento terral de Irlanda casi ninguna ola arriva a la península de Macrihanish.

1. Balephetrish

A large pebble and sand beach with good sand bars.

Une grande plage de sable et de galets avec des bars animés.

Se trata de una larga playa de arena y guijarros que dispone de unas barreras de arena favorables en su boca.

2. The Hough

Faces W/NW. Beach waves receive some protection from "The Hough Skerries". A left reef break warrants further investigation.

Ces vagues sont protégées par les "Hough Skerries". Une gauche de reef d'abord qui vous assure le déplacement si vous cherchez.

Orientada al O/NO. Estas olas playeras están protegidas del "Hough Skerries". Un pico que rompe a la izquierda merece ser chequeado.

3. The Maze

The most popular spot on the island for windsurfing and scene of The British Nationals. A long sandy beach open to all W swell. Long, fast peaks break on the beach and off the point. If you climb the remnants of a World War II radar station at Ben Hough, all will be revealed.

Maze est une longue plage sableuse ouverte à tous les swells d'Ouest. De longs murs cassent sur une plage à partir du "point". Si vous escaladez les ruines du poste d'observation de la deuxième guerre mondiale à Ben Hough, vous verrez tout le panorama.

La playa es larga y de arena y está expuesta a cualquier marejada del oeste. Las olas rápidas y largas rompen en la playa a la altura del pico. Si te sube mundial que aun perdura, podrás controlar toda la zona.

4. Port Bharrapol

A magnificent rock and sand bay at the bottom of high cliffs. Faces west and catches heaps of swell. From "The Glassery", (a restaurant between Bharrapol and Middleton) you can see the coast.

Une baie splendide de roches et de sable, au pied de hautes falaises. Regarde L'ouest et chope un max de houle. Depuis "The Glassery" (un restaurant avec une vue imprenable entre Bharrapol et Middleton) on peut voir la côte de haut en bas.

Es una magnífica bahía de arena y roca que se encuentra al pie de unos acantilados. Se encuentra orientada al oeste y coge montones de marejadas. Desde "The Glassery" (un restaurante situado entre Bharrapol y Middleton) se domina toda la costa.

5. Balephuil

2km shell sand beach picks up good amounts of swell. Peaks on the beach and Kenavara Point could also hold secrets. There are many other places of interest left for further discovery.

Plus de 2 kms de sable blanc qui fait face au Sud Sud-Ouest en récupérant bizarrement pas mal de houle. Gauches et droites cassent sur la plage et Kenavara Point peut aussi cacher quelques spots secrets. Plein d'autres endroits à voir mais on les laisse tranquilles.

Esta es una playa de dos Km de arena de concha en la que entra la marejada. Los picos de la playa y de Kenavara pueden tener sus secretos. Hay también muchos otros lugares de interés pero los dejamos para su descubrimiento.

6. Ardnave Bay

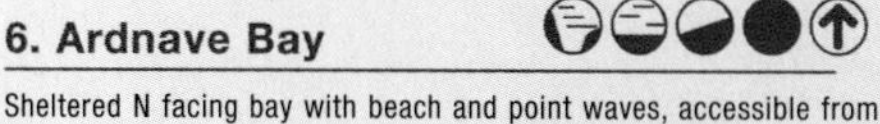

Sheltered N facing bay with beach and point waves, accessible from Ardnarch House and Loch. Needs a good swell to work.

Baie abritée exposée nord avec des plages et des points, accessibles depuis Ardnarch House. Il faut que ça rentre bien pour fonctionner.

Es una bahía protegida y orientada al norte, con picos de playa y de roca. Se puede llegar desde Ardnarch House y desde Loch. Necesita de una buena marejada para sus mejores condiciones.

7. Saligo Bay

Heavy W facing bay with strong currents. The waves are thick and sucky, lefthanders to the south and rights to the north. Take a good look before paddling out.

Baie impressionante exposée ouest avec des panneaux de mise en garde pour les courants. Les vagues sont d' épaisses et insidieuses gauches au sud et droites au nord.

Es una ruda bahía con fuertes corrientes y mirando al oeste. Las olas son densas y chupan bastante, presenta izquierdas al sur y derechas al norte. Echale un buen vistazo antes de salir.

Saligo Bay - *Photo: Andy Bennetts*

8. Machir Bay

The north works well with rights off the point. To the south the beach shelves more steeply forming powerful lefts. Good for camping.

4kms de sable divisé du nord au sud par une rivière. La partie nord marche bien avec des droites depuis le "point". Au sud, la plage se creuse pour former de puissantes gauches.

Los 4 Km de arena de norte a sur se encuentran separados por la boca del rio. El extremo al norte funciona bien con las derechas que salen del pico. Más al sur la playa se encuentra distribuida más escalonadamente habiendo contundentes izquierdas.

Machir Bay - *Photo: Andy Bennetts*

9. Lossit Bay

Lies at the bottom of high cliffs. Good waves if you can get down. Take the track to Lossit farm and there it's likely you'll have to park, so be courteous. It's a three mile walk around and down the cliffs.

Se situe au pied de hautes falaises et vous pouvez choper de bonnes vagues si vous arrivez à descendre. Prendre le chemin de la ferme Lossit où il faudra probablement se garer, soyez polis. Pas moins de 5 kms de marche pour descendre à moins que vous ne sautiez.

Se situa al pie de unos empinados acantilados que si logras bajar podras coger unas olas muy buenas. Coge la pista hasta la granja de Lossit donde seguramente tendrás que aparcar, así que compórtate. El camino que queda es de unos tres Km.

10. Laggan Bay

The biggest beach on the island stretches for miles and works on all tides. Access is to the south of the golf course. Park outside the Machrie hotel and follow the stream to the beach.

La plus grande plage de l'île qui s'étend sur plusieurs kms et comme c'est orienté sud-ouest avec les vents dominants, ça marche par toutes les marées. L'accés se fait au sud par le terrain de golf. Se garer à l'extérieur de l'hôtel Machrie et suivre le ruisseau jusqu'à la plage.

Esta es la playa más larga de toda la isla a lo largo de unas cuantas millas, En la zona orientada al S.O. cara al viento predominante, funciona con todas las mareas. La forma de llegar es por la parte sur del campo de golf. Lo mejor es aparcar afuera del hotel Machrie y seguir a la marabunta hasta la playa.

11. Caravans

Best at low to mid tide, its usually surfed when Westport's too big...seldom classic but can do its thing. Predominantly a right forming at the rivermouth, with shorter hollower lefts. Beware of submerged sea stacks which can pop up unannounced at any time.

Mieux de marée basse à mi-marée, souvent surfé quand Westport est trop gros. Rarement transcendant mais peut être correct. Souvent une droite en sortie de rivière, avec des gauches plus courtes mais plus creuses. Attention aux cailloux immergés qui peuvent apparaître soudainement à n'importe quel moment.

Lo mejor sale de baja a media marea y se suele coger cuando Westport está muy grande, algunas veces parece un lugar clásico pero normalmente será corriente. Predomina una derecha que se forma en la boca del rio, con izquierdas más cortas y cerronas. Cuidado con los maderos sumergidos que pueden aparecer sin previo aviso.

12. Graveyards

The next access down from caravans, also shares similar waves but more intense rocks in the lineup. Not for beginners. There are numerous other peaks along this stretch of coast, getting smaller the closer you get to the pub at Bellochanty. Better above mid tide.

L'accés suivant aprés Caravans qui partage les mêmes caractéristiques de vagues mais avec encore plus de cailloux au line-up. Débutants s'abstenir. On trouve plein d'autres spots sur cette côte dont les vagues se rapetissent quand on se rapproche du pub de Bellochanty. Mieux au-dessus de la mi-marée.

Es el siguiente acceso pasado caravans, las olas son parecidas aunque hay más rocas en la zona. Principiantes abstenerse. Hay un buen número de picos a lo larga de esta costa, tanto más pequeños cuanto más te acercas al pub de Bellonchanty. Mejor con mareas más altas que bajas.

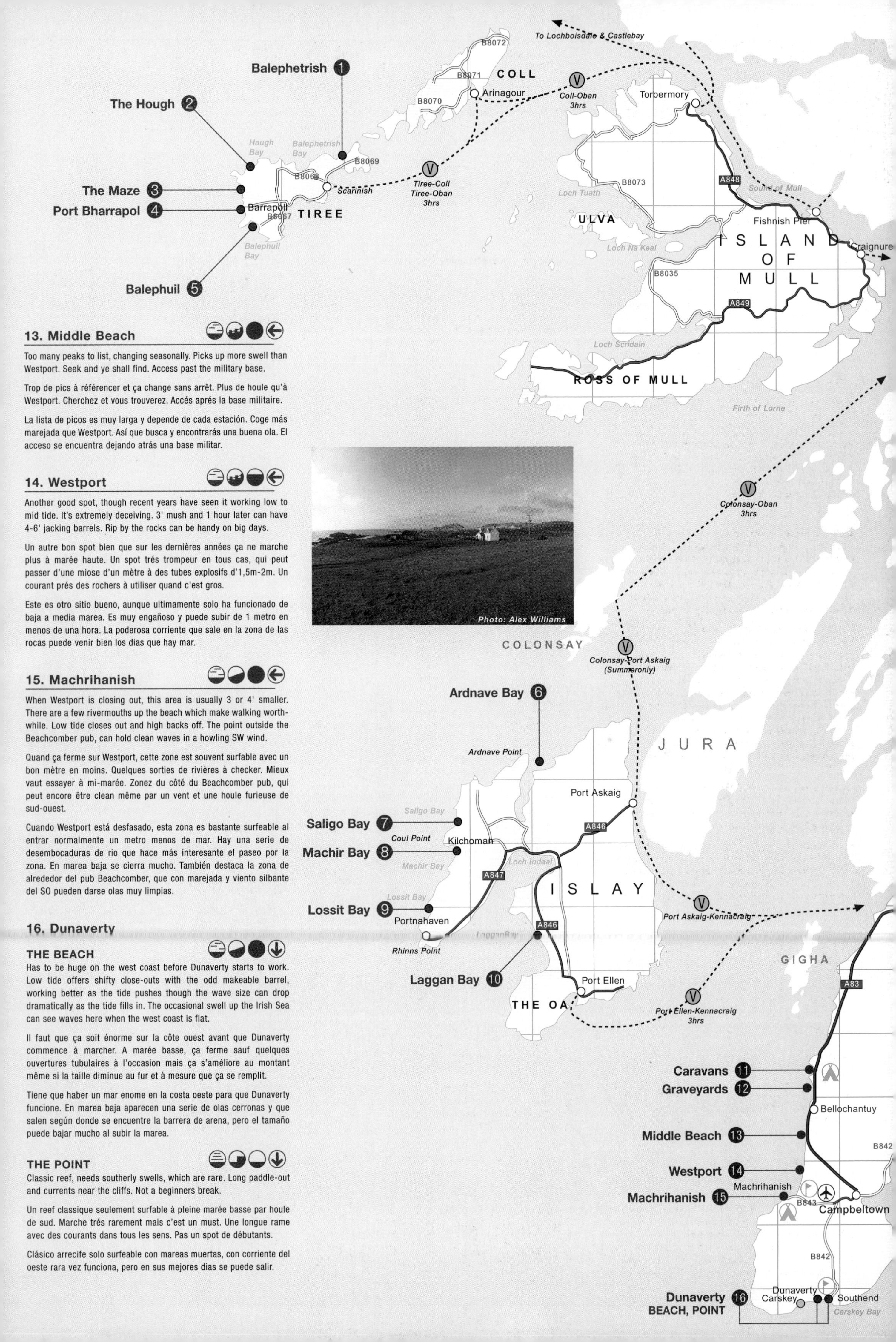

13. Middle Beach

Too many peaks to list, changing seasonally. Picks up more swell than Westport. Seek and ye shall find. Access past the military base.

Trop de pics à référencer et ça change sans arrêt. Plus de houle qu'à Westport. Cherchez et vous trouverez. Accés aprés la base militaire.

La lista de picos es muy larga y depende de cada estación. Coge más marejada que Westport. Así que busca y encontrarás una buena ola. El acceso se encuentra dejando atrás una base militar.

14. Westport

Another good spot, though recent years have seen it working low to mid tide. It's extremely deceiving. 3' mush and 1 hour later can have 4-6' jacking barrels. Rip by the rocks can be handy on big days.

Un autre bon spot bien que sur les dernières années ça ne marche plus à marée haute. Un spot trés trompeur en tous cas, qui peut passer d'une miose d'un mètre à des tubes explosifs d'1,5m-2m. Un courant prés des rochers à utiliser quand c'est gros.

Este es otro sitio bueno, aunque ultimamente solo ha funcionado de baja a media marea. Es muy engañoso y puede subir de 1 metro en menos de una hora. La poderosa corriente que sale en la zona de las rocas puede venir bien los dias que hay mar.

15. Machrihanish

When Westport is closing out, this area is usually 3 or 4' smaller. There are a few rivermouths up the beach which make walking worthwhile. Low tide closes out and high backs off. The point outside the Beachcomber pub, can hold clean waves in a howling SW wind.

Quand ça ferme sur Westport, cette zone est souvent surfable avec un bon mètre en moins. Quelques sorties de rivières à checker. Mieux vaut essayer à mi-marée. Zonez du côté du Beachcomber pub, qui peut encore être clean même par un vent et une houle furieuse de sud-ouest.

Cuando Westport está desfasado, esta zona es bastante surfeable al entrar normalmente un metro menos de mar. Hay una serie de desembocaduras de rio que hace más interesante el paseo por la zona. En marea baja se cierra mucho. También destaca la zona de alrededor del pub Beachcomber, que con marejada y viento silbante del SO pueden darse olas muy limpias.

16. Dunaverty

THE BEACH

Has to be huge on the west coast before Dunaverty starts to work. Low tide offers shifty close-outs with the odd makeable barrel, working better as the tide pushes though the wave size can drop dramatically as the tide fills in. The occasional swell up the Irish Sea can see waves here when the west coast is flat.

Il faut que ça soit énorme sur la côte ouest avant que Dunaverty commence à marcher. A marée basse, ça ferme sauf quelques ouvertures tubulaires à l'occasion mais ça s'améliore au montant même si la taille diminue au fur et à mesure que ça se remplit.

Tiene que haber un mar enome en la costa oeste para que Dunaverty funcione. En marea baja aparecen una serie de olas cerronas y que salen según donde se encuentre la barrera de arena, pero el tamaño puede bajar mucho al subir la marea.

THE POINT

Classic reef, needs southerly swells, which are rare. Long paddle-out and currents near the cliffs. Not a beginners break.

Un reef classique seulement surfable à pleine marée basse par houle de sud. Marche trés rarement mais c'est un must. Une longue rame avec des courants dans tous les sens. Pas un spot de débutants.

Clásico arrecife solo surfeable con mareas muertas, con corriente del oeste rara vez funciona, pero en sus mejores dias se puede salir.

The North Shore is divided between the counties of Caithness and Sutherland, and stretches from John'o'Groats to Sandwood bay, on a coastline as beautiful as it is varied.

Caithness is flat and lies on beds of hard grey stone. These stones, jutting into the Atlantic in huge flat slabs, are the breaking surface for some of Europe's hairiest waves. There are beautiful beaches in Caithness, however it is the reefs which make this such an intense surfing area.

Travelling west from Melvich one enters the district of Sutherland and the Caithness flagstones disappear. Great glacial river valleys rake down into the ocean and their remains form boulder reefs and sandy beaches, and much of the coastline offers empty surf.

La côte nord de l'Ecosse est séparée en deux contés de Caithness et Sutherland.

Caithness est situé sur un lit de cailloux gris qui sont plats et se brisent facilement. Ces cailloux, se jettant dans l'Atlantique par grosses plaques, constituent les fonds de certaines des vagues les plus craignos d' Europe. On trouve aussi de superbes plages à Caithness; même si ce sont les reefs qui en font une zone de suf de premier ordre.

En voyageant vers l'ouest à partir de Melvich, on rentre dans le canton de Sutherland et les dalles de cailloux disparaissent. D' imposantes vallées creusées par les rivières descendent jusqu'à l'océan en formant des moraines qui donnent des reefs de rochers et des plages de sable. Quand on regarde une carte trés détaillée, on devine un fort potentiel de vagues vierges.

La zona N esta dividida por 2 condados el de Caithness y Sutherland y se extiende desde John 'o' Groats hasta la bahía de Sandwood a lo largo de la costa con una bonita vista.

Caithness es llano con piedras grises. Estas piedras sobresalen hacia el Atlántico en enormes bloques haciendo de esta rompiente una de las más peligrosas de Europa. Hay bonitas playas en Caithness, de todas formas lo importante de esta zona de surfing son las rompientes de reef.

Viajando en el O desde Melvich una vez que se entra en el distrito de Sutherland desaparecen las piedras de Caithness. Grandes rios atraves de los valles desembocan en el oceano dejando piedras redondas y playas de arena donde la mayoria de las costas no son aptas para el surf.

Swells are generated by intense low pressure systems moving high in the North Atlantic. In summer, you can surf all day and most of the night, if there's swell - it's only briefly dark around 3am! Several of the breaks, Brims Ness in particular, experience strong currents and tidal water movements as the Atlantic charges along the coast to meet the North Sea. The tidal reach is also vast, especially on full moons and spring tides. Often it is the tide and current pushing into a swell which gives the waves their extra power. It pays to exercise extreme awareness, as there are few people around to help should you encounter difficulties, easily compounded by cold water conditions.

Thurso is the main town and source of facilities including good supermarkets, hotels, garages, pubs, B&B's and a heated public pool. Going west, traces of man thin considerably. It's a spooky experience - the knowledge that you're on a latitude comparable to Alaska, the big seals in the line-up, the lack of surfers, the reefs... the North Shore has a presence all of its own which demands respect.

Les houles sont générées par des systèmes dépressionnaires réguliers qui se forment dans les hautes latitudes, tout au long de l'année sauf en été, où l'on peut d'ailleurs surfer pratiquement 24H/24 puisqu'il ne fait sombre que vers 3 heures du matin! Nombre de reefs, comme Brims Ness en particulier, subissent l'effet de courants violents et de marnages importants là où l'Atlantique vient à la rencontre de la mer du Nord. Ce marnage est bien sûr au summum aux vives eaux , à savoir les pleines lunes ou l'equinoxe de printemps. Souvent, la marée montante renforce la puissance du swell et il s'agit de faire attention surtout quand c'est gros. Il n'y a que peu de gens autour si vous êtes en danger, ce qui peut arriver compte tenu du froid.

Les vagues y sont hantées si l'on considère la couleur vert sombre de l'eau, l'isolement latent de la campagne, le fait d'être à la même latitude que l'Alaska, les méga-otaries dans l'eau, le manque de surfers ou l'absence de gens en général, les reefs ...la côte nord a une identité bien à elle qui invite au respect.

Los swells son generados por las intensas bajas presiones que se forman en el norte Atlántico. Durante el verano se puede surfear durante tode el dia y parte de la noche, si el swell lo permite - la noche tiene fuertes corrientes en los cambios de mareas por la fuerza que tiene el Atlántico a lo largo de la costa Norte. El cambio de marea es muy fuerte sobre todo con luna llena y las mareas de primavera. Amenudo con marea y con fuertes corrientes empujando el swell da olas super potentes. Se debe ser conscientede que en esta zona hay muy poca gente que te puede ayudar en caso de dificultad, donde el agua esta muy fria.

Thurso es la ciudad más importante y da todo tipo de facilidades como supermercados, hoteles, garajes, pubs, bed and breakfast, y piscina climatizada. Es una experiencia alucinante, parece que estas en un sitio comparado a Alaska, las grandes focas, la escasez de surfers, las rocas... La costa norte tiene una presencia por si misma que demanda respeto.

the

Brims Ness - *Photo: The Gill*

north shore

"It's a spooky experience - the knowledge that you're on a latitude comparable to Alaska, the big seals in the line-up, the lack of surfers, the reefs... the North Shore has a presence all of its own which demands respect."

Thurso Castle - *Photo: Tim Rainger, LP*

Cut Peat - *Photo: Alex Williams*

David McKay, Thurso East - Photo: Malcolm MacWatt,

North Shore

1. Oldshoremore

A sheltered bay facing SW, receives waves on a strong W or even N swell, better at higher tides. A useful indicator- if Oldshoremore is on Sandwood is on. Just north of Kinlochbervie.

Une baie abritée exposée S-O, chope des vagues par grosse houle d'ouest et même de nord, mieux à marée haute. Un indicateur utile pour Sandwood: les deux marchent en même temps. Just au nord de Kinlochbervie.

Es una bahía refugiada orientada hacia el SO a la que llegan olas con marejadas tanto del O como del N. Mejora con la pleamar. Un buen criterio es el siguiente: si en Oldshoremore hay 1 pie, en Sandwood hay buenas olas.

2. Sandwood Bay

This mile long beach facing NW is one of Britain's finest, with no fewer than nine different breaks. It has reefs at both ends, and rock clusters marking its length. Save for birds and an occasional walker, it is deserted. High cliffs offer protection from N and S winds. It receives as much swell as any other Scottish beach but the only access is a four mile track located just north of Blairmore. The first two miles are navigable by car in summer-otherwise its strictly a walk through the peat bog. The walk is as stunning as the beach.

Cette plage d'1,5 km, qui regarde le N-O, est une des plus belles de Grande-Bretagne avec pas moins de 9 vagues. Elle a des reefs de chaque côté, avec deux groupes de rochers qui définissent sa longueur et des hautes falaises qui empêchent les vents de nord et du sud de s'y engouffrer. Mise à part les oiseaux et les promeneurs éventuels, c'est désert. Reçoit la même houle que n'importe quelle autre plage d'Ecosse. Le seul accès se fait par un chemin de 6 kms juste au nord de Blairmore. Les 3 premiers kilomètres sont carross-ables en été sinon il faut marcher tout le long dans les tourbières. La balade est aussi hallucinante que la plage.

Esta playa de una milla de largura es una de las mejores y más seguras playas británicas. Excepto pájaros y turistas ocasionales, es casi desierta. Hay nada menos que nueve barras/arrecife. La bahía da al NO con picos a ambos lados, los dos diques de roca con su longi-tud impresa y los altos acantilados proporcionan la protección nece-saria de los vientos del N y S. Recibe tanta marejada como cualquier otra playa escocesa. El único acceso es una pista de unas cuatro mil-las algo al norte de Blairmore. En las primeras dos millas todavía podemos usar el coche en verano, si no es necesario caminar por el borde de un lago. Este paseo es tan alucinante como la playa.

3. Balnakiel Bay

A sweeping sandy beach facing W into the Kyle of Durness. Picks up W and NW swell that may miss other breaks further east. Protected from N winds and swells.

Une plage de sable instable exposée ouest dans le Kyle de Durness. Chope les houles d'ouest et nord-ouest qui peuvent manquer les autres spots à l'est. Abritée des vents et houles de nord.

Esta playa extensa de arena está orientada al oeste hacia Kyle of Durness. Aprovecha las marejadas del O y NO que no cuadran en los picos más al este. Se encuentra protegido de los vientos del N y de las marejadas.

4. Durness (Sango Bay)

Below the town of Durness, sheltered by the limestone bluffs lies a small sandy beach facing NE. It picks up N swell with offshores from the SW, protection from W wind.

Sous Durness, abritée par les a-pics de calcaire se trouve une petite plage de sable exposée N. Ca récupère les houles de nord avec de l'off-shore par vents de sud, à l'abri des vents d'ouest. Les autres spots s'appellent Ceannabeine beach (Rispond Bay) et Rabbit Island.

Está situado debajo de la ciudad de Durness, refugiada entre unos riscos pedregosos se encuentra está pequeña playa de arena orienta-da al NE. Coge las marejadas del norte con vientos terrales del sur, está protegida de los vientos del O.

5. Kyle of Tongue

A Sheltered glacial inlet, works in huge swells, offering protection from all but northerly winds. An area surfed very rarely, waves are rideable for hundreds of metres up both sides in the right conditions.

Une baie protégée et glaciale qui marche quand ça rentre gras, abritée de tous les vents sauf ceux de nord. Une zone rarement sur-fée ou des vagues de plusieurs centaines de mètres sont surfables des deux côtés quand ça rentre bien.

Es una ensenada glacial protegida que funciona para enormes mare-jadas, está a salvo de todo menos de los vientos del norte. Es una zona poco surfeada, se puede ir en las olas hasta cientos de metros pero cuando las condiciones son buenas.

6. Torrisdale

Beach break with a good righthand rivermouth. The best bars are near the river; check for sinking sands along the bank. Low to mid tide is generally the best.

Beach break avec une bonne droite à la rivière. Les meilleurs bancs sont prés de la rivière mais attention aux sables mouvants le long des berges. Off-shore par vents de sud, de préference de marée basse à mi-marée.

Rompe en la playa con una buena derecha en la boca del rio. Las mejores barras se ponen cerca del rio; comprueba las aguas de desagüe a lo largo de este banco de arena. Lo mejor se da general-mente de baja a media marea.

7. Farr Bay

Due to its NE aspect Farr picks up swell that may miss Thurso. Lefts, are better at high tide, and rights at low. Walk through the dunes after taking a turn off at the Farr Bay Inn. Don't forget to close the gate as it is farmed land.

A cause de son orientation NE, Farr Bay chope des houles qui peuvent manquer Thurso. Les gauches sont meilleures à marée haute et inversement à marée basse. Traversez les dunes aprés avoir tourné à Farr Bay Inn. Ne laissez pas le portail ouvert car ce sont des champs cultivés.

Por su aspecto NE recibe la marejada que no ha llegado a Thurso. Las izquierdas son mejores con marea alta y las derechas con baja. Se llega por las dunas después de girar en Farr Bay Inn. Acuerdate de cerrar la valla al ser ésta tierra granjera.

8. Armadale Bay

Beach break, better at high tide. Either follow the rivermouth or walk from town.visible from the main road.

Exposé nord, visible depuis la route principale. Un beach break avec des pics meilleurs à marée haute. Suivez la rivière ou marchez depuis le village.

Se trata de un pico de playa que funciona en pleamar. Se llega siguiendo la desembocadura del rio o a pata desde el pueblo. Está a la vista desde la carretera principal.

9. Strathy Bay

Rivermouth with a good high tide right off the rocks at the eastern end of the bay. Well protected from westerly winds but also from westerly swell. Take the road to the graveyard, then walk over the dunes to the beach. Paddle out in the river or off the beach.

Une embouchure avec une bonne droite à marée haute sur les rochers à l'extrémité est de la baie. Bien protégé des vents d'ouest mais des swells d'Ouest aussi. Prenez la route jusqu'au cimetière et marchez sur les dunes. Ramez depuis la plage ou dans la rivière.

En esta desembocadura de rio sale una buena derecha al lado de unas rocas en marea alta en el este de la bahía. Bien protegido de los vientos del oeste así como de las marejadas del oeste. Dirigirse por la carretera al cementerio, y para llegar hasta la playa hay que caminar por unas dunas. Para salir, lo mejor es remar por el rio o por la playa.

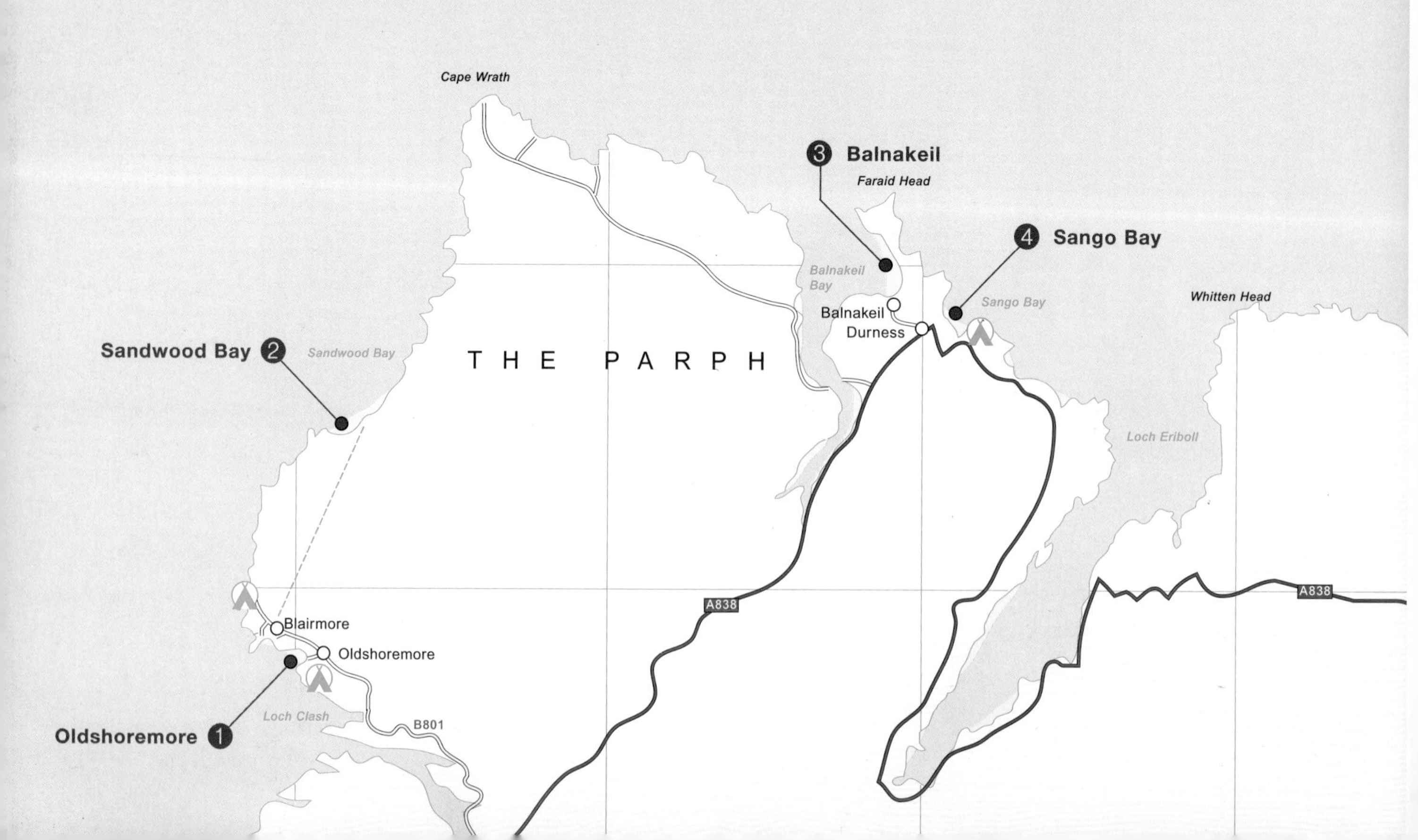

Sango Bay - *Photo: Alex Williams*

10. Melvich

Deserted bay with a river dominating the sandbar formations. Good lefts break best from mid to high tide. Park with consideration at the end of the access road to the house. The definition between public and private land appears uncertain. Sunbathing seals are common.

Une baie déserte avec une rivière qui influe sur la formation des bancs . De bonnes gauches cassent au mieux entre mi-marée et marée haute . Se garer avec précaution au bout de la route d'accés à la grosse maison . La définition entre le domaine public et privé n'a rien d'évident . On voit souvent des otaries qui se dorent la pillule .

Es una bahía desierta con un rio que influye en la formación de las barreras de arena. Las mejores izquierdas rompen de media a alta marea. Aparca cuidadosamente al final de la carretera de acceso a la casa. No se distingue muy bien entre propiedad pública y privada en la zona. Es frecuente ver a las focas tomando el sol.

11. Sandside Bay

A classic beach/reef setup. Sandside faces north. Lefthanders break into the bay from the harbour with occassional left and right bars on the beach. It works on an average north or big west swell, best at mid to high tide (the left gets rocky at low). It's within a stones throw of the reactor at Dounreay.

Une formation plage/Reef classique. Sandside est exposée au nord. Des gauches cassent dans la baie depuis le port avec des bancs pour droites et gauches de temps à autre. Ca marche par houle moyenne de nord ou un gros swell d'ouest, de préférence de mi-marée à marée haute (pas mal de cailloux sur la gauche à marée basse). Sandside Bay se situe à 18 Kms à l'ouest de Thurso, juste aprés le village de Reay, à portée de hallebarde du réacteur de Dounreay.

Una ola de playa arrecife constituida de forma clásica y orientada al norte. Las izquierdas rompen en la bahía a partir del puerto con algunas barras que rompen ocasionalmente en la playa tanto de derecha como de izquierda. Funciona con marejadas normales del norte así como las más grandes del oeste. Dentro del alcance de las piedras del reactor de Dounreay.

Sandside Bay / Dounreay - *Photo: Andy Bennetts*

8 Armadale Bay
9 Strathy Bay
Sandside Bay 11
10 Melvich
6 Torrisdale
7 Farr Bay
5 Kyle of Tongue
Armadale Bay
Strathy Bay
Melvich
Melvich Bay
Sandside Bay
Dounreay
Armadale
Strathy
Reay
Torrisdale Bay
Farr Bay
Farr
Bettyhill
Talmine
Melness
Kyle of Tongue
Coldbackie
A836
A897
B871
Helmsdale

Thurso & Orkneys

1. Brims Ness (Graveyards)

Brims Ness is Nordic for surf point and that's what it is! Whilst the long walk over the paddocks takes a bit of effort, especially in the cold, this point catches most of the swell in the area, and can be overhead when Thurso is flat. When seen from the road, size can be misleading. Turn right just after you see the silos and the waves are on the point 3 miles west of Thurso. Go down to the farm and park respectfully amongst the machinery and sheds; it's private property!

Brims Ness signifie Nordic comme spot de surf et c'est rien de le dire ! Alors que la longue marche à travers les enclos demande un petit effort, surtout quand ça pèle, ces trois spots peuvent choper le plus de houle dans les environs .puisque ça peut faire un bon mètre cinquante quand il n'y a rien à Thurso.Depuis la route, on se rend pas bien compte de la taille . Tournez à droite aprés avoir vu les silos et les vagues sur le spot à 5 Kms par la route . Descendez jusqu'aux bâtiments de la ferme et garez-vous soigneusement entre les machines et les hangars, c'est une propriété privée.

Brims Ness es nórdico como lugar de surfeo. Mientras el paseo a traves de los prados es un poco costoso, especialmente con frio, estos tres picos acaparan casi toda la marejada de la zona, y puede estar muy grande cuando en Thurso no hay casi nada. Al mirar desde la carretera, no se aprecia bien el tamaño. Gira a la derecha cuando veas las ensiladoras, y tendrás olas a lo largo de tres millas por la carretera de Thurso. Baja hasta las granjas y aparca entre los cobertizos y la maquinaria, cuidado, que es propiedad particular.

THE BOWL

As the name suggests, a bowly right breaking in shallow water. The swell comes out of deep water fast before unloading on the reef. Best on mid to high tide, on the push, up to 8ft.

Comme son nom l'indique, c'est une droite en bol qui casse dans peu d'eau. La houle arrive rapidement en eau profonde avant d'exploser sur le reef. Mieux de Mi-marée à marée haute, au montant, jusqu'à 2,5m.

Como el nombre indica, se trata de una derecha redonda que rompe en aguas poco profundas. La marejada sale de las aguas profundas para descargar contra el arrecife. Lo mejor sale de media marea a pleamar pudiendose alcanzar los tres metros.

Brims Bowl - *Photo: Andy Bennetts*

THE COVE

A similar set up to The Bowl, but not as fast. Located 50 yards down the point.

Ressemble au Bowl mais en moins rapide . A 50 m en bas du "point".

Una disposición parecida a la de la bola, pero no tan explosiva como ésta. Se encuentra a unos 50m debajo del pico.

THE LEFT / THE POINT

A classic lefthand point-break, rideable for 100 metres or more in the right conditions. Easily blown out.

Une gauche qui s'enroule parfaitement, jusqu'à 100 m ou plus avec les bonnes conditions. Ne supporte pas le vent.

Es el clásico pico que rompe de izquierdas, donde se puede ir en la ola hasta más de 100m con buenas condiciones (se desfasa fácilmente).

2. The Shit-Pipe

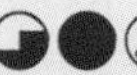

A N facing reef breaks right and left in a small swell directly adjacent to the main breakwater at Thurso harbour. Access is off the beach at low tide or the harbour wall at high. It's called the shit-pipe for obvious reasons and water quality can be marginal. You can see the seagulls congregating about 400 metres from the low water mark.

Par petite houle, ce reef exposé nord casse en gauche-droite. Directement relié à la jetée principale du port de Thurso. On y va depuis la plage à marée basse ou depuis le mur du port à marée haute. Ainsi nommé pour des raisons évidentes puisque l'eau y est détestable. On peut voir des hordes de mouettes à 400 mètres depuis le repère de marée basse.

Es un escollo orientado al norte, rompe tanto a la izquierda como a la derecha con poco mar. Está situado justo al lado del rompeolas del puerto de Thurso. El acceso es por la playa en marea baja y por el puerto en alta. El nombre de "zona de la mierda" le viene por razones obvias, así el agua es asquerosa. Se pueden ver gaviotas congregadas a unos 400 metros de la orilla del mar.

3. Thurso East

Long tubes break over a flat kelp covered reef. A slowish take-off and long barrel subside into a fast, smaller inside section. Can work at all stages of the tide, but considered best on an incoming from mid tide. An unsurfed bombora breaks in the middle of the bay, but when it's big enough to break, outside sets can close out from the shit- pipe to the castle, so even a brave paddle out in the river could be a terminally bad move. The water always looks brown here due to peat flowing out the mouth of the river.

De longs tubes qui cassent sur un reef plat couvert de kelp. Un take-off mollasson suivi d'une longue section tubulaire s'affaissent pour reprendre à l'inside sur un mur rapide mais plus petit. Ca peut marcher à toutes les marées mais l'idéal semble être sur une marée montante à partir de mi-marée, avec un vent de SE. Un récif au large, que personne ne surfe, peut casser au milieu de la baie mais quand c'est assez gros pour casser, les séries au large peuvent fermer de Shit-Pipe jusqu'au château; ainsi même une rame courageuse depuis la rivière peut mal se terminer. L'eau y est toujours marron à cause de la tourbe charriée par la rivière.

Sobre un arrecife cubierto de quelpo rompen unos tubos largos. Un suave take-off y una barra larga que te meten en una sección interior más pequeña y mucho más rápida. Funciona con todo tipo de mareas, aunque con media marea subiendo, viento en dirección sudeste, se dan las mejores olas. Una ola insurfeable rompe en el medio de la bahía, pero cuando está grande como para romper, las secciones de fuera te pueden cerrar desde la zona de desagües hasta el castillo, así que hasta una rápida salida remando por el rio puede ser la mala toma. El agua siempre está marrón por toda la turba que flota en la desembocadura del rio.

4. Murkle Point

Several rock formations lie between Thurso and Dunnet Bay. A beautiful left breaks off 'the spur' into the bay on a big swell.

Plusieurs groupes de rochers se trouvent entre Thurso et Dunnet Bay . Une superbe gauche casse à partir de "l'éperon" dans la baie avec une grande houle d'ouest ou de nord. Une petite route en sens unique y mène depuis le village de Murkle.

Se trata de una zona rocosa entre Thurso y Dunnet Bay.Con las fuertes marejadas del norte o del oeste sale una izquierda muy bonita que rompe desde "el espoleón" hacia la zona de la bahía. La forma de llegar es a traves de una carretera de un solo carril desde el pueblo de Murkle.

5. Nothing Left, Silos, The Pole

Three NE facing reefs provide thick left peaks in a N or big W swell. Rarely surfed as access is tricky...find them and surf them if you can.

Trois reefs exposés Nord qui donnent des gauches épaisses avec un swell de nord ou un bon swell d'ouest . Rarement surfé parce que difficilement accessible. Trouvez les et surfez les si vous pouvez.

Son tres picos de fondo rocoso que dan al norte, en los que sale una izquierda muy fuerte cuando la marejada es del norte o del oeste. Pocas veces se ha surfeado aquí ya que el camino tiene truco... así que trata de encontrarlo y cogete unas olas si puedes.

6. Dunnet Bay

Three mile long stretch of beach facing NW. Average sandbars along its length, and excellent rights on the reef at the northern end.

Une étendue de 5 Kms de plages exposées N-O. Bancs de sable moyens tout le long mais de super droites à l'extrémité nord.

Sobre una extensión de tres millas esta playa está orientada al noroeste. Cuenta con barreras de arena a lo largo, las derechas son muy buenas en su borde más septentrional.

7. Ham

Lefthand reef breaking into deep water around the harbour. From Ham you can see other reefs in the area.

Gauche de reef cassant en eau profonde autour du port. Depuis Ham, on peut voir d'autres reefs aux alentours.

Es un pico de izquierda que rompe sobre un fondo de roca y muy profundo cerca del puerto. Desde Ham puedes encontrar más picos en los alrededores.

8. Kirk o' Tang, Scarfskerry, The Haven

A series of reefs visible at various points from the main road.

Une série de reefs visibles à plusieurs endroits depuis la route principale.

Son una serie de picos de acantilado localizables a varias alturas de la carretera principal.

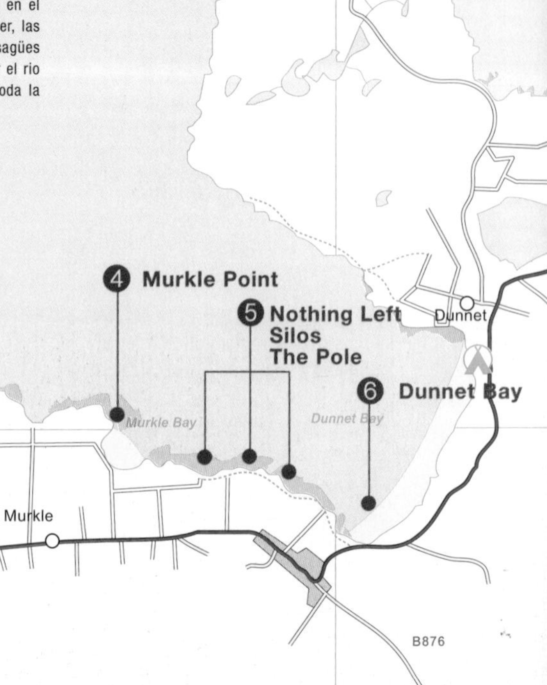

9. Tang Head

A mid to high tide reef facing NW. Turn off the A836 at May village.

Un reef qui marche de mi-marée à marée haute, exposée N-O. Tournez sur l'A836 au village de May.

Es un arrecife orientado al noroeste, las mejores olas se dan con media marea subiendo. Para llegar aquí has de salirte de la A836 a la altura de May.

10. Gills Bay

The most easterly spot on the Nth coast, Gills has lefts at the western end of the bay and rights at the Ness of Quoys. Park near the graveyard and walk over the fields.

L'endroit le plus à l'est sur la côte nord. Gills a une gauche à l'extrémité ouest de la baie et des droites à Ness of Quoys. Garez- vous prés du cimetière et marcher à travers les champs.

El spot más este de la costa Norte, Gilles tiene picos izquierdas al lado oeste de la bahía y derechas en la 'Ness de Quoys'. Aparca cerca del cementerio y cruza por el campo andando

11. The Orkney Islands

The Orkney Islands have steaming surf potential. Large portions of the coast consist of cliffs, but very often they flatten out creating rock reefs. There are also some sandy beaches. For large parts of the year, the islands are relentlessly battereded by wind.The tidal range is up to several metres. In general the surf seems to be at its best from mid to high tide coming in. There are a few local surfers and only on very rare occassions do surfers visiting Thurso take the ferry, but there are spots on most of the islands.The most popular is the Bay of Skail. Further north is Outshore Point which works when Skail is too small. It's a short but powerful reef break. North of here is Mar Wick a fast right. Needs a large swell. On the NE of Mainland, numerous lefts reefs catch N swell. Fisk Hellia is one of these. If the swell is clean it can break sectionless for more than 100 metres. There are many other spots which, if you go up there and meet local guys, you'll be introduced to.

Orkneys - *Photo: Jan Erik Jensen*

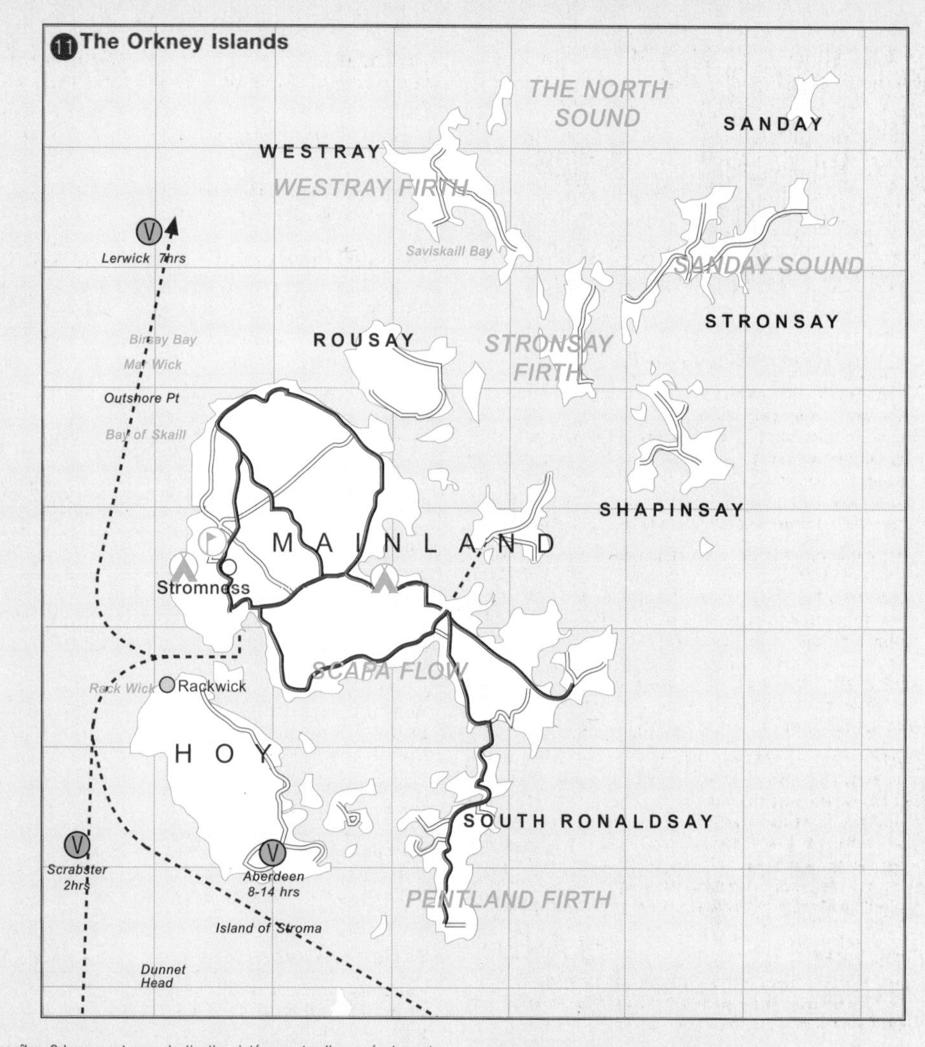

Les îles Orkney sont une destination intéressante. Il y a également quelques plages de sable. Pendant une grande partie de l'année, les îles sont sans arrêt battues par les vents. Le marnage va jusqu'à plusieurs mètres et les spots près des détroits sont les plus concernés. De façon générale, c'est plus gros et meilleur de la mi-marée à la marée haute. Il y a quelques surfeurs locaux et ce n'est qu'en de très rares occasions que les surfeurs prennent le ferry pour Thurso; il y a des spots sur la plupart des îles. Le plus réputé est celui de la baie de Skail sur la côte ouest. On peut trouver une droite et une gauche sur, respectivement, la partie nord et la partie sud. Plus loin, au nord, se trouve Outshore Point qui marche alors que Skail est trop petit.Ce reef break est court mais puissant. Juste au nord une droite rapide déroule, c'est Marwick. Il lui faut un plus gros swell que Skail. Sur la côte nord-est de l'île principale s'étendent de nombreuses gauches qui captent la houle du nord. La plupart d'entre-elles déferlent sur un récif de roches plates. C'est le cas pour Fisk Hellia. Si la houle est propre, cela peut dérouler sur plus de 100 m. Il y a beaucoup d'autres spots qui, si vous vous rendez là-bas et vous mêlez aux locaux, vous seront révélés.

La Isla de Orkney tiene un gran potencial de surf. Gran parte de la isla son acantilados, pero amenudo se llanan creando rompientes de reef. Tambien hay algunas playas de arena. Durante gran parte del año el viento pega en la Isla. La marea sube unos cuantos metros y suele cerrar afectando la mayoria de los spots. Se supone que la mejor marea para surfear es de marea media a alta, subiendo. Hay muy pocos surfers locales y en rara ocasión es visitado por surfers, que tienen que coger el ferry, pero hay spots por toda la isla. Es spot más popular es Bay of Skail en la costa oeste. Tanto en el Norte como en la zona Sur hay izquierdas y derechas. En la zona Norte hay un pico outshore que rompe cuando Skail esta muy pequeño. Es una rompiente corta pero con fuerza. Más al Norte se encuentra Marwick, una derecha rápida. Necesita más swell que Skail. Al N-O de la costa de Mainland se encuentran numerosas izquierdas que atraen el swell del N. La mayoria de los picos rompen sobre rocas planas. Uno de los picos es Fisk Hellia. Cuando el swell es claro pueden romper secciones de hasta 100 metros. Hay un montón de spots que para conocerlos debes hablar con los locales.

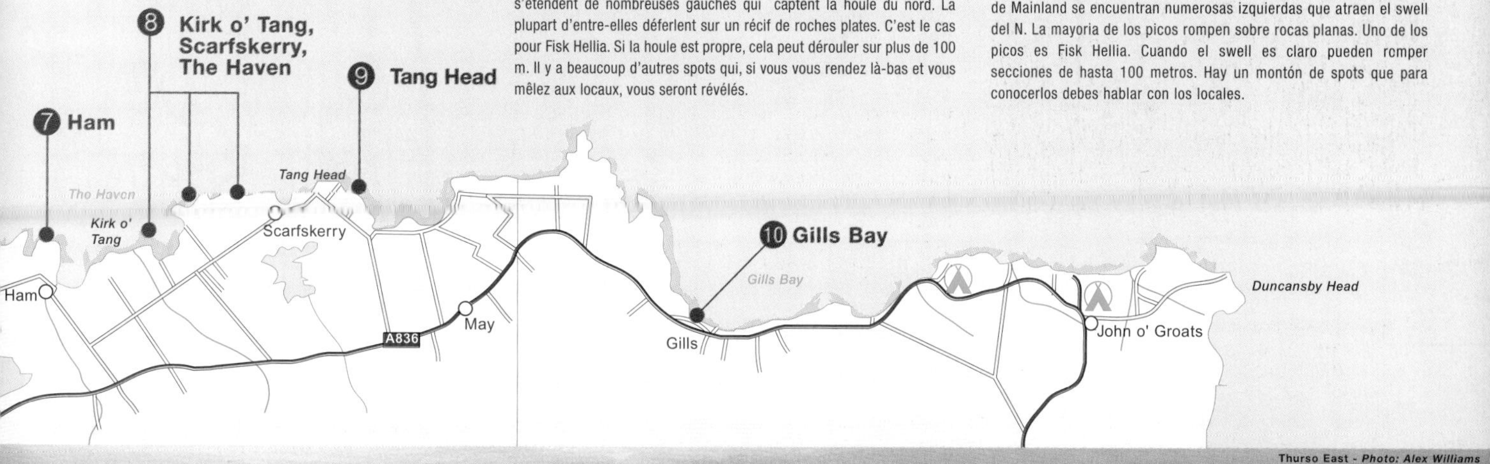

Thurso East - *Photo: Alex Williams*

Stüssy
DON'T BITE OFF SOMETHING THAT YOU CAN'T CHEW.... DON'T TRAIL BEHIND WHEN WE COME THRU!!
THE NEW STÜSSY U.K. CREW SEZ:
C-YA
Stüssy UK·LTD
071·224·2656

Banff evening glass - *Photo: Andy Bennetts*

east coast

The Nth Sea coasts of Scotland recieve roughly the same N, E and S swells and also share consistent offshore winds, though the various areas can have vastly different surf due to local orientation. Conditions are similar to those of the English and other North Sea coastlines and the water temperature is always 1-2 degrees cooler than the North Atlantic so don't forget your boots, and a wee dram for afters. Whilst not the ultimate surf travel destination, should you stray this way, you're sure to find surf, and a wave to yourself all day is very much a thing of the present. No guide to Europe would be complete without noting the lashing given to this coast by deep Lows in the long winter months and the dedication and hardiness of the locals, who surf in conditions as extreme as any. The folk here come from a long sea faring tradition, so its not surprising that the sport is gaining newcomers every year.

La côte Mer du nord de l'Ecosse reçoit grosso modo les mêmes houles de nord, d'est et de sud avec des vents off-shore consistants, bien que de nombreuses zones puissent avoir localement des orientations différentes. Les conditions sont similaires de celles des côtes anglaises et de la Mer du Nord, ça veut donc dire que vousn'oubliez pas vos chaussons et une bonne liqueur pour ensuite. Bien que ce ne soit pas une destinations idéale, si vous écumez aux alentours, vous trouverez certainement du surf et avoir une vague à soi reste encore tout à fait possible. Aucun guide en Europe ne pourrrait être complet sans parler du défilé des perturbations qui circulent incessamment pendant les longs mois d'hiver et du courage des locaux qui surfent dans des conditions extrêmes. Les gens ici ont une longue tradition maritime et il n'est donc pas surprenant que ce sport attire des passionés de la mer.

"A wave to yourself all day is very much a thing of the present..."

Pease Bay - Photo: Andy Bennetts

La costa Norte de Escocia recibe igualmente swell del N, E y S, y parte del offshore, aunque las distintas áreas pueden tener diferentes condiciones debido a su orientación. Las condiciones son similares a las de Inglaterra y la Costa Norte, donde el agua siempre esta 1 ó 2 grados más fria que en el Norte Atlantico, por lo tanto, no te olvides los escarpines, y un poco de calor para la salida. No olvidarse de este sitio para surfear. Aqui encontraras buen surf y buenas olas. Ningun guia de Europa estará completa sin conocer el azote dado en esta costa por las profundas bajas presiones en los largos meses de invierno y la dedicación y fuerza de voluntad de estos habitantes con tradición marinera. No es raro que este deporte atraiga nuevos turistas cada año.

Skirza Harbour - *Photo: Alex Williams*

Moray Firth

Brothers MacWatt - *ESP*

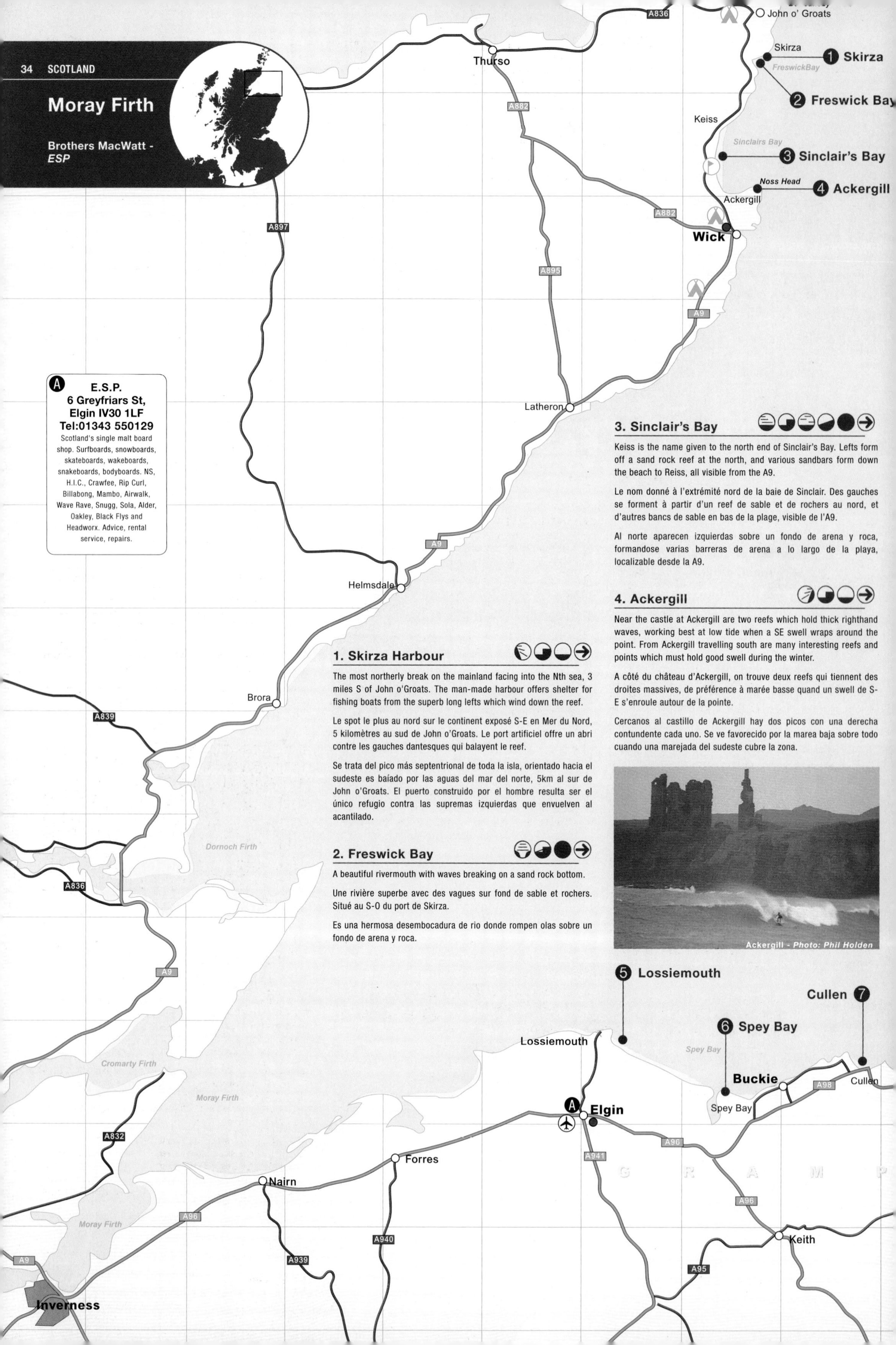

A E.S.P.
6 Greyfriars St,
Elgin IV30 1LF
Tel:01343 550129

Scotland's single malt board shop. Surfboards, snowboards, skateboards, wakeboards, snakeboards, bodyboards. NS, H.I.C., Crawfee, Rip Curl, Billabong, Mambo, Airwalk, Wave Rave, Snugg, Sola, Alder, Oakley, Black Flys and Headworx. Advice, rental service, repairs.

1. Skirza Harbour

The most northerly break on the mainland facing into the Nth sea, 3 miles S of John o'Groats. The man-made harbour offers shelter for fishing boats from the superb long lefts which wind down the reef.

Le spot le plus au nord sur le continent exposé S-E en Mer du Nord, 5 kilomètres au sud de John o'Groats. Le port artificiel offre un abri contre les gauches dantesques qui balayent le reef.

Se trata del pico más septentrional de toda la isla, orientado hacia el sudeste es baíado por las aguas del mar del norte, 5km al sur de John o'Groats. El puerto construido por el hombre resulta ser el único refugio contra las supremas izquierdas que envuelven al acantilado.

2. Freswick Bay

A beautiful rivermouth with waves breaking on a sand rock bottom.

Une rivière superbe avec des vagues sur fond de sable et rochers. Situé au S-O du port de Skirza.

Es una hermosa desembocadura de rio donde rompen olas sobre un fondo de arena y roca.

3. Sinclair's Bay

Keiss is the name given to the north end of Sinclair's Bay. Lefts form off a sand rock reef at the north, and various sandbars form down the beach to Reiss, all visible from the A9.

Le nom donné à l'extrémité nord de la baie de Sinclair. Des gauches se forment à partir d'un reef de sable et de rochers au nord, et d'autres bancs de sable en bas de la plage, visible de l'A9.

Al norte aparecen izquierdas sobre un fondo de arena y roca, formandose varias barreras de arena a lo largo de la playa, localizable desde la A9.

4. Ackergill

Near the castle at Ackergill are two reefs which hold thick righthand waves, working best at low tide when a SE swell wraps around the point. From Ackergill travelling south are many interesting reefs and points which must hold good swell during the winter.

A côté du château d'Ackergill, on trouve deux reefs qui tiennent des droites massives, de préférence à marée basse quand un swell de S-E s'enroule autour de la pointe.

Cercanos al castillo de Ackergill hay dos picos con una derecha contundente cada uno. Se ve favorecido por la marea baja sobre todo cuando una marejada del sudeste cubre la zona.

Ackergill - Photo: Phil Holden

5. Lossiemouth

The first real surf spot east of Inverness, an average but polluted beach that needs a big swell to work well.

Le premier vrai spot à l'est d' Inverness: une plage moyenne qui exige un gros swell pour bien marcher.

Es el primer lugar al este de Inverness donde realmente se puede surfear. Una playa corriente que necesita de una buena marejada para que la ola cuadre.

Lossiemouth - Photo: Roy Major

6. Spey Bay

Conditions similar to Lossiemouth.

Mêmes conditions que Lossiemouth.

Se dan las mismas condiciones que en Lossiemouth.

7. Cullen

Fast breaking lefts and rights visible from the A90

Des droites et gauches rapides visibles depuis l'A90.

Izquierdas y derechas muy rápidas, se pueden ver desde la A90.

8. Sandend Bay

Small village with harbour to the west of the bay. Beach with three main peaks, the most recognised being the left which breaks from the rocky point beside the harbour. Access is by paddling off the sewer pipe. The middle peak and the right at the far side of the bay work on a similar swell but at higher tide.

Petit village avec un port à l'ouest de la baie. Beach break avec trois pics principaux, le plus reconnaissable étant la gauche qui casse sur la pointe rocheuse à côté du port. L'accés se fait en marchant le long d'un tuyau d'égoûts et une petite rame jusqu'au pic . Le pic du milieu et celui de droite au bout de la baie marche avec la même houle mais avec une marée plus haute.

Un pequeño pueblo con puerto al oeste de la bahía en cuya playa rompen tres picos. El de más renombre es una izquierda que rompe en un fondo de roca muy cerca del puerto. El pico más al centro, así como la derecha en la zona más alejada de la bahía, funcionan con la misma marejada aunque con mareas más altas.

9. Byondie Bay

Beach west of the point, with shifting peaks over a sand bottom. A small reef at the N end sucks like f@*% in a big swell, water okay.

Plage à l'ouest du point, avec des pics sur fond de sable . Une petite droite de reef au nord suce par gros swell comme pas possible. Parking et accés corrects, l'eau moyenne.

La playa da al oeste del pico, el fondo de arena hace que sea un pico movedizo. En un pequeño arrecife a la derecha del extremo norte chupa rompe una ola con maretón.

10. Sunnyside Bay

A hard spot to find as it's signposted as a cliff walk, but if you get there you'll find a triangular reef in the middle of a sheltered bay. It's a bit of a mission, so few have surfed this spot. Same conditions as, Sandend. Water very good.

Petit village avec un port à l'ouest de la baie. Beach break avec trois pics principaux, le plus reconnaissable étant la gauche qui casse sur la pointe rocheuse à côté du port. L'accés se fait en marchant le long d'un tuyau d'égoûts et une petite rame jusqu'au pic. Le pic du milieu et celui de droite au bout de la baie marche avec la même houle mais avec une marée plus haute.

Un pequeño pueblo con puerto al oeste de la bahía en cuya playa rompen tres picos. El de más renombre es una izquierda que rompe en un fondo de roca muy cerca del puerto. La mejor forma de llegar allíes a través del paseo a lo largo de una tubería de deshechos, para luego entrar remando hasta el pico. El pico más al centro, así como la derecha en la zona más alejada de la bahía, funcionan con la misma marejada aunque con mareas más altas.

11. Banff

POINT

A good right point breaking over a triangular reef at the east end of Banff Links beach. Fickle but worth checking, as it can handle solid, hollow barrels at mid-high tide.

Une bonne droite qui casse sur un reef triangulaire à l'extrémité est de la plage de Banff Links. Capricieux mais vaut le détour parce que ça peut envoyer des tubes solides à mi-marée.

Una buena derecha rompe sobre un pico de arrecife triangular al extremo este de la playa Banff Links. No es consistente pero merece la pena echarle un vistazo, ya que nos puede sorprender con una ola tubera muy contundente de media a alta marea.

BANFF BEACH

You can find different peaks near Banff harbour to the west of the river. Hollow and powerful at low tide. Go down some metal stairs which also lead to the harbour. Water quality is bad here.

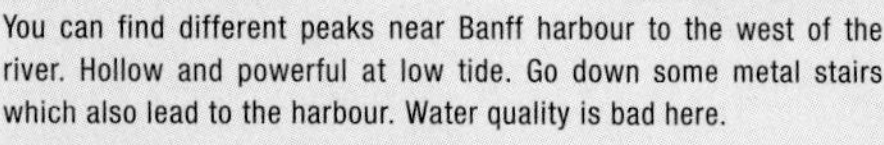

Différents pics prés du port de Banff, à l'ouest de la rivière . Un spot particulièrement creux et puissant à marée basse . Il faut descendre des échelles en fer depuis le mur qui fait route aussi dans le port . La qualité de l'eau laisse à désirer.

Se pueden encontrar varios picos a lo largo del puerto de Banff, al oeste del rio. Sale un tubo especialmente poderoso en marea baja. El acceso es por una escalera de hierro que desciende el espigón / carretera. Escasa calidad del agua.

12. Palmer Cove

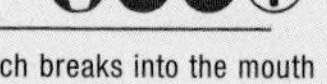

Long, fast and occasionally hollow right which breaks into the mouth of the river Devoran, best at dead low.

Une droite longue et rapide et parfois creuse casse dans l'embouchure de la rivière Deveran, le meilleur étant à l'étale basse. Marche à toutes les marées quand c'est gros.

Predomina una larga derecha ocasionalmente tubera que rompe en la desembocadura del rio Deveran, generalmente con poca fuerza.

13. Pennan

Small village perched on top of steep cliffs with a harbour. A variety of reef waves in the small bay work on various tides and swells. Easy paddle out through the harbour, even in a big swell. Beware of rips.

Petit village et port avec la plupart des maisons perchées au sommet de falaises abruptes. Une palette de vagues de reef marchent dans la baie avec des marées et des houles différentes. Rame fastoche depuis le port, même quand ça rentre épais. Attention aux courants.

Presenta una diversidad de olas de arrecife que salen según las distintas mareas y marejadas. Es factible salir remando a través del puerto, incluso con maretón.

14. Wisemans

A short heavy left which breaks beside Sandhaven harbour. A hollow, chucking peak and barrel section before the wave peels onto the inside "stone zone". Breaks on a solid north swell. No place for faint hearts. Water quality is poor.

Une droite courte et craignos qui à casse à côté du port de Sandhaven. Un pic creux qui jette au tube avant d'arriver à l'inside appelée la "zone cailloux". Par bon swell de nord, pour les téméraires seulement; L'eau est pas terrible.

Se trata de una corta pero contundente izquierda que rompe cerca del puerto de Sandhaven. El pico levanta la ola en forma de tubo hasta llegar a la zona de rocas más al interior. Rompe con la marejada del norte.

15. Phingask

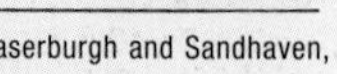

A long peeling left breaking between Fraserburgh and Sandhaven, in the same rocky bay as West Point.

Une longue droite entre Fraserburgh et Sandhaven, dans la même baie rocheuse que West Point.

Es una larga izquierda que rompe entre Fraserburgh y Sandhaven, situada en la misma bah´a que West point.

16. West Point

Two righthand point waves which break on the outskirts of town, west of Fraserburgh. A local fish factory discharges waste nearby so water quality is fishy. A flock of seagulls marks the spot.

Deux droites qui cassent sur les abords de la ville, à l'ouest de Fraserburgh . Une usine de poissons locale rejete ses déchets dans l'eau à côté. Une horde de mouettes situe le spot.

Dos picos con olas de derecha rompen en las afueras del pueblo, al oeste de Fraserburgh, una cofradía de pescadores arroja sus desperdicios en la zona , por lo que el agua de los alrededores huele a pescado, una bandada de gaviotas marcan dicha zona.

Fraserburgh Point - Photo: Andy Bennetts

17. Fraserburgh

Locally known as the "Broch", Fraserburgh is home to many of Scotland's best surfers with a hard core crew dating back to the seventies. The Point, beside the river produces good lefts in a N swell over a rock and sand bottom. The beach east of town is home to various quality waves; the town end faces east, while the eastern end (known as Philorth) faces N and picks up any N swell. It also works in massive southerlies, when the East coast is blown out.

Bien que Thurso soit connu pour avoir la vague la plus spectaculaire d' Ecosse, Fraserburgh abrite nombre des meilleurs surfers écossais avec une équipe de durs des années soixante-dix. Localement, la ville s'appelle "Broch" et on voit aussi de bons spots sur la plage à l'est de la ville.

A pesar de que sea popularmente la ola de Thurso la más espectacular de toda esta zona, Fraserburgh es la localidad de donde han salido muchos de los mejores surfistas escoceses, y ha existido un gran núcleo de surfistas desde los años setenta. El nombre autóctono del pueblo es el "Broch", y en la playa al este del pueblo se dan varios tipos de olas.

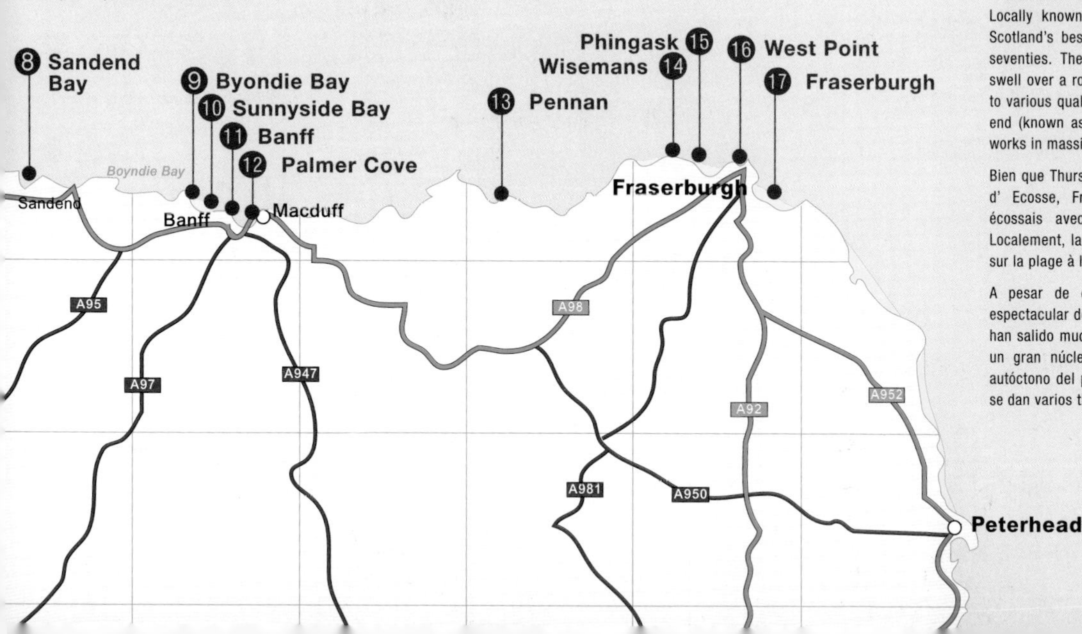

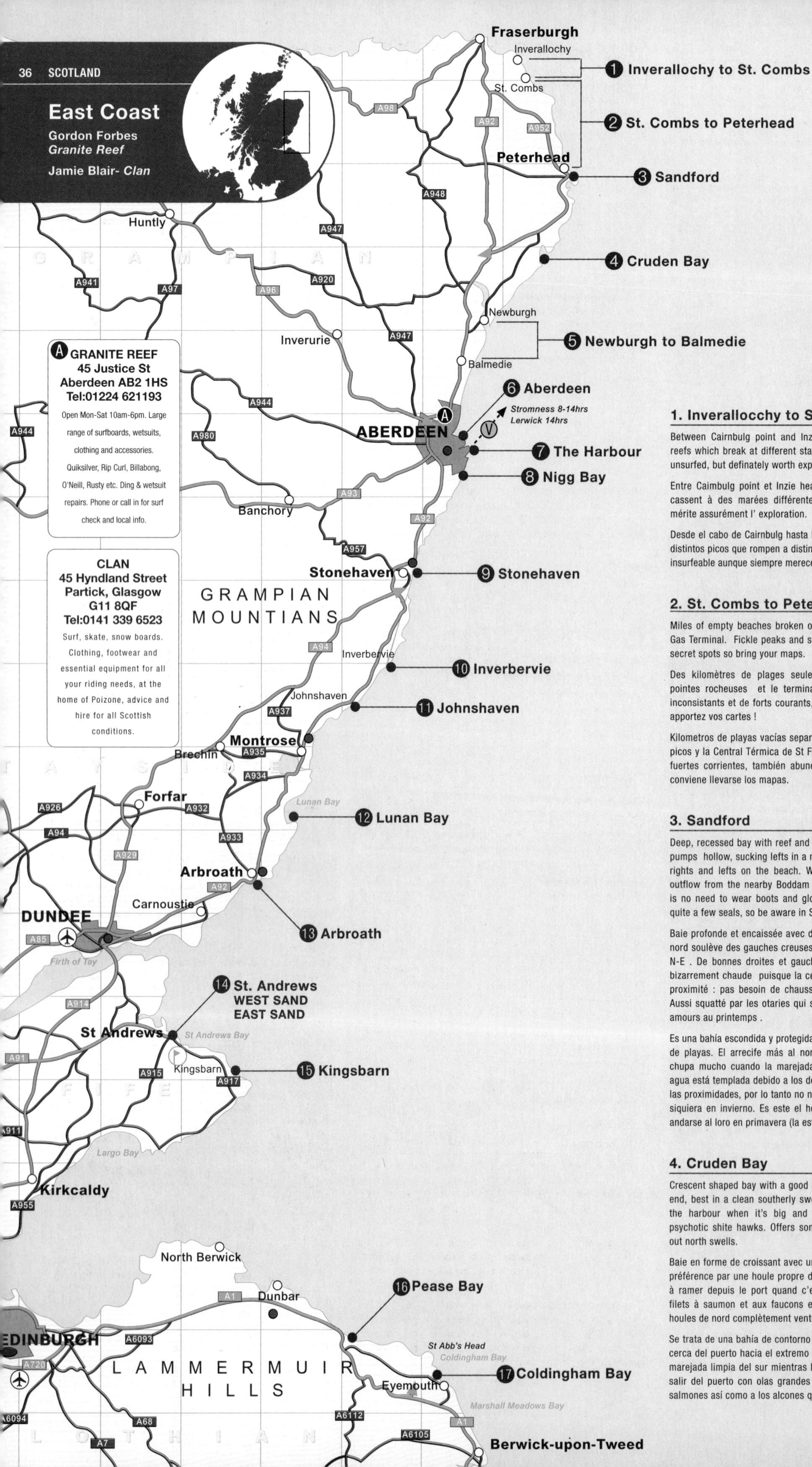

1. Inverallocchy to St Combs

Between Cairnbulg point and Inzie head the coast is littered with reefs which break at different stages of the tide. The area is largely unsurfed, but definately worth exploring.

Entre Caimbulg point et Inzie head, la côte est gavée de reefs qui cassent à des marées différentes. La zone est peu surfée, mais mérite assurément l' exploration.

Desde el cabo de Cairnbulg hasta Inzie la costa se halla salpicada por distintos picos que rompen a distintas mareas, la zona es mayormente insurfeable aunque siempre merecerá la pena echarle un vistazo.

2. St. Combs to Peterhead

Miles of empty beaches broken only by a few points and St Fergus Gas Terminal. Fickle peaks and strong currents, but there are a few secret spots so bring your maps.

Des kilomètres de plages seulement interrompues par certaines pointes rocheuses et le terminal de gaz de St-Fergus. Des pics inconsistants et de forts courants, mais il y a des secret spots alors apportez vos cartes !

Kilometros de playas vacías separadas únicamente por unos cuantos picos y la Central Térmica de St Fergus. Los picos son móviles y hay fuertes corrientes, también abundan los picos secretos por lo que conviene llevarse los mapas.

3. Sandford

Deep, recessed bay with reef and beach peaks. The reef to the north pumps hollow, sucking lefts in a north or north east swell. Also good rights and lefts on the beach. Water is suspiciously warm due to outflow from the nearby Boddam power station, consequently there is no need to wear boots and gloves even in winter! Also home to quite a few seals, so be aware in Spring (mating season).

Baie profonde et encaissée avec des plages et des reefs . Le reef au nord soulève des gauches creuses qui sucent bien par houle de nord N-E . De bonnes droites et gauches aussi sur la plage . L'eau est bizarrement chaude puisque la centrale électrique de Boddam est à proximité : pas besoin de chaussons ni de gants même en hiver . Aussi squatté par les otaries qui sont trés curieuses à la saison des amours au printemps .

Es una bahía escondida y protegida con picos de acantilados así como de playas. El arrecife más al norte saca una izquierda tubera que chupa mucho cuando la marejada es del N o NO. Curiosamente el agua está templada debido a los desagües de una central electrica en las proximidades, por lo tanto no necesitarás escarpines ni guantes ni siquiera en invierno. Es este el hogar de bastantes locales, así que andarse al loro en primavera (la estación de la copulación).

4. Cruden Bay

Crescent shaped bay with a good peak near the harbour at the north end, best in a clean southerly swell at lower tides. Paddle out from the harbour when it's big and watch out for salmon nets and psychotic shite hawks. Offers some protection from massive blown out north swells.

Baie en forme de croissant avec un bon pic prés du port au nord , de préférence par une houle propre de sud à marée basse. Commencez à ramer depuis le port quand c'est gros tout en faisant gaffe aux filets à saumon et aux faucons excités . Quelque peu protégé des houles de nord complètement ventées.

Se trata de una bahía de contorno ladeado en la que destaca un pico cerca del puerto hacia el extremo norte, las mejores olas se dan con marejada limpia del sur mientras la marea está baja. Se recomienda salir del puerto con olas grandes siempre atentos a las redes para salmones así como a los alcones que por allí merodean.

5. Newburgh to Balmedie

Average stretch of beach picking up the same swell as Aberdeen, not surfed often. Take care for salmon nets along this stretch of coast... longshore drift is common.

Morceau de plage correct qui chope le même swell qu'Aberdeen, mais moins souvent surfé. Attention aux filets à saumon qui peuvent dériver, ça arrive !

Es una extensión playera típica que se aprovecha de las mismas condiciones que Aberdeen, aunque no se surfee normalmente. Tener cuidado con las redes de salmones que abundan por estas costas.

6. Aberdeen

From Footdee, the beach runs north for two miles to the mouth of the river Don. Groins run the entire length, and hold good sandbars, producing clean, hollow waves. Donmouth goes off with excellent rights. Parking the length of the foreshore. Beware the Chief, our local longboarder. Water quality isn't great, but o.k.

Depuis Footdee, la plage s'étend au nord sur 3 bornes jusqu'à l'embouchure du Don. La construction d'épi s'étire sur toute la longueur et renferme de bons bancs sur lesquels cassent des vagues propres et creuses. Y'a une droite d'enfer à l'embouchure. Se garer directement sur la plage. Faites gaffe au chef, le longboarder local. L'eau n'est pas transcendante mais correcte.

Las urbanizaciones corren paralelas a lo largo de la playa, lo que supone una buena barrera para la arena, produciendose una ola tubera y muy limpia. La desembocadura del Don se caracteriza por unas buenas derechas. Hay parking a todo lo largo de la playa. Al loro con Chief, el longboarder de la zona. La calidad del agua no es la mejor pero está normal.

Footdee Beach - *Photo: Granite Reef*

7. The Harbour

Rarely surfed, perfect barreling right, sketchy due to ridiculous currents. In a huge swell, waves break inside the breakwater, but hazards include the Shetland ferry which sails through the lineup and hassly harbour police. Water quality is pretty gnarly.

Rarement surfé alors que c'est une droite tubulaire et parfaite mais délicate aussi à cause de courants démentiels . Quand ça rentre énorme, les vagues cassent à l'intérieur de la jetée . Attention au ferry des Shetland qui navigue sur le pic et aux garde-côtes qui font chier .L'eau est complètement gerbique.

Raramente surfeable, se trata de una barra de derecha aunque bastante fofa debido a las corrientes que allí se forman. Con grandes marejadas las olas llegan a romper dentro del espigón, existe el riesgo de que el ferry de Shetland pase por el mismo pico, y también hay que andarse al loro con la bulliciosa policia del puerto. La calidad del agua es asquerosa.

8. Nigg bay

Probably the best spot in the Grampian area, with hollow rights and killer lefts. Can be good at higher tides in big swells. Deep, hollow barrels to be had when conditions are right. The car park in the bay is often frequented by travellers (lock your car!), alternatively park on the grass hill to the south of the bay. Water quality unfortunately not good, especially after an east wind.

Probablement le meilleur spot dans la région de Grampian, avec des droites creuses et des gauches de folie. Peut bien fonctionner à des marées plus hautes mais avec de la taille. Des tuyaux profonds à choper quand les conditions sont optimales. Le parking est fréquemment visité par des voyageurs, il faut donc tout fermer à clé, ou garez-vous sur l'herbe sur la colline au sud de la baie. L'eau y est malheureusement polluée, surtout par vent d'est.

Probablemente sea el mejor sitio de toda la zona de Grampian, salen derechas tuberas así como una mortal izquierda, aprovechando de baja a media marea. Cuando las condiciones son buenas, puede tener una sección tubera muy profunda. El parking de coches de la zona suele ser frecuentado por numerosos viajantes, así que asegurate de cerrar bien tu coche, hay un parking alternativo en una loma al sur de la bahía. La calidad del agua no es buena desafortunadamente, especialmente cuando sopla viento del este.

Nigg Bay - *Photo: Granite Reef*

9. Stonehaven

Sand and pebble beach with a good right reef at the south end. Small river mouth makes for an easy paddle out. Works in S and larger N swells. Good spot to check when Aberdeen is blown out.

Plage de sable et de galets avec une bonne droite de reef au sud. Une petite rivière peut vous aider à passer la barre. Marche par houle de sud ou grosse houle de nord. A checker quand Aberden est trop venté.

Playa de arena y guijarros con un buen pico de derecha en su extremo sur. La desembocadura de un pequeño rio hace que sea facil salir del pico. Funciona con marejadas del sur así como con las del norte cuando son fuertes.

10. Inverbervie

Pebble beach that normally breaks left off the point near the car park, best on a clean south swell.

Plage de galet qui casse normalement en gauche sur la pointe à côté du parking, de préference par houle de sud sans vent.

Playa de guijarros donde normalmente rompe una izquierda en un pico cercano al parking de coches. Mejor cojerlo con marejada limpia del sur.

11. Johnshaven

Fickle exposed reef break needs a big, clean swell to work. Many other reef and point breaks in this area

Vague de reef rare qui exige un swell gros et propre. Plein d'autres reefs et point breaks dans le coin.

Son unos picos inconsistentes que necesitan de una enorme y limpia marejada, para que salgan buenas olas. Además también hay otros cuantos picos de arrecife donde rompe en esta zona.

12. Lunan Bay

Beautiful bay sheltered by high cliffs at both ends with a river mouth and big dunes giving it an isolated feel. Three main spots: North end has good lefts off the point (beware of rips). Shifty rights and lefts break in the middle of the bay, and the south end also gets waves, though it's often messy. It can be classic surfing with friends, watching the sun set behind the ruins of Red Castle. Lunan is a small village. Drive slowly and park respectfully behind the dunes.

Superbe baie protégée par de hautes falaises aux extrémités avec une embouchure et des dunes massives au milieu où on se sent isolé. Trois spots principaux: La partie nord a des bonnes gauches sur le point mais attention au jus. Des gauches et droites sont au milieu de la baie; la partie sud reçoit aussi quelques vagues mais c'est souvent brouillon. On peut vraiment s'y éclater avec des potes, en regardant le coucher de soleil sur les ruines du Red Castle.

Se trata de una hermosa bahía rodeada de altas colinas por sus extremos, la desembocadura de un rio así como sus grandes dunas hacen que parezca un lugar aislado. Hay tres zonas importantes: La más al norte es un pico del que salen buenas izquierdas. Suaves picos rompen en el medio de la bahía, y en la zona más al sur también salen olas, aunque normalmente suela estar desordenado.

13. Arbroath

3 km Beach break known as Elliot, located on the southern outskirts of town, best on an incoming to high tide. The rock point North of the bay works well in northerly swells, but shallow rocks mean experienced surfers only! Elliot is located directly in front of the Elliot caravan park.

3kms de beachbreak qu'on appelle Elliot, situé dans la banlieue sud de la ville, mieux à marée montante jusqu'à marée haute . La pointe rocheuse au nord de la baie marche bien par houle de nord, mais vu le peu de fond, vous avez intérêt à assurer!

Situada en las afueras hacia el sur del pueblo, las mejores olas rompen mientras la marea sube hasta en pleamar. Un pico de roca al norte de la bahía cuadra bien con marejadas del norte, pero sus rocas poco profundas hacen que este pico esté reservado para los surfistas más experimentados.

14. St Andrews

WEST SANDS

Shifty beach peaks, better at low-mid tide. The central peak is usually better and water quality is o.k.

Des pics changeants, mieux de marée basse à mi-marée. Le pic du milieu est souvent le meilleur où la qualité de l'eau est satisfaisante .

Playas con picos móviles, es mejor de media marea a alta. El pico del medio es generalmente el mejor y la calidad del agua es buena.

EAST SANDS

Good peaks break off the harbour wall. Get out on the rip. Usually closes out on outgoing tide. Town sewage affects water quality.

De bonnes droites et de bonnes gauches prés de la jetée du port . Sortir avec le courant, en général ça ferme à marée descendante . Les égoûts de la ville sont visibles.

Salen buenas derechas y las izquierdas rompen directamente contra la pared del puerto. Cuidado con la corriente. Los desechos del pueblo afectan a la calidad del agua.

15. Kingsbarns

Reef and beach breaks, working only in a big swell. Hasn't been surfed much, but worth checking out.

Du reef et du beach break qui marche uniquement par gros swell. Pas beaucoup surfé mais mérite le coup d'oeil.

Es una zona de playa y arrecife, funciona unicamente con grandes marejadas. No es un sitio donde se surfee a menudo, pero merece la pena echarle un vistazo.

Gullane Point, near North Berwick - *Photo: Andy Bennetts*

16. Pease Bay

Classic beach faces due north and nestles at the foot of high cliffs. The most consistent and accessible bay for miles, although it can get blown out easily. Under these conditions the southern end cleans up faster and is generally better. Facilities include holiday caravans, parking, loos and a shop. There are other spots nearby.

Plage renommée faisant face au nord et située au pied de hautes falaises. La baie la plus consistente et la plus accessible sur des kilomètres. "S'il y a une vague quelque part, c'est sûrement à Pease Bay" bien que ça ne supporte pas bien le vent. Dans ce cas, la partie sud redevient lisse plus rapidement tout en étant meilleure. Il reste d'autres spots à découvrir dans les alentours.

La clásica playa orientada al norte y situada al pie de unas altas colinas. Se trata de la más accesible y consistente bahía de los alrededores. "Si existe un sitio donde pillar una ola, ese lugar es Pease Bay" a pesar de que se pueda fastidiar fácilmente. Bajo estas condiciones la zona mís al sur se arregla antes con lo que generalmente es mejor. Existen más picos por descubrir en la zona.

Pease Bay - *Photo: Andy Bennetts*

17. Coldingham Bay

Faces due east, and is an alternative to Pease, with the advantage of two small hotel/pubs but no campsite.

Exposé à l'est, c'est une alternative à Pease, avec l'avantage d'avoir deux petits hôtels/Pubs mais pas de camping .

Orientada hacia el este, es una alternativa a la zona de Pease, con la ventaja de contar con dos pequeños hotel/pubs aunque no dispone de camping.

ENGLAND

ENGLAND

Despite its island status, English people are of mixed stock. The earliest immigrants were often refugees from tribal warfare and unrest (the Belgic tribesmen escaping from Imperial Rome, the Romans themselves, the Angles, Saxons, Jutes, Danes and Normans, all in turn brought genetic variety. Under Roman rule the population of the British Isles numbered about half a million. By the time of the Doomsday Census (1086) it had doubled and over the next 900 years it became, and remains one of the most densely populated countries in the world.

Despite physical proximity to Europe, England's people have maintained a strong sense of cultural separation in the past. The surrounding seas have served the English well, protecting them from casual invasion, providing them with food and trade, and being the starting point for their exploration and exploitation of far-flung lands. The British Empire was, for over 200 years, the most powerful in the world and it wasn't until the end of the WW2 that it began to disintergrate. In 1947 India and Pakistan became independent and by 1970 nearly every other commonwealth country had done the same.

Today it retains its place amongst the world's leading nations. English literature, music, fashion and other cultural influences continue to permeate global affairs, and her colonial history has created one of the world's most multi-cultural societies. Deeper integration with Europe should increase its cosmopolitan nature.

ANGLETERRE.

Malgré son statut insulaire, l' Anglais a des origines diverses. I es premiers immigrants furent souvent des réfugiés des guerres tribales et des invasions, comme les Belgres échappant à l'Empire romain, les Romains eux-mêmes, les Angles, les Saxons, les Jutes, les Danois et les Normands qui contribuèrent done à cette variété génétique des Anglais. Sous i'empire romain, on comptait environ un demi-million d'habitants. Au recensement de 1086, cette population avait doublé et en 900 ans, elle devint une des nations les plus importantes du monde.

Malgré ls poximité physique avec i'Europe, les Anglais ont toujours maintenu dans le passé un sentiment vif de différenciation culturelle. Les mers environmentes ont bien serve en les protégeant des invaions, en leur apportant i'approvisionement et le commerce, en étant le point d'anerage de leurs explorations et eploitations des pays lointains. L'Empire britannique fut pour plus de 200 ans le plus puissant au monde en ne se désagrégeant qu'à partir de la deuzième guerre mondiale. En 1947, L'Inde et le Pakistan devinrent indépendant mondiale. En 1947, l'Inde et le Pakistan devinrent independant et en 1970, presque tous les pays de la Couronne britannique s'étaient émancipés.

Aujourd'hui, i'Angleterre garde sa place parmi les nations en pointe. Sa littérature, sa musique, sa mode et d'autres influences culturelles continuent à pénétrer les cultures du monde, son héritage colonial lui laissant une des sociétés multi-raciales les plus colorées. L'intégration croissante avec l'Europe devrait accroitre cette touche cosmopolitaine.

ENGLAND

Inglaterra Pese a tratarse de una isla, la población inglesa es de variada procedencia. Los primeros en llegar fueron refugiados de guerras tribales (tribus Belgas huyendo del Imperio Romano, los Anglos, los Sajones, los Jutos, Daneses y Normandos) dando una extraordinaria variedad genética. En la época del dominio romano, la isla estaba habitada por medio millón de personas. En 1086 se había duplicado la población y en los 900 años posteriores llegaría a ser uno de los paises más densamente poblados del planeta.

Pese a su proximidad con el continente, los ingleses han mantenido un poderosa sentido de separación cultural. El carácter insular ha permitido a los ingleses protegerse de una eventual invasión, dedicarse al comercio y ser la base de sus exploraciones y colonización de tierras lejanas. Durante más de 200 años el Imperio Britanico fue el más poderoso y sólo comenzó a desintegrarse tras la II G.M. En 1947 India y Pakistán consiguieron su independencia, y para 1970 prácticamente todos los paises de la Commonwealth habian hecho lo mismo.

En la actualidad sigue una de las naciones lideres. Su literatura, música, moda y otras influencias culturales alcanzan a todo el mundo, y su historia colonial ha contribuido a crear una sociedad multicultural. Una mayor integración con Eúropa aumentará este caracter cosmopolita.

Capital:	London
Population:	5,090,000
Area:	32,714km²
Time:	GMT (summer GMT+1)
Language:	English

"Her colonial history has created one of the world's most multi-cultural societies"

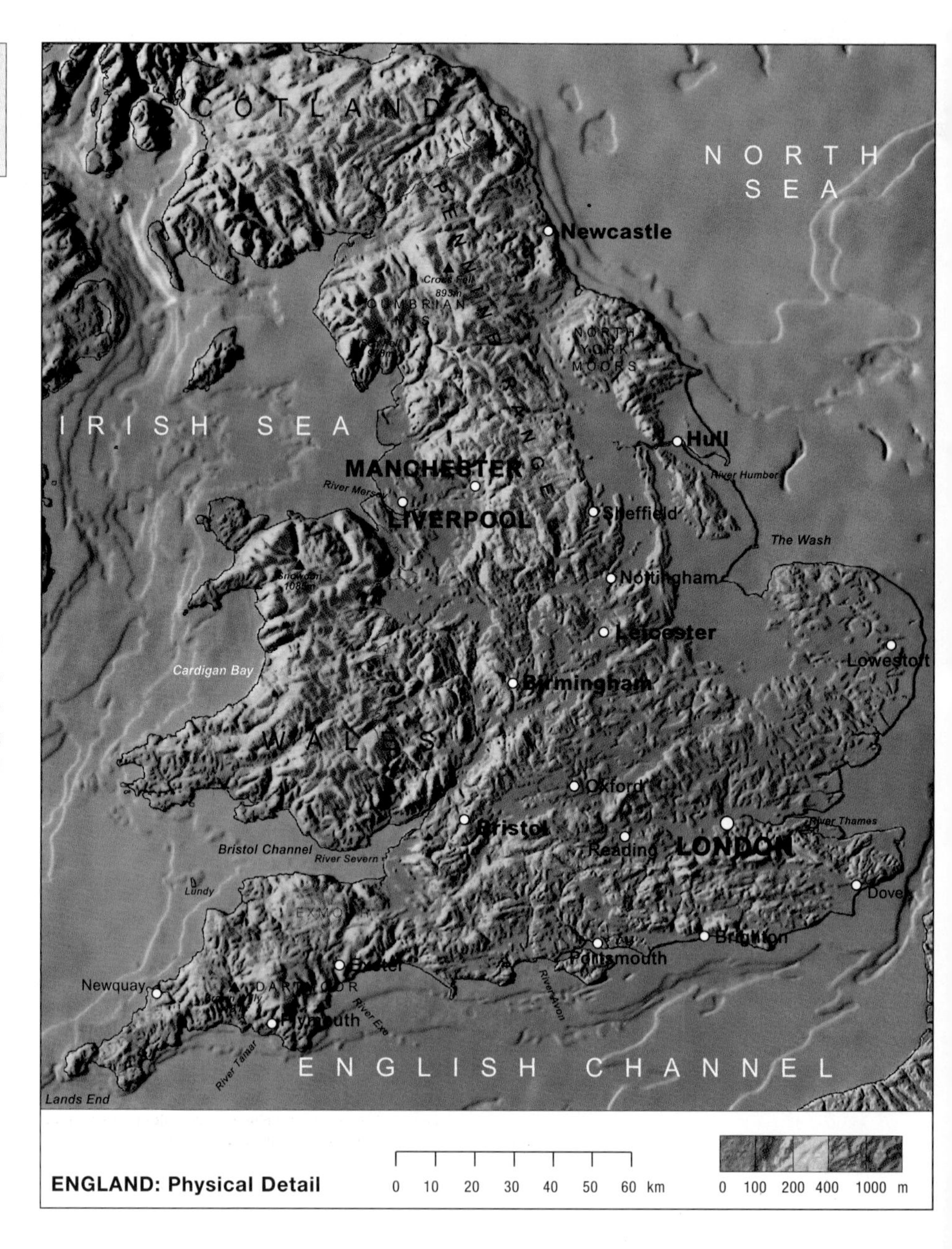

ENGLAND: Physical Detail

Rod Sumpter - *Photo: John Sumpter*

Porthleven - *Photo: Simon McComb*

English Surfing Federation
Neil Harris
23 Edgcumbe Gardens, Newquay, Cornwall, TR7 2QD
(44) 0637 875 853

Surf History

Like many other countries, surfing in England had its birth in the surf lifesaving movement, with paddle-skis first being ridden in 1959 and in 1960 the first crude wooden mals ('logs") appeared. The first foam and fibreglass boards were brought in and ridden by four Aussie lifeguards (Bob Head, Ian Tiley, John Campbell and Warren Mitchell) in spring of1962. Watergate and the Newquay town beaches were the most ridden then. As Doug Wilson says in his book, You Should Have Been Here Yesterday, " ...it was around this time that a clean-cut, surf-riding band called the Beach boys were taking surf to the suburbs. Suddenly, every city kid without a wave to his name tuned into a youth cult which stormed out of the west coast and rushed around the world. A new era had arrived, flower power was around the corner, and being a surfer meant plugging into a happening of indescribable fun."

By 1965 Bllbo had started life, quickly growing into a big part of the national and European surf scene, which was also growing fast. Since then, continual contact with foreign surfers, films, and magazines have kept the vibe strong. New spots were discovered and standards improved. By the mid 70s there were large numbers of hard core surfers in Cornwall and the emerging areas of Devon and Wales. Today there are around fifty thousand surfers in the U.K. and that numbrer is growing daily.

Surf and Weather

No part of England is more than 80 miles from its 7,000 miles of coastline, consequently the English are an instinctively seafaring nation. It's weather remains predictable only by its unpredictability and surfing conditions naturally share this changeability, making knowledge of weather forecasting that much more necessary.

The coast can be divided into three main surfing regions, all of which get more swell in autumn, winter and spring than in summer.

L'Historique

Comme beaucoup d'autres pays, le surf a commencé en Angleterre avec les maître-nageurs, avec les premiers paddle-skis surfés pour la première fois en 1959. En 1960, les premiers malibus basiques en bois (les troncs) apparurent. La première mousse et fibre de verre furent apportées par 4 maître-nageurs australiens (Bob Head, Ian Tiley, John Campbell et Warren Mitchell) au pritemps 1962. Watergate et les environs de Newquay étaient alors les plus surfés. Comme Doug Wilson le précise dans son bouquin, Il fallait être là hier, " c'était à ce moment qu'un groupe de surfers, bien coiffés, nommés les Beach Boys amenèrent le surf da¨ns les banlieues. Tout d'un coup, chaque gamin de la ville sans une vague à son nom se mit sur la fréquence de ce jeune culte qui déferlèrent sur la côte ouest et se propagèrent à travers le monde. Une nouvelle ère était née, l'époque hippie était au coin de la rue, être un surfer signifiait qu'on pouvait se brancher sur un mouvement de fun indescriptible."

Vers 1965, Bilbo était née, se développant rapidement comme un incontournable de la scène nationale et internationale, qui elle aussi se transformait rapidement. Depuis lors, des contacts continuels avec des surfers, des films et des magazines étrangers ont gardé l'ambiance aussi vivante. De nouveaux spots furent découverts et le niveau s'élevait. Au milieu des années 70, on trouvait plien de surfers purs et durs dans le Cornwall et les endroits qui montaient comme le Devon et le Pays de Galles. Aujourd'hui, on dénombre environ 50,000 surfers au Royaume-Uni et ce chiffre augmente continuellement.

Le Surf et le Climat

Aucun endroit en Angleterre n'est à plus de 120 kilomètres des 10,000 kms de côtes, c'est pourquoi les anglais ont toujours un attrait instinctif vers la mer. La seule chose prévisible sur son climat est son imprévisibilité, les conditions de surf partagent donc cette versatilité, ce qui rend la connaissance de la météorologie marine d'autant plus essentielle.

La côte a été divisée en 3 régions principales pour surfer, qui prennent toutes le moins de houle en été.

Surf and Weather

Historia del surf Como en muchos otros países, el origen del surf inglés está en los socorristas y las tablas que usaban para remar. En los años 1959 y 1960 aparecieron los primeros tablones de madera, pero no fue hasta la primavera de 1962 cuando aparecieron cuatro socorristas australianos (Bob Head, Ian Tiley, John Campbell y Warren Mitchell) surfeando en tablas de foam y libra de vidrio. Las playas de Watergate y Newquay eran las mas frecuentadas. Como cuenta Doug Wilson en su libro "Tenías que haber estado aquí ayer": en esta época los Beach Boys estaban acereando el surf a las ciudades, de un modo espontáneo, una forma de vida procedente de la costa oeste norteamericana se habia propagado por todo el mundo, anticipando la llegada de una nueva era en la que ser surfer significaba poder disfrutar de sensaciones difíciles de describir.

En 1965 nació creciendo rápidamente y alcanzando una importante cuota del mercado nacional y del europeo, ambos en fuerte expansión. Desde entonces, el contacto con surfers extranjeros, las revistas y las peliculas, junto con el descubrimiento de nuevos picos y la mejora del nivel han mantenido vivo el fenómeno. A mediados de los setenta, habia ya un gran número de practicantes en Cornwall y en las áreas emergentes de Devon y Gales. En la actualidad hay 50,000 surfers en Gran Bretaña y su número aumenta a diario.

Surf y Climatologia

Ningún lugar de Inglaterra dista más de 120kms de sus más de 10,000kms de costa, Consecuentemente los ingleses están habituados a ir de surfari. Lo único predecible del clima es que es imprevisible, y lo mismo ocurre con las condiciones surferas que son de gran variabilidad. Pero en cualquier caso es fundamental un buen conocimiento de los partes meteorológicos.

La costa se subdivide en tres regiones principales, cualquiera de ellas recibe más mar en otoño, invierno y primavera, que en verano.

east coast

Gabriel Davies

Tynemouth, Day of the British Cup - *Photo: Gabriel Davies*

Yorkshire envelope - *Photo: The Gill*

East Runton with traditional Norfolk crab boats - *Photo: Neil Watson*

"Blessed with many reef breaks and quality beaches, there are still miles of unexplored coastline...t"

The NE coast is a wild destination. Surfing started here in the mid 60's and by the 80's the surfing population was thriving. Pockets of local surfers exist in each coastal town, with surf shops in all the key locations (Seahouses, Tynemouth, South Shields, Hartlepool, Saltburn, Whitby and Scarborough). The rural coastaline of small fishing villages and castles is beautiful, but at the same time there's the throbbing night life of cities like Newcastle, and a heavily industrial surfing back drop.

The best waves come from Low Pressures off Scandinavia, but the coast also gets SE swells up the channel and the surf can be great, with prevailing SW winds offshore. Blessed with many reefs and quality beaches, there are still miles of unexplored coastline, but the best time to catch surf is through autumn, winter and spring, so bring a warm wetsuit.

Hardened by cold weather, polluted and freezing seas and inconsistent swells, the local guys are some of the keenest, most competitive and yet friendliest surfers anywhere, and define the term hard-core. There's an independent spirit and a strong local pride, particularly of the more special spots, that has been built on close friendships and a surfing network which exists along the coast, enriched by the discovery of new breaks. Surfers who wait all winter for classic swells will not stand for visitors who arrive with a disrespectful attitude.

Veitch, the East Coast legend, was one of the UK's first professional surfers and he paved the way for others. He charged everything he did and has inspired a talented generation of young surfers. These surfers are now flying. H'way the lads.

La côte nord-est est une destination "sauvage". Le surf a débuté ici au milieu des années 60 et depuis les années 80 la population surfeur se multiplie. On voit apparaître des bandes de surfeurs locaux dans chaque ville de la côte, avec des surf-shops dans tous les endroits stratégiques (Seahouses, Tynemouth, South Shields, Hartlepool, Saltburn, Whitby et Scarborough). La ligne côtière et rurale constituée de petits villages et de châteaux est charmante; et, en plus de posséder une industrie du surf florissante, certaines villes comme Newcastle sont victimes d'une certaine fièvre nocturne!

Les meilleures vagues proviennent des dépressions au large de la Scandinavie, mais la région reçoit également les houles de sud-est du"Channel" et le surf peut être super bon,lors de vents offshores de sud-ouest. Gâtée par de nombreux reefs et par des plages de qualité, il y a encore des kilomètres de côte inexlplorés, mais, puisque les meilleures périodes sont l'automne, l'hiver et le printemps, une épaisse combinaison est de rigueur.

Endurcis par le temps rude, une mer glaciale et polluée et enfin par l'iirégularité du swell, les locaux sont parmi les plus enthousiastes et les plus compétitifs tout en étant les plus sympathiques; ils sont l'illustration même de la notion d'"hard-core" (pur et dur). Il y règne un esprit d'indépendance et une forte fierté, ce qui est particulièrement vrai sur des spots spéciaux, qui se sont construits autour de fortes amitiés et un réseau de surf qui est présent le long de la côte, nourri par la découverte de nouvelles perles. Les surfeurs qui attendent tout l'hiver les super jours, ne supportent pas les touristes qui s'aménent avec une attitude irréspectueuse.

Veitch, la légende de la côte est, était parmi l'un des premiers surfeurs professionnels du Royaume-Uni et il balisa le chemin pour les autres. Il faisait à fond ce qu'il entreprenait et il servit de modèle à une génèration talentueuse de jeunes surfeurs. Ces surfeurs volent,maintenant, de leurs propres ailes. Bonne chance les gars.

La Costa Nordeste es un destino hardcore, garantía de un buen surfari. Es un bello paisaje costero y rural, de pequeños pueblos pesqueros y castillos. Simultáneamente existe un ambiente surfero post-industrial y una vibrante vida nocturna en ciudades como Newcastle. Endurecidos por el frío, por las gélidas y contaminadas aguas y por soportar marejadas inconsistentes, los locales son la mejor definición de lo que es ser hardcore en surfing, son de los más avezados, competitivos y amistosos que pueda encontrarse. Existe entre ellos un fuerte espìritu de independencia y un poderoso orgullo local, particularmente en los spots más especiales. Los surfers que aguantan todo el invierno la llegada de los días clásicos no están dispuestos a soportar visitantes poco respetuosos.

Las olas pueden ser magníficas, soplando terral el predominante Suroeste. Las mejores marejadas provienen del Norte, de las borrascas situadas cerca de las costas escandinavas. Pero la costa recibe también mares del Sureste. La mejor temporada son las estaciones de primavera, otoño e invierno, pero llévate un traje abrigadito. Abundantes arrecifes y playas de calidad bendicen una costa en la que permanecen sin explorar kilómetros de litoral. Grupitos de surfers existen en cada localidad costera, estando las tiendas de surf en los puntos clave de Seahouses, Tynemouth, South Shields, Hartlepool, Saltburn, Whitby y Scarborough.

El surf comenzó aquì a mediados de los sesenta y en los ochenta la población surfera estaba creciendo sobre las bases de una sólida amistad y una red de contactos surferos a lo largo de la costa, enriquecida por el descubrimiento de nuevas rompientes. Veitch, la leyenda de la Costa Nordeste, fue uno de los primeros profesionales del Reino Unido y allanó el terreno para los siguientes. Todo lo que hizo fue de un modo entusiasta que sirvió de inspiración a una nueva generación llena de talento.

North East

Gabriel Davies

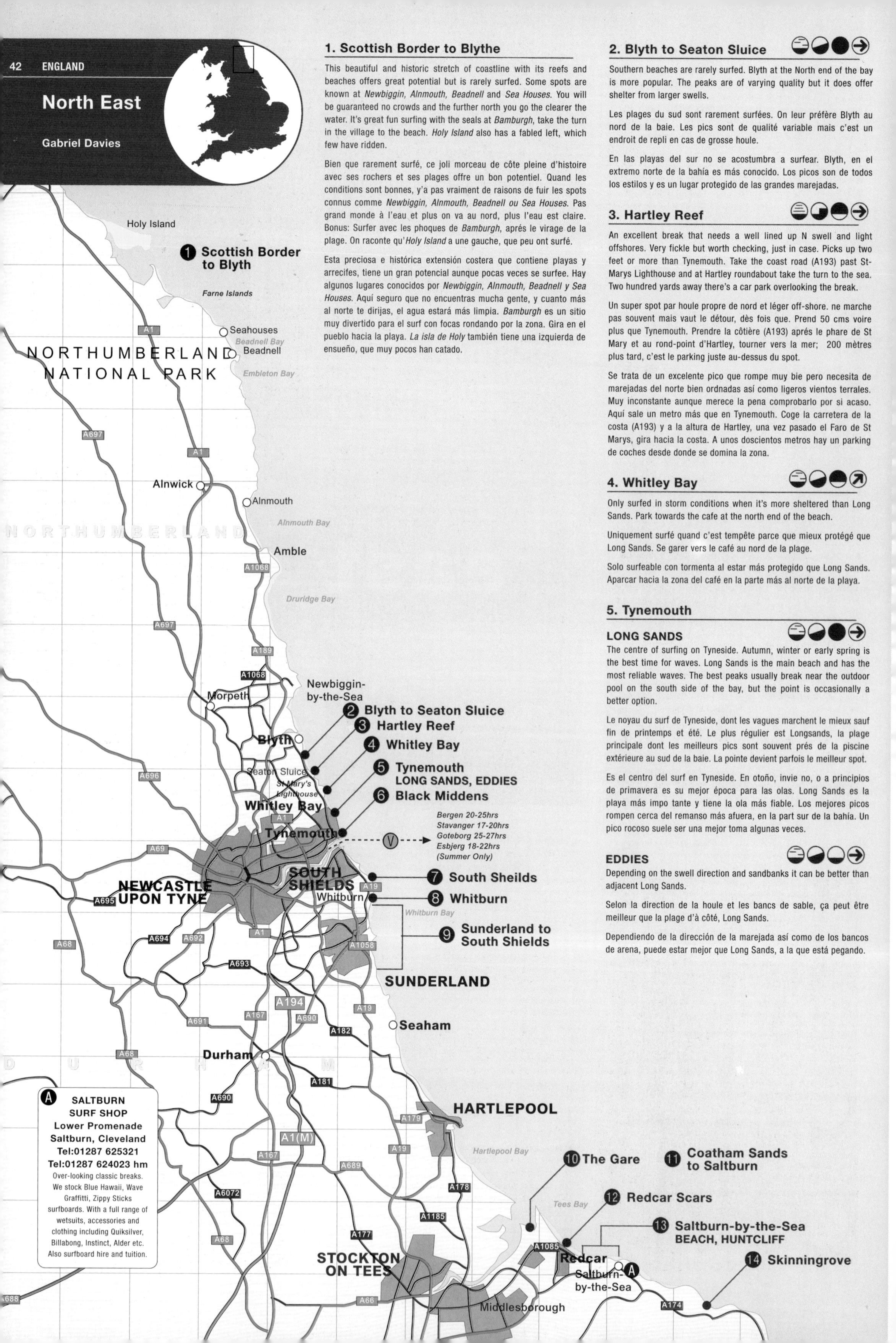

1. Scottish Border to Blythe

This beautiful and historic stretch of coastline with its reefs and beaches offers great potential but is rarely surfed. Some spots are known at *Newbiggin, Alnmouth, Beadnell* and *Sea Houses*. You will be guaranteed no crowds and the further north you go the clearer the water. It's great fun surfing with the seals at *Bamburgh*, take the turn in the village to the beach. *Holy Island* also has a fabled left, which few have ridden.

Bien que rarement surfé, ce joli morceau de côte pleine d'histoire avec ses rochers et ses plages offre un bon potentiel. Quand les conditions sont bonnes, y'a pas vraiment de raisons de fuir les spots connus comme *Newbiggin, Alnmouth, Beadnell ou Sea Houses.* Pas grand monde à l'eau et plus on va au nord, plus l'eau est claire. Bonus: Surfer avec les phoques de *Bamburgh*, aprés le virage de la plage. On raconte qu'*Holy Island* a une gauche, que peu ont surfé.

Esta preciosa e histórica extensión costera que contiene playas y arrecifes, tiene un gran potencial aunque pocas veces se surfee. Hay algunos lugares conocidos por *Newbiggin, Alnmouth, Beadnell y Sea Houses.* Aquí seguro que no encuentras mucha gente, y cuanto más al norte te dirijas, el agua estará más limpia. *Bamburgh* es un sitio muy divertido para el surf con focas rondando por la zona. Gira en el pueblo hacia la playa. *La isla de Holy* también tiene una izquierda de ensueño, que muy pocos han catado.

2. Blyth to Seaton Sluice

Southern beaches are rarely surfed. Blyth at the North end of the bay is more popular. The peaks are of varying quality but it does offer shelter from larger swells.

Les plages du sud sont rarement surfées. On leur préfère Blyth au nord de la baie. Les pics sont de qualité variable mais c'est un endroit de repli en cas de grosse houle.

En las playas del sur no se acostumbra a surfear. Blyth, en el extremo norte de la bahía es más conocido. Los picos son de todos los estilos y es un lugar protegido de las grandes marejadas.

3. Hartley Reef

An excellent break that needs a well lined up N swell and light offshores. Very fickle but worth checking, just in case. Picks up two feet or more than Tynemouth. Take the coast road (A193) past St-Marys Lighthouse and at Hartley roundabout take the turn to the sea. Two hundred yards away there's a car park overlooking the break.

Un super spot par houle propre de nord et léger off-shore. ne marche pas souvent mais vaut le détour, dès fois que. Prend 50 cms voire plus que Tynemouth. Prendre la côtière (A193) aprés le phare de St Mary et au rond-point d'Hartley, tourner vers la mer; 200 mètres plus tard, c'est le parking juste au-dessus du spot.

Se trata de un excelente pico que rompe muy bie pero necesita de marejadas del norte bien ordnadas así como ligeros vientos terrales. Muy inconstante aunque merece la pena comprobarlo por si acaso. Aquí sale un metro más que en Tynemouth. Coge la carretera de la costa (A193) y a la altura de Hartley, una vez pasado el Faro de St Marys, gira hacia la costa. A unos doscientos metros hay un parking de coches desde donde se domina la zona.

4. Whitley Bay

Only surfed in storm conditions when it's more sheltered than Long Sands. Park towards the cafe at the north end of the beach.

Uniquement surfé quand c'est tempête parce que mieux protégé que Long Sands. Se garer vers le café au nord de la plage.

Solo surfeable con tormenta al estar más protegido que Long Sands. Aparcar hacia la zona del café en la parte más al norte de la playa.

5. Tynemouth

LONG SANDS

The centre of surfing on Tyneside. Autumn, winter or early spring is the best time for waves. Long Sands is the main beach and has the most reliable waves. The best peaks usually break near the outdoor pool on the south side of the bay, but the point is occasionally a better option.

Le noyau du surf de Tyneside, dont les vagues marchent le mieux sauf fin de printemps et été. Le plus régulier est Longsands, la plage principale dont les meilleurs pics sont souvent prés de la piscine extérieure au sud de la baie. La pointe devient parfois le meilleur spot.

Es el centro del surf en Tyneside. En otoño, invie no, o a principios de primavera es su mejor época para las olas. Long Sands es la playa más impo tante y tiene la ola más fiable. Los mejores picos rompen cerca del remanso más afuera, en la part sur de la bahía. Un pico rocoso suele ser una mejor toma algunas veces.

EDDIES

Depending on the swell direction and sandbanks it can be better than adjacent Long Sands.

Selon la direction de la houle et les bancs de sable, ça peut être meilleur que la plage d'à côté, Long Sands.

Dependiendo de la dirección de la marejada así como de los bancos de arena, puede estar mejor que Long Sands, a la que está pegando.

6. The Black Middens

The good news is that this is one of the best waves on the East Coast. The bad news is that it's polluted and seldom works. It is sited at the mouth of the river Tyne on the north bank. Two piers built to protect shipping from winter storms clean up the waves. Needs a large swell to get between them. It can be seen from the coastguard's cottages or Lord Collingwood's monument.

La bonne nouvelle, c'est que c'est une des meilleures vagues de la côte est. La mauvaise: ça marche rarement et c'est pollué. Situé sur la rive nord de la rivière Tyne. Les deux jetées prévues pour protéger le transit des bateaux des tempêtes ont aussi l 'avantage de lisser les vagues à l'intérieur, ce qui n'est le cas qu'avec une houle bien grasse . Visible depuis les cottages des garde-côtes et du monument de Lord Collingwood.

La buena noticia es que se trata de una de las mejores ola de la costa este. La mala hace referencia a la contaminación y a que casi nunca funciona. Está situado en la boca del rio Tyne en el banco del norte. Los dos muelles construidos para proteger la pesca de las tormentas invernales, suavizan las olas, sin embargo necesita de una fuerte marejada para poder meterse entre los dos muelles. Es visible desde las casas de los Guardias-Costeros así como desde el monumento a Lord Collingwood.

7. South Shields

Beach break of varying quality. Local surfers tend to surf in the middle of the beach in front of the lifeguard station. Better waves may be found at the south end.

Vagues de beach break sans qualité particulière. Les surfers locaux ont tendance à surfer au milieu de la plage en face du poste des MNS. Peut-être de meilleures vagues au sud et aprés les falaises.

La calidad con que la ola rompe en esta playa varía mucho. Los surfistas locales suelen coger olas en el medio de la playa, frente a la estación de los socorristas. En el extremo sur salen mejores olas.

8. Whitburn (Razor Blades)

3 lefthand reefs produce good but fickle waves. Restricted access, particularly at weekends, across a firing range to the cliff path.

3 gauches de reef: bien mais rare. L'accés se fait par un pare-feu sur le chemin longeant la falaise parfois interdit surtout le week-end.

Salen tres izquierdas de arrecife que son buenas aunque inconstantes. Se llega a través de un coto de caza hasta un camino de acantilado, por lo que es restringido, particularmente los fines de semana.

9. Sunderland to South Shields

Some sheltered breaks for the heavy winter storms - Cats and Dogs by Roker Pier, Sunderland and the beach at Whitburn.

Voilà des spots abrités pour les bonnes vieilles tempêtes d'hiver: Cats and Dogs vers la jetée de Roker, Sunderland et la plage de Whitburn.

Hay algunos picos protegidos de las fuertes tormentas invernales - Cats and Dogs hacia Rocker Pier, Sunderland y la playa de Whitburn.

Photo: The Gill

Saltburn - *Photo: The Gill*

10. The Gare

Just inside the mouth of the River Tees on the south bank about 300yds upstream from the light house. Works only on an E swell of a moderate size or above. Swell wraps around the headland producing a very fast wave which breaks over a man-made boulder dump. Dangerous due to the nature of the bottom and pollution! A world class wave at its best. Access is from Redcar along the Warrenby road and on past British Steel out to the headland. Park by the lighthouse compound gates and walk over the grass bank to check it out.

A l'intérieur de la rivière Tees sur la rive sud à peu prés 300 mts en amont du phare. Marche seulement par houle d'Est de taille moyenne et au-dessus, qui s'enroule autour du petit cap pour donner des vagues ultra-rapides qui cassent sur fond de rejet de graviers: chaud dessous! Une vague épique quand tout est parfait, malgré la pollution. L'accés se fait depuis Redcar le long de Warrenby Rd, passé l'usine British Steel vers le cap. Se garer vers le portail du phare et marcher sur la rive herbeuse pour jeter un oei.

Se encuentra justo dentro de la boca del rio Tees, en el banco que se forma al sur a unos 300m corriente arriba desde el faro. Funciona de marejadas medias para arriba. Estas rodean el promontorio resultando una ola muy rápida que rompe contra un depósito de cascajo construido por el hombre. Este fondo, as¿1¿ como la contaminación, hacen que sea peligroso! Los mejores dias hace que parezca una ola de categoría mundial. La forma de llegar es desde Redcar por la carretera de Warrenby pasando British Steel tirar hacia el promontorio. Aparcar al lado de las puertas del faro para caminar por el banco de arena para echar un vistazo.

11. Coatham Sands to Saltburn

Five miles of beach, broken at its mid-point by Redcar scars. Waves can be found at most points with swell from SE to NW. Accessible by walking over the 'Stray' (dunes).

8km de plage, séparée au milieu par les dalles de reef de Redcar, où il y a généralement des vagues prés de tous les accés avec un swell de NO à SE. Accessible partout en marchant sur le 'Stray', à savoir les dunes.

5 millas de playa, salpicada en su mitad por un paraje rocoso, donde pueden aparecer numerosos picos con marejada del sudeste hacia el noroeste. Se accede a ella paseando por el "Stray" (zona de dunas).

12. Redcar Scars

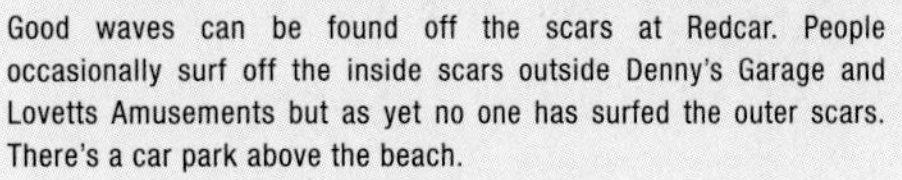

Good waves can be found off the scars at Redcar. People occasionally surf off the inside scars outside Denny's Garage and Lovetts Amusements but as yet no one has surfed the outer scars. There's a car park above the beach.

De bonnes vagues à côté des dalles de Redcar. Ca surfe parfois à l'intérieur de ces dalles en face du garage de Denny ou de la salle de jeux Lovetts. Pour l'instant, personne n'a surfé au large. Parking au-dessus de la plage.

Pueden darse buenas olas en este paraje rocoso en Redcar. La gente surfea ocasionalmente en las rocas más al interior, justo fuera del garage de Denny y de la casa recreativa de Lovetts. Mientras que en las rocas de afuera todavía no ha nacido el valiente que se atreva. Hay aparcamiento para coches encima de la playa.

13. Saltburn-By-Sea

BEACH

The most popular surfing beach in the NE but not that good a break. It's a flat beach, waves tend to lose power a long way from shore.

Le spot le plus célèbre du nord-est bien que pas terrible . Comme le fond est plat, les vagues perdent de leur puissance au large .

Es la playa surfera más conocida del noroeste, aunque tampoco se pueda decir que sea la ola que mejor rompe. Al ser una playa plana, las olas pierden fuerza bastante lejos de la orilla.

HUNTCLIFF

A point break at the southern end of the beach breaking off the huge scar lying beneath Huntcliff. A fast powerful right when it's working.

Un point break au sud de la plage qui casse sur la méga-dalle situé sous Huntcliff: une droite puissante et rapide quand ça marche.

Es un pico que rompe en el extremo sur de la playa colindante a un paraje rocoso asentado debajo de Huntcliff. Esta ola es una poderosa derecha cuando funciona.

14. Skinningrove

There are two beaches here, one to the north of the jetty and one to the south. The southern beach is sheltered to some extent from a W wind by a large stone jetty. To the south of Skinningrove Beck lies the long Hummersea Scar and a right which breaks off the Skinningrove end of the scar. The water quality here is some of the most disgusting possible. Only head out here if you're totally desperate and have had all the jabs.

Deux plages ici de part et d'autre de la jetée. Celle du sud est quelque peu protégée des vents d'ouest par un gros épi rocheux. Au sud de Skinningrove Beck s'étend la longue dalle de Hummersea avec une droite qui casse au bout de cette dalle.

Aquí hay dos playas, Una al norte del embarcadero y la otra al sur. En la del sur hay una zona protegida de los vientos del oeste debido a un muelle de piedra. Al sur del arrayo de Skinningove se encuentra la zona pedregosa de Hummersea, y en el límite del Skinningrove que da a esta zona suele romper una derecha.

Local Crew - *Photo: Gabriel Davies*

N.Yorks & Humberside

Roger Povey- *Secret Spot*

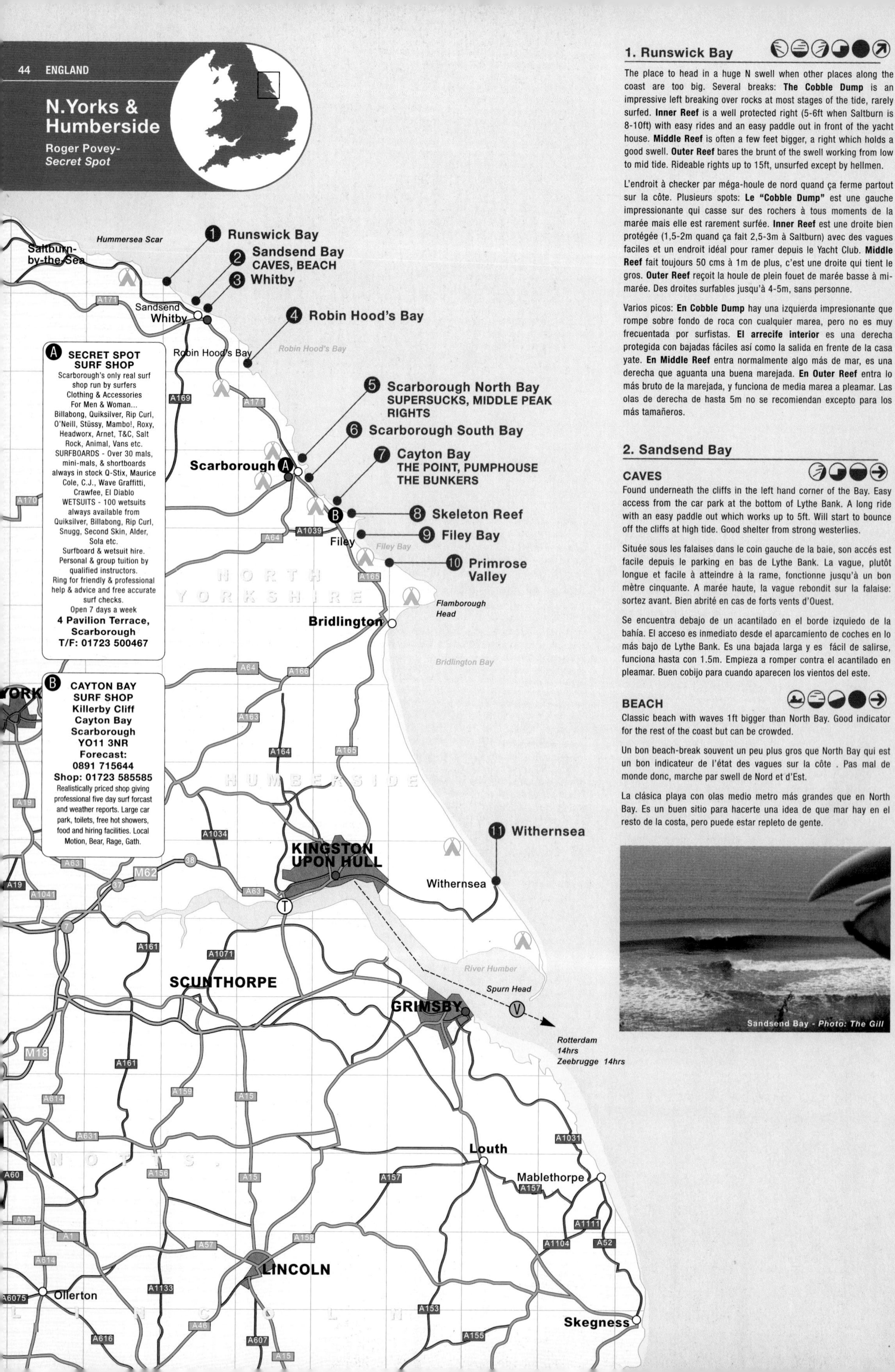

1. Runswick Bay

The place to head in a huge N swell when other places along the coast are too big. Several breaks: **The Cobble Dump** is an impressive left breaking over rocks at most stages of the tide, rarely surfed. **Inner Reef** is a well protected right (5-6ft when Saltburn is 8-10ft) with easy rides and an easy paddle out in front of the yacht house. **Middle Reef** is often a few feet bigger, a right which holds a good swell. **Outer Reef** bares the brunt of the swell working from low to mid tide. Rideable rights up to 15ft, unsurfed except by hellmen.

L'endroit à checker par méga-houle de nord quand ça ferme partout sur la côte. Plusieurs spots: **Le "Cobble Dump"** est une gauche impressionante qui casse sur des rochers à tous moments de la marée mais elle est rarement surfée. **Inner Reef** est une droite bien protégée (1,5-2m quand ça fait 2,5-3m à Saltburn) avec des vagues faciles et un endroit idéal pour ramer depuis le Yacht Club. **Middle Reef** fait toujours 50 cms à 1m de plus, c'est une droite qui tient le gros. **Outer Reef** reçoit la houle de plein fouet de marée basse à mi-marée. Des droites surfables jusqu'à 4-5m, sans personne.

Varios picos: **En Cobble Dump** hay una izquierda impresionante que rompe sobre fondo de roca con cualquier marea, pero no es muy frecuentada por surfistas. **El arrecife interior** es una derecha protegida con bajadas fáciles así como la salida en frente de la casa yate. **En Middle Reef** entra normalmente algo más de mar, es una derecha que aguanta una buena marejada. **En Outer Reef** entra lo más bruto de la marejada, y funciona de media marea a pleamar. Las olas de derecha de hasta 5m no se recomiendan excepto para los más tamañeros.

2. Sandsend Bay

CAVES

Found underneath the cliffs in the left hand corner of the Bay. Easy access from the car park at the bottom of Lythe Bank. A long ride with an easy paddle out which works up to 5ft. Will start to bounce off the cliffs at high tide. Good shelter from strong westerlies.

Située sous les falaises dans le coin gauche de la baie, son accés est facile depuis le parking en bas de Lythe Bank. La vague, plutôt longue et facile à atteindre à la rame, fonctionne jusqu'à un bon mètre cinquante. A marée haute, la vague rebondit sur la falaise: sortez avant. Bien abrité en cas de forts vents d'Ouest.

Se encuentra debajo de un acantilado en el borde izquiedo de la bahía. El acceso es inmediato desde el aparcamiento de coches en lo más bajo de Lythe Bank. Es una bajada larga y es fácil de salirse, funciona hasta con 1.5m. Empieza a romper contra el acantilado en pleamar. Buen cobijo para cuando aparecen los vientos del este.

BEACH

Classic beach with waves 1ft bigger than North Bay. Good indicator for the rest of the coast but can be crowded.

Un bon beach-break souvent un peu plus gros que North Bay qui est un bon indicateur de l'état des vagues sur la côte . Pas mal de monde donc, marche par swell de Nord et d'Est.

La clásica playa con olas medio metro más grandes que en North Bay. Es un buen sitio para hacerte una idea de que mar hay en el resto de la costa, pero puede estar repleto de gente.

Sandsend Bay - *Photo: The Gill*

3. Whitby

Works on similar conditions as Sandsend with a consistent left. Can have a hollow right breaking down the west side of the pier on an easterly swell.

Cette gauche consistente marche dans les mêmes conditions que Sandsend. Une droite bien creuse peut casser sur le côté Ouest de la jetée avec un swell d'est.

Funciona bajo las mismas condiciones que Sandsend con una izquierda consistente. Puede salir una derecha tubera que rompe al oeste del dique con marejada del este.

4. Robin Hood's Bay

Can be the only place working on the east Coast. Rarely surfed due to a long walk across the reef.

A essayer si rien ne marche ailleurs. Un marche pénible sur le reef limite le nombre de candidats.

Puede ser el único sitio surfeable de toda la costa este. Pero pocas veces se surfea aquí debido al largo trecho a recorrer por un arrecife.

5. Scarborough North Bay

SUPERSUCKS

All three waves are along a half mile stretch of sand and work on any swells. Supersucks is a short fickle wave at the north end of the bay. Swell: Large SE

Ces 3 vagues marchent par n'importe quelle houle sur une étendue de sable de moins d'un km, contrairement à Supersucks, une vague courte et aléatoire à l'extrémité nord de la baie, à checker par grosse houle de SE.

Las tres olas se encuentran a lo largo de una extension de playa de media milla, funciona con cualquir tipo de marejada. Supersucks es una pequeña ola inconstante situada lo más al norte de la bahía.

MIDDLE PEAK

Good fun wave for beginners to intermediate surfers.

La vague préférée des débutants car sympa et facile.

Una ola divertida para principiantes así como para surferos intermedios.

RIGHTS

On large, lined-up north swells a wave breaks off the kelp-covered point. Access is through the tunnel south of the bay.

En général recouvert d'algues, ce pic fonctionne jusqu'à deux mètres avec un gros swell de nord bien rangé. L'accés se fait par un tunnel à l'extrémité sud de la baie.

La ola rompe sobre un fondo cubierto de quelpo con una fuerte y bien alineada marejada del norte. El acceso es a través de un túnel al sur de la bahía.

6. Scarborough Sth Bay

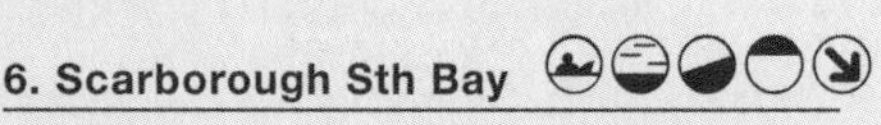

When it's onshore at North Bay, South Bay tends to clean up northerly swells as they wrap around the harbour. On a SE swell peaky high tide lefts and rights are popular with boogie boarders, and further crowded at weekends. Unsurfed reefs can be found at the far end of the bay. Parking on the Foreshore, the Spa, and Valley Road.

Quand le vent est onshore sur North Bay, South Bay a tendance à s'arranger avec les houles de nord qui s'enroulent autour du port du bout de la baie. Si ça vient du SE, on trouve des pics de gauches et droites à marée haute. Appréciée des jeunes en bisottes et donc pas mal fréquenté le week-end. Des spots plus tranquilles au bout de la baie. Laissez la caisse sur la Foreshore Rd, le Spa et Valley Rd.

Cuando el viento sopla hacia la tierra en North Bay, En South Bay la marejada del norte entra más ordenada rodeando el puerto. Con marejada del sudeste aparecen izquierdas fofas y las derechas que salen en pleamar son las más solicitadas por los jóvenes boogie boarders, y por tanto se llena de gente en fines de semana. Se pueden encontrar picos insurfeables en el extremo más alejado de la bahía. Hay parkings en Foreshore, Spa, y Valley Road.

Carwyn Williams, Secret Yorkshire Left - *Photo: The Gill*

Cayton Bay, Pumphouse & Bunkers - *Photo: The Gill*

7. Cayton Bay

THE POINT

Even on the messiest of days swell wraps around the point into a calm bay producing a fast hollow ride. Works up to 10ft on huge northerly swells and can be world-class, but strong rips, long paddles, wide sets, sewage, access and parking difficulties often put off all but a few local crew.

Même les jours les plus pourris, cette vague s'enroule dans une baie calme pour donner des sections creuses et rapides. Fonctionne jusqu'à 3 mètres sur une houle énorme de Nord. Ce peut être un must mais queqlues inconvéninets du style: forts courants, rame démente, des séries qui décalent et un accés et un parking pas évidents. En décourage beaucoup sauf une poignée d'irréductibles locaux.

Incluso en los dias más desordenados habrá una ola que ronde el pico hasta la bahía, se suele tratar de una derecha tubera muy rápida. Podría ser una ola mundial pero debido a las fuertes corrientes, largas remadas, series abiertas, aguas residuales, el acceso, y las dificultades para aparcar hace que la mayoría de gente se eche para atrás, excepto los locales.

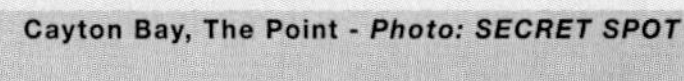

Cayton Bay, The Point - *Photo: SECRET SPOT*

PUMPHOUSE

A fickle wave which breaks with a huge clean northerly swell, over a shallow suck rock in front of the old pump house. Can produce a wave at low-tide but with a SE swell. Park at the surf shop above the break.

Une vague capricieuse qui marche plutôt par une houle propre et énorme de nord. Casse dans peu d'eau et suce pas mal en face d'une ancienne station de pompage. Peut aussi marcher à marée basse mais avec swell de SE.

Esta es una ola inconstante que rompe con las mejores marejadas del norte, se situa en un fondo de roca poco profundo y muy succionador frente a una vieja casa de bombeo de agua. Sale una ola en marea baja, aunque con marejada del sudeste.

BUNKERS

A horseshoe shaped sandbar produces hollow lefts and rights on a clean N swell. Often packed at weekends and holidays.

Un banc de sable en forme de fer à cheval produit des vagues creuses par une houle de nord bien nette. Gavé aux heures de pointe.

Es una playa de arena con forma de herradura donde salen izquierdas tuberas y también aparecen derechas con marejadas limpias del N.

8. Skeleton Reef

Recently discovered secret spot five miles south of Scarborough. An intense heaving wave, popular with transvestites and cross dressers. Watch out for the odd submerged motorbike. A local named Dennis rules the spot, don't cross him, you have been warned. Secret of secret spots, respect expected.

Récemment découvert, ce secret spot se trouve à 5 miles au sud de Scarborough. Une vague intense. Faites gaffe d'abord à une vieille moto submergée mais surtout à Dennis, un local pas fin qui sévit souvent; ne le droppez pas sinon... Secret spots parmi les secret spots, profil bas!

Un sitio secreto descubierto recientemente 5 millas al sur de Scarborough. Es una ola muy agitada, popular entre travestidos y gentes que gustan de vestir a lo fémina. Cuidado con una vieja moto sumergida. Un local llamado Dennis ronda la zona, será mejor que no te lo cruces, no digas que no te advertimos. Es el más secreto de entre los lugares secretos, se espera un respeto.

9. Filey Bay

Usually only surfed by locals under heavy wind and storm swell conditions. Not a quality wave but fun peaks hold up due to the protection of Filey Brigg.

Encore une vagues de locaux qui a quand même l'avantage d'être protégée des tempêtesgrâce à Filey Brigg. Pas une super vague mais de quoi s'amuser.

Normalmente frecuentado por locales que surfean con fuertes vientos y marejadas tormentosas. No es que sea una ola de muy buena calidad aunque sí hay unos picos muy divertidos debido a la protección que le proporciona Filey Brigg.

10. Primrose Valley

This semi-secret spot is rarely surfed as it only works under perfect conditions. Best on a clean large northerly swell. Beware of strong rips and the 'old guys' who rule it.

Un peu au Sud de Filey BAY, ce spot à moitié secret est rarement surfé car ne fonctionnant qu'avec des conditions optima, à savoir un bon swell nickel de nord. Attention aux courants et aux vieux locaux qui font la loi.

En este lugar recóndito pocas veces se puede surfear al requerir unas condiciones perfectas. Mejor con marejadas potentes del N. Al loro con las corrientes así como con los veteranos que rulan por la zona.

11. Withernsea

Only surfed when a huge swell is running and the rest of the east coast is blown out. Tends to produce mainly lefts. Parking by beach.

Le dernier recours et seulement en cas d'énorme houle quand toute la côte sature. Plutôt des gauches. Parking directement sur la plage.

Solo surfeable con enormes marejadas cuando el resto de la costa está pasada de mar. Suelen salir muchas izquierdas.

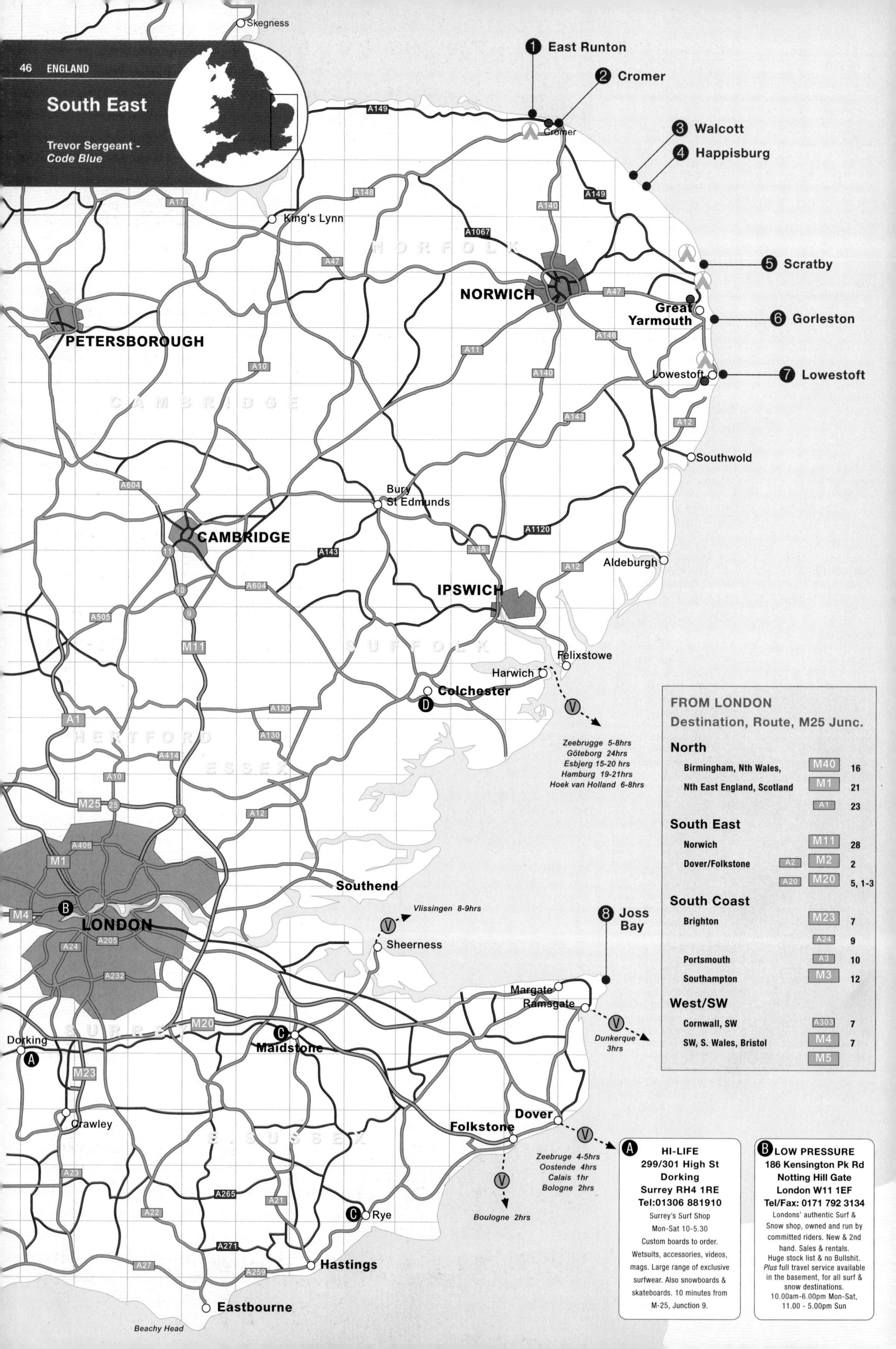
46 ENGLAND
South East
Trevor Sergeant - Code Blue
1 East Runton
2 Cromer
3 Walcott
4 Happisburg
5 Scratby
6 Gorleston
7 Lowestoft
8 Joss Bay
Skegness
King's Lynn
Cromer
NORWICH
Great Yarmouth
Lowestoft
Southwold
PETERSBOROUGH
CAMBRIDGE
Bury St Edmunds
IPSWICH
Aldeburgh
Felixstowe
Harwich
Colchester
Southend
LONDON
Sheerness
Margate
Ramsgate
Dorking
Maidstone
Crawley
Folkstone
Dover
Rye
Hastings
Eastbourne
Beachy Head
NORFOLK
CAMBRIDGE
SUFFOLK
HERTFORD
ESSEX
SURREY
E. SUSSEX
A149
A148
A17
A1067
A140
A47
A146
A11
A10
A143
A12
A604
A1120
A45
A505
M11
A1
A120
A130
A414
M25
A406
M1
M4
A205
A24
A232
M20
M23
A23
A265
A21
A22
A271
A27
A259
Zeebrugge 5-8hrs
Göteborg 24hrs
Esbjerg 15-20 hrs
Hamburg 19-21hrs
Hoek van Holland 6-8hrs
Vlissingen 8-9hrs
Dunkerque 3hrs
Zeebruge 4-5hrs
Oostende 4hrs
Calais 1hr
Bologne 2hrs
Boulogne 2hrs
FROM LONDON
Destination, Route, M25 Junc.
North
Birmingham, Nth Wales, M40 16
Nth East England, Scotland M1 21
A1 23
South East
Norwich M11 28
Dover/Folkstone A2 M2 2
A20 M20 5, 1-3
South Coast
Brighton M23 7
A24 9
Portsmouth A3 10
Southampton M3 12
West/SW
Cornwall, SW A303 7
SW, S. Wales, Bristol M4 7
M5
A HI-LIFE
299/301 High St
Dorking
Surrey RH4 1RE
Tel:01306 881910
Surrey's Surf Shop
Mon-Sat 10-5.30
Custom boards to order.
Wetsuits, accessories, videos, mags. Large range of exclusive surfwear. Also snowboards & skateboards. 10 minutes from M-25, Junction 9.
B LOW PRESSURE
186 Kensington Pk Rd
Notting Hill Gate
London W11 1EF
Tel/Fax: 0171 792 3134
Londons' authentic Surf & Snow shop, owned and run by committed riders. New & 2nd hand. Sales & rentals.
Huge stock list & no Bullshit.
Plus full travel service available in the basement, for all surf & snow destinations.
10.00am-6.00pm Mon-Sat,
11.00 - 5.00pm Sun

1. East Runton 

The premier surfing beach on the East Anglian coastline produces reliable quality waves over a shingle-sand bottom. The break has three peaks: the westernmost is a long right. The second is a left and slow right split by a sewage pipe. The third breaks over a reef made up of flint and rock and is mainly a left with a slower right. All need a northerly swell to work. At high tide the shorebreak falls onto sharp flintstones; care should be taken as cuts can easily become infected by the high rates of pollution in the area. Untreated sewage from the short outfall pipe has been polluting this break for thirty years. Anglian water has promised to remove it and build the region's first ever treatment plant. Many local surfers will obviously be happy to see water quality improve, but are sceptical as to how the pipes removal will affect the break. Only time will tell. Park above break.

Le berceau du surf de la région d'East Anglia offre des vagues plutôt régulières sur un fond de sable et de galets. Trois pics: le plus à l'ouest est une longue droite, celui du milieu une gauche et une droite molle séparée par une canalisation d'égoût. Le dernier casse sur un reef constitué de pierre et de silex, plutôt en gauche avec une droite plus lente. A marée haute, le shore break explose sur de silex tranchants, attention aux coupures qui peuvent facilement s'infecter à cause des risques élevés de pollution. Marche par swell de Nord, avec des courants quand c'est gros. Parking au-dessus du spot. Les rejets d'égoûts polluent ce break depuis 30 ans. On promet d'enlever tout ça bientôt et de construire une station de retraitement, ce que les locaux apprécieront sûrement sauf si l'enlèvement des tuyaux modifie le break, qui vivra verra.

La primera playa surfera de la costa este anglicana produce una buena calidad de olas sobre un fondo de cascajo. Rompe en tres picos diferentes, el situado más al oeste es una larga derecha. El segundo se trata de una izquierda así como una suave derecha separadas por una tubería de desechos. El tercero rompe sobre afilados peñascos, con lo que se deben tomar precauciones, ya que el elevado grado de contaminaión de la zona facilita la infección de los cortes. Necesita marejada del norte para funcionar y se pueden formar corrientes cuando está grande. Hay parking para coches sobre la playa. Los residuos no tratados de un desagüe de la proximidades han contaminado esta playa durante treinta años. Las autoridades han prometido limpiarla, así como construir la primera planta de tratamiento de desechos de la región. Muchos surfistas locales se alegrarán al comprobar la mejor calidad del agua, pero permanecen escepticos sobre como afectará a los picos esta eliminación de desechos. El tiempo lo dirá.

2. Cromer 

A popular family seaside resort, busy with tourists during the summer, in winter returns to being a retirement stronghold for the elderly. Another sand and shingle beach, with two breaks, one on either side of the pier, working on northerly swells, both best at mid to high tide. Again at high tide there are sharp stones to mash up your feet in the shorebreak. The water is horrendous. Cromer pier cunningly disguises yet another sewage outfall pipe which turdinates at the end of the pier. Solids, sanitary towels and contraceptives are frequently seen in the water. Many local surfers have vowed never to surf this break again after experiencing the repulse first hand. With onshore conditions the evidence is there for all to see, scattered a few hundred yards down the beach.

Petite station familiale agitée en été par le tourisme, elle retourne à son état de citadelle pour les vieux en hiver. Une autre plage de galets et de sable avec deux spots de part et d'autre de la jetée. Marche par swell de nord, préférablement de mi-marée à marée haute, même si le shore-break de marée haute peut vous lacérer les pieds sur les quelques tas de cailloux tranchants. La jetée de Cromer sournoisement dissimule une sortie d'égoûts, dont les rejets donnent la gerbe dans l'eau: tampons, capotes et autres délices font souvent partie du décor. Certains locaux se sont jurés de ne plus se remettre à l'eau après une expérience malheureuse. Avec des vents de mer, les délices s'éparpillent sur quelques centaines de mètres sur la plage.

Este famoso lugar familiar de veraneo, lleno de turistas durante el verano, se convierte en sitio de retiro para la tercera edad durante el invierno. Es otra playa de cascajo con dos picos, a los dos lados del muelle, funciona con marejada del norte, preferiblemente de marea media a alta. Una vez más en pleamar se encuentran pilas de afilados peñascos dispuestos a cortarte los pies. La calidad del agua es horrenda. El muelle de Cromer esconde astutamente más vertidos incontolados que salen por el final del mismo. Desechos sólidos, material sanitario y anticonceptivos se encuentran fácilmente en el agua. Muchas surfistas locales han jurado no volver a surfear aquí despues de entrar por la primera vez. Con viento del mar la prueba de esta suciedad está allí esparcida a lo largo de cientos de metros por toda playa.

Photo: Neil Watson

3. Walcott 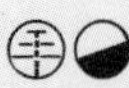  

Short beach with a succession of wooden groynes. It's inconsistent and as with other East Anglian waves, heavily affected by wind conditions. The best surf breaks on the outer sandbars at low tide.

Petite plage avec une succession d'épis de bois. Le spot manque de consistance et dépend terriblement des conditions de vent. Le meilleur spot est sur les bancs du fond à marée basse.

Esta es una pequeña playa con sucesivos diques de madera como defensa contra el agua. La ola no rompe de forma consistente, y como otras de la costa este anglicana, se ve muy afectada por las condiciones del viento. La mejor ola sale en marea baja y se da en el pico más lejano de la playa. La carretera corre paralela a la playa.

4. Happisburgh   

Another north facing sand and shingle beach. Fickle peak with a longer right. Heavily affected by wind conditions. Works best at mid tide. Water quality is bad.

Une autre plage de sable et de galets avec un pic capricieux et des droites plus longues, qui marchent mieux à mi-marée. Ne supporte pas le vent, l'eau est criticable.

Se trata de otra playa de fondo cascajo orientada al norte. El pico no tiene siempre la misma localización. ya que varía debido a su fondo de arena, dejando una derecha más larga. Afectada duramente por las condiciones del viento. La mejor ola rompe a media marea. La calidad del agua es mala.

5. Scratby    

From the small clifftop car park, two peaks become apparent. The first produces quality rights on strong southerly swells, the other a decent left on northerly swells a short walking distance away. The take-off is critical followed by a short hollow wall with plenty of push. The shorebreak can also be heavy. Can also work on easterlies at low to mid tide after which wave quality deteriorates rapidly.

Depuis le parking en haut de la falaise, deux pics se détachent. Le premier offre de bonnes droites avec un forte houle de Sud. L'autre qu'on rejoint rapidement en marchant, est une gauche correcte par houle de nord . Take-off raide et petite épaule creuse et puissant. Le shore-break peut être carton. Marche aussi par vents d'Est et de marée basse à mi-marée après quoi la vague se pourrit rapidement.

Desde un elevado parking para coches se diferencian dos picos distintos. El primero produce una buena derecha con condiciones de marejada del sur. El otro se encuentra a poca distancia andando, es una izquierda decente necesitando marejada del norte. El take-off es crítico seguido de una pared hueca muy enérgica. La orillera puede ser muy contundente. También funciona con vientos del este de baja a media marea, tras la cual la calidad de la ola se deteriora rápidamente.

6. Gorleston

A popular but inconsistent beach which produces slow peaks. From the clifftop you can see 'Scroby Sands' a vast offshore sandbar which blocks much of the swell. Needs a strong swell, northerlies being the most reliable, at mid to high tide. The promenade with its clusters of cafes, bars and amusement arcades has ample parking space. Water quality is bad as the port services the oil and gas industry and the accumulated pollution from this and sewage outfalls in the River Yare combine to make a heavy situation.

En haut des falaises, on peut voir 'Scroby Sands', un méga-banc de sable au large qui bloque la houle. Il faut donc un méga-swell, nord de préférence, de mi-marée à marée haute. Le transit de déchets des industries pétrolières et autres ajouté aux rejets d'égoûts dans la rivière Yare rend l'eau vraiment gerbique.

Una popular e inconsistente playa que tiene unos picos lentos. Desde lo alto se puede distinguir 'Scroby Sands' una basta linea de arena que contiene la marejada. Necesita de un fuerte maretón, rompe de media a alta marea, con viento del N. La calidad del agua es muy mala. Los servicios portuarios, las industrias del gas y del aceite, y la contaminación acumulada de éstos así como los vertidos incontrolados en el Rio Yare, se combinan haciendo muy delicada la situación.

7. Lowestoft

Popular with tourists, surfers and boogie boarders, Lowestoft has numerous peaks producing waves of varying quality, depending on swell direction and strength. Peaks on either side of the Claremont are favoured. Rides are often cut short by wooden groynes. Again a vast offshore sandbar which extends to Kessingland takes much of the power out of the waves. Rips become a problem on bigger swells.

Lowestoft a pas mal de pics, de qualité variable en fonction de la direction et de la puissance de la houle, mieux de part et d'autre de Claremont. Les vagues sont souvent interrompues par des jetées de bois. Encore une fois, un vaste banc de sable au large qui s'étend jusqu'à Kessingland absorbe l'essentiel de la houle.

Es una playa conocida para turistas, surfistas y corcheros. Lowestoft tiene numerosos picos, con olas diversas calidades, dependiendo de la dirección y fuerza de la marejada. Los picos de ambos lados del Claremont de ven favorecidos. La ola se ve acortada por la presencia de diques de madera. De nuevo una extensa barrera de arena que se extiende hasta Kessingland quita mucha fuerza a las olas.

8. Juss Day   

Most Popular beach in the area giving beach break peaks mainly in big northerly winter swells. Mid to high incoming generally best.

La plage le plus populaire avec un beach break surtout avec les grosses houles de nord en hiver.

Playa más popular en este área dando picos en swell grande del N.

Lowestoft - *Photo: Neil Watson*

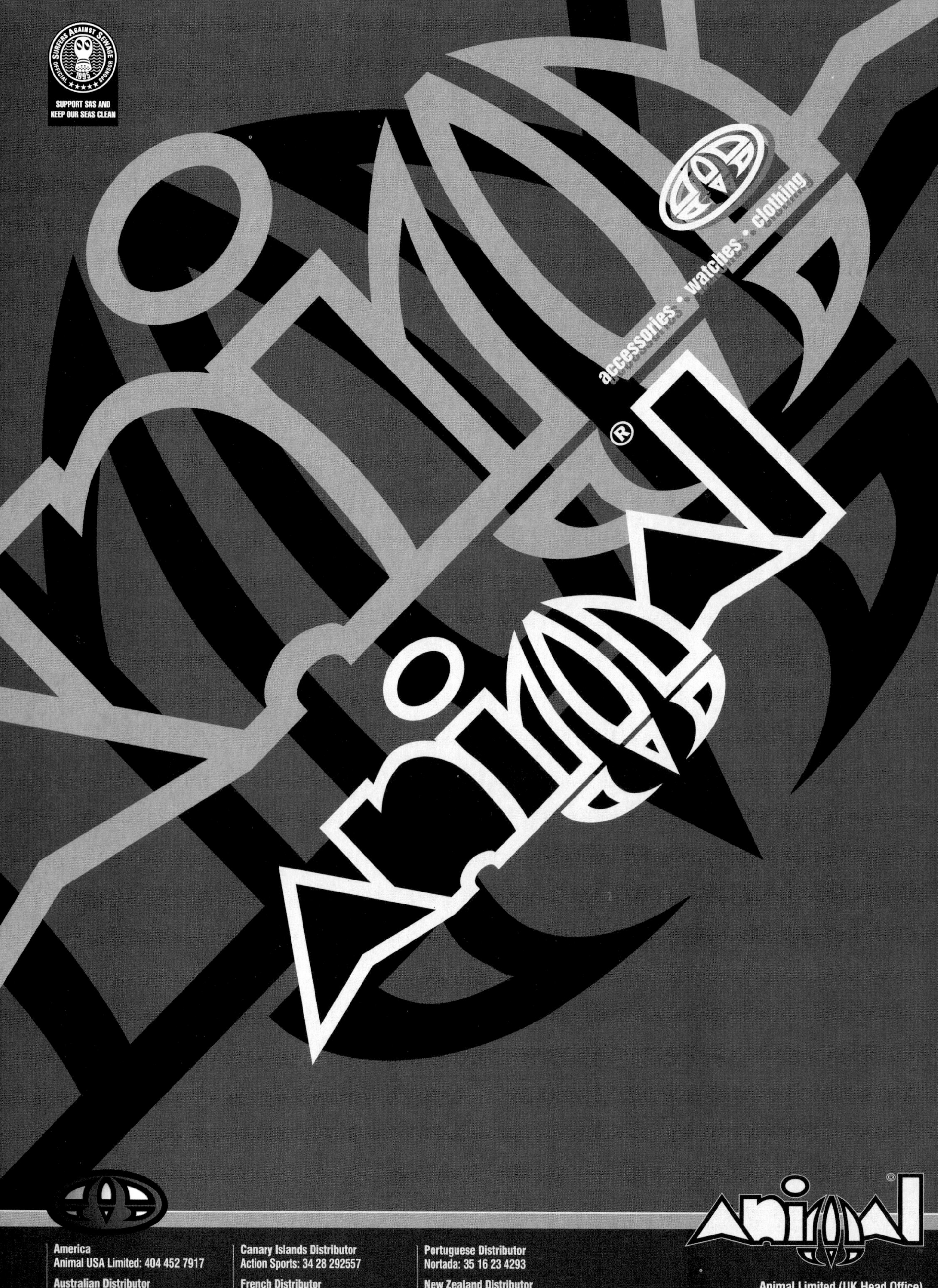

SURFERS AGAINST SEWAGE
OFFICIAL SPONSOR
1995
SUPPORT SAS AND
KEEP OUR SEAS CLEAN
accessories • watches • clothing

Infrequent and short duration swells, accompanied by onshore winds, typify the South Coast surf experience. The best sessions can be had with the presence of Biscay Lows, or Atlantic lows below or around Lands end. Despite this grim appraisal, classic days can be had and the busy surf population, centered around the main areas of Brighton, The Witterings, The Isle of Wight and Bournemouth is often augmented by Londoners on a quick dash away from town. The area from Paington to Weymouth is also reputed to have quite a few spots which work well a few times a year.

Houles éphémères et rares, accompagnées de vents onshores, caractérisent le surf sur la South Coast. Les meilleures sessions correspondent au passage des dépressions de la Baie de Biscay ou de l'Atlantique aux alentours de Landsend. Malgré cette appréciation quelque peu sinistre, quelques jolis surfs sont possibles, attirant les surfeurs de Brighton, des Witterings, de l'île de Wight et de Bournemouth tout en n'oubliant pas les Londoniens qui ne sont vraiment pas loin. La région de Paington à Weymouth est également reconnue pour avoir quelques bons spots qui marchent bien quelques fois par an.

La experiencia surfera tìpica que proporciona la costa sur de Inglaterra se caracteriza por marejadas infrecuentes y de corta duración acompañadas por vientos de mar. Las mejores sesiones pueden darse con bajas presiones situadas en el Golfo de Vizcaya, o depresiones atlánticas cercanas a Landsend. Pese a este panorama desalentador, hay dias clásicos y existe una activa comunidad surfera centrada en las principales áreas: Brighton, las Witterings, la isla de Wight y Bournemouth, que a menudo se ve reforzada por londinenses haciendo una rápida escapada de la ciudad. En la zona que va de Paington a Weymouth existen algunos buenos spots que pueden funcionar en condiciones apropiadas unas pocas veces al año.

south coast

Kimmeridge Bay, dawn patrol *Photo: Phil Holden*

South Coast

Guy/John- *Hot Rocks*
Grant- *Ocean Sports*
Pauly Gabriel- *Neptunes Revenge*
Simon/Duncan- Shoreboards

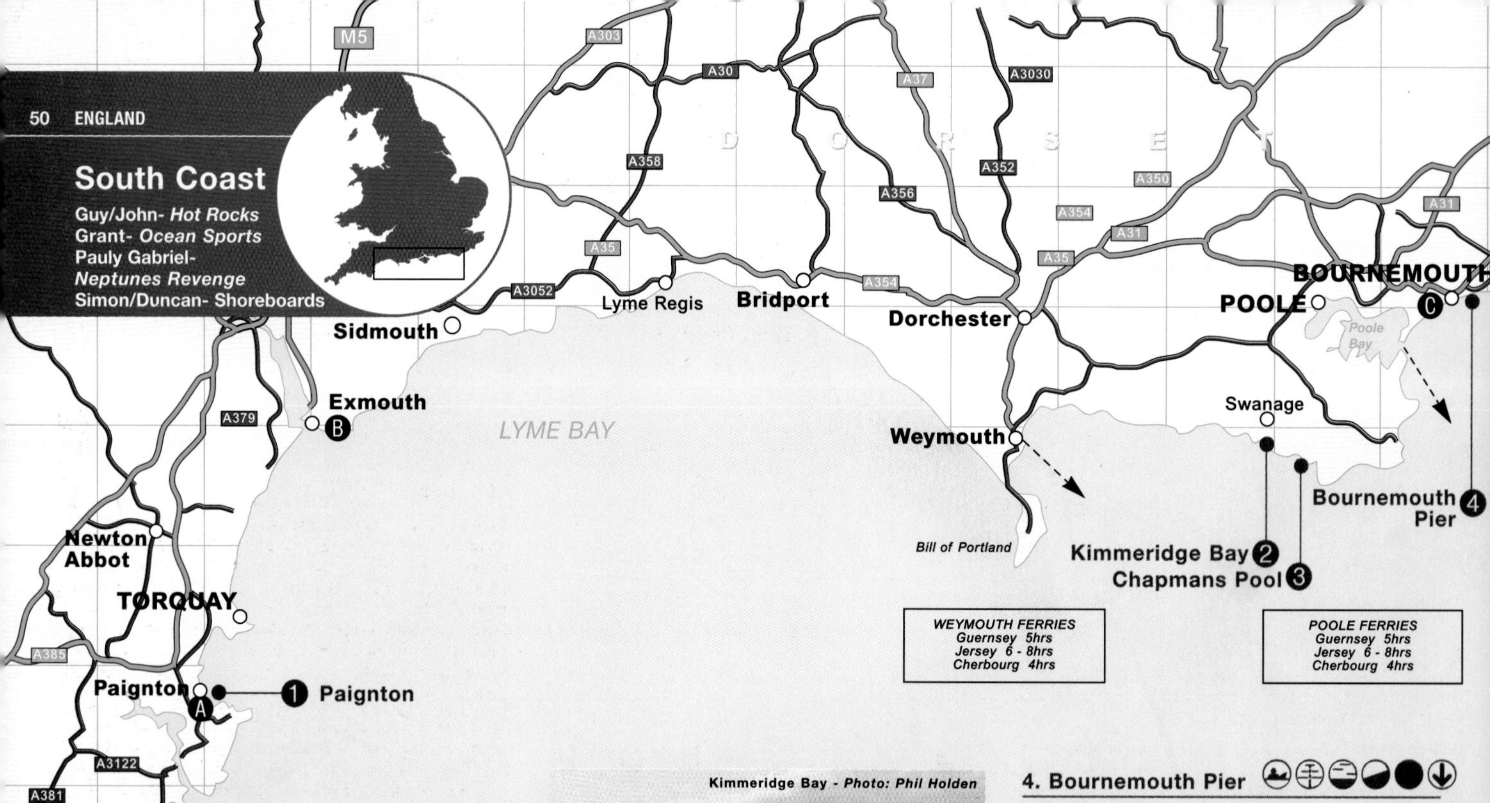

1. Paignton

E or NE winds blow wind swell in from the Channel. When winds turn offshore it will work for a few hours. Towards Lyme Regis there are a number of other spots which work in the same conditions.

Les vents d'est ou nord-est soulèvent une houle de vent en Manche. Lorsque les vents tournent offshore, le spot marchera pendant quelques heures.

Los vientos del E y NE traen el swell del Canal. Cuando el viento cambia a terral, funcionará durante varias horas.

2. Kimmeridge Bay

THE LEDGES

Classic well covered reefs which hold waves upto 8ft with a ground swell in the Channel. Its a mellow wave which can break a mile out to sea on big days, though prone to blowing out easily, mainly a left athough rights are also good. Crowded, especially with longboarders.

Des reefs "classiques" avec pas mal d'eau qui tiennent jusqu'à 2,5m avec un swell en Manche. C'est une vague douce qui peut péter à 1,5 km du bord les jours de gros. Elle ne dure cependant pas très longtemps. Même si la gauche est meilleure, les droites sont pas mal. Bondé tous les jours; les longboarders y sont particulièrement nombreux.

Son unos clásicos reefs bien cubiertos que aguantan olas de hasta 2 metros y medio con un swell y tormenta en el canal. Es una ola muy atractiva que en los mejores dias puede romper hasta a una milla de la costa, aunque se desfase fácilmente. Lo mejor es una izquierda aunque las derechas que aparecen tampoco están mal. Hay mucha gente todos los dias.

THE BAY

Located in the middle of the bay, it breaks a long way out. Similar to "The Ledges" but has more power and is never as crowded. Occasionally good if its onshore and big - an underrated wave!

Située au milieu de la baie, elle casse loin du bord. Ressemble à "The Ledges" mais a plus de puissance et n'est jamais aussi peuplée. Parfois bon lorsque c'est onshore et gros. Une vague sous-estimée!

Se encuentra en el medio de la bahía esta ola que rompe lejos de la orilla. Es parecido a "The ledges" pero más contundente y no se llena tanto de gente.

Kimmeridge Bay - *Photo: Phil Holden*

BROAD BENCH

A long powerful right with a short ultra-hollow and shallow left. Long walk to the break. Restricted access Monday to Friday as it's situated in an army firing range. Do not attempt to surf if off limits! Hardcore locals are bored with drop in artists!

Une droite puissante et longue avec une courte gauche ultra creuse avec très peu de fond. L'accès est limité du lundi au vendredi étant donné que la vague se situe sur un champ de tir. Ne surtout pas tenter de surfer hors des limites! Les locaux "purs et durs"ont en marre des artistes de la taxe.

A long powerful right with a short ultra-hollow and shallow left. Long walk to the break. Restricted access Monday to Friday as it's situated in an army firing range. Do not attempt to surf if off limits!Hardcore locals are bored with drop in artists!

3. Chapman's Pool

Secret lefthand reef break which can have a long ride, with the odd rock sucking dry. To get there it's a long walk through the conservation area. From here two other breaks are visible, one a right, as yet unsurfed. The other Cloudbreak, breaks a quarter of a mile out to sea.

Une gauche de récif prétendue secrète qui peut dérouler sur une longue distance, avec un étrange rocher "aspirant" à fond. Pour s'y rendre une longue marche à travers la zone protégée est nécessaire. De cet endroit, deux autres spots sont visibles, notamment une droite, pas encore surfée à ce jour. L'autre Cloudbreak, déferle à 400m du bord.

Es una derecha larga y poderosa y una izquierda cerrona de fondo poco profundo. Hay un buen paseo hasta la rompiente. El acceso está restringido de lunes a viernes por ser una zona de prácticas de tiro de la armada. año???? intentes ni surfear si los locales más engorilados empizan a derribar a los que no conocen!

4. Bournemouth Pier

A crowded spot with the most popular peak on the east side of the pier. Don't use the pier to get out back-if you can't paddle out, you shouldn't be out. Drop-ins are inevitable. Park in front of the peak.

Un spot bondé avec le pic le plus connu sur le côté est de la jetée. Ne pas emprunter la jetée pour sortir - si vous n'êtes pas capable de ramer, c'est que votre place n'est pas au large. C'est la guerre au pic. Il y a un parking en face du pic.

Este spot está siempre lleno de gente, el mejor pico sale en el lado este del dique. No intentes salir por el dique si ves que no puedes remar para salirte. Mete para adentro. Aparca enfrente del pico.

5. Boscombe Pier

A carbon copy of Bournemouth pier, but not as crowded.

La copie conforme de Bournemouth Pier, mais moins de monde.

Es una copia exacta de Bournemouth pier, pero con menós aglomeraciones.

6. Southbourne

A succession of groynes between Boscombe and Hergistbury Head, can produce hard breaking waves, picking up more swell than both piers but badly affected by the wind. If there's groundswell here K-bay will be going off. Lots of young local bodyboarders.

Une succession d'épis de cailloux entre Boscombe et Hergistbury Head, peuvent donner des vagues très franches, recueillant plus de swell que les deux jetées mais elles sont plus gâchées par le vent. S'il y a un bon swell ici, K-bay sera parfait. Beaucoup de jeunes locaux qui font du bodyboard.

Una serie de diques de contención de madera situados entre Boscombe y Hergistbury, donde salen unas olas fuertes que pillan más swell que los dos diques anteriores, aunque las condiciones de viento le perjudican. Caso de tormenta en los alrededores K-bay estará desfasado. Muchos jóvenes bodyboarders locales presentes.

7. Highcliffe Area

Picks up more swell than the piers but breaks a long way out and rolls for a long way. A slow right can be good if it's small at the piers. No protection from the wind.

Accepte plus la houle que les jetées mais casse au large et déroule sur une longue distance. Une droite un peu lente qui peut s'avérer bonne lorsque c'est petit près des jetées. La vague n'est pas abritée du vent.

Recoge más swell que los diques aunque tarda mucho en romper y lo hace bastante lejos. La derecha es suave y puede estar bien si en los diques está pequeño. No hay ninguna protección para el viento.

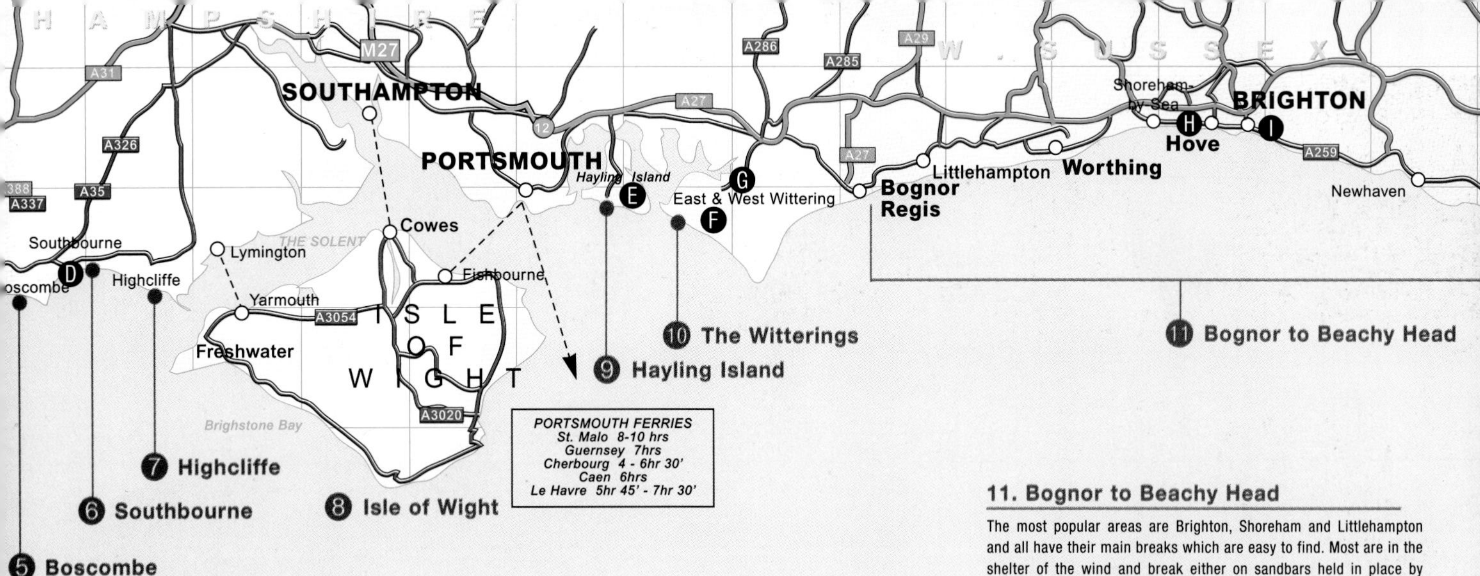

8. Isle of Wight

From Freshwater and Compton Bay down to St Catherine's Point are various SW facing breaks which can get pretty good.

De Freshwater et Compton Bay jusqu'à St Catherines's Point, on peut trouver toutes sortes de spots exposés sud-ouest qui peuvent se révéler plutôt bons.

Desde Freshwater y Compton Bay hasta St Catherine's Point hay una serie de picos orientados hacia el SO que se pueden poner bastante bien.

9. Hayling Island

More popular with windsurfers offering some of the best conditions on the South Coast. For surfing there are two spots, one at either end of the island.

Plus connue des windsurfeurs, elle offre parmi les meilleures conditions de la côte sud. On recense deux spots de surf, chacun à une extrémité de l'île.

Muy frecuentada por windsurfers, presenta de las mejores condiciones de la Costa Sur. Hay dos spots donde surfear, uno a cada extremo de la isla.

10. The Witterings

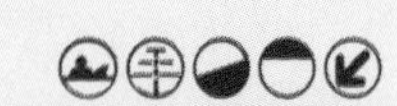

This 4 mile stretch is one of the most popular areas on the south coast with waves breaking between wooded groynes. Access to the waves is at East and West Wittering, Bracklesham Bay and Selsey. All breaks work on Channel swells and are best on the incoming tide. Rips can be strong.

Cette zone qui s'étend sur 6 kms est une des plus réputée de la côte sud avec des vagues cassant entre des pontons de bois. L'accès aux vagues se fait par Wittering Est ou Ouest, Bracklesham Bay et Selsey. Tous les spots marchent avec des swells provenant de la Manche et sont meilleurs avec la marée montante.

Esta extensión de 4 millas es una de las más populares de la costa sur con sus olas rompiendo entre los diques de madera. El acceso a las olas es por el este o el oeste de Wittering, Bracklesham Bay y Selsey. Todos los picos funcionan con el swell del Canal y lo mejor es con marea subiendo.

11. Bognor to Beachy Head

The most popular areas are Brighton, Shoreham and Littlehampton and all have their main breaks which are easy to find. Most are in the shelter of the wind and break either on sandbars held in place by jetties and piers, or over chalk reef beds, giving surfable conditions for most of the year. Also in between the main breaks lies miles of rarely surfed coastline. Due to the narrowing of the English Channel and the large tidal range this stretch can miss out on some of the clean groundswells but those strong enough to make it this far up the Channel unload their power with some well shaped waves.

Les régions les plus cotées sont celles de Brighton, Shoreham et Littlehampton et toutes leurs meilleures vagues qui sont faciles à trouver. La plupart sont à l'abri du vent et cassent sur des bancs de sable bien stabilisés par des jetées, ou sur des reefs de craie; elles sont surfables pratiquement toute l'année. Et, entre les breaks principaux s'étirent des kilomètres de côte rarement surfés. En raison de l'étroitesse de la Manche et du marnage important, cette région peut éviter quelques beaux swells de l'Atlantique nord mais si les dépressions arrivent jusqu'en Manche, les vagues pourront gonfler et avoir fière allure.

Las zonas más conocidas son Brighton, Shoreham y Littlehampton y todos los picos más importantes son fáciles de encontrar. La mayoría están protegidos del viento y pueden romper sobre bancos de arena que son aguantados por los rompeolas y diques o sobre asentamientos de reefs, disponiendo de buenas condiciones surfísticas durante la mayoría del año. Debido a lo estrecho de el Canal y el cambio de nivel de marea, esta zona puede perderse parte de la influencia del swell, pero con un swell capaz de llegar hasta aquí arriba descarga todo su poder resultando unas olas perfectas.

Bournemouth Pier - *Photo: Chris Power*

the channel islands

GUERNSEY

Guernsey is not the most consistent surf spot on the globe. If you live here and watch the weather and tides you will occasionally get some excellent waves, but arrive here for a two week holiday, hell bent on surfing every day, and you could be disappointed. Access to all the bays is simple. They all have parking facilities and most have beach side cafes or beach kiosks. Despite one of our surf breaks being nicknamed "Pooh Pooh's", this refers to one of the island's many land drainage pipes situated near the break and not a sewer pipe. Water quality is generally good.

Guernsey n'est pas le spot le plus consistant du globe. Si vous vivez ici et observez le temps et les marées, vous aurez de temps en temps quelques vagues excellentes, mais en arrivant ici pour des vacances de 2 semaines pour du surf acharné, vous risquez d'être déçu. Le windsurfeur de passage a plus de chance de passer du temps à l'eau. L'accés à toutes les baies est simple. Elles ont toutes des parkings et la plupart ont des cafés et des boutiques de plage. Un de nos spots porte le nom de "Pooh Pooh's"; ce n'est pas en raison d'une conduite d'égout mais à la présence d'une des nombreuses conduites de drainage situées près du spot. La qualité de l'eau est généralement bonne.

Esta isla no es el destino surfero más consistente del planeta. Si vives aquí y prestas atención al tiempo y a las mareas puedes disfrutar sesiones clásicas, pero si llegas para pasar un par de semanitas con la esperanza de surfear a diario, te puedes llevar un disgusto. Las condiciones para el windsurf son más regulares. Todas las bahías son de fácil acceso, disponen de buenos aparcamientos y tienen bares y kioskos playeros. La calidad del agua es buena, aunque hay un spot denominado "Pooh-Pooh's" donde hay una serie de tuberías cerca del pico, pero no vierten aguas contaminadas.

St. Ouen's Bay - *Photo: Pete Journeaux*

Watersplash - *Photo: Pete Journeaux*

JERSEY

Jersey is the largest and most southerly of the Channel islands and has a rich surfing history dating back to the 60's. Nearly all the surf can be found along the west coast, with the spectacular St Ouen's Bay providing 5 miles of beach and reef break waves (restricted during summer months). Access to all the breaks is very easy and like Guernsey, water quality is generally good.

Jersey est la plus grande et la plus au sud des îles Anglo-Normandes et posséde une histoire riche en surf remontant aux années 60. La majeure partie des vagues se trouvent le long de la côte ouest, avec la spectaculaire baie de St-Ouen proposant 8 kms de plages de sable et de récifs (dont certaines parties sont interdites en été). L'accés aux vagues est très facile et, comme pour Guernesey, la qualité de l'eau est généralement bonne.

Jersey es la más grande y meridional de las Islas del Canal, tiene una rica historia surfera que data de los años 60. Prácticamente todas las olas se hallan en la Costa Oeste, donde se encuentra la espectacular Bahía de St Ouen con sus ocho kilómetros de rompientes de playa y de arrecife (la práctica del surf está limitada durante el verano). El acceso es fácil.

The Channel Islands

Steve & Andy - *Freedom*
Chris Mason - *Nautifun*

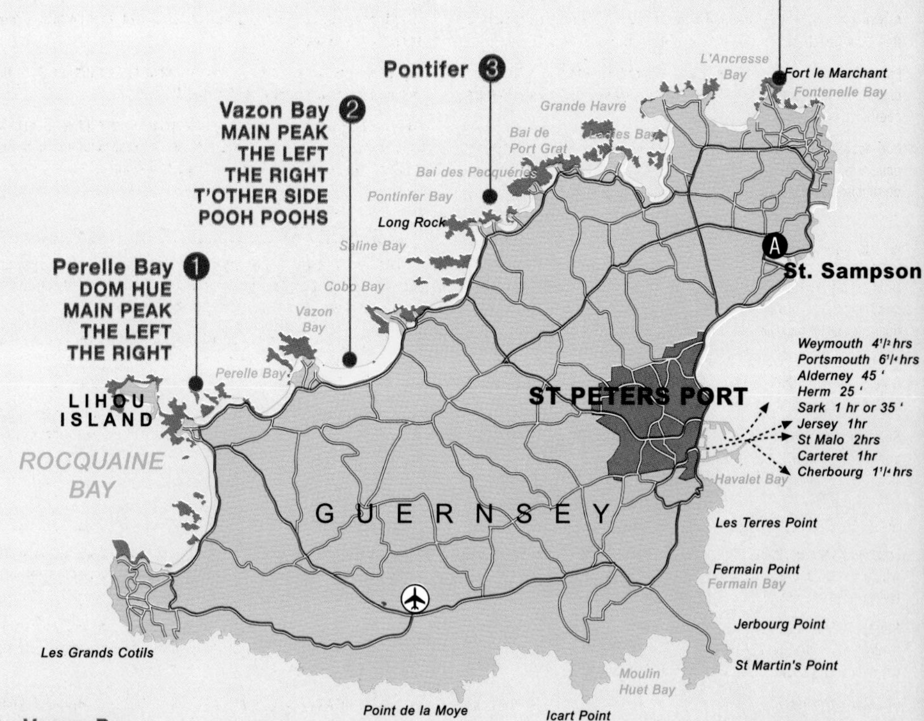

1. Perelle Bay

DOM HUE

The jewel in the crown of Guernsey surf, including a variety of waves at mid to high tide and the big wave spot on the island. Far out to sea, and very rocky surfing, Perelle is generally left to the 'experts' and can be a daunting prospect.

La petite merveille du surf de l'île, comprenant une grande variété de vagues de la mi-marée à marée haute; c'est également le spot de gros de l'île. Vague au large et de rocher, Perelle est le plus souvent une gauche (d'après les habitués) et peut devenir une aventure intrépide.

La joya de la corona del surf de Guernsey. Incluye varias olas (para marea media y alta) y un spot tamañero. Rompen mar adentro sobre rocas. Es un sitio para expertos que te puede intimidar.

THE PEAK

This big right breaks a long way out in the centre of Perelle Bay and is reached from the Islet of Dom Hue. The peak is very shifty and on a big day it's hard to suss the take-off point. To get there you have to pass two excellent breaks behind the island so it's not surfed much.

Cette grosse droite casse un long moment au centre de la baie de Perelle; on l'atteint par l'îlôt de Dom Hue. Le pic est traître et, un jour de gros, il est dur de repérer le take-off. Pour s'y rendre il faut passer deux excellentes vagues derriére l'îlot, relativement peu surfées.

Es una derecha tamañera que rompe alajada de la orilla en el centro de la bahía de Perelle. Se accede desde el islote de Dom Hue. El pico se mueve mucho y en los días grandes es difícil adivinar el take-off. Como para llegar al pico tienes que dejar atrás dos olas excelentes no se suele surfear muy a menudo.

THE LEFT

This is the wave that's ridden most at Perelle. It generally picks up more swell than other breaks on the island. Because it's 300m out to sea, it can suffer if the wind is blowing, but provides the best shaped and longest rideable left on the islands. Breaking off or around a rocky outcrop, one can catch long walling waves well into the shallows. Best on a smaller tide, it can hold a swell up to10ft. Due to the rocks and position, this is only for the most experienced surfers. Get caught on a big day and the rip can wash you to the other side of the island. On a small day you can lose a fin on the rocks below the surface as the tide recedes.

C'est la vague la plus surfée à Perelle. Elle reccueile plus de houles que les autres vagues de l'île. Parce qu'elle est située à 300 m du bord, elle peut pâtir du vent, mais c'est la plus belle et la plus longue gauche des îles. Déferlant le long de rochers à fleur d'eau, on peut y surfer de longs murs sur des hauts-fonds. Meilleur lors de petites marées, la vague tient une houle de 3 m. En raison des rochers et de son emplacement, la vague est réservée aux surfeurs confirmés. Un jour de petit, on risque de perdre une dérive lorsque la marée descend.

Es la ola más surfeada de la bahía, porque es la que más mar recibe de toda la isla. Al estar 300m mar adentro, no aguanta bien el viento. Empieza a romper alrededor de una formación rocosa y proporciona olas largas y bien formadas que se pueden surfear hasta que la roca queda en la superficie. Aguanta tres metros y se coge mejor con mareas muertas. Es sólo para surfers con experiencia. En un día grande la corriente te puede llevar al otro lado de la isla, y en uno pequeño puedes romper una quilla sobre las rocas al bajar la marea.

THE RIGHT

Probably the best wave on Guernsey, which breaks on a big swell, with a large tide. A sucking take-off, right next to a group of rocks, propels you onto a powerful peeling wave, over a couple of large rocks which emerge as the tide drops. Don't get caught on the inside.

Certainement la meilleure vague de Guernsey, qui ne casse que par gros swell, lors d'une grosse marée. Un take-off aérien, tout près d'une barre de rochers, vous propulse dans une vague plutôt décoiffante, au dessus de deux gros rochers qui affleurent lorsque la marée descend. Ne vous faites pas avoir dans l'inside! Bonne chance!

Para algunos la mejor ola de la isla. Requiere marejadas fuertes y mareas vivas. La bajada es chupona y se realiza al lado de un grupo de rocas, la ola se enrosca con fuerza por encima de rocas que emergen al bajar la marea. Procura que no te atrape la serie al final de la ola..

3 Vazon Bay

MAIN PEAK

The centre of Guernsey's surfing; predominantly a righthander breaking from the centre of the bay diagonally towards the land drainage pipe. Usually at its best from half tide up to the start of the backwash (caused by waves hitting the wall), which makes surfing impossible. Occasionally excellent just before the tide becomes high.

Le pôle du surf à Guernsey; une droite déferle en travers du centre de la baie vers la conduite d'égoût. Normalement, la vague est au meilleur de sa forme de la mi-marée jusqu'au début du backwash (dû au fait que les vagues rebondissent sur un mur), qui rend le spot impossible à surfer. De temps en tempsc'est parfait uste avant que la marée ne devienne trop haute.

El centro de la movida surfera de Guernsey, una derecha que rompe diagonalmente desde el medio de la bahía hacia la tubería de desagüe. Funciona de marea media hasta justo antes de la alta (en ocasiones perfecta), que es cuando comienza la contraola que rebota en el muro de la orilla imposibilitando surfear.

LEFT

When the tide is too high for the beach, the left on the reef starts to break. It can offer an exhilarating drop with a fast occasionally spitting section. Increase your adrenaline by a confrontation with Nipple Rock smack in the middle of the reef.

Quand la marée devient trop haute pour la plage, la gauche du récif commence à fonctionner. Cela peut donner un super drop avec, de temps à autre, une section rapide qui en jette. Le "Nipple Rock", en plein milieu du récif, vous permettra d'avoir des montées d'adrénaline tout à fait honorables!

Cuando la marea est· demasiado alta para surfear la playa, se puede coger el arrecife. Es una bajada intensa y rápida con secciones tuberas ocasionales. La posibilidad de chocar con una roca (Nipple Rock) a mitad de recorrido, aumenta la adrenalina.

RIGHT

This wave needs a spring tide to cover the bigger rocks sufficiently. Better than the left, and provides a sucking take-off followed by a longish ride into the shallows. The right only works up to about 6ft....

Cette vague a besoin d'une marée d'équinoxe pour recouvrir suffisamment les rochers les plus gros. Elle est meilleure que la gauche et commence par un take-off dans le vide suivi par un long surf sur les hauts-fonds. Cette droite marche jusqu'à environ 2 m..

Requiere una marea muy viva que cubra las rocas. Es aún mejor que la izquierda. Tiene bastante recorrido y una bajada muy vertical. Sólo aguanta dos metros porque a partir de ese tamaño se junta con...

T'OTHER SIDE

...the other side of the reef comes into its own on a big swell when the beach and the reef are closing out. It can provide long rights from the reef diagonally across the beach. There is no doubt that when everything gels this break can be classic.

L'autre côté du reef prend la relève lors des gros swells quand la plage et le récif ferment. La vague peut se transformer en de longues droites puis à travers la plage. Cela peut devenir un must quand les conditions sont réunies. L'absence de courants puissants la transforme en un surf pépère.

Este lado del arrecife funciona cuando las olas anteriores cierran. Proporciona largas derechas y tiene sus días clásicos. Además no hay corrientes apreciables.

POOH POOH'S

A wave breaks over sand, with a peak that can be ridden left or right. The rides are usually short, very fast and break predominantly right. Rarer, equally fast and hollow lefts also wind across the beach into one of the ubiquitous land drainage pipes.

Une vague déferle sur du sable, avec un pic qui part en droite et en gauche. La vague est habituellement courte, très rapide et la droite marche plus souvent. Plus rare, également rapide et creuse, la gauche s'enroule le long d'une conduite de drainage; encore une!

Rompe en arena con salida de derechas y de izquierdas. Son olas cortas, muy rápidas y predominan las derechas, aunque hay días en que salen izquierdas huecas junto a una de las abundantes tuberías de desagüe.

3. Portinfer

A popular bay which picks up more swell than Vazon, offering a consistent half tide break. At half tide a peak in the centre provides lefts and rights. As the tide drops the waves break more powerfully on the northern headland to provide a right across the narrow part of the bay. On a small tide, a respectable left can be found breaking off the rocks just below the port.

Une baie réputée qui chope plus de swell que Vazon, offrant un break consistant à mi-marée. A mi-marée aussi, un pic au centre fournit des gauches et des droites. Quand la marée baisse, les vagues déferlent avec plus de puissance au nord du promontoire et balacent une droite à travers la partie étroite de la baie. Lors d'une petite marée, une gauche correcte peut casser sur de la caillasse juste en dessous du port.

Recibe más mar que Vazon. Con marea media hay un pico en el centro, es consistente y con salida a ambos lados. Según baja la marea las olas tienen más fuerza en la parte norte dando derechas. Con mareas muertas, se puede surfear una izquierda de roca junto al puerto.

4 Fort le Marchant

A difficult rock reef break wrapping around a headland, and throwing just off the rocks with a shoulder walling up into deep water. This wave wraps through 90 degrees. When everywhere else is totally huge, and blown out, head here and watch probably the best wave on the island break.

Un spot de récif difficile qui s'enroule autour d'un promontoire, et se jette sur des rochers avec une épaule venant mourir en eau profonde. Cette vague tourne à 90 degrés.Quand toutest énorme et impraticable, c'est certainement la meilleure vague de l'île.

Una ola difícil que cae en fondo rocoso alrededor de una punta de roca, comenzando justo al lado de las rocas levantando su brazo hasta llegar a aguas profundas. La ola se tuerce en un ángulo de noventa grados. Es la mejor ola de la isla y funciona cuando todo lo demás está desfasado.

1. Greve De Lacq

A few times in winter, normally when the swells are huge, a visit to this little beach can be a good move. Only works on a 32ft.

Parfois en hiver, normalement quand le swell est énorme, cette petite plage vaut le déplacement. Marche seulement lors des marées à forts coefficients.

Con ocasión de los grandes maretones invernales, puede merecer la pena visitar esta pequeña playa, que sólo funciona con mareas vivas de mucho coeficiente.

2. Plemont Beach

Only on big swells will one find worthwhile waves here. When these conditions are present it can be rewarding with good waves in beautiful surroundings

On trouvera des vagues valables seulement lors des gros swells. Quand les conditions sont réunies, on peut être récompensé par de bonnes vagues dans un joli cadre.

Sólo merece la pena con fuerte marejada, te encontrarás buenas olas enmarcadas en un paisaje de gran belleza.

3. Stinky Bay

Located at the northern end of St Ouen's Bay. Works like a point and will always be crowded. The name Stinky Bay comes from rotting seaweed in the gulley where you paddle out.

Située à l'extrême nord de la baie de St-Ouen. Marche comme un "point" et sera toujours bondée. Le nom Stinky Bay ("baie puante") est due à la présence d'algues pourissantes dans lesquelles on rame.

Situado en la parte N de la Bahía de St Ouen, es un point donde siempre vas a encontrar mucha gente. El nombre de bahía hedionda procede de las algas en putrefacción que se encuentran en el lugar por donde se entra al agua.

4. Secrets

Long tubey, reef quality rides, surfable up to10ft. A left starts to work when the swell is over 4ft.

Vagues de reef avec un long tube, surfable au dessus de 3 m. Une gauche commence à marcher à partir d'1 m.

Proporciona olas largas, tuberas y de calidad similar a las de arrecife, pese a romper en arena; aguanta 3 metros. Además, hay una izquierda que empieza a funcionar a partir del metro.

5. Watersplash

If there's no swell at Watersplash then there is no swell anywhere. This makes this spot the most popular on the island. Watch out for rocks at low tide and beware of rips when it's big.

S'il n'y a pas de swell à Watersplash alors il n'y a rien nulle part. C'est pourquoi c'est le spot le plus populaire de l'île. Faites gaffe aux rochers à marée basse et des chutes lorsque c'est gros.

Si no hay olas en Watersplash, no las hay en ningún lugar de la isla. En consecuencia. es el spot más frecuentado. En marea baja presta atenciÓn a las rocas y si está grande vigila las corrientes.

6. Les Brayes

A medium to big wave spot, the waves here can pack a punch. The dropping tide is best and there's a rip running from south to north. Easy paddle out around the tower.

Un spot de vagues moyennes à grosses où les vagues percutent à max. La marée descendante est la meilleure et il y a une courant du sud au nord. Facile de sortir au niveau de la tour.

Olas de tamaño medio a grande, con una fuerza considerable. Se coge mejor con la marea bajando. Es fácil entrar rodeando la torre, existe una corriente del sur al norte de la playa.

Les Brayes - Photo: Pete Journeaux

7. Corbière Reef

Only starts to work when the swell reaches 15ft. Its only ever been surfed by a handful of experienced locals and it's unlikely as a travelling surfer that you will have the right equipment. If you do decide to tackle it ask the locals for advice which they will be more than happy to provide. Access is the same as Petit Port.

Ne daigne marcher que lorsque le swell atteint 4 à 5 m.N'a été surfé que par une poignée de locaux expérimentés et il est rare qu'un surfeur de passage ait l'équipement adéquat. Si vous décidez d'aller la taquiner, faites-vous conseiller par les locaux qui seront plus que ravis de vous renseigner. Même accés que pour Petit Port.

Empieza a funcionar a partir de cuatro metros. Sólo lo surfean un puñado de veteranos locales. Es difícil que el surfista de paso tenga una tabla adecuada para una ola de este tamaño, pero si decides intentarlo pregunta a los locales, que gustosamente te ofrecerán los consejos necesarios. Se accede del mismo modo que a Petit Port.

8. Petit Port

Jerseys' big wave spot. The righthander provides quality barrels up to 15ft. The lower the tide the more dangerous it becomes. To get out jump off the slipway, a rip will take you to the lineup, timing is crucial. There is a car park next to the slipway.

Le spot de grosses vagues de Jersey. La droite envoie des tubes jusqu'à 4 à 5 mètres. Plus la marée est basse et plus cela devient dangereux. Le timing est crucial pour se jeter du chantier de construction, un courant vous poussera jusqu'au lineup. Il y a un parking près du chantier.

Es el spot de ola grande de Jersey, la derecha proporciona tubos de calidad hasta casi los cinco metros. Cuanto más baja la marea más peligroso se pone. La entrada es difícil, se realiza a través del embarcadero, siendo crucial la elección del momento oportuno. La corriente te llevará al pico.

9. St Brelade's Bay

A popular tourist beach with windsurfing throughout the year. Waves only on the biggest swells when the west facing breaks are closing out. The best peaks are found by the pier and it will be crowded when it's working.

Un lieu touristique branché où l'on pratique le windsurf tout au long de l'année. Il y a des vagues seulement lors des gros swells quand les spots exposés à l'ouest ferment. Les meilleures pics se trouvent près de la jetée et ils seront bondés lorsque ça marche.

Las olas sólo aparecen en las grandes marejadas cuando los spots orientados al Oeste están desfasados. Los mejores picos están junto al espigón. Cuando funciona se llena de gente.

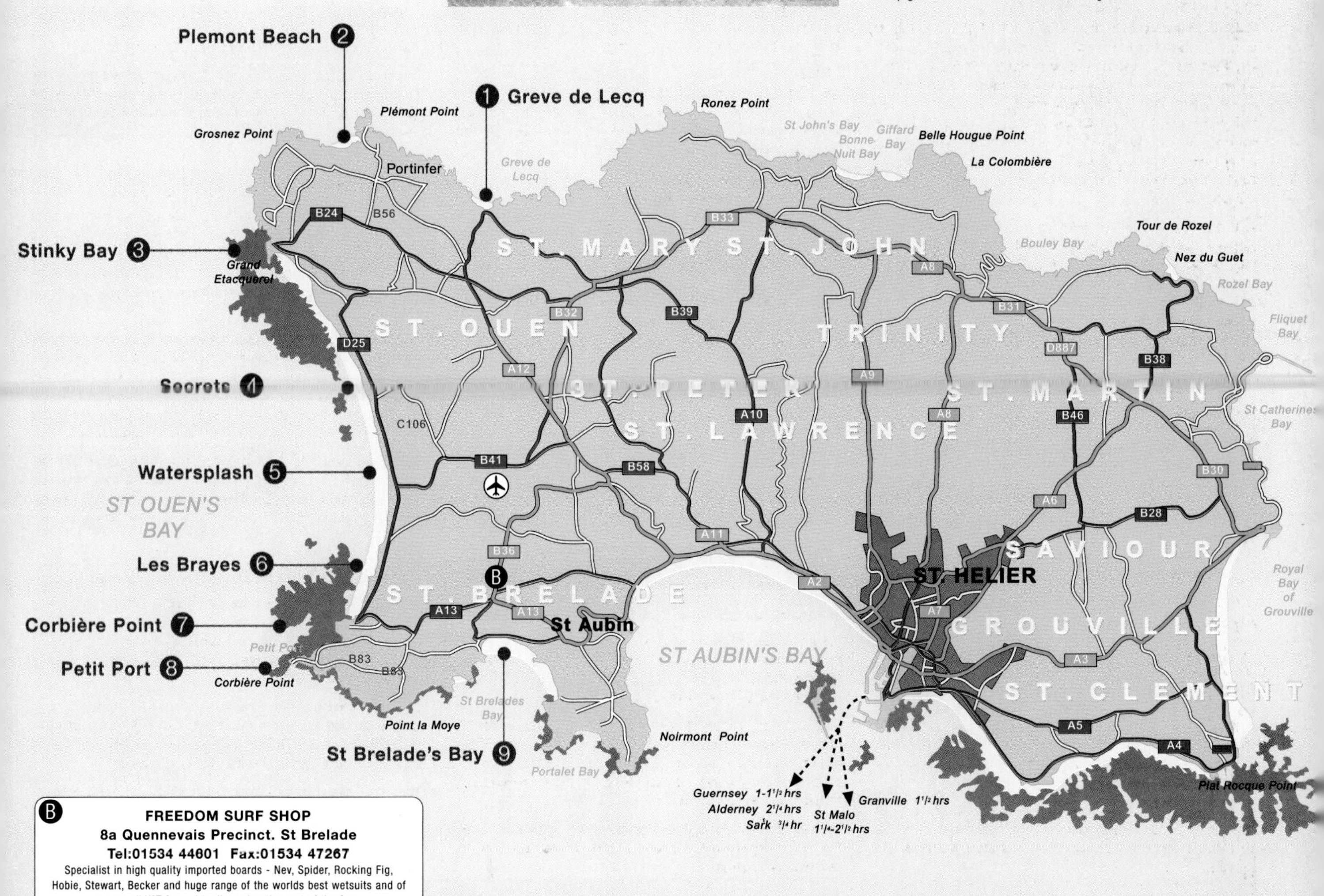

power
performance
&
COMPLETE
control.

Surfer: Keith Sasaki - Hawaii

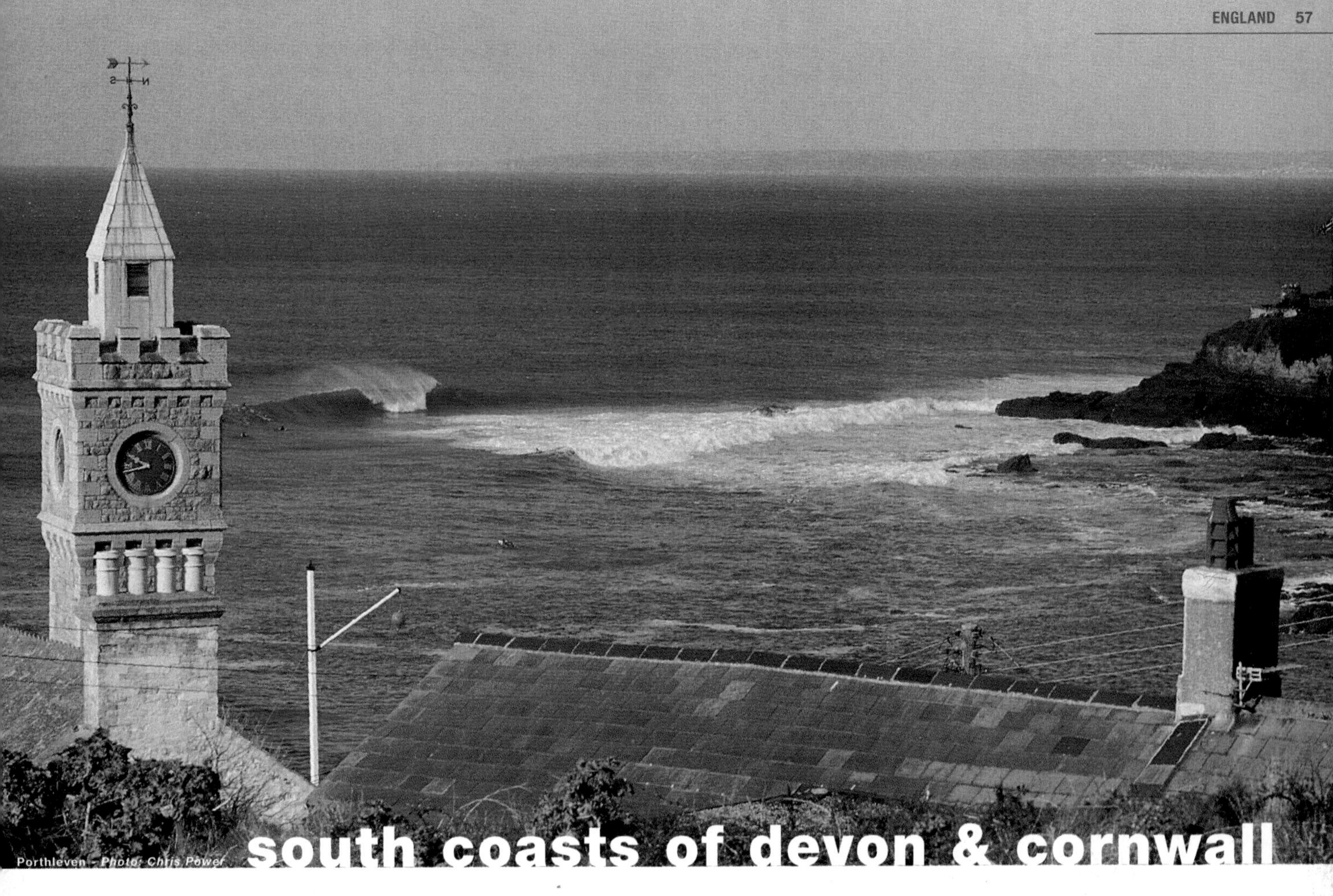

Porthleven - *Photo: Chris Power*

south coasts of devon & cornwall

"Southerly storms in the Bay of Biscay or in the sea area of Finistere produce short-lived but powerful waves on the south coast of Devon and Cornwall"

Falmouth Reef - *Photo: Simon McComb*

Southerly storms in the Bay of Biscay or in the sea area of Finistere produce short-lived but powerful waves on the south coast of Devon and Cornwall. An E, N or NW wind will provide the best conditions. Unfortunately, south coast swells are often accompanied with S or SW winds which drastically reduces the number of 'real' surfing days available.

Ironically, England's premier reef break, Porthleven, is on the south coast, making the rideable tubes rare jewels indeed. Quite often, a strong SW wind will turn NW for a time - so if a beach faces true south, such as Portwrinkle, the conditions will often clean up very quickly. The south coast is at its best between January and April when the winter storms take a more southerly track across Europe.

Les tempêtes du sud dans la baie de Biscay ou près du Finistère produisent des vagues pendant une courte période mais puissantes, elles déroulent sur la côte sud du Devon et di Cornwall. Un vent d'est,du nord ou nord-ouest fournissent les meilleures conditions.Malheureusement, les swells qui touchent la côte sud sont souvent accompagnés de vents du sud ou sud-ouest qui réduisent très fortement le nombre de jours réellement intéressants.

Curieusement, la première vague de reef d'Angleterre, Porthleven, est sur la côte sud, produisant des petits bijous de tubes. Assez souvent, un fort vent de sud-ouest fini par passer nord-ouest - ainsi si une plage est exposée plein sud,telle que Portwrinkle, les conditions s'améliorent très rapidement. La côte sud est au sommet de sa forme entre janvier et avril quant les tempêtes d'hiver prennent un chemin plus au sud à travers l'Europe.

Las borrascas del sur situadas en el Golfo de Vizcaya o en la zona marítima de Finisterre producen oleajes poderosos, aunque de corta duración, en las costas del sur de Devon y Cornwall. Los vientos de componente norte, del noroeste al este, proporcionan las mejores condiciones. Desafortunadamente, los oleajes procedentes del sur a menudo llegan acompañados con vientos de la misma dirección reduciendo de forma drástica los días disponibles para surfear en condiciones mínimas.

Irónicamente, Porthleven, la mejor ola de arrecife de toda Inglaterra, se encuentra en esta costa sur lo que provoca que sus tubos sean apreciados como joyas. Es bastante usual que el fuerte viento del suroeste role al noroeste, ordenando el mar rápidamente en las playas directamente orientadas al sur, como Portwrinkle. La mejor temporada para esta costa va de Enero a Abril que es cuando las borrascas siguen una trayectoria ligeramente más meridional en su ruta a través de Europa.

Portwrinkle - *Photo: Peter Cade*

Porthleven - *Photo: Peter Cade*

South Cornwall & Devon

Peter Cade
Alex Williams

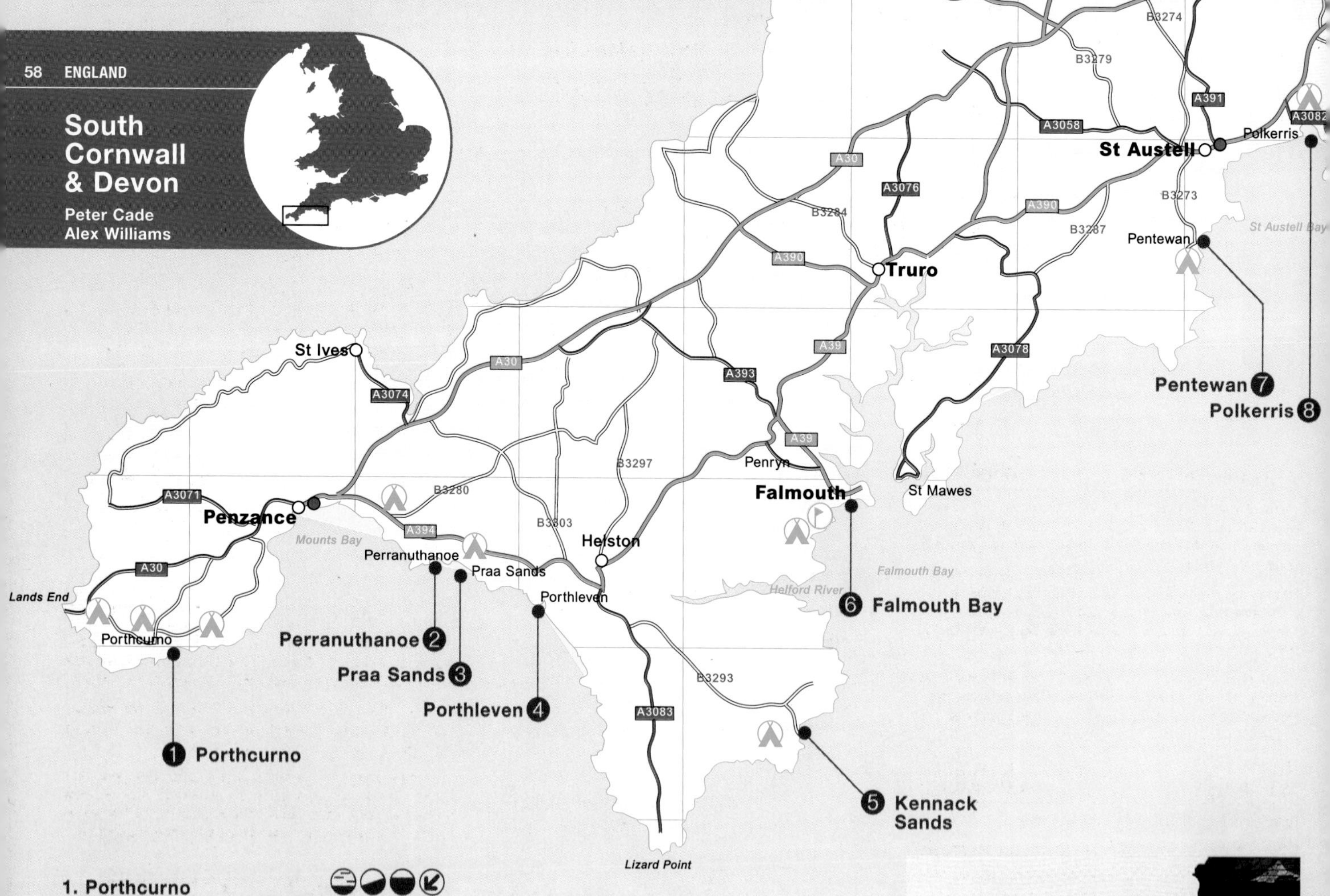

1. Porthcurno

A nice spot which can have some good waves when there's a big SW swell. There's a large car park by the beach.

Un bon spot qui peut bien marcher avec un gros swell de Sud-ouest. Méga-parking à côté de la plage.

Es un lugar precioso donde pueden salir buenas olas con una fuerte marajada del sudoeste. Hay un gran parking de coches por la playa.

2. Perranuthanoe

Sometimes a good righthander breaks near the rocks at the northwest end of the beach. Good to check when Praa Sands is too big, and doesn't get as crowded. Good for beginners.

Parfois une bonne droite à côté des rochers au nord-ouest de la plage. A checker quand Praa Sands est trop gros ou qu'il y a trop de monde. Bien pour les débutants.

Algunas veces rompe una derecha por las rocas del extremo noroeste de la playa. Es un sitio a tener en cuenta cuando Praa Sands está muy grande, y encima no se llena tanto de gente.

3. Praa Sands

One of the most popular beaches in the area, with surfers and holiday makers. Picks up more swell than Perranuthanoe. The northern end recieves some protection from W winds by the point, off which a fast right sometimes breaks. Eastern end can have dangerous rips in a big swell. Car park by beach.

Une des plages les plus populaires du coin pour les surfers et les touristes. Prend mieux la houle que Perranuthanoe. L'extrémité nord est abritée des vents d'ouest par le cap, au bout duquel une droite rapide casse de tempe en temps. De l'autre côté, attention aux courants violents quand c'est gros. Parking sur la plage.

Es una de las playas más famosas de la zona en la que conviven surfistas con veraneantes. Entra más mar que en Perranuthanoe. El límite del norte está protegido de los vientos del oeste al tiempo que una derecha muy rápida suele romper. Con fuertes marejadas pueden aparecer grandes corrientes en el extremo este.

Praa Sands - *Photo: Peter Cade*

4. Porthleven

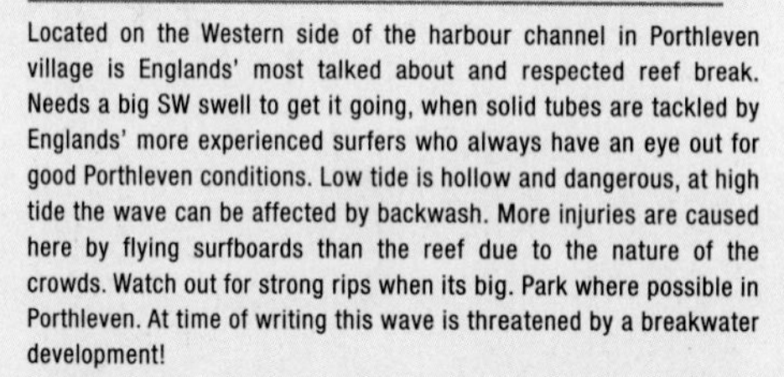

Located on the Western side of the harbour channel in Porthleven village is Englands' most talked about and respected reef break. Needs a big SW swell to get it going, when solid tubes are tackled by Englands' more experienced surfers who always have an eye out for good Porthleven conditions. Low tide is hollow and dangerous, at high tide the wave can be affected by backwash. More injuries are caused here by flying surfboards than the reef due to the nature of the crowds. Watch out for strong rips when its big. Park where possible in Porthleven. At time of writing this wave is threatened by a breakwater development!

Situé à l'ouest de l'entrée du port du village de Porthleven, le reef le plus respecté d'Angleterre, dont on parle souvent dans les chaumières. Exige un gros swell de sud-ouest pour marcher: ses tubes caverneux sont taquinés par les meilleurs surfers anglais qui gardent toujours un oeil attentif sur les conditions locales. A marée basse, c'est creux et dangereux tandis qu'il y a du backwash à marée haute. Les accidents sont plus souvent dûs aux planches perdues qu'au reef à cause de la foule. Méfiance quand c'est gros, il y du jus. Garez-vous dans Porthleven. On parle d'un projet de développement du port: encore un spot menacé!

Porthleven es uno de los picos máscomentados y respetados de Inglaterra. Necesita de una gran marejada del SO para funcionar, al tiempo que los surferos más experimentados de Inglaterra intentarán entrar en sus contundentes tubos ya que es este un sitio de cuyas condiciones todo el mundo está pendiente. La ola en marea baja es cerrona y peligrosa, mientrás que en pleamar hay que tener en cuenta a la contracorriente. Se producen más heridas en este lugar debido a las tablas que salen despedidas que al arrecife propiamente dicho debido a la multitud. Aparcad en Porthleven. En el momento en que se está escribiendo está revista, esta ola se encuentra amenazada por el proyecto de construcciónde un rompeolas!

5. Kennack Sands

Two beaches join at low tide to make one of the longest beaches on the eastern side of the Lizard Peninsula. Will only have waves in the biggest of swells.

Deux plages qui se joignent à marée basse pour faire une des plus longues plages du côté oriental de la Péninsule de Lizard. Des vagues seulement avec des conditions énormes.

Dos playas que se unen en marea baja para formar una de las playas más largas del lado oeste de la península de Lizard. Saldrán olas solo con las mayores marejadas.

Porthleven - *Photo: Alex Williams*

6. Falmouth Bay

A number of waves working best on storm or SW swells. Maenporth, Swanpool and Gyllyngvase beaches all have waves on their day but word gets out quick and they are always crowded. Gyllyngvase reef lies between Swanpool and Gyllyngvase beaches and about twice a year offers a good left with a fast take-off and short walling section as the tide covers the reef.

Un certain nombre de vagues qui marchent mieux quand c'est la tempête ou des houles de S-O. Les plages de Maenporth, Swanpol et Gyllyngvase ont toutes des vagues certains jours mais ça se sait vite et il y a pratiquement toujours du monde. Le reef de Gyllyngvase se trouve entre Swanpol et la plage de Gyllyngvase et donne deux fois par an une bonne gauche avec un take-off raide et des petits murs quand la marée recouvre le récif.

Son una serie de olas que cuadran con tormentas o con marejadas del SO. Las playas de Maenporth, Swanpool y Gyllyngvase, todas tienen olas en sus buenos dias. El arrecife de Gyllyngvase se halla situado entre las playas de Swanpool y Gyllyngvase y unas dos veces al año aparece aquí una excelente izquierda con un rápido take-off y una pared de sección corta al cubrir la marea el arrecife.

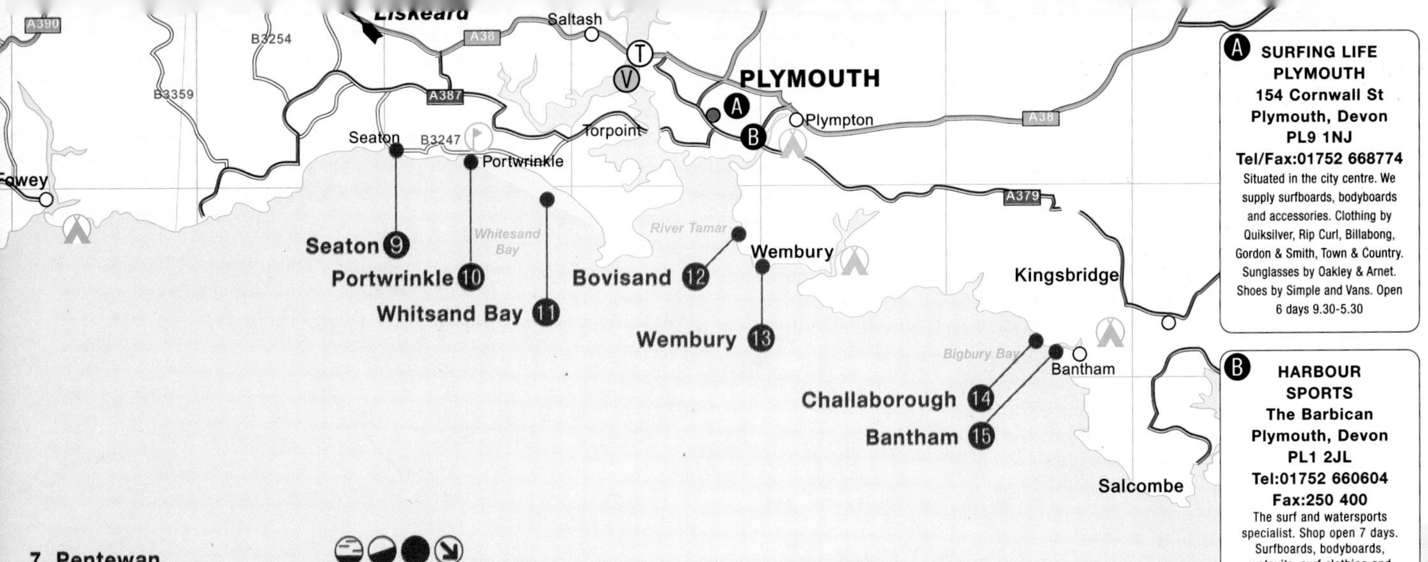

A SURFING LIFE PLYMOUTH
154 Cornwall St
Plymouth, Devon
PL9 1NJ
Tel/Fax:01752 668774
Situated in the city centre. We supply surfboards, bodyboards and accessories. Clothing by Quiksilver, Rip Curl, Billabong, Gordon & Smith, Town & Country. Sunglasses by Oakley & Arnet. Shoes by Simple and Vans. Open 6 days 9.30-5.30

B HARBOUR SPORTS
The Barbican
Plymouth, Devon
PL1 2JL
Tel:01752 660604
Fax:250 400
The surf and watersports specialist. Shop open 7 days. Surfboards, bodyboards, wetsuits, surf clothing and accessories. Over 10,000 different items stocked. Friendly, fast and efficient service.

7. Pentewan

Sheltered beach about four miles south of St Austell. Only works on a huge south coast swell and consequently is unlikely to work in the summer. The waves can get quite hollow at high tide when a fast beach break develops.

Plage abritée environ 6 Km au sud de St-Austell. Marche seulement par énorme swell de sud, cherchez pas en été. Les vagues peuvent y être assez creuses à marée haute quand un beach-break rapide se forme.

Es una playa protegida a unas 4 millas al sur de St Austell. Solo funciona con las más grandes marejadas costeras por lo que rara vez funcionará en verano. Las olas pueden volverse tuberass en marea alta al romper mucho más rápido.

8. Polkerris

Popular beach which needs a big swell to work.

Encore une plage conrue de tous, qui ne marche que pas gros swell.

Es una playa popular que necesita de una fuerte marajada para funcionar.

9. Seaton

Three miles to the east of Looe, this beach is quite sheltered. If Whitsands is 5ft expect 2ft waves at Seaton.

5 Kms à l'Est de Looe, cette plage est abritée. Si Whitsands fait 1,5 m, ça ne fera que moins de la moitié à Seaton.

Tres millas al oeste de Looe, esta playa se halla bastante a cubierto. Las olas son aproximadamente de la mitad de tamaño que en Whitsands.

10. Portwrinkle

At the east end of Whitsand Bay and usually a foot or two smaller. Favoured in big swells. A number of rocks get covered at high tide so watch your fins. Park above the beach and walk down the cliff path.

A l'extrémité Est de Whitsand Bat et normalement 50 cms de moins, mieux quand c'est gros donc. Pas mal de rochers sont recouverts à marée haute, faites gaffe aux ailerons. Garez-vous au-dessus de la plage et cherchez le petit chemin qui descend.

Se encuentra en el extremo este de Whitsands Bahía, y normalmente las olas son medio metro más pequeñas aquí. Sale favorecido con las grandes marejadas. Una serie de rocas se cubren con la pleamar así que ten cuidado con los pinreles. Hay un aparcamiento para coches encima de la playa con un camino de acceso hasta la misma.

11. Whitsand Bay

This four mile long beach is much visited by Plymuoth based surfers. Tregantle in the middle of the beach works quite well at high tide, but access is restricted by the army who seem to know when the surf is good and always close the path for shooting! Rips are particularly strong here. No parking near the beach - a ten minute walk down the road is needed.

Cette plage, longue de 6 Kms, est souvent visitée par les surfers de Plymouth. Tregantle au milieu de la plage marche plutôt bien à marée haute mais l'accès est restreint par l'Armée qui semble fermer pour les tirs seulement quand le surf est bon. Attention aux courants! Pas de parking prés de la plage, soyez prêts pour une bonne marche de 10 minutes.

Esta playa de 4 millas de largura suele estar concurrida por surfistas de Plymouth. En la mitad de la playa, Tregantle funciona bastante bien en pleamar, pero el acceso se halla restringido por el ejercito que parace saber cuando hay buenas condiciones surfísticas para cerrar el paso y áponerse a disparar! Las corrientes son particularmente fuertes aquí. No se permite aparcar cerca de la playa por lo que habrá que recorrer un camino de unos10min desde la carretera.

12. Bovisand

Small beach located inside Plymouth Sound. Hollow reef break only works on huge S/SW swell. Very steep take-off, very rare event.

Petite plage situes dans Plymouth Sound, qui marche avec une grosse houle de S/SO. Un take-off bien raide. Ne marche que rarement.

Pequeña playa situada dentro de Plymouth South. Pico de arecife hueco que solo funciona con un swell enorme de S/SO.

Bovisand - *Photo: Peter Cade*

13. Wembury

On smaller swells low to mid tide is best. The best waves of the bay are often the lefts off Blackstone Rocks. Swell is normally 1-2ft smaller than Bantham. A popular place for Plymouth based surfers.

Quand c'est tout petit, de marée basse à mi-marée. Les meilleurs vagues de la baie sont souvent les gauches de Blackstone Rocks. Ca fait en général 50 cms de moins qu'à Bantham.

Las mejores olas se dan con marejadas medias y a media marea. Las mejores olas de esta bahía suelen ser izquierdas y rompen contra Blackstone Rocks. Normalmente entra medio metro menos que en Bantham. Es un sitio frecuentado por los locales de Plymouth.

14. Challaborough

Beach break surf, lefts off the cliffs when the sand banks are right. Low tide righthand point works to the right of beach and can be good. Can handle SW or W winds.

Beach break qui donne des gauches vers les falaises quand les bancs sont favorables; Une droite à marée basse marche à droite de la plage, ça peut même être bon. Tient les vents de sud-ouest et ouest.

En esta playa las derechas rompen contra el acantilado cuando los bancos de arena se encuentran perfectos. El pico a mano derecha en marea baja funciona de derecha y puede ser excelente.

15. Bantham

Bantham catches most swell in the area with good beach peaks and tubing rights breaking into the mouth of the river Avon. Pushing tide.

Bantham chope la plupart des houles dans le coin avec de bons pics et des droites qui tubent en sortie de la riviere Avon.

Un lugar conocido de la costa sur, en Bantham sale una muy buena ola playera, con una derecha tubera que rompe contra la boca del rio.

Bantham - *Photo: Alex Williams*

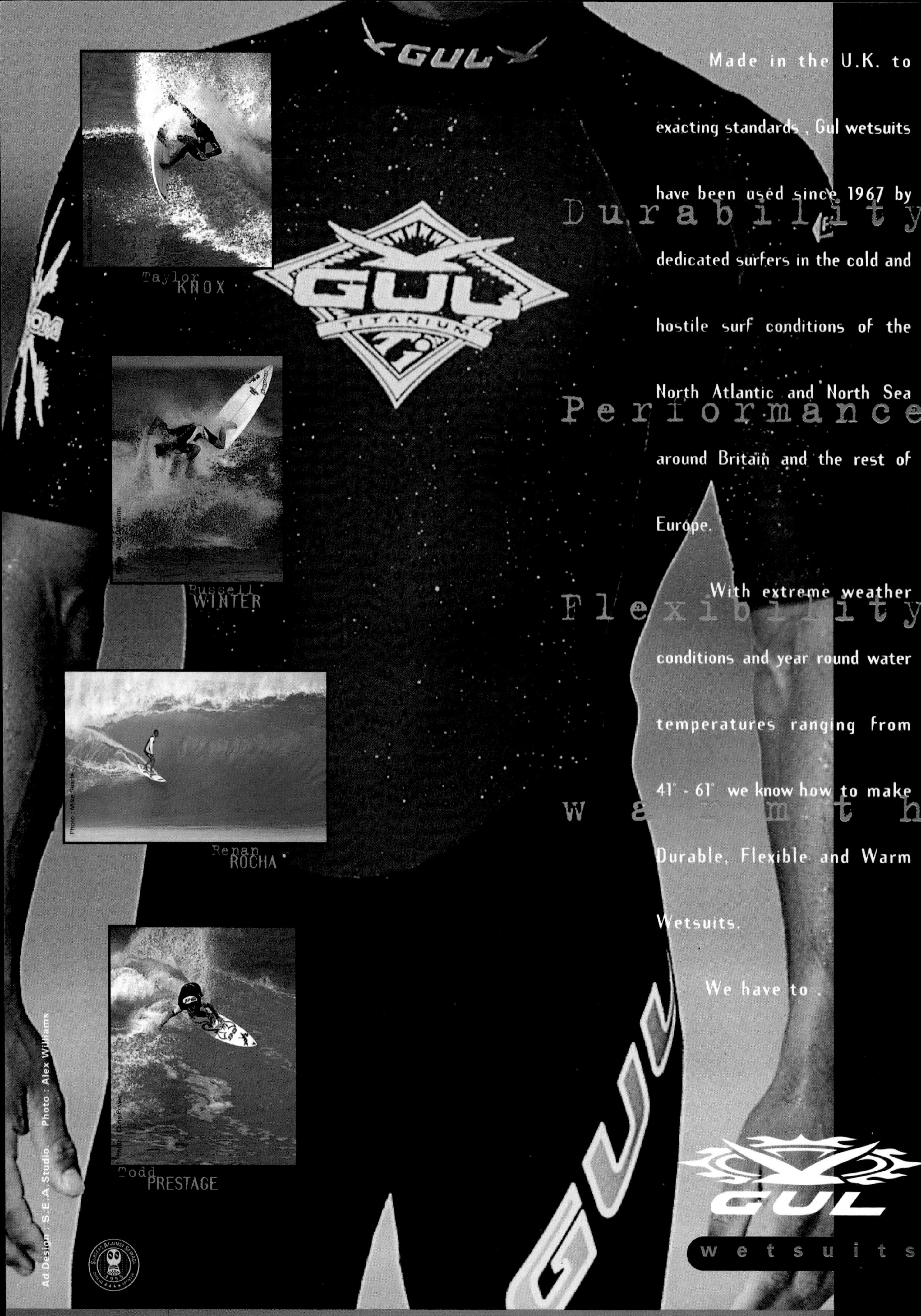
Made in the U.K. to exacting standards, Gul wetsuits have been used since 1967 by dedicated surfers in the cold and hostile surf conditions of the North Atlantic and North Sea around Britain and the rest of Europe.
Durability
Performance
Flexibility
warmth
With extreme weather conditions and year round water temperatures ranging from 41° - 61° we know how to make Durable, Flexible and Warm Wetsuits.
We have to.
Taylor KNOX
Russell WINTER
Renan ROCHA
Todd PRESTAGE
Photo : Mike Searle
Ad Design : S.E.A. Studio Photo : Alex Williams
GUL TITANIUM
GUL
GUL wetsuits

This area is often referred to as The Badlands for a number of reasons, not least the insularity and intensity of local spirit here, which can be challenging to outsiders. Not surprisingly, S.A.S. were born in the badlands and now they knock heads in Europe as well as at home.

The weather is usually milder than the rest of the U.K. and swells are as consistent as any other locations. Especially in winter, some of the most spectacular coast in Britain is left exclusively for the Cornish and a few travellers who have worked out that winter is the best surf season here with rideable 6-8' waves for days on end. A big variety of spots present themselves, and it is usually possible to find offshore waves on the north facing beaches (like Harlyn, St Ives and St Agnes), in the prevailing S.W. winds. Flat spells are common in summer, but easy to predict. Many of the spots also get very crowded in summer, and sewage problems are obvious at most of them. Even in winter some are pretty foul.

Cette région est souvent comparée aux Badlands pour un certain nombre de raisons, notamment pour son esprit insulaire et l'intensité du localisme, qui peuvent rérouter les étrangers. Pas étonnant que S.A.S soit né dans les Badlands et qu'ils sévissent aussi en Europe.

Le temps est habituellement plus doux que dans le reste de l'Angleterre et les swells sont aussi consistants que n'importe où en Angleterre. Particulièrement en hiver, l'un des bords de mer les plus spectaculaires est le Cornish, de plus certains surfeurs ont pris conscience que l'hiver est la meilleure saison pour le surf avec des vagues surfables de 2-3 m durant des jours. Une grande variété de spots existe; il est très possible de trouver des vagues offshore sur les plages orientées au nord (par exemple Harlyn, St Ives et St Agnes), avec les vents de sud-ouest dominants. Les périodes de calme sont fréquentes en été mais faciles à prévoir. La grande majorité des spots est surpeuplée en été, et les problèmes de pollution sont flagrants. Même en plein hiver certains spots sont immondes.

Está región es conocida como las Malas Tierras por diversas razones como su insularidad y la existencia de un fuerte espíritu local que puede manifestarse en actitudes desafiantes hacia los foráneos. No es, por tanto, sorprendente que la S.A.S (Surfers Against Sewage) nacieran en estas "Badlands".

La climatología es habitualmente más benigna que en el resto de Inglaterra y las marejadas son tan consistentes como puedan serlo en cualquier otro lugar de Inglaterra. Especialmente en invierno esta costa, que es de lo más espectacular del país, queda para el uso exclusivo de los locales de Cornualles y unos pocos viajeros que han tenido en consideración que el invierno es la mejor temporada con incontables días de olas de un tamaño de dos a tres metros. Hay una gran variedad de spots, siendo habitual encontrar olas con viento terral en las playas orientadas al norte (Harlyn, St Ives, St Agnes y otras) cuando sopla el predominante viento del suroeste. En verano abundan los días sin olas que son fáciles de pronosticar. Asi mismo bastantes spots se saturan y surgen problemas de vertidos contaminantes, que también se dan ocasionalmente en invierno. En las descripciones de los spots se incluye la información disponible referida a la contaminación existente.

west cornwall

Photo: Mike Searle

John Sumpter, Perranporth - Photo: Rod Sumpter

West Cornwall

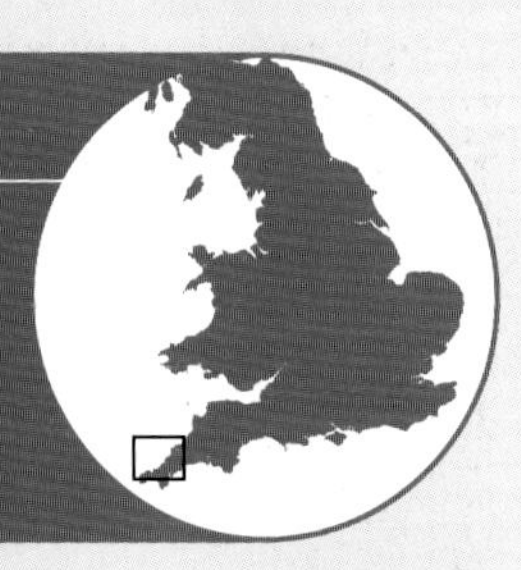

1. Sennen Cove

Britain's most westerly beach is located just to the north of Lands End. Can be crowded in Summer but for the rest of the year the waves are mostly empty. Sennen is well signposted and there's a car park and campsite by the beach.

La plage anglaise la plus à l'ouest juste au nord du Lands End. Peut être bondée en été mais c'est tranquille le reste de l'année. Sennen est bien indiquée et posséde un parking.

Es la playa Británica situada más al oeste y se encuentra al norte de Lands End. Puede estar abarrotado en verano aunque el resto del año las olas están más vacias de gente. Sennen está bien señalizado y hay un parking en la playa.

2. Gwenvor

One of Cornwall's most consistent beaches. Faces west and is exposed to all swell - if there's no swell here there's no swell anywhere. This point/reef works best at 3-6ft, the peak shifting with tidal movement. The rips can be strong. Either walk from Sennen Cove or turn right down Escalls Lane off the A30 followed by a 15 minute walk down cliff paths.

Une des vagues les plus consistantes de Cornwall.Exposée à l'ouest, elle reçoit tous les swells-s'il n'y a pas de vagues là, il n'y en a nulle part.Ce spot marche entre 1 et 2m, le pic bouge en fonction de la marée. Les courants peuvent être forts. Soit vous marchez à partir de Sennen Cove ou vous tournez à droite de Escalls Lane jusqu'à l'A30 suivi d'une marche de 15 minutes par des chemins jusqu'en bas de falaises.

Una de las playas más consistentes de Cornwall. Al estar orientada hacia el oeste coge todo el swell si no entra swell aquí no hay swell en ningún otro lado. Cuando mejor funciona este point/reef es de 1 a 2 metros. El pico se mueve según la marea. Hay fuertes corrientes. Para llegar o caminas desde Sennen o bajas hacia Escalls saliendo de la A30 por la derecha seguido de una caminata de unos 15 minutos por acantilados.

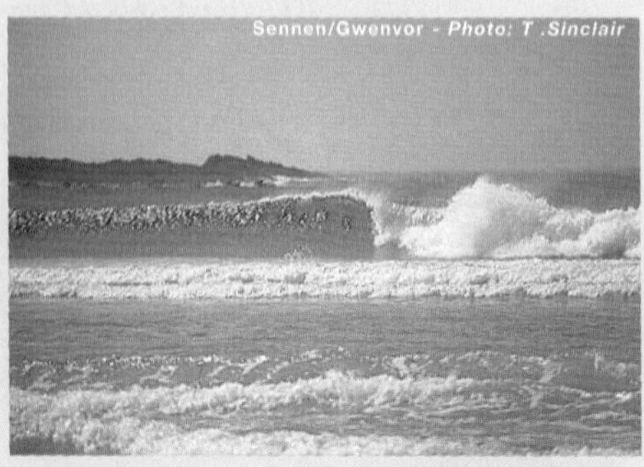

Sennen/Gwenvor - Photo: T .Sinclair

3. Porthmeor

Most popular beach with St.Ives locals. Reasonably consistent, with good peaks in a S-SW wind. If Porthmeor is 1ft then Gwenvor to the south will be 2-3ft as will Gwithian to the north. Car park by beach.

C'est la vague des locaux de St Ives. Vague relativement consistante, avec de bons peaks par vent de sud ou sud-ouest. Si Porthmeor fait 30 cm alors Gwenvor, au nord, fera le double ou le triple comme Gwithian, plus au nord. Il y a un parking sur la plage.

Es la playa más conocida con los locales de St Ives siempre presentes. Consistente con buenos picos cuando sopla de SO. Si en Porthmeor hay 1 pie en Gwenvor, más al sur, habrá de 2 a 3 pies así como en Gwithian al norte. Aparcamiento para coches en la playa.

4. Carbis Bay

Only works on the largest swells. At high tide entry is off the rocks at the end of a steep wooded path, which crosses the railway tracks. Limited parking.

Ne marche que lors des gros swells. A marée haute, l'accés se situe au niveau de rochers à la fin d'un sentier escarpé et boisé, qui traverse la voie de chemin de fer. Petit parking.

Solo funciona con los swells más grandes. en pleamar se entra por unas rocas al final de un escarpado paso de madera, que cruza las vias del tren. Parking limitado.

5. Hayle River

Turn off to the north of Hayle town centre on the road to Gwithian. Rivermouth wave that works inbig swell badly affected by wind.

Prendre au nord du centre de Hayle town sur la route de Gwithian. La vague de l'embouchure peut être très défigurée par un vent trop fort.

Gira al norte en el centro urbano de Hayle por la carretera a Gwithian. El viento enseguida desfasa la ola de la boca del rio.

6. Gwithian/Godrevy

This spot picks up the most swell in the area. Gwithian, the peaks below the car-park are less powerful and hence more suited to beginners. At high tide this area is cut off by rocks and then only Godrevy to the north works. Access is via a turn off south of Gwithian Village leading to an extensive car park.

A l'extrême nord-est dans la baie de St Ives, ces spots reçoivent la plupart des houles de la région. Gwithian, qui déferle en bas d'un parking, est moins puissant et par conséquent plus adapté aux débutants. A marée haute, la vague est interrompue dans son élan par les rochers, c'est alors que Godrevy plus au nord se met à marcher. L'accés se fait via un embranchement au sud de Gwithian Village jusqu'à un imposant parking.

En el límite más al noreste de St Ives Bay, se aprovecha de casi todo el swell de la zona. Los picos en Gwithian de debajo del parking de coches son los menos contundentes y más apropiados por tanto para los más principiantes. En marea alta aparece la zona de rocas y solo Godrevy más al norte funcionará. El acceso es por un cruce hacia el sur en el pueblo de Gwithian que conduce a un enorme parking.

Gwithian - Photo: Tim Rainger, LP

7. Portreath

HARBOUR WALL

On a decent sized swell this is the best wave breaking at the northern end of the beach.

Lorsque la houle est convenable, c'est la meilleure vague cassant au nord de la plage.

Con un swell de tamaño considerable es la ola que mejor rompe en la zona norte de la playa.

BEACH

Beginners should avoid the right and surf the beach break. This gets crowded in the summer months.

Les débutants devront éviter la droite et surfer le beach break. Beaucoup de monde à l'eau pendant l'été.

Los principiantes deberían de evitar la derecha y meterse en la playa. Se llena de gente durante los meses de verano.

8. Porthtowan

Good quality beach break that can suffer crowds. High tide can benefit from protection by the cliffs from SW winds. Easy parking by the beach.

Un beach break de qualité mais que de monde à l'eau parfois. La vague à marée haute peut se retrouver abritée.

Es una ola playera de buena calidad que se llena de gente. En marea alta se encuentra protegida de los vientos del SO por sus próximos acantilados. Fácil aparcamiento.

9. Chapel Porth

More powerful than many of Cornwall's other beaches. At high tide it is completely submerged, and at low conects with Porthtowan to the south. Signposted from St. Agnes, there is a national trust car park by the beach.

Les vagues sont plus puissantes que la plupart des autres vagues du Cornwall. A marée haute il n'y a plus de plage, et à marée basse la connection est possible avec la plage au sud qui s'appelle Porthtowan. Indiqué à partir de St.Agnes, il y a un parking sûr près de la plage.

Las olas son bastante más fuertes que en resto de las playas de Cornwall. En marea alta está todo sumergido y en baja conecta con Porthtowan por el sur. Se encuentra señalizado desde St Agnes y hay un parking, explotado por la hacienda pública, en la playa.

Chapelporth - Photo: Alex Williams

10. St Agnes

Can have some good, powerful surf especially at mid tide, although it needs a fair size swell to work. One of the few spots to work in the prevailing SW wind and hence tends to get crowded. There's a small parking area above the beach. Bad water quality, set to improve.

A mi-marée surtout, on peut avoir un bon surf bien puissant, bien que cela nécessite une houle honorable pour que cette vague donne sa pleine mesure. Un des rares spots qui marche par vent de sud-ouest dominant et a ainsi une fâcheuse tendance à être bondé. Il y a un petit parking au dessus de la plage.

Puede practicarse un surf muy poderoso especialmente a media marea, aunque en realidad dependa de que halla un swell potente en la zona. Se trata de uno de los pocos spots que funcionan cuando sopla del SO, por lo cual está muy abarrotado con estas condiciones. Arriba de la playa hay un pequeño parking.

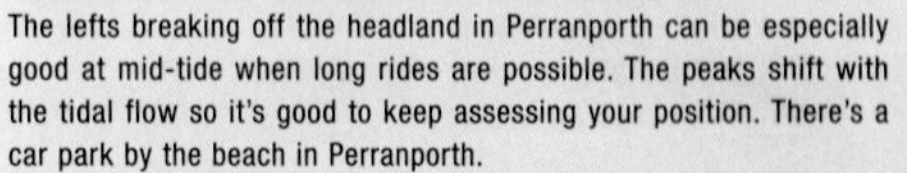

11. Droskyn/Main Beach

The lefts breaking off the headland in Perranporth can be especially good at mid-tide when long rides are possible. The peaks shift with the tidal flow so it's good to keep assessing your position. There's a car park by the beach in Perranporth.

Les gauches cassent au niveau d'un promontoire. Cela peut être particulièrement bon à mi-marée avec de longues vagues. Les pics se déplacent en fonction de la marée, ainsi est il judicieux de bien observer ce qui se passe.

Las izquierdas que rompen en el promontorio pueden ser especialmente bonitas en media marea con paredes muy largas. Los picos cambian con la marea, así que disfruta del que más te guste.

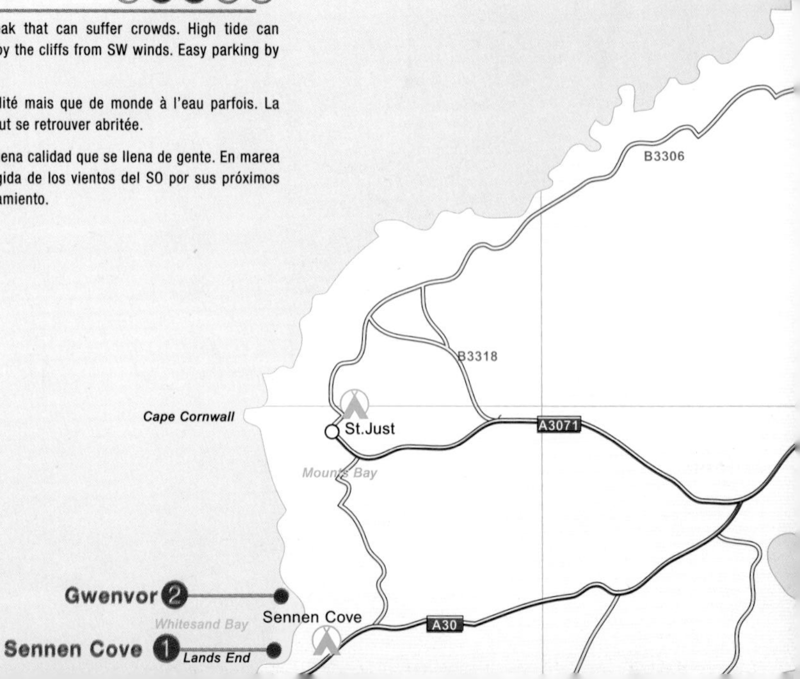

Perranporth, Droskyn & Penhale - *Photo: Alex Williams*

Crantock - Photo: Rod Sumpter

12. Penhale

Long walling rights peel off the rocks at the north end, with heaps of other peaks down the beach. Drive through Perran Sands Holiday Park, and walk across the dunes.

Des droites formant de longs murs se levant devant des rochers à l'extrême nord du spot, également d'autres pics plus vers la plage. Traverser le Perran Sands Holiday Park, et marcher dans les dunes. Présence d'un parking à Perranporth près de la plage.

Paredes de derecha muy largas bordean las rocas en el extremo norte, y aparte hay más picos por la playa. Dirígete por Perran Sands Holiday Park, y camina por las dunas. Hay un parking en la playa de Perranporth.

13. Holywell Bay

Average beach break. From the car park it's a 5-10 minute walk over the dunes. The south end receives some protection from SW winds.

Un beach break moyen. Il faut marcher 5 à10 mns à travers les dunes. La partie sud est protégée des vents sud-ouest.

Se trata de la típica ola playera. Desde el parking de coches queda un paseo de unos 5-10 minutos por las dunas. La zona del sur está resguardada de los vientos del SO.

14. Crantock

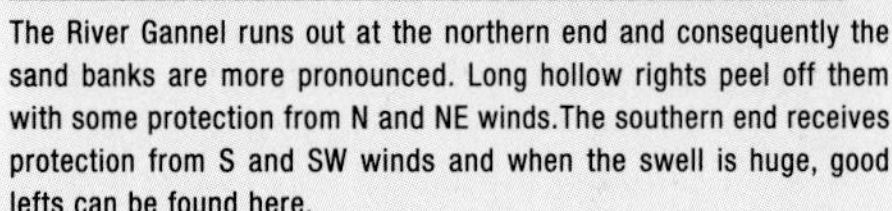

The River Gannel runs out at the northern end and consequently the sand banks are more pronounced. Long hollow rights peel off them with some protection from N and NE winds.The southern end receives protection from S and SW winds and when the swell is huge, good lefts can be found here.

Le sud de la plage est prémuni des vents du sud et du sud-ouest, et par swell énorme, on peut trouver de bonnes gauches. Le River Gannel vient se jeter au nord de la plage, ce qui permet la formation de bancs de sable intéressants. De longues droites creuses se soulèvent, abritées des vents de nord et nord-est.

El extremo más al sur se encuentra protegido de los vientos del S y SO y cuando el swell es muy grande aparecen unas izquierdas excelentes. El rio Gannel transcurre por la zona norte con lo que se forman más y mayores bancos de arena. Aquí salen unas derechas tuberas que están protegidas de los vientos del N y NE.

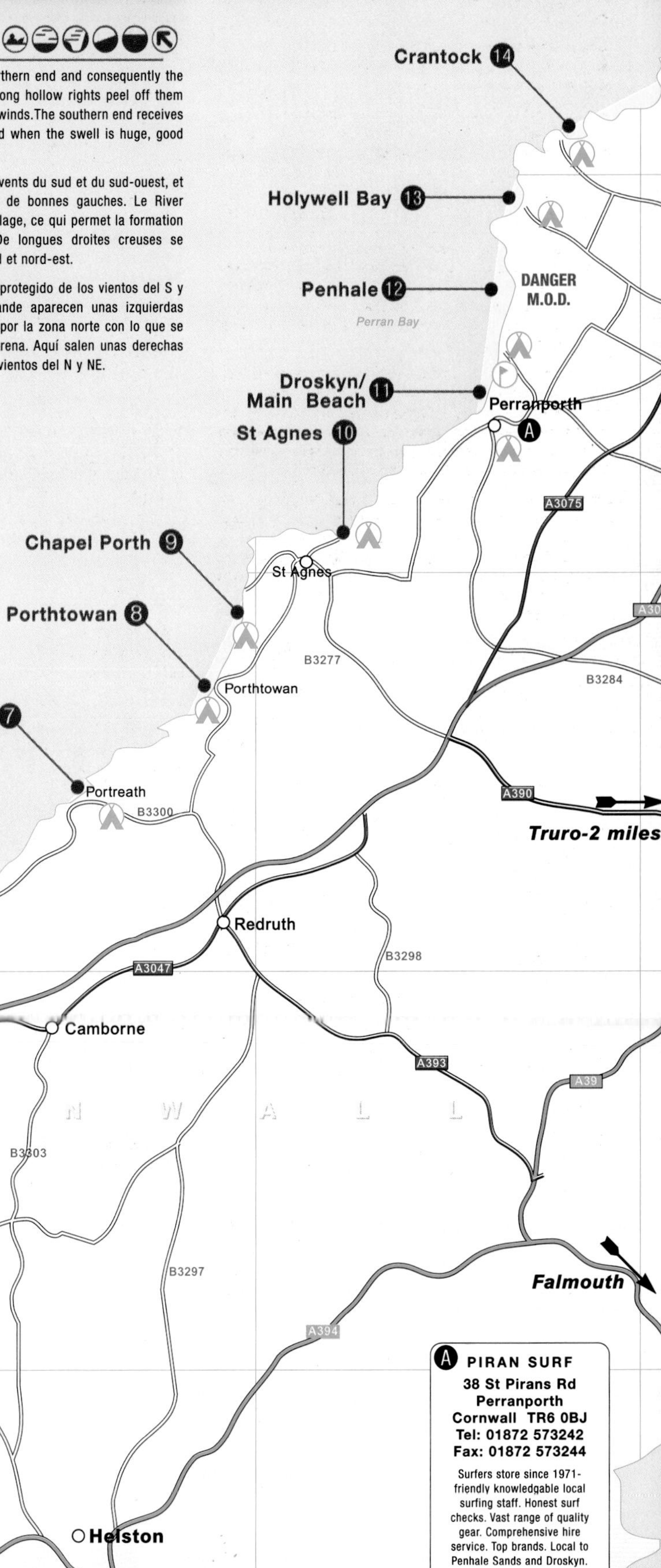

Newquay

1. Fistral

England's most famous beach holds three world class sets of peaks, and has seen all the major U.K. surf competitions. It's fame makes it a consistent crowd puller, which in summer turns into a bit of a mad house; though colder winter months and bigger swells thin the crowds considerably. All spots pick up loads of swell and are reknowned for peaky, tubing lefts and rights. **South Fistral** breaks left, usually better at higher tides, while both **Nth Fistral** and **Little Fistral** break both ways. Though Nth Fistral breaks at high tide, it's undoubtedly the low tide barrels that have made the waves at the Nth End so famous.

La plage la plus célèbre d'Angleterre recèle trois spots de classe mondiale, qui ont vu les plus grandes compétition s'y dérouler. Sa réputation attire beaucoup de monde, et ça devient la Chine sur les vagues l'été. Au contraire, l'hiver avec ses mois plus froids et ses grosses vagues réduit considérablement la foule. Tous les spots prennent bien la houle et sont réputés pour avoir des pics droites-gauches tubulaires. Le **sud de Fistral** casse en gauche, en général meilleur à marée haute, tandis que **Fistral-nord** et **petit Fistral** n'ont pas vraiment de préférence. Alors que Fistral-nord casse à marée haute, c'est sans aucun doute les tubes à marée basse de l'extrême-nord qui lui ont donné ses lettres de noblesse.

Es la playa más famosa de Inglaterra en la que hay tres picos de nivel mundial, a la vez que por aquí han pasado los mejores surfistas de R.U. Debido a su fama, se encuentra abarrotado de gente, lo que en verano hace que se convierta en una locura de sitio; Aunque por los meses más frios de invierno y con las marejadas más grandes la gente no acude en masa. Todas sus olas se aprovechan de las distindas marejadas, y son famosas tanto por ser grandes como tuberas, izquierdas o derechas. En el **sur de Fistral** rompe una izquierda, normalmente con mareas altas. Mientras que tanto en **Norte de Fistral** como en **Little Fistral** rompe de ambos lados.

2. The Cribber

One of England's big wave spots! Rarely ridden but much discussed. Many locals have a board in the shed waiting for the right day. Rips and other obvious dangers associated with this kind of wave make it a venue for big wave surfers only.

Une des vagues de gros en Angleterre. Rarement surfée mais souvent un sujet de discussion: beaucoup de locaux ont un gun dans un coin attendant le bon jour. Les courants et autres dangers évidents associés à ce genre de spot en font un rendez-vous privilégié des surfers de gros.

Es uno de los sitios en Inglaterra donde hay maretón. Se ha hablado más de este sitio de lo que en realidad se ha probado. Muchos locales poseen una tabla en su cobertizo a la espera del dia en que cuadre el mar. Hay peligros asociados a este tipo de olas como las corrientes... lo que lo convierten en punto de encuentro solo para tamañeros.

Little Fistral - *Photo: Roy Major*

North Fistral - *Photo: Roy Major*

South Fistral - *Photo: Roy Major*

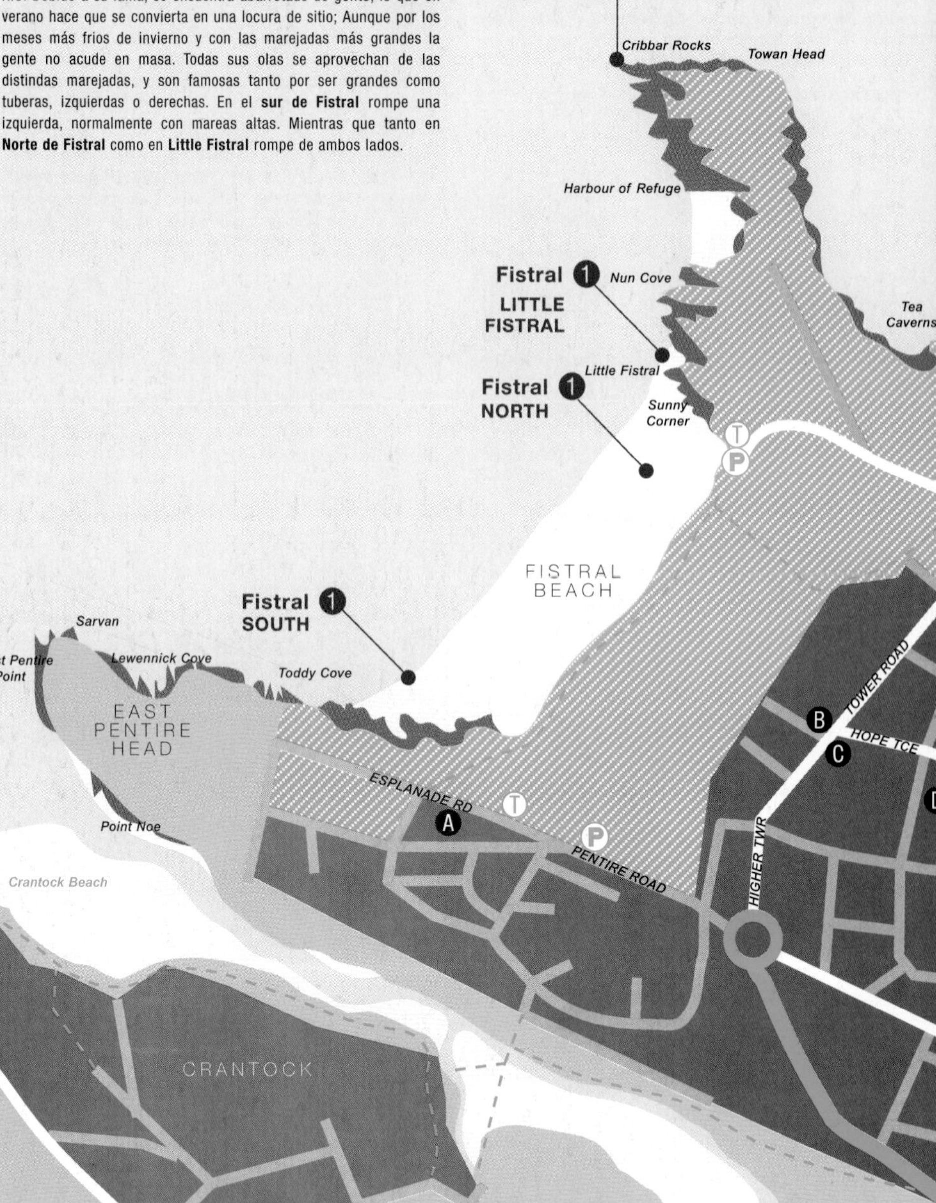

3. Town Beaches

At low tide the four beaches of Lusty Glaze, Tolcarne, Great Western and Towan link up to make a single mile long stretch. At high tide each beach becomes its own cove surrounded by high cliffs. At Towan, the most protected of them, lefts break off the Harbour Wall. On rare days this can be the only rideable wave in Newquay. The rest share the same sheltered characteristics and appeal especially to grommets and holiday makers learning to surf. Local surfers head here only when there is no other choice.

A marée basse, les 4 plages de Lusty Glaze, Tolcarne, Great Western et Towan se rejoignent pour faire une seule plage d' 1,5Km. A marée haute, chaque plage devient une anse entourée par des hautes falaises. A Towan, la plus protégée des 4, des gauches déroulent depuis la jetée du port . Il arrive que ce soit la seule vague surfable de Newquay. Les autres plages sont également protégées et plaisent particulièrement aux vacanciers et aux débutants. Les locaux ne surfent qu'ici qu'en dernière limite.

En marea baja las playas de Lusty Glaze, Tolcarne, Great Western y Towan se unen formando una extensión de una milla de largura. Mientras que en pleamar cada playa vuelve a aislarse rodeada por sus acantilados. En Towan, la más protegida de todas ellas, rompen unas izquierdas contra la pared del puerto. En los dias extraños esta puede ser la única ola que salga en Newquay. El resto de playas tambien están protegidas contra la climatología más adversa y atraen especialmente a aquellos que están aprendiendo a surfear.

4. Porth Beach

Average beach break, popular in the summer when the town beaches become unbearably crowded. Receives protection from Porth Island. Park above the beach and walk down the steps to the water.

Beach-break moyen, fréquenté pendant les mois d'été quand les plages de la ville saturent de monde. Abrité de la houle par Porth Island. Garez-vous au-dessus de la plage et descendez les marches jusqu'à la mer.

Se trata de la típica ola que rompe en las playas, popular en los meses de verano cuando todas las playas del pueblo se llenan de gente. Se encuentra protegida por la isla de Porth. Aparcad encima de la playa y llegad al agua por las escaleras.

Towan Beach - *Photo: Phil Holden*

Water Quality

In peak summer months, raw sewage from Newquay's entire population goes into the ocean on the north side of Towan Head. In the prevailing SW winds, Newquay's holiday makers, on the town beaches, swim in severely polluted water. Fistral is somewhat better in some winds, but the local council and South West Water should be ashamed of the current state of the ocean at England's premier surfing and bathing location.

Qualité de l'eau

Pendant les mois d'été, toutes les eaux usées de la population entière de Newquay s'écoulent dans l'océan au nord de Towan Head. Avec les vents dominants de Sud-Ouest, les touristes nagent en pleine merde sur les plages de la ville. Fistral est un peu mieux lottie avec les vents, mais la municipalité et la Compagnie des Eaux locale devraient avoir honte de l' état de l'océan de ce haut-lieu du surf et de la baignade.

Calidad del Agua-

En plenos meses de verano, tanto los residuos como los deshechos sin tratar de toda la población de Newquay son lanzados al oceáno por la zona norte de Towan Head. Los veraneantes de Newquay, que disfrutan en las playas del pueblo, y mientras soplan los vientos predominantes del oeste, se bañan en aguas mayormente contaminadas. Fistral está algo mejor con ciertos vientos, pero el Consejo local y la South West Water, deberían de estar avergonzados por el estado actual del oceano en la primera localidad de toda Inglaterra en cuanto a surf y baño se refiere.

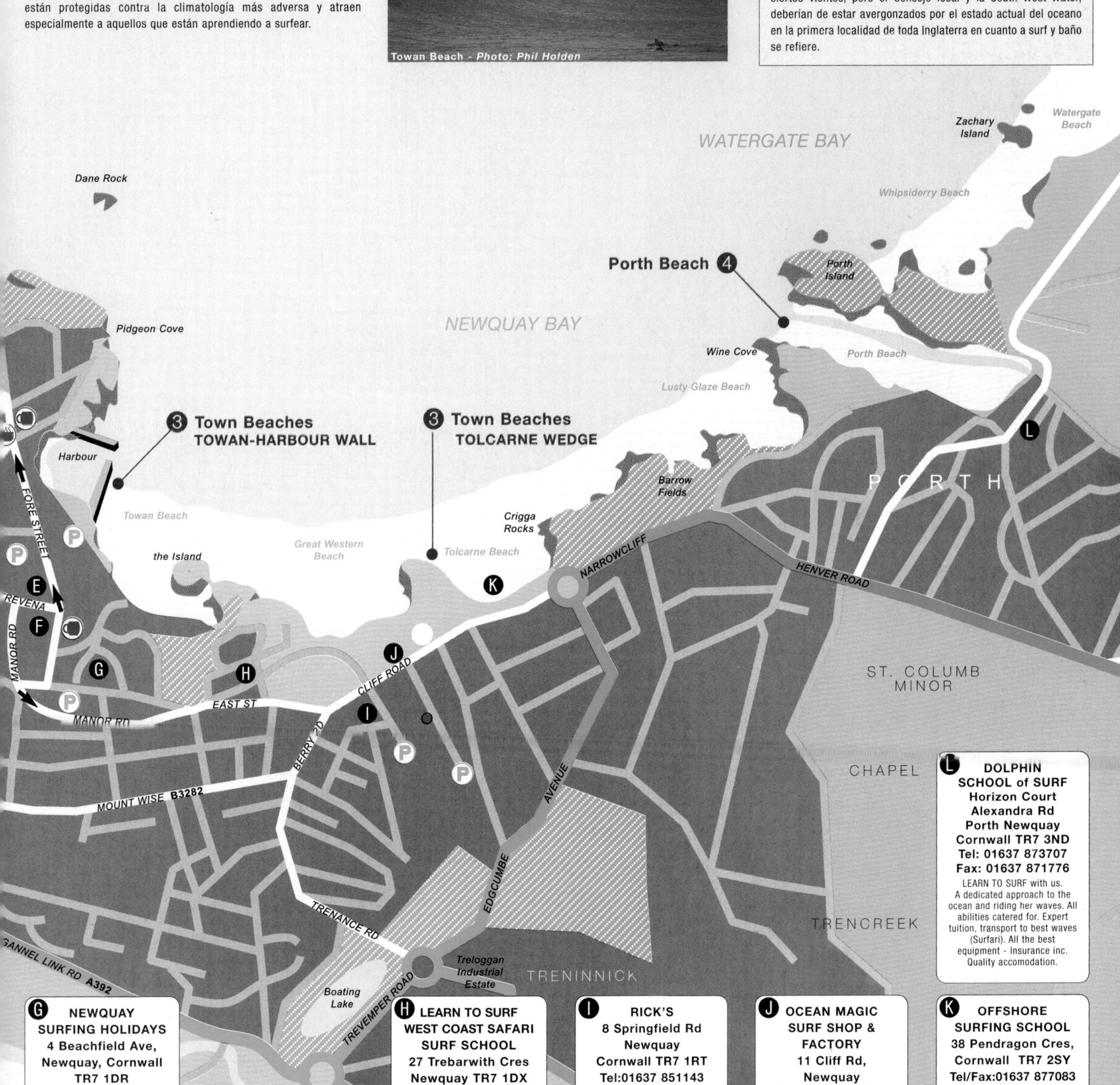

L DOLPHIN SCHOOL of SURF
Horizon Court
Alexandra Rd
Porth Newquay
Cornwall TR7 3ND
Tel: 01637 873707
Fax: 01637 871776
LEARN TO SURF with us. A dedicated approach to the ocean and riding her waves. All abilities catered for. Expert tuition, transport to best waves (Surfari). All the best equipment - Insurance inc. Quality accomodation.

G NEWQUAY SURFING HOLIDAYS
4 Beachfield Ave,
Newquay, Cornwall
TR7 1DR
Tel Fax: 01637 82756
Learn to surf Newquay Cornwall. All qualified British Surfing Association instructers. All equipment provided. All types of accommodation available. Weeks and weekends, groups and schools catered for.

H LEARN TO SURF
WEST COAST SAFARI SURF SCHOOL
27 Trebarwith Cres
Newquay TR7 1DX
Tel:01637 876083
Learn with the most qualified and experienced coaches in Europe. We guarantee success. Week & weekend holidays, day surfaris and half day lessons. For brochure and information

I RICK'S
8 Springfield Rd
Newquay
Cornwall TR7 1RT
Tel:01637 851143
Open all year, Rick's specialises in accommodation for surfers, and has a friendly atmosphere. Showers, bedding, cooking facilities included in the price. M.T.V. Clean comfotable bedrooms from £5 per night.

J OCEAN MAGIC SURF SHOP & FACTORY
11 Cliff Rd,
Newquay
Cornwall TR7 2NE
Tel/Fax:01637 850071
World class surfboards by Nigel Semmens, Maurice Cole, T & C, Aloha, Gash. Custom orders our priority. Clothing, wetsuits and accessories by Rip Curl, Aloha, T & C, Low

K OFFSHORE SURFING SCHOOL
38 Pendragon Cres,
Cornwall TR7 2SY
Tel/Fax:01637 877083
Learn to surf with Britains' longest established surfschool, situated on Tolcarne beach. We offer week holidays, weekends, day surfaris, half day lessons. Groups catered for. Write or Phone for information.

ASP top 44 Pro Jake Spooner ripping on a NS at Hossegor. Photo: Joli

north cornwall

Bude - *Photo: Phil Holden*

The coastline of Nth Cornwall is backed almost entirely by National Trust land, with very little development marring its windswept beauty. The region extends from Hartland point to Newquay and is one of the most wave rich in Britain. A maintained, world reknowned coastal path runs almost its entire length, offering extensive and unspoilt coastal views of its reefs, beaches and points, some of which are known to hold large swells. Secret spots abound.

La côte de Nth Cornwall fait partie presque entièrement du National Trustland, petite beauté sauvage balayée par les vents. La région s'étend du Hartland Point à Newquay et est un des endroits qui regorgent le plus de vagues en Angleterre. De célèbres sentiers côtiers, bien entretenus, s'étirent sur presque l'ensemble de la côte, offrant des points de vue magistraux et imprenables de ses reefs, plages et avancées, dont certains ont la réputation de tenir de grosses houles. Les spots secrets sont légion.

El litoral costero del norte de Cornwall está cubierto casi enteramente por un Parque Natural, existiendo poca explotación de esta belleza natural barrida por los vientos. La región que se extiende de la punta de Hartland hasta Newquay es una de las más ricas en olas de Gran Bretaña. Una ruta costera bien conservada y de renombre mundial recorre toda su longitud, ofrecienda amplias vistas de las playas, arrecifes y points (algunos de los cuales aguantan maretones considerables) que constituyen este salvaje litoral en el que abundan los spots secretos.

Trebarwith Strand - *Photo: Peter Cade*

Photo: Chris Power

Photo: Phil Holden

North Cornwall

Nigel - *Zuma Jays*

1. Watergate Bay

2 mile long stretch of sands. Good beach break waves that are popular with Newquay locals.

Une étendue de 3kms de sable. Bon beach break bien connu des locaux de Newquay.

Esta es una extensión de arena de 3km. Buenas olas que atraen especialmente a los locales de Newquay.od beach break waves that are popular with the Newquay locals.

Watergate Bay - *Photo: Roy Major*

2. Mawgan Porth

Typical beach break which can favour lefts breaking into the river Menalhyl. Beacon Cove to the south also has waves but tends to be less crowded.

Beach break typique qui favorise les gauches entrant dans la rivière Manalhyl. Beacon Cove au sud a aussi des vagues et tend à être moins populeux.

Es la típica playa donde las izquierdas son favorecidas por la presencia del rio Menalhyl contra el que rompen. La cueva Bacon, al sur, también saca olas, pero suele estar menos concurrido.

3. Treyarnon

Picks up a good amount of swell, and is popular from mid to high tide. Various peaks break at either end and along the 1km beach.

Récupère aussi pas mal de houle et plus fréquenté de mi-marée à marée haute. Plusieurs pics cassent des deux côtés et le long de cette plage d'un Km.

En este sitio entra mucho mar, y es conocido por sus buenas condiciones de media marea hasta pleamar. Varios picos rompen a lo laego de esta playa de 1Km.

4. Constantine

One of the best swell pullers in North Cornwall. In the middle of the bay there are lefts and rights. At the south end a left will break off the reef. Booby's Bay to the north has a good but fickle righthand reef break from low-mid tide. Strong rips so beginners beware.

Un des meilleurs "aimants à houle" du nord-Cornwall. gauches et droites au mileiu de la baie. Au sud se trouve une gauche de reef. Booby's Bay au nord a une droite rare de marée basse à mi-marée. Débutants, méfiance, il y a du jus.

Es uno de los lugares donde mejor encaja la marejada en North Cornwall. En medio de esta bahía aparecen tanto izquierdas como derechas. En el límite del sur sale una izquierda contra un arrecife. En Booby's bay, al norte, puede encontrarse un pico de derecha, aunque inconstante, de baja a media marea.

5. Harlyn Bay

A horseshoe shaped bay which is one of the most popular spots when there are strong south-west winds and a good sized swell. Incoming tide can increase the size of the wave. Newtrain Bay to the East can be worth checking.

Une baie en forme de fer à cheval qui est un des spots les plus populaires quand c'est la tempête de SO. La marée montante peut augmenter la taille des vagues. Newtrain Bay à l'Est peut valoir le coup d'oeil.

Se trata de una bahía con forma de herradura que resulta ser uno de los lugares más concurridos cuando soplan los vientos del SO y hay bastante tamaño de olas. Con marea subiendo, la ola alcanza su mayor grandeza.

6. Polzeath (Hayle)

Very popular beach break picking up most available swell. There can be a righthander at the northern end breaking off Pentire Point on bigger days. Parking by the beach.

Beach break super consistent et super fréquenté. Quand ça rentre, il peut y avoir une droite au nord qui casse à Pentire Point. Parking à proximité.

Es una ola muy conocida que abarca toda la marejada disponible. Puede aparecer una derecha en el extremo N rompiendo en Pentire Point los dias de más mar.

7. Lundy Bay

A good spot to check when big swells and strong south-west winds are blowing out other breaks. The ten minute walk from the car park keeps the beach crowd free.

Un bon spot à checker quand ça rentre gros et que de violents vents de S-O bousillent les autres spots. Les 10 minutes de marche depuis le parking éloigne la foule.

Es un buen sitio a controlar con fuertes marejadas y recios vientos del SO soplando y desfasando otros lugares, el paseo de 10 min desde el parking de coches mantiene esta playa libre de gente.

8. Trebarwith Strand

Consistent beach with average waves. The sorthern end has a good left which receives some protection from N winds. The beach is completely submerged at high tide.

Spot consistent avec des vagues moyennes. Le côté nord est protégé des vents de nord. La plage est complètement recouverte à marée haute.

Una playa consistente con olas corrientes. El extremo norte esté protegido de los vientos N. La playa se encuentra completamente sumergida en marea alta.

9. Crackington Haven

Good waves but tends to back off at high tide. Sheltered from north winds. Holds big swells. Coombe Barton Inn serves good food and ales. Excellent camping field.

Bonnes vagues qui ont tendance à s'affaiblir à marée haute. Protégées des vents de nord et tient le gros. L'auberge Coombe Barton sert des bonnes bières et de la bonne bouffe. Excellent camping.

Buenas olas pero se suaviza al subir la marea. Está a cubierto de los vientos del N. Aguanta las fuertes marejadas. Buena comida y cervezas. Buena zona para acampar.

Unmaxibles, Crackington Haven - *Photo: Tim Rainger LP*

10. Widemouth Bay

A famous English beach break with various sand reef setups at each end. Works best up to 6ft and the reefs (Wanson, Black Rock) tend to get good. though the banks shift continuously.

Un des meilleurs beach breaks anglais avec des reefs recouverts de sable à chaque extrémité. Marche mieux jusqu'à 2 mètres et les reefs de Wanson ou Black rock ont tendance à bien fonctionner bien que les bancs changent sans arrêt.

Playa donde rompen olas contra varios arrecifes de arena a cada lado de la misma. Funciona hasta con 2m y los arrecifes (Wanson, Black Rock) suelen cuadrar aunque los bancos estén cambiando contínuamente.

11. Upton

A semi-secret spot that's part reef part sand. Good rights and lefts on the North and South side. Best on a 4-6ft swell. Access is by a dangerous descent down the cliff. No parking.

Un spot presque secret sur fond de sable et cailloux. De bonnes gauches et droites au nord comme au sud. Mieux par houle d'1 à 2 mètres. La descente par la falaise réserve parfois quelques frayeurs. Pas de parking à proximité.

Es este un lugar semi-secreto parte arrecife parte arena. Buenas izquierdas y derechas tanto en el lado norte como en sur. El acceso es por un descenso vertiginoso de un acantilado. No hay parking.

12. Bude

SUMMERLEAZE

Hollow lefthander works at low tide off 'The Barrel'. Holds most swell. From Mid-high tide a right breaks into the harbour which can handle big swells and SW winds. Take-off can be steep and dangerous with strong rips.

Cette gauche creuse marche à marée basse en face du "Barrel" et supporte la plupart des houles. De mi-marée à marée haute, une droite casse dans le port et peut tenir de gros swells ainsi que des vents de S-O. Le take-off peut être raide et dangereux à cause des courants.

Es una ola tubera de izquierdas que rompe en marea baja contra "la barrera". Aguanta cualquier marejada. De media a alta marea aparece una derecha en el puerto que puede aguantar bastante maretón y los vientos del SO.

MIDDLE BEACH

Between Crooklets and Summerleaze. Excellent lefts and rights often crowded with locals. Swells up to 6ft.

Entre Crooklets et Summerleaze. Des gauches et des droites d' excellente qualité mais souvent peuplées de locaux. Jusqu'à 2 mètres.

Se situa entre Crooklets y Summerleaze. Buenas derechas e izquierdas pero hay muchas aglomeraciones con los locales.

CROOKLETS

Some hollow sandbank peaks and Wrangles Rocks to the north work at low tide. At high tide Tower Rock produces a good, if shallow, wave. The infamous Crooklets shorebreak also holds swell up to 6ft.

Des pics creux sur fond de sable et Wrangles Rocks au nord qui marche à marée basse. A marée haute, Tower Rock offre une bonne vague, si elle est creuse. Le shorebreak infâme de Crooklets tient la houle aussi jusqu'à 2 mètres.

Se trata de algunos picos de banco de arena que producen una ola cerrada, así como Wrangles Rock más al norte, los cuales funcionan en marea baja. En pleamar, el sitio a dirigirse será Tower Rock en el caso de que el fondo sea poco profundo. La orillera de la infame Crooklets tambien aguanta mares de hasta

13. Northcott Mouth

The banks at low tide produce some heavy hollow waves. Tends to back off at high tide, except on a big swell which produces a good righthander on the north side.

Les bancs à marée basse balancent de gros paquets. Tendance à mal casser à marée haute, sauf si la houle est massive auquel cas on trouve une bonne droite sur le côté nord.

Los bancos que aparecen en marea baja hacen que se forme una contundente ola tubera. Tiende a suavizarse para mareas más altas, aunque siempre quede la zona más al norte donde con buenas marejadas sale una exquisita derecha.

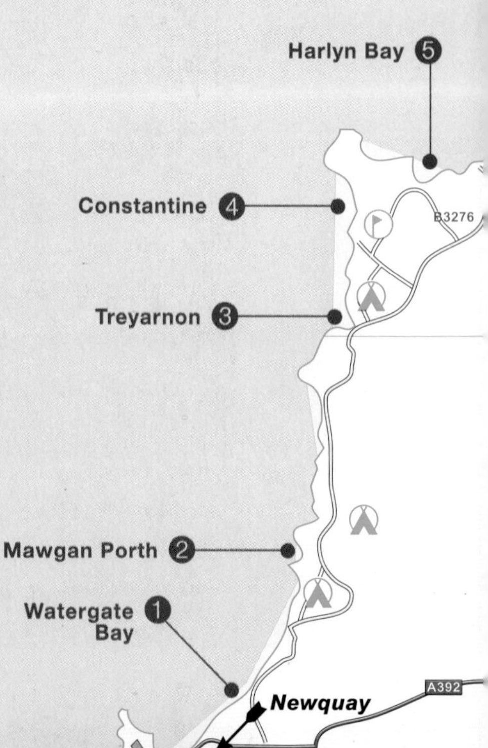

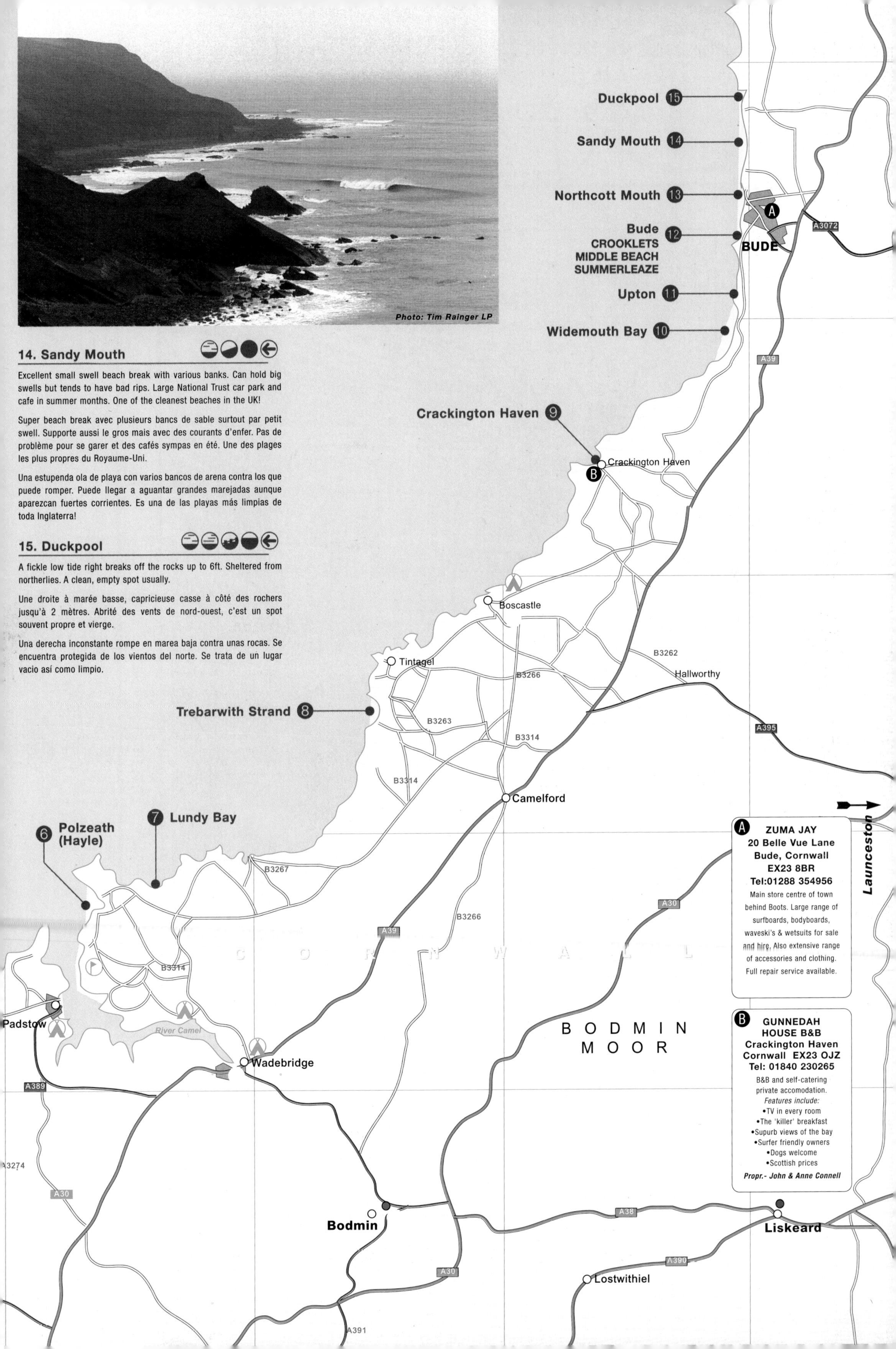

14. Sandy Mouth

Excellent small swell beach break with various banks. Can hold big swells but tends to have bad rips. Large National Trust car park and cafe in summer months. One of the cleanest beaches in the UK!

Super beach break avec plusieurs bancs de sable surtout par petit swell. Supporte aussi le gros mais avec des courants d'enfer. Pas de problème pour se garer et des cafés sympas en été. Une des plages les plus propres du Royaume-Uni.

Una estupenda ola de playa con varios bancos de arena contra los que puede romper. Puede llegar a aguantar grandes marejadas aunque aparezcan fuertes corrientes. Es una de las playas más limpias de toda Inglaterra!

15. Duckpool

A fickle low tide right breaks off the rocks up to 6ft. Sheltered from northerlies. A clean, empty spot usually.

Une droite à marée basse, capricieuse casse à côté des rochers jusqu'à 2 mètres. Abrité des vents de nord-ouest, c'est un spot souvent propre et vierge.

Una derecha inconstante rompe en marea baja contra unas rocas. Se encuentra protegida de los vientos del norte. Se trata de un lugar vacio así como limpio.

Croyde Bay - *Photo: David Bateson*

north devon

Rick Abbot

The bulk of the good surf arrives on the west facing beaches between Woolacombe in the north and Westward Ho in the south. A moderate swell in conjunction with a light easterly wind will offer widespread and excellent conditions, however the wind rarely stays light easterly for all that long! It is for those days of cross winds, and very small or very big swells that this guide is intended. Not only does the nature of the surf depend on the swell size and wind direction, it also depends on the sea bed and tides in this area are extreme. The tidal flow up and down the Bristol Channel is similar to the current in a huge river – moving eastwards during the flood and westwards during the ebb. The 'push' effect of the incoming tide, by helping a weak swell on its way, can be significant. Because of the vast range, there is also a considerable difference in water level between say, low spring-tide and low neap-tide. This affects the quality of some of the low tide breaks. A local tide table is a crucial investment.

The worst winds are westerlies and north-westerlies, although in the summer when it's often flat, even these may give rideable waves for the desperate. North Devon has proved extremely popular in spring, summer and Autumn with surfers from the big cities in the midlands, and some spots like Croyde and Putsborough have been struggling to handle the crowds but the vibe remains friendly.

"A moderate swell in conjunction with a light easterly wind will offer widespread and excellent conditions"

La majeure partie des bons jours ont lieu sur les plages exposées à l'ouest entre Woolacombe au nord et Westward Ho au sud. Un swell correct assorti d'un léger vent d'est offriront d'excellentes conditions sur toute la côte, cependant le vent reste rarement un doux vent d'est très longtemps! C'est pour les jours de vent de travers, et les jours de très petit ou très gros swells , que ce guide a été conçu. La qualité du surf ne dépend pas seulement de la taille du swell et de la direction du vent, elle dépend aussi des fonds marins et des marées qui ont des amplitudes extrêmes dans ces régions. Le courant qui descend et remonte le Bristol Channel est comparable à celui d'une grosse rivière - se déplaçant vers l'est lors de la marée montante et vers l'ouest lors du reflux. L'effet de poussée du flux, en aidant au passage une houle faiblarde, est loin d'être négligeable.En raison d'un marnage important, il existe aussi une différence colossale entre lee mortes et les vives eaux. Cela nuit à la qualité de certains spots à marée basse. Une table locale des marées est un investissement vital.

Les pires vents sont les vents d'ouest et nord-ouest, bien qu'en été cela soit souvent plat, il se peut qu'il y ait des vagues surfables. North Devon est très couru au printemps, été, automne par les surfeurs des grandes villes du Midlands, et quelques spots tels que Croyde et Putsborough doivent admettre une imposante foule mais, malgré tout, l'ambiance reste bonne.

Las mejores y más constantes condiciones se encuentran en las playas orientadas al oeste situadas entre Woolacombe en el norte y Westward Ho en el sur. Un oleaje de tamaño medio asociado a vientos suaves del este proporciona excelentes condiciones en la mayoría de los spots, sin embargo los vientos del este no suelen soplar largos periodos de tiempo. En aquellos días de viento cruzado, con marejadas enormes o diminutas, es cuando cobra sentido el propósito de esta guía. Por supuesto que las olas no van a depender sólo de la dirección del viento y del tamaño de la marejada, también la naturaleza del fondo y las mareas que son muy extremas en este área juegan un papel esencial. El flujo mareal en el Canal de Bristol es semejante a la corriente en un río caudaloso, moviéndose hacia el este cuando sube la marea y hacia el oeste cuando baja. El efecto empujón de la marea ascendente combinado con una marejada, aunque sea débil, puede ser significativo. Dada la enorme amplitud de las mareas, la diferencia entre una marea viva y una muerta afecta de un modo crucial a los spots, sobre todo a los de marea baja. Por tanto, se hace necesario adquirir una tabla de mareas.

Los peores vientos son el oeste y el noroeste, aunque en verano pueden producir olas de viento que pueden surfearse si estas muy desesperado. North Devon es un destino muy popular en primavera, verano y otoño, acudiendo surfers de las principales ciudades del interior, y en algunos spots como Croyde y Putsborough existen verdaderos problemas de saturación, afortunadamente el ambiente es amistoso.

Downend Point - ***Photo: David Bateson***

North Devon

Rick Abbott

Photo: Roy Major

1. Speke's Mill

Can have a rideable wave when everywhere else is flat. Can have lefts. Not for beginners. Difficult access. Respect the locals.

Peut avoir une vague surfable quand c'est le lac ailleurs. Des gauches par exemple. Par pour débutants. Accés difficile.

Aquí puede salir una ola considerable cuando todo lo demás está fofo. No es el sitio indicado para principiantes y el acceso es un tanto complicado.

2. Buck's Mill

An attractive small village of thatched cottages which overlooks a rock strewn shingle and sand beach. The wave breaks along a rocky phalloid called 'The Gore'. One of North Devon's best spots in strong S or SW winds when huge swells are closing out North Devon and Cornwall's west facing breaks.

Un petit village attrayant de fermes de chaume qui surplombent cette plage graveleuse gavée de cailloux aussi. La vague casse sur un "doigt" rocheux appelé "The Gore". Un des meilleurs spots du coin avec des forts vents de sud ou sud-ouest quand ça ferme à maximum sur les plages exposés ouest.

Se trata de un pueblo pequeño y atractivo de cabañas con tejados de paja desde el que se domina una singuera de rocas esparcidas así como una playa de arena. La ola rompe a lo largo de un garito rocoso conocido como "The gore". Es uno de los mejores sitios del norte de Devon con fuertes vientos del S o SO al tiempo que las grandes marejadas han fastidiado toda la costa oeste de N Devon y Cornwall.

3. Westward Ho

Average quality waves only really surfed by locals from Westward Ho and Bideford. Easy parking.

Vagues moyennes seulement surfées par des locaux de Westward Ho et Bideford. Parking facile.

Son unas olas de calidad corriente donde solo surfean lacales Westward Ho y Bideford. Fácil aparcar.

4. Saunton

Three miles of extensive sands, backed by Braunton Burrows. Gets some protection from northerly winds and is the perfect place for learner surfers and windsurfers due to its length and the slow breaking nature of the waves it receives. Easy parking at the north end of the beach.

5kms de sable avec Braunton Burrows en toile de fond. Protégé des vents de nord, c'est un endroit idéal pour les débutants et les windsurfers grâce à sa longueur et au déroulement lent des vagues. Parking facile au nord de la plage.

Está al refugio de los vientos del norte y es el lugar perfecto para los que están aprendiendo tanto surf como windsurf ya que esta es una ola muy larga y rompe lentamente.

5. Croyde

DOWNEND POINT

Good wave offering a fast take-off and long walls, in a large swell. One should practice caution - the rocks are jagged and the peak has a habit of shifting around. Entry and exit points should be closely looked at. With good timing gulleys on either side of the point can save the pain of a damaged board or body.

Une bonne vague avec un take-off sportif et de longs murs, avec une bonne houle. Attention! Les rochers sont tranchants et le pic n'a rien de stable. Se mettre et sortir de l'eau n'ont rien d'évident, trouvez des channels entre les pierres, un bon timing devrez éviter des contacts éventuels avec la planche ou le corps.

Una buena ola que ofrece un rápido take-off y una larga pared los dias de gran marejada. Es un sitio donde se debe de tener cuidado - las rocas son puntiagudas y el pico está cambiando constantemente de emplazamiento©, Se debe de vigilar los lugares de entrada y de salida, con un buen cálculo de cada lado del pico se puede salvar el daño de una tabla averiada o bien de un cuerpo.

BEACH

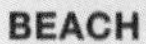
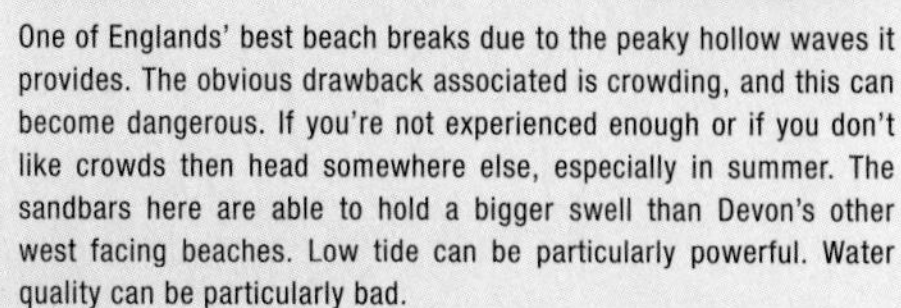

One of Englands' best beach breaks due to the peaky hollow waves it provides. The obvious drawback associated is crowding, and this can become dangerous. If you're not experienced enough or if you don't like crowds then head somewhere else, especially in summer. The sandbars here are able to hold a bigger swell than Devon's other west facing beaches. Low tide can be particularly powerful. Water quality can be particularly bad.

Un des meilleurs beach breaks du Pays Grace aux vagues creuses en pic. L'in convenient est le monde qui peut etre dangereux. Si vous n'etes pas assez fort ou vous n'aimez pas la foule, auez ailleurs surtout en ete. Les bancs peuvent tenir des plus grosses houles que les autres plages du Devon exposees ouest. A marée basse, c'est carrément puissant. Il faut que la houle soit bien grasse pour que ça marche. Si oui, le plus important est la premiere section en bol, rapide et creuse. Casse dans peu d'eau, ne convient qu'aux bons surfers.

Es una de las mejores playas surferas de toda Inglaterra debido a la ola tubera pero inconstante que proporciona. El consiguiente bajón es la cantidad de gente que se amontona, lo cual se puede volver peligroso. Si no le tienes el suficiente callo, o si no gustas de las multitudes, entonces éste no es tu sitio, especialmente durante el verano. La marea baja es especialmente poderosa.

Croyde Bay - Photo: ESTPIX

REEF

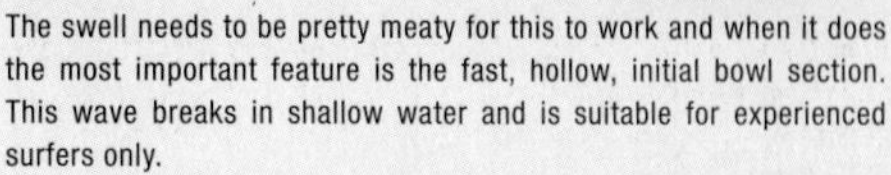

The swell needs to be pretty meaty for this to work and when it does the most important feature is the fast, hollow, initial bowl section. This wave breaks in shallow water and is suitable for experienced surfers only.

Le swell ici doit tabasser pour ce reef fonctionne, mais il present un bowl section initial qui est rapid et creuse. Cette vague casse en mer peut profond et est seulement pour surfers avec experience.

Necesita de una marejada bastante sólida para funcionar, y cuando lo hace resulta ser una ola rápida y de sección tubera nada más romper. Rompe en aguas poco profundas y es adecuada solo para surfistas ya experimentados.

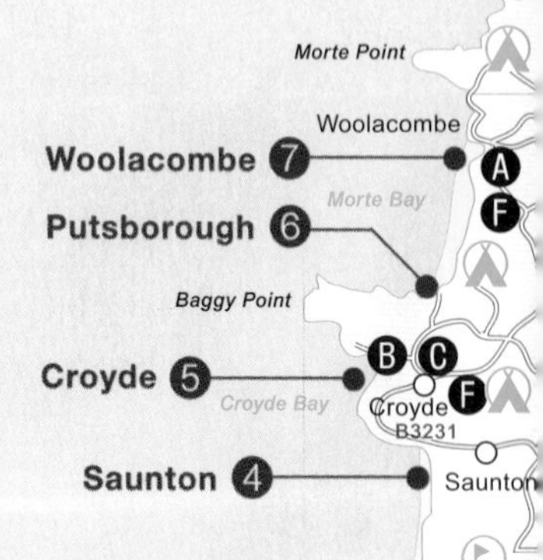

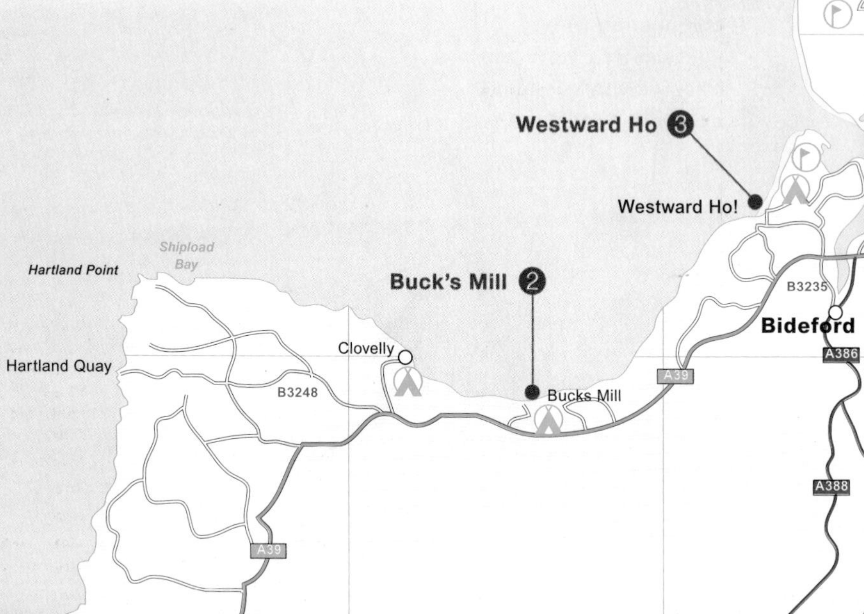

6. Putsburough

Baggy point protects the southern end of this beach from S or SW winds. The higher the tide, the more protected it becomes. This makes Putborough a worthwhile destination when Croyde and other North Devon breaks are blown out. Popular with all forms of surf craft. Parking and camping by the beach.

Baggy point protège la partie sud de cette plage des vents de sud et sud-ouest. Plus la marée est haute, plus c'est protégé. Cela fait de Putborough une alternative à considérer quand ça ferme sur Croyde et les autres spots de la région. On y trouve tous les genres d'utilisateurs de vagues. Parking et camping prés de la plage.

Se trata de un sitio espacioso donde el extremo sur de esta playa se encuentra protegido de los vientos del S y del SO. Cuanto más alta se encuentre la marea, más refugiado se encontrará. Esto hace de Putborough un lugar que merece la pena cuando Croyde y otros picos del norte de Devon están desfasados.

7. Woolacombe

In the longboard days this was the hub of the surfing scene. Now that the emphasis has shifted to Croyde, Woolacombe is left as a relatively unspoilt and mellow place to surf. The rocks at the northern end of the main beach can produce some interesting rights above half-tide. Barricane, known locally as Combesgate, can have some nice peaks at low tide, and receives protection from N winds. Park by beach.

Dans les années longboard, c'était le centre du surf. Maintenant que l'attention s'est déplacée vers Croyde, Woolacombe est redevenu un endroit relativement peinard pour surfer. Les rochers au nord de la plage principale peuvent donner des droites intéressantes au dessus de la mi-marée. Barricane, aussi appelée localement Combesgate, peut avoir des pics sympas à marée basse, protégés des vents de nord. Parking prés de la plage.

En los dias de los tablones, éste era el centro de la escena surfística. Ahora que la marabunta se ha pasado a Croyde, Woolacombe se ha convertido en un lugar intacto y tranquilo donde surfear. Las rocas en el extremo norte de la playa principal pueden producir unas interesantes derechas con media marea subiendo. En Barricane, conocido autóctonamente como Combesgate, pueden aparecer unos divertidos picos en marea baja, así mismo esta protegido de los vientos del norte.

8. Lynmouth

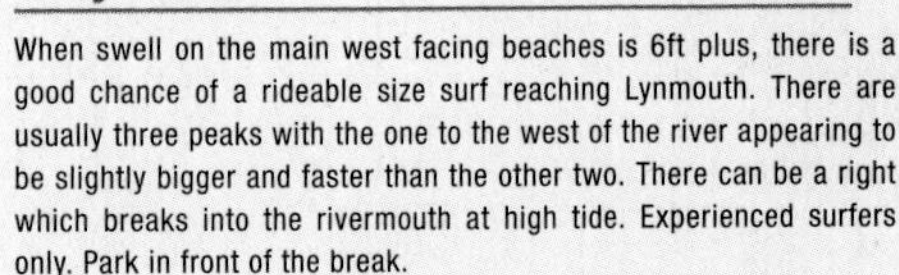

When swell on the main west facing beaches is 6ft plus, there is a good chance of a rideable size surf reaching Lynmouth. There are usually three peaks with the one to the west of the river appearing to be slightly bigger and faster than the other two. There can be a right which breaks into the rivermouth at high tide. Experienced surfers only. Park in front of the break.

Quand ça fait plus de 2m sur les plages exposées ouest, il est fort possible que des vagues tout à fait surfable atteignent Lynmouth. Trois pics en général: celui à l'ouest de la rivière semble souvent plus gros et plus rapide que les 2 autres. On peut trouver une droite dans l'embouchure à marée haute. Seulement pour surfers avertis. Se garer en face du spot.

Cuando el mar llega a los 2m en las playas más importantes orientadas al oeste, hay bastantes posibilidades de que la ola que llega a Lynmouth tenga un tamaño más asequible para surfear. Normalmente hay tres picos, siendo el que aparece al oeste del rio algo más contundente y rápido que los otros dos. También puede salir una derecha que rompe en la boca del rio en pleamar, solo para surferos con experiencia.

Lynmouth - *Photo: Rick Abbott*

9. Porlock Wier

Can Provide some excellent fast waves when huge swells are closing out most of North Devon's and Cornwall's other breaks. Park in village.

Peut avoir de super vagues rapides quand une houle énorme fait fermer la plupart des spots du nord-Devon et du Cornwall. Se garer dans le village.

Puede proporcionar unas olas rápidas y excelentes al tiempo que la gran marejada ha desfasado el resto de lugares de North Devon y Cornwall donde normalmente se surfea.

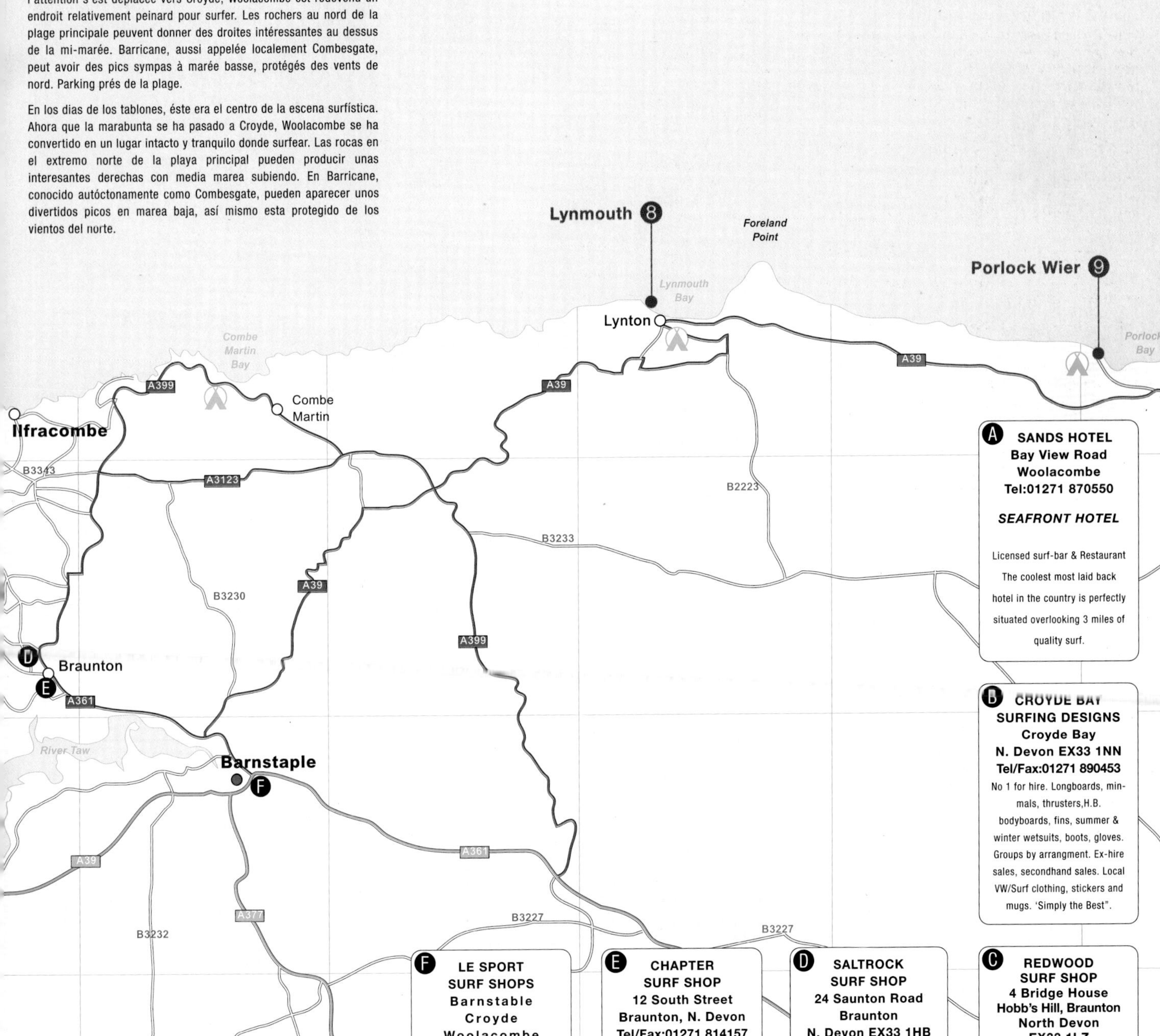

Lynmouth 8
Foreland Point
Porlock Wier 9
Lynmouth Bay
Lynton
Combe Martin Bay
Porlock Bay
Combe Martin
Ilfracombe
A399
A39
A3123
B3343
B2223
B3233
B3230
A361
Braunton
River Taw
Barnstaple
A377
B3227
B3232
B3217
B3220
Oakhampton
A SANDS HOTEL
Bay View Road
Woolacombe
Tel:01271 870550
SEAFRONT HOTEL
Licensed surf-bar & Restaurant
The coolest most laid back hotel in the country is perfectly situated overlooking 3 miles of quality surf.
B CROYDE BAY SURFING DESIGNS
Croyde Bay
N. Devon EX33 1NN
Tel/Fax:01271 890453
No 1 for hire. Longboards, min-mals, thrusters,H.B. bodyboards, fins, summer & winter wetsuits, boots, gloves. Groups by arrangment. Ex-hire sales, secondhand sales. Local VW/Surf clothing, stickers and mugs. 'Simply the Best".
F LE SPORT SURF SHOPS
Barnstable
Croyde
Woolacombe
Everything the surfer needs stocked, plus a full range of hire equipment including custom boards and winter wetsuits etc. in season.
Enquiries: 01271 79675
Surf Check:
01271 890147
E CHAPTER SURF SHOP
12 South Street
Braunton, N. Devon
Tel/Fax:01271 814157
We hire boards and wetsuits for singles or parties. Everything you need to go surfing including custom longboards. Ring for a surf check. Ding repairs. Open 7 days a week
D SALTROCK SURF SHOP
24 Saunton Road
Braunton
N. Devon EX33 1HB
Tel:01271 815619
A friendly shop with the full range of Saltrock clothing and accessories. Boards made to our renowned top quality. There is also 100's of seconds at factory prices.
C REDWOOD SURF SHOP
4 Bridge House
Hobb's Hill, Braunton
North Devon
EX33 1LZ
Tel/Fax:01271 890999
Redwood is owned by former English & British champion Richard Carter with over 20 years surfing experience. Richard is available to advise surfers of any standard. Open all year. Hire always available.

WALES

Capital:	Cardiff
Population:	2,798,200
Area:	20,760km²
Time:	GMT (summer GMT+1)
Language:	English, Welsh

Arguments for self-rule are not strong now as they are in Scotland or Ireland, but some people still have a desire for independence.

WALES

Wales is Britain's smallest country, surrounded on three sides by ocean. It is predominantly mountainous though coastal areas, especially around The Gower and Dyfed are also noted for their beauty. Another nation of Celtic origins, the Welsh continually fought off the Romans and then the English until 1282, when Edward 1 defeated the last native Welsh prince Llewyn ap Gruffyd, at which point Wales passed into English rule. Trouble flared in the 15C and when the Welsh Prince Henry Tudor defeated Richard III at the Battle of Bosworth he paved the way for the 1536 Act of Union which tied the Welsh and English in an uneasy but lasting relationship. It was once one of the great mining areas in the world though it has greatly diminished, replaced by Tourism, farming, light industry and the dole. The passing centuries have watered down Welsh culture but the language is still widely used. It can be seen on bi-lingual road signs all over the country and mostly heard in N and central Wales. Arguments for self-rule are not strong now as they are in Scotland or Ireland, but some people still have a desire for independence.

PAYS DE GALLES

Le Pays de Galles est le plus petit pays du Royaume-Uni, entouré sur trois côtés par l'océan. C'est en majorité une zone montagneuse bien que certaines zones côtières comme Gower ou Dyfed soient pittoresques. Encore une nation aux origines celtiques, les Gallois ont continuellement lutté contre les Romains et les Angalis jusqu'en 1282, lorsqu'Edouard I battit le dernier prince gallois Llewyn ap Gruffyd et c'est alors que le pays tomba sous la loi anglaise. Des troubles sont apparus au XV siècle quand le prince gallois Henry Tudor infligea une défaite à Richard III à la bataille de Bosworth, il préfigurait alors l'acte d'Union de 1536 qui scella les relations anglo-galloises d'une façon difficile mais durable. C'était alors une des grandes nations minières dans le monde, activité qui a maintenant beaucoup perdu au profit du tourisme, de l'élevage de l'industrie légère et du chômage. Les siècles passant ont dilué quelque peu la culture galloise sauf la langue qui est toujours largement parlée surtout dans le nord et au centre du pays. Pour exemple, les panneaux sur la route sont bilingues dans tout le pays. Les désirs d'indépendance ne sont pas aussi forts qu'en Ecosse ou en Irlande bien que présents dans les mentalités.

GALES

Gales es el país más pequeño de Gran Bretaña, rodeado en tres cuartas partes por el océano. Las zonas costeras especialmente Gower y Dyfed son de gran belleza, siendo el resto del territorio montañoso. Sus orígenes son célticos, los galeses lucharon primero contra Roma y luego contra los ingleses hasta 1282, fecha en que Eduardo I derrotó al último principe nativo Llewyn ap Gruffyd, pasando Gales al dominio inglés. En el siglo XV resurgieron los problemas, y la victoria en la Batalla de Bosworth del príncipe galés Enrique Tudor sobre Ricardo III allanó el camino para el Acta de Unión que ligaba a ingleses y galeses en una compleja, pero duradera relación. En el pasado fue una de las principales regiones mineras del mundo, pero su importancia se ha reducido drásticamente, siendo sustituida por el turismo, la agricultura, la industria ligera y el paro. El paso de los siglos ha diluido la cultura galesa, pero su idioma es todavía ampliamente utilizado. Se puede apreciar en las señales de carretera biling¸ es, y oir principalmente en el norte y el centro de Gales. Los deseos de autogobierno no son de importancia, como sucede en Escocia o Irlanda, pero en algunos grupos aún perviven.

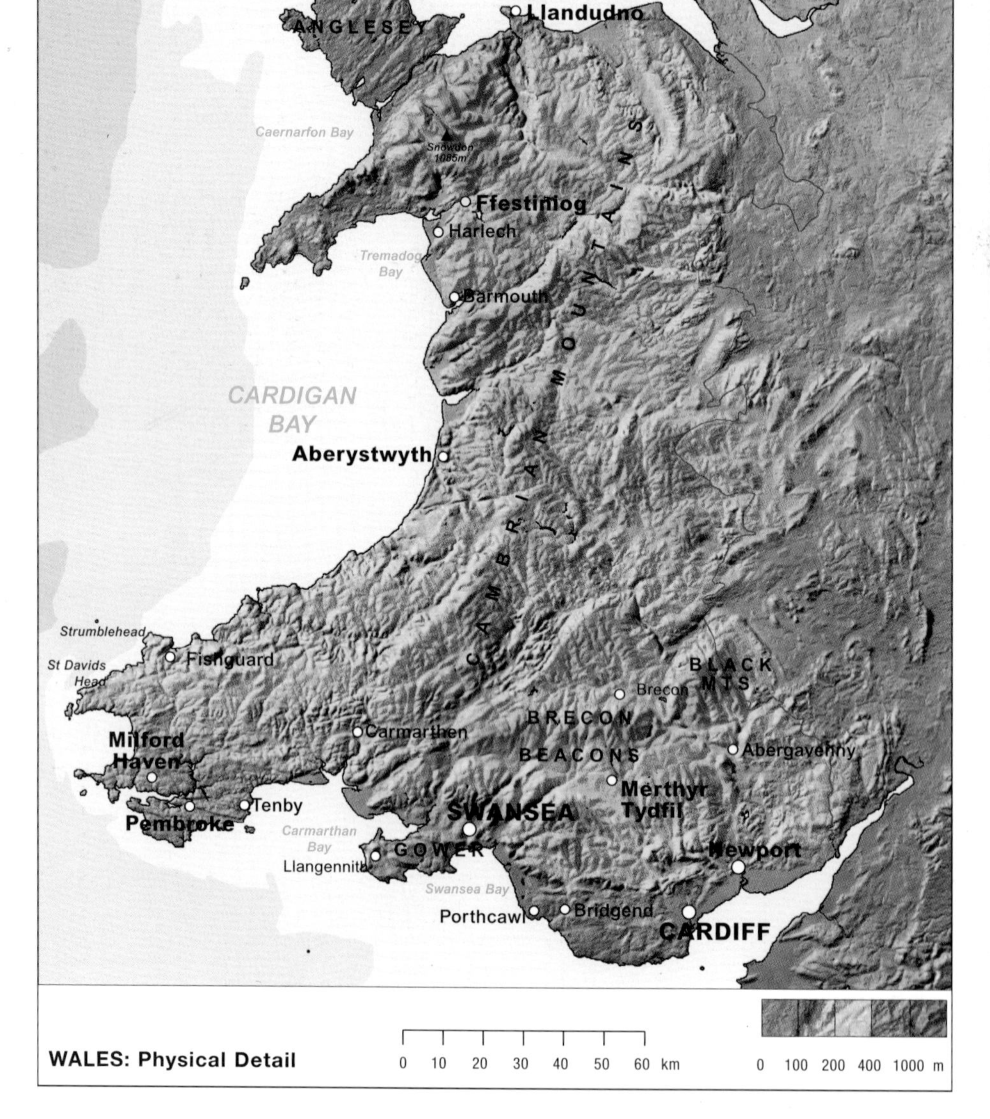

WALES: Physical Detail

"It is predominantly mountainous though coastal areas...are also noted for their beauty."

"...this place holds swell to 10ft" - *Photo: Phil Holden*

Welsh Surfing Federation
Linda Sharp (Committee Wales)
71 Fairway, Port Talbot, S. Wales, SA12 7HW, Wales
Tel: (44) (01639) 88 62 46
Fax: (44) (0656) 64 78 51

"You hear people say that it always rains when they visit Wales, but we don't mind as long as there's swell."
Carwyn Williams

The Surf

Surfing in Wales began in the early sixties, but it wasn't until 1967, when Australian surf champion Keith Paul came to the Gower, that it took off. During a classic late summer swell at Langland, he ripped up the shore-break in his silver baggies and the locals gawked in amazement. International surfing had arrived. During the sixties surfing was mainly confined to the beaches at Langland, Caswell and Llangennith. Heavy boards and the risk of damage to board and body (leashes only came into use in late 1972), meant the more inaccessible reefs and points were only surfed by the most hard-core. Keith Paul, Howard Davies and John Goss were the first to surf Crab Island and other pioneers include Viv Ganz, Dave Friar, Robin Hansen, Paul Connibear and myself. By the mid 70's, most of the Gower reefs had been surfed but during the early eighties, a few 'secret' spots were added to the map by Carwyn Williams and Rob and Phil Poutney.

The longest surviving board factory in Wales is Crab Island Surfboards, still spearheaded by 'technical-guru' Pete Phillips. By the late seventies Crab Island boards were used by most of Wales top surfers and during this time, Kiwi airbrusher and shaper Craig Hughes worked there. Craig, who later founded Wave Graffitti surfboards, provided the catalyst needed to enhance the talents of a young Langland surfer Carwyn Williams, who became Britain's most successful pro of the eighties. By then, locally made boards were able to match the imports from Newquay and abroad, and surfing in Wales had come of age.

The Weather

Like the rest of Britain, Wales has a mild, damp climate. The high regions are cooler than the lowlands and have a heavy rainfall (over 200 days a year). Says Carwyn Williams," You hear people say that it always rains when they visit Wales, but we don't mind as long as there's swell. We must be one of the few bunches of guys who get excited when the forecast is for gale force winds and rain. I think this breeds the hard-core element into Welsh surfing."

Le Surf

Le surf a commencé au Pays de Galles dans les années 60 mais c'est en 1967 que Keith Paul, un champion de surf australien vint sur la Gower et ça commença vraiment. Lors d' une houle parfaite de fin d'été à Langland, il fracassa sur le shore-break dans son short argenté et les locaux furent médusés. Le surf international était arrivé. A cette époque, le surf se confinait aux plages de Langland, Caswell and LLangennith. Les planches lourdes et les risques de dommages et de blessures (on n'utilisa des leashes qu'à partir de 1972) signifiaient que les reefs et les pointbreaks les plus inaccessibles n'étaient surfés que par une poignée de fous furieux. Keith Paul, Howard Davies et John Goss furent les premiers à surfer Crab Island avec d'autres pionniers comme Viv Ganz, Dave Friar, Robin Hansen, Paul Connibear et moi-même. Au milieu des années 70, la plupart des reefs de la Gower avaient été découverts. Cependant, pendant les années 80, quelques spots secrets furent ajoutés sur la carte par Carwyn Williams, Rob et Phil Poutney.

L'atelier de shape le plus ancien est Crab Island Surfboards, encore managé par le gourou de la technique. Pete Phillips. Pendant les années 70, les planches Crab Island étaient utilisées par la plupart des meilleurs surfers du pays et à cette époque, le décorateur et shaper Craig Hughes y bossait. Craig, qui lanca plus tard, Wave Graffitti Surfboards a apporté le soutien aux pointures locales comme Carwyn Williams qui devint le surfer anglais professionnel le plus compétitif. C'est alors que les planches locales atteignaient le niveau de qualité des importations depuis Newquay ou d'ailleurs. Le surf avait donc atteint sa majorité.

Le temps

Comme ailleurs en Angleterre, le Pays de Galles a un climat doux et humide. Les régions hautes sont plus fraîches que les plaines avec de fortes précipitations (plus de 200 jours par an). Comme le souligne Carwyn Williams: on entend toujours les gens dire qu'il pleut toujours quand on visite le Pays de Galles, peu importe du moment qu'il y a de la houle. On doit être les seuls à être excités quand les prévisions sont des vents à décorner les boeufs et de la pluie. Je crois que ça développe la fibre de forcené qui existe dans le surf gallois.z

El Surf

Comenzó al inicio de los sesenta, pero no despegó hasta 1967, año en que el campeón australiano Keith Paul llegó a Gower. En un día clásico de finales de verano en Langland, surfeó la orillera con su traje de baño plateado dejando flipados a los locales. Supuso la llegada del surf internacional. Los reductos surferos de los sesenta eran las playas de Langland, Caswell y Llangennith. El peso de las tablas, la inexistencia de inventos (no llegaron hasta 1972) y el consiguiente riesgo de roturas y accidentes, implicaba que sólo los más duros surfeaban los arrecifes y points apartados. Keith Paul, Howard Davies y John Goss fueron los primeros en surfear Crab Island. Otros pioneros ilustres fueron Viv Ganz, Dave Friar, Robin Hansen, Paul Connibear y Pete Jones. A mediados de los setenta, la mayoría de los arrecifes de Gower habìan sido surfeados, pero todavía en los primeros ochenta Carwyn Williams y Rob y Phil Poutney añadieron unos pocos spots secretos al mapa.

Crab Island es el taller de tablas superviviente más antiguo de todo Gales, a cuya cabeza se mantiene el guru Pete Phillips. A finales de los setenta, los mejores surfers iban en tablas Crab Island, shapeadas y pintadas por el neozelandés Craig Hughes, que más tarde fundaría Wave Graffitti, proporcionando el impulso necesario para el talento emergente de un joven surfer de Langland. Carwyn Williams que ha sido el surfer profesional inglés de más éxito en los años ochenta. En esa época, el surf galés llegó a su mayorìa de edad, siendo las tablas de fabricaciÛn local del mismo nivel que las de Newquay o las importadas.

El Clima

Como en el resto de Gran Bretaña, el clima de Gales es húmedo, triste y apacible. En las zonas altas hace más frío y llueve más que en las bajas (más de 200 días al año). Ya lo dice Carwyn Williams, "La gente que visita Gales se queja de que siempre está lloviendo, pero a nosotros nos da igual mientras haya olas. Somos unos pocos los que nos emocionamos al ver que la previsión del tiempo es de vientos huracanados y lluvia. Esta es la forma en que ha crecido el espíritu hardcore del surf galés".

Severn Estuary

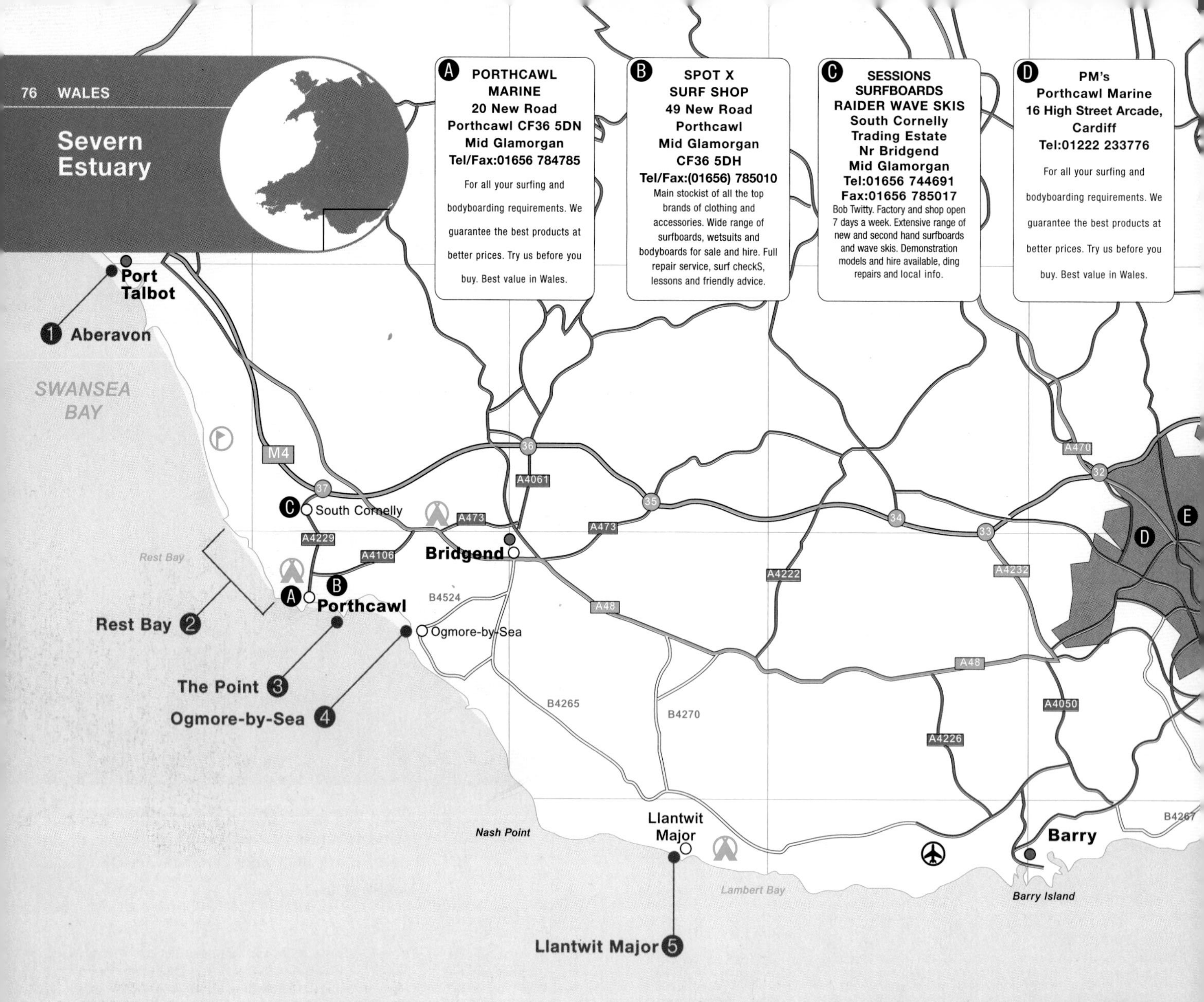

1. Aberavon

One of south Wales' best and most polluted waves is under threat due to the planned construction of a massive breakwater. The local crew who've surfed this wave for over 20 years are fighting to save the waves in what is seen by some as a test case in the UK. The left is the better wave being longer and hollower but the right is still a lot of fun. Aberavon is one of the only spots that will work on a SE wind.

Une des meilleures vagues du sud du Pays de Galles mais super polluée et menacée par la construction prévue d'une grosse jetée. Les locaux qui surfent cettevague depuis 20 ans luttent pour sauver cette vague, ce qui est considérée comme un exemple-test au Royaume-Uni. La gauche est une meilleure vague étant plus longue et plus creuse mais on peut taper quelques rollers sur la droite. Aberavon est un des seuls spots à marcher par vents de SE.

Es una de las mejores y más contaminadas olas del Sur de Gales, además se encuentra amenazada por un proyecto de construcción de un enorme rompeolas. Los locales que llevan surfeandola más de veinte años están tratando de salvarla, en Gran Bretaña este caso es contemplado como una prueba de la capacidad de presión de los surfers para proteger las olas. La mejor ola es la izquierda, más hueca y de mayor recorrido que la derecha, aunque esta última es una ola muy divertida.

Aberavon - *Photo: Phil Holden*

2. Rest Bay

Can have good rights and lefts all the way to Margam sands, but is often badly affected by common W winds. Pollution can be bad due to the heavy industrial site of Port Talbot to the north.

On peut trouver de bonnes droites et gauches tout le long jusqu'à Margam sands mais c'est souvent gavé de vents d'ouest. La pollution peut y être alarmante à cause de la proximité de Port Talbot.

Puedes encontrar buenes picos llegar al arenal de Margam, sin embargo los vientos habituales del O le pegan mal. La fuerte concentratión industrial situada al N causa que el agua esté seriamente polucionada.

3. The Point

Can be excellent but only works in big swells. Always crowded. Located between Sandy bay and Trecco Bay to the S of Porthcawl.

Ca peut être fantastique mais seulement quand ça rentre balaise. Allez voir Sandy Bay ou Trecco Bay au sud de Porthcawl.

Puede sur excellente pero soloen mareas grandes. Siempre hay mucha gente. Está situado entre Sandy Bay y Trecco Bay.

The Point - *Photo: J. Newman, SESSIONS SURFBOARDS*

4. Ogmore-by-Sea

On the southern side of the river there's a good left with rides of up to 100mtrs. Needs a clean swell and works best from mid to high tide. Polluted due to the river, which also causes strong rips. The beach can have good peaks, depending on the state of the sand banks. Beginners should definitely avoid the left at the river mouth!

Au sud de la rivière, une bonne gauche déroule sur prés de 100 mètres, avec une houle propre et de préférence de mi-marée à marée haute, débuitants s'abstenir. Pollué à cause de la rivière et attention aux courants. Ensuite, la plage peut avoir de bons pics, selon l'état des bancs de sable.

En la parte Sur del rio se halla esta buena izquierda de hasta cien metros de recorrido. Requiere una marejada ordenada y funciona mejor con la marea de media a alta. El agua del rio baja contaminada y provoca una fuerte corriente que los principiantes deben evitar a toda costa. En la playa puede haber buenos picos si las barras est·n en condiciones.

5. Llantwit Major

Needs a fair sized swell to work, but can be well worth a visit. The best wave is a right at low tide to the left of the beach, which can be long and fast. As the tide comes in, lefts and rights break along the beach. Beginners should take care of rocks and rips and try not to swallow too much of the water which can be badly polluted.

Il faut une houle correcte pour que ça marche mais ça vaut le coup d'oeil quand même. La meilleure vague est une droite à marée basse sur la gauche de la plage, qui peut être longue et rapide. Quand la marée monte, des gauches et des droites cassent le long de la plage Les débutants doivent faire attention aux rochers et aux courants et attention aussi à ne pas trop avaler l'eau: ça craint !

Necesita una marejada considerable, pero puede merecer un vistazo. La mejor ola es la derecha de marea baja situada en la izquierda de la playa, puede ser larga y rápida. Al subir la marea, rompen derechas e izquierdas a lo largo de la playa. Los novatos tienen que tener cuidado de las rocas y de las corrientes y evitar tragar agua que puede estar muy contaminada.

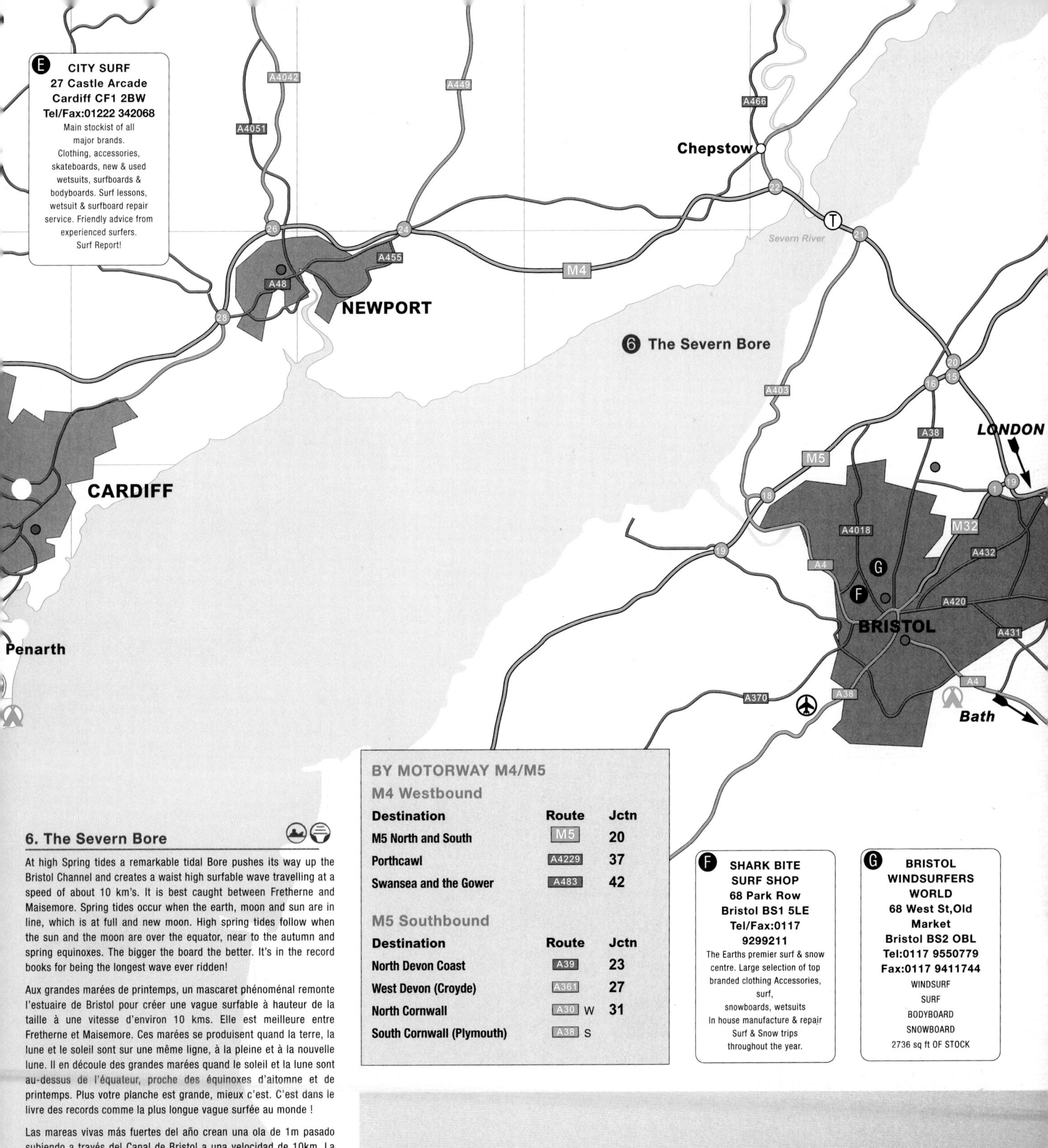

E CITY SURF
27 Castle Arcade
Cardiff CF1 2BW
Tel/Fax:01222 342068
Main stockist of all major brands. Clothing, accessories, skateboards, new & used wetsuits, surfboards & bodyboards. Surf lessons, wetsuit & surfboard repair service. Friendly advice from experienced surfers. Surf Report!

6. The Severn Bore

At high Spring tides a remarkable tidal Bore pushes its way up the Bristol Channel and creates a waist high surfable wave travelling at a speed of about 10 km's. It is best caught between Fretherne and Maisemore. Spring tides occur when the earth, moon and sun are in line, which is at full and new moon. High spring tides follow when the sun and the moon are over the equator, near to the autumn and spring equinoxes. The bigger the board the better. It's in the record books for being the longest wave ever ridden!

Aux grandes marées de printemps, un mascaret phénoménal remonte l'estuaire de Bristol pour créer une vague surfable à hauteur de la taille à une vitesse d'environ 10 kms. Elle est meilleure entre Fretherne et Maisemore. Ces marées se produisent quand la terre, la lune et le soleil sont sur une même ligne, à la pleine et à la nouvelle lune. Il en découle des grandes marées quand le soleil et la lune sont au-dessus de l'équateur, proche des équinoxes d'aitomne et de printemps. Plus votre planche est grande, mieux c'est. C'est dans le livre des records comme la plus longue vague surfée au monde !

Las mareas vivas más fuertes del año crean una ola de 1m pasado subiendo a través del Canal de Bristol a una velocidad de 10km. La mejor zona para cogerla es entre Fretherne y Maisemore y cuanto mayor sea la tabla mejor. Las mareas vivas se dan cuando se alinean la tierra, la luna y el sol, es decir con luna llena y luna nueva. Cerca de los equinoccios de otoño y primavera, la luna y el sol se encuentran sobre el Ecuador, es en esos períodos cuando las mareas vivas alcanzan su mayor amplitud y se forma esta ola, que está en los libros de records por ser la más larga jamás surfeada.

Severn Bore - *Photo: Phil Holden*

BY MOTORWAY M4/M5

M4 Westbound

Destination	Route	Jctn
M5 North and South	M5	20
Porthcawl	A4229	37
Swansea and the Gower	A483	42

M5 Southbound

Destination	Route	Jctn
North Devon Coast	A39	23
West Devon (Croyde)	A361	27
North Cornwall	A30 W	31
South Cornwall (Plymouth)	A38 S	

F SHARK BITE SURF SHOP
68 Park Row
Bristol BS1 5LE
Tel/Fax:0117 9299211
The Earths premier surf & snow centre. Large selection of top branded clothing Accessories, surf, snowboards, wetsuits
In house manufacture & repair
Surf & Snow trips throughout the year.

G BRISTOL WINDSURFERS WORLD
68 West St,Old Market
Bristol BS2 OBL
Tel:0117 9550779
Fax:0117 9411744
WINDSURF
SURF
BODYBOARD
SNOWBOARD
2736 sq ft OF STOCK

Nick Gammom (watching) Johno (surfing), Crab Island - *Photo: The Gill*

Matt Stephens, Gower Reef - *Photo: The Gill*

the gower peninsula

Carwyn Williams

"...the rugged, scenic coastline offers a wide variety of breaks, most withln sheltered bays providing waves which smugglers rode in on centuries ago..."

Gower View - *Photo: Chris Power*

The Gower Peninsula is Wales' premier surfing area, ideally located to receive swells generated by mid and south Atlantic Low Pressure systems. The rugged, scenic coastline offers a wide variety of breaks, most within sheltered bays providing waves which smugglers rode in on centuries ago. These bays now offer secrets for the dedicated surfer to find.

Surfing on the Gower has a great heritage. I grew up in a spot called Langland Bay where I had to learn respect for the locals who were, by rights, the best surfers in the country. You would never paddle out onto the best breaks in the bay unless you did it early in the morning, or you were encouraged by the crew. The surf can sometimes be brilliant, but we must be one of the few bunches of surfers who get excited when the forecast is for gale force winds and rain. We don't mind that at all as long as there's surf. This breeds the hard-core element into Welsh surfing. When the surf is flat at Langland we normally go to Llangennith. This is the most consistent of all the breaks on the Gower and if there's no wind and you know the tides, there's some nice reef breaks to be found. It's touch and go whether you'll get perfect waves if you come to the Gower, but there are a few characters to meet, the night life in Mumbles is classic and the sheep are friendly!

La Gower Peninsula est la région de surf d'origine du Pays de Galles, idéalement placée pour recevoir les houles génèrées par les systèmes dépressionnaires du sud et du centre de l'Atlantique. La côte accidentée et panoramique offre une large variété de spots, la plupart à l'intérieur de baies protégées fournissant des vagues sur lesquelles "surfaient" les contrebandiers il y a des siècles. Ces baies offrent maintenant leurs secrets au surfeur prêt à les trouver.

Le surf sur le Gower est empreint d'un grand héritage . J'ai grandi sur un spot appelé Langland Bay où j'ai dû apprendre à respecter les locaux qui étaient, sans problémes, les meilleurs surfeurs du pays. On n'allait jamais surfer les meilleurs spots de la baie si ce n'était tôt le matin ou si on n'y était pas encouragé par la "bande".Le surf peut parfois être excellent, mais nous devons être un des rares groupes de surfeurs qui se réjouissent lorsqu'il est annoncé de forts coups de vents et de la pluie. Cela nous était complétement égal du moment qu'il y a du surf. Cela rend compte de l'aspect "pur et dur" du surf gallois. Quand c'est calme à Langland, nous allons normalement à Llangennith. C'est le plus consistent de tous les spots sur le Gower et s'il n'y a pas de vent et si on connait les marées, il y a quelques jolis spots de récifs à trouver. On n'est pas certain d'avoir des vagues parfaites si on vient sur le Gower, mais il y a des personnages à découvrir, la nuit à Mumbles est un grand classique et les moutons sont sympathiques!

Es la principal zona surfera de Gales. Está orientada de un modo óptimo para recibir las marejadas generadas por las borrascas del centro y del sur del Atlántico. La accidentada y espectacular costa ofrece una amplia variedad de picos, la mayoría en bahías abrigadas, antaño frecuentadas por los contrabandistas. Ahora es el surfer inquieto quien puede encontrar los secretos que guardan estas bahías.

La herencia surfera de la zona es importante. Yo crecí en Langland Bay, donde aprendì a respetar a los locales, que eran los mejores surfers del país. Salvo a primera hora de la mañana o en el caso en que te animasen a ir, evitaba los mejores picos de la bahía. En ocasiones, las condiciones eran excelentes y contituiamos el único colectivo que se alegraba cuando el parte meteorológico anunciaba temporal. No nos importaba, siempre que hubiera olas. De este modo surgió el auténtico espíritu surfero galés. Cuando no había olas en Langland, îbamos a Llangennith (el spot más consistente). En Gower puedes surfear algunos buenos arrecifes, siempre que no haya demasiado viento y prestes atención a las mareas. No es seguro que en Gower encuentres olas perfectas, pero hay buena gente que vale la pena conocer, Mumbles tiene un excelente ambiente nocturno y el ganado es amistoso.

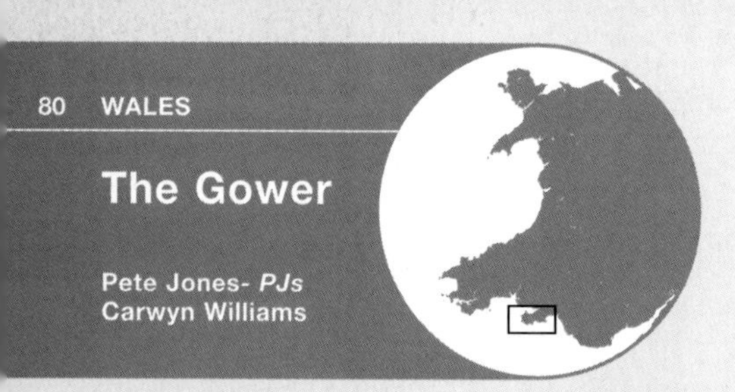

The Gower

Pete Jones- *PJs*
Carwyn Williams

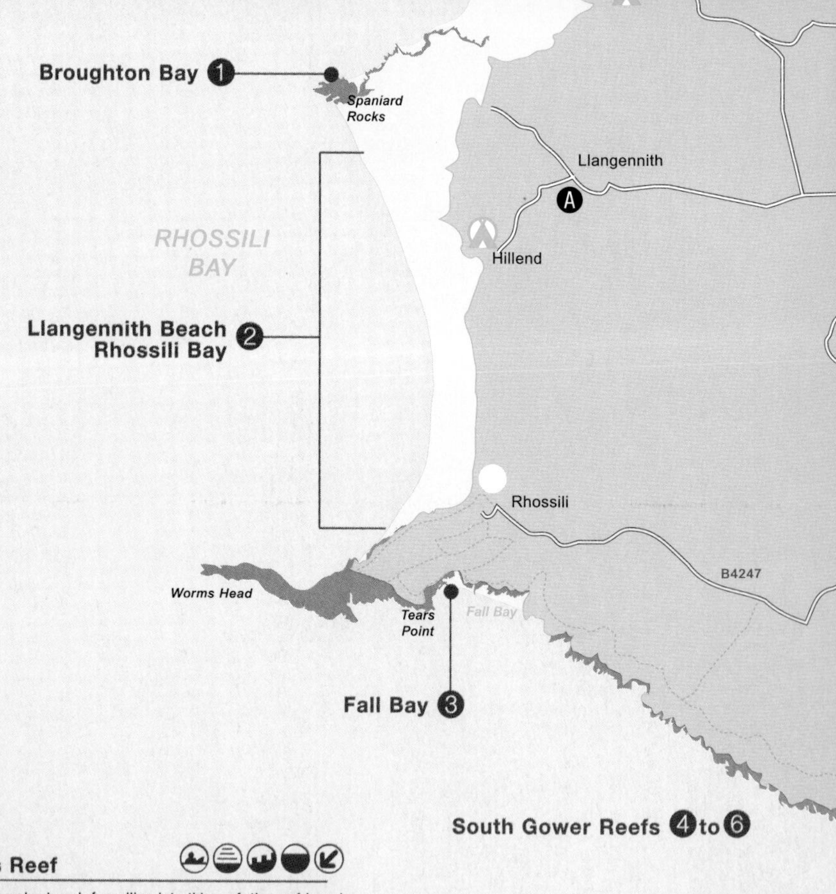

South Gower Reefs 4 to 6

1. Broughton Bay

In heavy SW storms it's one of the longest lefts in South Wales, especially suitable for longboards. Strong rips drag you away from the peak- not really for beginners. Access is through the village of Llangennith, straight past PJ's and remember to park outside the caravan park as the local site owner does not take kindly to surfers!

Par grosse tempête de sud-ouest, c'est une des plus longues gauches du sud du Pays de Galles, idéal pour les longboards. De forts courants vous éloignent du pic, pas vraiment pour les débutants. Allez-y par Lalngennith, en passant PJ's et n'oubliez pas de vous garer à l'extérieur du caravaning parce que le proprio n'apprécie pas les surfers.

Con poderosas tormentas del Suroeste esta es una de las izquierdas mas largas del Sur de Gales, especialmente adecuada para tabloneros. Potentes corrientes te alejan del pico, no siendo recomendable para principiantes. Se llega por el pueblo de Llangennith, sigue directo pasando PJ's y aparca fuera del parking para caravanas, ya que al propietario no le agradan los surfers.

2. Llangennith Beach

The indicator for the Gower area, three mile beach picks up any swell. When big, its one of the hardest places in Britain to paddle out, with few rips to help. When its 4ft or less,'Three Peaks' at the northern end of the beach can have excellent waves from mid to high tide. When swell is huge and the wind from the sth quadrant, sheltered waves can be found at Rhossili. 'The Kings'pub is renowned for its raves.

Le spot indicateur de la zone de Gower: une plage de 5 kms qui récupère toutes les houles. Quand c'est gros, c'est un des endroits les plus durs du pays pour passer la barre, avec peu de courants pour s'aider. Quand ça fait moins d'1,5m, le spot de "Three Peaks" au nord de la plage peut avoir d'excellentes vagues de mi-marée à marée haute. Quand c'est énorme et le vent de sud, on peut surfer abrité à Rhossili.

Cuando está grande es uno de los sitios más duros de toda Gran Bretaña para conseguir entrar, además las corrientes no ayudan nada. Cuando hay olas de un metro o algo menos, en 'Three Peaks' al final del lado Norte de la playa puede haber olas excelentes, siempre que la marea esté de media a alta.

Llangennith - *Photo: Phil Holden*

3. Fall Bay

Only works when the swell is big. Access is a very long walk through fields from Rhossili.

Seulement quand ça rentre gros. Une trés longue marche à travers champs depuis Rhossili.

Sólo cae con marejadas fuertes. Para llegar hay que darse una buena caminata campo a través desde Rhossili.

Fall Bay - *Photo: Phil Holden*

4. Pete's Reef

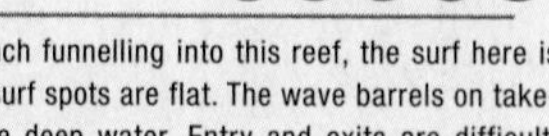

Due to a deep water trench funnelling into this reef, the surf here is 2-3ft when all the other surf spots are flat. The wave barrels on take-off and breaks into ankle deep water. Entry and exits are difficult. Works well on small summer swells. Strong rip on an incoming tide.

Due à une fosse profonde qui précède ce reef, les vagues peuvent faire un bon mètre quand les autres spots sont flat. Une vague qui tube au take-off avec de l'eau aux chevilles. Difficile d'y aller et d'en sortir. Marche bien avec les petits swells d'été. Fort courant à marée montante.

Debido a un cañón submarino, este arrecife puede tener de medio a un metro cuando el resto de los spots están plato. Forma tubo en la bajada y rompe sobre un palmo de agua. Funciona bien con los mares pequeños de verano, la corriente es fuerte según sube la marea.

5. Boiler Reef

Breaks into a deep water gully. Watch out for the take-off, any hesitation and you'll be picking barnacles out of your back! Strong rip constantly pulls you away from the impact zone. Don't be late leaving the water. As the bay fills, waves slam against the rocks. Difficult access.

Casse dans un goulet d'eau profonde. Attention au take-off car si vous hésitez une seconde, vous irez ramasser les bernacles avec votre dos! Un courant incessant vous tire hors de la zone d'impact. Ne sortez pas de l'eau trop tard car à marée haute, les vagues pètent sur les rochers. Accés difficile.

Rompe en un profundo canal. Atento en la bajada, cualquier duda y comes fondo. Una fuerte corriente te aleja constantemente de la zona de impacto. Vigila la marea, según se llena la bahla la ola termina cayendo sobre rocas expuestas. Se accede difícile.

6. Sumpter's

The easiest of the Gower reefs to surf. A deep water gully makes the paddle out easy, even when the swell is huge. Difficult access, park respectfully.

Le plus facile des reefs de la Gower à surfer. Un chenal en eau rpofonde rend la rame facile même quand ça rentre énorme.Accès difficile et garez-vous correctement.

Es el arrecife de Gower más sencillo de surfear. Un profundo canal permite entrar al pico con facilidad, incluso con olas muy grandes. Se

7. Port Eynon Point

Picks up more swell than the breaks to the east. A sucky peak breaking in shallow water, the take-off and first section are best. As the wave peels into deeper ocean it flattens off.

Chope plus de houle que les spots à l'est. Un pic qui suce cassant sur trés peu d'eau, le take-off et la première section étant les meilleurs parce qu'aprés la vague va mourir en eau profonde.

Es un pico chupún que rompe con poca agua, lo mejor es la bajada y la primera sección, en la parte final del recorrido la ola se queda fofa al caer sobre aguas más profundas.

8. Horton

Llangennith needs to be about 6ft for Horton to get going when it can produce good shore break barrels. Excellent for beginners, as it's usually uncrowded. Horton and Port Eynon Beach are two great Gower sailing spots.

Il faut que ça fasse 2m à Llangenith pour qu'Horton puisse envoyer des bonnes vagues de shore-break. Parfait pour les débutants car souvent tranquille. Horton et la plage de Port Eynon sont aussi deux super spots de funboard.

Cuando hay un par de metros o más en Llangenith, se pueden encontrar tubos orilleros en Horton. Es un sitio adecuado para principiantes que es poco frecuentado. Horton y Port Eynon Beach son dos importantes spots windsurferos de la península de Gower.

9. Slade Bay

Needs a solid swell. Access is via Horton followed by a pleasant walk around the coast path below the cliffs.

Encore par grosse houle. Allez à Horton et marchez le long de la côte en bas des falaises, c'est sympa.

Requiere una marejada potente. Se llega atravesando Horton y continuando con un agradable paseo por un sendero costero que desciende por el acantilado.

10. Oxwich Bay

A beautiful, crescent shaped bay. Calm most of the year it comes alive during big winter storms, handling howling westerlies, always bigger as the tide turns back. When it's working, word gets around quick and its usually crowded. Access is via an expensive, privately owned beach car park.

Une baie superbe en forme de croissant, calme le plus souvent sauf en hiver pendant les tempêtes; ça supporte les vents d'ouest déchaînés, toujours plus gros quand la marée descend. Attention, l'accés par la plage est payant car c'est privé.

Una preciosa bahía en forma de media luna. La mayor parte del año está en calma, pero toma vida durante los grandes maretones de invierno, recibiendo fuertes vientos del Oeste, y cayendo más grande con pleamar empezando a bajar.

11. Threecliff Bay

Picture postcard bay which needs a big swell. Dangerous currents close to the cliffs. Access is through Penmaen with limited parking.

La baie style carte postale où il faut encore pas mal de houle pour espérer des vagues. Courants dangereux à côté de la falaise. Pour y aller, visez le petit parking de Penmaen.

Este paisaje de postal requiere una fuerte marejada. Cerca de los acantilados hay corrientes peligrosas. Se accede por Penmaen y el aparcamiento es limitado.

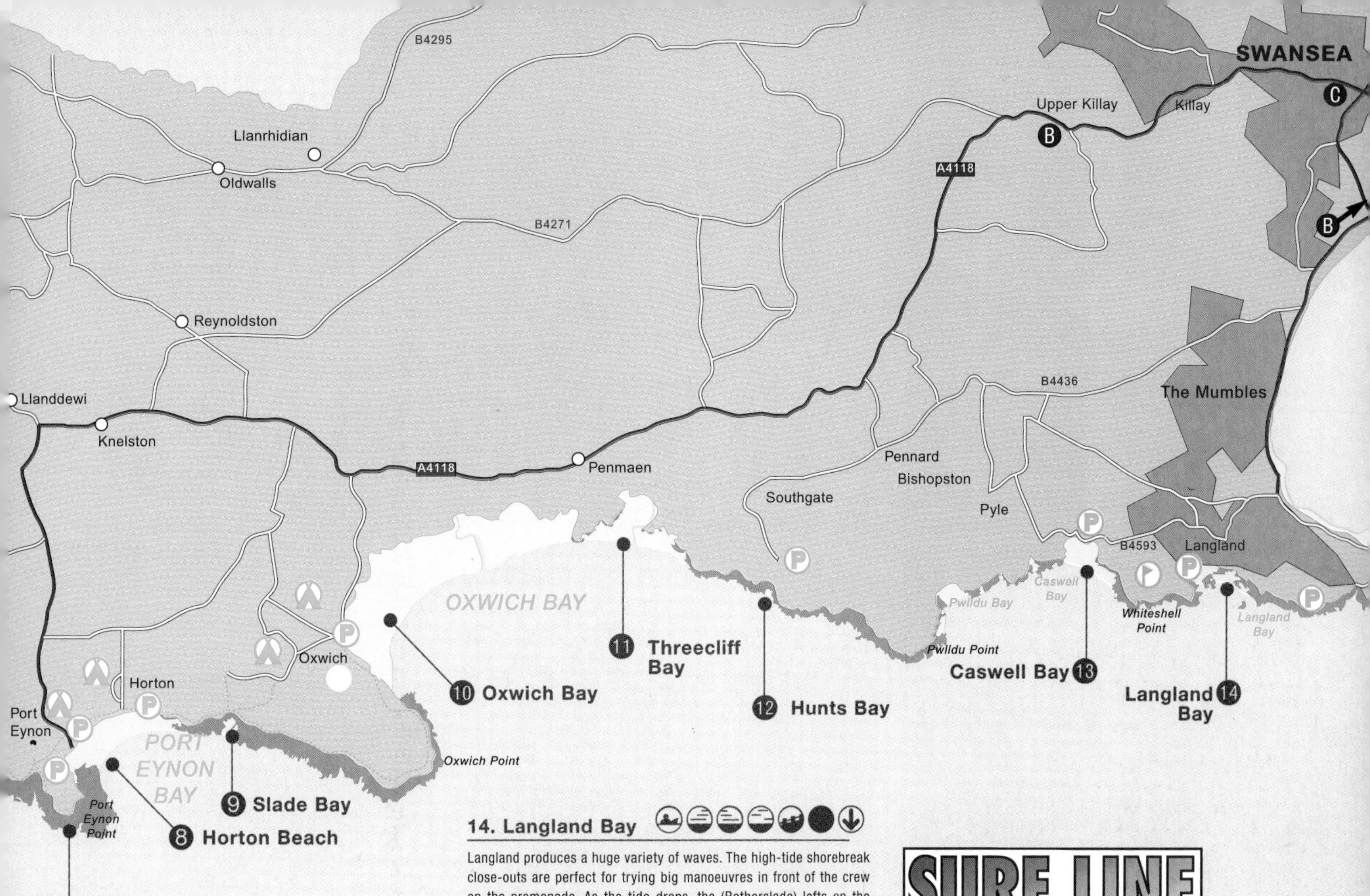

12. Hunts Bay

Needs a solid 5-6ft swell to work properly, usually uncrowded. Access is through Southgate village.

Exige au moins deux mètres de houle pour fonctionner correctement. Peu de monde en général. On y va par Southgate.

Necesita una marejada sólida de un par de metros para caer en condiciones, habitualmente sin gente. Acceso a través del pueblo de Southgate.

13. Caswell Bay

A stone's throw from Langland, the best wave is the left at the westerly end of the beach. Only works in a strong SW swell, always smaller than Langland.

A une portée de fusil de Langland, la meilleure vague est une gauche à l'extrémité ouest de la plage. Ne marche que par bonne houle de sud-ouest, toujours plus petit que Langland.

A un tiro de piedra de Langland, su mejor ola es la izquierda de la zona Oeste de la playa. Solo rompe con mar fuerte del Suroeste, siempre está más pequeño que en Langland.

14. Langland Bay

Langland produces a huge variety of waves. The high-tide shorebreak close-outs are perfect for trying big manoeuvres in front of the crew on the promenade. As the tide drops, the (Rotherslade) lefts on the reef start to work; slow but pretty perfect. This often turns into what is known as the reef, a right and left normally crowded and pretty slow. As the tide goes out, the middle of the bay might start to work along with the lefts and the shit pipe. At low tide Crab Island starts to become visible and a nice right-hander peels off the back of it. It's a great wave but has a heavy crew of older surfers on big boards, along with some of the younger whipper snappers and you should stay away unless you catch it with no one out (you may live in hope). The other option is the point, a nice right with not too many people surfing it.

Une large variété de vagues. Le shore-break qui ferme à marée haute est idéal pour tenter des grosses manoeuvres devant la foule sur le remblai. Quand ça descend, les gauches de Rotherslade sur le reef se mettent à fonctionner; c'est lent mais c'est parfait. Ca se transforme souvent en ce qu'on appelle le "Reef", un pic droite-gauche assez facile avec du monde d'habitude. Quand la marée descend vraiment, le milieu de la baie se met à marcher avec des gauches et "Shit Pipe". A marée basse, Crab island commence à être visible avec une belle droite qui déroule dessus. C'est une super vague mais attention aux vieux locaux avec des grosses planches et aux jeunes grommets qui fracassent, il ne faut démarrer que s'il n'y a personne au pic! Vous pouvez toujours essayer le Point, une droite sympa pas trop fréquentée.

Una enorme variedad de olas. Las orilleras de marea alta cierran de manera perfecta para intentar maniobras radicales frente a la multitud situada en el paseo. Según baja la marea, las izquierdas comienzan a funcionar, lentas pero perfectas. A menudo, esto se transforma en lo que se conoce como el reef, un pico con salida de izquierda y de derecha habitualmente lleno de gente y muy lento. Más tarde y con la marea aún más baja, empieza a funcionar el medio de la bahía junto con las izquierdas y la tubería de desagüe. En marea baja se hace visible Crab Island donde rompe una buena derecha en su parte posterior. Es una ola muy buena, pero la frecuentan un montón de locales, surfers veteranos con sus tablones junto con jóvenes con ganas de llamar la atención, por eso es mejor no entrar salvo que no haya gente, lo que es prácticamente imposible.

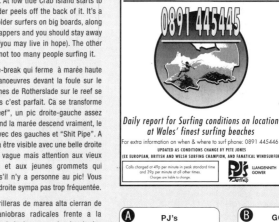

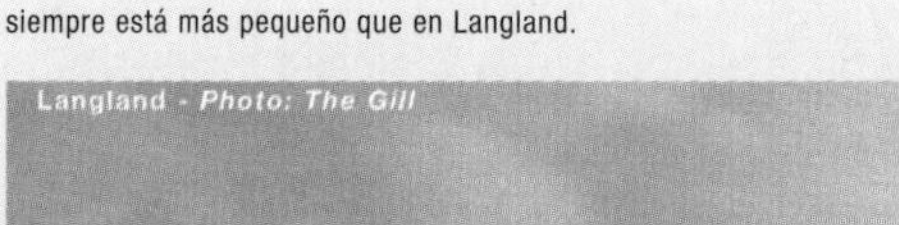

Langland - *Photo: The Gill*

Dyfed

Phil Holden
Alf Anderson

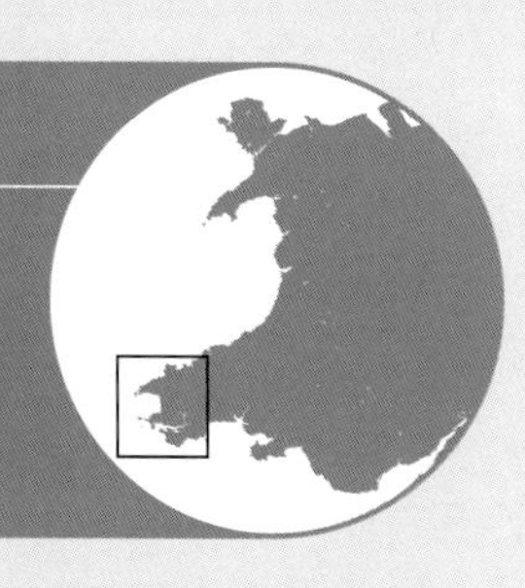

Little or no development has taken place to spoil the sand dunes and red sandstone cliffs that shelter the beaches and the surrounding National Parks that make up Dyfed. The wild wide openness of Freshwater West extends in both directions. Between Milford Haven and Abereiddy, there are numerous beaches and coves that require only a moderate swell to provide excellent surfing conditions. Many have remained unchanged for centuries. The occasional ice cream van is often the only source of sustenance here and local surfers are both keen and friendly. The South Pembrokeshire Surf Club has been running for 20 years. Whitesand Bay is the focus for most surfing in North Dyfed while Freshwater West is the main spot in the south.

L'industrie peu développée de cette région n'a pas endommagé les dunes de sable et les falaises de grès rouge qui recouvrent les plages et les parcs nationaux alentours. L'occasionnelle camionette de glaces est souvent la seule source de nourriture et les surfeurs locaux sont à la fois enthousiastes et sympathiques. Le South Pembrokeshire Surf Club fonctionne depuis 20 ans. La large ouverture sauvage de Freshwater West s'étend dans les deux directions. Entre Milford Haven et Abereiddy, il y a de nombreuses plages et criques qui n'exigent qu'une houle modérée pour fourrnir des conditions de surf excellentes. Beaucoup sont restées les mêmes depuis des siécles. Whitesands regroupe l'essentiel du surf dans le nord et Freshwater West est le spot principal pour le sud.

Las dunas y acantilados de arenisca roja que protegen las playas y zonas adyacentes (Parques Nacionales) permanecen salvajes. A menudo la única fuente de alimento es una furgoneta de helados. Los locales son amistosos y competitivos. El surf club de Pembrokeshire tiene 20 años de antiguedad. La amplia y salvaje Freshwater West se extiende en dos direcciones. Entre Milford Haven y Abereiddy hay abundantes playas y calas que con una marejada moderada proporcionan sesiones excelentes. Muchos de estos lugares no han cambiado en siglos. Whitesands es el nucleo surfero al norte de Dyfed y Freshwater West el del sur.

Freshwater West - *Photo: Phil Holden*

Freshwater West - *Photo: Phil Holden*

Freshwater West - *Photo: Phil Holden*

1. Abereiddy

Has great scenery but with none of the crowds found at Whitesand Bay. A bed of rock at the southern end of the beach can produce a hollow left at mid tide. Good protection from all winds except a westerly, check on a SW to SE wind. Car park by the beach.

Un panorama splendide sans commune mesure avec la foule de Whitesand Bay. Une langue de rochers au sud de la plage qui envoie une gauche creuse à mi-marée. Offre une bonne protection des vents sauf ceux d'ouest. Checker par vents de sud-ouest ou de sud-est.

El fondo de roca del final Sur de la playa da forma a una izquierda hueca en marea media, enmarcada en un bello paisaje. Es un lugar bien protegido de todos los vientos, salvo del Oeste. Merece un vistazo con vientos del Suroeste al Sureste. Aparcamiento fácil.

2. Whitesand Bay

Works up to 8ft. The water is clean, the locals friendly and the setting impressive. It gets crowded however (with seals often waiting in the line-up), but when it's working there are plenty of waves. To get out back when it's big there's a useful rip at the north end of the beach. A good beginners spot. Easy parking.

Marche jusqu'à 2,5m. L'eau est propre, les locaux sont sympas et le paysage est à couper le souffle. Cela dit, y'a du peuple et des phoques aussi qui attendent au pic mais quand ça marche, y'a plein de vagues. Pour sortir quand c'est gros, il faut utiliser un courant au nord de la plage. Un bon spot pour débutants. Parking à proximité.

Emplazada en un escenario de gran belleza, los locales son amistosos y el agua está limpia. Sin embargo suele llenarse de gente, a'n asì cuando funciona hay olas suficientes para todos. Una corriente en el Norte de la playa resulta muy útil para entrar cuando está grande. Es un buen sitio para principiantes y sin problemas de aparcamiento.

3. St Brides Bay

Five miles of consistent beach waves. Newgale gets the most swell and is the most surfed. Broadhaven gets protection from SW wind but is usually half the size of Newgale. Druiston is not so accessible but good for some solitude. Suitable for beginners. Easy parking.

8 kms de vagues consistantes. Newgale chope le plus de houle et c'est l'endroit le plus surfé du coin. Broadhaven reçoit une bonne protection des vents de SO mais c'est souvent deux fois plus petit que Newgale. Druiston n'est pas aussi accessible mais parfait si l'on veut être seul. Parfait pour les débutants. Parking facile.

8 kms de consistentes olas playeras. En Newgale entra más mar y es la zona más surfeada. Broadhaven está bien protegido del viento Suroeste, pero entra la mitad de tamaño que en Newgale. Druiston es de dificil acceso pero adecuado si buscas soledad. Apropiado para principiantes.

4. Marloes Sands

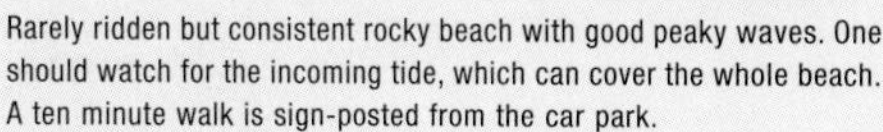

Rarely ridden but consistent rocky beach with good peaky waves. One should watch for the incoming tide, which can cover the whole beach. A ten minute walk is sign-posted from the car park.

Rarement surfé mais consistant avec de bons petits pics. Il y des rochers éparpillés sur la plage et il faut faire gaffe à la marée montante, qui peut couvrir toute la plage. Une marche de 10 minutes est indiquée depuis le parking.

Buenos y consistentes picos en este consistente spot. Hay rocas dispersas a lo largo de la playa. Cuidado con la marea alta pues puede cubrir toda la playa. Desde el aparcamiento tienes que andar diez minutos siguiendop las indicaciones para llegar a la playa.

5. Freshwater West

Dyfed's most consistent and popular break. A series of reefs link two bays with particularly good sand bars at the extremes of the tides. Best waves break on the ragged rocks at the southern end, giving hollow rides up to 100 metres. The beach is MOD and firing times are indicated by red flags. Rips can be strong, so beware. Easy Parking.

Le spot le plus connu et le plus consistent de la Dyfed, où beaucoup de compétitions se sont déroulées. Une série de reefs joint les deux baies avec des bancs de sable particulièrement bons en été aux marées extrêmes. Les meilleures vagues cassent sur des rochers sauvages du côté sud, donnant des vagues creuses de prés de 100 mètres. Cependant, cette vague est une zone militaire dont les tirs sont indiqués avec des drapeaux rouges. Les courants peuvent être forts, méfiance. Parking fastoche.

Es el spot más popular y consistente de todo Dyfed. Un conjunto de arrecifes une dos bahías, donde en verano se forman unas excepcionales barras de arena, mejores en los dos extremos de la marea. Las mejores olas caen sobre un desigual fondo de roca en el lado Sur, dando un recorrido hueco de hasta 100m. El principal problema de esta playa es que es campo de tiro militar, unas banderas rojas avisan de los períodos de disparo.

6. Broadhaven (Bosherton)

Good wedgy lefts are the speciality. Needs a decent swell but closes out above 6ft. Handles a strong W or SW wind. Park by the beach.

De bonnes gauches en coude qui sont la spécialité du coin mais il faut une houle de bonne taille et ça ferme au-dessus de 2 mètres. Peut tenir de forts vents d'ouest ou de sud-ouest. Parking sur la plage.

Aquí encontrarás unas buenas izquierdas cóncavas. Necesita que haya bastante mar, pero cierra a partir de los dos metros.

Secret Spot - *Photo: The Gill*

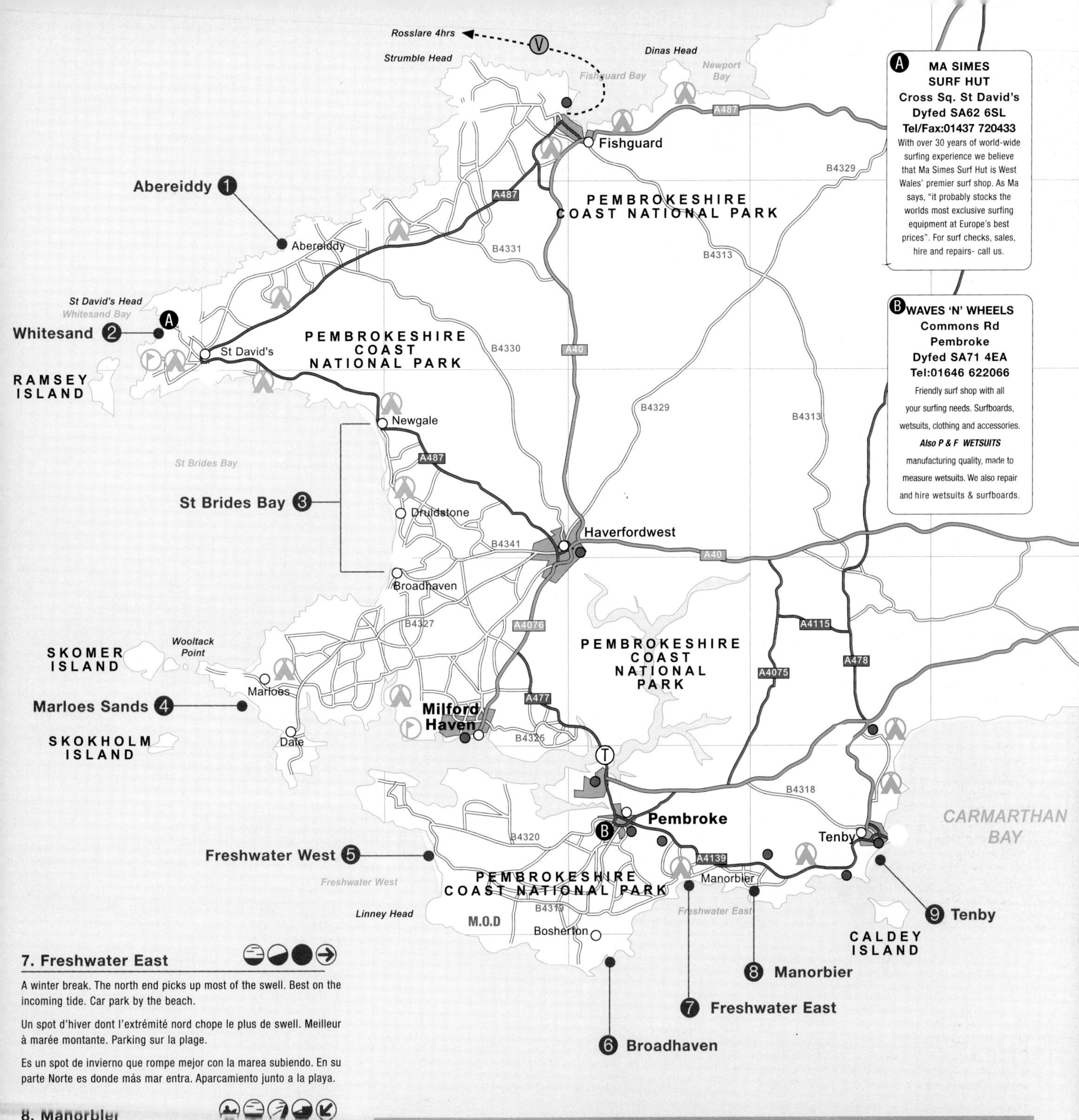

7. Freshwater East

A winter break. The north end picks up most of the swell. Best on the incoming tide. Car park by the beach.

Un spot d'hiver dont l'extrémité nord chope le plus de swell. Meilleur à marée montante. Parking sur la plage.

Es un spot de invierno que rompe mejor con la marea subiendo. En su parte Norte es donde más mar entra. Aparcamiento junto a la playa.

8. Manorbier

A lovely sand and rock beach with an impressive 12th century Norman castle standing guard over consistent quality waves. Though it can get very crowded, it works well even in onshores. Car Park by beach.

Une charmante plage de sable et de rochers avec un impressionant château Normand du XII° siècle qui monte la garde sur des vagues souvent de qualité. Bien que ça puisse être bondé, sachez quand même que ça marche aussi avec de l'on-shore. Parking sur la plage.

Un impresionante castillo Normando del siglo XII domina esta preciosa playa de arena y rocas junto con sus olas, consistentes y de gran calidad. Funciona bien incluso con viento de mar, la única pega es que suele saturarse de surfers.

9. Tenby (South Beach)

Can be worth a visit in a storm swell when all the other spots are blown out. Gets crowded with tourists in the summer, but for the rest of the year it's fine. Popular with beginners and windsurfers.

Peut valoir le détour si c'est la tempête quand tous les autres spots sont balayés par le vent. Est gavée de touristes en été, mais le reste de l'année, c'est cool.

Merece una visita en caso de que haya tal maretón que el resto de los spots se encuentran desfasados. Se llena de turistas, pero el resto del año es un lugar tranquilo, adecuado para principiantes y popular entre los windsurferos.

Manorbier - Photo: Phil Holden

North West

Alex Badley-
Abersoch Watersports

The coastline of Mid and North Wales, including the Lleyn Peninsula and Anglesy, is not renowned throughout the world for its surf. But, with patience decent waves can be found.

Le littoral nord et central du Pays de Galles, avec la péninsule Lleyn et Anglesy n'est pas renommé de par le monde pour ses vagues. Patience et vous trouverez !

El litoral de la zona central y norte de Gales (incluyendo la Península de Lleyn y Anglesey) no es especialmente famoso por su surf, pero con paciencia, se pueden hallar olas decentes.

1. Llandudno

Only works in a large westerly gale. Popular seaside resort with badly polluted water.

Marche seulement en présence d'un fort coup de vent d'ouest. Station balnéaire à la mode avec une eau très polluée.

Sólo funciona con una borrasca poderosa del Oeste. Es un sitio vacacional muy popular. El agua está muy contaminada.

2. Anglesey

The Southwest coast between Rhosneigr and Aberffraw has a number of different waves breaking when SW winds push swell up the Irish Sea. A popular windsurfing venue with easy access to the beaches.

La côte Sud-Ouest enntre Rhosneigr et Aberffraw regorge de nombreuses vagues différentes déferlant quand les vents de Sud-Ouest soulèvent la mer d'Irlande. Un lieu connu pour le windsurf avec un accés facile aux plages.

La costa Sudoeste entre Rhosneigr y Aberffraw dispone de bastantes rompientes cuando los vientos del SO impulsan la marejada hacia el Mar de Irlanda. Es un lugar frecuentado por los windsurferos.

3. Whistling Sands/Porthor

Needs at least force 8 gales to get going. A wrap around right is the best wave, popular with boogie boarders. Best at high tide from 2-4ft.

A besoin d'un vent à décorner les boeufs pour marcher. Une droite qui s'enroule bien, fréquentée par les body boarders, c'est la meilleure vague. Meilleure à marée haute à partir d'1 m.

Necesita un viento de al menos fuerza 8 para funcionar. Una envolvente derecha frecuentada por bugueros es la mejor ola. Mejor en marea alta.

4. Aberdaron

Consistent and attractive beach, deserted for much of the year. Waves break right over the boulders. Good pub overlooking the beach.

Vague consistante et intéressante, désertée depuis pas mal d'années. Des "droites" déroulent sur des rochers.

Bonita playa, desierta la mayor parte del año. Las olas rompen sobre bloques de roca. Hay un buen pub.

5. Fisherman's/Rhiw

Strong localism, difficult access and big boulders keep this spot relatively uncrowded.

Un "localisme" affirmé, un accés difficile et de gros rochers permettent à ce spot d'être relativement peu fréquenté.

Spot poco frecuentado debido al fuerte localismo, el difÌcil acceso y las grandes rocas.

6.Hell's Mouth

DUCKBOARDS

4 miles of beach and probably the busiest spot in North Wales. Waves are generally better from mid to high tide from 1-4ft. Good for beginners.

6 kms de plages et certainement le spot du nord le plus surfé. Les vagues sont généralement meilleures de la mi-marée à marée haute pour de petites vagues. Bon pour les débutants.

Más de seis kilómetros de playa con olas mejores si la marea es de media a alta y el oleaje no supera con mucho el metro. Buen sitio para novatos.

Hells Mouth - *Photo: TURTLE*

THE REEF

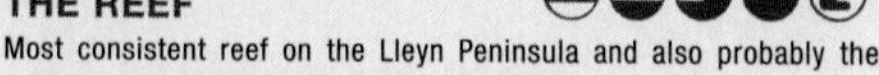

Most consistent reef on the Lleyn Peninsula and also probably the most crowded. Best either side of high tide.

Le récif le plus consistant se situe sur la "Lleyn Peninsula" mais c'est aussi le plus bondé. Meilleur avant et après la marée haute.

El arrecife más consistente de la Península y probablemente el más saturado de surfers. Su mejor punto es justo antes y justo después de la marea alta.

THE CORNER

Starts breaking on rock and finishes over sand and holds the biggest surf in the area. Can link up with the reef and will handle a South wind. Tends to be quite a fat wave.

Commence à dérouler sur du rocher et finit sur du sable. Tient la grosse houle. Peut rejoindre le récif et marchera avec un vent du sud. A tendance à être une vague épaisse.

Aguanta las mayores olas de la zona, empieza a romper sobre rocas y finaliza en arena. Suele ser una ola fofa que puede llegar a unirse con el "reef". Soporta el viento Sur.

7. Porth Ceriad

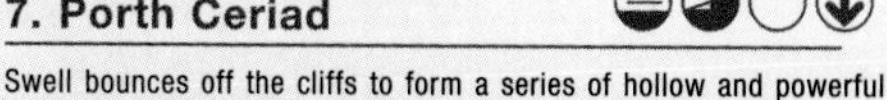

Swell bounces off the cliffs to form a series of hollow and powerful peaks. Good spot which works to about 6ft. There's a car park and camping on the cliff edge overlooking the break.

La houle rebondit sur les falaises pour former une succession de pics creux et puissants. Bon spot qui marche jusqu'aux alentours de 2 m. Il y a un parking et un camping sur le bord de la falaise surplombant le spot.

El mar rebota en el acantilado perfilando series de picos huecos y poderosos. Es una buena ola que funciona hasta los 2m. Hay aparcamiento y camping en la parte superior del acantilado desde donde se divisa la rompiente.

Chris Hookes, Porth Ceriad - *Photo: TURTLE*

8. Harlech

4 miles of beach with a classic castle worth a look on one of the many flat days.

6 kms de plages avec un château d'époque qui vaut une visite lors d'un des nombreux jours calmes.

Más de seis kilómetros de playa cerca de un majestuoso castillo que merece la pena visitar en alguno de los abundantes días sin olas.

9. Llandanwg to Barmouth

15 mile stretch of exposed beach break waves.

Des vagues de sable bien exposées qui s'étendent sur 20 km.

Veintidós kilómetros de playa abierta al mar. Olas playeras.

10. Llwyngwril

Can be the best wave in mid-Wales when there's a big swell pushing up the Irish Channel. Experienced surfers only.

Peut-être la meilleure vague du centre du Pays de Galles quand une grosse houle remonte le "Channel" irlandais.Pour surfeurs confirmés seulement.

Puede ser la mejor ola de la zona central de Gales cuando hay una fuerte marejada subiendo por el Canal de Irlanda. Sólo para surfers con experiencia.

11. Borth

Popular seaside resort with 2 miles of beach, best on the pushing tide. No crowds. An ideal small beginners waves.

Station balnéaire renommée possédant 3 kms de plage, meilleure à la marée montante. Peu de monde à l'eau et idéal pour les surfeurs de petites vagues et les débutants.

En esta zona vacacional hay una playa de 3km. Suele haber poca gente y sus olas pequeñas son ideales para aprender.

Alex Badley, Hells Mouth - *Photo: TURTLE*

Porth Neigwl - *Photo: TURTLE*

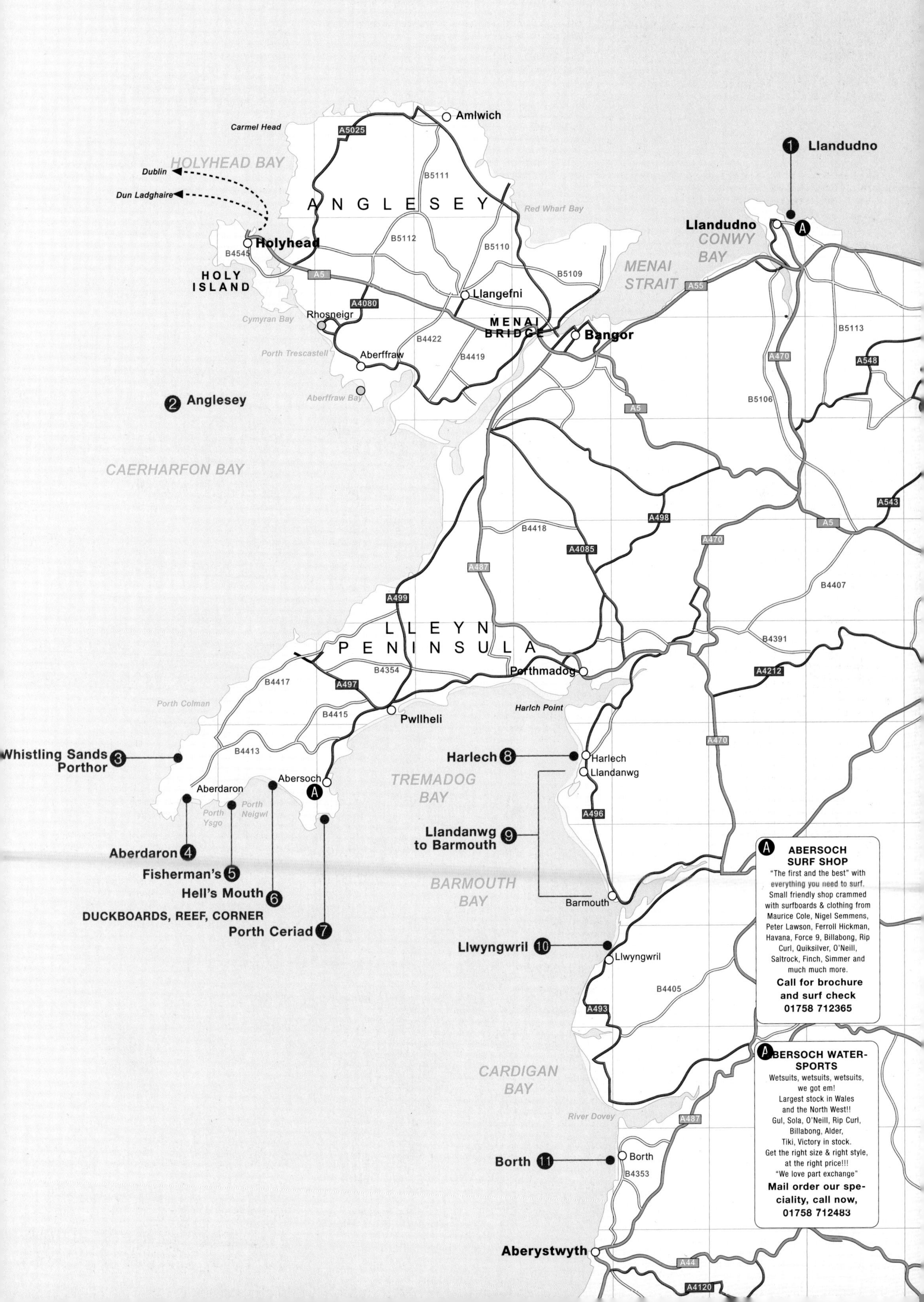

Carmel Head
HOLYHEAD BAY
Dublin
Dun Ladghaire
Amlwich
A5025
B5111
ANGLESEY
Red Wharf Bay
Holyhead
B4545
HOLY ISLAND
B5112
B5110
A5
B5109
MENAI STRAIT
A55
Llangefni
A4080
Cymyran Bay
Rhosneigr
MENAI BRIDGE
Bangor
B4422
Porth Trescastell
Aberffraw
B4419
Aberffraw Bay
2 Anglesey
1 Llandudno
Llandudno
CONWY BAY
A
B5113
A470
A548
B5106
CAERHARFON BAY
A498
A543
B4418
A4085
A487
A499
B4407
LLEYN PENINSULA
B4391
B4354
Porthmadog
A4212
B4417
A497
Porth Colman
B4415
Pwllheli
Harlch Point
Whistling Sands Porthor 3
B4413
Harlech 8
Harlech
Llandanwg
Aberdaron
Abersoch
TREMADOG BAY
Porth Ysgo
Porth Neigwl
A496
Llandanwg to Barmouth 9
Aberdaron 4
Fisherman's 5
Hell's Mouth 6
DUCKBOARDS, REEF, CORNER
Porth Ceriad 7
BARMOUTH BAY
Barmouth
Llwyngwril 10
Llwyngwril
B4405
A493
CARDIGAN BAY
River Dovey
Borth 11
Borth
B4353
Aberystwyth
A44
A4120
A ABERSOCH SURF SHOP
"The first and the best" with everything you need to surf. Small friendly shop crammed with surfboards & clothing from Maurice Cole, Nigel Semmens, Peter Lawson, Ferroll Hickman, Havana, Force 9, Billabong, Rip Curl, Quiksilver, O'Neill, Saltrock, Finch, Simmer and much much more.
Call for brochure and surf check
01758 712365
A ABERSOCH WATER-SPORTS
Wetsuits, wetsuits, wetsuits, we got em!
Largest stock in Wales and the North West!!
Gul, Sola, O'Neill, Rip Curl, Billabong, Alder, Tiki, Victory in stock.
Get the right size & right style, at the right price!!!
"We love part exchange"
Mail order our speciality, call now,
01758 712483

EIRE & NORTHERN IRELAND

IRELAND

Ireland is the whole island west of Britain. N.Ireland comprises the 6 counties that have remained part of the UK since the Anglo-Irish treaty in 1921. The Republic of Ireland (Eire) comprises the 26 counties governed from Dublin. For the purpose of this guide, Ireland is being treated as one country. The first settlers arrived around 6000BC from N.E. Scotland. The next were Celtic tribesmen who came through around 700BC. The Romans considered it not worth invading so the tribes warred amongst themselves. Centuries later Christianity arrived. Wars continued and the Vikings were followed by Norman and British invaders. Oliver Cromwell marched through with a bloodied sword, strengthening the English hold. Laws were enforced forbidding Catholics to hold mass or to buy or inherit land. The failure of the potato crops in 1845, 1846 and 1848 threw the people into appalling famine. In less than ten years the population was reduced by two million. Half died, the other half left forever.

Long standing resentment deepened in Easter1916, when a group took control of public buildings in Dublin. They were overrun and executed, but this only strengthened sympathy for the Republicans. In 1921 the Anglo-Irish treaty was signed which did little but plunge the country deeper into civil war. In 1938 a new constitution came into effect, finally declaring Ireland's complete independence and renouncing British sovereignty. This free state became known as Eire but even though a truce exists today, the troubles in Ireland remain its most reported topic.

IRLANDE

L'Irlande est l'île à l'ouest de l'Angleterre. L'Irlande du nord comprend les 6 comtès qui font partie intégrante du Royaume-uni depuis le traité anglo-irlandais de 1921. La république d'Irelande (Eire) comprend les 26 comtès gouvernés par Dublin. Dans le cadre de ce guide, l'Irelande est traitée comme un seul pays. Les premiers habitants arrivèrent il y a environ 8000 ans du nord-est de l'Ecosse. Ls suivants provenaient de tribus celtiques originaires d'Europe. Les Romains ne trouvaient pas intéressant de les envahir, alors les tribus se contentaient de s'entre-tuer sur place! Des siecles plus tard, le christianisme apparut. Les affrontements continuèrent et les Vikings précèdèrent les Normands et les envahisseurs venus d'Angleterre. Le temps passa et Olivier Cromwell défila avec une épée pleine de sang, renforçant la mainmise anglaise. Les lois interdirent aux catholiques de se réunir, d'acheter ou d'hériter. Les mauvaises récoltes de pommes de terre de 1845, 1846 et 1848 plongèrent la population dans une famine épouvantable. En moins de 10 ans, l'Irlande ne comptait plus que 2 millions d'habitants. Parmi ces deux millions, la moitiè mourrut, l'autre moitiè quitta le pays à jamais.

Le profond ressentiment s'accentua quand lors du lundi de Pâques 1916, un groupe prit le contrôle d'un nombre d'édifices publiques à Dublin. Ils furent maîtrisés et exécutés mais cela renforça la sympathie envers les Républicains et leur cause. Le 6 décembre 1921, le traité anglo-irlandais fut signé qui, l'air de rien, plongea encore plus pronfondément le pays dans la guerre civile. En 1938, une nouvelle constitution prit effet, déclarant la totale indépendance de l'Irlande et la renonciation à la souveraineté anglaise. Cet état libre porta le nom d'Eire et à ce jour, même s'il existe une trêve, les troubles en Irlande restent d'actualité.

IRLANDA

Los bosques han sido ampliamente reemplantados por pequeños campos de hierba divididos por setos. Irlanda es la isla situada al oeste de Gran Bretaña. El norte de Irlanda está compuesta por 6 comunidades que han venido a formar parte de UK desde el tratado Anglo-Irlandes en 1921. La República de Irlanda, Eire, está compuesta por 16 comunidades gobernadas desde Dublin. Para esta guia, Irlanda ha sido tratada como un país. Los primeros colonos llegaron desde el Noreste de Escocia hacia el año 6000 a.C. Los siguientes fueron los celtas que llegaron sobre el año 700 a.C. Los romanos consideraron que no valía la pena invadirlo por lo tanto las tribus vivian tranquilas. Siglos despues llegó el cristianismo. Las guerras continuaron y los vikingos fueron seguidos por los Normandos y invasores británicos. Oliver Cromwell atravesó con una espada sangrienta, fortaleziendo el poderío ingles. Las leyes fueron impuestas prohibiendo a los católicos crear comunidades ni comprar o heredar tierras. El fracaso del cultivo de la patata en 1845, 1846 y 1848 llevó a las personas al hambre. En menos de 10 años la población se redujó en 2 millones. La mitad muertos y la otra mitad se fueron.

La gente empezó a establecerse a partir de Semana Santa de 1916 cuando un grupo tomó el control de los edificios públicos de Dublin. Fueron capturados y ejecutados pero esto solo fortaleció la simpatía por los republicanos. En 1921 el tratado Anglo-Irlandes fue firmado que hizo poco pero empujó al país a la Guerra Civil. En 1938 una nueva constitución hizo efecto, finalmente declarando Irlanda completamente independiente y renunciando a la soberanía británica. Este estado libre es conocido como Eire. Aunque todavia existe una tregua, los problemas en Irlanda estan al orden del dia.

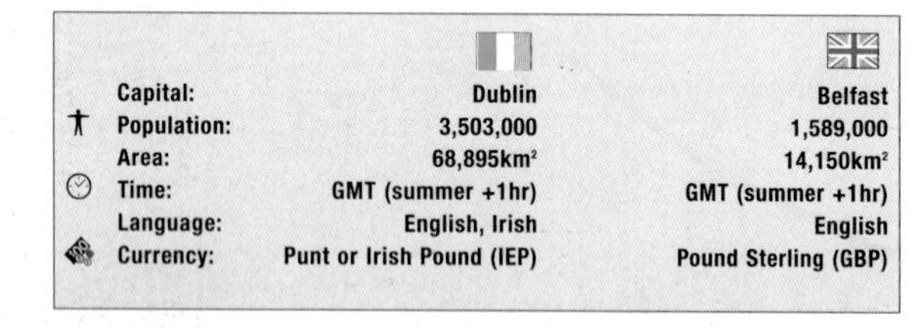

	Eire	N. Ireland
Capital:	Dublin	Belfast
Population:	3,503,000	1,589,000
Area:	68,895km²	14,150km²
Time:	GMT (summer +1hr)	GMT (summer +1hr)
Language:	English, Irish	English
Currency:	Punt or Irish Pound (IEP)	Pound Sterling (GBP)

Killarney - *Photo: Alex Williams*

...The forests have been largely replaced by a patchwork of small grass fields divided by hedgerows,

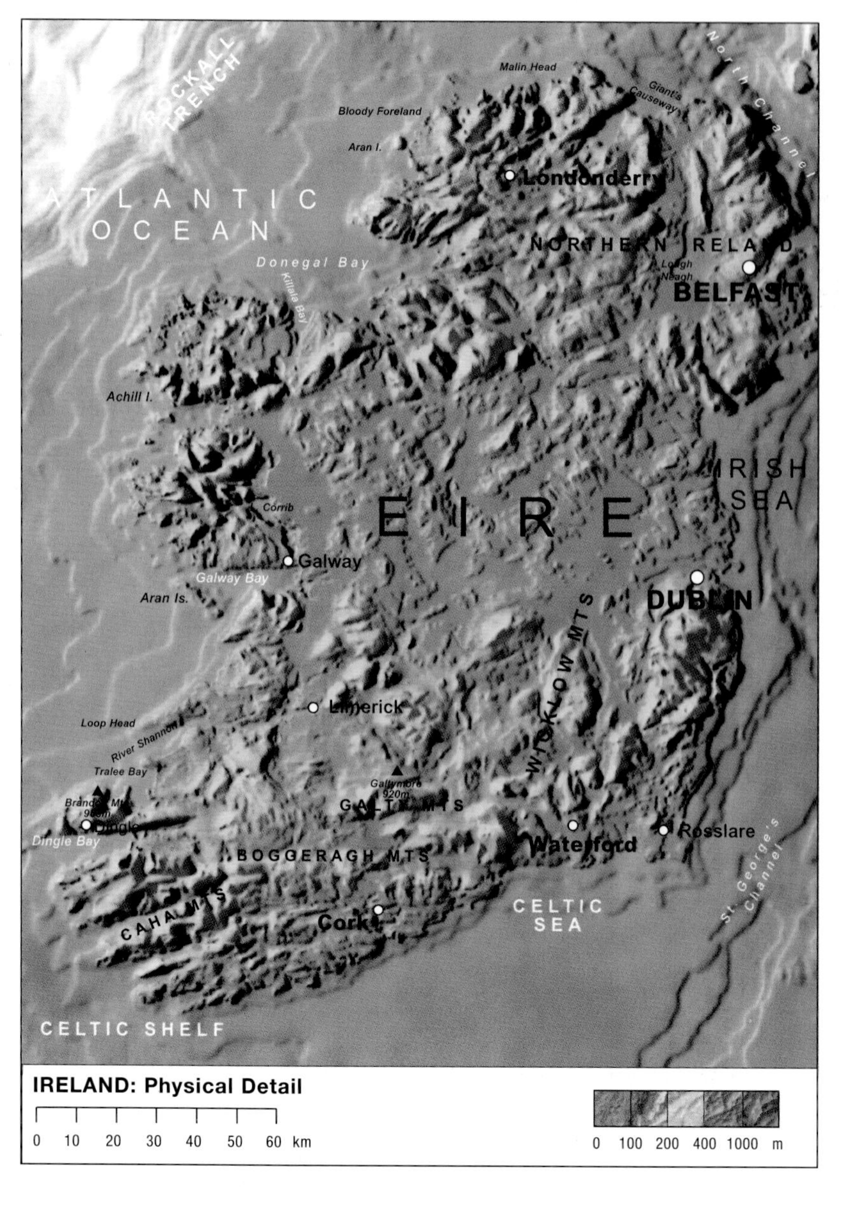

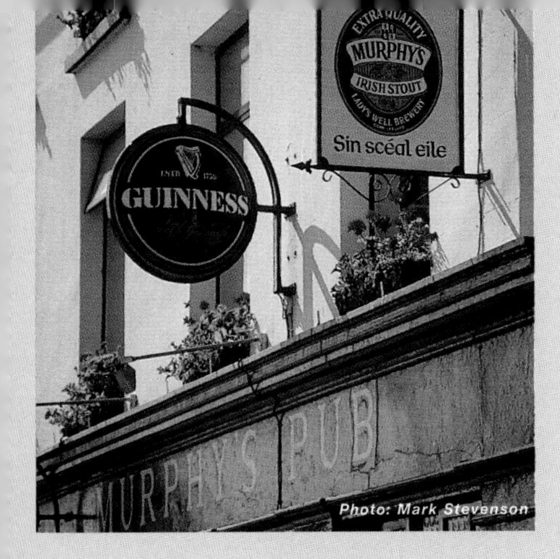

Photo: Mark Stevenson

Telephoning

	Ireland	UK
Ireland	353	00+
Ireland	353	44 +
Directory Enquiries	190	192
International Directory	114	153
Operator	10	100
INT. Operator	114	155
Emergency	999	999

Cost of Living

Restaurant *	IR£ 10
Bed & Breakfast	IR£ 10-15
Camping	IR£ 3-5
Pint of Guinness	IR£ 2

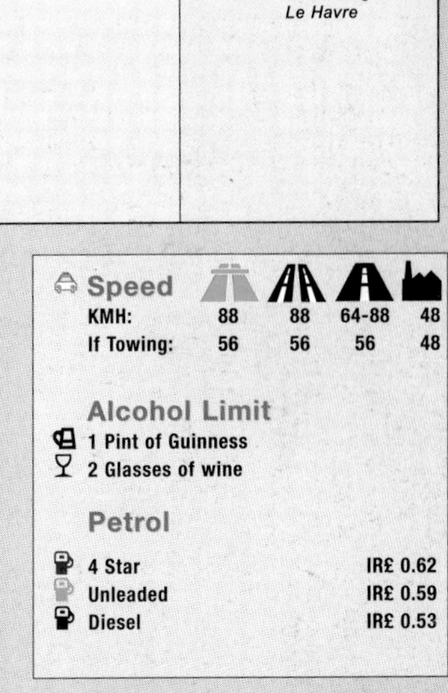

Ireland is not a cheap place to travel, If anything more expensive than the U.K.. It's hard to live cheaply, but it can be done by renting a cottage between friends and cooking your own food. Camping is easy and obviously the cheapest way to live, although Ireland's wet climate it's not for everyone. Farm cottages and B&B's are numerous and usually extremely comfortable. No visit to Ireland is complete without a visit to a pub! Especially in rural areas, the pub is far more than just a place to drink, it's the heart of the village and often the political centre too. For food, advice, conversation, local entertainment (especially music), the pub is the place to head.

Driving

Ireland's roads cater for drivers who are prepared to take their time. You can't get anywhere fast, so it's best not to try. Savour the pace of life and don't try to cover too large an area in too short a time. Petrol is expensive and petrol stations in some of the more remote areas are few and far between, but driving from one great reef break to the next is one of Ireland's greatest delights. As in Britain you drive on the left and most other road signs and markings are similar

Ferry Services

Prices vary considerably depending on which season you travel in and outside of the summer period they can be good value. The main advantage of travelling by ferry is that you can bring your car...vital if one is going to get the best out of Ireland's swell pounded coasts.

Visas

British nationals do not need a passport to enter the Republic or the North, but it is useful to carry one in case you use the medical services. If you don't take a passport, be sure to have some other form of convincing ID. Other EC nationals, travellers from the USA, Canada, Australia, New Zealand and Commonwealth countries simply need a passport and can stay for up to three months.

L'Irlande n'est pas une destination bon marché. Cela revient plus cher qu'un voyage en Angleterre. Cependant on peut limiter la casse en louant un cottage à partager à plusieurs et en faisant sa propre cuisine. On peut facilement camper et c'est bien sûr la manière la plus économique de vivre bien que cela ne soit pas évident. Les cottages et les B&B's sont nombreux. On ne peut visiter l'Irlande sans avoir fait un tour dans un pub! Tout particulièrement dans les campagnes, le pub est bien plus qu'un débit de boissons. C'est là où l'on entend battre le coeur du village Irlandais, et souvent il fait office de forum politique. Pour les conseils culinaires et la conversation, le pub est presque toujours l'endroit qu'il faut et très souvent ce sera le lieu de rendez-vous pour les divertissements locaux, particulièrement pour la musique.

En voiture!

Il vaut mieux se souvenir que les routes irlandaises satisfont ceux qui ont du temps. Aucune route ne permet d'aller vite,alors ce n'est pas la peine d'essayer. Il faut savourer le rythme de vie particulièrement lent et il faut savoir prendre son temps. Ne pas oublier que l'essence est chère (2,80 livre IR. par galon) et les stations d'essence dans les régions reculées sont rares et espacées. Pourtant, rouler de super spot en super spot posséde un charme intense et procure une joie immense. Comme en Angleterre, on conduit à gauche; la signalisation et le marquage sont similaires.

Les ferry

L'Irlande est desservie par un certain nombre de compagnies de ferry qui partent de France et d'Angleterre. Les prix, très variables, sont fonction de la saison et, en dehors de l'été, peuvent être intéressants. Prendre un ferry posséde l'avantage de permettre de prendre sa voiture... Ce qui est vital si on souhaite exploiter à fond les côtes irlandaises et ses houles.

Irlanda no es un sitio barato para viajar, cualquier cosa es más cara que en Gran Bretaña. Es difícil vivir barato pero se puede hacer alquilando una casa de campo entre amigos y cocinando tu propia comida. Hacer camping es fácil y la manera más barata de vivir aunque el clima húmedo de Irlanda no es para todo el mundo. Abundan las granjas y los bed and breakfast los cuales generalmente son muy confortables. Una visita a Irlanda no es completa si no visitas uno de sus pubs. Especialmente en áreas rurales, un pub es más que un sitio donde beber, es el corazón del pueblo y en muchas ocasiones el centro político. Para comida, consejo, conversación, entretenimiento local (especialmente música), un pub en un buen sitio donde dirigirse.

Carreteras

Las carreteras de Irlanda están llenas de conductores que están preparados para tomarse el tiempo con calma. No se puede llegar a cualqier sitio rápido, por lo tanto en mejor no intentarlo. Saboreala vida y no intentes de convertir un tramo largo en un corto periodo. La gasolina es cara y en algunos puntos las estaciones de servicio son escasas e lejos entre ellas, pero conducir desde un gran pico de reef haste el siguiente es una de los grandes placeres irlandeses. Como en Gran Bretaña se conduce a la izquierda y la mayoria de las señalizaciones son similares.

Ferry

Los precios varian considerablemente dependiendo de la temporada en la que viajes y fuera del periodo del verano puedes conseguir un buen precio. La mayor ventaja que hay de viajar en ferry es que te puedes llever el coche...vital si quieres conocer los mejores sitios de la costa irlandesa.

Speed

	Motorway	Dual carriageway	Road	Town
KMH:	88	88	64-88	48
If Towing:	56	56	56	48

Alcohol Limit

- 1 Pint of Guinness
- 2 Glasses of wine

Petrol

4 Star	IR£ 0.62
Unleaded	IR£ 0.59
Diesel	IR£ 0.53

Ferries

Larne - P&O:	01574 274321
North Irish Ferries:	[illegible] 770000
Dublin - B&I Line:	01 797977
Rosslare - Irish Ferries:	053 33158
Rosslare - Sealink:	053 33115
Cork - Brittany Ferries:	021 277801
Swansea-Cork Ferries:	01792 456116

Airports

Belfast:	018494 22888
Galway:	091 55569
Shannon:	061 61660
Cork:	021 313131

Train Stations

Belfast:	230310 / 235282
Dublin:	787777
Galway:	091 61444
Waterford:	051 73401
Cork:	021 506766

Bus Stations

Dublin:	366111
Galway:	091 63555
Waterford:	051 79000
Cork:	021 508188

"...as there is no real problem with crowds, little time is given to searching for new spots."

Easky Right - *Photo: Tim Rainger, LP*

the surf & weather

by Brian Britton

Surfing began in Ireland in the mid '60's with 3 groups starting simultaneously on the Causeway Coast, in Rossnowlagh and in Tramore. The Surf Club of Ireland formed in1967, though it remains relatively undeveloped by European standards.

The majority of waves come from lows tracking from the US to Iceland, deepening as they go. Surf comes from the SW to N, as the lows approach, with winds from the lows generally blowing SW. This means that the N and NW facing breaks, angled to catch the swell, enjoy predominant cross/offshore winds. The best times to visit are spring and autumn, as during summer swells are sporadic and flat periods can last two weeks. During winter, surf is continuous but the water is colder and winds can be very strong. Spring is often blessed with the best weather, the water is still cool, but the swells start to settle and the surf is consistent. September to November is prime time with winter swells rolling in and fairly warm water. If youre usedc to wearing a wetsuit, you'll find the temperatures acceptable up to late November.

Most of the surfers tend to use the better known breaks and most locals will give you a list of places they plan to check soon, and this generosity should be appreciated. Show respect, drive with consideration and be friendly. Things go slowly here so be patient. If you are, you will fully enjoy yourself.

Le surf débuta en Irlande au milieu des années 60 avec 3 groupes qui commencèrent simultanément sur la Causeway Coast, à Rosnowlagh et à Tramore. Le surf club d'Irelande se forma en 1967, bien que cela reste le pays d'Europe où le surf s'est développé le moins.

La majorité des vagues est le résultat des dépressions qui se déplacent des Etats-unis à l'Islande, se creusant au fur et à mesure qu'elles se rapprochent. Le swell provient du sud-ouest au nord au moment où les dépressions se rapprochent de l'Islande avec des vents à dominante sud-ouest. Cela signifie que les spots orientés nord ou nord-ouest, orienté pour recevoir la houle, ont des vents offshores prédominants. Les meilleures périodes pour venir surfer sont le printemps et l'automne. Pendant l'hiver, on peut surfer tout le temps mais l'eau est plus froide et les vents peuvent être violents. Pendant l'été les swells sont rares et les périodes sans vagues peuvent durer 2 semaines. Le printemps profite d'un temps clément, l'eau est toujours à température acceptable et les swells sont présents et le surf est plutôt consistant.La meilleure période se situe entre septembre et novembre. Les houles d'hiver se préparent et l'eau est encore plutôt bonne.

La plupart des surfeurs ont tendance à surfer sur les spots les plus connus et comme le monde n'est pas un problème, ils consacrent peu de leur temps à la recherche de nouvelles vagues. D'une façon générale, le local donnera une liste des endroits qu'il connait, geste généreux s'il en est. Il faut montrer du respect, conduire avec prudence et être sympathique. Les choses vont doucement ici, il faut faire preuve de patience. Dans ce cas, vous aurez bien des raisons de vous réjouir. Vous serez plus que bienvenu.

Irish Surfing Assoccation
President: Brian Britton
3 Jocelyn Place, Dundalk, Co. Louth
Tel:042 32700 Fax:042 37512

Cead mile failte -
A hundred thousand welcomes

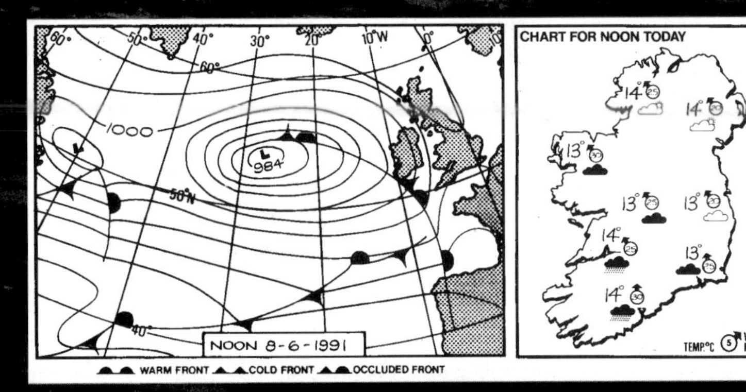

Ireland escapes extremes of weather with the enveloping Atlantic producing a mild, damp climate. Summers are rarely hot, winters rarely cold and in parts of the west it rains two days out of three and coastal areas are often pounded by big swells and strong winds. This mild, rainy climate is good for the growth of grass and moss and it's this that led William Drennan to name it 'The Emerald Isle' in the 18C.

L'Irlande échappe aux conditions climatiques extrêmes grâce à l'Atlantique qui favorise un climat doux et humide. Les étés sont rarement chauds, les hivers rarement froids et, dans l'ouest, il pleut deux jours sur trois et les régions côtières sont souvent battues par de gros swells et des vents violents. Ce climat doux et pluvieux est bon pour l'herbe et la mousse et c'est pourquoi William Drennan la nomma "l'île d'émeraude" au 18 éme siècle.

Irlanda escapa de los extremos climatológicos envuelta por el atlántico produciendo un clima templado y húmedo. En verano raramente es frio y en zonas del oeste llueve dos de cada tres dias y las costas amenudo son golpeadas por grandes swells y fuertes vientos. El clima templado y lluvioso es apropiado para el crecimiento de la hierba y todo lo demás y es por esto por lo que William Drennan la llamó "Isla Esmeralda".

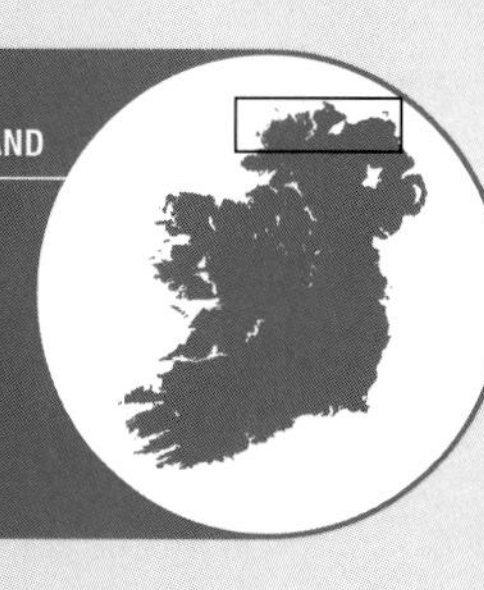

Causeway Coast

Ian & Andy Hill - *Troggs Surf Shop*

"The Causeway Coast" stretches from Ballycastle to Magilligan Point. Surfing first started here in Easter 1963 when Ian Hill entered the water at Castlerock with a 'Bob Head' board from Mawgan Porth, Cornwall. Three years later a group of youngsters led by Alan Duke (to be many times Irish champion) started surfing the Portrush/Portstewart area and began travelling to the west coast where they met up with other surfers. For 20 years the number of Northern Irish surfers stuck at around 20. The advent of body boarding opened up the sport to a younger age group and a proportion of these youngsters progressed to stand-up surfing. Today local surfers number about 120, mainly from Portrush/Portstewart. A few travellers come up from Belfast on the weekends attracted by both the surf and the night life! 'Kellys' in Portrush is the biggest disco in Ireland. The main surfing season on the north coast is from mid August to mid May. In the summer months the lows tend to be a lot further south in the Atlantic and Malin Head tends to stop swell getting round to the Causeway Coast.

La côte du Causeway s'étend de Ballycastle à Magilligan Point. Le surf a commencé ici au printemps 63 quand Ian Hill entra dans l'eau à Castlerock avec une planche "Bob Head" de Mawgan Porth dans le Cornwall. Trois ans plus tard, un groupe d'ados mené par Alan Duke (qui sera plusiuers fois champion d'Irlande) débuta le surf entre Portrush et Portstewart, en commençant à voyager vers la côte ouest où ils rencontrèrent d'autres surfers. Pendant 20 ans, le nombre des surfers en Irlande du Nord plafonna autour de 20. L'arrivée du bodyboard ouvrit ce sport aux plus jeunes et une partie de ces ados se mit au surf aprés et encore aujourd'hui. On compte maintenant environ 120 surfers, surtout entre Portrush et Portstewart. Quelques voyageurs viennent ici en week-end de Belfast, attiré par le surf et la vie nocturne! Kellys à Portrush est certainement la plus grosse discothèque. La saison de surf principale sur la côte nord se situe de la mi-août à la mi-mai. Pendant les mois d'été, les dépressions ont tendance à se retrouver trop au sud dans l'Atlantique et Malin Head a tendance à barrer la houle avant la côte du Causeway.

The Causeway Coast va desde Ballycastle hasta el pico Magilligan. Se surfeó por primera vez en las vacaciones de Semana Santa de 1963 cuando el socorrista Ian Hill entró por primera vez en Castlerock con un "Bob Head Board" hecho en Mawgean Porth en Cornwall. Tres años más tarde un grupo de jóvenes liderado por Allan Duke (campeón de Irlanda en muchas ocasiones) empezaron a viajar hacia la costa oeste donde se encontraron con otros que acababan de surfear en Rossnowlagh, Waterford y en el área de Tramore. Durante veinte años, el número de surfistas de la costa norte de Irlanda se quedó estancado en veinte. La facilidad del bodyboarding impulsó este deporte que lo empezó a practicar un grupo de jóvenes y algunos, más tarde, se pasaron al surf. Hoy en dia el número de surfistas ronda los ciento veinte, la mayoria de Portrush/ Portstewart; también hay algunos surfistas de Belfast que llegan atraídos por el surf y la diversión nocturna, donde pasan los fines de semana. La discoteca "Kelly's" es la más grande de Irlanda en la zona de Portrush. La mejor época del año para surfear la costa norte es la de mediados de agosto hasta mediados de mayo.

North and West Donegal

There are only a few coastal areas left in Europe where the possibility of finding perfect undiscovered waves still exists. North and West Donegal is one of these places! It receives so much swell that more often than not one's only real concern will be the wind conditions. These winds can often be very strong and they will generally blow from the north and west. The relentless forces of nature have slowly carved up the desolate coastline around Donegal, consequently little protected bays and islands have become abundant. Such places offer unlimited potential, all they need is time and energy to explore! Donegal is sparsely populated due its harsh climate and inhospitable landscape, accessability is therefore limited. Bloody Foreland, Magheroaty, Dunfanaghy, Gweebarra and Loughros Beg have been surfed in the past, beyond these breaks you will very possibly be surfing virgin territory.

Il existe peu de zones côtières en Europe où la possibilité de trouver des vagues vierges et parfaites existe encore. La partie ouest et nord du Donegal en est une! Cela chope tellement de houles que la plupart du temps le seul souci sera les conditions de vent. Ces vents peuvent souvent être trés forts en soufflant plus souvent du nord ou de l'ouest. Les forces infatigables de la nature ont lentement découpé les côtes sauvages autour du Donegal, c'est pourquoi des petites baies protégées et des îles se sont multipliées. Ces endroits offrent un potentiel illimité, tout ce qu'il faut est du temps et de l'énergie pour les explorer. Le Donegal est peu habité à cause de son climat difficile et de son paysage inhospitalier, son accessibilté est donc limitée. Bloody Foreland, Magheroaty, Dunfanaghy, Gweebarra et Loughros Beg ont été surfés par le passé, au-delà de ces spots vous trouverez certainement des territoires de vagues plutôt vierges.

Es una de las únicas zonas de Europa donde se pueden descubrir nuevos spots surfeables. North y West Donegal es una de ellas. En esta zona el swell entra con más fuerza donde el único inconveniente es el viento. En esta zona generalmente el viento es de componente norte u oeste. Es una costa especial con pequeñas bahías y abundantes islitas, donde se pueden explorar nuevos spots.

1. Benowe/Magilligan

The longest beach in Ireland...ten miles of peaks. Access is via Downhills and Benowe. A superb view from 'Bishops road' above the beach to Donegal and Londonderry.

La plage la plus longue d'Irlande...15 kms de pics. L'accés se fait par Downhills et Benowe. Une vue superbe de "Bishops road" au-dessus la plage jusqu'à Donegal et Londonderry.

La playa más larga de Irlanda con miles de picos. Se llega via Downhills y Benowe. Con una estupenda vista desde "Bishops Road" arriba de la playa, hacia Donegal y Londonderry.

2. Castlerock

A little way east of Castlerock is a long stone jetty. The presence of this jetty has helped to create a consistent sandbank. This bank is best surfed around mid tide when it can produce an excellent, long righthander, best from 3-6ft. Any bigger and it will close out. From low to mid tide the sands are wide and firm and are safe for most vehicles to drive on. You can either drive from Castlerock or, alternatively, it is possible to drive along the beach from Portstewart and paddle out through the river, around the jetty, to the wave.

Un peu à l'est de Castlerock, y'a une grosse jetée de cailloux dont la présence a aidé à créer des bancs réguliers qui marchent mieux à mi-marée quand ça peut envoyer une droite longue et excellente, mieux de 1 à 2 mètres. Plus gros, ça ferme sévère. De marée basse à mi-marée, le sable est dur et permet derouler sans problème sur la plage. On peut arriver de Castlerock ou par la plage depuis Portstewart et ramer par la riivière, en contournant la jetée.

Se llega por un pequeño camino de piedras al este de Castlerock sigiendo un malecon. La presencia de este malecon a conseguido crear consistente bancos de arena. Para surfear este pico la media marea es la mejor, donde salen excelentes derechas, el mejor tamaño es de 3 a 6 pies, cuando está más grande cierra. Con marea media o baja se pueden meter la mayoria de los vehículos sin peligro. A este pico se puede llegar desde Castlerock o, la alternativa, cruzando la playa en coche desde Portstewart y remar por la ria a lo largo del malecon hasta el pico.

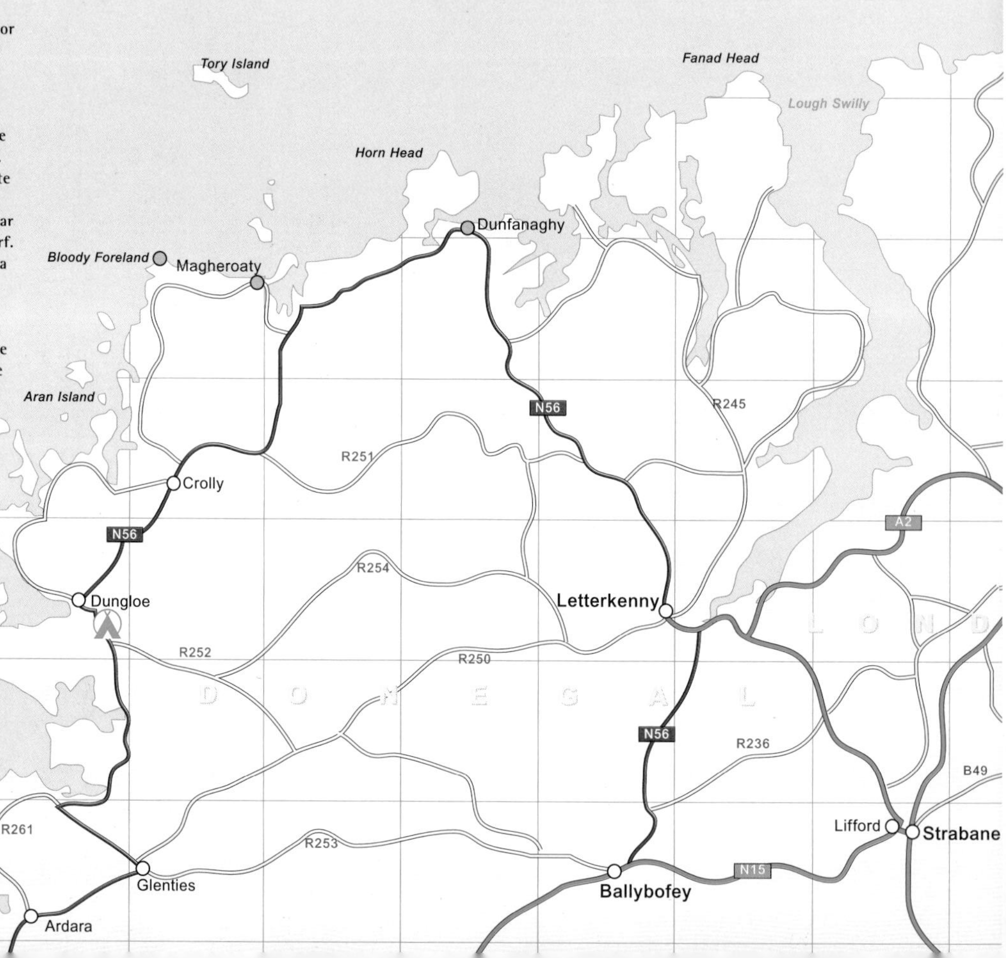

3. Portstewart Strand

Portstewart itself, is a busy seaside resort which gets crowded during summer months. The beach here can provide some of Northern Ireland's gentler waves with good rights and lefts surfable up to around 8ft. Either park above the beach, or do as the locals do and park on the sands.

Portstewart en soi est une station plutôt animée où il y a foule l'été. La plage ici peut envoyer parmi les vagues les plus faciles d'Irlande du Nord avce des bonnes droites et gauches jusqu'à 2,5m. Soit vous vous garez au-dessus de la plage, ou comme les locaux directement sur le sable.

Portstewart es una ciudad con mucho moviemiento y duranto los meses de verano se abarrota de gente. Es un pico que deja una buena derecha e izquierda surfeable hasta 8 pies. Se puede aparcar cerca del pico o sino se puede meter el coche en la arena como lo hacen los locales.

4. Portrush

EAST STRAND

Portrush, like Portstewart is a popular holiday resort for people living in Northern Ireland. On the Eastern side of the peninsula, you'll find a good beach break which is also a good spot to check out on a big swell, when the other nearby beaches are closing out. Big car park next to the beach.

Portrush, comme Portstewart est une station balnéaire pour les gens qui vivent dans le nord de l'Irlande. Sur la partie Est de la peninsule, on trouve un bon beach-break qui est aussi un bon spot à checker en cas de gros swell, quand les plages d'à côté ferment. Méga-parking à côté de la plage.

Portrush, tanto como Portstewart, es un sitio de verano para la gente que vive en el norte de Irlanda. Al este de la peninsula se encuentra un buen point que se debe tener en cuenta con fuerte swell cuando las olas de las playas cercanas están cerrando. Tiene una gran parking junto a la playa.

WEST STRAND

Faces NW and catches swell when East Strand is too small. Waves increase in size from E to W. One of the most surfed spots in the N.

Exposé NO et reçoit la houle quand East Strand est trop petit. Les vagues augmentent en taille d'est en ouest. Un des spots les plus surfés dans le nord.

Da al noroeste y entra el swell del oeste cuando está pequeño las olas crecen desde el este al oeste. Es uno de los spots más surfeados del norte.

BLACK ROCKS/DHU VARREN

Located at the western end of West Strand is a lefthand reef which holds surf to 8ft. Drive under the railway bridge to the car park.

Situé à l'ouest de West Strand, cette gauche de reef tient jusqu'à 2,5m. Roulez sous la vois ferrée jusqu'au parking.

Situado al oeste rompe una izquierda que aguanta hasta 8 pies. Para llegar al parking pasar por debajo de las vias del tren.

Andy Hill, Portrush - Photo: Irish Surfing Association

5 White Rocks

Average beach break waves which gets crowded in summer but with tourists not surfers.

Beach break moyen qui se peuple en été de touristes, pas de surfers.

Es una playa que rompe regularmente y en verano se llena de turistas pero no de surfers. Fondo de arena y piedrilla.

6 Portballintrae

Just to the East of Portballintrae lies a consistent bay which is often a foot or two bigger, and more powerful than other nearby beaches. Quality will depend on the state of the sandbanks and wind direction; Too much west in it will mess up the swell. Good to 8ft. Park in Portballintrae, next to the SW corner of the beach. From here it's a short walk.

Juste à l'Est de Portballintrae se trouve une baie consitente qui est souvent un à deux pieds plus gros et plus puissant que les plages environnantes. La qualité dépendra de l'état des bancs et de la direction du vent: s'il est trop à l'ouest, il désorganisera la houle. Bon jusqu'à 2,5m. SE garer à Portballintrae, au SO de la plage. Depuis là, y'a peu à marcher.

Situada al este de Portballintrae, es una bahía de arena y piedrilla donde las olas rompen 2 pies más grandes y más potente que en las playa cercanas. La calidad de la ola depende de los bancos de arena y de la dirección del viento. El viento del oeste destroza el swell. Rompe hasta 8 pies. Se aparca en Portballintrae junta a la esquina suroeste de la playa. Desde aqui es corta la distancia andando.

7. White Park Bay

An attractive 2km beach which can make surfing here that much more worthwhile if the waves are good. The car park above the beach is 5 minutes walk from the sands.

Une plage sympa de 2kms qui peut rendre le surf d'autant plus agréable quand les conditions y sont. Le parking au-dessus de la plage est à 5 minutes à pied du sable.

Es una atractiva playa salvaje de 2 km, con fondo de arena y piedrilla, donde rompen buenas olas. El parking está a cinco minutos andando de la playa.

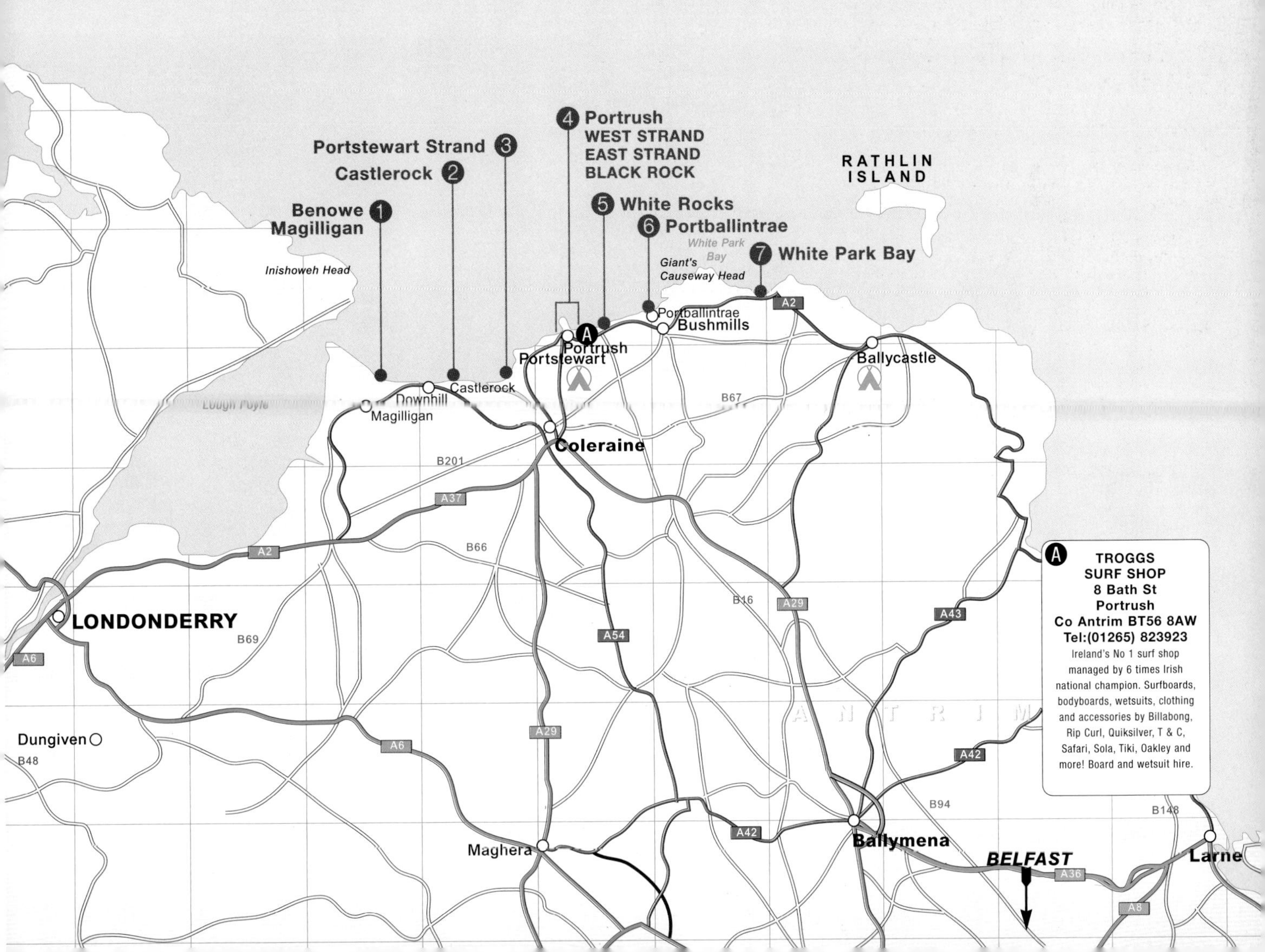

the northwest

by Roci Allen / Rossnowlagh Surf Club

Dave Malherbe, Kilcummin - *Photo: Alex Williams*

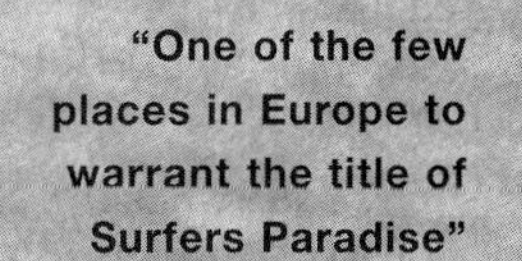

"One of the few places in Europe to warrant the title of Surfers Paradise"

Bundoran - ***Photo: Irish Surfing Association***

The North West might seem an unusual choice of location, but in Europe it is one of the few places to warrant the title 'a surfers paradise'. A large portion of its coast is north facing, so it works in the prevailing south west airstream. It presents numerous reefs, points and beaches to the wrath of the north Atlantic and picks up swell from the W and N.

It remains an uncrowded place to surf and the reasons it's remained so become obvious when looking at climatic tables. Co's Donegal and Sligo are wet and windy. As well compare the costs of a French and Irish surf holiday, and you'll get an idea of why people have left the NW to a select handful of surfers. But when you get there, you'll see waves which make all the cost comparisons not worth the paper they're written on.

A number of main focal points have emerged in the North West: Rossnowlagh and Bundoran in South Donegal, Strandhill and Easky in Sligo. Rossnowlagh is home to the biggest surf club in Ireland so look out for the crack in the surfers bar. Bundoran is also home to some semblance of surf culture, complete with a surf shop. The waves at Bundoran and Tullen are excellent and surrounding areas are beautiful. But it is the two breaks at Easky which have so far become the best known in Ireland and it's not uncommon to find people of six nationalities camping on the point. The town is small and friendly and accommodation is not difficult to find.

Le North West pourait donner l'impression d'être une destination peu habituelle, mais en Europe, c'est un des rares endroits à mériter le titre de "paradis des surfeurs". Une grande partie de cette côte est orientée nord, ainsi les vents favorables sont oriientés sud-ouest. On y trouve de nombreux reefs,caps et plages exposés aux tourmentes de l'Atlantique Nord en recevant la houle d'ouest, nord-ouest et nord.

Cela reste un endroit tranquille pour faire du surf et les raisons en sont évidentes lorsqu'on regarde les statistiques sur le climat. Co's Donegal et Sligo sont humides et venteux. Lorsque vous comparez les côuts d'un trip en France et en Irlande, on comprend pourquoi les gens ont abandonné le North West à quelques poignées de surfeurs, mais quand on est sur place, on peut voir des vagues qui supportent la comparaison; ce qui n'apparaissait pas évident sur le papier.

Quelques spots sortent du lot: Rossnowlagh et Bundoran à S. Donegal & Strandhill et Easky à Sligo. Rossnowlagh est le lieu du plus grand surf club d'Irlande. Bundoran est le berceau de la surf culture, et l'on trouve de nombreux surf-shops. Les vagues à Bundoran et Tullen sont excellentes et la nature y est belle, mais ce sont les deux spots de Easky qui sont devenus les plus connus et il est courant de trouver 6 nationalités différentes à l'eau. La ville est petite et sympathique. Le logement n'est pas difficile à trouver.

Puede parecer una eleccion poco comun. Pero es uno de los pocos sitios en Europa donde garantizan el "Paraiso Surfero". Una gran vientos del SO. Hay numerosos reefs, picos y playas abiertas al furioso Atlantico Norte, de donde recoge los swells del O, NO y N.

Todavia quedan sitios invadidos por poca multitud donde surfear y la razon es obvia al consultar el clima. Co's Donegal y Sligo son húmedos y con mucho viento. Al comparar los costes de un surfari por Francia o por Irlanda veras por que la gente ha cedido el NO a un selectivo puñado de gente, pero al llegar alli, veras las olas que hacen que esta comparacion de costes no este tan fundada como parecia.

Han aparecido un buen numero de points focales. Rossnowlagh y Bundoran en S. Donegal & Strandhill y Easky en Sligo. En Rossnowlagh esta el mayor club de surf de Irlanda. En Bundoran existe una amplia cultura surfista completada con las tiendas de surf. Las olas en Bundoran y Tullen son excelentes y los alrededores son bonitos, pero las dos olas de Easky son las mas famosas y es normal que haya gente de hasta 6 nacionalidades distintas. El pueblo es pequeño y acogedor y es facil de encontrar alojamiento.

Photo: ***Chris Power***

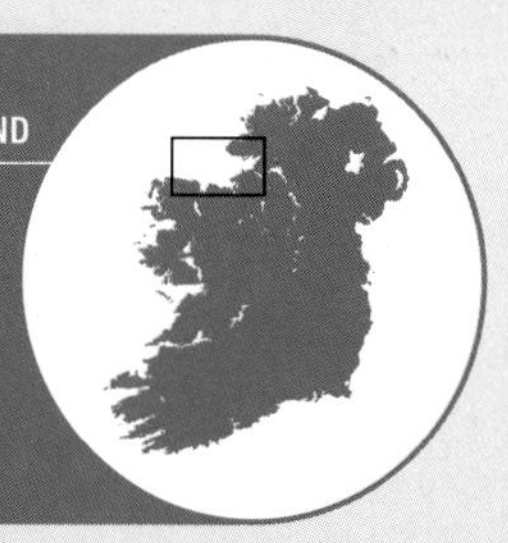

The North West

Brian Brittain

1. Bunatrahir Bay

A little way outside of Ballycastle is a road leading to a small unmarked harbour. A nice left breaks at the western side of Bunatrahir Bay. It needs a fair N swell to get it going and a S wind to clean it up.

Un petit chemin en dehors de Ballycastle est en fait la route menant à un petit port non répertorié. Une jolie gauche déroule du côté ouest de Bunatrahir Bay. Elle exige un swell de nord conséquent pour s'épanouir et un vent du sud pour être belle et propre!

Un pequeño camino por fuera del castillo de Bally te lleva a un pequeño puerto. Una buena izquierda rompe al O de la bahía Bunatrahir. Necesita bastante swell del N y vientos del S para que el swell sea claro.

2. Lackan Bay

Secluded bay which works under similar conditions as Kilcummin, but needs less swell. Follow the road from Kilcummin.

C'est une baie isolée dont la vague marche dans les mêmes conditions qu'à Kilcummin, mais elle réclame moins de houle. Possibilité de se garer.

Esta bahía apartada funciona con condiciones similares a las de Kilcummin pero necesita menos swell. Sigue la carretera de Kilcummin y aparca donde sea posible.

3. Kilcummin Harbour

In a big swell, an excellent long left breaks in front of the harbour wall. Although a S or SE wind is best, the shelter it receives means a W wind will not ruin it. Kilcummin is signposted from the main road.

Lors d'un gros swell, on pourra trouver une gauche longue excellente qui casse devant le mur du port. Bien que le vent de sud ou sud-est permettent les meilleures conditions, abritée comme elle est, cette vague supporte les vents d'ouest. Kilcummin est indiqué sur la route principale.

Con fuerte swell rompe una excelente y larga izquierda frente a la pared del puerto. Aunque los vientos del S y SE son los mejores, el estar protegido el viento del O no le afecta mucho. Kilcummin esta señalizado en la carretera principal.

Kilcummin - *Photo: Alex Williams*

4. Inishcrone

At the eastern end, near the harbour an excellent right will start to break when the swell is big enough. There's also a beach break with pretty mellow peaks.

A l'extrème est, près du port se trouve une excellente droite qui commence à péter quand la houle est assez grosse. Il y a aussi un beach break qui forme de jolis pics prêts à être consommés!

Al extremo este cerca del puerto rompe una derecha cuando el swell es lo suficientemente fuerte. Tambien hay una playa con picos bastante flojos.

5. Pollacheeny Harbour

A righthander tubes its way down the rock point at the mouth of Pollacheeny harbour giving fast rides up to 150mtrs in length. Like nearly all of Ireland's breaks it's rarely surfed, however If any of these waves were in Cornwall or SW France, they would always be crowded! Parking by the slipway.

Des tubes pour les normal foot. Il faut prendre le chemin pour descendre la pointe rocheuse à la sortie du port de Pollacheeny pour atteindre une vague qui peut faire 150 m de long. Comme la plupart des vagues irlandaises, elle est rarement surfée, alors que si elle était située dans le Cornwall ou dans le sud-ouest de la France, elle serait bondée! Parking près du chantier.

Una derecha rápida y tubera rompe cerca de las rocas en la boca del puerto de Pollacheeny dando rápidas olas con una longitud de hasta 150 metros. Como la mayoria de los picos de Irlanda raramente es surfeado, y si alguna de estas olas estuviesen en Cornwall o en el sur-oeste de Francia, estaría siempre lleno de gente. Se aparca junto a las gradas.

Pollacheeny Harbour - *Photo: Chris Power*

6. Easky

LEFT

The left breaking west of the harbour is a very good reason for spending time in Easky. It works under similar conditions as the right but breaks in a smaller swell. Paddle out off the harbour wall. Due to Easkys' popularity the council, with the I.S.A. have erected toilets and changing facilities beside the castle, overlooking the waves.

La gauche qui casse à l'ouest du port est une autre très bonne raison pour rester à Easky. Elle marche avec les mêmes conditions que la droite mais se contente d'un plus petit swell. Il faut ramer au-delà du mur du port. En raison de la fréquentation, le conseil municipal, en accord avec la I.S.A, a fait construire des toilettes et fait changer les installations à côté du château, surplombant les vagues.

Esta izquierda rompe contra el lado oeste de la pared del puerto, es otra buena razón para quedarse un tiempo en Easky. Funciona con las mismas condiciones que la derecha pero rompe con marejada más pequeña. Hay unas escaleras al final de la pared del puerto para entrar en el agua, y poder salir fácilmente. Debido a la popularidad de Easky, por decisión del Consejo del Condado Local junto con la Asociación Irlandesa de Surfing, se han construido nuevos inodoros y vestuarios al lado del castillo desde donde se dominan las olas.

Easky Left - *Photo: Tim Rainger, LP*

EASKY RIGHT

World class right breaking on a flat rock reef. Low tide is best. One of the major pluses for this break is its consistency and the amount of offshore winds you get here. These conditions provide perfect tubes and long fast walls up to 10ft. Very popular wave.

Droite de réputation mondiale déferlant sur un récif de rochers plats. Meilleure à marée basse. Cette vague est remarquable par sa consistance et la fréquence de ses vents offshore. On y obtient des tubes parfaits et des murs longs et rapides surfables jusqu'à 3 m. Vague très renommée.

Esta derecha de categoría mundial rompe en un fondo liso de roca. Lo mejor sale en marea baja. Una de sus ventajas está en su consistencia y en la cantidad de vientos terrales de que dispone. Con estas condiciones salen tubos perfectos y unas paredes muy largas y rápidas de hasta 3 metros. Es una ola muy popular.

7. Dunmoran Strand

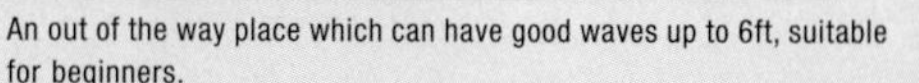

An out of the way place which can have good waves up to 6ft, suitable for beginners.

Un endroit hors des sentiers battus, qui peut révèler de bonnes vagues jusqu'à 2 m, convient aux débutants.

Este sitio está un poco a desmano aunque pueden salir buenas olas de hasta 2 metros. Está bien para principiantes.

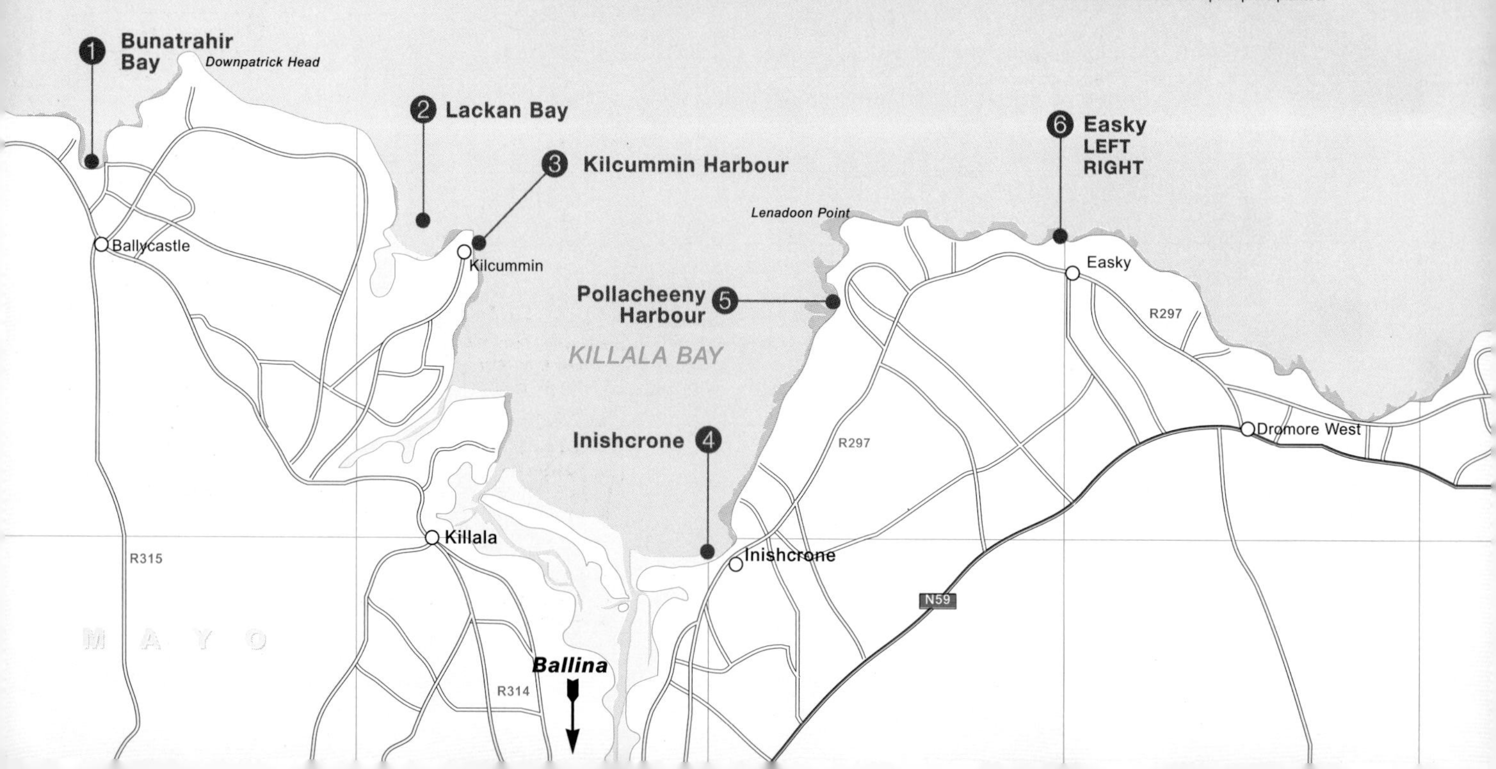

8. Strandhill

Either surf the main beach, or the sandbar (which involves a long paddle). If you enjoy surfing long rights you can surf 'Bluerock' an unforgiving 200m wave breaking at the end of the beach. One can rent a surfboard here, worthwhile remembering if yours has been chewed up by some of Ireland's hungry reefs!

Soit on surfe la plage principale soit le banc de sable (qui exige une longue rame). Si on aime surfer de longues droites, on peut surfer Bluerock, une incroyable vague de 200 m cassant à l'extrémité de la plage. On peut louer une planche sur place, utile si un des reefs irlandais a englouti la vôtre!

Se puede surfear tanto en la playa principal cpmo en la barreras de arena (hay que remar mucho antes de llegar). Si te gusta surfear largas derechas entonces tu ola es "Bluerock", una ola inolvidable de unos 200m que rompe al final de la playa. Se pueden alquilar tablas, no viene mal si has perdido la tuya en los feroces acantilados de Irlanda.

9. Streedagh Strand

Needs a fair sized swell to produce worthwhile waves, however if the sandbanks here aren't producing the goods, then your time spent getting here might not necessarily be wasted. Beyond Streedagh, all the way down to Ballyconnell are numerous unmarked roads leading to various coves and inlets. The possibillty of finding an unmarked reef or point break is high.

Exige une taille honorable de la houle pour former des vagues valables; cependant si les bancs de sable ne produisent pas de bonnes vagues, la journée n'est pas pour autant foutue. Après Streedagh, de nombreuses routes non balisées allant vers Ballyconnell ménent à divers criques et bras de mer. La probabilité de trouver un reef ou un point break non répertoriés est réelle.

Necesita de una marejada de tamaño respetable para que salgan olas que merezcan la pena, aunque si los bancos de arena no están bien, no es necesario malgastar el tiempoo viniendo hasta aquí. Más allá de Streedagh, bajando hasta Ballyconnell, hay muchas carreteras sin marcar que conducen a distintas ensenadas y cuevas, con lo que hay muchas posibilidades de topar con una buena ola por la zona.

10. Mullaghmore

With a SW wind and a big NW swell, clean lines push into the bay. It can also be worth a drive around Mullaghmore Head. Reputedly a lefthander breaks over shallow rocks that can hold a 20ft swell!

Avec un vent de sud-ouest et un gros swell de nord-ouest, on profite de lignes propres arrivant dans la baie. Mullaghmore peut valoir le détour. Une vague de goofy foot au-dessus de rochers à fleur d'eau; elle tient la houle jusqu'à 6 m!

Cuando sopla el viento del SO acompañado por una fuerte marejada del NO este es un buen sitio a comprobar. Así uno puede encontrarse con unas líneas bien definidas que empujan contra la bahía. También combiene merodear un poco por la zona de Mullaghmore Head ya que una izquierda muy regular rompe en un fondo de roca poco profundo aguantando marejadas de hasta 7m.

11. Bundoran

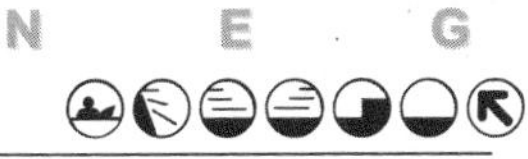

One of Ireland's most surfed waves, a low tide break at its best in the 4-6ft range. The peak gives a short and snappy right with a longer left peeling and tubing its way across the rocks on the northern side of the bay. When it's big, another more sheltered left starts to work.

Une des vagues les plus surfées d'Irlande; un spot de marée basse qui jette particulièrement entre 1,50 et 2 m. Le pic donne une courte droite qui a du punch avec une gauche plus longue se soulevant et tubant sur des rochers du côté nord de la baie. Quand c'est gros, une gauche plus abritée commence à marcher.

Es una de las olas más surfeadas de Irlanda. Del pico se desprende una rápida e instantánea derecha, y una izquierda más larga que bordea en su recorrido la zona rocosa en forma de tubo al norte de la bahía. Un pico en marea baja es lo mejor que hay de entre uno y dos metros. Cuando se pone grande, empieza a funcionar una izquierda más protegida.

12. Tullan Strand

A nice spot, considered to be some of the best and most consistent beach waves in Ireland. The southern end has the best shaped peaks. If it's flat along the rest of the coast, then there can still be a wave here. Take the first left north of Bundoran (it isn't signposted). You will come to an area for parking above the beach.

Un joli spot considéré comme un des meilleurs et des plus consistants en Irlande. La partie sud possèdent les pics les mieux formés. S'il n'y a rien sur le reste de la côte, alors il se peut qu'il y ait une vague ici. Il faut prendre la première à gauche à Bundoran (ce n'est pas indiqué). Un parking est disponible au-dessus de la plage.

Es un bonito lugar, y está considerada por algunos como la mejor y más consistente playa de olas de Irlanda. En el extremo sur se encuentran los picos con mejores secciones. Si está plato en el resto de la costa hay posibilidades de que aquí halla olas. Desviate a la izquierda en la primera al norte de Bundoran (no está señalizado) llegarás a una zona de aparcamiento encima de la playa.

13. Rossnowlagh

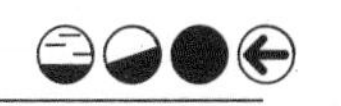

Home to Ireland's biggest surf club, housed in the 'Surfers Bar'. Here, along with Irish surfers and a pint of Guinness you can find surf memerobilia built up since the sixties. The waves can be good but will be smaller and less powerful than those at Tullen.

Lieu du plus important club de surf d'Irlande, situé au "Surfers Bar". Ici, avec les surfeurs irlandais et une pinte de Guiness, on peut trouver toute l'anthologie du surf depuis les années 60. Les vagues peuvent y être bonnes mais seront plus petites et moins puissantes que celles de Tullen.

Es el hogar del club de surf más grande de Irlanda, con su sede en "Surfers Bar". Aquí, además de surfistas irlandeses y una pinta de Guinness podrás encontrar surf memorable recopilado desde los sesenta. Las olas pueden estar bien aunque siempre más pequeñas y con menos fuerza que en Tullen.

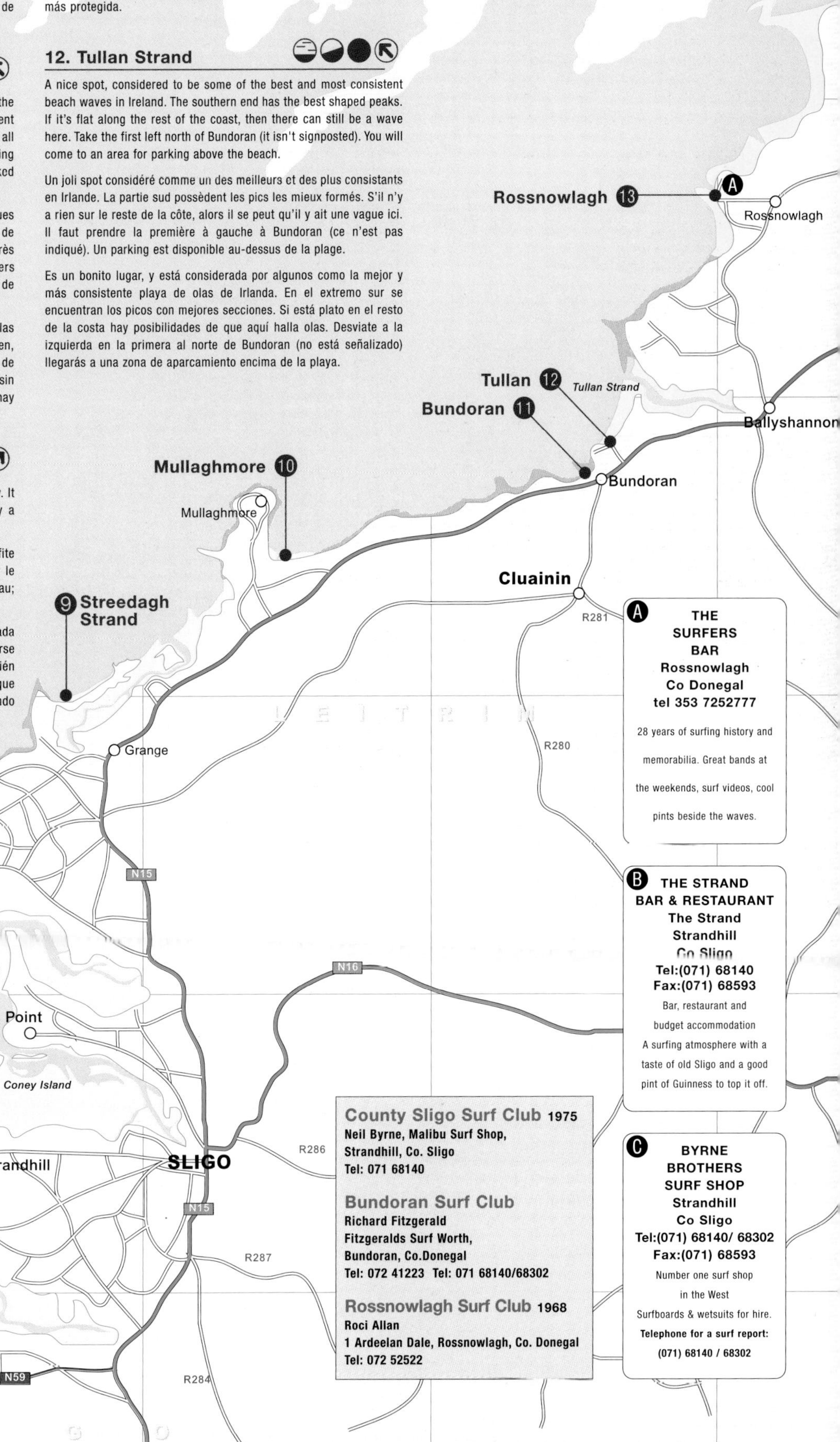

Photo: *Tim Rainger LP*

county clare

Photo: *Mark Stevenson*

"To stand above Lahinch and see the points break is a magnificent sight..."

County Clare is exposed to the full influence of the Atlantic and would be one of Europe's most popular surf destinations if the weather was more hospitable. It offers a huge selection of surf spots ranging from mellow reefs and beaches to the biggest, gnarliest tubes you could ever want to ride!

Offshores, being SE, aren't consistent so this area may be perfect less often than many north facing areas, but when it's on, it's right on. To stand above Lahinch and see the points break is a magnificent sight and though Lahinch is only one of many superb spots, it's the surf centre for good reasons, situated next to a long, white beach with three excellent left reefs at its northern end. There's a variety of accommodation available in town, also a hostel at Spanish Point, many in Doolin and two between Lahinch and the cliffs of Moher.

There are other breaks along the coast but access is a problem. If you insist on trying to find them you could antagonise the local farmers, which wouldn't endear you to the local surf community.

County Clare est exposée à l'influence de l'Atlantique et serait une des destinations d'Europe les plus en vue si le temps était plus clément. Cette région offre une imposante brochette de spots allant des récifs et plages offerts sur un plateau aux tubes les plus gros dans lesquels on puisse s'engouffrer!

Les vents offshores étant sud-est, ils ne sont pas fréquents; ainsi les vagues parfaites sont plus rares que dans la plupart des régions orientées au nord, mais quand c'est bon, c'est vraiment bon. Le point de vue est merveilleux lorsque l'on peut admirer les vagues au-dessus de Lahinch, et pourtant Lahinch n'est qu'un des nombreux superbes spots. Ce spot est digne de sa réputation de berceau du surf: il est situé à côté d'une longue plage de sable blanc avec trois excellents reefs qui partent en gauche du côté nord de la plage. La ville est très accueillante, il y a aussi une auberge à Spanish Point, plusieurs à Doolin et deux entre Lahinch et les falaises de Moher.

Il y a d'autres vagues le long de la côte mais elles sont difficilement accessibles. Si vous tentez l'aventure, vous risquez de contrarier les paysans locaux; et la communauté locale des surfeurs ne vous apprécierait guère.

County Clare esta abierto al Atlantico y podria ser uno de los mejores sitios para surfear en Europa si el clima acompañase. Hay una gran variedad de spots donde surfear, con picos de playa y rocas de todos los tamaños, hasta esos tubos con los que siempre has soñado.

El viento terral pega del SE, aunque no es muy habitual, por lo que esta zona funciona mucho menos que las que dan al N, pero cuando funciona esta muy bien. Desde Lahinch puedes ver los picos ya que hay una buena vista, aunque Lahinch es solo uno de los spots, es el centro del surf por distintas razones: esta situado tras una larga playa de arena blanca donde salen 3 excelentes izquierdas de roca al N. Hay bastante oferta de alojamiento en la ciudad, asi como un albergue en Spanish Point, otros tantos en Doolin y otros dos entre Lahinch y los.

acantilados de Moher. Hay otros picos dificiles de acceder a lo largo de la costa, pero si insistes en llegar a ellos acabaras enfadando a los granjeros locales, lo cual no sera del agrado de los surfistas locales.

Cregg Left - *Photo: Chris Power*

Mossies - *Photo: Simon McComb*

Inch Reefs - *Photo: Tim Rainger LP*

the dingle peninsula

Photo: *Mark Stevenson*

"The Dingle Peninsula is one of the most naturally beautiful areas of Ireland"

The Dingle Peninsula is one of the most naturally beautiful areas of Ireland. Even if there's no surf the area is worth a visit. Fortunately the breaks are also great. There is fishing for most tastes from deep sea angling to surf casting for Atlantic bass, from spinning for sea trout to trying to catch their wild mountain lake cousins.

Accommodation is no problem. There are camping and caravan parks of varying standards and many bed and breakfast establishments. It is also possible to rent holiday cottages by the week. A few pubs specialize in sea food Such as Spillanes, (Castlegregory) and particularly in Dingle there are excellent if expensive restaurants.

La Dingle Peninsula est une des régions les plus belles et les plus sauvages d'Irlande. Rassurez-vous les spots aussi valent le détour. Tous les types de pêche sont possibles; de la pêche à la ligne à la pêche au gros (bar), en passant par la pêche à la truite (de mer ou d'eau douce) à la cuiller.

Aucun problème pour le logement. Il y a des campings de différents standings et plein de bed and breakfast. Il est également possible de louer des maisons à la semaine. Quelques pubs (comme le Spillanes, le Castlegregory et particulièrement sur Dingle où il y a d'excellents restaurants même s'ils sont chers) proposent une belle carte de poissons et autres crustacés.

La peninsula de Dingle es una de las áreas más naturales y bonitas de toda Irlanda y, aunque no haya condiciones para surfear, es una visita obligada. Hay pesca para todo tipo de gustos, de altura o de bajura, y también se puede pescar trucha en el mar o en los lagos de las montañas. Afortunadamente tiene muy buenos picos.

No hay problemas de alojamiento. Hay camping y un parking para caravanas, también hay muchos bed and breakfast, con tarifas razonables. También hay la posibilidad de alquilar pequeñas casas, pero se deben de reservar con antelación. Unos pocos pubs especializan en pescados como Spillanes, Castlegregory y, sobre todo en Dingle, hay excelentes restaurantes aunque a menudo son caros.

County Clare

Thomas Buckley - *Lahinch Surf Shop*

1. Crab Island

Not to be taken lightly, firstly because of its distance from Doolin Pier (a long paddle), but mostly because of its size. It jacks up suddenly from deep water and can form very frightening tubes. Check your leash carefully. Great wave but few capable of handling it!

La vague ne doit pas être prise à la légère la première fois, d'une part en raison de la distance qui la sépare de la jetée de Doolin (qui demande un bon coup de rame) mais surtout en raison de sa taille. C'est une grosse droite qui se soulève d'un seul coup et peut engendrer des tubes effrayants si le vent vient d'est. Avant de partir à l'eau, vérifiez votre leash!

Es un point serio, no solo por la distancia que hay desde Doolin Pier (una gran remada), sino por el tamaño. La ola se levanta de golpe y forma tubos peligrosos. Revisa tu invento. Es una ola de gran calidad pero pocos son capaces de surfearla.

2. Doolin Point

A fast wave that can section, but with a clean swell long walling rides are possible. There are other waves further inside the bay if the point is not to your liking. Doolin is well signposted and there is a carpark in front of the wave.

Après le parking, on peut voir une droite rapide qui déroule sur du récif. Souvent des sections cassent sans prévenir, ce qui gâche la vague. Mais quand le swell est assez clean, on peut surfer de longs murs. Doolin est bien indiqué et il y a un parking devant la vague.

Es una ola rápida con secciones, con suave swell se pueden surfear largas paredes. Si en este point no es de tu gusto un poco más afuera de la bahía rompen otras olas. Doolin está bien señalizado y enfrente del pico se encuentra un parking.

3. Lehinch Area

BEACH

About the closest thing to a surfing town you will come across in Ireland. Many beginners practice on the excellent, slow beach break waves. A rip on the left will help you get out back. Easy parking.

Lahinch est la ville la plus "surf" de toute l'Irlande. Il y a un surf shop, pas mal de surfeurs et un large évantail de bonnes vagues. Les meilleurs surfent généralement le reef break alors que les nombreux débutants s'entrainent sur de lentes et excellentes vagues de beach break. Il y a un parking facile d'accés.

Cercano a la ciudad, hay que cruzar una isla para llegar al pico. Muchos principiantes practican en estas excelentes pero lentas olas de playa. A la izquierda hay una calma por donde podrás salir. Fácil de aparcar al lado de la playa.

LEFT

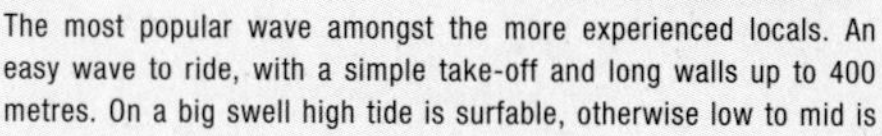

The most popular wave amongst the more experienced locals. An easy wave to ride, with a simple take-off and long walls up to 400 metres. On a big swell high tide is surfable, otherwise low to mid is best.

C'est de loin la vague la plus connue des locaux de Lahinch. C'est une vague très facile à surfer, avec un take-off tranquille et de longs murs surfables sur 400 m et jusqu'à 3m. Le parking est à Lahinch.

Desde hace mucho tiempo está considerada como la ola más conocida entre los locales expertos. Es una ola fácil de surfear con un fácil take-off y largas paredes haste de 400 metros.

CORNISH REEF

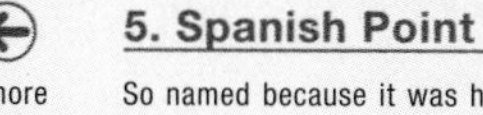

Works under the same conditions as the Left but it's a faster more tubey wave. It doesn't get as crowded. Fairly easy paddle out between Cornish and Lahinch Left.

Cornish Reef peut donner de bonnes, voire d'excellentes gauches. A besoin des mêmes conditions que Lahinch Left pour fonctionner mais c'est une vague plus rapide et plus tubulaire. Ramer jusqu'aux rochers entre Cornish et Lahinch Left, est relativement facile.

Funciona con las mismas condiciones que la izquierda pero es más rápida y más tubera. No suele haber mucha gente. Fácil para salir remando entre Cornish y Lahinch Left.

Cornish Reef - *Photo: Lahinch Surf Shop*

SHIT CREEK

The least surfed and most demanding of Lahinch's reefs. Main Ride is a left but the right is also good. Don't be put off by the name, Shit Creek is so called because of murky river water discolouring the sea. Beyond Cornish Reef.

C'est le reef de Lahinch le moins surfé et le plus exigeant. On y surfe surtout la gauche mais il y a aussi une bonne droite. Enfin, ne soyez pas rebuté par le nom, Shit Creek est appelé ainsi en raison des eaux troubles de la rivière et pas en raison de la pollution!

La menos surfeada y la más demandada entre los picos de Lahinch. La izquierda va mejor pero la derecha es también buena. Este pico es llamado Shit Creek por las aguas turbias que arroyan el rio y enturbian el mar. Está situado al final del Cornish Reef.

Silas, Shit Creek - *Photo: Lahinch Surf Shop*

4. Cregg/Moy Beach

A good spot to check when there's a big swell. You will find some fun waves, with the best size being 2-4ft. South of Lehinch, you'll see it from the road. Parking is possible for a few cars. SW of Cregg beach is an excellent reef break called Aussie Left, one of the longest waves in Clare. Turn off at the sign for Barr Tra Seafood Resturaunt.

Cette petite plage de galets peut être un bon spot à bien considérer quand il y a une grosse houle. Vous pourrez alors profiter de gauches et de droites particulièrement sympathiques entre 50cm et 1m. Située au sud de Lahinch, vous pourrez la voir de la route.

Es un buen spot tener en cuenta cuando hay fuerte swell, donde encontrarás unas olas divertidas. El mejor tamaño es de 2 a 4 pies. Está situado al sur de Lahinch, se ve desde la carretera. Tiene un pequeño parking.

Brendy, Lahinch Beach - *Photo: Lahinch Surf Shop*

5. Spanish Point

So named because it was here that survivors from wrecked Armada ships swam ashore. Unfortunately for them, the high Sheriff of Clare had them all executed. Now, these hazardous rocky reefs provide some excellent rights.

Ce spot s'appelle ainsi car on y a recueilli des survivants du naufrage des bateaux de l'Armada. Malheureusement pour eux, le Sheriff de Clare les avait fait tous exécuter. Maintenant, ces dangereux récifs de rochers peuvent générer d'excellentes droites.! Il y a aussi de bonnes vagues de beach break.

Conocido por el naufragio de un barco de la armada, donde desafortunadamente los supervivientes fueron ejecutados por el sheriff de Clare.

INSIDE POINT

A short fun wave that needs a big swell. Park at the car park above the north end of the beach.

Inside Point réclame une grosse houle avec un vent de sud-est, est ou nord-est pour produire de bonnes vagues. Pour l'Inside Point, il faut se garer au-dessus de l'extrémité nord de la plage.

Este arriesgado y rocoso point produce una excelente derecha.Para aparcar cerca del pico de dentro, pasa por encima del final de la zona norte.

MIDDLE POINT

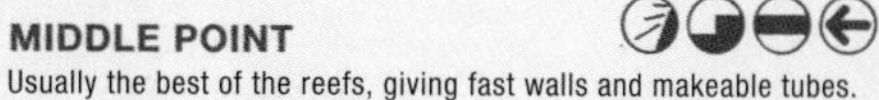

Usually the best of the reefs, giving fast walls and makeable tubes.

Middle Point est normalement le meilleur des trois reefs, offrant des murs rapides avec des tubes exploitables!

El pico de dentro necesita fuerte swell donde sale una corta y divertida ola. El pico de enmedio es el mejor de los tres, dejando largas paredes con posibles tubos.

OUTSIDE POINT

Takes the brunt of most swells and is rarely surfed due to its ferocity. Can hold a 15-20ft swell. For middle and Outside Point, take a small unmarked road about half km north .

Outside Point prend la plupart des houles et est rarement surfé car la vague est méchante. Peut tenir une houle de 5-6m. Pour Middle et Outside Point, prendre une petite route non répertoriée à environ1km au nord du parking.

El pico de fuera es el que acepta mayor swell y pocas veces suele ser surfeado por su ferocidad. Rompen olas de hasta 20 pies. Para aparcar cerca de los picos del medio y fuera hay que tomar una pequeña carretera no señalada recorriendo 1/2 km dirección norte.

6. Doughmore

When every other break is too small this works. If it's big it closes out right across the beach even in offshore winds. Access is a real problem, check with the local surf club before crossing anybody's land or you could find yourself in trouble.

Beach break avec un reef outside. Lorsque c'est tout petit sur les autres spots, cela marche ici. Quand le swell est gros, cela arrive droit sur la plage même par vent offshore. Mais l'accès est un problème épineux. Demandez auprès du surf club local si la traversée des propriétés privées a été reglé. Sinon, vous pourriez vous retrouver en situation très délicate.

Funciona cuando en todos los demás picos están muy pequeños. Si está grande cierra toda la derecha aunque haya off shore. El acceso es un problema, comprueba en el club local de surf antes de atravesar ninguna tierra ya que te puedes encontrar con problemas.

7. Doonbeg Castle

In a huge swell a nice wave can be found near the old ruined castle by the jetty in Doonbeg. Head here when all other breaks in Clare are closing out. Access is off the main coast road by the church.

Quand il y a un swell énorme avec un vent de sud-ouest, une très jolie gauche peut déferler près du vieux château en ruines au niveau de la jetée de Doonbeg. Cela casse sur un fond de rochers et c'est meilleur de la mi-marée à la marée haute. Cela vaut le coup lorsque tous les autres spots sont saturés. Il faut prendre la route côtière au niveau de l'église.

Donde hay fuerte swell se puede encontrar una buena ola cerca del viejo castillo de ruinas junto al jetty en Doonbeg. Acceso es en la carretera general junto a la iglesia.

8. Killard

Works under the same conditions as Doonbeg, with waves surfable to 4ft. Easy Parking by the beach.

Cette petite baie de sable marche dans les mêmes conditions que Doonbeg. Les vagues ici sont meilleures de marée basse à mi-marée et sont surfables jusqu'à 1,5 m. Il y a un parking facile d'accés au niveau de la plage.

Funciona con las mismas condiciones que Doonbeg, con olas surfeables hasta 4 pies. Con parking junto a la playa.

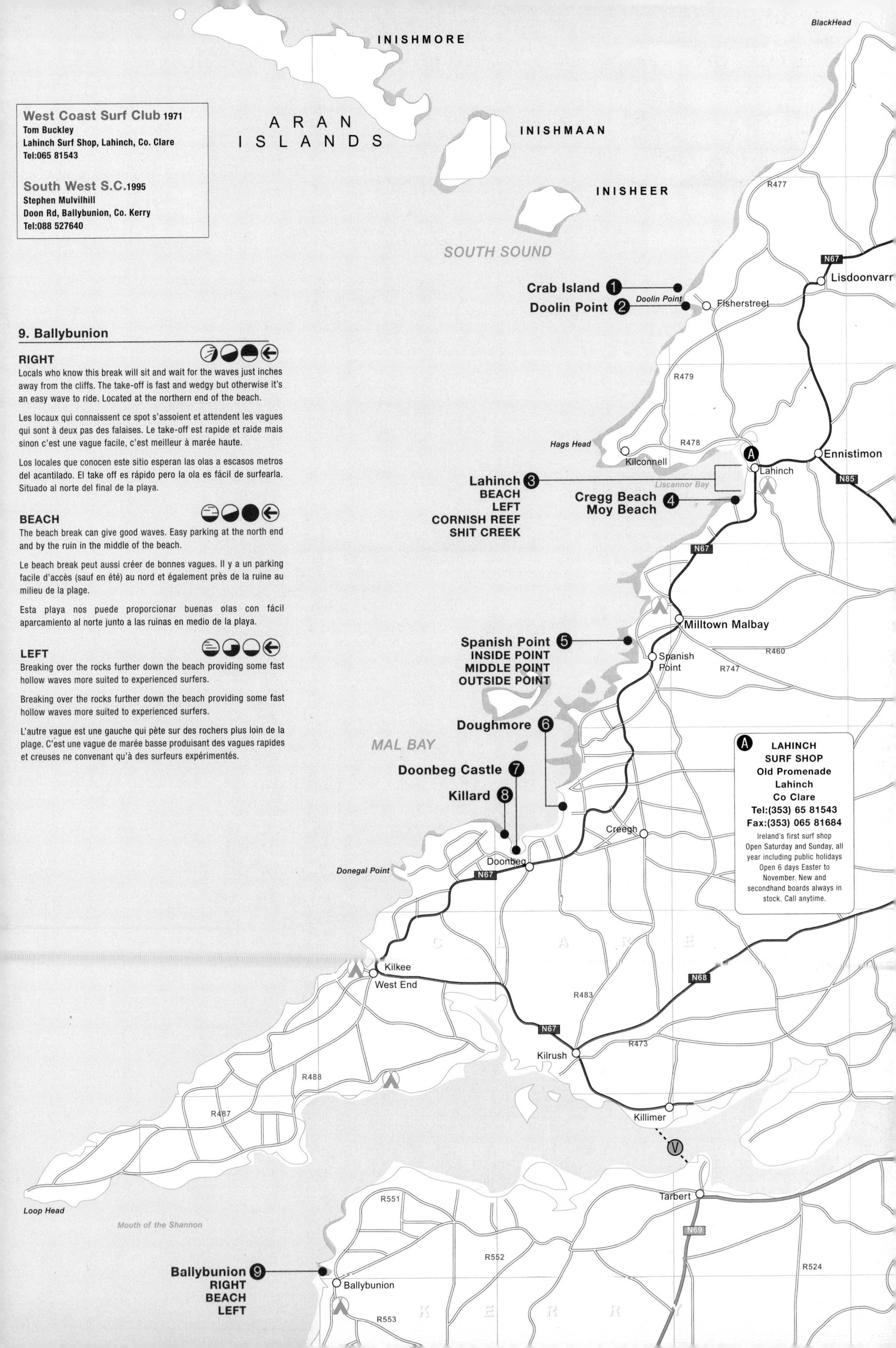

West Coast Surf Club 1971
Tom Buckley
Lahinch Surf Shop, Lahinch, Co. Clare
Tel:065 81543

South West S.C. 1995
Stephen Mulvilhill
Doon Rd, Ballybunion, Co. Kerry
Tel:088 527640

9. Ballybunion

RIGHT

Locals who know this break will sit and wait for the waves just inches away from the cliffs. The take-off is fast and wedgy but otherwise it's an easy wave to ride. Located at the northern end of the beach.

Les locaux qui connaissent ce spot s'assoient et attendent les vagues qui sont à deux pas des falaises. Le take-off est rapide et raide mais sinon c'est une vague facile, c'est meilleur à marée haute.

Los locales que conocen este sitio esperan las olas a escasos metros del acantilado. El take off es rápido pero la ola es fácil de surfearla. Situado al norte del final de la playa.

BEACH

The beach break can give good waves. Easy parking at the north end and by the ruin in the middle of the beach.

Le beach break peut aussi créer de bonnes vagues. Il y a un parking facile d'accès (sauf en été) au nord et également près de la ruine au milieu de la plage.

Esta playa nos puede proporcionar buenas olas con fácil aparcamiento al norte junto a las ruinas en medio de la playa.

LEFT

Breaking over the rocks further down the beach providing some fast hollow waves more suited to experienced surfers.

Breaking over the rocks further down the beach providing some fast hollow waves more suited to experienced surfers.

L'autre vague est une gauche qui pète sur des rochers plus loin de la plage. C'est une vague de marée basse produisant des vagues rapides et creuses ne convenant qu'à des surfeurs expérimentés.

Dingle Peninsula

Jamie Knox

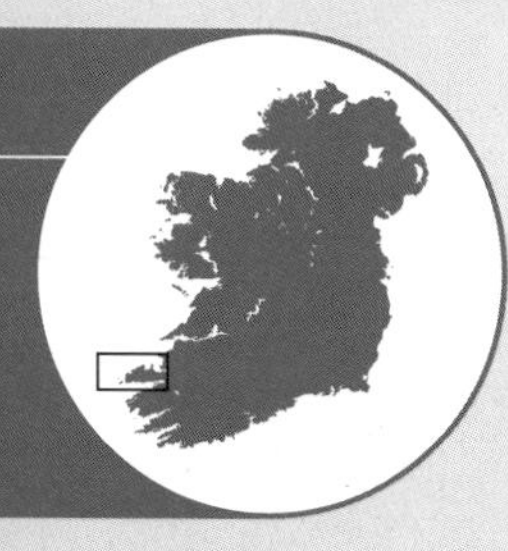

1. Garywilliam Point

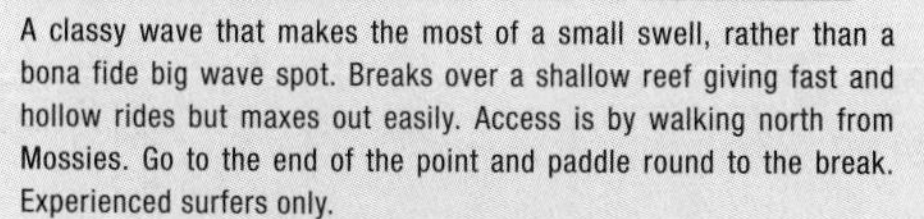

A classy wave that makes the most of a small swell, rather than a bona fide big wave spot. Breaks over a shallow reef giving fast and hollow rides but maxes out easily. Access is by walking north from Mossies. Go to the end of the point and paddle round to the break. Experienced surfers only.

Une vague classieuse qui maximise le moindre swell plutôt qu'un spot dé grosses vagues automatiques. Casse sur très peu d'eau en donnant des vagues rapides et creuses mais sature vite. On y va en marchant vers le nord depuis Mossie's. Allez jusqu'au bout de la pointe et ramez autour du cap. Uniquement pour surfers avertis.

Una ola mitica que coge la mayoria del poco swell, en vez de la genuina ola de mareton. Rompe sobre un reef poco profundo, produciendo una ola rápida y hueca que se deshace al final. Se llega andando hacia el N desde Mossies. LLega hasta el final del pico y rema hasta la rompiente. Solo para surfers con experiencia.

2. Mossies

Mellow reef break, nicknamed after the farmer who first saw surfers at this spot. Unless you like a long paddle out access is easiest from Garywilliam Point by driving to the end of the road, walking between the houses and down the cliff. Respect the locals!

Reef tranquille d'excellente qualité, ainsi nommé après qu'un paysan ait vu pour la première fois des surfers sur ce spot. A moins que vous ne préfériez ramer pendant 2 plombes, mieux vaut y aller depuis Garywilliam en roulant jusqu'au bout de la route et en marchant entre les maisons puis en bas de la falaise.

Es un pico clasico de roca que se ha quedado con este nombre desde que un granjero vio surfers en este spot. A no ser que quieras remar mucho para salir lo mejor es llegar por Garywilliam conduciendo hasta el final de la carretera, andando entre las casas y bajando por el acantilado.

3. Brandon Bay

From the top of Conner Pass you can see the horseshoe sweep of Brandon Bay facing NW. It picks up most swell except S and SW and even then some swell pulls around Brandon Head. Popular with windsurfers and longboarders.

En haut de Conner Pass, on peut voir l'étendue en fer à cheval de la baie de Brandon exposée nord-ouest. Elle prend presque toutes les houles sauf sud et sud-ouest même s'il y a alors quelques vagues à Brandon Head. Très prisé des winsurfers et des longboarders.

Desde lo alto de Conner Pass se puede ver la forma de herradura de Brandon Bay orientada al NE. Recoge todos los swells excepto los del S y SO, e incluso algunos swells de Brandon Head. Popular entre windsurfers y longboarders.

4. Ballydavid

Big wave spot that works very infrequently. A sucky take-off, an almighty drop, then a fast peeling wall that sucks harder down the line the bigger it gets. Needs to be 6ft to break. It gets good at 8ft and at 10-12ft it gets better. The Admiralty charts show 90 fathoms just off the harbour. Line up the old coast guard lookout post with the big radio mast at all stages of tide and all swell sizes. Just move up and down the line according to conditions.

Un point-break avec un take-off qui suce où il faut au moins 2 mètres pour que ça marche. Ca devient une bonne vague à 2,5m et à 3-4m, c'est carrément le pied avec un drop de tous les diables et un mur rapide qui aspire d'autant plus que c'est gros. Les cartes marines montrent 90 brasses de profondeur juste hors du port, ce qui explique ce topo. Ramez au line-up au niveau de l'ancien poste des garde-côtes avec la grosse antenne radio à toutes les périodes de marée et de tailles de houle. Il suffit de bouger le long de ce repère selon les conditions.

Un pico con un potente take-off que necesita como minimo de 6 pies para romper. Con 8 pies esta bien pero con 10-12 esta mejor. Tiene un drop peligroso y una rápida pared que chupa y se hace mas grande. Las cartas de navegacion del Ministerio de la Marina alcanzan hasta las 90 brazas de profundidad fuera del puerto. Permanece a la vista del puesto de guardacostas con torre radiofónica para cualquier marea y tamaño de ola.

Ballydavid - *Photo: Wilma Gammon*

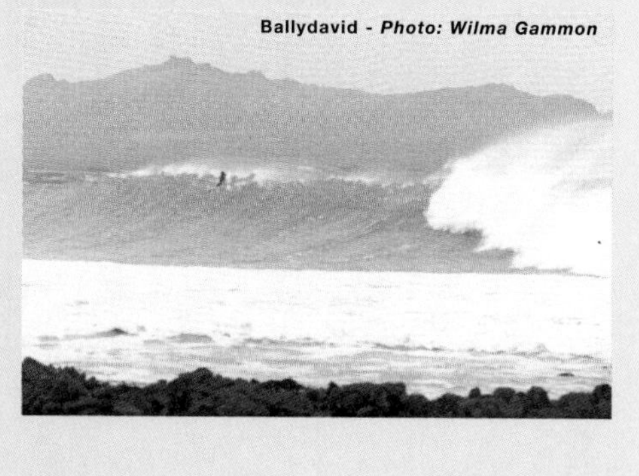

5. Reanough

An extremely shallow, very tubey, spitting reef, safest at low tide but can be surfed through depending on swell size. The beach here (Black Strand) can also have good peaks.

Un reef peu profond, hypra-tubulaire, crachant une droite, plus sûre à marée basse bien qu'on puisse y surfer jusqu'à marée haute selon les conditions. la plage ici (Black Strand) peut aussi avoir de bons pics.

Poco profundo, muy tubero, reef peligroso en la derecha, mas seguro en marea baja y surfeable segun las swells. La playa contigua (Black Strand) tambien tiene buenos picos.

Coumeenole - *Photo: Nick Gammon*

6. Coumeenole

Three peaks that work at low tide with the banks on the left being best. As the tide pushes in, a heavy right breaks in front of the shipwreck (note well!) and rocky reef. Fools rush in where angels fear to tread. Strong rips.

Trois pics qui marchent à marée basse avec les bancs de gauche qui marchent le mieux. Quand la marée remonte, des droites craignos cassent devant l'épave (Prenez en note) et une avancée rocheuse. Les idiots s'y précipitent alors que les anges ont peur d'y marcher. De puissants courants.

Tres picos que funcionan en marea baja, con unos bancos de arena a la izquierda que son los mejores. Cuando la marea sube, rompe una potente derecha contra el rompeolas junto a las rocas. Solo los mas

Garywilliam Point - *Photo: The Gill*

7. Annascaul Rivermouth

Good rivermouth with a faster take-off than Inch Reefs though the peak moves around a bit. As it wraps in you get a nice tube and a fast inside section. The paddle out is often difficult...good duckdiving needed. Best on incoming to mid tide. Needs a huge swell.

Bonne droite en sortie de rivière avec un take-off plus radical qu'Inch Reefs bien que le pic ait tendance à bouger. Pendant que ça s'enroule, on peut se taper un tube sympa et une section rapide à l'inside. Sortir est souvent difficile, on conseille de bien maîtriser le canard. Idéalement à mi-marée montante.

Esta es una desembocadura de rio con un take-off mas rapido que los reefs de Inch, aunque el pico es un poco movil. Una vez dentro puedes pillar buenos tubos y rapidas secciones. Salir remando suele ser costoso, ya que hay que bucear bastante. Lo mejor es con media marea subiendo.

8. Inch Strand

A beautiful spot which can provide some good quality surf. It's more of a longboard or beginners wave, best at mid tide. The N end is usually the best part of the beach.

Un spot superbe qui peut fournir des vagues de bonne qualité. Plutôt un spot de longboards ou pour les débutants, mieux à mi-marée. L'extrémité nord de la baie est souvent le meilleur endroit de la plage.

Un precioso spot con olas de buena calidad. Las olas son mas adecuadas para longboarders o principiantes, mejor en media marea.

El extremo del N suele ser el mejor.

9. Inch Reefs

P.J. said he knew there was a J Bay in Ireland somewhere. This Autumn I found it at Inch Reef. In 2 hours I caught 4 waves, but was surfing all the time, or paddling back. The next day I could hardly walk. I measured the distance on the mileometre, (the road runs along the cliff above), 1.2 miles! Killer paddle though, with a 0.5 knot rip pulling against you. Low tide is best, the bigger the swell the better. Take care getting in and out of the water and make sure you have a suitable exit point figured out before coming in. No clear access. Park beside the road and find a way down the cliff.

Quand P.J. vint habiter ici, il dit qu'il y avait un Jeffreys Bay en Irlande quelque part. Cet automne, je l'ai trouvé à Inch Reef. En deux heures, je pris 4 vagues mais je surfai tout le temps ou je ramai. Le jour d'après, je pouvais à peine marcher. Je mesurai la distance avec un appareil (la route suit le bord de la falaise au-dessus): presque 2 kms! La rame est carrément pénible à cause d'un contre-courant d'un demi-noeud. La marée basse est meilleure et plus c'est gros, mieux c'est. Attention à la mise et à la sortie de l'eau en vous assurant que vous connaissez une portie de sortie avant de prendre une vague. L'accès se fait où vous voulez. Garez-vous sur le bord de la route et trouvez un chemin pour descendre.

Cuando P.J vino para quedarse ya dijo que tenia que haber una J. Bay en algun sitio de Irlanda. Este otoño lo he encontrado en Inch reef, en 2 horas cogi 4 olas pero no paraba de surfear y de remar. Al dia siguiente no podia ni andar. Medí la distancia en el tacometro (la carretera corre paralela al acantilado). 1,2 millas. Remar aqui es mortal con una corriente de 0,5 nudos en contra. Mejor en marea baja, con mas swell mejor. Cuidado al entrar y salir del agua asegurandote un buen sitio de salida antes de coger la ola. Se entra por cualquier sitio. Aparca junto a la carretera y busca el camino de bajada.

Dingle Panorama - *Photos: Nick Gammon*

Southern Ireland

Henry Moore - *Attitude Surf Shop*
Fred Jump

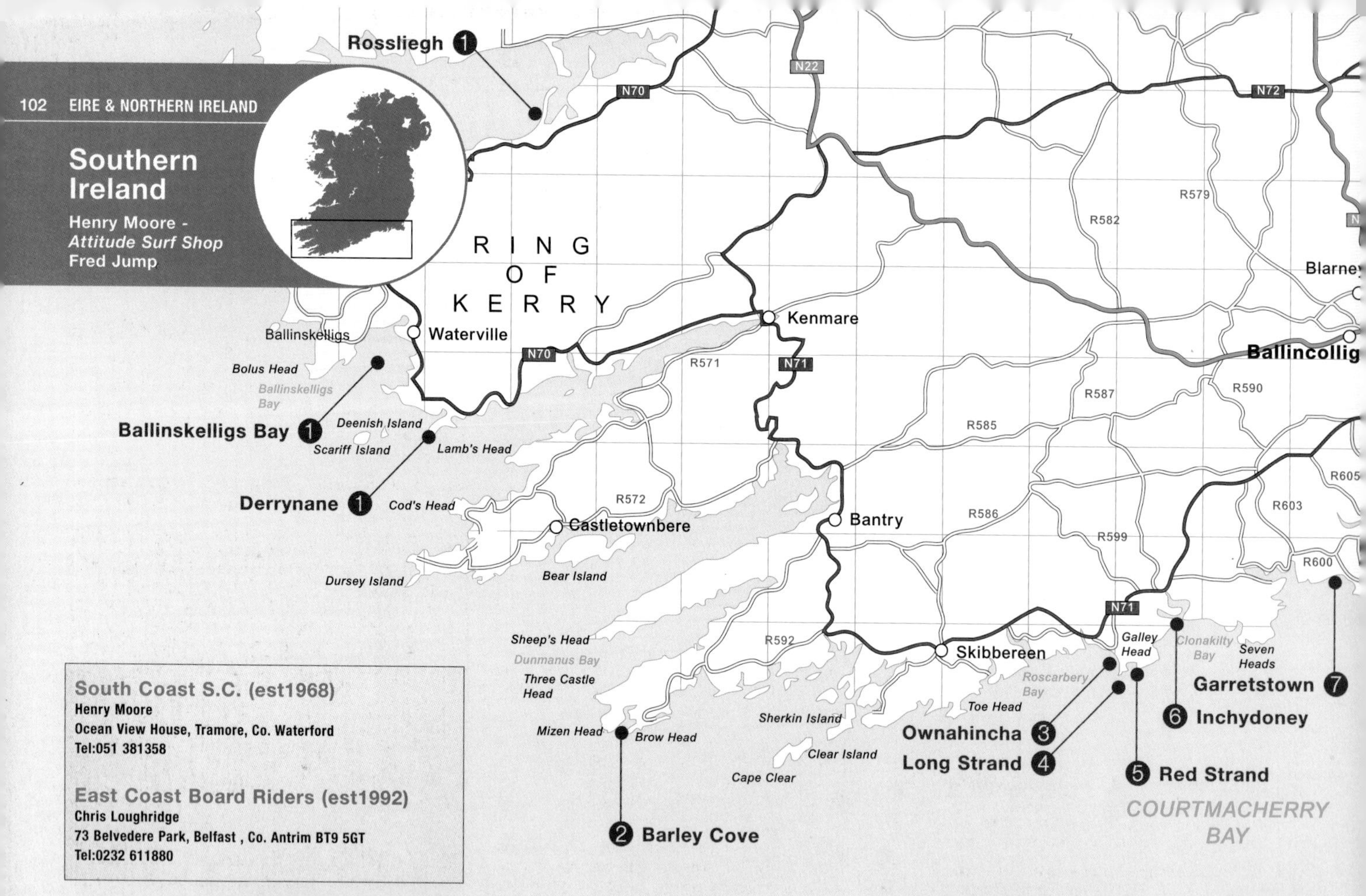

South Coast S.C. (est1968)
Henry Moore
Ocean View House, Tramore, Co. Waterford
Tel:051 381358

East Coast Board Riders (est1992)
Chris Loughridge
73 Belvedere Park, Belfast , Co. Antrim BT9 5GT
Tel:0232 611880

Simon Fernie - Photo: Simon Mcomb

Southern Ireland

Large variety of beach/reef breaks with small to medium and occasionally large surf. Prevailing winds are onshore, however but surf is uncrowded with a lot of undiscovered spots. Tramore is the centre for the southeast but there are a lot of surfers that "come out of the woodwork" in the Cork/Kerry area. The surfing community is very relaxed and emphisis is on having fun rather than getting every wave, be prepared to share waves and throw your watches away.

Cette région posséde une grande variété de vagues de sable et de récif avec essentiellement du surf petit à moyen mais du gros surf parfois. Les vents dominants sont onshore, mais il n'y a personne et de nombreux spots vierges. Tramore est le centre du surf dans le sud-est mais il y a beaucoup de surfeurs qui n'hésitent pas à faire le déplacement dans la région du Cork/Kerry. Les locaux sont très cool et sont sensibles au fun plutôt qu'à la compétition/agressivité dans les vagues. Soyez prêts à partager les vagues et à oublier votre montre.

Gran variedad de playas y picos de reef con olas pequeñas a medianas y ocasionalmente grandes para surfear. Los vientos dominantes son onshore, sin embargo no hay mucha gente surfeando con un montón de spots sin descubrir. Tramore es el centro del sureste pero hay un montón de surfers que aparecen en el área de Cork/Kerry. La comunidad surfera es muy relajado y lo importante es divertirse antes que querer coger todas las olas. Estate preparado para compartir las olas y tira los relojes.

1. Ring of Kerry

Rossleigh is 4 miles of beach break. Also a hollow left which requires a long paddle. Your next port of call should definitely be **Ballinskelligs Bay**. This sheltered bay contains a number of breaks ranging from gentle beaches to excellent reefs and points. With a SW swell, or a big W swell waves will show themselves. Different breaks work on different tides with different winds so something will nearly always be working here. Past Waterville is **Derrnane**, here there is a lovely beach with crystal clear waters which can, when the swell is big enough provide some pristine little waves. Even if there is no swell, then a trip around the Ring of Kerry can be considered a must for anyone who appreciates great countryside.

Rossleigh est 6 kms de beach break. De plus une gauche creuse qui exige un bon coup de rame. Votre prochaine escale devrait être sans aucun doute **Ballinskelligs Bay**. Cette baie protégée posséde de nombreux spots allant des gentilles plages de sable aux excellents reefs et autres pointbreaks. Avec une houle de sud-ouest, ou un gros swell d'ouest, les vagues atteindront leur maximum. Chaque spot a ses propres exigences de marée et de vents, ainsi il y aura toujours quelque chose qui marchera dans la région. Après Waterville,c'est **Derrnane**; ici, il y a une jolie plage avec des eaux cristallines qui peuvent être le theâtre, lorsque le le swell est suffisament gros, de charmantes?? petites vagues. S'il n'y a pas de houle, alors un voyage dans le Kerry s'impose pour quiconque apprécie les paysages grandioses.

Rossleigh es 4 millas de beach break. También una izquierda hueca donde se necesita remar mucho. El siguiente spot es **Ballinskelligs Bay**. Esta bahía protegida tiene muchas y diferentes olas que rompen en arena y en reef. Para que rompan buenas olas se necesita un swell del suroeste o fuerte swell del oeste. En este spot rompen olas durante todas las mareas y la dirección del viento no es lo más determinante. Pasando Waterville se encuentra **Derrnane**; aquí hay una preciosa playa con aguas cristalinas donde rompe una ola cuando el swell es lo suficientemente fuerte. en caso de no haber olas merece la pena darse una vuelta por este precioso paisaje natural.

2. Barleycove

A sandbar at the swell mouth creates nice lefts in a small swell. Breathtaking scenery.

Un banc de sable provoque de belles gauches par petit swell. Paysage à vous couper le souffle.

Una barra de arena en la boca del swell crea buenas izquierdas con swell pequeño. Un paisaje para tomar aliento.

3. Ownahincha

Two beaches seperated by a rocky outcrop, some nice waves can be had here mainly from sandbars.

Deux plages séparées par des rochers à fleur d'eau, quelques vagues sympathiques peuvent être prises essentiellement sur des bancs de sable.

Aquí se encuentran dos de las playas más abiertas al mar de todo la costa sur de Irlanda. La mejor marea es de media a alta.

4. Long Strand (Castlefreake)

Takes its name from a local castle and has some of the best surfing in Munster. Both ends of the beach have waves breaking off rocks and hold large waves. There are also several sandbars along the beach.

Tiens son nom d'un château des environs et est un des meilleurs endroits pour surfer de tout le Munster. Les deux extrémités de la plage ont des vagues cassant au-delà de rochers pouvant tenir de grosses vagues. Il y a aussi plusieurs bancs de sable le long de la plage.

Toma el nombre de un castillo local y es uno de los mejores sitios para surfear en Munster. Los dos extremos de la playa tienen olas que rompen sobre rocas y aguantan largas olas. También hay varias barras de arena a lo largo de la playa.

5. Red Strand (Dirk Bay)

When every other place is blown out and the swell is big Red Strand really works. A big reef in the middle of the bay breaks the large swells of winter (not surfable) and lets waves through on the reform where some nice 2-3ft lefts and 3-5ft hollow rights break on cliffs.

Quand tous les autres spots sont hors-contrôle et que le swell est gros, Red Strand se révèle. Un méga récif au milieu de la baie interrompt les larges houles d'hiver (insurfable) et filtrent les vagues à la reforme pour offrir de jolies gauches de 0,5-1 m et des droites creuses de 1-1,5 m cassant près des falaises.

Es una pequeña bahía bien protegida del viento. Está situada al este y cuando los fondos están bien rompe una buena izquierda. Puede ser surfeada hasta 4-5 pies. Red Strand está bien señalado con fácil aparcamiento.

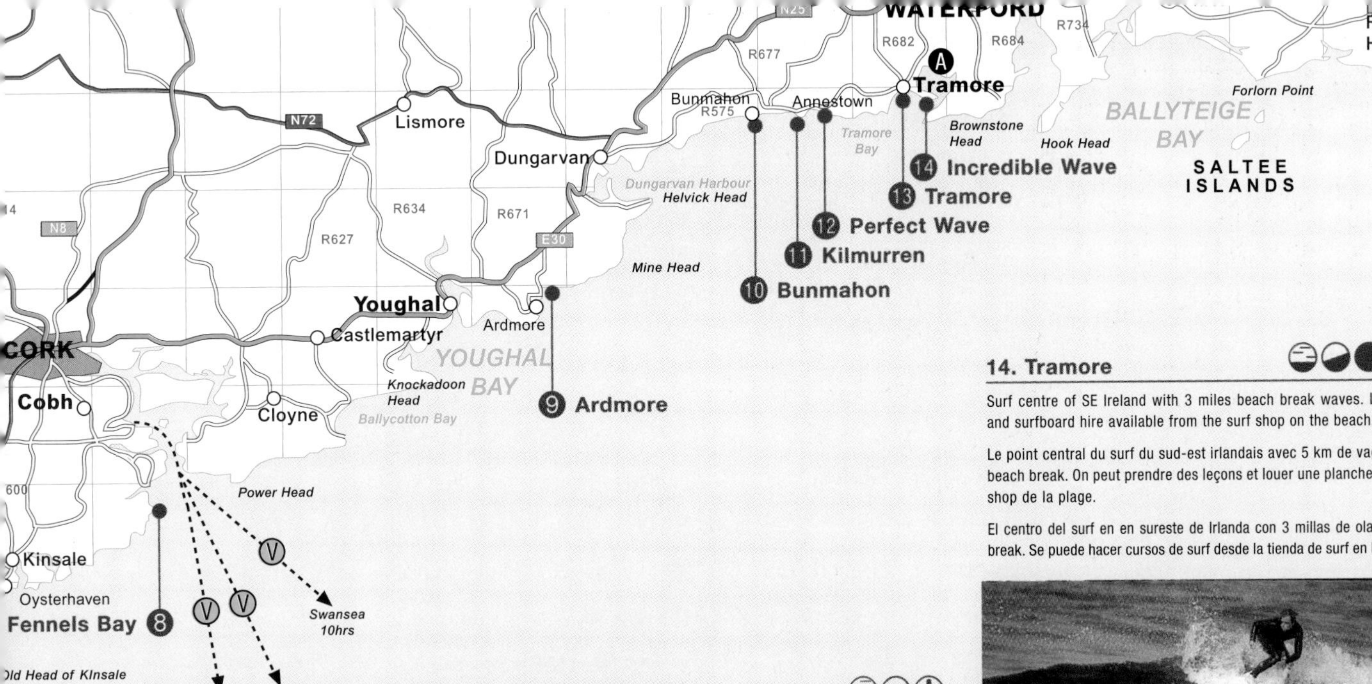

6. Inchedoney

An attractive beach with a headland in the middle and a river at each end. Waves can be excellent depending on swell size and direction.

Une plage attrayante avec un promontoire au milieu et une rivière à chaque bout. Les vagues peuvent être excellentes selon la taille du swell et sa direction.

Inchadoney es una playa con un saliente en medio y un rio al final de la playa. Por encima de la playa hay una vista fabulosa desde donde se pueden observar los diferentes bancos de arena.

7. Garretstown

Two beaches seperated by a rocky point. At the eastern beach there can be a nice right on large SW swell. Also good beach breaks ideal for beginners. The western beach (Coakleys) works on any swell from the East to West. Mainly beach breaks with an excellent right at the western end. Two groins in centre of beach neglected and dangerous when covered by high water.

Deux plages séparées par une pointe rocheuse. Sur la partie ouest de l'île, on peut découvrir une droite intéressante lors d'un swell sud-ouest conséquent. De bons beach breaks, idéals pour les débutants. La plage située à l'ouest (coakleys) marche avec n'importe quelle houle d'est à d'ouest. Principalement des beachs breaks avec une excellente droite à l'extrémité ouest. Deux aines au centre de la plage risquent d'être négligées et se révèler dangereuses quand la marée les recouvrent.

Dos playas separadas por un pico de roca. Al este de la playa puede romper una buena derecha con swell fuerte del suroeste. También hay una buena playa con buenos picos para principiantes. La playa del oeste (Coakleys) funciona con cualquier swell del E o O. La playa principal tiene una excelente derecha en el extremo O. Dos bloques que aparecen en el centro de la playa pueden convertirse peligrosos en marea alta.

8. Fennels Bay

A left reef that works on a SSE swell. Exit from the water can be difficult. Nice hollow wave from 2-4ft.

Un reef qui déroule en gauche et qui fonctionne avec un swell de sud/sud-est. Sortir de l'eau peut être difficile. Agréable vague creuse de 50 cm à plus d'1 m.

Una izquierda de reef que funciona con swell del SSE. Salir del agua puede ser difícil. Olas huecas cuando rompe de 2 a 4 pies.

9. Ardmore

Sheltered bay, waves generally half the size of prevailing swell, good on storm surf with N winds (very rare). Picturesque seaside village.

Baie protégée, où les vagues font généralement la moitié de la houle; bon dans des conditions de tempête avec du vent du nord (très rare). Pittoresque village de bord de mer.

Una bahía protegida donde entra la mitad del swell con buenas olas en condiciones de tormenta con vientos del N (muy raro). Con un pueblo pintoresco.

10. Bunmahon

Beach break with rips caused by small river mouth in the bay. One of the few waves in the SE that is good for bodyboarders. Always an option at the end of SW storms.

Beach break avec du courant dû à la présence, dans la baie, de l'embouchure d'une petite rivière. Une des rares vagues du sud-est du pays qui vale le déplacement pour les bodyboarders. Toujours une possibilité de se mettre à l'eau en fin de période de tempête de sud-ouest.

Una de las pocas playas del sur de Irlanda que necesita un swell del S/SE y viento de componente norte. Con estas condiciones pueden romper olas tan buenas como en cualquier otro sitio. Si encuentras la playa con buenos fondos, no pierdas el tiempo ya que el swell de sur no dura mucho tiempo.

Bunmahon - *Photo: Margaret O'Brien-Moran*

11. Kilmurrin

Last resort when storm surf is closing out elsewhere. Has a big drop with little else. Wave breaks at mouth of cove, don't venture out beyond it.

L'endroit où il faut aler lorsque ça sature ailleurs. Posséde un bon drop mais pas grand-chose après. La vague casse à l'entrée d'une crique; ne pas s'aventurer au-delà.

Cuando en todas las demás playas esta pasando de mar y el viento sea demasiado fuerte, en esta abrigada playa en la bahía de horseshoe podemos encontrar buenas olas. La ola tiene un fuerte drop en el pico seguido de una buena pared.

12. The Perfect Wave

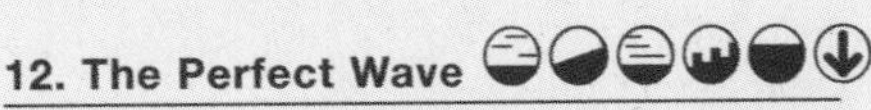

The beach offers good surf from 2-6ft and has a good left breaking outside on storm surf. The "Perfect Wave" is a small left reef to the left of the beach with access through a gap in the rocks. Good barreling surf from 3-6ft. Not for beginners due to proximity of exposed rocks.The most consistent quality wave on this coastline.

La plage offre un bon surf de 0,5 à 2 m et posséde une bonne droite déroulant outside lors des tempêtes. La "vague parfaite " est une petite gauche de récif à gauche de la plage que l'on atteint par une ouverture parmi les rochers. Bonne vague tubulaire de 1 à 2 m. Pas conseillé aux débutants en raison des rochers qui attendent patiemment leur proie! Belle vague qui est, en plus, la plus consistante de la côte.

Esta es una famosa rompiente al este de Annestown a la que se puede llegar andando entre las rocas a 100m de la playa. Aquí las olas suelen sur más grandes que en ningún otro sitio. Las rocas están cercan si no esta rompiendo a más de 4 pies. No es aconsejable para los principiantes.

14. Tramore

Surf centre of SE Ireland with 3 miles beach break waves. Lessons and surfboard hire available from the surf shop on the beach.

Le point central du surf du sud-est irlandais avec 5 km de vagues de beach break. On peut prendre des leçons et louer une planche au surf shop de la plage.

El centro del surf en en sureste de Irlanda con 3 millas de olas beach break. Se puede hacer cursos de surf desde la tienda de surf en la playa.

Tramore - *Photo: Margaret O'Brien-Moran*

13. Incredible Wave

Long left at eastern end of Tramore beach. Cars are parked at end of paved road. Good relations betwen local farmers and surfers as consideration and courtesy for their property is given. Works on med/large swell which often occur in February when the winds are particularly biting, a good wetsuit is necessary. When it's on it's top to bottom for as long as you can make it but quite fickle due to swell direction and tide height.

Longue gauche qui se trouve à l'extrémité est de Tramore Beach. On peut garer les voitures à l'issue d'une route pavée. Les fermiers locaux et les surfeurs entretiennent de bonnes relations (respect des propriétés). Marche par moyen et gros swell, ce qui corrrespond souvent au mois de février quand les vents sont particulièrement cinglants; une bonne combinaison est nécessaire. C'est alors vraiment bien du début jusqu'à la fin aussi longtemps que vous pouvez suivre la vague mais un peu inconstant car trop dépendant de la direction de la houle et des variations de profondeur duent aux marées.

Una larga izquierda rompe al extremo O de la playa de Tramore. Los coches aparcan al final de la carretera pavimentada. Hay una buena relación, consideración y cortesia entre los granjeros locales y los surfers. Funciona con swell de medio/fuerte lo cual se suele dar en febrero cuando pega el viento, se necesita un buen traje para surfear. Con buen swell se pueden coger largas olas pero suelen ser inconstantes dependiendo de la dirección del swell y la fuerza de la marea.

East Coast

The East coast of Ireland can occasionally have rideable waves. During winter strong south winds will generate some swell. These winds then need to swing round to a more westerly direction to make the swell clean. If you are in the area and these conditions are present, then Jack's Hole is worth a look. The Irish Sea is reputedly the most radioactive sea in the world, so even if it looks clean......?

La côte est de l'Irlande peut avoir des vagues surfables. Pendant l'hiver des vents forts du sud peuvent engendrer de la houle. Ces vents doivent pivoter vers l'ouest pour créer un swell propre. Si vous êtes dans les parages et si les conditions sont réunies, Jack's Hole vaut le détour. La mer d'Irlande a la réputation d'être la mer la plus radioactive du monde, alors même si cela paraît clean.....?

La costa este de Irlanda raramente tiene olas surfeables. Durante el invierno los fuertes vientos del sur pueden generar algo de swell. Los vientos tienen que coger más dirección O para que llegue un swell claro. Si estas en esta zona y se te presentan estas condiciones deberás mirar en Jack's Hole. El mar irlandes es el más contaminado por la radioactividad en el mundo asi que aunque parezcan las aguas limpias...

NORTH SEA NATIONS

NORWAY

Capital: Oslo
Population: 4,274,000
Area: 323,895km²
Time: GMT +1(summer time GMT+2)
Language: Norwegian & Lappish
Currency: Norwegian Krone (NOK)
1 Krone = 100 Ore

Telephoning:
Norway 095 +
Norway 47 +

NSA Norwegian Surfing Federation
Valldalvien 9, Sandnes, Norway

DENMARK

Capital: Copenhagen
Population: 5,100,000
Area: 43,075km²
Time: GMT+1 (summer time GMT+2)
Language: Danish
Currency: Danish Krone (DKK) 1
Krone = 100 Ore

Telephoning:
Denmark 45 +
Denmark 009 +

DSA Danish Surfing Association
Hegensvej 20, Naerum,
2850, Denmark

NETHERLANDS

Capital: Oslo
Population: 4,274,000
Area: 323,895km²
Time: GMT +1(summer time GMT+2)
Language: Norwegian & Lappish
Currency: Gulden (Guilder) (NLG)
1 Gulden = 100 Cents

Telephoning:
Netherlands 00 +
Netherlands 31 +

HSA Holland Surfing Association:
PO Box 84007, 2508 AA
The Hague, The Netherlands

SWEDEN

Capital: Stockholm
Population: 8,644,000
Area: 449,790km²
Time: GMT+1 (summer time GMT+2)
Language: Swedish, Finnish, Lapish
Currency: Swedish Krona (SEK)
1 Krona = 100 cents

Telephoning:
Sweden 009+(Telia) 007 + (Tele 2)
Sweden 46 +

GERMANY

Capital: Berlin
Population: 79,000,000
Area: 356,840km²
Time: GMT+1 (summer time GMT+2)
Language: German
Currency: Deutschmark (DEM)
1 Mark = 100 Pfennings

Telephoning:
Germany 00 +
Germany 49 +

DWV Deutscher Wellenreit Verband
Honenstauffenring 23,
50674 Khöln, Germany

BELGIUM

Capital: Oslo
Population: 4,274,000
Area: 323,895km²
Time: GMT +1(summer time GMT+2)
Language: Norwegian & Lappish
Currency: Belgian Franc (BEF)
1 Franc = 100 Centimes

Telephoning:
Belgium 00 +
Belgium 32 +

BSA Belgium Surfing Federation
Ijzerwaglaan 72, 9050 Ledevberg
(Gent) Belgium

Surfing In the North Sea

The coastlines which share the Nth Sea are seeing some remarkable growth in surf culture. There is even surf in the Baltic sea of Sweden, and where there are waves, someone will end up riding them, testament to the unceasing pull of the sport. Holland and Norway are probably the most advanced countries, though Germany, despite its tiny coast, has the biggest volume of afficionados, who more often surf in France or the Canaries than they do at home.

Les surfers de la Mer du Nord

Les côtes qui se partagent la Mer du Nord connaissent une expansion rapide de la culture surf. On trouve même des surfers sur la Baltique en Suède et partout où il y a des vagues, on finira par trouver quelqu'un qui les surfe, ce qui prouve l'essor phénoménal de ce sport. Les Pays-Bas et la Norvège sont probablement les pays les plus développés, bien que l'Allemagne malgré sa portion de côte réduite, ait le plus grand nombre d'adeptes, qui surfent plus souvent en France ou aux Canaries que chez eux.

El Surf en el Mar del Norte

Las costas que circundan el Mar del Norte están comenzando a ver el crecimiento de la movida surfera. Incluso los suecos surfean en el Báltico y alli donde haya olas alguien terminará surfeándolas, fruto del imparable ascenso de este deporte. Holanda y Noruega son los países punteros, pero es en Alemania, cuya costa es bastante escasa donde existe el mayor número de aficionados, anque éstossurfean más a menudo en Francia o en Canarias que en casa.

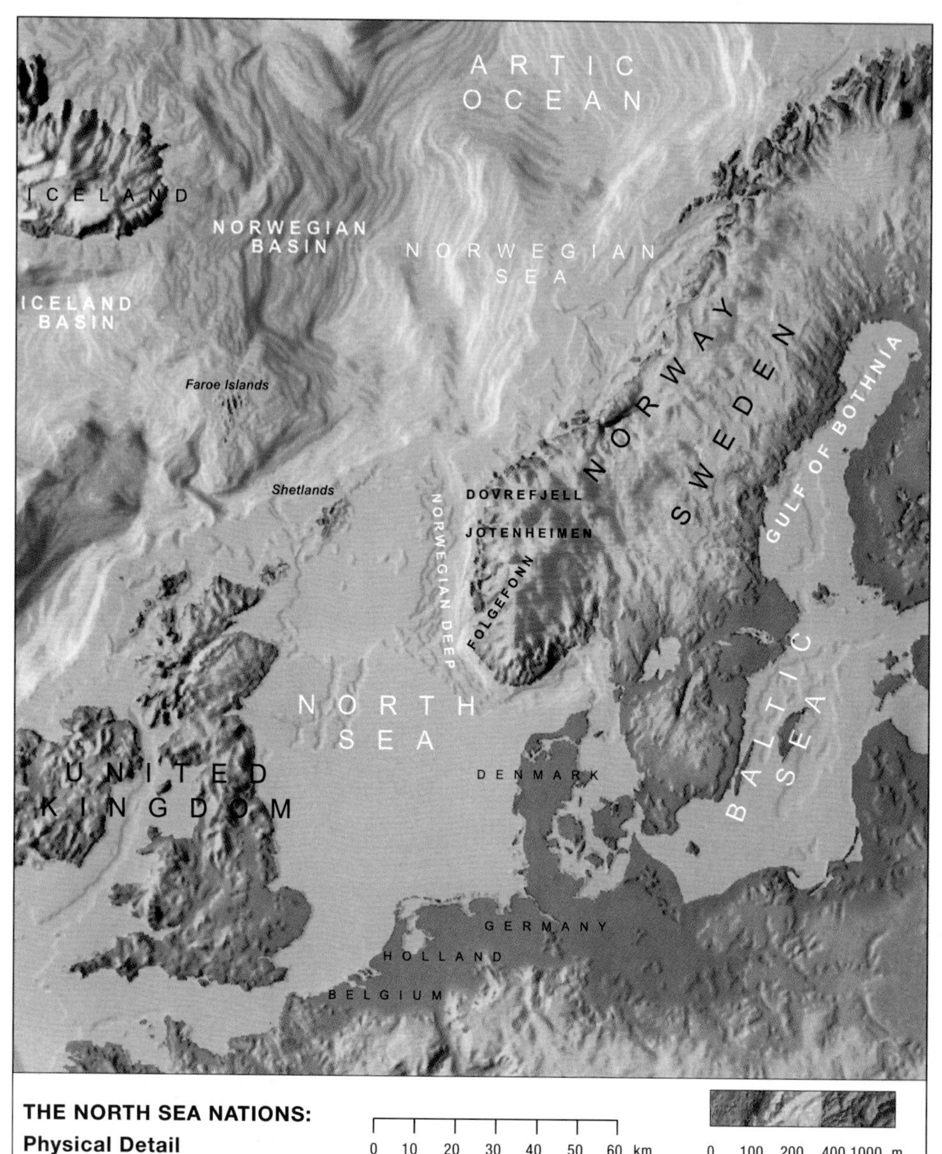

Photo: BINGE

Scheveningen Noord, Netherlands - Photo: Robby Buttner

North Sea Waves

The North Sea is a relatively shallow body of water but all through the year, winds blow from south-westerly to north-westerly directions creating swell. These winds are generated by Low Pressure systems travelling from Iceland to Scandinavia or forming in the Channel and Nth Sea, and provide the North Sea surfer with waves ranging from one to six feet, sometimes bigger. The best waves occur from late August to April when the water temperature can drop to a mighty crisp 2 degrees C (in Norway). A typical winter swell is overhead and the quality can be very good when its offshore. Unfortunately this also coincides with rather chilly weather when continental high pressure keeps the lows some distance from the coast. This can mean sub-zero temperatures and powder snow on the beach! You'll understand why thick wetties, booties, gloves and hood are a must.

Summertime (May until August) can be very flat, with only the occasional classic day. A passage of weather fronts can give good conditions when the prevailing onshore winds turn offshore and there are still the remains of swell. This gives rise to short sessions and requires that you head for the beach as soon as the wind changes. Water temperatures can rise to eighteen degrees Celsius in summer in Holland, and surfing in a springy is possible in southern areas.

Water Quality

Generally worst at river outlets, harbours and near industrial sites. Scary evidence of pollution was found recently by some Belgian surfers who collected a sample of North Sea water in a beer bottle and placed it on their TV-set. After two days it exploded. Although spots near rural areas seem o.k., the quality of the North Sea is not great due to its history of abuse by industry.

Les conditions de surf

La Mer du Nord est une étendue d'eau peu profonde mais tout au long de l'année, les vents soufflent du sud-ouest au nord-ouest en créant de la houle. Ces vents sont générés par les systèmes dépressionnaires voyageant depuis L'Islande en Scandinavie ou qui se forment en Manche et dans la Mer du Nord. Ils produisent des vagues de 30 cms à 2m, parfois plus. Les meilleures vagues arrivent de fin août à avril où la température de l'eau peut descendre à un 2 degrés polaire en Norvège. Une houle typique hivernale fait un bon mètre cinquante et ça peut être bon si le vent est off-shore. Malheureusement, ces houles correspondent aussi avec le temps glacial quand les autres pressions continentales gardent les dépressions à distance de la côte. Cela signifie des températures négatives avec de la poudreuse sur la plage! Vous comprendrez alors pourquoi une combinaison épaisse, des botillons, des gants et une cagoule sont indispensables.

L'été de mai à Août peut être désespéramment flat avec très peu de bons jours. Un passage de fronts dépressionnaires peut apporter de bonnes conditions quand les vents on-shore dominants tournent à 180° et qu'il reste encore de la houle. Ca donne lieu à de courtes sessions mais ça veut dire qu'il faut aller checker la plage dès que le vent tourne. La température de l'eau peut monter jusqu'à 18°C en été en Hollande, on peut donc sortir le springsuit dans cette partie méridionale.

La qualité de l'eau

En général pitoyable en sortie de rivière, des ports et à proximité des zones industrielles. Des preuves affolantes de pollution furent récemment découvertes par des surfers belges qui firent une ponction en Mer du Nord dans une bouteille de bière qu'ils mirent sur une télévision. Après 2 jours, elle explosa. Bien que les spots en zones rurales semblent satisfaisants, la moyenne générale en Mer du Nord n'est pas géniale vu les abus commis par l'industrie.

Olas en el Mar del Norte

El Mar del Norte es poco profundo comparado con otros mares, pero a lo largo del año es barrido por vientos del cuadrante oeste que generan marejadas. Estos vientos proceden de las borrascas que pasan desde Islandia hacia Escandinavia o que se forman en el mismo Mar del Norte o en el Canal. Las olas resultantes van del medio a los dos metros, en ocasiones algo más grandes. Las mejores olas rompen desde finales de Agosto hasta Abril, y la temperatura del agua en ese periodo puede bajar hasta los 2°C en Noruega. Una sesión típica de invierno trae olas de más de metro y medio y buena calidad si sopla offshore. Lo único malo es que esto suele coincidir con tiempo gélido al estar la borrasca alejada de la costa por el anticiclón continental, por lo que las temperaturas suelen ser bajo cero con la nieve cubriendo las playas. Esto supone que el equipamiento es esencial, requiriéndose guantes, capuchas, botines y muchos milímetros de neopreno.

El verano (de Mayo a Agosto) suele implicar mar plato, exceptuando la sesión clásica ocasional. Tras pasar un frente, si el viento deja de soplar de mar y aún queda algo de oleaje, se puede surfear buenas pero muy cortas sesiones con una temperaturas del agua que puede ascender a 18°C en Holanda, haciendo posible surfear en un primavera.

Calidad del agua

Suele ser muy mala en las salidas de ríos y cerca de los puertos y aglomeraciones industriales. Un ejemplo de lo contaminada que esta, es el caso de unos surfers belgas que cogieron un frasco de agua del mar y lo pusieron junto al televisor. Al cabo de dos dias el frasco explotó. En las zonas rurales la calidad es bastante buena, pero la densidad y la larga historia industrial de los paises ribereños ha deteriorado mucho la calidad del agua del Mar del Norte en general.

Norway

Jan Erik Jensen

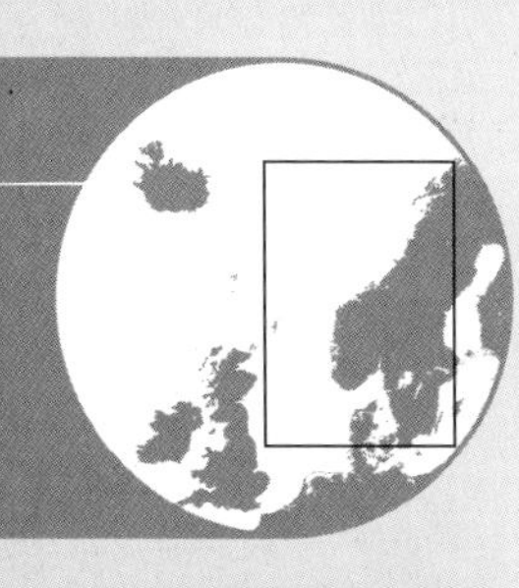

Photo: Jan Erik Jensen

NORWAY

Norway is one of the last surfing frontiers in Europe and there are waves along a significant proportion of the coastline. Despite this, only a few places are surfed regularly because the coast is generally rocky and fringed with islets and skerries. Getting around is time consuming when deep fjords and high mountains have to be crossed.

The Jaeren area has the highest density of spots and extends from Stavanger to Eigersund. The coastline here is unusually open and almost 30 spots are surfed within an hours drive of Stavanger. A good winter season will give two or three days of relatively good surf a week. Summer swells are rare and wave quality is generally poor. Areas further north around Molde and on Stat-landet are frequently visited by surfers from Oslo. The tidal range is small in the south, but further north it reaches several meters. Water quality is good at all locations described.

NORVEGE

La Norvège est une des dernières frontières du surf en Europe avec des vagues sur une partie non négligeable de la côte. Malgré tout, seulement quelques spots peuvent être surfés régulièrement parce que cette côte est généralement rocheuse et entourée d'îlôts et de cailloux. Rouler prend pas mal de temps quand il faut contourner les fjords profonds ou certaines montagnes assez élevées.

La zone de Jaeren qui possède la plus grande concentration de spots va de Stavanger à Eigersund. Le littoral y est anormalement ouvert avec presque 30 spots surfables à moins d'une heure de Stavanger. Pendant une bonne saison d'hiver, on peut surfer deux à trois jours par semaine. Les houles d'été sont rares et la qualité des vagues plutôt décevante. Les zones au nord aux environs de Molde jusqu'à Stat-Landet sont souvent fréquentées par les surfers d'Oslo. Le marnage des marées est minîme dans le sud alors qu'il atteint plusieurs mètres dans le nord. La qualité de l'eau est bonne sur tous les spots mentionnés.

NORUEGA

Noruega es una de las últimas fronteras del surf en Europa y dispone de olas en una buena porción de sus costas. A pesar de esto, solo se surfea regularmente en unos pocos sitios debido a que es una costa rocosa salpicada de innumerables islas pequeñas. Adentrarse en esta tierra lleva mucho tiempo debido a los profundos fiordos y altas montañas que hay que cruzar.

La zona de Jaeren presenta la más alta densidad de spots y se extiende desde Stavanger hasta Eigersund. Aquí la costa se encuentra muy abierta y a unas horas de coche de Stavanger hay unos 30 spots surfeables. En un buen invierno saldrán de 2 a 3 dias semanales de buen surf. Los swells no abundan en verano por lo que la actividad surfística será pobre. Las zonas más al norte alrededor de Molde y Stat-landet son frecuentadas por los surfistas de Oslo. El rango de mareas es menor en el sur, pero más al norte es de varios metros. La calidad del agua es buena en todos los sitios descritos.

SURF SHOPS

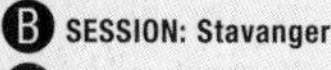

A SURFSENTRUM: Stavanger, Tel: 47 51531122

B SESSION: Stavanger

C BERNHARD SPORTS: Oslo

1. The Lofoten Islands

A largely undiscovered surf zone, though this region has a huge swell catchment area. One of the most scenic places in Norway with steep mountains rising from sea level with a coastline of boulder and sand beaches facing into large fetches of Atlantic and Arctic ocean.

Une zone de surf encore mal connue alors qu'elle reçoit un paquet de houles. Un des endroits de Norvège les plus spectaculaires avec des montagnes à pic qui surgissent tout droit de l'océan entrecoupées de plages de sable et de galets exposées aux méga-fetchs de l'Atlantique et de l'Artique.

Es uno de los paisajes más bonitos de Noruega con escarpadas montañas surgiendo desde el nivel del mar, con una costa de cantos rodados y playas de arena orientadas hacia la inmensidad de los oceanos Atlántico y Artico.

2. Molde

Some powerful waves break on a rock reef near the village of Bud. Locals claim it is too hollow to be considered a hot-dog wave. A deep trench points at the reef, contributing to its power and consistency.

Un certain nombre de vagues puissantes sur du reef aux alentours de Bud. Les locaux les considèrent comme trop creuses pour être des vagues de hot-dog.

Unas olas poderosas rompen contra un reef de roca cerca del pueblo de Bud. Los locales creen que la ola es muy hueca para considerarla "hot-dog wave".

3. Godøy

An island off Aalesund, Godøy is known to produce a good right.

Une île au large de Aalesund, on sait que Godøy peut donner une droite.

Esta isla frente a Aalesund, es conocida por la derecha que produce.

4. Stat-Landet Peninsular

3 bays, two of them sandy, regularly visited by surfers from Oslo. **Fossarevet** is a reef north of Ervika that receives N swell when other spots are sheltered. The most hollow wave in the region can produce A-frame barrels. **Hoddevika** picks up SW to W swell best and is known for good beach peaks, especially at the north end. If the swell is from the NW **Ervika** will be better but beware, there's a ship wreck in the bay, most of which is hidden at high tide, but clearly visible at low.

Fossarevet est un reef au nord d'Ervika qui chope les houles de nord tandis que les autres spots sont protégés. La vague la plus creuse de la région peut devenir des pics parfaits et tubulaires. **Hoddevika** prend mieux les swells de sud-ouest à ouest, avec de bons beach-breaks surtout au nord. Si la houle vient du nord-ouest, le mieux sera à **Ervika** mais attention, y'a une épave dans la baie pratiquement immergée à marée haute ,qui se découvre bien à marée basse.

Fossaveret es un reef al norte de Ervika que recibe el swell del N cuando otros spots estén resguardados. Es la ola más tubera de la zona que puede formar barreras en forma de A. **Hoddevika** recoge el swell del SO y O y destaca por sus picos playeros especialmente en el norte. Si el swell es del NO **Ervika** estará mejor pero cuidado con las ruinas de un barco que hay en la bahía, que permanece oculto en marea alta y visible en baja.

5. Refsnes (North)

Named Norway's "most scenic beach" in the early nineties, the coast here is characterised by high hills, fjords and islands. Little surfable territory is known south, before Stavanger.

Cette côte se caractérise par de hautes collines, des fjords et des îles. Peu de surf répertorié au sud avant Stavanger.

En la costa destacan sus altos acantilados, fiordos e islas. El escaso territorio surfeable se encuentra al sur antes de Stavanger.

6. Hellestø

Hellestø has shifting peaks which close-out more than Bore. Still, at the north there is often a good sandbar.

Hellestø a des pics irréguliers qui ferment plus que Bore. Cependant, y'a souvent un bon banc au nord.

Produce unos picos móviles que se cierran más que en Bore. Al norte suele haber una buena barrera de arena.

7. Sele

A small point break and probably Norway's most crowded surf spot. Up to 20 surfers have been recorded here on a 2' day!

Un petit "point-break" qui est probablement le spot le plus couru. On y déjà vu jusqu'à 20 surfers sur des vagues de 50 cms.

Este pequeño pico es el más concurrido de toda Noruega. Se han contado hasta 20 surfistas en dias de medio metro.

8. Bore

Most consistent spot in the region, surfed frequently in summer. Sometimes the sandbars here create good waves. It's signposted, with camp-sites at the south end. The dunes are susceptible to erosion, so use the established paths.

Le spot le plus consistant de la région souvent surfé en été. Souvent les bancs y font de bonnes vagues. Bien signalisé avec des campings au sud. Les dunes sont fragiles, merci pour elles de marcher sur les sentiers battus.

Es el spot más consistente de la región y más surfeable en verano. La barrera de arena produce algunas veces unas olas guapas. El lugar está señalizado y hay sitio para acampar al sur. Como las dunas tienden a erosionarse, procura utilizar los caminos circundantes.

9. Steinen

There are several peaks from here S to Reve havn and the most regularly surfed spot is Steinen. There are two spots between Steinen and Foglingane (the name given to two rocks outside the southern end of Bore beach). Racetrack is a short, fast ride against some boulders sticking well above the water surface. Kick out in time here! Lefthanders consists of large close-out sections unless there's a classic swell when it can be ridden through its length. This may happen once or twice through winter.

Plusieurs pics depuis Steinen au sud à Revehavn, le spot le plus surfé étant Steinen. On trouve deux spots entre Steinen et Foglingane. Racetrack est une vague courte et rapide sur des galets qui émergent de la surface. Faites votre kick-out au bon moment. Lefthanders consiste en une méga-section qui ferme à moins qu'une houle parfaite ne vienne arranger les choses, à savoir une ou deux fois dans l'hiver.

Hay varios picos desde aquí hacia el sur hasta Reve Havn, y el spot más surfeado es Steinen. Entre Steinen y Foglingane hay un par de spots. Racetrack es una corta y rápida que acaba encima de unos peñascos a bastante profundidad, ándate al loro! Lefthanders consiste en una gran sección cerrona a no ser que el swell permita recorrerla a todo lo largo, lo cual ocurre una o dos veces en invierno.

10. Reve havn

Reve havn produces tubes but is unfortunately very inconsistent.

Revehavn peut être tubulaire mais ça ne marche pas souvent.

Produce tubos pero es muy inconsistente.

Reve havn - *Photo: Jan Erik Jensen*

11. Ghosthouse

Usually a close out close to the shore, however it can produce one of the hollowest waves in the area. Lined-up sand bars or messy swell can also make it surfable. Just north of Pigsty.

Souvent un close-out immonde sur le bord bien que ca puisse être une des vagues les plus creuses de la zone. Des bancs de sable bien formés ou un swell désordonné peuvent le rendre surfable.Juste au nord de Pigsty.

Es normalmente una orillera, pudiendo convertirse, sin embargo, en una de las olas más huecas de la zona. Las barreras de arena alineadas o un swell revuelto pueden hacerla surfeable. Justo al norte de Pigsty.

12. Pigsty

Pigsty is a one man wave 500 m south of Reve havn, and even the locals create crowds here! Though inconsistent, Pigsty is a quality wave, even by international standards and picks up north swell better than other spots nearby.

Pigsty est une vague pour un seul surfer à 500m au sud de Revehavn tant et si bien que les locaux arrivent à saturer le pic. Bien qu'inconsistant, Pigsty est une bonne vague, même avec des critères internationaux.

Es una ola para poca gente a unos 500 metros al sur de Reve Havn, donde incluso solo con los locales se producen aglomeraciones. Aunque algo inconsistente, Pigsty es una ola de calidad incluso a nivel internacional, y recoge el swell del norte mejor que el resto de spots de la zona.

Pigsty - Photo: Jan Erik Jensen

13. Jarens Rev

Jaerens rev is a long shallow water zone extending a mile offshore producing a swell shadow south of it. The coast north of Jaerens rev is referred to as the "North Shore" and the locals named Jaerens rev "Phantoms" because it breaks bigger than any other spots nearby. High risks due to its distance from shore and strong currents. No locals have surfed it yet.

Jaerens Rev est une zone avec peu d'eau qui s'étend un mile au large, qui coupe le swell au sud. La côte au nord de Jaerens Rev est connu comme le "North Shore" ou "Phantoms" parce que ça casse toujours plus gros que les autres spots. Assez risqué parce que loin du bord et parce que les courants y sont forts. Aucun local n'a surfé ici encore.

Es una zona de poco fondo que se adentra hasta una milla en el oceano produciendo una aureola de swell hacia el sur. La costa al norte de Jarens Rev es conocida como "North Shore" y los locales conocen a Jarens Rev como "Phantoms" por que rompe más grande que en los alrededores. Hay peligro por la distancia que lo separa de la orilla y las fuertes corrientes. Ningún local se ha atrevido a surfearla todavía.

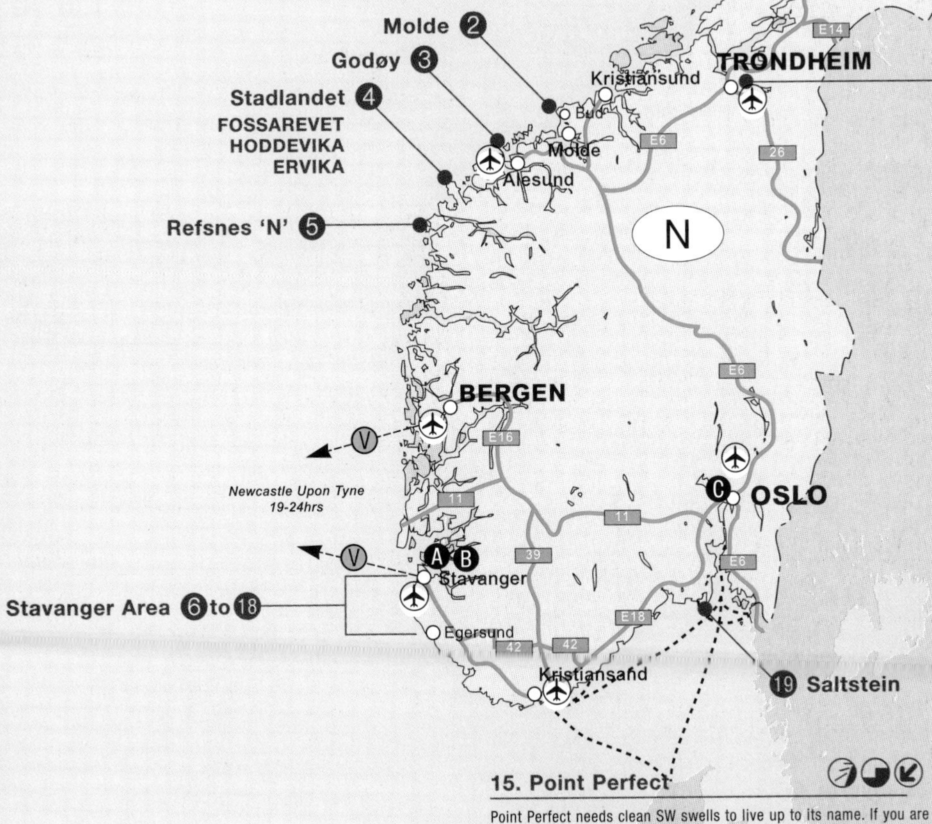

Flowrider, Trondheim - *Photo: Skip Snead*

14. Orre Beach

At the south end are two good boulder reefs that require a solid swell before they work. During an average season they are surfed a handful of times. Camping facilities in the vicinity.

Au sud, on trouve deux reefs sur des gros galets qui exigent une bonne houle pour fonctionner. Ca se surfe environ 4-5 fois dans la saison. Des possiblités de camping dans le coin.

En la zona sur hay dos reefs peñascosos que necesitan de un buen swell para funcionar. Durante una estación normal se cuentan con los dedos de una mano los dias de buen surfing. Hay facilidades para acampar en los alrededores.

15. Point Perfect

Point Perfect needs clean SW swells to live up to its name. If you are travelling by car, turn off along a dust road after the sign indicating Refsnes as a swimming beach. Park at Vik airfield.

Il faut une houle décente et propre pour que Point Perfect mérite son nom. Si vous conduisez, il faut tourner sur un chemin de terre après le panneau indiquant Refsnes comme une plage.

Necesita de un swell limpio del SO para merecer su nombre. Si vas en coche, gira por una carretera empolvada después de ver la señal indicando Refsnes, playa de nadar.

16. Refsnes Beach

Important windsurfing spot. Also a good surf spot on the peninsular S of the beach. Raunen holds large swells but is susceptible to winds.

Un super spot de windsurf d'abord mais y'a aussi un bon spot de surf sur la péninsule de Raunen, au sud de la plage. Raunen tient le gros.

Spot conocido para el windsurfing pero también hay una buena zona en Raunen peninsular para el surf, al sur de la playa.

17.Kvassheim

Classic point-break which holds its shape, even during the largest swells, giving rides up to 150m. It's the best spot in the region in south-west swell, located on the other side of the bay from the Kvassheim lighthouse.

Un point-break typique qui ne se déforme pas même avec les méga-houles de sud-ouest. Situé de l'autre côté de la baie avec le phare de Kvassheim.

Este es el clásico point que aguanta el tipo hasta con los mayores swells con olas de hasta 150 metros. Es el mejor spot de la región con un swell SO, Se encuentra al otro lado de la bahía del faro de Kvassheim.

18. Brusand

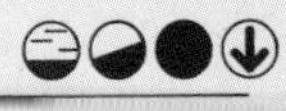

The southernmost beach in Norway picks up south swell. The sandbars change, but the east end usually produces the best surf. Camp-sites and cottages for rent.

La plage la plus au sud de Norvège prend les houles de sud. Les bancs y changent mais le bout à l'est produit souvent les meilleures vagues. Des campings et des cottages à louer.

Es la playa situada más al sur de Noruega, recoge el swell del sur. Las barras de arena suelen cambiar de emplazamiento aunque la mejor ola se da en la zona este. Se alquilan lugares de acampadas y pequeñas casa.

19. Saltstein

A small bay facing south-east, and home to a few local surfers, as well as being the closest spot to Oslo. During summer, chop produced by afternoon sea-breezes can create rideable surf.

Une petite baie qui regarde le sud-est avec quelques surfers locaux, le spot le plus proche de d'Oslo. En été, les ondulations poussées par les thermiques de l'aprés-midi peuvent être surfables.

Es una pequeña bahía orientada hacia el sudeste, y hogar de unos pocos surfistas locales ya que se trata del spot más cercano de Oslo. En verano, la agitación que produce la brisa de poniente hace bueno el surf que se desprende.

Sweden

Niklas Långström - *Wave Life*

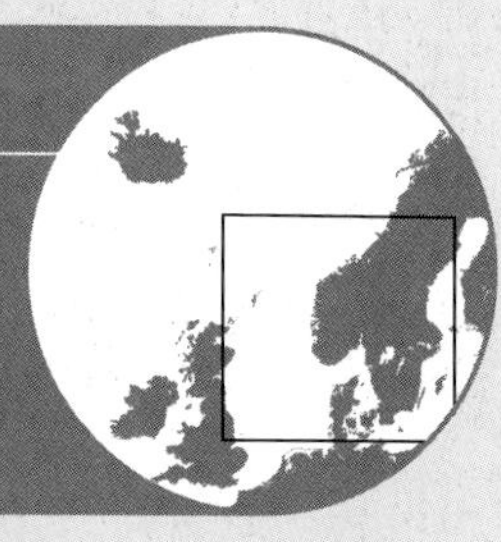

SWEDEN

Sweden is not well known for its surf, but the Swedish Surfing Association was formed in 1985 by Janne Ekstedt, and Swedish surfers have participated in the European Championships every year since then. The swell is best during autumn and winter when the storms are blowing, though there is some good waves during the summer also. All you have to do is wait for Low Pressure. More people have started surfing every year, especially since the snowboard boom of the last few years. Some think it's impossible to ride waves up here, but there are some really great spots, so when you come to Sweden, don't forget your board!

Water Quality. The water quality is generally good in Swedish waters, though there were problems in the 1980's, concerning the lack of oxygen in the water on the westcoast. Our coasts have also been affected by oil discharges. The question of water quality is very important and deserves more discussion than this.

SUÈDE

La Suède n'est pas franchement réputée pour ses vagues mais la fédé suédoise fut constituée en 1985 par Janne Ekstedt, ce qui a permis, entre autre, aux suédois de participer à tous les championnats depuis. La houle est la meilleure en automne et en hiver quand les tempêtes soufflent, bien qu'il puisse y avoir quelques coups de surf en été où la seule chose à faire est d'attendre les dépressions. Chaque année, de plus en plus de gens se mettent au surf, surtout depuis le boom du snowboard ces dernières années. Certains pensent qu'il est impossible de surfer des vagues ici bien qu'il y ait quelques bons spots. Alors, si vous passez par la Suède, n'oubliez pas votre planche.

Qualité de l'eau: Elle est généralement bonne par ici, bien qu'il y eut quelques problèmes dans les années 80 à cause du manque d'oxygène dans les eux occidentales. Les côtes ont été aussi affectées par les vidanges d'huile. Le problème de la qualité de l'eau est crucial et demande plus d'attention que ces quelques lignes.

SWEEDEN

Suecia no es muy conocida por su surf aunque la Asociación Sueca de Surfing fue fundada en 1985 por Janne Ekstedt, y los surfistas suecos han participado en los campeonatos europeos desde entonces. El mejor swell es en otoño e invierno con las mejores tormentas, aunque también salen buenas olas en verano. Hay que esperar a las bajas presiones. Cada año empieza a surfear más gente, especialmente tras el boom del snowboard de los últimos años. A algunos les parece mentira que se cojan olas aquí arriba pero lo cierto es que hay unos spots muy buenos, así que cuando te acerques a Suecia tráete tu tabla.

Calidad del agua. Las aguas de Suecia son generalmente de buena calidad, a pesar de los problemas que hubo en los 80 debido a la falta de oxígeno en las aguas de la costa oeste. También ha habido problemas por el vertido de aceites en nuestras costas. Este tema de la calidad del agua es más importante de lo que parece y debiera discutirse más que ésto.

Photo: BINGE

1. Åsa - Stenudden

A right point between Gothenburg and Varberg. Needs a strong SE wind.

Un pointbreak qui casse en droite entre Gothenburg et Varberg. Il faut un fort vent de sud-est.

Es un buen point entre Gothenburg y Varberg. Funciona con fuerte viento de SE.

2. Träslövsläge

Left point break. Best wind direction S.

Un pointbreak de gauche. Le meilleur vent vient du sud.

Es un point donde rompe de izquierda, viento del S.

3. Apelviken

The most famous windsurf location in Sweden was "found" as a surf spot at the beginning of the 1980's, and now people live here just for the surf. Best wind direction is NE. Talk to the guys working in the surf shop "Surfers Paradise" in Varberg. They have information about other places that are worth a visit on the westcoast. The waves are o.k. in the south part of the bay when the wind is blowing from the SE.

Le spot de windsurf le plus célèbre en Suède a été trouvé comme un surfspot au début des années 80 et maintenant certains y habitent uniquement pour surfer. Le meilleur vent vient du nord-est. Allez discuter le bout de gras avec les gars du surf shop "Surfers Paradise" à Varberg. Ils ont des infos sur des autres spots de la côte ouest qui valent le coup. Les vagues y sont correctes au sud de la baie quand le vent vient du sud-est.

Es la localidad windsurfista más famosa de Suecia donde se empezó con el surf a principios de los 80, y ahora la gente solo vive para el surf. Mejor dirección del viento NE. Si preguntais a los tipos que trabajan en la tienda de surf "Surfers Paradise" en Vargberg os informarán sobre otros sitios a los que merece la pena echar un vistazo en la costa oeste. Las olas son buenas en la zona al sur de la bahía al soplar el viento del SE.

4. Glommen

Point break. Best wind direction N.E.

Point Break. Le meilleur vent vient du nord-est.

Lo mejor con viento NE.

5. Mellbystrand

All wind directions can be good, but north-west, west and south are the best. Very good windsurfing. To get the best waves, come when it's blowing from the north-west, common during the summer. It's located about 20 km south of Halmstad, in Laholmsbukten.

Toutes les directions de vent sont propices mais ceux de nord-ouest, ouest et sud sont les meilleurs. Pour aller sur les meilleures vagues, venez-ici quand ça souffle au nord-ouest, ce qui est fréquent en été. Situé à environ 20 kms au sud d'Halmstad, à Laholmsbukten.

Cualquier viento es bueno, pero los del NO, O y S son los mejores. Buenas condiciones para el windsurfing. Para las mejores olas el mejor viento es el del NO, que se da mucho durante el verano. Se halla situado a unos 20 Km al sur de Halmstad, en Laholmsbukten.

6. Vik

A great surf spot located just north of Simrishamn in Skåne. I really recommend a visit to this point break when the wind is blowing from the South East or East.

Un super spot situé juste au nord de Simrishamn à Skåne. On recommande vraiment le détour sur ce point break quand le vent souffle au sud-est ou à l'est.

Es un buen spot para surfear situado justo al norte de Simrishamn en Skane. Sinceramente se recomienda echarle un vistazo a este point cuando el viento sopla del SE o E.

7. Grönhögen

Oland is an island on the east coast. To get here you go to Kalmar then take the bridge across Kalmarsund. The island is a small one, and is easy to travel around. Gronhogen is a great spot on the south-west part with good surf between the camp site and the harbour. Best wind-directions are south-west and south-east. You can get three to four metres waves here.

Oland est une île sur la côte est. Pour y aller, il faut aller à Kalmar et prendre le pont jusqu'à Kalmarsund. L'île est petite et il y est facile de bouger. Gronhogen est un super spot au sud-ouest avec de bonnes vagues entre le camping et le port. La meilleure direction de vent est au sud-ouest ou sud-est. On peut y surfer des vagues de 3 à 4 mètres.

Olan es una isla situada en la costa este. Para llegar hasta aquí tienes que pasar por Kalmar y coger el puente que cruza Kalmarsund. La isla es pequeña, así que es fácil recorrersela. Gronhogen es un buen spot situado en el sudoeste y con un excelente surf por descubrir entre las praderas y el puerto. Los mejores vientos son SO y SE. Puedes pillar olas de tres a cuatro metros acá.

8. HagaPark

On the west of the island you find this fine spot. You go to Färjestaden and then drive south about 7 km towards Mörbylånga. Best wind directions are south and south-west, when the waves break over a sandstone reef. You can park about 25 metres from the spot.

A l'ouest de l'île, vous trouverez ce spot sympa. Il faut aller jusqu'à Färjestaden et rouler environ 7 kms vers Mörbylånga. Idéal par vent de sud et sud-ouest, quand les vagues cassent sur du sable et du rocher. On peut se garer à environ 25m du spot.

Este spot se encuentra al oeste de la isla. llegas primero hasta Farjestaden y tiras hacia el sur unos 7 Km hacia Morbylanga. Los mejores vientos son S y SO, al romper las olas en un reef de roca y arena. Se puede aparcar a unos 25 metros del spot.

9. Ängjärnsudden

Sand beach on the north part of the island which holds waves up to 2 metres. Easy parking.

Une plage de sable au nord de l'île qui tient des vagues jusqu'à deux mètres. Parking facile.

Playa de arena situada al norte de la isla y con olas de hasta 2 metros. Fácil aparcamiento.

10. Tofta

The bigger of the two islands on the east coast. Since it's an island, you can find good surf with almost every wind direction. Gotland is a popular place during summer, so be prepared for a party if you come here. Tofta is a spot on the west coast of Gotland. Best winds from south to north-west.

La plus grande des deux îles sur la côte est. Comme c'est une île, on peut trouver des vagues avec n'importe quelles conditions de vents. Gotland est une destination connue en été, soyez donc prêts à vous faire la fête si vous passez par là. Tofta est un spot sur la côte ouest de Gotland. Les meilleurs vents viennent du sud ou du nord-ouest.

Es la mayor de las 2 islas en la costa este. Al tratarse de una isla, cualquier viento será bueno para encontrar un buen spot. Como Gotland es un sitio muy popular durante el verano, preparate para la fiesta. Tofta se encuentra en la costa oeste de Gotland. Mejores vientos son del S y NO.

11. Ireviken

On the north-west part of Gotland you'll find this wave paradise. Gets big when the wind is blowing from north to west.

Au nord-ouest de Gotland, on trouve cette vague paradisiaque. Ca peut être gros quand ça souffle du nord à l'ouest.

Este paraiso de las olas se situa al noroeste de Gotland. Se pone grande cuando el viento es del NE.

12. Fåro

When the wind is strong, you'll find some really good surf on this little island located just north of Gotland. Drive around and look for spots like: **Aursviken** when the wind is blowing from West to North, you'll find a quick left here. **Ekeviken** is best when it's blowing from the NW. Go here after a storm...you'll find that the waves stay around for a while.

Quand le vent est fort, on peut choper du bon surf ici sur cette petite île située juste au nord de Gotland. Roulez et cherchez des spots comme Aursviken avec des vents d'ouest à nord, ce sera une gauche rapide ici, ou Ekeviken, idéal par vents de N-O. Venez ici après une tempête, vous verrez que les vagues peuvent durer quelques temps.

Cuando el viento sopla fuerte, se puede practicar excelente surf en esta pequeña isla al norte de Gotland. Muevete por la zona y darás con sitios como: Aursviken cuando el viento es del SO aparece una izquierda muy rápida en este spot. Ekeviken Lo mejor con viento del NO. Si llegas aquídespués de una tormenta comprobarás que las olas duran un buen tiempo.

13. Torö

One of the most famous Swedish surf spots 20 km south of Stockholm. You take Torövägen to Herrhamra gård and then turn to the right on a gravel road taking you down to the beach. It's a beach break with left and right waves. The best wind direction is strong SE-SW. The Swedish surfing association have held a couple of competitions here.

Un des spots suédois les plus célèbres du pays, à 20 kms au sud de Stockholm. Il faut prendre direction Torövägen Gård en prenez à droite sur un chemin de gravier qui vous amène jusqu'à la plage. C'est un beach-break avec des gauches et des droites. Le meilleur vent est un fort vent de SE-SO. La Fédé suédoise a organisé quelques compétitions ici.

Es uno de los spots más famosos, situado a unos 20Km al sur de Estocolmo. Vas desde Torovagen hasta Herrhamra gard y giras hacia la derecha por una carretera de grava que te baja hasta la playa. Rompe en una playa con derechas e izquierdas. El mejor viento es SE-SO. Se han celebrado un par de campeonatos de surf en esta localidad organizados por la Asociación sueca de surfing.

Toro - Photo: BINGE

14. Sikhjälma

Good surf when the wind is blowing from NW to NE. You find this spot south of Gävle.

De bonnes vagues avec des vents de NO à NE. On trouve ce spot au sud de Gävle.

Buen surf cuando el viento sopla del NO al NE. Este spot se encuentra al sur de Gavle.

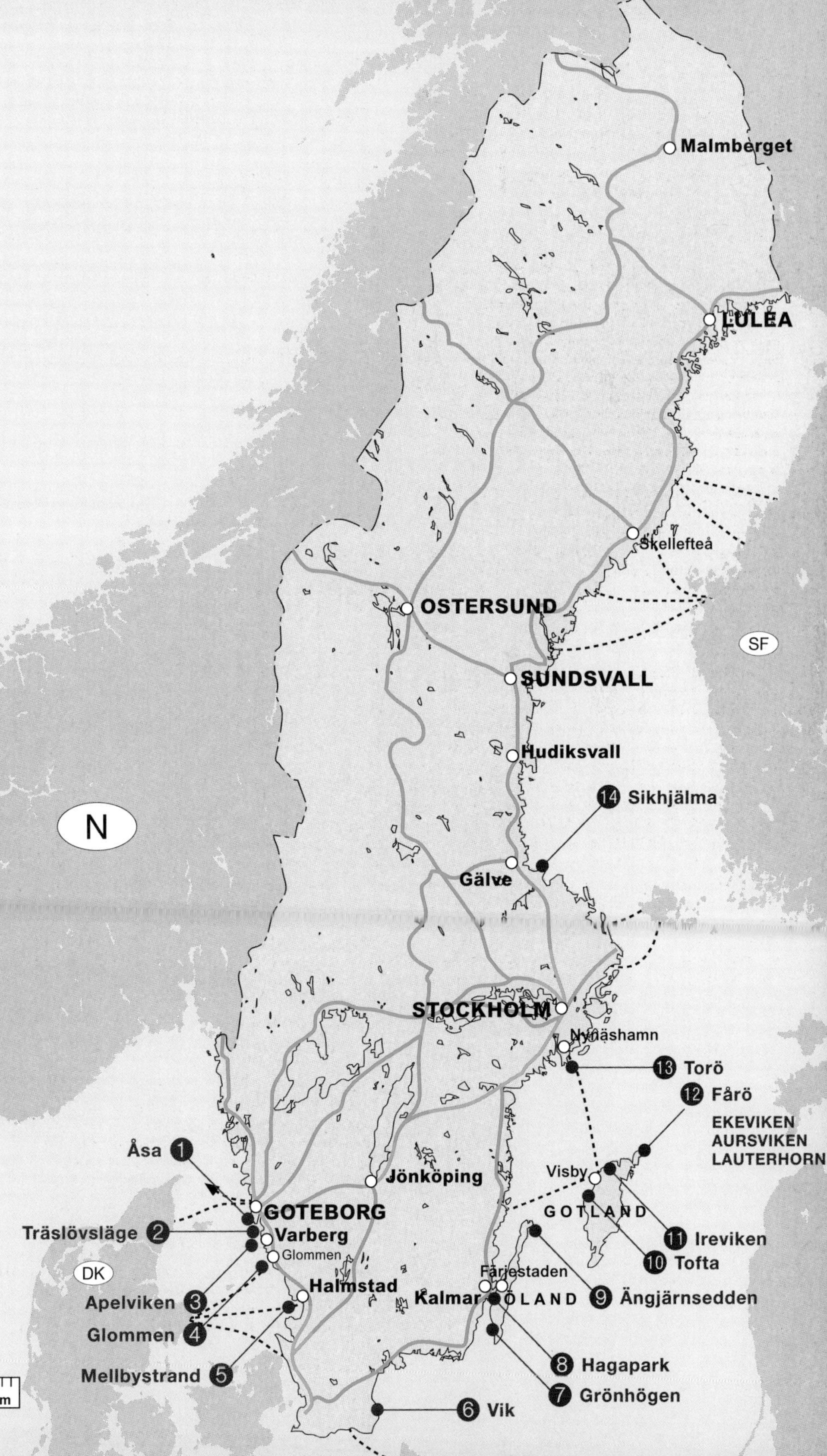

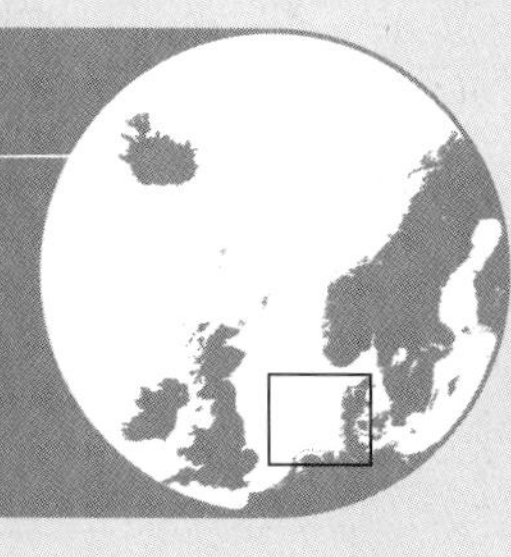

Germany & Denmark

Norbert Hoischen - DWV

GERMANY

Surfing in Germany began in the mid-60's when lifeguards from Sylt heard about the waves in Biarritz. After their experiences in France, they were so stoked they began making boards and searching for spots on their island. This was the beginning. During the '70's, a student called Uli Richter began giving lessons in Hendaye. He wrote a book and his school became well known. The Sylt community grew and travellers from other areas caught the bug. Also, in the mid-80's, when wind surfing was fashionable, some of the young people tried surfing without sails. Fathers passed it on to their sons and daughters and we already have a second generation.

In 1988 a group of 12 guys formed a team to participate in the World Amateurs in Costa Rica and in 1991 the German Surfing Federation (DWV) was formed. Since then, numbers of German surfers in European and World champs has grown, and our first local competition was held in 1993 in Sylt. The surf was 2ft but we had a great time. Most waves are from wind swells, though ground swells occasionally come from the English Channel. There are now 3 surf magazines and more than 10,000 surfers, including a good proportion of girls. Many travel the world avoiding our winter but from time to time we hear about new spots in both the North & Eastern Sea. The water is cold but the stoke is big.

ALLEMAGNE

Le surf en Allemagne débuta dans le milieu des années 60 quand les maître-nageurs de Sylt entendirent parler de surf à Biarritz. Après avoir essayé en France, ils trouvèrent ça tellement génial qu'ils fabriquèrent des planches et chercher les spots sur l'île. C'était le début. Pendant les années 70, un étudiant nommé Uli Richter donnait des leçons de surf à Hendaye. I l écrivit un livre et son école devint célèbre. La communauté des surfers de Sylt se développa avec des voyageurs d'autres régions qui attrapèrent le virus. Ensuite, dans les années 80, quand le windsurf devint à la mode, certains adeptes essayèrent de surfer sans la voile. Les pères apprirent à leurs enfants et on en est maintenant à la deuxième génération.

En 1988, un groupe d'une douzaine de gars formèrent une équipe pour participer aux championnats du Monde amateurs et en 1991, la fédé allemande (DWV) fut constituée. Depuis, le nombre de surfers allemands aux compétitions européennes et modiales a cru et en 1993, la première compète locale fut organisée sur Sylt. Y'avait 50 cms de vagues mais c'était top. La plupart des vagues sont générées par les vents bien que parfois de vraies houles passent par la Manche. Il y a maintenant 3 magazines de surf et plus de 10,000 surfers incluant une large proportion de filles. Beaucoup voyagent à travers le monde pour éviter l'hiver, de temps en temps on entend parler de nouveaux spots sur la mer du Nord ou de l'est. L'eau est froide mais la motivation est profonde.

GERMANY

El inicio del surf en Alemania fue a mediados los 60 cuando socorristas de Sylt tuvieron noticia de las olas en Biarritz. Quedaron tan impresionados tras su experiencia en francia que empezaron a construirse sus tablas y a buscar olas en su isla. Durante los 70 un estudiante conocido como Uli Richter empezó a dar clases en Hendaya, escribió un libro y sus cursos se hicieron famosos. La comunidad de Sylt creció y viajeros de otras zonas continuaron con la expansión. A mediados de los 80 cuando el windsurfing estuvo tan de moda, algunos de los jóvenes intentaron surfear sin velas. Los padres lo transmitieron a sus hijos e hijas y ya tenemos la segunda generación.

En 1988 un grupo de 12 tios hicieron un equipo para participar en los Campeonatos mundiales Amateurs en Costa Rica, y en 1991 se formó la Federación alemana de Surf (DWV). Desde entonces el número de alemanes en Campeonatos europeos y mundiales ha aumentado, y la primera competición local se celebró en Sylt en 1993. Las olas no pasaron del medio metro pero lo pasamos muy bien. La mayoria de las olas vienen con los swells de viento aunque puede llegar el swell de tormenta del Canal inglés. Hoy en dia se editan tres revistas de surf y hay más de 10.000 surfistas, incluyendo un buen numero de chicas. Muchos viajan por ahí sobre todo para evitar el crudo invierno pero de cuando en cuando se encuentra algún nuevo spot en los mares del Norte y del Este. El agua está fria pero las ganas son muchas.

1. Borkum

The most westerly island in Germany with good wind waves and North Sea ground swells when there've been westerly winds for 3-4 days. 2 spots: Jugendbad and FKK Strand (nudist beach) both of which are uncrowded and have good water. For more information drop into 'Wind surfing Borkum' on the west side. Catch the ferry from Emden.

L'île la plus à l'ouest d'Allemagne qui fonctionne avec de bonnes vagues de vents et les houles de la Mer˝ du Nord quand y'a eu des vents d'ouest pendant 3-4 jours. 2 spots: Jugendbad et FKK Strand (plage nudiste) où pas grand monde surfe. L'eau est impeccable. Pour plus d'infos, arrêtez-vous à Windsurfing Borkum du côté ouest. Prendre le ferry depuis Emden.

Es la isla más al oeste de Alemania con buenas olas como fruto del swell en el Mar del Norte y de 3 a 4 dias seguidos de vientos del oeste. 2 spots: Jugenbad y FKK Strand (playa nudista), en ambos suele haber poca gente y presentan buena calidad de agua. Para más información preguntar en "Wind surfing Borkum" en la zona oeste. Coger el ferry desde Emden.

2. Norderney

A long thin island which works under the same conditions as Borkum but is more popular due to the shorter and cheaper ferry from Norddeich. Mainly a tourist spot but increasingly one will find surfers in the water at Januskopf (which has a surfers café), Café Cornelius, Weiße Dune (Close to Happy Windsurfing School) and Strandsauna. The water around the island is generally of good quality.

Une île longue et étroite qui marche dans les mêmes conditions que Borkum avec plus de monde à l'eau parce que le ferry est plus court et moins cher depuis Norddeich. Principalement un endroit touristique mais on trouve de plus en plus de surfers à Januskopf (avec un café branché surf), Café Cornelius, Weiße Dune, et Strandsauna. L'eau est souvent de bonne qualité.

Es una isla larga y estrecha que funciona con las mismas condiciones que Borkum aunque está más concurrida ya que el viaje en ferry desde Norddeich es más corto y barato. Se trata fundamentalmente de un lugar turístico aunque te encontrarás surfistas en el agua en Januskopf (tiene un café surfístico), Café Cornelius, Weiße Dune y Strndsauna. El agua de la isla es por lo general de buena calidad.

3. St Peter Ording

Various sandbar peaks, popular with surfers and windsurfers. The area is busy with holiday makers, with heaps of campsites near the coast. Water quality ok.

Un paquet de pics, bien connu des surfers et des windsurfers. Pas mal de touristes en saison avec des campings partout.

Varios picos de arena lo hacen conocido entre surfers y windsurfers. La zona se llena de veraneantes, con sus trastos y tiendas de campaña cerca de la costa.La calidad del agua está bien.

Sylt

The best surfing area in Germany with various spots having waves along its 35km length. Starting in the north:

La meilleure zone de surf en Allemagne avec une brochette de spots le long des 35 kms de côtes. En aprtant du nord:

Es la mejor zona para surfear en Alemania, cuenta con varios spots con olas a lo largo de sus 35 Km de costa. Empezando

Sylt - Photo: Guido Brebach

4. Buhne 16 Kampen

Pretty fat beach break that has waves when there have been strong west winds for a few days. Not too crowded due to the walk through the dunes.

Un beach-break plutôt épais avec des vagues quand ça a soufflé d'ouest pendant quelques jours. Pas trop de monde parce qu'il faut marcher à travers les dunes.

Una playa con una rompiente bastante tosca que se favorece de los fuertes vientos del oeste. No suele llenarse de gente debido a la larga caminata que hay que pegarse por entre las dunas.

Thomas Lange - *Photo: Guido Brebach*

5. Sturmhaube Kampen

A sand and rock bottom spot with good rights between the stone jetties. Easy access.

Un spot de rochers et de sable avec de bonnes droites entre les jetées de pierre. Accès facile.

Este spot es de fondo de roca y arena y salen buenas derechas entre los diques de contención. Fácil acceso.

6. Nordseeklinik Westerland

Popular spot with waves when everywhere else is flat. Favourite spot for windsurfers in a south wind.

Spot fréquenté avec des vagues alors que tout le reste est flat. Beaucoup de windsurfers par vent de sud.

En este sitio conocido salen olas cuando en el resto no hay nada. Con viento sur es el sitio preferido para windsurfistas.

7. Brandenburg Westerland

The most popular area in Germany with powerful waves. The shoreline has a kink so waves break both ways. Best at mid tide.

Le spot le plus branché d'Allemagne avec des vagues relativement puissantes. La côte fait un coude aussi les vagues cassent-elles en droite et en gauche. Meilleur à mi-marée.

Es la zona más famosa de Alemania por sus contundentes olas. La costa presenta un desnivel así que las olas rompen en ambas direcciones. Mejor en media marea.

8. Oase zur Sonne Westerland

Shorebreak with killer waves up to 6ft. Broken boards are a common sight. Works on all tides and like Nordseeklinik gets crowded.

Gros shore-break avec des vagues d'enfer jusqu'à deux mètres. On y voit souvent des planches cassées. Marche à toutes les marées et devient encombré comme Nordseeklinik.

Aquí aparecen una olas mortales de hasta 2 metros. Que se rompan tablas es algo normal. Funciona con todas las mareas pero enseguida se llena de gente.

9. Sansibar Rantum

A few km's down from Westerland. Not as crowded but can have little tubes in an offshore wind. Easy access.

Quelques kms au sud de Westerland. Pas aussi encombré et des petits tubes avec off-shore. Accès facile.

Se encuentra unos Km debajo de Westerland. No suele haber tanta gente y si sopla terral puede haber suculentos tubos. Fácil acceso.

10. Kilometerstein Vier Hörnum

Located at the very southern end of Sylt. A good place for those who want to avoid the crowds at Westerland.

Situé complètement au sud de l'île. Un bon endroit pour ceux qui veulent éviter la foule de Westerland.

Se encuentra en el extremo más al sur de Sylt. Es un buen sitio si quieres librarte de las aglomeraciones de Westerland.

11. Eastern Sea

DAMP, HOHWACHTER BUCHT, FEHMARN & PELZERHAKEN.

Not quite Hawaii, but small wind swells during the winter months provide waves for a hardy, select group of surfers.

Pas vraiment Hawaii mais les petits swells de vents pendant l'hiver produisent quelques vagues pour un petit groupe de surfers élitistes.

No tan Hawaii, pero con un poco de swell durante los meses de invierno salen olas aptas para un reducido grupo de recios surfistas.

Schiermonnikoog
N357
N357
GRONINGEN
A7
E22

DENMARK.

Surfing in Denmark is still a bit mysterioso, but her coast is open to a wide fetch of North Sea, and undoubtedly receives similar swells to Germany's premier wave region. In fact Sylt itself is only just within German borders. Denmark has a surfing association and a few hundred keen surfers who, like their German neighbours, travel a lot.

DANEMARK

Le surf au Danemark est encore un peu mystérieux bien que la côte soit bien exposée aux fetchs de la Mer du Nord en recevant sans aucun doute les mêmes swells que la meilleure région allemande. En fait, Sylt est sur la frontière. On trouve une association de surfers danois et quelques centaines d'accros qui , comme leurs voisins allemands, voyagent beaucoup.

DENMARK.

El surf en Dinamarca es tadavía un tanto desconocido aunque sus costas están abiertas a las aguas del mar del norte. Recibe los mismos swells que la región más surfística de Alemania. De hecho el propio Sylt se encuentra justo dentro de los límites alemanes. En Dinamarca hay una asociación surfística cuyos cientos de aficionados, como en Alemania, gustan de viajar mucho.

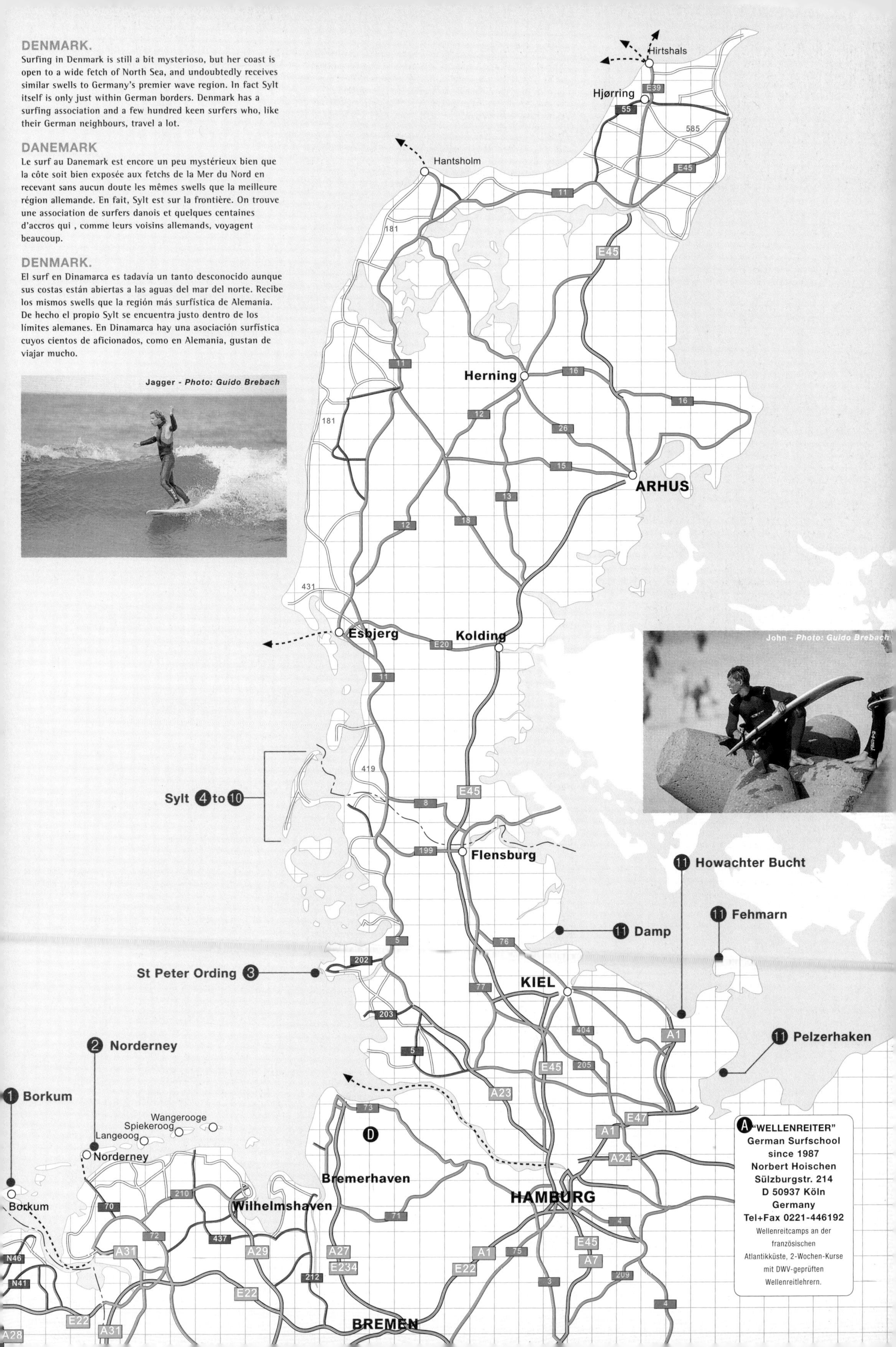

Jagger - *Photo: Guido Brebach*

John - *Photo: Guido Brebach*

PHOTO: BOB BARBOUR SURFER: WINGNUT

Slufter - *Photo: Robby Buttner*

Map: Volkskrant

Verwachting voor morgen

Nederland	zaterdag	zondag	maandag	dinsdag	woensdag
temp. min.	5/6 °C	1/3 °C	-1/3 °C	-3/1 °C	-5/1 °C
max.	6/7 °C	4/6 °C	2/5 °C	3/6 °C	1/4 °C
wind	WNW 5-8 Bft	N.V 4-8 Bft	NW 4-7 Bft	NW 2-4 Bft	Z 3-4 Bft

netherlands & belgium

Martijn Drenth

"Surfing is only allowed in specially assigned areas during summer"

HSA Crew - *Photo: Nathalie van der Hoeven*

Jan Willlem Coenraads Nederveen begon voor het eerst met surfen in Nederland in de jaren 30, veelal alleen tot aan het eind van de jaren 50. De 2de generatie van de jaren zestig bestond uit: Go Klap, Albert van Garderen, Arie Verbaan en Jaap van der Toorn. Een vriend die in de V.S. was geweest, leende Go een "Harbour" longboard, gedurende een periode waarin de meeste jongens zelfbouw planken bereden. Go opende zijn winkel in 1973 en de sport groeide nu snel. In België begon het allemaal met een Belg die luistert naar de naam Kobbe. In 1983 verbleef hij acht maanden in Marokko. Eenmaal thuis, begon hij de Noordzee dijning te surfen.

Het gaat niet gemakkelijk. De winter omstandigheden zijn erg zwaar en in steden zoals Den Haag (met zijn haven Scheveningen) in Nederland, en in de meeste Belgische kustplaatsen, is surfen alleen toegestaan in speciaal toegewezen gebieden in de zomer. Om de beste plekken te kunnen surfen, moesten de Nederlandse en Belgische surfers zich organiseren als wettelijk erkende clubs. De Holland Surfing Association (HSA) werd opgericht in 1973 en de Belgian Surf Association (BSA) aan het begin van de jaren negentig. Beide verenigingen organiseren surf evenementen en publiceren club bladen. Onderhandelingen met de gemeente van Den Haag heeft geleid tot vaste surf stekken in de zomer en in Belgische kustplaatsen zijn er speciaal aangewezen "surf zones". Gedurende de Nederlandse winter (wanneer de golven het best zijn), is de kust ongelimiteerd, maar in België kan je nog steeds uit het water worden gehaald. Respecteer de verboden gebieden. Wanneer je uit het water wordt gehaalt door de politie of kustwacht, verlaat het water. Doe je dit niet, dan breng je de vergunningen voor de aangewezen gebieden van de HSA en BSA in gevaar en het bespaart ook jezelf een hoop narigheid.

Het totaal aantal Nederlandse en Belgische surfers wordt geschat op ongeveer 500. De HSA heeft meer dan honderd leden en wanneer je in Nederland of in België woont, sluit je dan aan en maak je sterk voor deze organisaties.

Jan Willlem Coenraads Nederveen surfed for the first time in the Netherlands in the 30's, mostly on his own until the late fifties. The 2nd generation of the sixties included: Go Klap, Albert van Garderen, Arie Verbaan and Jaap van der Toorn. A friend who visited the U.S. lent Go a "Harbour" longboard at a time when most of the other guys were riding home made planks. Go opened his shop in 1973, and the sport is still growing fast. In Belgium it started when a guy called Kobbe spent eight months in Morocco during 1983. Once back home, he started riding the North Sea swells.

It doesn't come easy. The winter conditions are very harsh and in cities like The Hague (with its harbour Scheveningen) in the Netherlands, and in most Belgian seaside towns, surfing is only allowed in specially assigned areas during summer. To be able to surf the best spots, Dutch and Belgian surfers had to organise legally registered clubs. The Holland Surfing Association (HSA) was formed in 1973 and the Belgian Surf Association (BSA) in the early nineties. Both clubs organise surf events and publish magazines. Negotiations with the local government of The Hague, have resulted in designated summer surf areas and in most Belgian seaside towns there are specially assigned "surf zones". In the Dutch wintertime (when the waves are best), the coast is unrestricted, but in Belgium you can be called from the water anywhere and at any time. Respect the restricted areas. If you do get called out by the police or the coast guard, leave the water. If not, you jeopardise HSA or BSA licenses for the assigned areas and you'll have hassles yourselves.

The combined number of Dutch and Belgian surfers is estimated at around five hundred. The HSA has over one hundred members, if you live in the Netherlands or Belgium get involved and join.

Jan Willem Coenraads Nederveen surfa pour la première fois aux Pays-Bas dans les années 30, généralement tout seul jusqu'à la fin des années 50. La seconde génération des années 60 comptait dans ses rangs: Go Klap, Albert Van Garderen, Arie Verbaan et Jaap Van Der Toorn. Un ami qui séjourna aux E-U prêta un longboard "Harbour" alors qu'à l'époque la plupart des autres surfeurs se fabriquaient leur propre planche. Go ouvrit une boutique en 1973, et le surf se développa rapidement. En Belgique, le coup d'envoi fut donné lorsque qu'un gars s'appelant Kobbe passa 8 mois au Maroc en 1983. De retour chez lui, il commença à surfer les swells de la Mer Du Nord.

Le surf n'avait rien de facile. Les conditions en hiver sont très dures et pour des villes comme La Haye (avec son port Schevingen) aux Pays-Bas, ou la plupart des villes du bord de mer en Belgique, le surf n'est autorisé que dans des zones bien déterminées pendant l'été. Afin de pouvoir surfer les meilleurs spots, les surfeurs hollandais et belges durent s'organiser en clubs officiels. La Holland Surfing Association (HSA) fut crée en 1973 et la Belgian Surfing Association (BSA) au début des années 90. Chacun des deux clubs organisent des compétitions et publie des magazines. Des pourparlers avec les autorités de La Haye, ont abouti à des zones réservées de surf pour l'été; sur la plupart des stations balnéaires belges, elles portent même le titre de "zones de surf". En hiver (quand les vagues sont les meilleures) il n'y a pas de limites, mais en Belgique vous pouvez être rappelé au bord n'importe où, n'importe quand. Ne pas plaisanter avec ces zones réservées. SI vous êtes rappelé au bord par la police ou un MNS, quittez l'eau. Sinon, vous compromettez les autorisations HSA ou BSA pour les zones réservées et vous pouvez vous-mêmes avoir des problèmes.

Le nombre de surfeurs hollandais et belges est estimé à environ 500. La HSA a plus de 100 membres, et si vous avez l'occasion de vivre aux Pays-Bas ou en Belgique, rejoignez les.

Netherlands & Belgium

Martijn Drenth

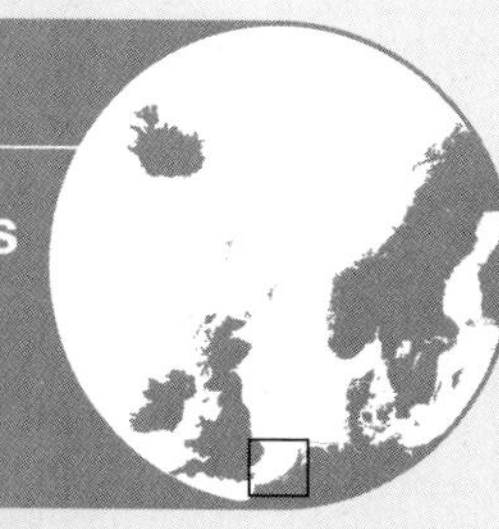

1. Waddeneilanden

Er is nog niet veel bekend over de golven op de Waddeneilanden. De stroming kan sterk zijn door het grote tij verschil. De "Slufter" op Texel is een goede stek.

Not much is known about surf on the Wadden Islands. The currents can be strong due to big tidal differences. The "Slufter" on the island of Texel is a good break.

On ne sait pas grand chose des iles Wadden, sauf que les courants y sont forts á cause des marnages importants. Cependant, Slufter'sur l'île de Texel est un bon break.

2. Camperduin & Hargen

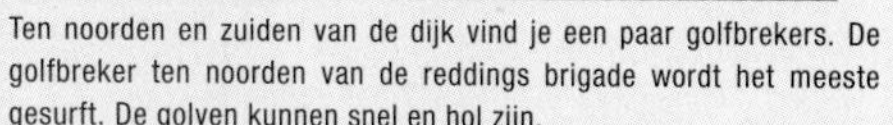

Ten noorden en zuiden van de dijk vind je een paar golfbrekers. De golfbreker ten noorden van de reddings brigade wordt het meeste gesurft. De golven kunnen snel en hol zijn.

North and south of the dike here there are a number of breakwaters. The breakwater, north of the life-saving club Hargen, is the most frequently surfed. It can be fast and hollow.

On peut trouver quelques jetées au nord et au sud de la digue, mais sachez que celles au nord du poste de secours d'Hargen ont les vagues les plus fréquentées, les plus creuses et les plus rapides.

3. Bergen/Egmond aan Zee

Twee kustplaatsen met kleine surfgemeenschap. Middelmatige zandbanken, waarover de golven breken, met sterke stroming.

Two seaside villages that have small surfing communities. Average beach breaks with strong currents.

Deux villages côtiers pourvus d'une petite communauté de surfers et de beach-breaks moyens balayés par de puissants courants.

4. Wijk aan Zee Noordpier

Eén van de beste stranden voor golven in de provincie N-Holland, recht tegenover de "Hoogovens". Met sterke Zuidelijke of ZW wind is de golf langzaam en wordt vaak overgenomen door windsurfers. Gebruik niet de stroming naast de haven... dan kom je op de blokken. Surf info: Egbert Visser (02517) 5826.

One of the best beach breaks in the province of NTH Holland in front the massive "Hoogovens" steel mill. In strong southerly or SW wind it becomes kind of slow, and is often invaded by windsurfers. Do not use the rip by the harbour wall... you can get slammed. Surfcheck: Egbert Visser (02517) 5826.

Un des meilleurs beach-breaks au nord de la province de Hollande en face de l'imposante acierie Hoogovens. Par fort vent de sud, sud-Ouest surtout, ça devient un peu mou et ça grouille de windsurfers. N'utilisez pas le courant de la jetée pour remonter ou vous risquez de vous ramasser. Infos surf: Egbert Visser (02517) 5826

5. Zandvoort to Katwijk

Drie kleine kustplaatsen twintig minuten buiten Amsterdam, met niet veel zeggende golven, maar aardige locals.

Three little beach resorts twenty minutes from Amsterdam with unspectacular waves, but friendly locals.

Trois petites stations balnéaires á 20 minutes d'Amsterdam avec des vagues pas terribles mais des locaux plutôt accueillants.

6. Scheveningen

PIER

Naar het noorden van de haven vind je de pier met restaurant. Sterke stroming. Werkt met W deining.

A pier with a restaurant about a mile to the north of the harbour. Watch out for strong currents. Works in W swell.

Une jetée avec un restaurant environ 1.5 km au nord du port Attention aux courants qui sont forts .Marche par houle d' ouest

NOORD

Verschuivende zandbank golven. Linkse vaak langer. Op zijn beste met noord tot west dijning. Werkt ook met zuidwesterlijke winden. Respecteer de locals!

Shifting sandbar waves. Lefts are usually longer, best with north to west swell. Also works in southwesterly winds. Respect the locals.

Les bancs de sable bougent. Les gauches sont souvent plus longues, idéalement avec une houle de nord à ouest. Ca matche aussi avec des vents de sud-ouest. Respectez les locaux.

ZUID

Heeft meer dijning nodig om goed te lopen, maar één van de betere plekken in Holland die hogere golven kan houden. De haven beschermd tegen sterke noordelijke wind. Niet zo veel surfers als op de Noord. Aan de kant een leuke rechtse over een zandbank gevormd door een kleine golfbreker.

Needs more swell than Noord to work well, but one of the better spots in Holland which can handle sizable waves. The harbour wall protects against strong northerly winds. Usually not as crowded as the Noord. Inside a nice right is produced by a sandbar formed over a submerged jetty.

Exige plus de houle que le nord mais ça peut être un des meilleurs spots du pays et ça tient le gros. La jetée du port protège des vents de nord et dans le port casse une droite sur un banc formé sur un épi submergé Souvent moins de monde qu'au nord.

Scheveningen, Zuid - *Photo: Eric de Roode*

7. Kijkduin

Badplaats ongeveer tien minuten ten zuiden van Scheveningen. Goede plek om naar toe te gaan, wanneer Scheveningen niet goed loopt met laag tij. De banken hebben noorderlijke dijning nodig voor rechtse golven en sterke zuidwesterlijke wind voor linkse golven, die breken naast de golfbrekers.De golven hier kunnen hol zijn en de stroming sterk.

Small beach town situated ten minutes south of Scheveningen. A good spot to check out when Scheveningen is not working well at low tide. This beach break needs a north swell to create a right and a strong SW wind for long lefthanders breaking off rock jetties. The waves here can be very hollow and currents can be strong.

Petite station à 10 minutes au sud de Scheveningen. A checker quand Scheveningen ne marche pas à marée basse. Ce beach break a besoin d'une houle de nord pour créer une droite ou de forts vents de sud-ouest pour des gauches qui cassent prés d'epis de cailloux. Les vagues peuvent y être trés creuses mais encore une fois, les courants sont violents.

8. Ter Heyde

Leuke badplaats met een ontspannen atmosfeer. De banken worden gevormd tussen korte golfbrekers.

A nice beach town with a relaxed atmosphere. The sandbars are formed between small rock jetties.

Une petite station bien cool avec des bancs de sable entre des mini-jetées de cailloux.

9. Maasvlakte Area

MAASEXPRESS

Breekt over een stenen bodem, in het ondiepe gedeelte van de riviermond van de Nieuwe Waterweg. Krachtige en snelle golf - kan board brekend zijn. Er zijn drie golfbrekers. De hoofd piek begint vanaf de meest westerlijke golfbreker. Het begin van de golf is recht voor of naast de tweede golfbreker. Impossibles is een kort gedeelte van hoofd piek die naast de derde golfbreker breekt. De golf wikkeld recht voor de stenen af (neem korte leashes mee). De aanleg van een pijpleiding heeft de kwaliteit van de golf aangetast en de golf loopt alleen nog met sterke noord deining. Stroming kan er sterk zijn.

Breaks over a packed cobblestone bottom in the shallow part of the rivermouth Nieuwe Waterweg. Powerful, fast wave - can be board breaking. There are three jetties. The main peak starts from the western jetty. The take-off is in front of or beside the second jetty. 'Impossibles' is a short section breaking off the third jetty. It peels straight in front of the rocks (bring short leashes). Pipeline construction has decreased the quality of the wave. Needs strong north swell. Rips can be severe.

Casse sur des gros galets dans la partie peu profonde de l'embouchure de la Nieuwe Waterweg. On a vu des planches cassées sur ces vagues puissantes et rapides. Trois jetées: le pic principal casse sur celle à l'ouest; la zone de take-off est en face ou à côté de la jetée du milieu Impossible est une section courte de ce pic qui commence depuis la troisième jetée, juste en face des rochers, un petit leash est conseillé. La construction d'un oléoduc a amélioré la qualité de cette vague.

Maasexpress - *Photo: Robby Buttner*

BLOKKEN

Zeven minuten rijden vanaf de Maasexpress. Beschermde plek met zand bodem. Koelwater van een elektriciteits-centrale zorgt ervoor, dat het water vijf graden Celsius warmer is dan elders - lekker in de winter. Werkt tijdens sterke noord dijning. Verschillende pieken en meerdere uitpaddel zones. De rechtse, die breekt vanaf de hoofd piek, is het beste. Naar het ZW is er een kleine linkse en hier kan je het makkelijkst uitpeddelen, wanneer de golven hoog worden. De Blokken kan elke maat deining houden.

Seven minute drive from the Maasexpress. A sheltered spot with a sandy bottom. Cooling water from a power plant causes the water to be five degrees Celsius warmer then else where, which is nice in winter. In strong northerly swells. There are various peaks and several paddle out zones. The right from the main peak is best. To the SW there is a small left and here you find the easiest paddle out when it is big. The Blokken can hold all swells.

A 7 minutes de route du Maasepress, on trouve ce spot abrité avec un banc de sable. Une centrale thermique peut réchauffer l'eau jusqu'à 5°C en hiver. Avec un gros swell de N, on peut trouver quelques pics et des channels pour aller au fond. La droite est souvent la meilleure. Au SO, il y a une petite gauche et le meilleur channel quand ça rentre gros. Ca devrait tenir toutes les tailles.

Sheveningen Noord & Pier - *Photo: Robby Buttner*

SLUFTER 

Verderop en zichtbaar vanaf de Blokken. Vanaf de Blokken moet je helemaal met de auto omrijden, om bij dit stuk strand te komen. De zandbanken worden ondiep tijdens hoge dijning en de golven hol. Stroming met sterke side shore wind.

Further down and visible from "the Blokken", a stretch of beach called the Slufter. By car from the Blokken you have to drive all the way around to get to the Slufter. The sandbars can get ultra shallow in bigger swells and very hollow. Rips in strong side shore winds.

Plus au sud des Blokken, on peut voir une partie de la plage qu'on appelle le Slufter Pour y aller, il faut faire tout le tour. Ca peut casser sur trés peu d'eau quand c'est gros , c'est creux donc. Du courant par forts vents de côté.

Maasvlakte, Slufter - Photo: Robby Buttner

10. Domburg 

Klein dorpje in de provincie Zeeland, dichtbij Middelburg. Wind vanuit het noorden is aflandig en brengt tevens de dijning.

Domburg is a small village in the province of Zeeland, near the city of Middelburg. This beach break works best during low tide. Wind from the north is offshore and it also brings swell.

Petit village de la province de Zeeland, près de Middleburg, Dombourg est un beach-break qui marche mieux à marée basse .Ici, les vents de nord sont off-shores et amènent la houle.

11. 't Swin 

Wanneer je bereid bent om op onderzoek uit te gaan, dan is dit een mooie plek om naar toe te gaan. Rij naar de laatste parkeer plaats - vlakbij een oud zwembad - en loop vijftien minuten door het natuur reservaat. Beste met noord dijning.

The first break in Belgium. If you are into some exploring this is a great place to go. Drive to the last parking lot (near an old swimming pool) and walk another 15 minutes through the nature reserve. Best on Northern swells.

Le Premier spot en Belgique. Pour ceux qui se sentent une âme d'explorateur, c'est ce qu'il vous faut. Roulez jusqu'au dernier parking près d'une piscine et marche 15 min à travers la réserve naturelle. Meilleur par houle de N.

12. Blackenberge 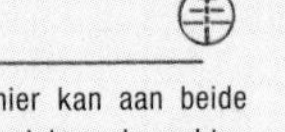

Net buiten de haven van Zeebrugge. De pier hier kan aan beide kanten worden gesurfd. De noord kant heeft drie pieken, de rechtse zijn het best. De stroming kan het moeilijk maken om uit te paddelen, maar dan kan je van de pier springen.

Blankenberge just next to the main port of Zeebrugge has a pier. Both sides of the pier can be surfed. The north side has three peaks and the righths are favorite. The rip can make it hard to paddle out, but you can jump from the pier.

Juste à côté du port de Zeebruge, allez à Blackenberge dont la jeté se surfe des deux côtés. Au nord, trois pics qui favorisent les droites. Si le courant rend la rame difficile, sautez de la jetée.

13. Oostende 

De grootste kustplaats langs de Belgische kust, met een levendig nachtleven. Hier vind je verschillende zand banken, middenin windsurf zones. Werkt het best met noordwest dijning. Beperkt surfen gedurende zomer seizoen.

Oostende is the biggest seaside town along the Belgian coast with a lively nightlife. Here you can find several beach breaks, which work best in Northwest swell, in the middle windsurf zones. Restrictions on surfing during summer.

La plus grande station balnéaire de la côte belge qu'on appelle la Reine de stations grâce à une vie nocturne intense. On y trouve pas mal de beach-breaks, au milieu de la zone de windsurf, quand la houle vent de nord-ouest. Restrictions de surf en été.

14. Oostduinkerke to Mariakerke

Goede zandbanken tussen de vele golfbrekers langs dit gedeelte van de kust. Er zijn surfzones in plaatsen zoals Oostduinkerke, Nieuwpoort Bad, Middelkerke Bad en Mariakerke. In het algemeen is surfen alleen toegestaan in deze surfzones, maar betere golven kunnen ook buiten deze zones worden gevonden.

This beach has some good sandbars, formed between the numerous jetties along this part of the coast. At places like Oostduinkerke, Nieuwpoort Bad, Middelkerke Bad and Mariakerke there are surfzones. In general surfing is only allowed in these zones during summer, but better surf can also be found outside these areas.

Bons bancs qui se forment entre les nombreuses jetées le long de cette partie de la côte. Aux endroits comme Oostduikerke, Nieuwpoort Bad, Middelkerke Bad et Mariakerke, on trouve des spots. En général, le surf n'est permis que dans les zones de surf en été, bien que de meilleures vagues puissent être trouvées en dehors.

Editor's note: Thanks to Go Klap, Robby Buttner, Erik de Roode, Rik Uiterwijk, Ron Visser en Guy Fierens for information and great photos.

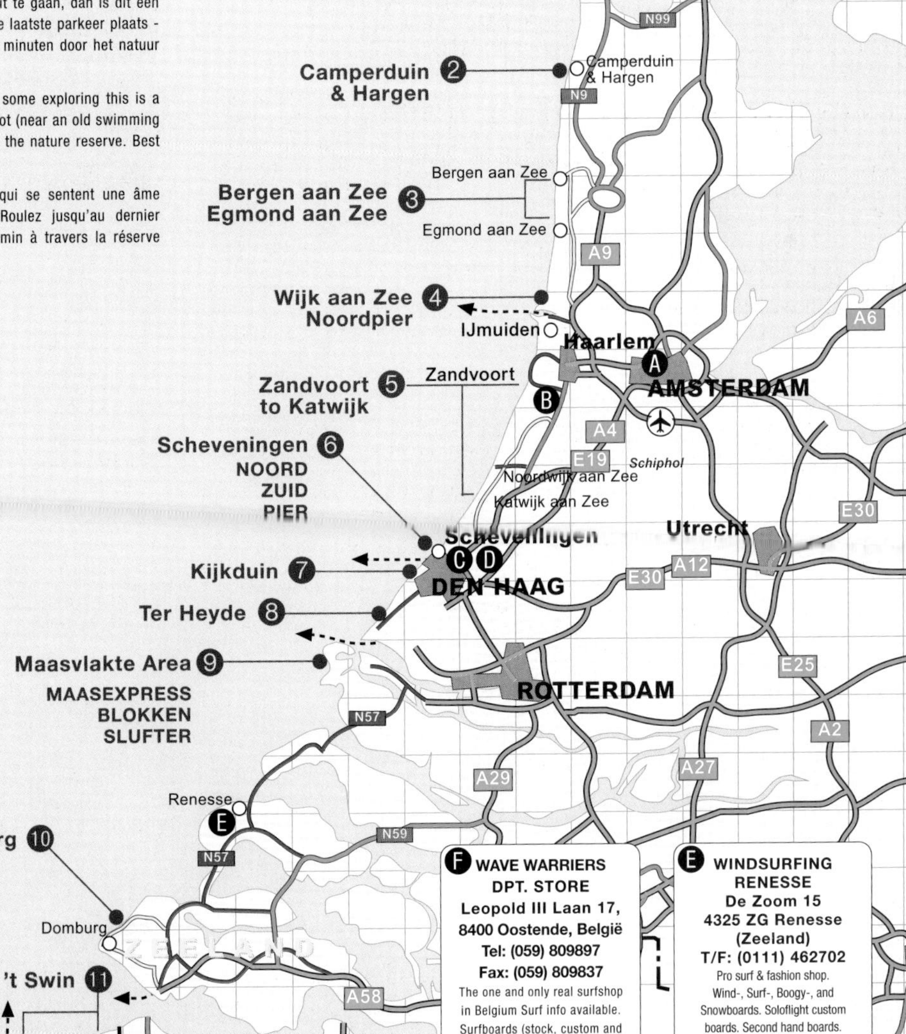

FRANCE

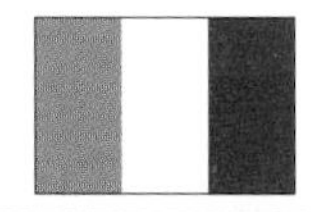

Capitale:	Paris
Population:	56,823,000
Superficie:	543,965km²
Fuseau Horaire:	GMT+1 (GMT+2)
Monnaie:	1 Franc (FF) = 100 centimes

Mont St. Michel - *Photo: Peter Cade*

FRANCE:
Carte physique

0 100 200 300 km

0 100 200 400 1000 2000 4000 m

Les massifs montagneux

383 stations de ski répertoriées.

❶ Vosges:	750m/1350m
❷ Jura:	880m/1680m
❸ Les Alpes du Nord (Savoie):	650-3840m
❹ Les Alpes centrales (Dauphine):	900-3600m
❺ Les Alpes du Sud:	1200m-2800m
❻ Massif Central:	1150m/1850m
❼ Pyrenees:	1350m/2500m

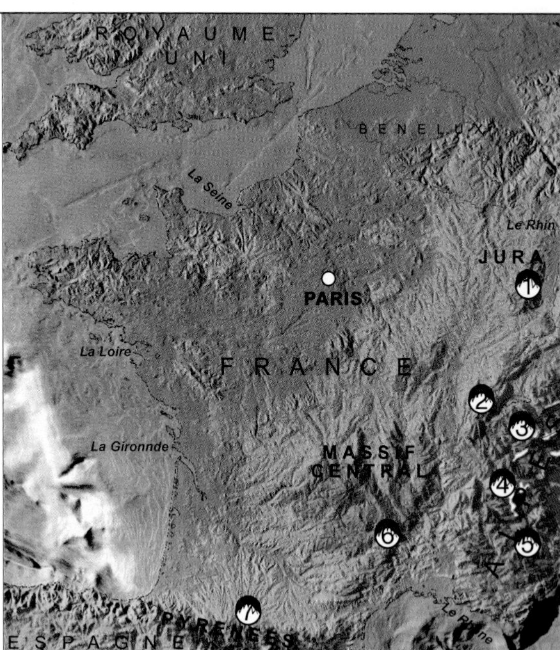

FRANCE

La France est le plus grand pays d'Europe et contient une incroyable diversité à l'intérieur de ses frontières, allant des plus hautes montagnes d'Europe de l'ouest à certaines des plus grandes rivières en passant par de trés longues plages et des collines verdoyantes. La côte plane au nord fait face à la Manche tandis que l'ouest sauvage fait front à l'Atlantique. Le sud est séparé de l'Espagne et l'Afrique par les Pyrénées; la Méditérannée et les frontières orientales sont partagées par l'Italie, la Suisse, l'Allamagne, le Luxembourg et la Belgique. Un haut-plateau au centre (le massif Central) annonce les Alpes.

Comme ses voisins en Europe, la France posséde une histoire richissime. Les premier habitants étaient les hommes descavrenes, peintres et chasseurs. Alors que les galciers au nord se rétractèrent environ 1500 ans avant J-C, une société agricole se développa. Les gaulois en étaient leurs descendants de l'âge du fer et ils étaient environ 11 millions quand les romains arrivèrent en 52 avant J-C. Les contestations politiques et sociales depuis lors ont été variées avec une succession de personnalités qui ont marqué l'histoire, comme Jeanne d'Arc, Louis XIV et Napoléon, dont les conquêtes militaires restent légendaires. La France a été envahie plusieurs fois par une succession de peuplades, commençant avec les Francs. Le pays conserve une des cultures européennes les plus importantes, au milieu de ses voisin les plus redoutables. Les principaux agents qui ont formaté la culture française durant les derniers siècles furent la révolution de 1789, les deux guerres mondiales et la naissance de la CEE. L'influence française s'étend sur la Méditerrannée, l'Afrique, l'Indochine et le Pacifique (ce qui n'est pas sans poser problème) avec un"art de vivre" omniprésent dans les arts, l'artisanat, la cuisine... Il en résulte une toile de fonds culturelle partout où l'on va.

FRANCE

France is Western Europe's largest state and contains an incredible diversity within its borders, ranging from W.Europes highest mountains, some of its biggest rivers, longest beaches and luscious hill land. The flat North coast faces La Manche and the wild West confronts the Atlantic. The South is separated from Spain and Africa by the Pyrenees and the Mediterranean and Eastern boarders are shared with Italy, Switzerland, Germany, Luxembourg and Belgium. A high inland Plateau (The Massif Central) steps up to the Alps.

As with all of Europe, the history of France is an immense topic. The first inhabitants were hunters, cave dwellers and painters. As the Northern ice-cap receded around 1500 BC, an agricultural and pastoral society developed. The Gauls were their iron age descendants and there were roughly 15 million of them when the Romans invaded in 52 BC. The social and political contortions since then have been many and varied and a succession of outrageous characters have asserted their place in history, notably Louis 14, Joan of Arc and Napoleon, whose military achievements were legendary. France has been invaded by a long succession of expansionist societies, starting with the Francs themselves, yet it remains one of Europe's strongest cultures, placed centrally between some tough neighbours. The main events which have shaped French culture over the last few centuries are the Revolution of 1789 the two world wars, and the birth of the E.C. neither of which need explanation here. French influence extends through the Mediterranean, Africa, Indo China and The Pacific (currently a source of great debate) though the Gaelic "Art de Vivre" is unique and thoroughly physical and their capacity for the arts and cuisine is legendary. The general feeling is one of cultural vibrancy in all areas.

FRANCIA

Francia es el mayor país de Europa Occidental, albergando una increíble diversidad dentro de sus fronteras: algunos de los más altos montes y ríos más largos de Europa, las playas más largas y una enorme sucesión de suaves colinas. Desde la Costa de la Mancha en el norte, la salvaje Costa Oeste batida por el Atlántico, pasando por los Pirineos (frontera natural con España) y el Mediterráneo, hasta sus regiones fronterizas con Italia, Suiza, Alemania, Luxemburgo y Bélgica, y por último su meseta central (Massif Central) y de los Alpes, conforman una espectacular diversidad y riqueza natural.

Como ocurre con la del resto de Europa, la historia francesa está repleta de tópicos. Sus primeros moradores fueron cazadores, habitantes de cavernas en las que dejaron sus pinturas. Tras la retirada de la capa de hielo, cerca de 1500 antes de Cristo, se desarrolló una sociedad agrícola y ganadera. Los galos fueron sus descendientes en la edad de hierro, y cuando los romanos comenzaron su invasión en el 52 a.c., eran ya unos 15 millones de habitantes. Las transformaciones sociales y cambios políticos han sido desde entonces tantas y tan variadas y los personajes históricos como Luis XIV, Juana de Arco y Napoleón tan sobradamente conocidos que no hay espacio en estas páginas para glosar toda su historia. Francia ha sido multitud de veces invadida por distintos pueblos comenzando por los mismos francos. Su cultura se mantiene como una de las principales de Europa. Los principales acontecimientos históricos de los últimos siglos han sido la Revolución Francesa (1789), las dos guerras mundiales y el nacimiento de la Comunidad Europea, no hace falta comentar su trascendencia. La influencia francesa se manifiesta en importantes zonas del Mediterráneo, Africa y el Pacífico (actual fuente de controversia), siendo su Art de Vivre algo único que se manifiesta en el gusto por la buena vida, las artes y la buena cocina. En general, se trata de un país donde las vivencias culturales son extraordinarias.

Ferries

Brittany Ferries- Roscoff:	99 29 28 28
Brittany Ferries- Caen:	31 36 36 00
P&O- Calais:	21 46 10 10
P&O- Cherbourg:	33 44 20 13
Hoverspeed- Calais:	05 26 03 60
Stena Sealink- Paris:	05 43 20 20
SNCM- Marseille-Corse:	91 56 32 00

Aeroports

Paris- C.de Gaulle:	(1) 48 62 22 80
Paris- Orly (S):	(1) 49 75 15 15
Bordeaux:	56 34 50 00
Biarritz:	59 43 83 83

Trains-SNCF

Paris Info (English):	(1) 42 82 50 50
Bordeaux- Gare St. Jean	56 92 50 50
Bayonne:	59 50 19 19

Autobus

Paris- Eurolines:	(1) 49 72 51 51
Bayonne- Sud Ouest:	59 59 19 33

Ferries

De loin la méthode la plus utilisée par les anglo-saxons est eclle du ferry. Les traversées nocturnes (en général moins chères) Plymouth-Roscoff et Porstmouth-St-Malo peuvent vous amener tout frais à quelques heures des vagues. Les prix varient en fonction de la saison qui va de la mi-juillet à début septembre. Les prix hors-saison peuvent être avantageux surtout si vous êtes en groupe dasn un van. Quelques compagnies assurent la liaison Douvres-Calais jour et nuit. C'est de loin le plus court et le moins cher pour traverser la Manche (surtout de minuit à l'aube) bien que ça rallonge le trajet par la route et surtout un bon pactole pour l' essence.

Trains

La réseau de la SNCF est rapide et efficace surtout avec le TGV qui relie Paris à toutes les côtes dans des temps record. Pas toujours trés pratique avec les planches, il permet quand même à beaucoup de parisiens d'aller surfer en week-end. Renseignez-vous pour les abonnements parce que le tarif plein est assez lourd.

Ferries

By far the most popular method of travelling to France from the UK is by car ferry. The overnight crossings (usually cheaper) (Plymouth–Roscoff, and Portsmouth–St Malo) can leave you rested and ready to hit the water within a few hours. Prices vary, with the peak season running from mid July to the beginning of September. Off peak prices can be good if you're a group travelling in a campervan. Several companies ply the Dover - Calais route leaving hourly, day and night. It's the shortest and therefore cheapest way of crossing the Channel (especially from midnight to dawn), although it adds quite a few hours to your driving time and many pounds to the fuel bill.

Trains

The French national train network (SNCF) has a reputation for efficiency and speed. The T.G.V (France's hi-speed train) runs (amongst other destinations) from Paris to Bayonne and can be an excellent way to get to the coast from the north.

Ferries

Son el medio más utilizado para trasladarse del Reino Unido a Francia. Los trayectos (Plymouth-Roscoff y Portsmouth-St Malo) nocturnos suelen ser los más baratos y te permiten descansar y estar preparado para en pocas horas darte tu primer baño. Los precios fluctuan, siendo la temporada alta de mediados de julio a septiembre. Incluso en esa época, si viaja un grupo en furgoneta no sale demasiado caro. Bastantes navieras cubren regularmente la ruta Dover-Calais. Es el itinerario más corto y más barato para cruzar el Canal (sobre todo por la noche); las pegas son que implica conducir durante más tiempo con el consiguiente mayor gasto de combustible.

Trenes

La red de ferrocarriles francesa (SNCF) tiene una buena reputación por su rapidez y eficiencia. Uno de los recorridos del tren de alta velocidad (TGV) une París con Bayona, resultando óptimo para desplazarte desde el norte a la costa suroeste.

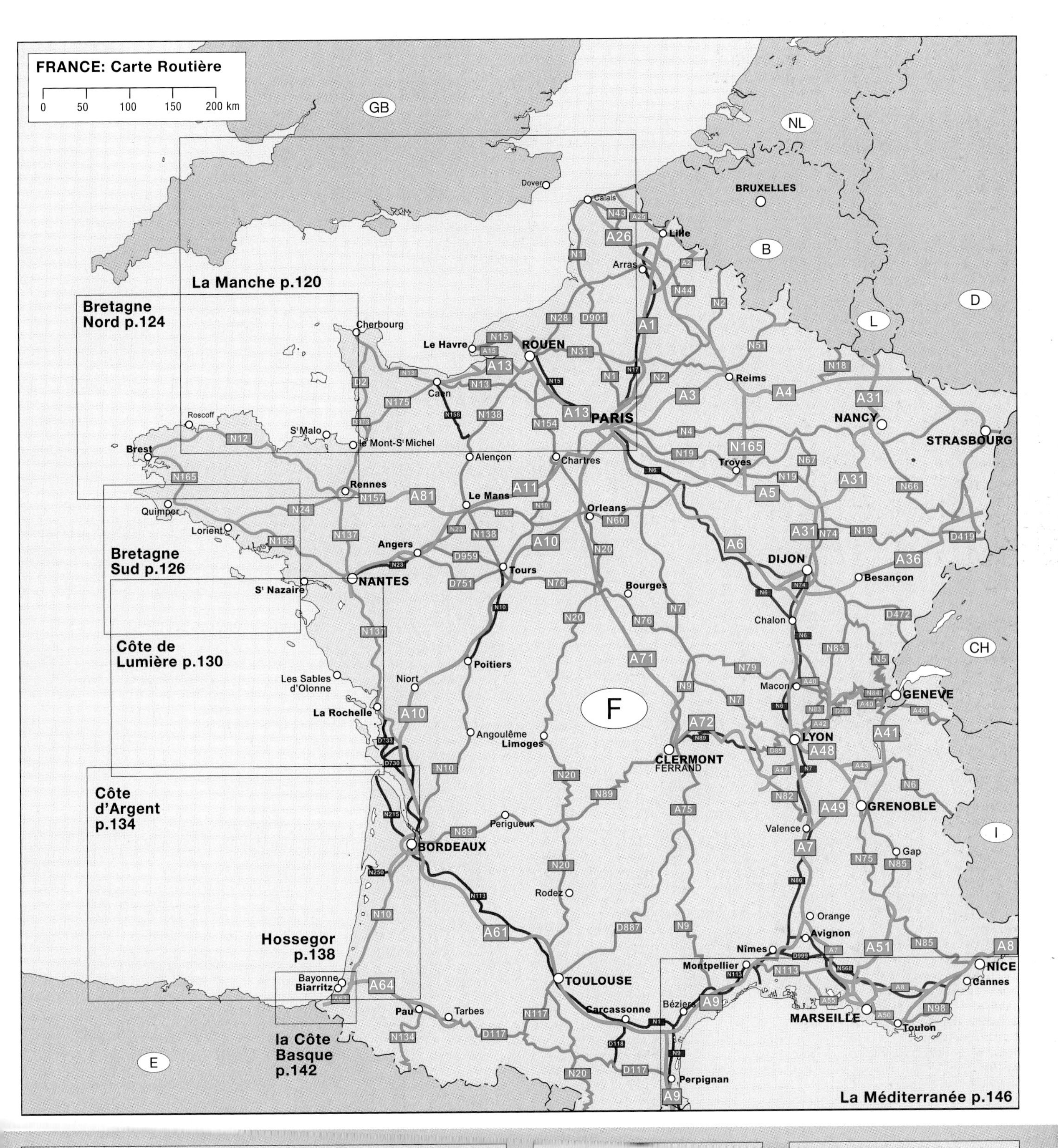

Vitesse

	Autoroute			Ville
KMH:	130	110	90	50
Pluie:	110	100	80	50

Ivresse

2 Pressions — 2 Verres de vin

Essence

		SUPERMARCHE
Super	FF6.20/ l	FF5.70/ l
Diesel	FF4.20/ l	FF3.80/ l

Autoroutes Informations

Tel: (1) 47 05 90 01

Cost of Living

Restaurant *	FF70-100
Hotel **	FF150-250
Camping	FF50
Demi	FF12
Cafe	FF5.00
Baguette	FF4.00

Telephone

Telecarte Conseillée	*40FF 96FF*
France	19 +
France	33 +
INT. Operateur	193311
NAT. Operateur	10
NAT. Annuaire	12
Police	17
Medical	15
Pompiers	18
APRES OCT. 96	
France	00 +
Paris	01
Nord-Ouest	02
Nord-Est	03
Sud-Est	04
Sud-Ouest	05

La Route

Les routes françaises sont parmi les meilleures du monde en ayant souvent le choix entre une route natioanle (RN) et les autoroutes à péages (cher). Roulez à droite et n'oubliez pas non plus la priorité à droite, sauf indication contraire comme sur les rond-points qui ont tendance à se miltiplier. Les prix à la pompe sont les plus élevés d'Europe avec une différence notable (jusqu'à 80 centimes) entre les stations sur l'autoroute et celles des supermarchés où avoir une carte de crédit permet de faire le plein 24h/24. En été, pas mal de routes côtières sont encombrées, les parkings saturent et les flics sont partout, mieux vaut être en règle avec tous les papiers nécessaires.

Driving

French roads are some of the best in the world. You nearly always have the choice between the high speed Péage (which can work out expensive) or very good A roads (R.N Routes Nationales). Two road rules of the road are [1]drive on the right and [2]always give way to traffic coming from the right (unless indicated). Petrol prices are amongst the highest in Europe, most expensive on the peage. Buy gas from the supermarkets! French roads get very full at the beginning and ends of August and long drives should be avoided if possible at these times. One must carry vehicle registration documents, insurance, license and passport with you at all times on French roads.

Carreteras

Las carreteras francesas son de las mejores del mundo. Puedes elegir entre autopistas de peaje (suelen resultar caras) o carreteras nacionales (R.N./Routes Nationales). Las normas de tráfico son similares a las españolas. El precio de la gasolina es de los más altos de Europa, siendo más elevado en las autopistas de peaje. ¡Reposta en los supermercados!. A ser posible no te desplaces ni a comienzos ni a finales de Agosto, porque se forman largas caravanas. Es obligatorio llevar en el vehículo la documentación del mismo, su seguro, tu carnet de conducir y tu pasaporte.

le surf et les temps

Avec l'Espagne, c'est le seul pays à avoir deux côtes surfables. Bien que le surf en Méditerranée soit désormais accepté comme une réalite, c'est bien sûr la côte Atlantique de la Manche à la baie de Biscay qui possède le meilleur potentiel de vagues. C'est cette dernière zone qui correspond grosso modo à l'Aquitaine où les vagues ont une puissance phénoménale due à la fosse au large qui empêche le plateau continental de freiner l'arrivée des houles et à une exposition ouest/nord-ouest optimale. Une autre caractéristique est la formation de baïnes, mini-lagons qui font des beach breaks aquitains un trésor de belles vagues quand la houle est propre. Les côtes plus au nord n'ont certes pas ces deux caractéristiques mais offrent des angles différents avec un littoral rocheux qui permet encore de surfer quand ça sature dans le sud. C'est dans le Pays Basque que le surf a commencé en Europe lorsque Peter Viertel vint à Biarritz en 1956 où, il se fit envoyer une planche. Les locaux furent vite inspirés par ses exhibitions, comme Georges Hennebutte (qui inventa le leash sans déposer le brevet) ou Barland/Rott qui shapèrent les premières planches. La France à l'automne devient dans les années 60 un rendez-vous des surfers dans le monde avec la superbe vague de la Barre avant la construction de la digue. Cependant, le surf resta marginal jusqu'à ce que la première étape professionnelle à Lacanau en 79 et les championnats du monde amateur en 80 donnent un nouveau souffle. Le développement fut aidé par la relance du skate et surtout la frénésie du snowboard. Actuellement, le business lié au surf en dit long sur son développement à l'heure actuelle. 3 magazines de surf, une soixantaine de surf-shops, 8000 planches de surf vendues par an, et eviron 45,000 surfers, réguliers comme occasionnels. Bien évidemment, ça fait du monde à l'eau bien que l'encombrement des spots soient restreint aux week-ends et aux vacances scolaires. Evitez ces périodes et vous n'aurez pas à batailler. On cite souvent Septembre-Octobre comme la meilleure saison, ça ne veut surtout pas dire qu'il faille exclure Novembre et Décembre qui peuvent réserver d'excellentes surprises. La période de Janvier à Mars est réservée aux hard-cores prêts à braver de grosses vagues avec d'épaisses combinaisons. Le printemps peut être consistant mais finalement plus aléatoire que l'automne avec une eau plus froide.

La position dans ces latitudes tempérées rend les statistiques trés aléatoires dans la mesure ou les variations de températures sont considérables. En moyenne, les hivers oscillent de 5 à 10°C du nord au sud. On estime que les pluies sont plus fréquentes de Novembre à Mars aussi mieux vaut éviter cette période si l'on campe. Cependant, avec 170 à 180 jours de pluie par an, on ne peut que difficilement l'éviter. Aux demi-saisons, il fait environ 15°C avec des printemps plus secs au nord et des automnes plus souriants au sud. En été, il n'est pas rare d'avoir des jours de canicule à plus 25°C surtout en juillet-Août. Quant à la température de l'eau, on compte 3 à 5 degrés de différence du nord au sud. Pour le sud, comptez 12°C en hiver, 14°C jusqu'en Mai, 20°C voire plus jusqu'à mi-Septembre et 16°C jusqu'en Novembre. Les vents dominants sont de sud-ouest en hiver et de nord-ouest en été, ceci n'exclue pas une bonne fréquence de matinées off-shore et de quelques jours avec des vents de terre réguliers.

In 1956, Hollywood scriptwriter Peter Viertel was on The Basque coast shooting an adaptation of Hemingways novel The Sun Also Rises. Amazed by the waves, he sent for a surfboard from California, but he was a strict beginner and shared his apprenticeship with a couple of Biarritz locals, George Hennebutte and Joel de Rosnay. His wife, the actress Deborah Kerr, became the patroness of Frances first surf club, "The Waikiki". Within a year the sport had grown and Hennebutte, together with Phillipe Barland and Jaques Rott had began to make longboards under the Barland name. Phillipe became a great innovator and has been credited, amongst other things, with designing the first pre-shape machine.

The 60's saw the first surf films containing European content shot here. The first was "Wave of Change" by Greg MacGillivary and Jim Freeman, starring Billy Hamilton, Keith Paull and Mark Markinson. The most famous was "Evolution" a film by Paul Witzig starring Nat Young and Wayne Lynch, shot principally at La Barre.

Despite the media attention, surfing in France remained a marginal sport till the end of the 70's. The Lacanau Pro was created in 1979 and France hosted the World amateurs in 1980. From that moment surfing gained considerable recognition and a new generation of surfers were born. The surfers of the 60s, who never went anywhere without 5 or 6 guys in the car, were replaced by a generation of individualists. France still has very few surfers (45,000), though with three A.S.P. competitions (at Lacanau, Hossegor and Biarritz), it's a crucial stop on the A.S.P. world tour. At the Andre Malraux college in Biarritz, it has been introduced as a sporting option and there is a diploma course at the Technical College near Lacanau. The French surf Federation now has a technical director and surfers are accepted as top level athletes at home.

The Climate is as varied as the landscape. Whilst the N experiences similar rainfall and temps to S. England, as one heads South it gets warmer and drier. During summer the N.Atlantic feeds remarkably warm water along the West coast and regular morning winds blow offshore, a result of consistent high pressure over the S.W. In winter the same E wind gets freezing, coming off the snow covered Alps. Snow falls on the beaches on rare occasions but summer is long and warm to balance the intensity of winter.

Correia el año 1956 cuando el guionista de Hollywood Peter Viertel se encontraba filmando una adaptación de la novela de Hemingway "The Sun Also Rises" en la Costa Vasca. Alucinado por las olas, encargó que le trajeran una tabla desde California. Como se trataba de un principiante compartió su aprendizaje con dos locales de Biarritz, George Hennebutte y Joel de Rosnay. La famosa actriz Deborah Kerr (esposa de Viertel) fue la madrina del primer Surf Club "El Waikiki". En un año se había desarrollado el deporte y Hennebutte, junto con Phillipe Barland y Jacques Rott empezaron a hacer tablones bajo la marca Barland. Phillipe pasó a ser un gran innovador, atribuyendosele entre otros avances la primera máquina de pre-shapes.

En los 60 se filmaron aquí algunas escenas para películas surferas. La primera fue "Wave of Change" de Greg Mac Gillvary y Jim Freeman, protagonizada por Billy Hamilton, Keith Paull y Mark Markinson. La más famosa fue "Evolution" de Paul Witzig, filmada principalmente en La Barre y protagonizada por Nat Young y Wayne Lynch.

A pesar de la atención de los medios de comunicación, el surf era en Francia un deporte marginal a finales de los 70. La creación en 1979 del Lacanau Pro y el Campeonato Mundial Amateur del 80 supusieron un considerable reconocimiento del surf y el nacimiento de una nueva generación de surfers. A diferencia de los de los 60, que se movían en grupos de 5 o 6, éstos iban a ser mucho más individualistas. En la actualidad habrá de 50,000 surfers en Francia y la etapa francesa del circuito ASP es esencial, con campeonatos en Lacanau, Hossegor y Biarritz. En el colegio Andre Malraux de Biarritz puede escogerse el surf como deporte escolar y en un Colegio Técnico cercano a Lacanau se imparte un curso sobre surf. La Federación Francesa de surf cuenta con un director técnico y los surfers ahora son aceptados como atletas de élite.

Es tan variado como el paisaje. Mientras que el clima del Norte se asemeja al del Sur de Inglaterra (fresco y húmedo), las regiones sureñas son mucho más cálidas y secas. El verano es considerablemente templado y bonancible en la costa atlántica donde las altas presiones situadas en el suroeste hacen que el viento matinal sople predominantemente terral. En invierno ese mismo viento Este sopla gélido proveniente de los Alpes. En alguna ocasión llega a nevar en las playas, pero en contraposición el verano es prolongado y apacible para contrarrestar el intenso invierno.

ESF/FFSS
Francis Distinguin
BP 28 Plage Nord, Hossegor 40150, France
Tel: (33) 56 09 12 08 Fax: (33) 37 81 34 033 020

La Manche

Nicolas Dejean

Le Havre - Photo: J.M.Herbert

Partagée entre la France et l'Angleterre, cette partie de l'Europe manque sans doute de puissance et de consistence mais mérite un détour pour deux raisons: ce sont les vagues les plus proches pour toute la région parisienne et la Normandie offre un cadre agréable pour les visiteurs débarquant à Calais ou à Cherbourg. N'oublions pas non plus un potentiel intéressant pour le windsurf ou le speed-sail . Deux zones principales: le NO du Cotentin qui prend raisonnablement les houles d'ouest à sud-ouest et la haute-Normandie avec Etretat comme fer de lance. Les marées hautes amènent souvent les plus grosses vagues. Les courants et les marées y sont particulièrement violents et les jours de surf se concentrent principalement sur les jours de tempête, où il fait froid et humide. Surf austère avec peu de spots donc mais surf quand même!

Split between France and England, the waves in this part of Europe clearly lack power and consistency but the region is surfed firstly because these are the closest waves to Paris area and secondly because Normandy offers charming scenery for visitors disembarking at Calais or Cherbourg. Basically two main surf zones: the NW of Cotentin Peninsula that picks up W/SW swells similarly to the Channel Isles, and Upper-Normandy with Etretat being the focal point. High tides and stormy conditions often bring the strongest waves. Rips and tides are particularly violent, and though the surf is harsh, with few spots, there is still surf!

En el lado francés del canal las olas carecen de fuerza y consistencia, pero de surfea porque es una zona cercana a París y porque atrae el turismo que desembarca en Calais o Cherburgo. Hay dos áreas surferas: el Noroeste de la Peninsula de Cotentin que recibe marejadas del Oeste y del Suroeste, semejantes a las de las Islas del Canal y la parte alta de Normandía, siendo Etretat el lugar más relevante. Con marea alta y condiciones tormentosas, se suelen coger las olas más potentes. Las corrientes y las mareas son muy pronunciadas. Pese a las condiciones desapacibles y los escasos spots, al menos queda el consuelo de que se puede surfear.

1. Carteret

D'abord un spot de fun-board, l'endroit s'est révélé avoir quelques vagues correctes. Le front de mer de Barneville au sud permet de voir pas mal de possibilités.

Primarily a wave-sailing spot but waves means surfers. A good stretch of beach is visible from the beach-front road south of the cape.

Primero, un spot de windsurfers, pero con olas correctas. Desde la avenida marítima de Barneville al sur, se ven las otras posibilidades.

2. Le Rozel

La D62 vous emmène tout droit vers les pics les plus puissants de la presqu'ile du Cotentin. Pas de quoi sortir le gun quand même! Respectez les locaux.

Take the D62 straight towards Cotentin peninsula's most powerful waves. No need to ride a gun, but some hollow sections. Respect to the locals.

La D62 te lleva directo a los picos más potentes de la península del Cotentin. Pero no necesitas el gun ! Respecta a los locales.

3. Diélette

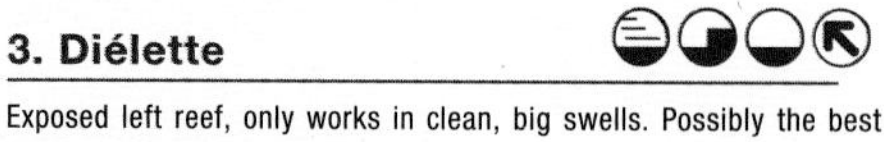

Exposed left reef, only works in clean, big swells. Possibly the best wave on this section of coast.

Exposed left reef, only works in clean, big swells. Possibly the best wave on this section of coast.

Spot de arrecifes, con una izquierda que funciona solo con un oleaje importante y limpio. Probablemente la mejor ola de esta zona.

4. Vauville

L'embarras du choix avec cette plage de 15 kms, chère aux glisseurs en tous genres de Cherbourg. On conseille vivement le Sud vers Siouville.

15 km long beach which picks up loads of swell, popular with the Cherbourg crew. Best waves can be found south around Siouville.

La elección es tuya con esta playa de quince kilómetros, muy popular entre los surfistas de Cherbourg. Las mejores olas quedan al sur hacia Siouville.

5. Anse du Brick

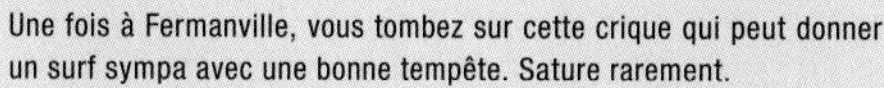

Une fois à Fermanville, vous tombez sur cette crique qui peut donner un surf sympa avec une bonne tempête. Sature rarement.

Once in Fermanville, you'll find this cove. Can produce nice conditions in a strong West swell. Good spot to check when other spots are closed-out.

Caleta en Fermanville. Funciona muy bien con un oleaje potente de oeste cuando los otros spots cierran.

6. D-Day Beaches

Pas de surf d' habitude sur ces plages,sauf en de rares occasions comme le débarquement. En effet, le 6 juin 1944, une méga-tempête venait surprendre les soldats avec des vagues de 50 cms.

Usually no surf on this stretch of coast, except on rare occassions such as the D-Day landings. On 6th June 1944 Huey created a huge storm in the Atlantic created 2ft perfection to greet the soldiers.

No se suele hacer surf sobre estas playas excepto en raras ocasiones, como durante el desembarcamiento del 6 de junio de 1944, con olas de 50 centímetros para acoger a los soldados !

7. Trouville

Sur la plage principale, on trouve une vague prés de la jetée à marée basse. Seulement par vents de sud-est et un gros swell de N-O.

On the main beach waves break close to a jetty at low tide. Only with a SE wind and big NW swell.

Sobre la playa principal, rompe una ola en maÔrea baja al lado de la escollera. Solo con viento de Sureste y grande oleaje de Noroeste.

8. Etretat

Même si ça ne rentre pas suffisamment gros pour soulever une vague, il faut voir au moins une fois dans sa vie les falaises d'Etretat et la plage de l'Aiguille Creuse. Pas mal de monde à l'eau quand ça marche. Meilleur au descendant pendant 2 heures. Shore-break carton à marée haute.

Found at the feet of L'Aguile Creuse, the most publicised spot in Normandy and the scene of many competitions. .A consistent and sometimes crowded break, best on the outgoing tide for 2 hours . Pounding shore-break at high tide.

Aunque no haya olas, vale la pena para ver la playa de L'Aiguille Creuse y los acantilados de Etretat. Buen pico, con mucha gente, durante dos horas de reflujo. Orilleras fuertes en marea alta.

Etretat - Photo: J.M.Herbert

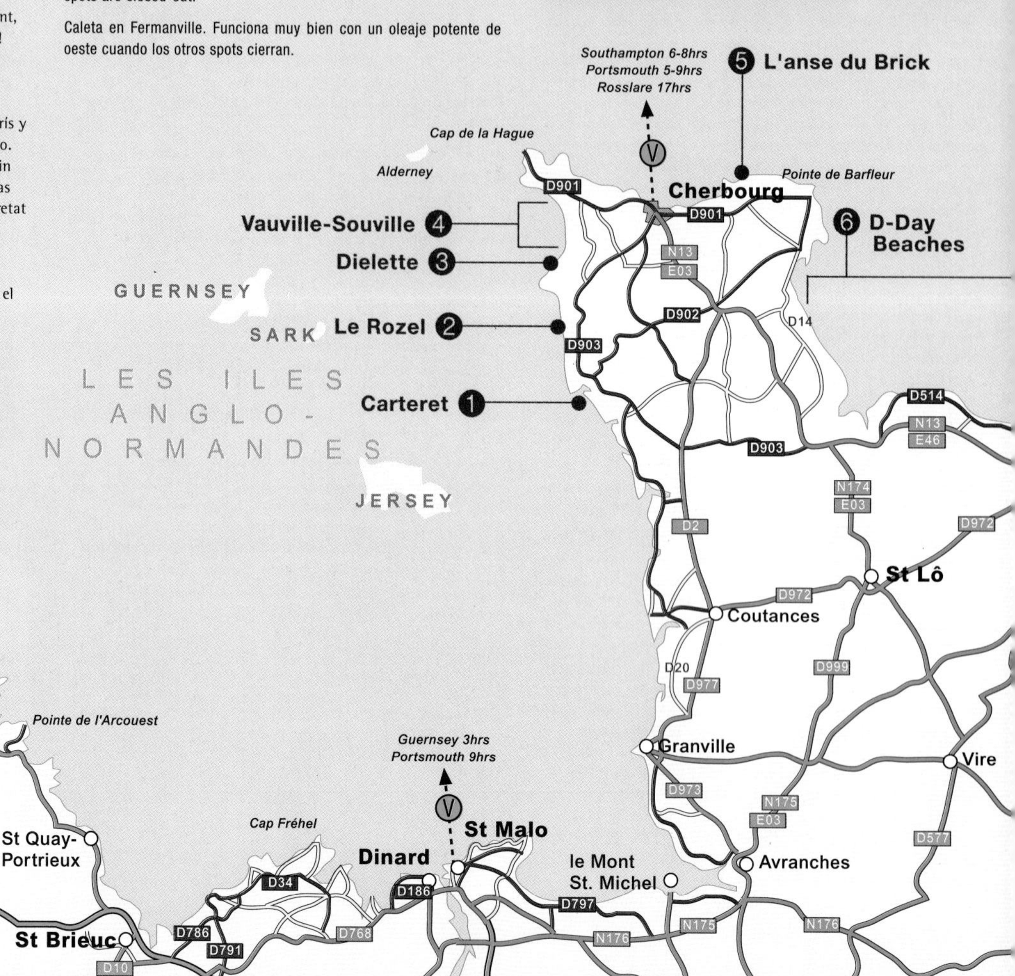

9. Yport

Dans les mêmes conditions qu'Etretat, la plage de Vaucottes se réveille avec les tempêtes. Les courants y sont violents.

Same requirements as Etretat. Vaucottes gets rideable at times but has heavy rips.

Igual que en Etretat. A veces funciona. Mucha corriente.

10. Fécamp

Un spot fréquenté par les windsurfers. Peut marcher jusqu'à 2m, plus souvent 2 cms.

Popular spot for windsurfers. Waves upto 6ft. 6 inches is more likely.

Un spot para windsurfers. Funciona hasta 2 metros (2 centímetros más probables !)

11. Les Petites Dalles

Pour ceux qui ont une grande faim de vagues, contrairement à ce que dit le panneau. Pas toujours fabuleux donc.

A few peaks when on. Not epic.

Unos picos cuando funciona. Mediocre.

12. Pourville

Au Nord de Wimereux, on peut trouver des droites et des gauches avec une grande houle en Manche. Quelques rochers à éviter.

Just North of Wimereux, rights and lefts with a strong W-SW swell. Pay attention to the rocks.

Justo al norte de Wimereux se puede encontrar derechas y izquierdas con mucho oleaje en la Manche. Cuidado al las rocas.

13. La Pointe aux Oies

Au nord de Wimereux on trouve cette plage bordée de rochers. Des gauches et des droites à mi- marée des deux côté de la plage .

North of Wimereux is this beach bordered by rocks. Mid-tide rights and lefts on either side of the beach.

Al norte de Wimeraux, izquierdas y derechas con importante oleaje de Oeste/Suroeste. Cuidado con las rocas !

14. Cap Gris-Nez

Le meilleur spot du Nord avec des options autour comme Cap Blanc-Nez et Wissant, par la D940, orientés différemment. Ca n' est pas l'Indonésie mais une bonne houle de SO vous garantit des vagues.

The best spot in the North with other nearby options such as Cap Blanc-Nez, Wissant and Wimeraux. Nothing like Indonesia but a good size SW swell guarantees rideable waves.

El mejor spot del Norte con opciones alrededor como Cap Blanc-Nez, Wissand y Wimeraux. No es Indonesia, pero un buen oleaje de Suroeste te garantiza olas.

15. La piscine d'Etampes

Vous vouliez connaître la limite entre une vqgue et une surface lisse : la voici ! Casques et pansements de rigueur.

You'd like to know the borderline between an even surface and a wave: here it is ! Don't forget your helmet and some plasters!

Querías conocer la frontera entre una ola y una superficie lisa : ya la tienes ! Cascos y vendajes imprescindibles !

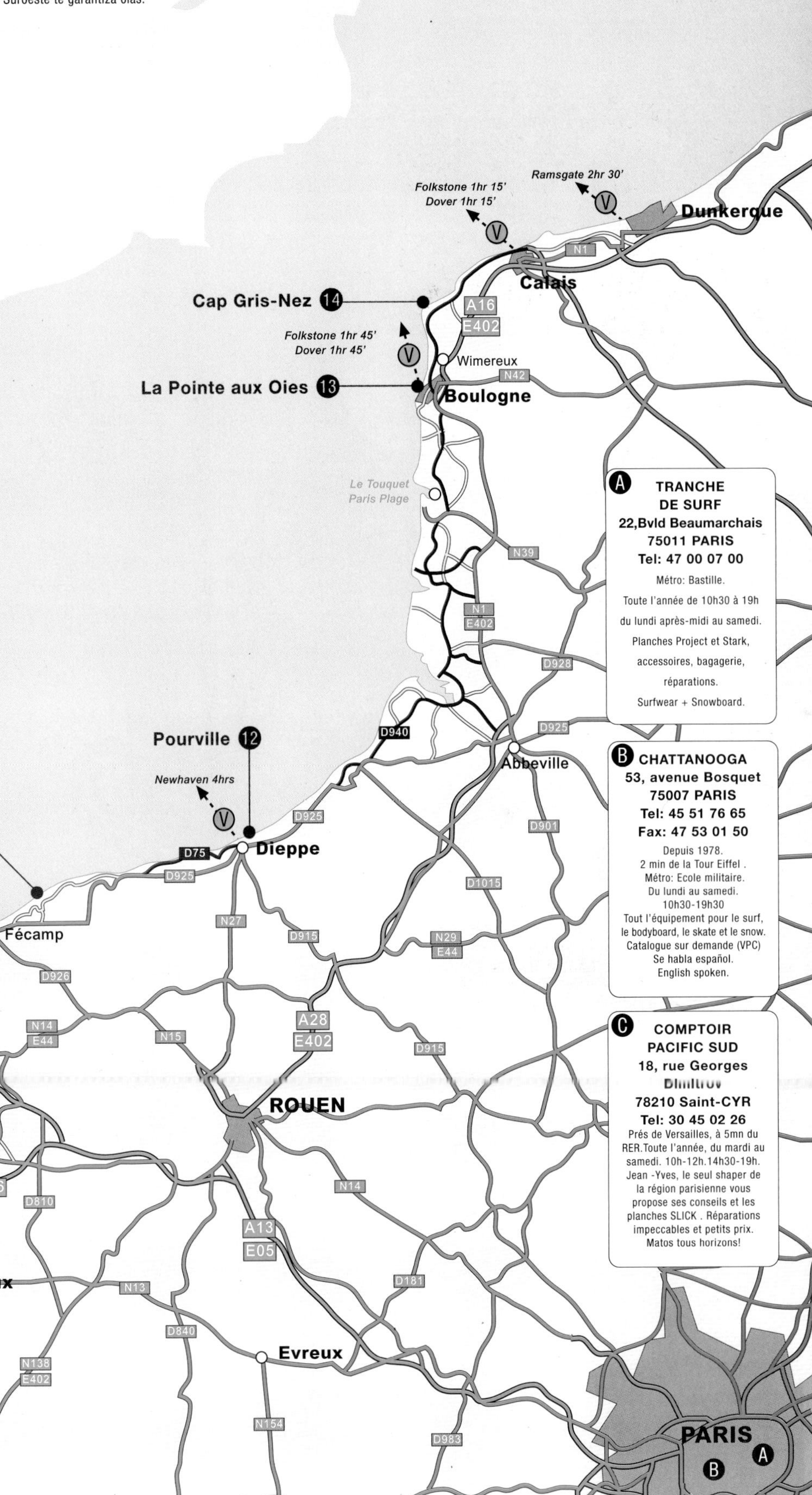

MEUH!...
kandibeach
kb.
découvrez la BRETAGNE et son folklore...

Photo: Serge Morin

bretagne

Photo: Serge Morin

Jesus est un Surfer - Photo: Serge Morin

"...Si c'est trop gros et que vous en vouliez plus, allez voir du coté du Cap de la Chèvre. guns et grand leash obligatoire..."

Cap de la Chevre - Photo: Serge Morin

La Bretagne a une place à part dans le coeur de beaucoup de surfers qui la connaissent, qui dépasse le cadre de ses vagues: une atmosphère unique issue de ses côtes déchiquetées (1200kms), de son héritage celtique (dolmens, tumulus, menhirs), de ses gens courageux (grands voyageurs, marins insatiables) et chaleureux (fest-noz, tavernes) et de son identité originale (langue bretonne, crêperies, patisserie, cidre. Arrosée certes mais moins que le Pays Basque par exemple, elle offre des possibilités multiples en fonction de la houle et des vents. où le surfer averti peut quasiment surfer tous les jours s'il est prêt à tailler la route . La fréquence des coups de vents en fait aussi une terre de prédilection pour les windsurfers surtout dans la partie nord où restent encore des spots vierges qui n'attendent que vous .

Brittany has a special place in the heart of most surfers who've visited there, disproportionate to the quality of the surf: a unique atmosphere a result of 800 miles of rugged coastline, its Celtic heritage (dolmens, tumulus, menhirs), its ancestral legends (King Arthur, the Korrigans), its courageous people (great travellers, intrepid sailors), hearty local bars (fest-noz) and original identity (vernacular, pancakes, sweats and cider). Tides of up to forty feet have been measured on the Nth coast, and its rugged cliffs, islands, rocks and winds give a strong feel to the surroundings, reflected in many place names e.g. Baie des Trepasses (Bay of the Dead), Fromveur (The Channel of Great Fear). For sure it gets lots of rain (though less than the Basque country, for example), but one can take advantage of the varying orientation of the coastline, depending on swell and winds, and surf virtually every day. Virgin spots still wait to be discovered.

Bretaña deja un recuerdo especial en el corazón de todos los surfers que la han visitado. Desproporcionado a la calidad de su surf. Sus más de mil kms de accidentada costa producen una atmosfera única, sus orígenes célticos (dólmenes, túmulos, menhires), sus leyendas ancestrales (el rey Arturo, los Korrigans), sus valientes habitantes (navegantes intrÈpidos y grandes viajeros), su hospitalidad y su original identidad vern·cula (sidra y otros productos tradicionales) hacen que sea un lugar distinto. Mareas de m·s de doce metros se han medido en su costa Norte y sus impresionantes acantilados, islas, parajes rocosos y fuertes vientos producen una sensación poderosa que de refleja en sus topónimos: Bahia de los Muertos, Estrecho del Miedo... Aún siendo una región lluviosa, lo es menos que el País Vasco, por ejemplo, y su perfil litoral permite surfear casi a diario en función de la dirección del viento y del mar. Aún permanecen spots vírgenes por explorar.

Bretagne Nord

Joel H.

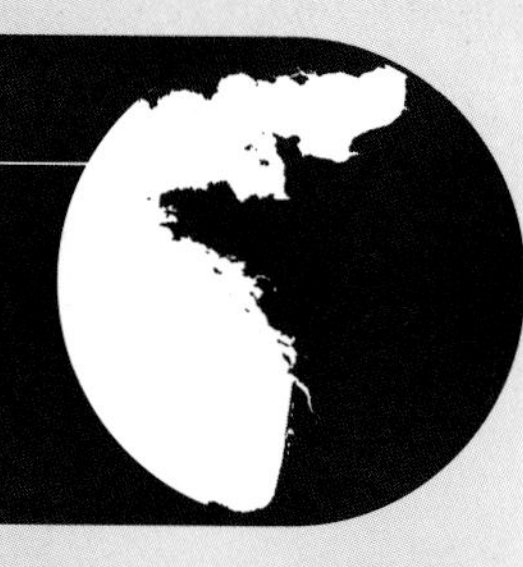

1. Baie de Douarnenez

"Pors ar Vag" bon beach break pour les débutants et par vents d'ouest. "Le Riz" encore plus mou que le premier, mais des falaises la protegent des vents de sud ouest. Avant d'arriver à Douarnenez."Pointe de Leydé" ou "Roches Blanches" dues à la couleur des rochers qui embrasseront votre planche au take off raté. Très belle gauche qui pète à raz la callaisse. Nécessite une très grosse houle d'ouest, idéal par tempêtes de sud-ouest. Dans Douarnenez prendre les Sables-Blancs et suivre la côte sur 500m. Attention aux locaux.

"Pors ar Vag" good beach break for beginners . Follow signs for Plomodiern. "Le Riz" is more mellow and protected from stormy SW winds by high cliffs. "Pointe de Leydé" or "Roches Blanches" is a very good left. If you miss the take off, your board will kiss the big rock. Needs a big swell; perfect in a SW storm. In Douarnenez take the road for Les Sables Blancs and follow the coast for 500m. Respect the locals!

"Pors ar Vag" : buena ola de arena para principiantes. Ir hasta Plomodiern. "Le Ritz" es aun mas flojo pero es protegido de los vientos de Suroeste por los acantilados. "Pointe de Leydé" o "Roches Blanches : buena izquierda. Si fallas el take off, tu tabla besa ̈rá las rocas ! Necesita un oleaje muy importante, perfecto con una tormenta de Suroeste. En Douarnenez, toma por Les Sables Blancs y sigue la costa durante 500 metros. Respecta a los locales.

2. La Palue

Spot le plus consistent et le plus populaire de la presqu'ile de Crozon. Marche mieux à marée haute et Losmach' à marée basse tient la houle jusqu'a 3m. Par tempêtes les vagues par dessus le "Guéneron". Si c'est trop gros et que vous en vouliez plus, allez voir du coté du cap de la Chèvre, guns et grand leash obligatoire. Les orques sont fréquents, attention. Le soir rendez-vous à Morgat au "ti ar pesketer" puis au "keep cool". Prendre Crozon, Morgat puis la Palue.

The most consistent and popular of the spots on the Crozon peninsular. Works better at high tide and at low tide check 'Losmach', rideable up to 3m. If it's big and you want more, check out "Cap de la Chevre". Guns and long legrope necessary. Dolphins are frequent visitors. At night go to Morgat. There are a couple of bars..."Ti ar Pesketer" and later go on to "Keep Cool".

El spot más consistente y popular de la península de Crozon. Funciona mejor en marea alta y "Losmach" en marea baja aguanta hasta 3 metros. Si quieres más grande aún, vete a ver al Cap de la Chèvre : Guns y cordones grandes necesarios. Delfines pueden visitarte. De noche, varios bares en Morgat como el "Ti ar Pesketer", y después el "Keep Cool".

La Palue - *Photo: Serge Morin*

3. Pointe De Dinan

Très panoramique, belle droite sur du reef, par bonnes conditions, surfable sur 200 m quand c'est petit on fait du slalom entre les rochers. La gauche plus facile, casse sur du sable à marée haute; spot protégé des vents de nord. Si vous aimez le sable allez voir "Goulien" ou "Kerloch'", peut réserver des surprises.

Very scenic, good right on the reef. With good conditions you can ride for 200 m; when it's small you do some slalom betwen the rocks. Protected against N winds. If you like beach breaks go see "Goulien" or "Kerloch". You can get a good surprise.

Muy pintoresco, buena derecha sobre las rocas. Con buenas condiciones, surfeable 200 metros. Con pequeñas olas, haz gambetas entre las rocas. Spot protegido de los vientos de Norte. Si prefieres la arena, puedes tener buenas sorpresas en "Goulien" o en "Kerloch".

4. Pointe Du Toulinguet

Beach break creux exposé plein ouest, la houle et la foule y sont toujours plus petites qu'a "la Palue", attention aux courants. Prendre Camaret puis la pointe du Toulinguet.

Hollow beach break exposed to the west. The swell and the crowds are less than at "La Palue". Be carefull of the rip.

Ola de arena hueca expuesta al Oeste. Menos oleaje y gente que en "La Palue". Cuidado con las corrientes.

5. Le Petit Minou

Beach break creux, ne marche qu'à marée basse. Body-boards et grommets vous feront regretter de vous y être attardé . Allez plutôt voir "deolen", "talbosse" ou "le trez-hir", tous ces spots sont protégés des vents de N et NO.

Hollow beach break, working only at low tide. Body boarders and grommets in your face. It's better to go surf "Deolen", "Talbosse" or "le Trez-Hir". These three spots are also protected from N winds.

Unicamente en marea baja, ola de arena hueca con muchos bodyboarders y grommets. Es mejor ir a "Deolen", "Talbosse" o "Le Trez-H–ir" que quedan protegidos de los vientos de Norte y de Noroeste.

Le Petit Minou - *Photo: Serge Morin*

6. Blancs-Sablons

Beach break mou qui ferme, pour debutants. Prendre le Conquet.

Sloppy beach break which closes-out easily. Good for beginners. Take the road for Le Conquet.

Olas de arena flojas que cierran fácilmente. Para principiantes. Pasar por Le Conquet.

7. Le Gouerou

Vague trés creuse et courte près du bord. Prendre Lampaul-Plouarzel.

Short, hollow wave, breaking close to the shoreline. Follow signs for Lampaul-Plouarzel.

Orillera muy hueca y corta. Pasar por Lampaul-Plouarzel.

8. Penfoul

Trés mou, aller plutôt chercher les reefs secrets"La Chapelle", "Le Triangle". Prendre Ploudalmézeau puis Penfoul.

A pretty sloppy spot. It's better to find the secret reefs "La Chapelle" & "Le Triangle". Go to Ploudalmézeau and follow signs for Penfoul.

Muy flojo. Busca mejor los secret spots "La Chapelle", "Le Triangle". Tomar por Ploudalmézeau hasta Penfoul.

9. Le Dossen

Un paradis de Winsurfer; tres mou et venté pour les surfers, aller plutôt a la Mauvaise Gréve (reef populaire) ou si vous aimez le surf hard core, allez a L'Ile de Sieck, droite puissante et creuse sur un reef craignos.Entre Le Dossen et Penfoul, une des regions les plus riches de reefs, les surfers qui connaissent sont avares d'indications.

Winsurfers paradise; very sloppy and exposed to the wind. It's better to surf at "La Mauvaise Greve" (a popular reef), or if you like hard core waves, go to "L'Ile de Sieck", a hollow and powerful right breaking on a shallow reef. Betwen Le Dossen and Penfoul you'll find one of richest areas of reefbreaks in Brittany. Surfers who know won't speak too much.

El paraíso de los windsurfers ; muy flojo y con mucho viento. Ir mejor a "La Mauvaise Grêve" (muy popular) o si te gusta el surf hard core, vete a "L'Ile de Sieck", una derecha potente y hueca que rompe sobre rocas peligrosas. Entre Le Dossen y Penfoul, encontrarás la zona más rica en olas de rocas de Bretaña. Los locales no te ayudarán a localizarlas.

10. Primel-Tregastel

Comme dans toute cette partie nord de la Bretagne, ça rentre rarement mais dès fois que vous soyez là au bon moment. Si la marée est basse, allez zoner du côté de St-Jean du doigt.

Not much happens in this part of Brittany, but if you are here at the right time; at low tide, look around the area of St-Jean du doigt.

En toda la parte norte de Bretaña, el oleaje entra muy raramente, pero por si acaso... vete a ver a los alrededores de Saint-Jean-Du-Doigt en marea baja.

11. Beg Leguer

Littéralement "embouchure de la Leguer". Consistent pour la région.

Litteraly means "mouth of the Leguer". Consistent for the région.

Traducción : desembocadura del Legueĩr. Consistente para la zona.

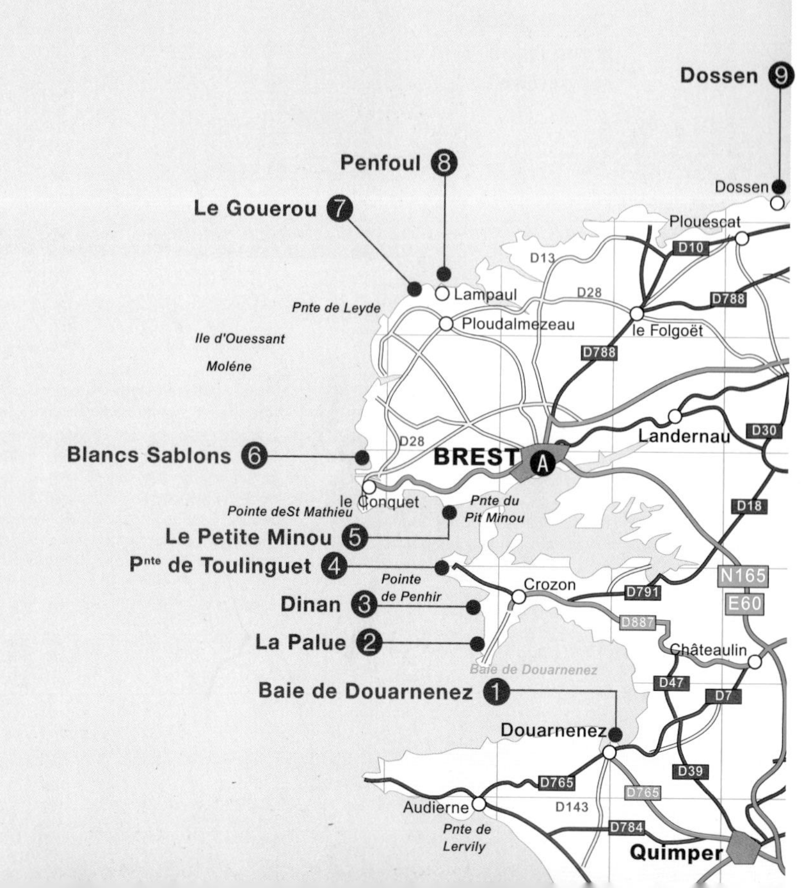

12. Locquirec

Une des meilleures places en Bretagne pour passer l'hiver. Les locaux y sont encore sympas. Un paquet de spots protégé des tempêtes de sud-ouest, 'Pors Ar Villec' le plus consistent 'Poul Rodou', 'Moulin La Rive'. Prendre morlaix puis Locquirec .

One of the best places to spend the winter in Brittany. The locals are cool and there are a couple of good spots protected from SW storms: "Pors Ar Villec" (the most consistent), "Poul Rodou" & "Moulin La Rive". Take the road for Morlaix and follow the signs for Locquirec.

Uno de los mejores lugares para pasar el invierno en Bretaña. Los locales son simpáticos y unos spots quedan bien protegidos de las tormentas de Suroeste : "PORS AR VILLEC" (el mas consistente), "POUL RODOU" y "MOULIN LA RIVE". Tomar por Morlaix hasta Locquirec.

Photo: Serge Morin

13. Tregastel Plage

Entre la côte et l'île deTomé, quelques vagues de temps en temps.

Between the coast and Tomé island, a few waves once in a while.

Entre la costa y la isla de Tomé, unas olas de vez en cuando.

14. Pleherel

3 kms à l'ouest de la plage du Vieux-Port. Poussez jusqu'au Cap Fréhel et ses falaises colorées. Point de vue pour mater Plevenon et le reste aussi.

3 kms west of the Vieux-Port beach. Drive up to Cap Fréhel to take a look at its coloured cliffs. Perfect viewpoint to check the surf at Plevenon and around.

3 kilómetros al Oeste de la playa del Vieux-Port. Conducir hasta el Cap Fréhel y sus acantilados colorados. Punto de vista perfecto para buscar las olas en Plevenon y sus alrededores.

15. La Garde-Guerin

Direction St-Lunaire et la plage de Longchamps, on trouve le spot de surf du coin: des vagues assez creuses pour glisseurs en tous genres.

Heading towards St-Lunaire and Longchamps beach, you"ll find one of the only real surfspot around. Fairly hollow waves for any wave users.

Tiene que ir por St-Lunaire and la playa de Longchamps para encontrar el mejor spot alrededor. Olas son bastante huecas com todos tipos de corredores das olas.

16. La Plage du Sillon

Entre Paramé et St-Malo, on trouve quelques vagues le long du remblai, le plus souvent par tempête de Sud-Ouest.

Between Paramé and St-Malo break mushy waves close yo the promenade, more often with a SW storm.

Entre Paramé y St-Malo, se encuentran algunas olas por la pared de rocas, a menudo con ventos fuertes de SO.

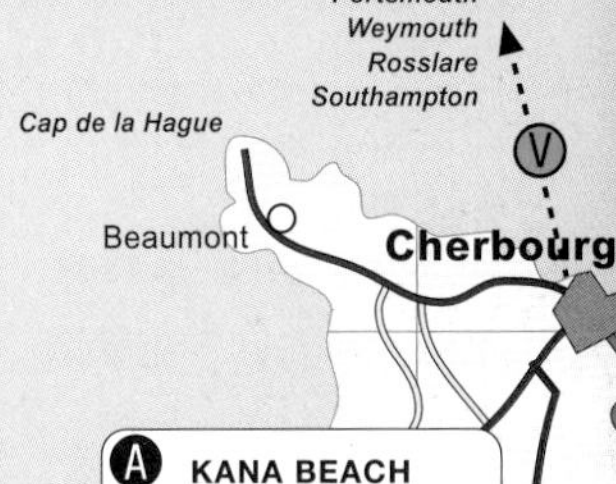

A KANA BEACH
10,Place de la Liberté, 29000 BREST
Tel: 98 43 31 64
Fax:98 48 92 44
Centre ville, toute l'année, tous les jours sauf lundi. 10h-12h.14h-19h
Longboards Superfrog et shortboard brésiliens + freezing hot + matos skate et accessoires. Toute la collection Kana Beach. Fluente anglishe !
Ocean Surf Report 36 68 1 360

B MAGIC SURF
Av du Sergent Maginot
35000 RENNES
Tel: 99 35 17 18
Fax: 99 35 09 10
Au bout des quais, dir. Sesson-Sévigné.Tous les jours sauf dimanche, 9h-12h/15h-19h
Le spécialiste des sports de glisse pour toute la Bretagne. Large choix d'accessoires. Réparation, dépôt-vente
Doors open for anyone.

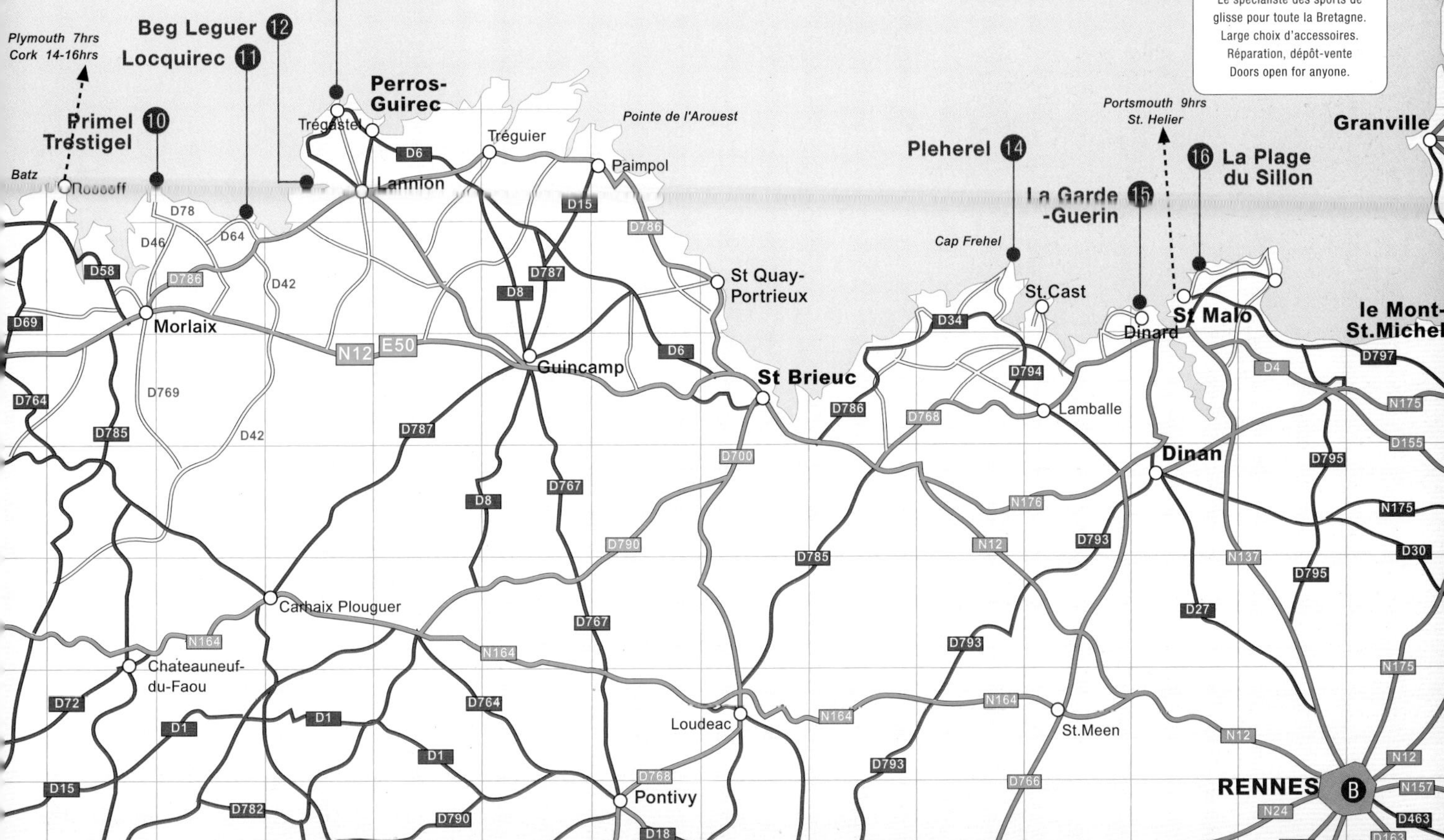

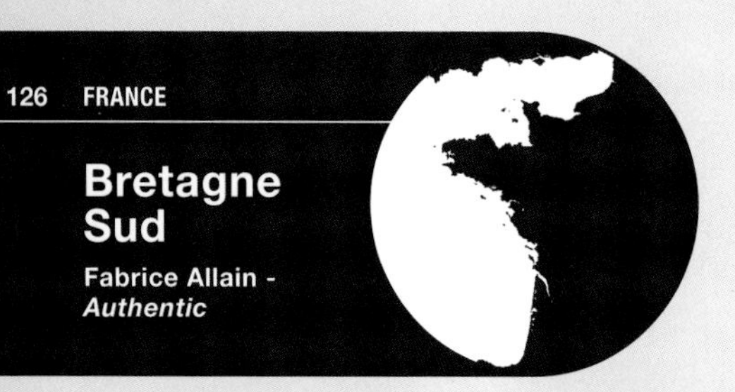

Bretagne Sud

Fabrice Allain - *Authentic*

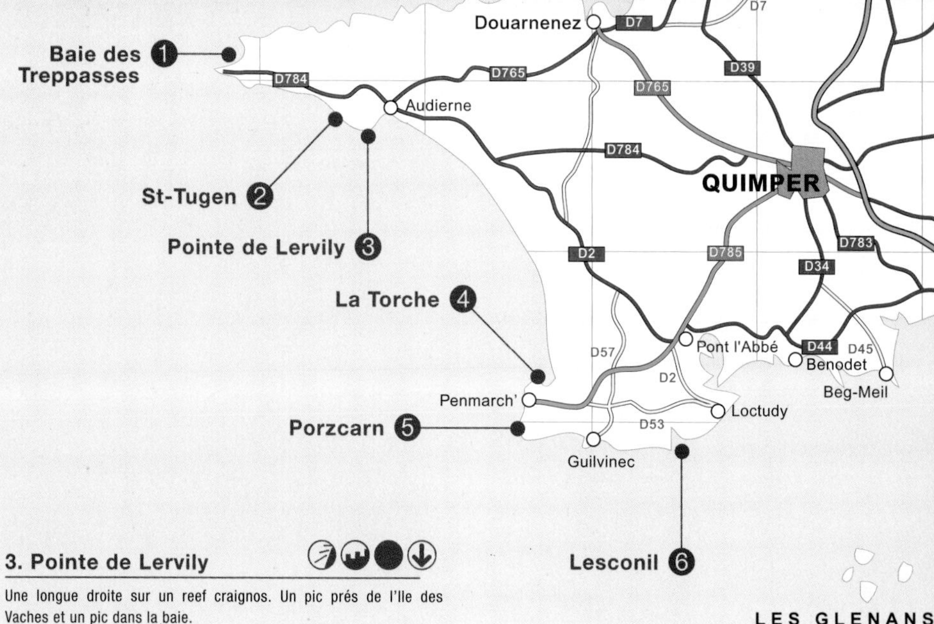

1. Baie des Trépasses

Avec de la chance vous en rencontrerez. Bon beach break, le vent de sud y tourne offshore dans la baie. Ne reçoit que les houles d'ouest et de nord ouest. Marche mieux à marée basse et avec de petites houles qui peuvent vous offrir de trés longs rides, c'est le spot le plus froid du Finistère. Si vous avez le temps, allez sur l'Ile de Sein, de bons reefs vous y attendent (prendre le bateau à Audierne)

(Bay of Death) The name says it all. Good beach break works in a West or North swell, better at low tide with a small swell. Some very long rides. The coldest spot on the Finistere. If you've got time, check out "Ile de Sein" where there's some good reefs (take the boat at Audierne).

(Bahía de los Muertos) Estás advertido ! Buena ola de arena. Funciona con oleajes de Oeste a Norte, mejor en marea baja con pequeños oleajes que ofrecen largos recorridos. El spot mas frío en el Finistère. Si tienes tiempo, toma el barco en Audierne para buenas olas de rocas sobre la isla de Sein.

Baie des Treppasses - *Photo: Serge Morin*

2. Saint Tugen

(ou Anse de Cabestan) La perle du Cap Sizun, trés bon beach break, ne marche qu'à marée basse, à plus de 2m vous rentrez debout dans le tube. La plage est orientée plein sud. Prendre 'la Pointe du Raz' et tourner au niveau de Primelin à 'la Chapelle st Tugen'.

The pearl of Cap Sizun, a good south facing beach break, working only at low tide. If the wave is more than 2m...stand up barrels. Follow signs for 'la Pointe du Raz' and turn-off near Primelin at 'Chapelle St Tugen'.

La perla del Cap Sizun. Ola de arena muy buena que funciona únicamente en marea baja. Más de 2 metros, tubo garantizado. Tomar "La Pointe du Raz" y girar al nivel de Primelin hacia "La Chapelle Saint Tugen".

3. Pointe de Lervily

Une longue droite sur un reef craignos. Un pic prés de l'Ile des Vaches et un pic dans la baie.

A long right breaking on a shallow reef. A peak close to the Island of Cows and another peak in the bay.

Una derecha larga sobre rocas peligrosas. Un pico cerca de "l'Ile des Vaches", otro en la bahía.

4. La Torche

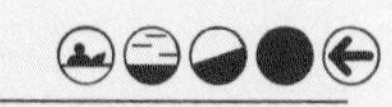

Beach-break trés populaire, éviter les week-ends. Trés belle droite à la Pointe, beaucoup de monde aussi. Si vous aimez le soul surfing remontez la plage jusqu'a Tronoên, Penhors ou Guendrez des vagues de qualité vous y attendent.

Very popular beach break, crowded at weekends. Very good right on the point, a lot of people also. In a SW wind go to Pors Carn (to the left). If you like the soul surfing, go up the beach to "Tronoen", "Penhors" ou "Guendrez". You'll find some good quality waves.

Ola de arena con demasiada gente durante los fines de semana. Bonita derecha en la punta. Si te gusta el "soul surfing", sube la playa hasta "Tronoen", "Penhors" o "Guendrez" para correr olas de buena calidad.

La Torche - *Photo: Serge Morin*

5. Porzcarn

Une droite à marée basse, une érosion rapide sur la dune. Au sud, on trouve les Etocs, des reefs parfaits au large pour les couillus du gros surf, jusqu'à 6 m.

Low tide right with dune erosion. South are les Etocs, perfect offshore big wave reefs for daredevils. 8-18ft.

Derecha en marea baja con la erosión de la duna. Al Sur, Les Etocs : ola perfecta con un viento offshore, sobre las rocas, para los ariesgados. (8-18ft).

Porzcarn - *Photo: erge Morin*

6. Lesconil

Excellent conditions for windsurfing between Benodet and Beg Meil. Occasional waves with big SW, W swells. The reef favours lefts on an incoming low to mid-tide close to the harbour.

Excellent conditions for windsurfing between Benodet and Beg Meil. Occasional waves with big SW, W swells. The reef favours lefts on an incoming low to mid-tide close to the harbour.

Condiciones excelentes para los windsurfers entre Benodet y Beg Meil. Algunas olas con oleaje muy consistente de Suroeste y Oeste. Izquierdas sobre todo en marea baja a media, cerca del puerto.

7. Guidel

PLAGES

Des vagues de sable et de rochers. Quelques bons bancs, la plage du Loch étant la plus surfée.

Reef and beach breaks. A few good banks, the plage of Loch being the most popular waves.

Olas de arena y arrecife. La Playa de Loch es mas popular.

Ronan Chatain, La Torche - *Photo: Serge Morin*

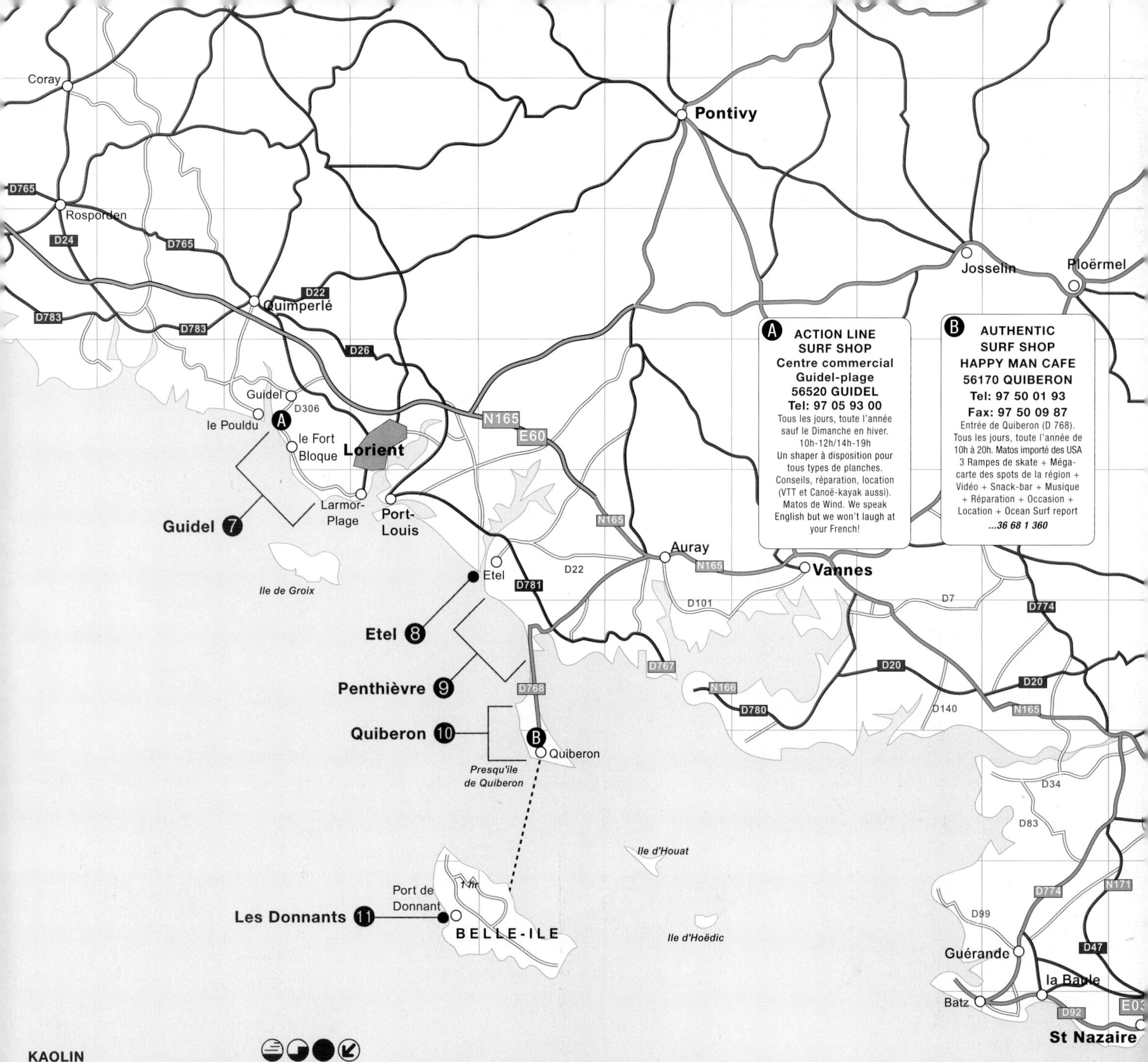

KAOLIN

Des droites rapides et tubulaires sur peu d'eau . Rare mais parfait !

Tubular and fast rights on a shallow bottom. Rare but perfect!

Derechas rapidas con tubazos sobre poco de agua. Raro pero perfecto!

P^NTE DU COUREGAN

Une vague très longue à environ 20 mns de rame, peut valoir l'effort.

A very long wave about 20min paddle off-shore. Can be great!

Una ola muy longa que se corre a 20 minutos afuera. Vale la pena.

8. Etel

Ressemble souvent à une immonde barre qui ferme mais parfois quand le vent de terre et les courants infernaux permettent de creuser la vague, les sections tubulaires sont exploitables: le turbo est de rigueur!

Often looks like an infamous close-out but sometimes when off-shore winds and vicious currents hollow the wave, some tubular sections are makable : better be fast !

Muy a menudo barras que cierran, pero, a veces, el viento offshore y la corriente ahuecan la ola y permiten surfear, siendo super rápido !

9. Penthièvre

Quand la marée est haute à Quiberon, cette zone peut marcher tout comme Kirminhy, Sainte-Barbe ou Le Fozo.

When the tide is high in Quiberon, this area might work together with other spots like Kirminhy, Sainte-Barbe or Le Fozo.

Cuando la marea esta alta en Quiberon, esta zona puede fonctionnar como Kirminhy, Sainte-Barbe or le Fozo.

10. Quiberon

La péninsule concentre au nord de la Côte Sauvage certains des meilleurs spots de Bretagne avec une consistence appréciable. Port-Blanc et Port-Rhu sont deux cales avec 2 gauches assez puissantes. Plus facile, la longue plage de Port-Bara parfois sature de monde ou ferme. D'autres spots plus au sud comme le Château.

The Peninsula concentrates north of the Côte Sauvage amongst the best spots in Brittany, whose consistency is kind of a proof of waves on a trip. Port-Blanc, Port-Rhu are two creeks with two powerful lefts. Easier is Port-Bara large beach that sometimes gets really crowded or close-outs. When the tide goes in, head north of Penthièvre.

La península concentra al norte de la Côte Sauvage unos de los mejores spots en Bretaña, bien consistentes. "Port-Blanc" y "Port-Rhu son dos diques con 2 izquierdas bastante potentes. Más facíl, en la larga playa de "Port Bara", a veces cierra la ola o hay demasiada gente. Cuando sube la marea, ir al norte de Penthièvre.

11. Les Donnants

Belle-ile mérite le détour car recèle certainement d'autres vaguesque celle du port des Donnants, qu'on soupçonne de marcher souvent.

Belle-ile deserves some kind of expedition since it certainly hides other waves. Les Donnants may be the most consistent one though.

'Belle Ile" merece la pena y ciertamente, tiene otras olas que las del puerto, que deben funcionar a menudo.

Port Bara, Quiberon - *Photo: Marc Fenies*

BODY GLOVE

Sables d'Olonne - *Photo: Thierry Organoff*

"Choper la 'Sauze' quand ça marche, ça veut dire des sections tubulaires et d'excellentes vagues en tous cas"

La Sauzaie - *Photo: Marc Féniès*

côte de lumière

La Sauzaie - *Photo: Thierry Organoff*

Partagée entre la Vendée et des Charentes, cette côte offre sur 600 kms le meilleur ensoleillement de la côte atlantique surtout au sud. Compromis entre les dunes du sud-Ouest et les criques de la Bretagne, cette côte offre un potentiel de vagues encore méconnu, certes moins exposé que le sud-ouest avec un plateau continental plus étendu mais qui permet de surfer des reefs de qualité notamment pendant les nombreuses tempêtes tout en ayant de bons beach-breaks suffisamment exposés pour les houles d'été. Les inconditionnels des îles trouveront Ré et Oléron pour s'évader . Malgré une desserte routière encore insuffisante et des paysages qui manquent parfois de relief, on ne peut que recommander cette zone qui possède peut-être la meilleure palette de vagues en France.

Lumière means light and the 400-mile Cote de Lumiere (including parts of the departments of Vendée and Charentes) recieves the most sunlight on the Atlantic coast, especially in the south. It's an interesting mix of Aquitaine's dunes and Brittany's creeks, with a great array of underrated waves. Despite a less convenient swell exposure than SW France and a somewhat extended continental shelf, there are many quality reefs which go off in big swells, as well as good beaches for summer swells. Island lovers can drive to Ré or Oléron for a getaway and though the road network is sometimes slow and the landscape kind of flat, we highly recommend this area and its cache of possibly the widest variety of waves in the country.

Los 600 kms de la Costa de la Luz (incluyendo parte de los departamentos de Vendee y Charantes) reciben el mayor número de horas de luz de la costa Atlántica, especialmente en su parte sur. Es una mezcla interesante de las dunas aquitanas y los arroyuelos bretones, con una gran gama del olas subestimadas. Pese a tener una peor orientación a las marejadas que el suroeste francés junto con una plataforma continental más extensa, existen muchos arrecifes de calidad que funcionan con grandes marejadas, así como buenas playas para el verano. Los amantes de las islas pueden hacer una excursión conduciendo a Ré o a Oléron, y pese a que la red de carreteras no permite desplazamientos rápidos y el paisaje es bastante plano, es una zona recomendable por ser posiblemente la de mayor variedad de olas del paìs.

Sauveterre - *Photo: Marc Fenies*

Photo: Marc Fenies

"... vous n'avez plus qu'à choisir entre le Pic du large et ou le PIc du Phoque..."

Côte de Lumière

Jean-Pierre
'Pitou' Vernhes

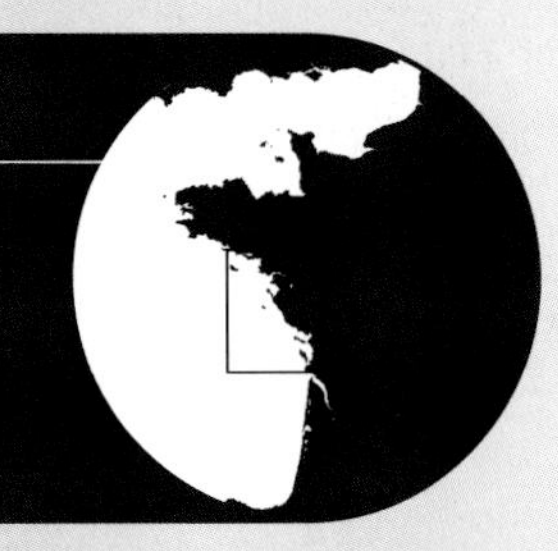

1. Batz/Mer

La Govelle est le rendez-vous privilégié des surfers de la Baule quand ça veut bien rentrer. Rien d'extraordinaire mais y'a de quoi faire surtout sur la droite.

La Govelle is the most famous cross-roads of La Baule surfers when there is a swell. Nothing stupendous but there can be good rides especially on the right.

La Govelle es la cita más famosa entre los surfistas de La Baule cuando hay oleaje. Nada de muy especial, pero muy correcto, sobre todo la derecha.

2. Saint-Marc

La petite plage de la Courance, parfois , avec beaucoup de houle s'agite et crache quelques vagues moyennes. A marée haute, de l'autre côté du cap à Ste-Marguerite, la droite du Grand Trait peut se réveiller. Ouvrez les yeux, y'a du rocher.

The little beach of La Courance gets a few average waves with much swell . At higher tides, on the other side is Ste-Marguerite, the Grand Trait right wakes up sometimes. Open your eyes, there is rock underneath.

La playita de La Courance tiene a veces, con mucho oleaje, unas olas regulares. En marea alta, por el otro lado del cabo en Sainte-Marguerite, la derecha del Grand-Trait puede funcionar. Ojo con las rocas escondidas !

3. Préfaille

Entre la Pointe St-Gildas et Préfaille, les surfers nantais écument les reefs et trouvent. A vos jumelles ! Dernière option au sud de la Loire: les beach-breaks des Rochelets ou de l'Ermitage.

Between the Pointe St-Gildas and Préfaille, surfers from Nantes have been roaming the reefs and found something. Get a pair of binoculars! Last option south of La Loire: Rochelets and Ermitage beach-breaks.

Entre la punta Saint-Gildas y Préfaille, los surfistas de Nantes buscan... y encuentran olas. No te olvides de tus gemelos ! Ultima opción al sur de la Loire : los spots de arena de Rochelets e Ermitage.

4. Saint-Gilles Croix-de-Vie

...Croix de Bois, Croix de fer, si c'est puissant , je vais en enfer ! Plutôt mou donc mais ne sature pratiquement jamais. Le remblai fait du back-wash à marée haute mais peut garantir un public attentif pour les frimeurs. Plus c'est gros, plus il faut se rapprocher de la jetée. Au nord, le plateau continental remonte et filtre mêmes les houles les plus puissantes.

Rather mushy beach-break that rarely closes out. The concrete promenade creates back-wash at high tide and guaranties a curious crowd for those who want to show off. When it gets bigger,it's more protected closer to the jetty. To the north, the continental shelf gets shallower and therefore filters even the most powerful swells.

Más bien flojo pero casi nunca cierra. El terraplén de cemento crea back-wash en marea alta pero te asegura un público atentivo. Cuanta más grande la ola, tanta mas cerca de la escollera ! Al norte subeå la meseta continental que filtra hasta el oleaje más potente.

5. La Sauzaie

La corniche offre une vue imprenable à marée basse sur cette dalle rocheuse recouverte d'algues. Choper la "Sauze" quand ça marche (assez souvent d'ailleurs), ça veut dire des sections tubulaires et d'excellentes vagues en tous cas. Supporte mal le vent et plus de trente surfers ou assimilés. N'oubliez pas la droite de Killer juste à côté.

The seaside road delivers an awesome view at low tide of this sea-weed covered reef. A classic "Sauze, is quite frequent and means tubular sections and brilliant waves. Holds a bit of wind and more than 30 surfers. Don't forget the Killer's right immediately to the N.

La cornisa ofrece una vista panorámica en marea baja sobre esta baldosa rocosa cubierta de algas. Correr la "Sauze" cuando funciona (bastante a menudo) significa tubos y excelentes olas. No soporta el viento y más de 30 surfistas. No te olvides de la derecha del Killer justo al norte.

La Sauzaie - *Photo: Thierry Organoff*

6. Les Dunes

Beach-break plutôt mou, qui a tendance à fermer au-dessus de 2 mètres. De bons murs pour le longboard. Bon spot de windsurf.

Somewhat mellow beach-break, that tends to close-out over 6'. Good walls for longboarding. Good wave-jumping spot.

Ola de arena, floja. Cierra con más de 2 metros. Buenas paredes para el longboard. Buen spot de surf a vela.

7. Sauveterre

Au beau milieu de la forêt d'Olonne, se trouvent pas moins de deux bons reefs et un beach-break bien exposé. Avec une houle moyenne et bien rangée, vous n'avez plus qu'à choisir entre le Pic du large et ou le PIc du Phoque: C'est long et c'est bon ! Sinon, le beach-break marche bien jusqu'au block-haus.

In the heart of the Olonne woods, are two good reefs and a well-exposed beach-break. With an average and clean swell, you just have to choose between Pic du Large and Pic du Phoque: long and easy rides!

En medio del bosque de Olonne, 2 olas de rocas y 1 de arena bien expuesta. Con oleaje mediano y ordenado, elige entre el pico de alta mar y el pico de la foca : largo y bueno ! La ola de arena funciona bien hasta el "block-haus".

Sauveterre - *Photo: Marc Fenies*

8. Les Sables d'Olonne

La Baie des Sables peut se surfer un peut partout mais ça ferme souvent. Meilleures ouvertures à Tanchet (pointe sud) et surtout à L'Aubraie, bien caché à la Chaume au Nord, entre cimetière et antenne télécom. Il faut marcher quelques minutes mais on ne le regrette pas tout le temps.

The Bay of Les Sables can be surfed pretty much everywhere but it often closes out. Best shaped waves can be found at Tanchet (south point) and especially at l'Aubraie, well hidden in La Chaume to the north, between a cemetary and a big transmitor. There is a bit of a walk but you won't often regret it.

La Bahía de Les Sables puede ser surfeada desde cualquier lugar pero cierra a menudo. Abre más en "Tanchet" (punta sur) y sobre todo en "La Chaume" al Norte, entre el cem‰enterio y la antena de telecomunicaciones. Hay que caminar un poco pero puede valer la pena.

9. Saint-Nicolas

Quelques secret spots en cas de grosse houle jalonnent la côte jusqu'aux Sables. La seule référence connue: les gauches de la plage de la Mine prés du Parc de la Grange. A vous de trouver les autres !

A few secret spots in case of a big storm scattered up to Les Sables . The only reference known : the lefts of Plage de la Mine close to Park de la Grange. You have to find the other ones!

Unos secret spots en caso de fuerte oleaje entre Saint-Nicolas y Les Sables. La única referencia conocida : las izquierdas de la playa de "la Mine" al lado del "Parc de la Grange". Busca las otras !

10. Longeville

Plusieurs plages qui rappellent la Côte d'Argent. Les vagues aussi d'ailleurs puisque creuses et puissantes. Trois choix: Les Conches au centre qui est le lieu de ralliement, Bud-Bud (mi-marée) au Nord ou La Terrière au Sud avec quelques cailloux.

Several beaches similar to the Côte d'Argent. So are the waves with definite power and hollowness. Three choices: Les Conches in the middle where most people meet, Bud-Bud (mid-tide) to the north and La Terrière to the South with a few rocks.

Varias playas que parecen a las de "La Côte d'Argent", así como las olas, huecas y potentes. 3 elecciones : "Les Conches" al centro que es el punto de reunión, "Bud-Bud"(media marea) al Norte o "La Terrière" al sur con unas rocas.

11. La Tranche/Mer

Lieu de repli pour les tempêtes, la jetée ou l'Embarcadère de la Tranche donne des droites molles idéales pour les malibus.Une option plus consistente: Le phare du Groin.

Storm option. The jetty of La Tranche named Embarcadère gives you mushy rights, best ridden with longboards. A more consistent option is the Groin lighthouse.

Mejor opción de tormenta, con derechas flojas, perfectas para los longboards. Otra opción : el faro del Groin.

12. Le Lizay

Puissant quand ça marche. Ca peut même bastonner sévère sur les rochers.

Powerful when on. It can be pretty severe bouncing on the rocks.

Potente cuando funciona. Muy espectacular cuando rompe sobre las rocas.

13. La Couarde/Mer

La vague qui marche le plus souvent sur Ré mais n'éxagérons rien , l'exposition est loin d'être idéale. Deux pics moyens de part et d'autre d'une jetée en bois devant le parking de La Pergola.

The wave that works most often on Ré island, but let's be honest, its exposition is not great. Two average peaks on both side of a wooden jetty in front of the Pergola parking.

La ola que más funciona sobre la Isla de Ré, pero no hay que exagerar, no tiene una exposición tan buena. Dos picos regulares en los dos lados de una escollera de madera frente al aparcamiento de La Pergola.

14. Chassiron

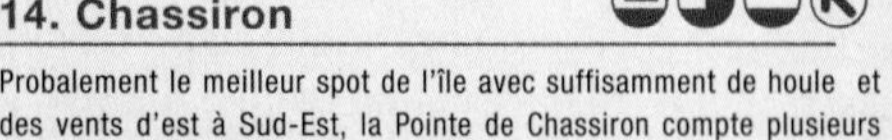

Probalement le meilleur spot de l'île avec suffisamment de houle et des vents d'est à Sud-Est, la Pointe de Chassiron compte plusieurs reefs. Attention aux cailloux donc et aux violents courants. En cas de grosse tempête, farfouillez vers St-Denis et la Pointe des Boulassiers, d'autres gauches peuvent vous attendre.

The Pointe de Chassiron has various reefs and is probably the best spot of the island when there is enough swell and SE winds. Beware of the rocks and rips. In case of a big storm, search towards St-Denis and the Pointe des Boulassiers, others lefts may a wait you.

Probablemente el mejor spot de la isla con suficiente oleaje y vientos de Este a Sureste, la punta de Chassiron cuenta con varias olas de rocas. Ojo : rocas y corrientes ! De tormenta, busca izquierdas hacia Saint-Denis y la "Pointe des Boulassiers".

15. Les Huttes

Souvent associé aux Trois Pierres, les Huttes est un shore-break assez massif, parfois tubulaire. Vous ne serez certainement pas seul à venir voir. Le spot se trouve en fait de l'autre côté des Huttes .

Often associated with Trois Pierres, les Huttes is quite a pounding shore-break, sometimes tubey. You probably won't be alone. The spot is actually located on the other side of les Huttes.

A menudo asociado con "Trois Pierres", "Les Huttes" es una orillera bastante masiva, a veces con tubo. Probablemente no vas a estar solo. El spot se ubica en realidad por el otro lado de "Les Huttes".

16. Les Alassins

Vert-Bois est le spot le plus consistant de l'île, le plus fréquenté aussi. Droites et gauches.

Vert-Bois is the most consistent spot of the island, the most surfed too. Pas mal de pics un peu partout. Heaps of peaks.

Vert-Bois es el spot más consistente y recorrido de la isla. Derechas y izquierdas.

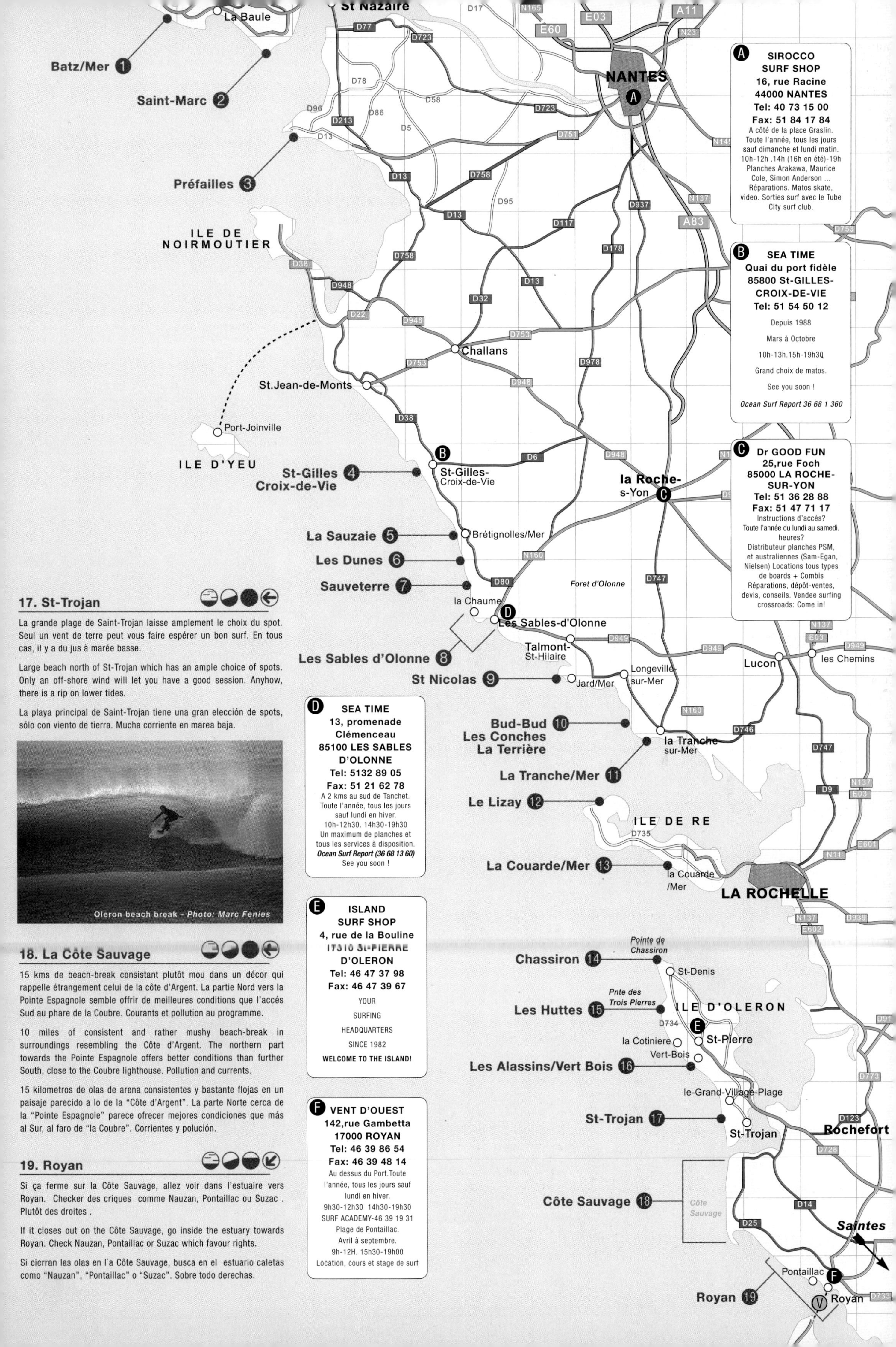

17. St-Trojan

La grande plage de Saint-Trojan laisse amplement le choix du spot. Seul un vent de terre peut vous faire espérer un bon surf. En tous cas, il y a du jus à marée basse.

Large beach north of St-Trojan which has an ample choice of spots. Only an off-shore wind will let you have a good session. Anyhow, there is a rip on lower tides.

La playa principal de Saint-Trojan tiene una gran elección de spots, sólo con viento de tierra. Mucha corriente en marea baja.

Oleron beach break - *Photo: Marc Fenies*

18. La Côte Sauvage

15 kms de beach-break consistant plutôt mou dans un décor qui rappelle étrangement celui de la côte d'Argent. La partie Nord vers la Pointe Espagnole semble offrir de meilleures conditions que l'accés Sud au phare de la Coubre. Courants et pollution au programme.

10 miles of consistent and rather mushy beach-break in surroundings resembling the Côte d'Argent. The northern part towards the Pointe Espagnole offers better conditions than further South, close to the Coubre lighthouse. Pollution and currents.

15 kilometros de olas de arena consistentes y bastante flojas en un paisaje parecido a lo de la "Côte d'Argent". La parte Norte cerca de la "Pointe Espagnole" parece ofrecer mejores condiciones que más al Sur, al faro de "la Coubre". Corrientes y polución.

19. Royan

Si ça ferme sur la Côte Sauvage, allez voir dans l'estuaire vers Royan. Checker des criques comme Nauzan, Pontaillac ou Suzac. Plutôt des droites.

If it closes out on the Côte Sauvage, go inside the estuary towards Royan. Check Nauzan, Pontaillac or Suzac which favour rights.

Si cierran las olas en la Côte Sauvage, busca en el estuario caletas como "Nauzan", "Pontaillac" o "Suzac". Sobre todo derechas.

A SIROCCO SURF SHOP
16, rue Racine
44000 NANTES
Tel: 40 73 15 00
Fax: 51 84 17 84
A côté de la place Graslin. Toute l'année, tous les jours sauf dimanche et lundi matin. 10h-12h .14h (16h en été)-19h Planches Arakawa, Maurice Cole, Simon Anderson ... Réparations. Matos skate, video. Sorties surf avec le Tube City surf club.

B SEA TIME
Quai du port fidèle
85800 St-GILLES-CROIX-DE-VIE
Tel: 51 54 50 12
Depuis 1988
Mars à Octobre
10h-13h.15h-19h3Q
Grand choix de matos.
See you soon !
Ocean Surf Report 36 68 1 360

C Dr GOOD FUN
25,rue Foch
85000 LA ROCHE-SUR-YON
Tel: 51 36 28 88
Fax: 51 47 71 17
Instructions d'accès? Toute l'année du lundi au samedi. heures? Distributeur planches PSM, et australiennes (Sam-Egan, Nielsen) Locations tous types de boards + Combis Réparations, dépôt-ventes, devis, conseils. Vendee surfing crossroads: Come in!

D SEA TIME
13, promenade Clémenceau
85100 LES SABLES D'OLONNE
Tel: 5132 89 05
Fax: 51 21 62 78
A 2 kms au sud de Tanchet. Toute l'année, tous les jours sauf lundi en hiver. 10h-12h30. 14h30-19h30 Un maximum de planches et tous les services à disposition.
Ocean Surf Report (36 68 13 60)
See you soon !

E ISLAND SURF SHOP
4, rue de la Bouline
17310 St-PIERRE D'OLERON
Tel: 46 47 37 98
Fax: 46 47 39 67
YOUR SURFING HEADQUARTERS
SINCE 1982
WELCOME TO THE ISLAND!

F VENT D'OUEST
142,rue Gambetta
17000 ROYAN
Tel: 46 39 86 54
Fax: 46 39 48 14
Au dessus du Port.Toute l'année, tous les jours sauf lundi en hiver.
9h30-12h30 14h30-19h30
SURF ACADEMY-46 39 19 31
Plage de Pontaillac.
Avril à septembre.
9h-12H. 15h30-19h00
Location, cours et stage de surf

côte d'argent

Photo: Peter Cade

Photo: C. Dimuille

Un cordon littoral parfaitement rectiligne exposé légèrement nord-ouest seulement interrompu par le Bassin dArcachon, le seul d'une guirlande d'étangs qui ne s'est pas encore refermé. Cette plage de 230 kms possède probablement le meilleur potentiel de bonnes vagues vierges entre Pâques et Toussaint. Une qualité de vague remarquable due à la formation de baïnes, des mini lagunes qui forment des bancs de sable en général meilleur de mi marée à marée haute. Compte tenu de marnages importants, la physionomie des vagues évolue à une vitesse parfois déroutante: un close-out immonde à midi peut devenir un pic parfait deux heures plus tard. Leur orientation favorise les droites bien que les gauches déferlant à contre-courant sont peut-être plus puissantes. Le chenal d'évacuation de l'eau n'est jamais très profond aussi les vagues au-dessus de 2m-2,5m auront tendance à fermer. Les baïnes sont rapidement défigurées par les tempêtes, il faut donc réexaminer les bancs après chaque hiver. Peu de spots de repli donc quand la mer est agitée: le nord de la Gironde, l'entrée du Bassin, Capbreton ou le Boucau sans garanties. Une population réduite à de petites villes côtières et une forêt de pins quasi-omniprésente rendent l'endroit merveilleusement sauvage sauf en été où les plages font le plein .Une destination d'été donc dont Lacanau et Hossegor sont les têtes d'affiches. Pour ceux que marcher dans le sable n'effraie pas...

The Silver Coast is an almost ruler straight, 160-mile beach with a slight NW exposure and between Easter and All Saint's Day has the best potential for good unridden barrels any where in Europe. The quality of waves is high due to the depth and funnel shape of the Bay of Biscay, and the "Baïne" (small lagoons) that shape good sand banks. The single significant interruption to the coast remains the Bassin of Arcachon, (the only one of a series of 20 lakes that flows into the sea), but many small rivers and stream mouths dot its length. Owing to the fact that offshores can change fast and tidal ranges can be large, waves evolve with incredible speed. Perfect spitting peaks can turn into shitty mush within two hours. Baïne orientation favours rights, however, the lefts being hollowed by fairly consistent N to S undertow, tend to be very hollow. Channels to get to the line-up rarely get deep (except for a few spots), so it tends to close-out over 8 foot and gets hard to surf. Good banks can get destroyed by winter storms and the main problem is the lack of shelter when the sea gets out-of-control. Only north Gironde, The Arachon Basin entrance, Hossegor (Le Nord), Capbreton or Boucau might be surfable with a low below 960mb. The local population is sparsely divided in villages amongst zillions of pine-trees. It's clearly wild and undeveloped but in summer the beaches fill up with Europeans of all nationalities. No doubt, it's one of the best summer trips in Europe with boardies worn for four months a year in consistent surf. Lacanau and Hossegor are the most famous; for those prepared to walk deep into the sandy forests...

Esta costa parece trazada con regla, más de 200 kms de playa ligeramente orientados al Noroeste. De Semana Santa al día de Todos los Santos es un litoral solitario con el mayor potencial tubero de toda Europa, la calidad de las olas es alta debido a la profundidad y forma de embudo del Golfo de Vizcaya. Los iBainesi, pequeños lagunas litorales proporcionan buenas barras arenosas. La única interrupción de importancia en el perfil costero está en Arcachon donde un lago el único, de un grupo de 20, desagua en el Océano; aunque un montón de reios y arroyos intercalan el trazado de la costa. Los cambios de viento y la amplia oscilación intermareal hacen que las condiciones cambien con inusual rapidez, bastan unas horas para que picos huecos y perfectos se afofen totalmente. La orientación de los Baines favorece las olas de derecha, aunque las izquierdas son especialmente huecas. En pocos spots hay canales profundos, por lo que a partir de dos metros y medio suelen cerrrar. Los principales problemas de esta costa son: la ausencia de lugares protegidos, y que los mejores bancos de arena son presa fácil de los maretones invernales. Sólo el norte de la Gironda, la entrada de la Basin de Arcachon, Le Nord en Hossegor, Capbreton y Boucau pueden surfearse con una borrasca de menos de 960 mb. La población local se dispersa en pueblecitos separados por incontables pinares. Excepto en verano, esta costa permanece salvaje y poco explotada, pero con el calor, europeos de todos los paises saturan sus playas. Es uno de los mejores destinos para un surfari veraniego, puedes estarte cuatro meses en bermudas. Lacanau y Hossegor se llevan la fama, pero algunos prefieren adentrarse entre profundos pinares y dunas..

Photo: Eric Chauché

Côte d'Argent

Thierry Fernandez - *Pacific Island*

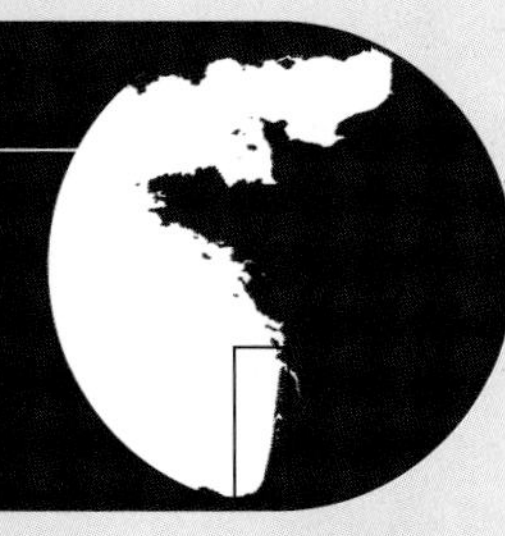

PICTOGRAMMES

De par leur ressemblance, les vagues correspondent toutes à ces pictogrammes.

Due to their similarity, these pictograms apply to all the breaks.

Como olas son parecidas sobre esa costa, usamos esos pictogrammos.

1. Le Mascaret de la Dordogne

Aux équinoxes, une vague d'environ 200-300m au Bec d'Ambes à St-Pardon. Longboard ou Bodyboard. Le record est de 15 minutes en Kayak surf.

Tidal bore which produces a very slow wave on the biggest spring tides. Rides of 200-300m for bodyboards or longboards, and up to 15 minutes riding a kayak.

Durante la marea más grande de los equinoccios, una ola de 200/300 metros, desde el "Bec d'Ambes" hasta "Saint-Pardon". Longboard o Bodyboard, y hasta 15 minutos de recorridos para un Kayak surf !

2. Verdon-sur-Mer

Compte tenu de la proximité de l'estuaire de la Gironde, ce spot ne marche que par grosse houle voire trés grosse en amont de la pointe de Grave. Courants et pollution au menu.

Due to the proximity of The Gironde Estuary, this spot only works with big swells. Even bigger swells required on the other side of Pointe de Grave. Drastic rips and pollution.

Como está al lado del estuario de la Gironde, el spot sólo funciona con un oleaje fuerte o muy fuerte arriba de la "Pointe de Grave". Corrientes y polución.

3. Soulac-sur-Mer

Vagues de repli en cas de tempête compte tenu de l'ensablement des fonds par la Gironde.

Rideable when everywhere else is closed-out, since the rivermouth creates offshore sandbanks that reduce the waves power.

Cuando hay una tormenta gracias a los bancos de arena que cubren la entrada del estuario.

4. L'Amelie

Depuis la D101, cet accés discret sans aucun aménagement ouvre une nouvelle option.

From D101, this tiny access gets to a non-developed spot.

Desde la D101, este acceso discreto puede desarrollar una nueva opción.

5. Le Gurp

On y a souvent vu des surfers bordelais ou canaulais venir ici choper des gauches tubulaires alors que ça sature complètement au Sud. Cherchez la plage de la Négade et Dépé prés d'un block-haus. Camp naturiste d'Euronat.

Best spot when it's out-of-control down south. Filthy tubing lefts. Look for beaches of Négade or Dépé with a german bunker. Nudist camp of Euronat.

Cuando cierra por todas partes al Sur. Izquierdas con tubos. Busca la playa de "La Négade" y "Dépé", cerca de un "block-haus". Campo naturista de Euronat.

6. Montalivet-les-Bains

Encore un haut-lieu du Naturisme au sud de la ville. Bonnes vagues et parking facile.

Another high spot for naked tourists south of the town. Good views of the peaks from the car park.

Otro spot importante ... de Naturismo, al Sur de la Ciudad ! Buenas olas y aparcamiento fácilÊ.

7. le Pin Sec

Si vous trouvez du monde ici, vous avez vraiment pas de bol. La zone 7-9 subit une érosion rapide qui découvre l'argile et l'alios à marée basse.

If you get a crowd here, you'll be very unlucky. The zone between spots 7-9 experiences rapid erosion and low tide uncovers clay and soft reef named Alios.

No tienes suerte si hay gente. De los spots 7 a 9, la zona sufre una erosión rápida que descubre en marea baja una mezcla muy dura de arcilla y de arena llamada "Alios".

8. Hourtin-Plage

Rendez-vous habituel des Britanniques l'été, on commence donc à trouver quelques pics saturés l'été. Plein de pistes cyclables entre lacs et forêts peuvent donner des idées pour les activités annexes.

Popular British hang-out which gets crowded at times during the summer. Heaps of biking tracks between the lakes and woods offer incentives for discovery.

Cita popular de los Británicos. Por eso, a veces, durante el verano, los picos pueden ser sobrepoblados. Puedes desarrollar otras actividades con las pistas para ciclistas, entre lagos y bosques.

9. Carcans-Plage

Alternative à Lacanau pour éviter les encombrements au pic.

Escape from the crowds at Lacanau when surf is perfect.

Alternativa a Lacanau cuando el pico está perfecto y sobrepoblado.

10. Lacanau-Ocean

Avec un front de mer qui permet de mater les vagues depuis la voiture, avec une compétition ASP depuis 1979 et Gary Elkerton qui sévit ici quelques mois dans l'année, avec un accés direct depuis Bordeaux, Lacanau est le noyau du surf girondin. Camping des Grands Pins.

With a beachfront that allows anyone to check the surf from the car; with an ASP contest since 1979 ; with Gary Elkerton a local and close to Bordeaux, Lacanau is the Gironde surfing center. Best camping at Les Grands Pins.

Con una avenida marítima que permite ver desde el coche donde están los picos, una competición ASP desde 1979, Gary Elkerton como local, una carretera directa desde Burdeos, Lacanau es el núcleo del surf girondino. Camping en "Les Grands Pins".

Lacanau-Ocean - *Photo: Simon McComb*

11. Le Porge

Peut-être la route la plus courte depuis Bordeaux mais deux minutes de marche pour traverser la dune.

The closest spot to Bordeaux. The beach is 2 minutes walk from the parking lots.

Tal vez la carretera más corta desde Burdeos pero con dos minutos de caminada por las dunas.

12. La Jenny

Sur la D3, tournez à Lauros au Nord de l'entrée du camp naturiste. Longue marche donc... pas de monde.

Turn off the D3 at Lauros, north of the nudist camp entrance. Long walk, so no crowd.

En la carretera D3, gira en Lauros al Norte de la entrada del campo naturista. Larga caminada ... poca gente !

13. Le Grand Crohot

Un des spots privilégiés des surfers bordelais ou d'Andernos.

Popular spot for surfers from Bordeaux or Andernos.

Uno de los spots privilegiados de los surfistas de Burdeos o Andernos.

14. Le Truc Vert & Le Petit Train

Primo, un camping branché surfer un peu a l'écart des trépidations estivales. Autre option pour camper aux Sables d'Or. Ca s'agite pas mal l'été et la jetée stabilise parfois des fonds corrects.

The first spot is surfer root style, well away from tourist attractions. If in need of more social life, camp at Sables d'Or. The wooden pole jetty helps to build decent sandbars.

Primero un camping de estilo surfista, un poco alejado de las trepidaciones veraneas. Otra opción : camping en "Les Sables d'or". Una escollera de madera que a veces estabiliza bancos de arena correctos.

15. Cap Ferret

Au bout de l'isthme à l'entrée du Bassin d'Arcachon, les courants sont violents surtout à la descendante mais ça peut rester surfable alors que ça sature au nord.

On the northern tip of the isthmus facing the Bassin d'Arcachon. Currents get powerful, especially on the outgoing tide, but there can be surf when it's big in the N.

Se puede surfear cuando cierra al Norte, al cabo del istmo en la entrada norte del "Bassin d'Arcachon". Corrientes violentas sobre todo cuando baja la marea.

16. La Salie

La Salie dépend terriblement des bancs de sable qui se détachent du bassin. Deux accés dont celui du Wharf mène aux spots les plus réguliers. Malheureusement, la jetée de fer crache des eaux pas trés rassurantes qui puent. Si c'est flat, on peut faire une reconstitution d'Endless Summer sur les hautes dunes (100m) du Pyla.

The sandbars shift incredibly fast. The best and the worst can be found at the 2 access points. Wharf one leads to the most reliable banks, it also releases stinking, suspicious foam. If it's flat, surf the highest dunes in Europe (110m).

La condiciones dependen mucho de los bancos de arena. Dos entradas, cuya una, el "Wharf", te guía a los spots más estables, con aguas sospechosas y que huelen mal por la culpa de la escollera de hierro. Si no hay olas, surfea la duna más alta de Europa, "La Dune du Pyla" (110 metros de altura).

17. Biscarrosse-Plage

Deux accés directs sur la plage et du monde à l'eau. Camping "Le Vivier" au Nord. Au sud commence une zone militaire dont l'accés est interdit jusqu'à Mimizan.

2 obvious access points to the beach with the usual crowds. Best campsite at Les Viviers. To the south, as far as Mimizan it's a military zone. Access is stricly forbidden.

Dos entradas directas hacia la playa y mucha gente en el agua. Camping "Le Vivier" al Norte. Al Sur, una base militar hasta Mimizan: acceso prohibido.

18. Mimizan-Plage

Mimizan-Plage a un front de mer de quelques centaines de mètres, un courant (rivière) qui donne certaines années de bons bancs avec finalement peu de surfers. Des jetées de bois sur la plage. Si vous sentez des bouffées d' activités papetières, le vent est à l'est.

Beach with a pole jetty and a rivermouth that some years can shape good sandbars. Several access points. Not that many surfers. If there's a foul smell from nearby paper factories, good news... it's offshore!

M¨imizan tiene una playa de unos cientos metros, un río que crea, ciertos años, buenos bancos, con un número de surfistas razonable, escolleras de madera. Si hueles a los olores de la planta de papel, el viento está offshore !

19. Lespecier

Jusqu'au spot 23 commence une "zone d'ombre" d'accés relativement long depuis les villes. Exemple flagrant ici.

From here to spot 23 is a remote zone with difficult access. This resort is no exception.

De este spot, hasta el 23ero, la zona, aislada, tiene un acceso difícil.

20. Contis-Plage

Débrouillez-vous pour visiter le phare de 183 marches par temps calme et bonne houle et mater avec des jumelles les environs, surtout vers la rivière au nord.. Vous verrez facilement les bons bancs.

Try to visit the lighthouse with binoculars during clear weather and clean swell to see what's happening with the sandbanks, especially those north, close to the rivermouth.

Cuando hay un buen oleaje y que el tiempo está claro, intenta visitar con tus gemelos el faro (183 escalones) para ubicar los bancos y los mejores spots. Sobre todo hacia el río, al Norte.

21. Cap de L'Homy

Pas vraiment de cap mais un isolement assuré.

Not really a cape but year round peace and quiet.

No es realmente un cabo, pero te aseguramos el aislamiento.

22. St-Girons Plage

Encore un camp naturiste bien qu'il y ait des nudistes partout sur la Côte d'argent.

Another nudist camp although you may find naked people almost anywhere along the silver coast.

De nuevo un campo naturista, a pesar de que encuentres a muchos nudistas sobre casi todas las playas de "La Côte d'Argent".

23. Moliets Plage

Une idée fun: descendez le courant d'Huchet avec votre planche depuis le lac de Léon. Vous arrivez peut-être sur le meilleur break à l'embouchure.

Let's have fun: paddle down the Huchet river from Leon lake. You may end up at the best break around.

Una idea divertida : baja "Le Courant d'Huchet" (un río) con tus aletas desde el lago de Léon. Tal vez encontraras buenas olas en la desembocadura.

24. Vieux Boucau-Port D'Albret

A partir d'ici, la D652 se rapproche du littoral, ce qui permet donc de checker plus de vagues . Avant d'arriver sur les vagues de Vieux-Boucau, vous traverserez Port- d'Albret, un bassin artificiel plutôt sympathique mais légèrement pollué par Soustons . Des bancs de sable intéressants qui méritent le détour.

From here the D652 gets closer to the coast. Port d'Albret is a man-made lagoon with nice surroundings in spite of some pollution. Vieux Boucau is definitely worth a look since its sandbars usually give good waves.

A partir de aquí, la carretera D652 se acerca a la costa, "lo que te permite chequear más olas. Antes de llegar a las olas de Vieux-Boucau, puedes pararte en Port D'Albret, una cuenca artificial simpática, pero un poco contaminada por Soustons, que tiene buenos bancos de arena.

25. Labenne-Ocean / Ondres Plage

Pas bien loin de la N10 et peu de surfers viennent traîner leurs slaps ici. Tendance à former des shore-breaks épais,

Close to the N10 but not really crowded. Pounding shore-breaks at high tide.

Al lado de la N10 con poca gente. En marea alta, orilleras potentes.

26. Tarnos Plage

La plage du métro n'a rien de transcendant contrairement au Boucau avec sa digue, sa grue et son bateau échoué qu'on ne voit plus mais qu'on devine. Ici, protégées des vent de sud, les gauches peuvent être tubulaires et rappeler l'époque d'avant la digue. Attention, les locaux sont chaud et le paysage industriel peu romantique.

Two spots. The Metro beach is nothing special, unlike Boucau, with its long jetty, crane, and submerged sunken ship that shapes perfect sandbanks and tubing lefts. Protected from southerlies. Localism is heavy here. An industrial area of dirty factories and unfriendly chimneys.

Dos spots : la playa del "Métro" (nada de muy especial) y Boucau, con su dique, su grua y su bote encallado (que ya no ves pero que puedes adivinar todavía), sus izquierdas con tubos, protegidas de los vientos del Sur. Localismo muy fuerte y un paisaje industrial muy poco romántico.

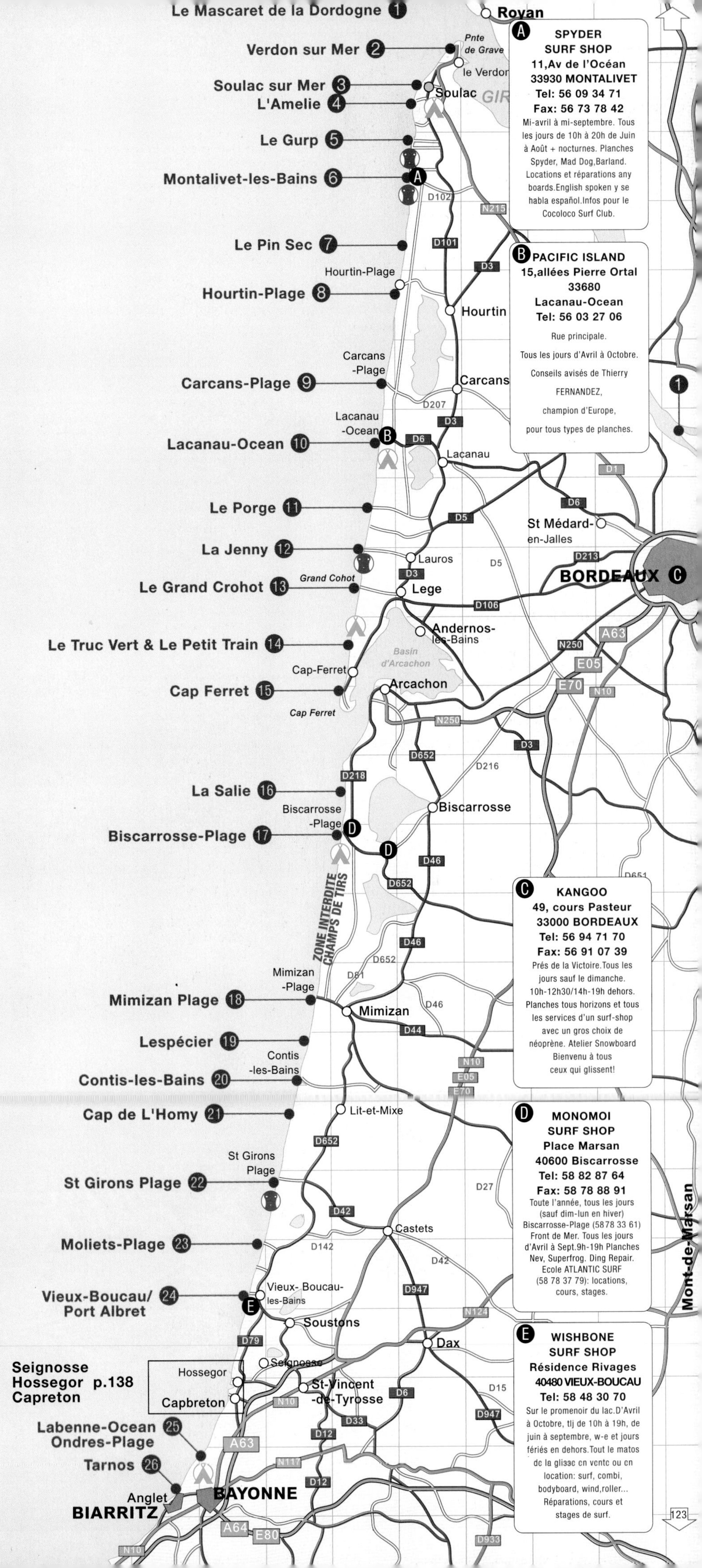

Boucau Tarnos - *Photo: Eric Chauché*

THE SEARCH
RIP CURL
Search Team Rider : Grishka Roberts
Photographe : C. Dimulle

l'Epi Nord - *Photo: Marc Fenies*

Une fosse trés profonde au large en forme de doigt pointe sur Hossegor . Le "Gouf" de Capbreton, ainsi nommé donc, est la cicatrice laissée par l' Adour pendant des millions d'années sur le fond, à l'époque où le puissant flot s'écoulait à Capbreton . C'est au XVIII siècle que Napoleon l'a déviée sur Bayonne pour créer un port sûr, à l'abri de ces côtes battues par les tempêtes . Cette initiative devait donner un résultat spectaculaire pour la communauté du surf dans le monde.

Hossegor a donc gagné ses lettres de noblesse dans le monde pour la puissance de ses vagues, sans que ça soit automatique bien sûr, comme partout ailleurs. L'été est malheureusement trés irrégulier et le plus peuplé d'où certaines tensions qui apparaissent .Faites vraiment gaffe, les étrangers ne sont pas toujours les bienvenus . Les sensibilités locales doivent être respectées : ceux qui squattent les parking avec un van ou qui campent doivent faire attention ."oublier" des ordures , se vider les intestins ou la vessie partout, faire du tapage nocturne peuvent attirer pas mal d'ennuis à commencer par la police . Ne droppez jamais sur les vagues, surtout si ça chauffe au pic ! Vous avez le temps, évitez les heures de pointe !

Les spots au nord des Estagnots ont tendance à être meilleurs aux marées hautes contrairement aux bancs de Capbreton et plus au sud . Les vagues varient terriblement en fonction des conditions, ce qui oblige à une attention constante. Attention aux baïnes , ces mini-lagons en forme de virgules qui favorisent la formation de bancs de sable parfaits mais qui en se vidant , génèrent de puissants courants . Un point noir: beaucoup de déchets sur la plage en hiver et une eau pas toujours appétissante.

Avec ses espaces verts, ses pistes cyclables, et toutes ses activités sportives, le coin se laisse facilement vivre en ajoutant en été une vie nocturne trépidante et des plages bondées de maillots plus timides que leurs propriétaires . A vous d'aller voir !

A finger of extremely deep water points directly at Hossegor. The "Fosse de Capbreton", as it is known, is the signature of the River Ardour on the ocean bottom, a deep scar formed over millions of years of powerful water flow. It used to come out at Capbreton but Napoleon re-directed it to Bayonne in the 18 century in an attempt to create a safer harbour, away from the tempestuous waves along this 10km stretch of coast. An incredibly grand vision has had spectacular results for the French and world surfing communities

Hossegor has become extremely well known due to its powerful waves, but it doesn't work all the time, like anywhere. Summer is unfortunately the most crowded and inconsistent and tensions are beginning to appear. Cut out all the shit...foreigners are guests of another society. Local culture and feelings should be deeply respected. Travellers in vans should park and camp with consideration. Littering makes no friends. Neither does loud drunken behaviour. Drop in rules should be strictly adhered to!

The main spots start north of the pier at Le Penon and extend south of Capbreton. All have individual characteristics which can change daily. Not surprisingly on such a long, deep beach, dominant north to south rips are a huge factor, especially in a big swell. Unfortunately, so is pollution, which can be pretty horrific.

The social atmosphere is relaxed, the night life good, and in summer the beaches become a writhing mass of sun-tanned bodies playing and surfing in the sun. Go see for yourself

Un profundo cañón submarino conocido como la 'Fosa de Capbreton' está situado frente a la costa de Hossegor. Durante millones de años las aguas del río Adour desembocaban en este lugar, pero Napoleón en el siglo XVIII modificó el cauce dirigiéndolo hacia Bayona en un intento de crear un puerto seguro,alejado del embravecido mar de estos 10 kms de litoral. Esa increíble decisión ha tenido consecuencias espectaculares para la comunidad surfera francesa e internacional.

Hossegor es un sitio muy famoso por el poder de sus olas, pero como sucede en todos los sitios no funciona a diario, especialmente en verano que es cuando más gente hay en el agua y aparecen las situaciones tensas. Es importante que el visitante respecte y el modo de vida local, que aparque su furgoneta en los sitios adecuados, que no deje basura ni monte bronca cuando se emborracha...y, por supuesto, que no se dedique a saltar olas

Los principales spots comienzan al norte junto al espigón de Le Penon y se extienden hacia el sur hasta Capbreton, cada uno tiene sus peculiaridades que además varían con frecuencia. Al ser una playa tan larga y tan expuesta, existe una corriente de norte a sur que con maretón es especialmente fuerte. Por otro lado, la contaminación está aumentando.

El ambiente es relajado, hay vidilla nocturna y durante el verano la playa se llena de los más bellos cuerpos bronceados. Merece la pena ir a verio.

Hossegor

Seignosse Hossegor & Capbreton

Rip Curl

Le Penon/Bourdaines- *Photo: Eric Chauche*

1. Le Penon

Le village le plus tranquille de la zone. Plus au nord, un parking largement squatté par les vans. Au sud, une petite jetée de bois favorise parfois de bons bancs.

Northern village with facilities and travellers car park to the north. A small wood jetty to the south sometimes creates good sandbars.

El pueblo más tranquilo de la zona. Más al Norte, un aparcamiento con muchos coches de viajeros. Al Sur, una pequeña escollera de madera favorece a veces buenos bancos de arena.

2. Les Bourdaines

Commence au sud d'une longue jetée en acier. Peut-être un peu moins de monde parce qu'on ne se gare pas aussi facilement qu'ailleurs et que les camps de vacances sont des propriétés privées.

Starts south of the long steel jeety. Thinner crowds because of small car parks and many holiday villages which are private property.

Empieza al Sur de una larga escollera de acero. Tal vez hay un poco menos de gente porque es más difícil aparcarse y que los campos de vacaciones son propiedades privadas.

Estagnots- *Photo: Thierry Organoff*

3. Les Estagnots

Un nom célèbre parce que médiatisé par le Rip Curl Pro et souvent squatté par les voyageurs. Des douches en été.

A stretch which always has consistent peaks and hosts the Rip Curl Pro contest. The car park is a notorious place for travellers to meet. Showers in summer.

Spot famoso por el Rip Curl Pro cuyo aparcamiento está lleno de coches de viajadores. Duchas de verano.

4. Les Culs Nuls

Le maillot de bains n'y est donc pas indispensable. Garez-vous sur les côtés et traversez la dune. A partir d'ici, le shore-break devient carton.

Hossegors' naturist beach and site of the 1995 Rip Curl Pro. The name litterally means 'bare-bums'. Park and cross over the dunes. Consistent hollow banks.

Traducción : "Los culos desnudos". Aparcate al lado y cruza la duna (por las escaleras!). Aquí, orilleras muy potentes.

Les Culs Nuls- *Photo: Eric Chauché*

5. La Gravière

La machine à tubes d'Hossegor avec des droites monstrueuses surfables quand les conditions sont propres. Toujours la Chine quand c'est bon: soyez prêts à attendre et à vous faire touiller.

Hossegor tube station with monster-barrels rideable in clean conditions. Always a crowd when on: be prepared to wait and get slammed.

La máquina de tubos en Hossegor con derechas monstruosas, surfeables cuando las condiciones están idoenas. Mucha gente cuando funciona: prepárate para esperar y sufrir.

La Gravière - *Photo: Eric Chauché*

6. l'Epi Nord

Spot de grosses vagues au large avec des droites surfables quand les bancs sont là. Le shore-break du Front de Mer est suicidaire. Plus au sud, y'a de bons shore-breaks à marée basse avec assez de houle.

In big swells the outside has huge rights rideable when sandbanks are shaped. Suicide shore-break on the beach, facing the 'Front de Mer'. Towards the pier are some low-tide shoreys with possible good peaks in big swell.

Spot de olas grandes en alta mar con derechas surfeables cuando los baµncos quedan bien colocados. La orillera es un suicidio. Más al Sur, buenas orilleras en marea baja con oleaje.

7. Capbreton/le Prevent

Les plages les plus accessibles entre des jetées. Le spot de repli quand c'est tempête ou que ça sature mais ça prend moins la houle et n'est foule pas sentimentale quand ça marche.

Accessible beaches between the jetties, which can be the only place to get surf when it's big and blown-out elsewhere. However, catches less swell than in the north and it gets packed when on.

Las Playas más acequibles entre dos escolleras. El spot de repliegue de tormenta. Capta menos oleaje. Sobrepoblado cuando funciona.

Le Prevent - *Photo: Eric Chauché*

8. la Piste/VVF

Au sud des block-haus se trouvent des plages un peu à l'écart qui balancent des vagues rapides et tubulaires aux marées basses . Plutôt des droites où il vaut mieux ne pas griller les priorités de ceux qui cherchent le tube, comme vous.

South of scattered german bunkers start remote beaches that often get fast and tubular at lower tides . Favors rights and don't drop-in attitudes amongst any tube-seeker around you.

Al sur de los "block-haus", encuentras playas con olas rápidas y con tubos en marea baja. Más bien derechas en donde hay que respectar la prioridad de los que buscan el tubo.

Capbreton/Le Prevent- *Photo: Thierry Organoff*

La Piste - *Photo: Alex Williams*

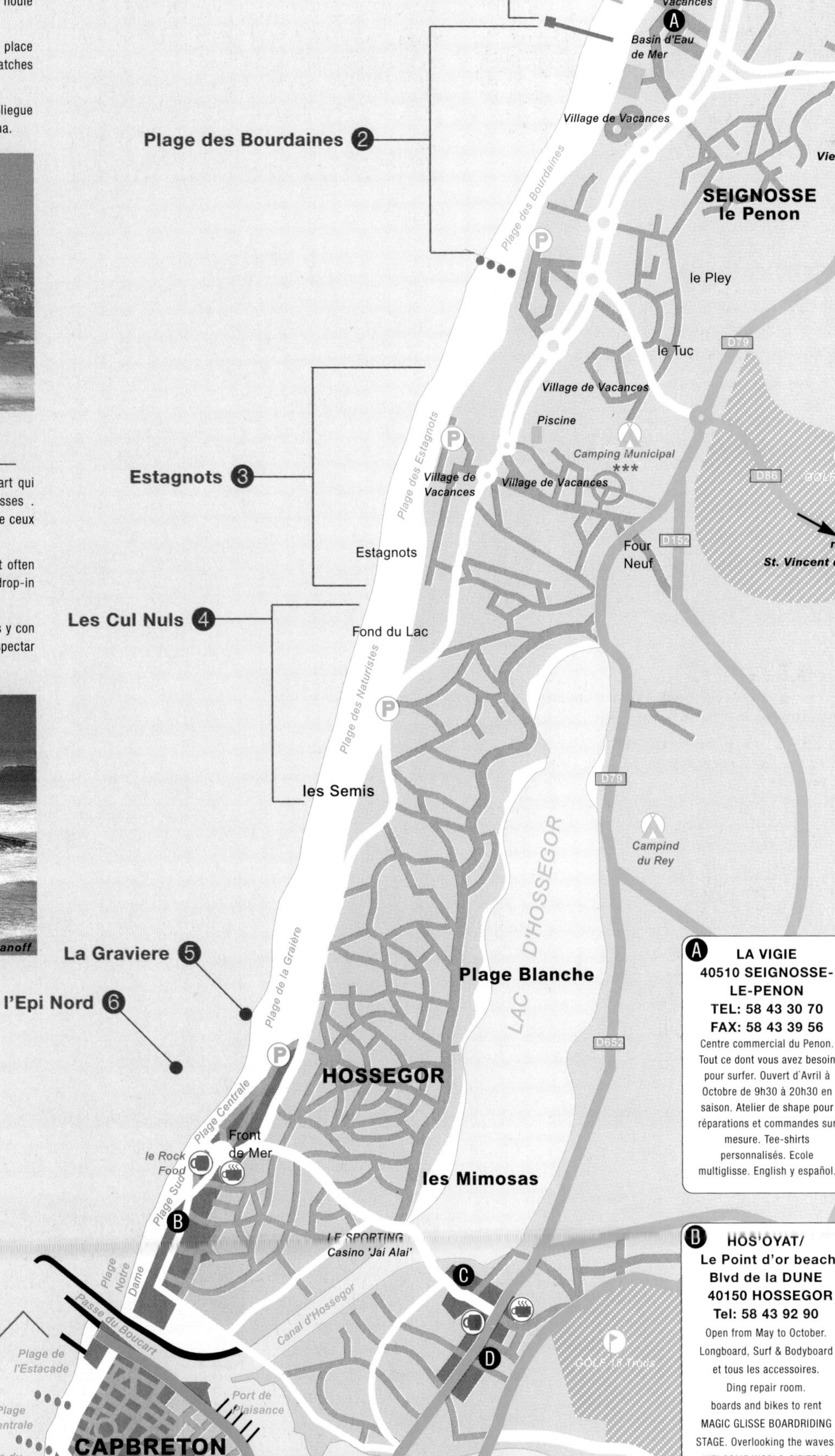

A LA VIGIE
40510 SEIGNOSSE-LE-PENON
TEL: 58 43 30 70
FAX: 58 43 39 56

Centre commercial du Penon. Tout ce dont vous avez besoin pour surfer. Ouvert d'Avril à Octobre de 9h30 à 20h30 en saison. Atelier de shape pour réparations et commandes sur mesure. Tee-shirts personnalisés. Ecole multiglisse. English y español.

B HOS'OYAT/
Le Point d'or beach
Blvd de la DUNE
40150 HOSSEGOR
Tel: 58 43 92 90

Open from May to October. Longboard, Surf & Bodyboard et tous les accessoires. Ding repair room. boards and bikes to rent MAGIC GLISSE BOARDRIDING STAGE. Overlooking the waves. WELCOME WORLD CITIZENS

C RIP CURL
AV DU TOURING CLUB
40150 HOSSEGOR
TEL: 58 43 93 94

Ouvert de 9h à 21h en saison, 10h-13h/15h-20h le reste de l'année. Toutes les planches, combinaisons et fringues Rip Curl. Ecole Tom et Jerry pour les petits, Seabird pour les bodyboarders et une école de surf pour cours et stages. Empreintes de pieds et de mains des pros. Ca sent la wax!

"Peu de fonds et un drop vraiment impressionnant"

Photo: *Eric Chauché*

Photo: *Eric Chauché*

Le berceau du surf en Europe était déjà célèbre de par le monde dans les années 60 avec La Barre à l'embroucure de l'Adour avant la contruction de la digue. Premier cailloux en arrivant du Nord, Biarritz sonne le glas des plages à perte de vue pour donner une côte rocheuse avec quelques excellents reefs (Guethary, Lafitenia) entrecoupées de quelques plages (Grande plage, Côte des Basques, St-Jean de luz, Hendaye) relativement protégées, sans oublier Anglet et ses digues. Territoire de vagues puissantes et rondes, la Côte Basque offre une variété de vagues se pliant à presque toutes les conditions. Seules ombres au tableau, les spots saturent de monde en été peut-être plus qu'ailleurs et la pollution peut y être alarmante. Tant que possible, evitez les jours de pointe et n'oubliez pas les activités environnantes: stations de ski entre une et deux heures, les paysages hallucinants de l'intérieur, les escapades en Espagne et la formidable culture basque qui force le respect.

"Bonne droite puissante et ronde qui tient jusqu' à 4-5 mètres..."

la côte basque

The Basque coast is the cradle of surfing in Europe, a region rich in surf and surf culture. Unlike on The Silver Coast further north, SW France is home to some excellent and hollow reefs, jetties and points (which hold huge swells), as well as her celebrated and variously orientated beaches. Although many spots are close to well populated towns, crowds for most of the year remain minimal. Unfortunately you can't say the same thing regarding the pollution problems. Summer can get a bit crazy, and localism can also be potent at some spots, but with such a variety of surf, snowfields two hours away, also easy trips to Spain and the hallucinatory countryside of the interior, it has been a lure for travellers from all over the world for many years. Not surprisingly, the French Basque are proud of their unique culture, as are their Spanish cousins.

La Costa Vasca fue la cuna del surf europeo. Es una región rica en olas y en cultura surfera. A diferencia de la Costa de Plata situada al Norte, este rincón del suroeste francés alberga olas de arrecife huecas y de gran calidad, olas en espigones y points (que aguantan fuertes maretones) asÌ como sus populares y variadas playas. Pese a que los spots están cerca de algunas ciudades populosas, las olas no están masificadas durante la mayor parte del año. Lamentablemente se dan algunos problemas de contaminación. En verano las cosas cambian, los picos se llenan de gente y en algunos lugares se enardece el localismo. Pero la variedad del surf, las estaciones de ski a tan sólo dos horas de trayecto, la cercanía de España y el alucinante paisaje del interior, han hecho que sea un destino favorito del turimo mundial durante muchos años. No es de sorprender que tanto los vascofranceses como sus vecinos espaÒoles estén orgullosos de su cultura única.

Côte Basque

Christophe Reinhardt -
Guethary

1. La Barre

Vague célèbre dans les années 60 à l'embouchure de l'Ardour dont la qualité s'est dégradée avec la construction de la jetée. Il reste encore de bonnes gauches avec suffisamment de houle, protégées des vents de Sud et Nord. Trop de back-wash à marée haute. Aprés de forte pluies, l'eau n'est pas franchement appétissante.

A famous wave at the Adour rivermouth whose quality has been reduced since the 1960's by jetty construction. A few lefts break in a big swell protected from cross-shore winds. Too much backwash at high tide. Water quality is suspicious due to effluent from the Adour.

Ola famosa durante los años 60 en la desembocadura de "L'Adour" cuya calidad se empeoró con la construcción del dique. Todavía quedan buenas izquierdas cuando hay lo suficiente oleaje, protegidas de los vientos de Sur y Norte. Demasiado back-wash en marea alta. Después de fuertes lluvias, la calidad del agua se degrada con lo que lleva el río.

2. Les Cavaliers

De l'autre côté de la Barre se trouve ce super spot dont les tubes à marée basse n'ont rien à envier à ceux d'Hossegor. Souvent, plus de taille que les autres plages de Anglet. Trop de back-wash à marée haute. Menacée par la construction d'une marina. Plusieurs pics mais il n'est malheureusement pas rare de voir une centaine de surfers à l'eau en été, voire plus.

On the other side of the jetty are several peaks. Their tubes rival those of Hossegor. Often bigger than other Anglet beaches. Heavy backwash at high tide. In summer 100 surfers in the water is not uncommon. Threatened by harbour development.

Por el otro lado de 'La Barre', super spot con tubos 'calidad Hossegor" en marea baja. A menudo, más tamaño que en las otras playas de Anglet. En marea alta, demasiado back-wash. Amenazado por la construcción de una marina. Mucha gente (a veces más de 100 surfistas!).

Les Cavaliers - *Photo: Simon McComb*

3. Les Plages d'Anglet

Bons beach-breaks. Plusieurs accès à ces plages d'Anglet, les deux premières proches de Chiberta sont moins fréquentées en raison de la marche depuis le parking. La Marinela est la plage du camping de Fontaine Laborde.

There are several access points to Anglets good beach breaks. L'Ocean and La Madrague are not as crowded due to a long walk from the car park. Good peaks break at all points between the jetties to check out the surf.

Buenas olas de arena con varias entradas : "L'Océan" y "La Madrague" con menos gente porque hay que caminar desde el aparcamiento.È Varios picos que chequear entre las escolleras.

4. Sables D'or/VVF

Ce sont les spots de la Chambre d'Amour directement visibles depuis la route et des parkings: du monde à l'eau donc. Marche aussi à marée haute Toujours un spot qui marche. Du côté de la falaise du phare casse une gauche correcte à marée basse.

These two spots are directly visible from the road and car parks of Chambre d'Amour and hence all have a crowd factor to consider. There's always a wave working somewhere. A wedging left breaks near the lighthouse cliffs with nice rides.

Se ven estos dos spots desde el aparcamiento y la carretera de "La Chambre d'Amour" : en consecuencia, mucha gente. En cualquier marea, siempre hay un pico que funciona. En marea baja, una izquierda al lado del acantilado del faro.

5. Grande Plage

La plage frime de la Cote Basque. protégée des vents de Sud qui prend moins la houle qu'Anglet. Seule la moitié sud est surfable. En été, cette moitié est reduite par la zone de baignade. En plus, il est difficile, en tous cas payant de se garer. Souvent peuplé mais éclairé la nuit.

The Basque Coasts most mythical beach is protected from S winds but has a narrower swell window than Anglet. Only the southern half gets surf with bathing zone restrictions in the summer. Difficult and expensive car parking. Often crowded and the water is not particularly clean. Can be surfed at night.

La playa de moda de la Costa Vasca, protegida de los vientos, menos expuesta al oleaje que Anglet. Se surfea unicamente en la mitad Sur, reducida de verano con la zona de baño. Difícil de aparcarse y hay que pagar. A menudo sobrepoblado, pero alumbrado de noche.

Grande Plage, Biarritz - *Photo: Eric Chauché*

6. Cote des Basques

Le berceau de surf en France et des Tontons surfers. Une atmosphère décontractée, très prisée des longboarders avec des vagues plutôt molles sans vraiment de bancs de sable. Vers le Sud, quelques reefs corrects dont la Mouscariette.

One of the spots where surfing first started in Europe, now poular with longboarders. Generally mushy waves which lack shape. To the South are some reefs which are worth checking, one is called La Mouscariette.

Uno de los primeros spots en que se surfeó en Europa, popular para el longboard. Ola floja, no hay verdaderos bancos de arena. Al Sur, unas olas de rocas correctas con "La Mouscariette" por ejemplo.

Bidart - *Photo: Alex Williams*

7. Ilbarritz

Les plages d'Ilbarritz (Marbella, Bora Bora, Edouard VII) peuvent mériter le coup d'oeil même si les reefs ne produisent pas de fonds particulièrement bons. Beaucoup de rochers donc.

The various beaches of Ilbarritz (Marbella, Bora Bora, Edouard VII) can produce good waves even thought the reefs don't look really good. A lot of rocks to look out for.

Olas correctas en Ilbarritz (Marbella, Bora Bora, Edouard VII) aunque los fondos de rocas no son muy buenos. Muchas rocas.

8. Bidart

La plage centrale n'est pas facilement accessible; quelques rochers mais peut réserver de bonnes surprises, contrairement à Ouhabia, visible depuis la N10, qui peut en réserver de trés mauvaises à cause des rejets de la rivière.

The central beach does not have a clear access and has a few rocks but has some good days. However, Ouhabia, visible from the N10, can be badly polluted by the river.

La playa central no tiene un acceso muy ˆfácil. Con unas rocas, puede ofrecer buenas sorpresas, al contrario de Ouhabia, que se ve desde la N10, con a veces rechazos del río.

9. Guéthary

Bonne droite puissante et ronde qui tient jusqu' à 4-5 mètres. La gauche peut être surfable mais on risque de bouffer la série au retour. L'inside peut être creux avec de bons murs à marée haute. Beaucoup de monde, beaucoup de longboards. Le port et le village de Guéthary valent le détour

Sunset-like right with a shifting peak and short shoulder that holds upto 15ft with clean NW swell. The left can be ridden but you will end up in the impact-zone. The inside wave has good walls at higher tides. Crowds and londboarders are a feature. Guethary harbour and village are worth a look.

Buena derecha potente y redonda que aguanta hasta 4-5 metros. Puedes correr la izquierda con el riesgo que rompa toda la tanda al regresar. En alta mar, intenta el inside con buenas paredes. Mucha gente, muchos longboards. El puerto y el pueblo de Guéthary merecen un vistazo.

Les Alcyons/Avalanche

Descendez la route de l'autre côté du port de Guethary. D'abord les Alcyons, une gauche courte et intense qui tient jusqu'à 4 m. Pas mal de courant en milieu de marée. Peu de fonds et un drop vraiment impressionnant. Pour les plus courageux, la vague du fond se surfe jusqu'à 6 metres, sortez le gun.

Down the road on the other side of Guethary harbour. The first spot is Alcyons, a short but powerful left that holds swell upto 12ft. A heavy current at mid-tide and shallow bottom makes these spots for big wave surfers only. The outside lefts can be ridden upto 20ft with the right board.

Por el otro lado del puerto de Guéthary abajo. Primero "Les Alcyons", una izquierda corta y muy potente que aguanta hasta 4 metros. Mucha corriente en marea media. Poco profundo. Las izquierdas que vienen de afuera, Avalanche, se corren hasta 6 metros. No te equivoques de tabla !

12. Lafitenia

Belle droite consistente qui peut être longue quand la section du milieu de la baie connecte avec le premier pic au niveau des remous. Marche d'escalier au take-off. Tubes à l'inside. Suivre Acotz pour trouver le parking et la baie de Lafitenia.

Beautiful and consistent right that can be long when the middle-bay peak connects with the first peak in the whirling waters that makes a step in the take-off. The inside gets tubes. Follow Acotz for parking lots and Lafitenia bay.

Linda derecha consistente que puede ser larga cuando la sección en la mitad de la bahía se conecta con el primer pico al nivel d e los remolinos. Una escalera durante el take-off. Tubos en el inside. Seguir Acotz para encontrar el aparcamiento y la bahía de Lafitenia.

Lafitenia - *Photo: Tim Rainger LOW PRESSURE*

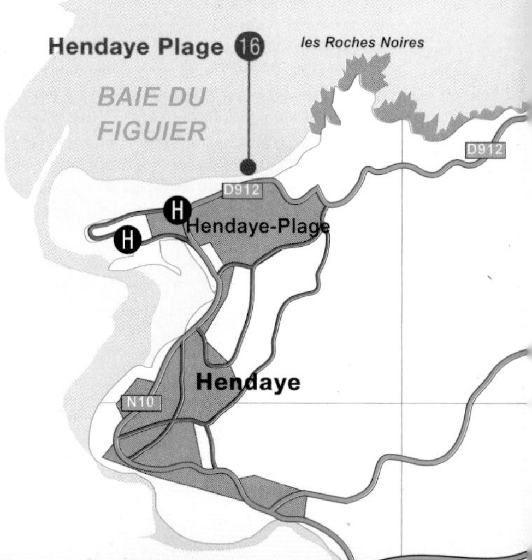

13. Erromardie

Les bonnes vagues y sont rares mais quelques gauches en face du poste de secours ou vers la falaise.

Good waves are rare but there are a few lefts facing the lifeguard house or towards the cliffs.

Las buenas olas son raras. Unas izquierdas en frente del puesto de auxilio o cerca del acantilado.

14. Sainte-Barbe

Cette longue droite déroule depuis la jetée nord de la baie. Le take-off y est radical. En bout de vague se trouve une deuxième section, 'les Flots Bleus' dans la baie qui devient un spot de fun-board quand ça souffle. Ce spot est menacé par des blocs de béton qu'on dépose pour ramener le sable sur la plage.

A long right wraps around the North jetty of the bay. Take-off is radical. At the end of the wave is 'les flots Bleus', a peaky point break. Many wave sailors when it's stormy. Concrete blocks for beach protection may destroy the wave.

Una larga derecha que empieza desde la escollera Norte de la bahía. El take-off es radical. Al final de la ola, hay una secunda sección, "les flots bleus". Muchos windsurfers de tormenta. Este spot se encuentra amenazado por los bloques de cemento que hunden para proteger la playa.

St Jean de Luz - *Photo: Eric Chauche*

15. Ciboure/Socoa

Quand ça rentre trés gros, plusiers spots marchent du port à la digue de Socoa en passant par la Bougie. Beaucoup de locaux et des vagues au compte-goutte: chaud devant!

When it gets very big, several spots work inside the bay from the harbour mouth towards Socoa jetty and passing through 'The Candle'. Many locals, few waves, respect due!

Cuando hay un oleaje muy fuerte, varios spots funcionan, del puerto al dique de Socoa, pasando por "la Bougie". Muchos locales, pocas olas : respecto !

16. Hendaye Plage

L'ultime solution quand tout sature. Longue plage qui offre le choix pour trouver un pic correct selon les marées, plutôt vers le casino. Vagues moyennes sauf vers les 'Deux Jumeaux' au Nord de la baie: une droite qui demande patience et détermination. Idéal pour débutants.

The ultimate solution when everything else is closing-out. Long stretch of average beach break that offers a wide choice of peaks, the best generally not far from the casino. The two rocks to the north hold a right that requires patience. Perfect for beginners.

La última solución cuando todo cierra. Larga playa que ofrece varios picos diferentes según la marea, más bien hacia el casino. Olas regulares, excepto hacia "les Deux Jumeaux", al Norte de la bahía : una derecha que necesita paciencia y determinación. Perfecto para principiantes.

A **AUBERGE DE JEUNESSE**
19 Route des Vignes, 64600 Anglet
Tel: 59 63 86 49 Fax: 59 63 38 92
Accueil hiver de 8h30 à 12h30 et 15h30 à 22h00. Éte de 8h30 à 22h00. Ouvert toute l'année (sauf 15/12-15/1), formules tous les budgets (Bed & Breakfast, demi-pension, pension complète en bâtiment ou en camping. ECOLE DE SURF et une ambiance unique au pub (concert, video surf...)

B **Hotel Residence Mer & Golf**
47, Boulevard de la Mer, 64600 Anglet
Tel: 59 52 70 00 Fax: 59 03 58 91
Face à la Mer. Vue imprenable sur les spots de la Chambre d'Amour. Location d'appartements, de studios et de deux piècespour 4 à 6 personnes. Kitchenette, lave-vaisselle, TV payante, telephone. Restauration possible sur place. Local planches de surf. Ouvert à l'année.

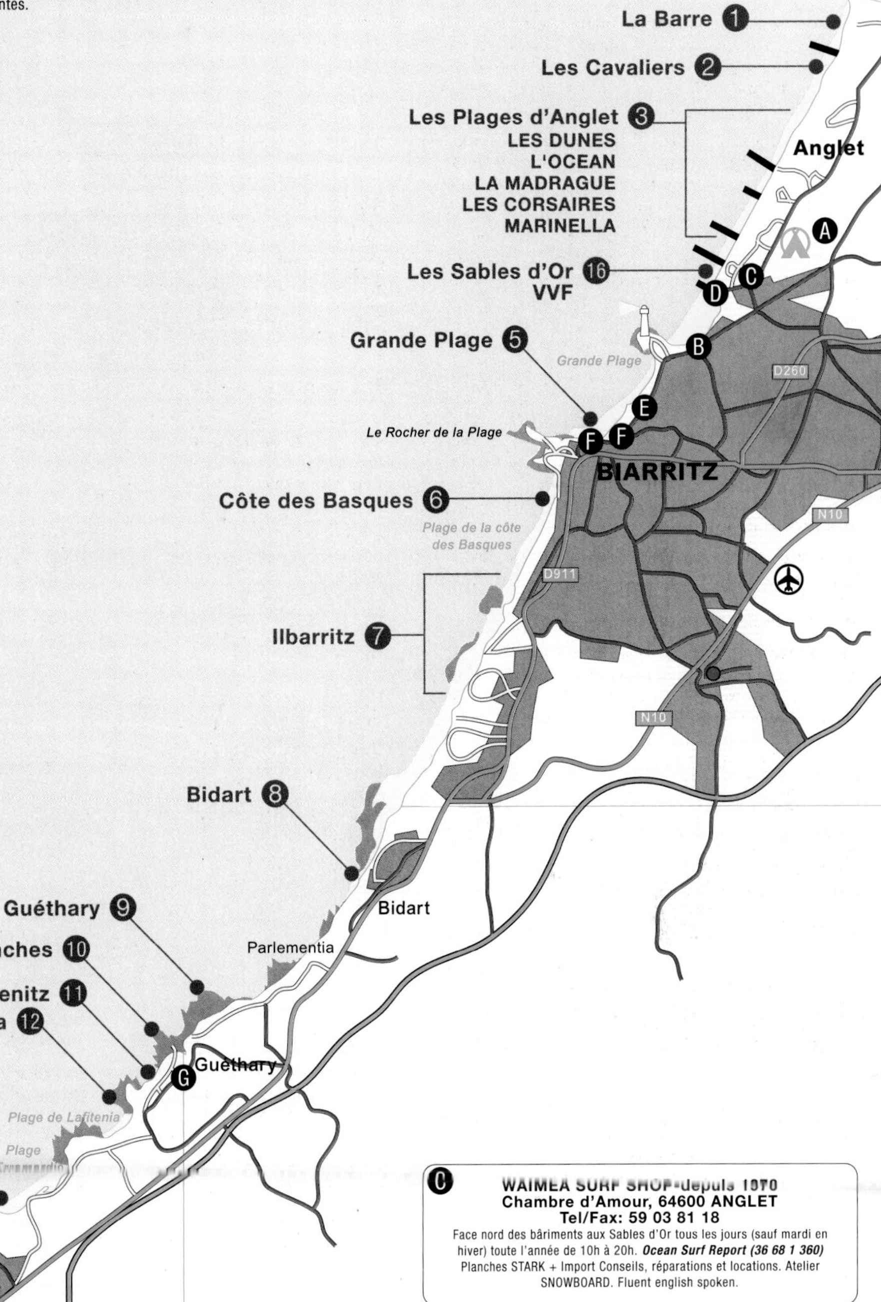

C **WAIMEA SURF SHOP-depuis 1970**
Chambre d'Amour, 64600 ANGLET
Tel/Fax: 59 03 81 18
Face nord des bâriments aux Sables d'Or tous les jours (sauf mardi en hiver) toute l'année de 10h à 20h. ***Ocean Surf Report (36 68 1 360)*** Planches STARK + Import Conseils, réparations et locations. Atelier SNOWBOARD. Fluent english spoken.

D **LINE UP SURF SHOP**
Plage de la Chambre d'Amour 64600 ANGLET
Tel: 59 03 51 22
Toute l'année, tous les jours (sauf de lundi en hiver). De 9h30 à 20h (Sauf en hiver 10h à 13h et 15h à 19h) Toute la collection et les planches Rip Curl et Sammy's.ECOLE DE SURF (pension possible) Info-Vagues (36 68 78 73) Welcome. Bienvenido

E **FREEDOM SURF SHOP**
2 Avenue Reine Victoria, 64200 BIARRITZ
Tel: 59 24 38 40 Fax: 59 28 28 25
En face de l'hôtel du Palais, Ouvert tous les jours sauf l'année, toute l'année de 9h à 19h. Toute la collection et les planches Rip Curl plus le reste. Location, reparation et Ecole de Surf.

H **FLUIDE SYSTEME**
4 Rue des Orangers, 64700 Hendaye Plage
Tel: 59 20 67 47
Atelier ouvert à l'année: Port de la Floride. Fabrication, Réparations et Location de tous types de planches. ECOLE DE SURF Boulevard de la Mer: cours et stages. Hébergement avec l'association Bilkua 59 20 51 39.

G **GUETHARY SURF SHOP**
Maison du Chef de Gare, Gare SNCF, 64210 Guethary
Tel: 59 54 71 58 Fax: 59 47 71 27
En face des spots des Alcyons et de Guethary. Christophe Reinhart, le spécialiste des guns hawaiien jusqu'à dix pieds: Gerry Lopez, Jeff Johnson, Mac Kee...Ouvert de Pâques à fin Novembre et les jours de gros swells. Le train s'arrête devant la porte de shop. Deux planches de tandem sont a louer.

F **QUIKSILVER Boardrider Club**
Grande plage 64200 BIARRITZ
T: 59 22 03 12 F: 59 24 32 44 +Place Bellevue (59 24 34 05)
Tous les jours , toute l'année de 9h30 à 19h30.
JEFF HAKMAN SURF SHOOL:location, cours et stages de perfectionnement. English spoken, se habla español...

la méditerranée

Vincent Chasselon, l'Arquet - *Photo: Philippe Chevodian*

Autrefois considéré comme une boutade, le surf en Méditerranée s'est affirmé en quelques années avec les windsurfers conscients des "coups de surf" brefs mais magiques générés par les vents locaux. A la première place, le Mistral de la vallée du Rhône qui dévie dès qu'il atteint la mer: de nord, il passe à nord-ouest puis à ouest. Il balance des vagues jusqu'à 1,5m selon la force et l'eloignement du spot (jusqu'à Toulon), quand il se calme, ça peut être propre surtout en cas de renverse. C'est le seul vent qui rime avec ciel bleu, les autres vents étant chargés d'humidité. Le vent d'Est, fréquent en hiver sur la Côte d'Azur donne quelques bonnes sessions. Les autres vents sont plus rares: Libeccio, le marin (SE) ou le coup de Labbé (S). Rappelez-vous qu'il n'y a pas de marées et que les vagues sont toujours trés rapprochées. Les vents étant étroitement liés à l'activité dépressionaire dans l'Atlantique nord, il faut donc éviter Juin-Septembre où il n'y a généralement que de faibles thermiques d'ouest. Restez vigilants et patients, les vagues sont ici trés capricieuses. Cela dit, outre son soleil, la Provence et la Côte d'Azur ont plein d'autres arguments pour vous tenir en haleine.

Photo: Xavier Gonzales

Formerly considered a bit of a joke, surfing in the Med has become a reality within a few years, mainly through windsurfers becoming conscious of surf conditions (which mostly depend on local winds), also a result of the general upsurge in the popularity of surfing in France. Swells are short, but they can be magic. The Mistral blows down the Rhône Valley, which deviates as it reaches the ocean. From a north direction, it curves north-west and then west. It can produce waves up to 6', depending on the fetch length (as far as Toulon) and the wind strength. When the wind drops, conditions can be clean, especially if the wind reverses. Mistral wind means blue sky, whereas the other winds bring showers. E winds, regular in winter especially on the eastern part (Côte d'Azur), can also provide some good sessions. Other winds are more scarce: Libeccio(SW), Marin (SE) or the Labbe (S). Remember there are no tides and that wave period is very short. Winds are deeply linked with North Atlantic lows so it's advisable to avoid June-September. To get surf here you have to be patient and aware; swell is inconsistent. However with everlasting sun and great history, Provence and Côte d'Azur have a lot of experience to offer.

Photo: Xavier Gonzales

Aunque al principio parecía una broma, el surf en el Mediterráneo ha llegado a ser una realidad en pocos años. Sobre todo cuando los windsurferos se dieron cuenta de las condiciones para el surf (dependientes de los vientos reinantes), y también fruto del resurgimiento general de la popularidad del surf en Francia. Las marejadas son muy cortas, pero pueden ser mágicas. El Mistral sopla por el Valle del Rhone desviándose al llegar al mar. De una dirección Norte, rola primero al Noroeste y después al Oeste. Puede producir olas de hasta dos metros, en función de la extensión sobre la que sople (puede llegar a Toulon) y de su fuerza. Al cesar el viento, puede ordenarse el mar, especialmente si el viento cambia de dirección. El Mistral trae consigo cielos despejados, al revés que los otros vientos que traen lluvia. Los vientos del Este, habituales en el invierno sobre todo en la Costa Azul (Cote d'Azur), también pueden traer buenas sesiones. Otros vientos son más escasos: Libeccio (Suroeste), Marin (Sureste) o el Labbe (Sur). Recuerda que no hay mareas y que los periodos de olas son de muy corta duración. Los vientos están asociados a las depresiones del norte del Atlántico, por lo tanto evita el período de Junio a Septiembre. Para surfear aquí hay que ser paciente y estar muy atento. Sin embargo, el sol garantizado y su larga historia hacen que Provenza y la Costa Azul tengan mucho que ofrecer.

"Autrefois considéré comme une boutade, le surf en Méditerranée s'est affirmé en quelques années"

Photo: Xavier Gonzales

Mediterranée

Vincent Chasselon

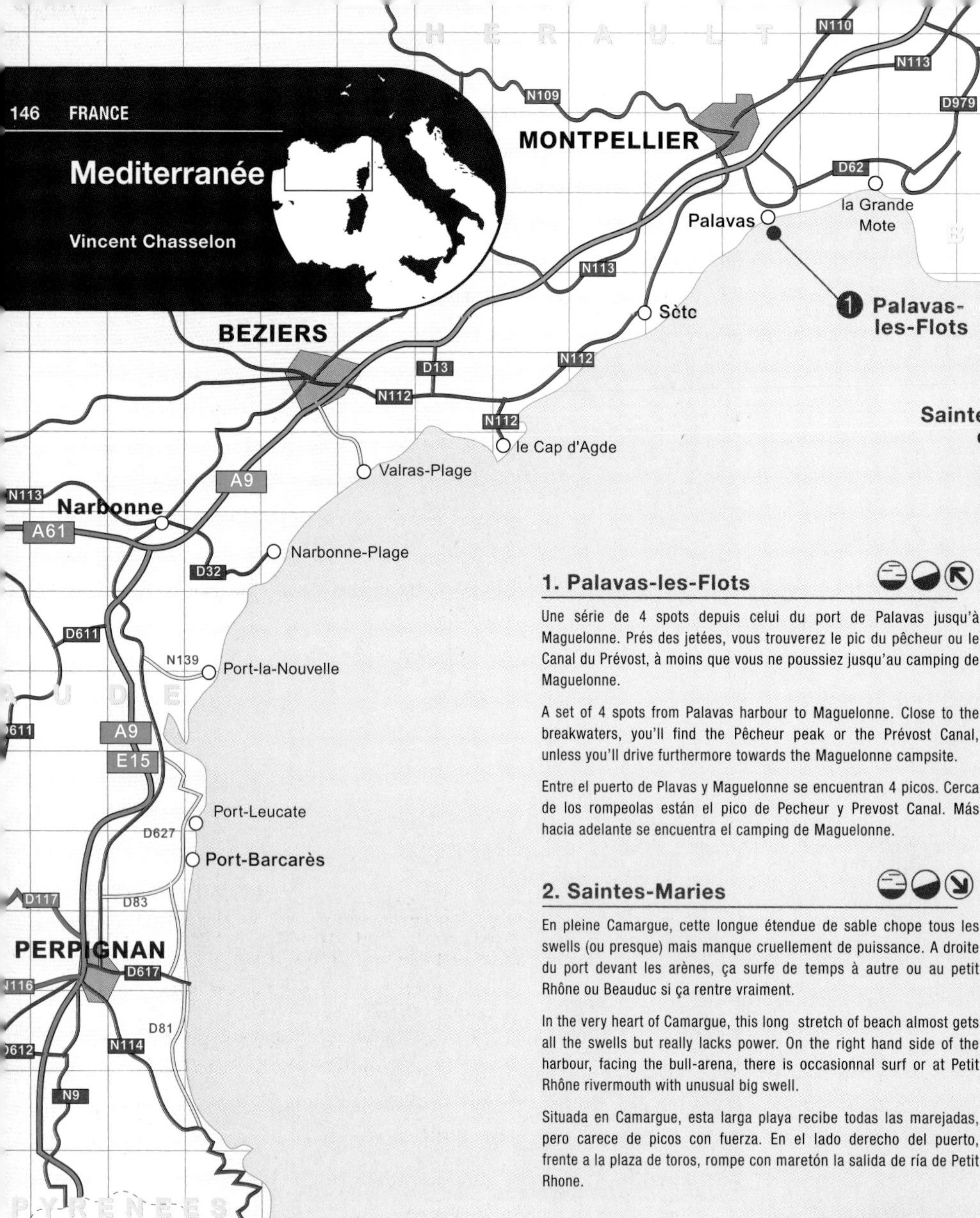

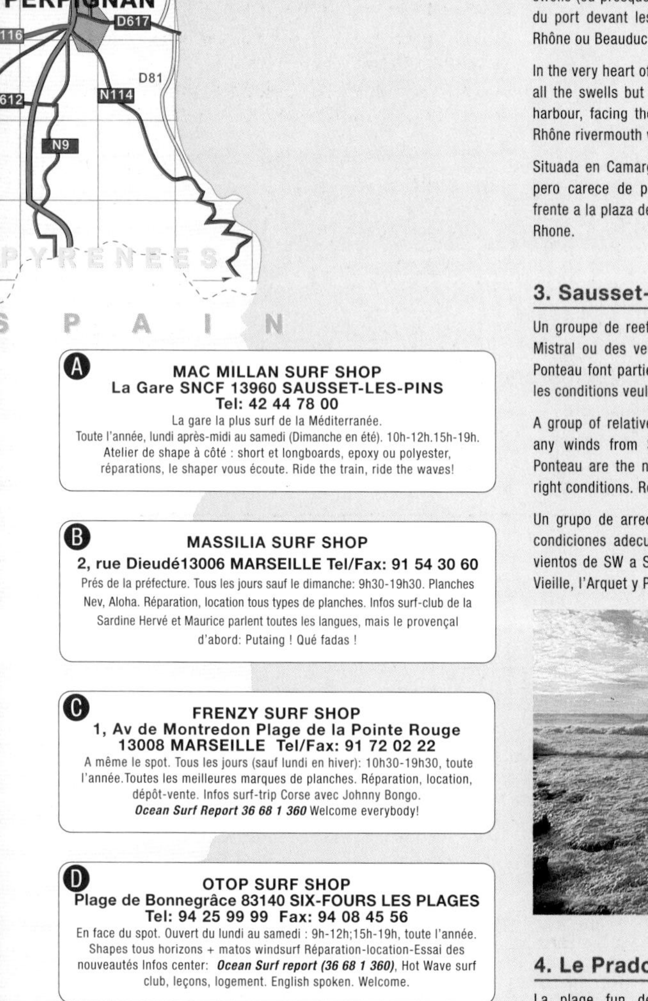

A **MAC MILLAN SURF SHOP**
La Gare SNCF 13960 SAUSSET-LES-PINS
Tel: 42 44 78 00
La gare la plus surf de la Méditerranée.
Toute l'année, lundi après-midi au samedi (Dimanche en été). 10h-12h.15h-19h.
Atelier de shape à côté : short et longboards, epoxy ou polyester, réparations, le shaper vous écoute. Ride the train, ride the waves!

B **MASSILIA SURF SHOP**
2, rue Dieudé13006 MARSEILLE Tel/Fax: 91 54 30 60
Prés de la préfecture. Tous les jours sauf le dimanche: 9h30-19h30. Planches Nev, Aloha. Réparation, location tous types de planches. Infos surf-club de la Sardine Hervé et Maurice parlent toutes les langues, mais le provençal d'abord: Putaing ! Qué fadas !

C **FRENZY SURF SHOP**
1, Av de Montredon Plage de la Pointe Rouge
13008 MARSEILLE Tel/Fax: 91 72 02 22
A même le spot. Tous les jours (sauf lundi en hiver): 10h30-19h30, toute l'année.Toutes les meilleures marques de planches. Réparation, location, dépôt-vente. Infos surf-trip Corse avec Johnny Bongo.
Ocean Surf Report 36 68 1 360 Welcome everybody!

D **OTOP SURF SHOP**
Plage de Bonnegrâce 83140 SIX-FOURS LES PLAGES
Tel: 94 25 99 99 Fax: 94 08 45 56
En face du spot. Ouvert du lundi au samedi : 9h-12h;15h-19h, toute l'année. Shapes tous horizons + matos windsurf Réparation-location-Essai des nouveautés Infos center: ***Ocean Surf report (36 68 1 360)***, Hot Wave surf club, leçons, logement. English spoken. Welcome.

E **SURF SAGA**
2,rue Sebastiani 20000 AJACCIO
Tel/Fax: 95 21 06 56
Face à la galerie Napoleon.Tous les jours sauf dimanche, 9h-12h/14h30-19h30 Tous types de planches pour glisser sur l'eau. Locations, réparations, école de surf. Renseignements ligue Corse pour licences, compétitions... (95 23 17 24)

1. Palavas-les-Flots

Une série de 4 spots depuis celui du port de Palavas jusqu'à Maguelonne. Prés des jetées, vous trouverez le pic du pêcheur ou le Canal du Prévost, à moins que vous ne poussiez jusqu'au camping de Maguelonne.

A set of 4 spots from Palavas harbour to Maguelonne. Close to the breakwaters, you'll find the Pêcheur peak or the Prévost Canal, unless you'll drive furthermore towards the Maguelonne campsite.

Entre el puerto de Plavas y Maguelonne se encuentran 4 picos. Cerca de los rompeolas están el pico de Pecheur y Prevost Canal. Más hacia adelante se encuentra el camping de Maguelonne.

2. Saintes-Maries

En pleine Camargue, cette longue étendue de sable chope tous les swells (ou presque) mais manque cruellement de puissance. A droite du port devant les arènes, ça surfe de temps à autre ou au petit Rhône ou Beauduc si ça rentre vraiment.

In the very heart of Camargue, this long stretch of beach almost gets all the swells but really lacks power. On the right hand side of the harbour, facing the bull-arena, there is occasionnal surf or at Petit Rhône rivermouth with unusual big swell.

Situada en Camargue, esta larga playa recibe todas las marejadas, pero carece de picos con fuerza. En el lado derecho del puerto, frente a la plaza de toros, rompe con maretón la salida de ría de Petit Rhone.

3. Sausset-La Couronne

Un groupe de reefs relativement consistants qui s'activent avec du Mistral ou des vents de SW-SE. Carro, Couronne-vieille,l'Arquet et Ponteau font partie des noms à retenir. Des sessions épiques quand les conditions veulent bien être là. Du monde et des rochers.

A group of relatively consistent reefs that get lively with Mistral or any winds from SW to SE . Carro, Couronne-vieille, l'Arquet et Ponteau are the names to remember. Some epic sessions with the right conditions. Rocks and crowds.

Un grupo de arrecifes rocosos de cierta consistencia, que con las condiciones adecuadas dan sesiones clásicas. Requieren Mistral o vientos de SW a SE. Los nombres a recordar son: Carro, Couronne-Vieille, l'Arquet y Ponteau. Bastante gente.

La Couronne - Photo: Philippe Chevodian

4. Le Prado

La plage fun de Marseille avec son lot de windsurfers, de bodyboarders et de détritus. Un spot de bodyboard à la Pointe-Rouge. Rien d'extraordinaire mais c'est frime!

Hip Marseille beach with tons of wave-sailors, sponges and trash. Nothing stupendous but chicks like it! Bodyboard spot at Pointe Rouge.

Es la playa más característica de Marsella. Está llena de windsurferos, corcheros y de basura. Nada estupendo, si no fuera porque es frecuentada por multitud de chicas.

5. Cassis

Rien de régulier ici mais ça peut bien rentrer en gauche avec une droite mollassonne à la plage de l'Arène. Bien abrité par Mistral, un décor dantesque. Parking difficile.

Fickle wave that can produce a surprising hollow left and much mellower right. Look for Arène beach. Sheltered with Mistral ,unreal scenery. Difficult parking.

Ola inconstante que puede producir una izquierda muy hueca y una derecha normalita. Busca Arene Beach.

6. La Ciotat

Rare aussi mais si ça souffle ou ça a souffle d'Est, les gauches valent le déplacement.

Rare, but with heaps of E winds can have some good lefts.

En ocasiones hay buenas izquierdas con vientos del Este.

7. Cap Saint-Louis

Certainement le meilleur spot à l'est de Marseille au prés du port des Lecques. Du monde, des oursins et parfois du courant mais la droite peut être longue et creuse.

Probably the best spot of E Marseille close to the harbour at Cape Saint-Louis. Crowds, urchins and occasionnal rips but the right can be really long and hollow.

Probablemente el mejor spot marsellés, cercano al puerto de Cape Saint-Louis. Muy frecuentado, erizos y corrientes en una derecha larga y hueca.

8. Bandol

A l'ouest de la plage centrale, une gauche courte, difficile à trouver. L'ile de Bendor à un reef aussi. Bonne rame!

To the west of the central beach is a short left, hard to locate. Try Bendor island right in front, that has a good reef. Good luck for the paddle!

Al oeste de la playa céntrica hay una izquierda corta de dificil localización. Intenta llegar a la isla de Bendor donde hay un buen arrecife. Larga remada.

9. Six-Fours les Plages

La péninsule offre certainement la meilleure palette de swell et de vent de toute la région. Difficile de louper Brutal Beach, souvent gavée de windsurfers. Tout prés se trouve la Coudoulière, une droite qui n'est bonne que sans vent. De l'autre côté, à la Seyne, aux Sablettes, il faut checker plage de la Verne ou de Saint-Asile à Pin-Rolland.

The peninsula certainly offers the widest swell and wind exposure. First, you can't miss La Coudoulière, a right-hander that gets good if the wind is nil. On the E side, La Seyne, drive to Les Sablettes to check Verne beach or Pin-Rolland.

La península ofrece la más amplia exposicíon al mar y al viento. La Condouliere es una derecha que puede estar bien si no hay viento. En el lado Este, están Les Sablettes, playa Verne y Pin-Rolland.

10. Gigaro

S'il n' y a pas de surf, vous pourrez au moins profiter d'un panaroma unique.

If you don't find any surf, you will certainly enjoy the unique scenery.

Un escenario único del que puedes disfrutar en caso de que no haya olas.

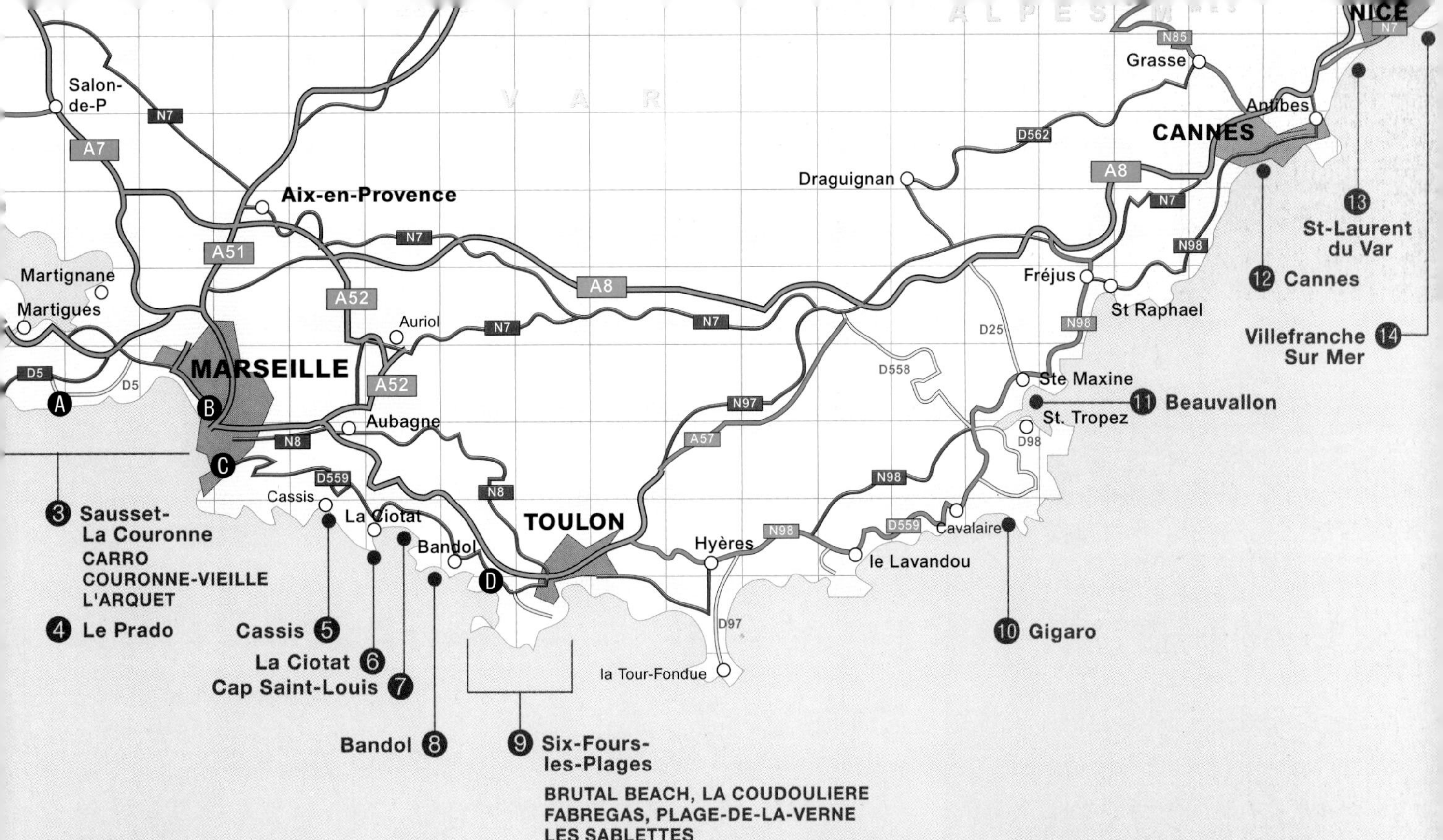

11. Beauvallon

Des vagues creuses et rapides abritées de quelques mauvais vents. Moins de monde qu'à St Tropez en face mais pas la solitude non plus.

Fast and hollow waves sheltered from nasty winds. Not as crowded as the hip resort of St-Tropez facing it but if it works, there should be people surfing around you.

Olas rápidas y huecas protegidas del mal viento. No tan masificado como St-Tropez, pero si funciona seguro que no surfeas solo.

12. Cannes

La plage peut donner des petits tubes avec du vent d'Ouest. Si ça vient de l'Est, passez de l'autre côté du cap de la Croisette en face du Palm Beach Casino. Peut-être un trip en bateau pour l'île de Sainte-Marguerite et les pointes du Batéguier et du Dragon.

Central beach can have small tubes with westerlies. If blowing from the E, get on the other side of the Croisette cape in front of the Palm Beach Casino. You may want to explore Sainte-Marguerite island, by ferry, Batéguier and Dragon points are the surfing reefs.

La playa central ofrece tubos pequeños con vientos del Oeste. Si sopla del Este, vete al otro lado del cabo Croisette frente al Casino Palm Beach. Cogiendo un ferry puedes explorar la isla de Sainte-Marguerite donde se encuentran dos arrecifes: Bateguier y Dragon.

13. St-Laurent du Var

Un spot relativement consistent à l'embouchure du Var, avec l'eau boueuse et froide de la rivière. Prés d'un centre nautique et d'une jetée.

Relatively consistent spot at the Var rivermouth, which makes the water cold and muddy. Next to a nautical center and a jetty.

En la boca de la ría de Var rompe con bastante consistencia esta ola. El agua está fría y cenagosa. Junto a un centro naútico y un espigón.

14. Villefranche/Mer

Même si c'est flat, il faut y aller. Au fond de la baie, le pic droite-gauche peut être puissant .

Even though the odds of finding it flat are high, the place is worth checking. Deep in the bay, the peaks can be powerful.

Pese a que lo más probable es que no haya olas, merece la pena echar un vistazo, porque el pico que rompe al fondo de la bahía puede dar izquierdas y derechas potentes.

15. Algajola

Probablement le spot le plus gros de Corse, bien connu des windsurfers: direction la plage d'Aregno!

Probably Corsica's biggest wave spot, famous amongst wave-sailors. Head for Aregno Beach.

Es el spot de ola grande de Córcega, famoso entre los windsurferos. Busca playa Aregno.

16. Capo di Feno:

Accés difficile mais ça rentre souvent.Roulez sur le route des Iles Sanguinaires et jetez un oeil aux CRS ou devant la maison de Tino Rossi.

Difficult access but it's quite consistent. Drive past Tino Rossis' house or CRS on the road towards the Sanguinaires Islands.

El acceso es difícil, pero este spot es bastante consistente.

Capo di Feno - *Photo: Xavier Gonzalez*

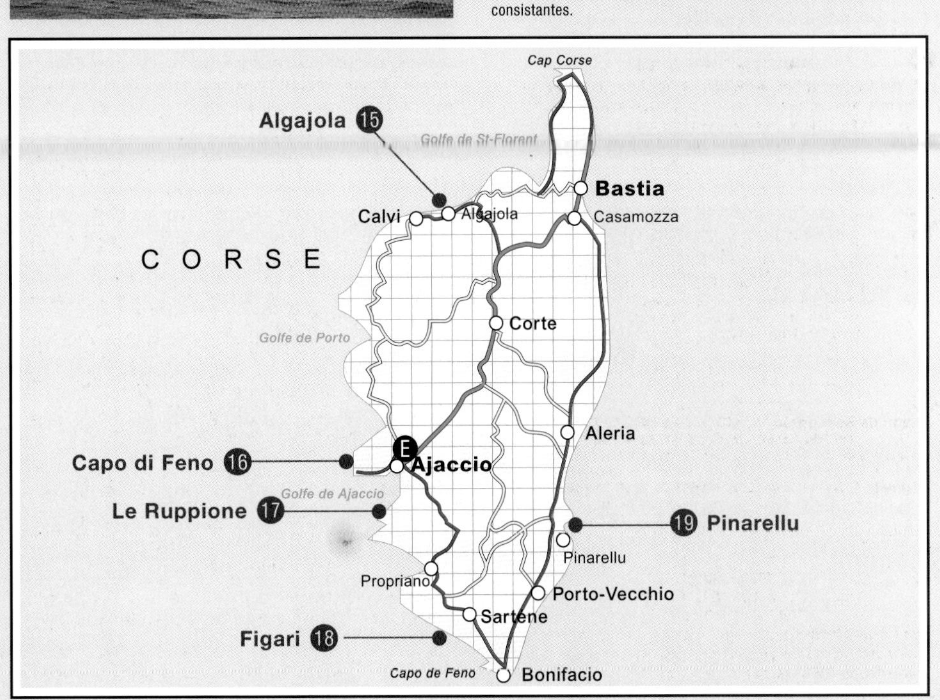

17. Le Ruppione

Passé Punta di Sette Nave, ce spot est un shore-break assez gras. La Castagne à quelques encablures est un reef digne de ce nom.

Past Punta di Sette Nave, this spot is a fat shore-break. Close by is La Castagne, a much better wave on a reef.

Ola orillera fofa, está pasando la Punta di Sette Nave. Cerca está La Castagne, una ola de arrecife mucho mejor.

18. Figari

De l'autre côté de la baie, on peut surfer de temps en temps. Surtout fréquenté par les windsurfers.

On the eastern side of the bay are waves to be found. Usually a windsurfing spot. North of Ste-Lucie de Porto-Vecchio.

19. Pinarellu

Au nord de Ste-Lucie de Porto-Vecchio, les vagues plus consistentes de la côte Est.

N of Ste-Lucie de Porto-Vecchio, most consistent waves on E coast.

Al norte de Ste-Lucie de Porto-Vecchio, son las olas más consistantes.

ITALIA

Capital:	Edinburgh
Population:	5,090,000
Area:	32,714km²
Time:	GMT (summer GMT+1)
Language:	English

Venice - Photo: Tim Rainger, LP

Telephoning

Italia	19 +	Italia	39 +
INT. Operator	12	Police	112
Medical	113	Pompiers	115

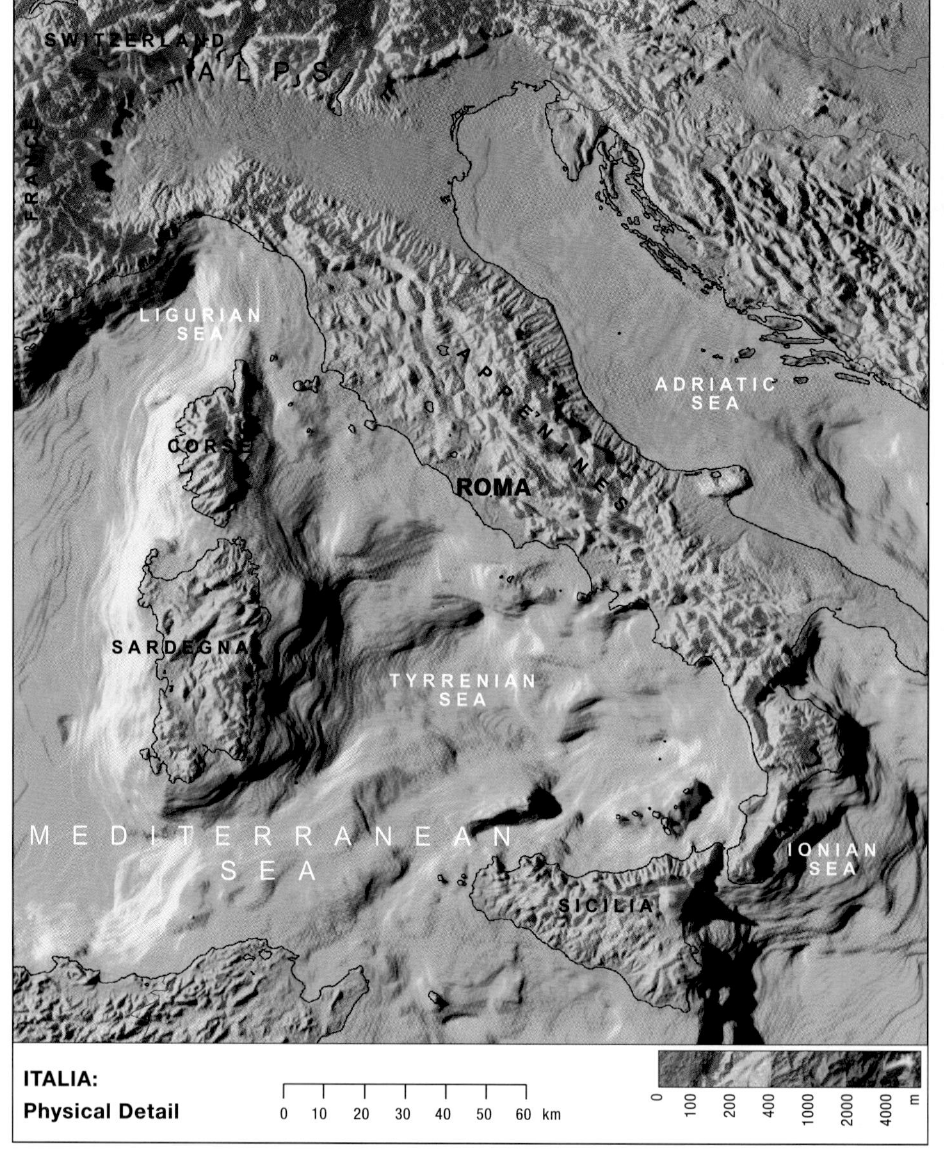

ITALIA: Physical Detail

Breve Storia del Surf Italiano

Nei primissimi anni ottanta assieme al grande boom del windsurf, compaiono in Italia i primi surfisti "da onda". Inizialmente il loro numero era molto esiguo ma nonostante la difficoltà a spiegare che anche i mari Italiani sono agibili per il surf, il numero di praticanti è continuamente cresciuto; attualmente vi sono circa 4.000 surfisti. Dai primi anni novanta ad oggi il numero di surf shops sale da 4 a 20 ed i giornali che trattano esclusivamente di surf passano da 0 a 3. Ci sono anche due federazioni di surf ISF, che organizano competizioni ufficiali e FISO. Con i suoi oltre 8.000 Km di coste l'Italia è certamente da considerarsi ancora ampiamente inesplorata specie nell'estremo Sud, dove ancora i surfisti sono visti come un fenomeno. Sino ad oggi la FISO ha censito e mappato oltre 100 spots, ma essi sono solo una piccola parte del patrimonio italiano.

A Brief History of Italian Surfing

In the early 80's with the windsurf boom, the first 'wave surfers' appeared. Initially numbers were small, but once the difficulty of explaining that Italian seas were surfable was overcome, the numbers of people practising the sport has increased steadily. At the moment there are about 4000 surfers. Since the early 90's the number of surf shops went from 4 to 20 and specialised magazines from 0 to 3. here are also two surfing federations: The ISF organise all official competitionsand FISO (see below). With 8000km of coast, Italy is largely unexplored, especially the extreme south, where surfers are still an unusual phenomena. To date FISO has located 100 spots, but they are only a start.

L'histoire du surf en Italie

Dans le début des années 80 avec le boom du windsurf, les premiers surfers "de vagues" apparurent. Au départ, les effectifs étaient minimes mais une fois que la difficulté d'expliquer que les eaux italiennes étaient parfaitement surfables fut surmontée, les adeptes se sont multipliés régulièrement. Actuellement, il y a peu près 4000 surfers. Depuis le début des années 90, le nombre de surf-shops est passé de 4 à 20 et les magazines spécialisés de 0 à 3. Il y a aussi deux federacion de surf. Le SFI qui organise les competitions. Avec 8000 kms de côtes, l'Italie reste encore largement inexplorée, surtout dans l'extrême sud, où les surfers sont encore une curiosité. Pour l'instant, la FISO a répertorié une centaine de spots mais ce n'est qu'un début.

Le notizie sono state fornite da:
FISO Federazione Italiana Surf da Onda
RIVIERA SURF CLUB, SURFER PLANET CLUB
SARDINIA SURFING ASSOCIATION
LIGURIA SURF DIVISION

Andrea Tazzari
& Ringraziamo per la collaborazione:
Monica Proietti, Carlo Marrazzi, Paolo Perucci, Gilberto Bonasegale, Carlo Azzarone, King Surfer Magazine, SURF NEWS magazine

Nel 1994 nasce la FISO (Federazione Italiana Surf da Onda) che coordina il lavoro e le iniziative di molti clubs surfistici Italiani che attualmente sono una dozzina. Inoltre dal 1994 la FISO gestisce l'unico SURF REPORT che fornisce informazioni 24/24 sulla situazione dei mari attorno all'Italia. La FISO è a disposizione di tutti coloro che sono interessati a visitare l'Italia "surfisticamente", contattateci per ogni informazione!

In 1994 FISO (Federazione Italiana Surf da Onda) was born and it co-ordinates the works and initiatives of many local surfing clubs, (currently 12).Futhermore FISO manages the only surf report which provides a 24hr information sevice on the sea situation around Italy. Anyone interested in visiting Italy "Surfistically", contact us for info and assistance.

En 1994, la FISO fut créée pour coordonner les initiatives et les actions des surf-clubs locaux (12 pour l'instant). De plus, la FISO gère le seul Surf Report qui fournit une info 24H/24 sur la situation marine autour de l'Italie. Quiconque intéressé à visiter l'Italie surfistiquement peut nous contacter pour info et assistance à.

Verazze - *Photo: Phillipe Chevodian*

Paolo Perucci, Banzai - *Photo: FISO*

Italian Surfing Federation (ISF)

Allesandro?? Dini
IWST Piza Palombari, Deil' Artiglio, Club Nautico, 55049
Viareggio (LU)
Tel/Fax:(39) 0584 395215

FISO

(main office) via A. Agnello, 20 48100 Ravenna Italy
Tel. +39 544 212-020/217-720

Condizioni Metio Italiene

Grazie alle favorevoli condizioni geo-climatiche, i mari circostanti l'Italia spesso si presentano mossi, con onde di buona qualità comprese tra gli 1 ed i 2 metri. In condizioni particolari in alcuni spots è possibile surfare onde che raggiungono anche i tre metri di altezza! La condizione meteorologica più frequente generante le onde, è l'attraversamento da (N/W verso S/E) di perturbazioni generate sul Nord Atlantico, che dopo aver varcato la Spagna e la Francia fanno irruzione sul bacino del Mediterraneo. Il contrasto di temperatura tra i mari circostanti l'Italia e l'aria arrivata dall'oceano genera vento di forte intensità con componente ciclonica che interessa tutte le coste italiane e le isole. Un'altra situazione meteorologica favorevole per generare le onde è la discesa di aria fredda dalla ex URSS che provoca forti venti da E-N/E sui mari Italiani.Vi è anche la situazione generata da aria fredda oceanica che entrano profondamente nel Nord Africa per reazione instaura venti sostenuti da S su tutti i mari Italiani anch'essi causa di onde.Solitamente le perturbazioni attraversano abbastanza velocemente l'Italia, facendo sì che nei giorni successivi vi siano onde di buona fattura e condizioni meteo favorevoli. Il periodo migliore per il surf è da settembre a giugno, quando sono più frequenti le perturbazioni che si avvicendano sul mediterraneo. Più raramente anche luglio ed agosto possono offrire onde. La frequenza dei giorni surfabili varia molto a secondo della collocazione geografica degli spots e va da un minimo di 60 giorni surfabili all'anno fino ad un massimo di 200.Il clima italiano è particolarmente favorevole per il surf: nei periodi più freddi sulla costa ovest della penisola e sulle due isole maggiori difficilmente la temperatura dell'aria scende sotto i 10°C mentre la temperatura dell'acqua rimane attestata attorno ai 12/14°C. La costa Est, più fredda nel periodo invernale, durante l'estate vede salire la temperatura dell'acqua in prossimità della costa, sino a 30°C.

La qualità dell'acqua dei bacini circostanti l'Italia e complessivamente buona. Solo in alcune aree altamente industrializzate o nei pressi di foci di fiumi essa decade. Da oltre 7 anni esiste uno stretto controllo effettuato da enti governativi tramite la "Green Schooner" che certifica la qualità dell'acqua.

The Italian Weather

Thanks to good climatic conditions, the seas surrounding Italy often have good waves from 3-6ft. On rare days it's possible to ride 8ft surf. The most frequent meteorological conditions are the crossing from the NW towards the south of general disturbances created in the north Atlantic. After the Low has crossed France and Spain it erupts in the Mediterranean Basin. The contrast of temperatures between the seas surrounding Italy, and the air arriving from the ocean, generates strong winds that affect the whole Italian coastline and islands. A favourable set of conditions for the generation of waves is the descent of cold air currents from the former Soviet block triggering strong E/NE wind on the Italian seas. There is also a situation caused by cold oceanic air that enters North Africa deeply and results in winds from the south, across all Italian seas, that in turn cause waves. Usually disturbances cross Italy swiftly, allowing waves and favourable conditions for a couple of days. The best surf period is September to June, when disturbances passing across the Med are most frequent. The frequency of surfable days varies greatly depending on the position of the spots; varieying from a minimum of 60 surfable days to a maximum of 200 a year. The Italian climate is particularly favourable. During the colder periods on the west coast and on the islands, the air temps rarely fall below 10c and water reaches 12-14c. The Eastern coast is colder during winter, but summer water temps rise up to 30c.

The water quality in the Italian Basin is o.k. though in industrialised areas and at the mouths of rivers the quality is poor. Seven years ago tight controls were imposed, funded by government agencies. The "Green Schooner" certifies the quality of the water.

La Meteo Italienne

Grâce à de bonnes conditions climatiques, les mers qui entourent l'Italie ont souvent un bon potentiel pour des vagues de 1 à 2 mètres. On peut même parfois surfer jusqu'à 2,5m. Les conditions météo les plus fréquentes sont le passage de perturbations du nord-ouest au sud depuis l'Atlantique nord. Après que la dépression a traversé la France et l'Espagne, elle heurte le bassin Méditerranéen. Le contraste de températures entre les mers entourant l'Italie et l'air arrivant de l'océan génére des vents violents qui affectent tout le littoral italien et ses îles. Un situation favorable pouur la formation de vagues est la descente de courants d'air froid depuis l'ex-bloc soviétique qui provoquent de forts vents d'est/nord-est sur le littoral italien. Il y a aussi la situation d'un air océanique froid qui entre violemment en Afrique du Nord, ce qui amène dÚes vents de sud sur toutes les mers italiennes et donc des vagues. Souvent, les perturbations circulent sur le pays rapidement, donnant des vagues et des conditions favorables pour un ou deux jours. La meilleure période pour surfer s'étend de septembre à Juin, quand ces dépressions sont les plus fréquentes. La fréquence des jours surfables varient énormément en fonction de la position des spots: de 60 au minimum à 200 jours par an. Le climat italien est particulièrement clément. Pendant les périodes les plus froides sur la côte ouest et les îles, les températures descendent rarement au-dessous de 10°c avec une eau entre 12°c et 14°c. La côte orientale est plus froide pendant l'hiver mais l'été, ça peut monter jusqu'à 30°c. La qualité de l'eau est correcte bien que dans les zones industrialisées et aux sorties de rivières, elle soit inquiétante. En 1988, des contrôles sévères furent imposés par des institutions gouvernementales. Le "Green Schooner" (bannière verte) certifie la qualité de l'eau.

Sardegna & Adriatico

FISO

Sardegna 1-7

La qualità dell'acqua in tutti gli spots Sardi è eccellente. I prezzi variano molto da zona a zona, ma restano comunque accessibili in autunno ed in primavera le stagioni migliori per il surf. Il numero dei praticanti è in continuo aumento ed il localismo è quasi inesistente. Rispetta le regole e sarai il benvenuto.

The best seasons are autumn and spring when good consistent swells bring waves to all Sardinia's coasts. The numbers of surfers is growing rapidly but if you're friendly, you will be warmly welcomed. The water quality is excellent.

Les meilleures saisons sont l'automne et le printemps quand les houles propres et consistantes amènent des vagues sur toutes les côtes de la Sardaigne. Le nombre de surfers y progresse rapidement mais si vous êtes amicaux, vous y serez chaleureusement reçus. L'eau y est irréprochable.

1. Costa Nord

ISOLA ROSSA

Stretta spiaggia circondata da rocce in cui frangono onde destre e sinistre da 1 a 3m molto potenti che tendono a tubare. Poco affollato.

Narrow beach surrounded by rocks. Can have powerful tubes.

Une plage étroite entourée par des rochers.

BADESI

Ampia spiaggia in cui frangono vari beach break. Lavora al meglio con swell da NO in scaduta.

Wide beach with various peaks best in a NW swell.

Une plage avec des pics variés meilleurs par houle de nord-ouest.

LA CIACCIA (VALLEDORIA)

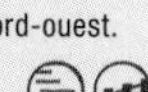

Parte iniziale della spiaggia di Valledoria. Anche qui il fondale è di roccia e sabbia genera sinistre da 1 a 3m molto lunghe. Lavora in prevalenza con swell da NO.

Can have good long lefts.

Peut avoir de longues vagues de qualité.

SOTTO IL CASTELLO

E' lo spot del paese di Castelsardo. Riparatissimo dal vento di NO lavora solo con grosse mareggiate. Picco prevalentemente destro dai 2 ai 3m. Le onde molto potenti ma non lunghe, terminano la loro corsa contro una scogliera a picco. Poco affollato.

A short but powerful peak breaks right. Needs a big swell.

Un pic court mais puissant qui casse en droite. Demande un gros swell.

LU BAGNU

Spot dal fondale di sabbia e roccia su cui rompono onde sino a 2m; lavora con swell da SO, O e NO meglio se in scaduta. La migliore condizione dello spot in cui surfarlo è con onde di 2 m sul picco sinistro su cui si genera un largo tubo. Poco affollato.

Works up to 2m with swell from the SW-NW. A tubing left peak.

Marche jusqu'à 2m avec une houle de SO à NO. Un pic en gauche qui donne un bon tube.

2. Alghero - Porto Ferro

Lo spot è situato a 15km da Alghero ed è una baia che lavora con swell da SO-N ma non con vento forte. Le onde vanno da 1 a 4m e rompono sia a destre che a sinistra. Facile la discesa in acqua.

A bay needing swell from SW-N and no wind. Works from 1-4m.

Une baie qui nécessite une houle de sud-ouest à nord mais sans trop de vents. Marche de 1 à 4 mètres!

3. Puzzu Idu

E' considerata la zona migliore della Sardegna (o del Mediterraneo?), si trova a trenta km a NO di Oristano. Lavora prevalentemente con vento di Maestrale (NO), vento dominante nell'isola, ma si può surfare anche con swell da SO, O e N.

Some of the best waves in the med break in an area 30km's northwest of Oristano. Works in Mistal conditions.

Parmi les meilleures vagues de la Mediterranée dans un rayon de 30 kms au nord-ouest d'Oristano.

CAPO MANNU

Lavora con Maestrale anche attivo. E' una baia esposta a SO in cui le onde penetrano seguendo il profilo della costa, formando un largo picco centrale. La destra molto lunga e potente tuba soprattutto nella sezione finale; la sinistra, più corta e ripida, tende al close out nell'ultima parte. L'altezza dell'onda va da 1.5 a 3m. L'entrata e soprattutto l'uscita dall'acqua possono creare qualche problema per il tavolato roccioso molto tagliente, i ricci e le correnti sottocosta. Si consiglia l'uso dei calzari.

A powerful peak gives a long powerful tubey right, and a shorter steeper left. Sharp rocks and urchins mean boots are a good idea.

Un pic puissant qui donne une droite puissante et tubulaire avec une gauche plus courte et plus raide encore. Des rochers coupants et des oursins, n'oubliez pas vos chaussons.

MINI CAPO

Questo spot è surfabile quando a CAPO MANNU le onde superano i 3m. Onde con picco centrale da 1 a 3m molto ripide e veloci tubanti in partenza in particolar modo la sinistra che però è più corta. Lo spot lavora anche con vento di forte intensità da NO. Molti surfisti preferiscono questo spot a CAPO MANNU che consente una facile discesa in acqua dalla piccola spiaggia a destra dello spot.

Starts to break when Capo Mannu is big. A good steep peak.

Commence à casser quand Capo Mannu est gros. Un bon pic bien creux.

LA LAGUNA (SA MESA LONGA)

Incantevole spiaggia col reef al largo a Nord del promontorio di CAPO MANNU. Ottimo spot quando il CAPO è inconsistente lavora con swell da SO, O, NO e N; buone sia le onde destre che le più lunghe e ripide sinistre che possono raggiungere anche i 4m.

Excellent spot when Capo is inconsistent. Holds big swell.

Excellent spot quand Capo est irrégulier. Tient bien le gros quand ça vient du nord au sud-ouest.

SU PALLO SU

Cala rocciosa confinante con la LAGUNA che lavora con le stesse condizioni. Sinistra non molto lunga ma potentissima e con un drop impegnativo.

Long and powerful wave works in the same conditions as La Laguna.

Une vague très longue et puissante marchant dans les mêmes conditions que la Lagune.

4. Buggeru

Lavora con swell da SO, O e NO e genera un'onda sinistra molto potente che tende a tubare in partenza. Facile l'entrata in acqua seguendo la corrente che costeggia il molo o tuffandosi dallo stesso.

Heavy left that tubes on take-off. Easy paddle out along the pier. Also waves at Porti Sceddu.

Une gauche carton qui tube au take-off. Il est facile de ramer le long de la jetée. Des vagues aussi à Porti Sceddu.

5. Cagliari (CHIA)

A 50 km da Cagliari è situato il migliore spots della costa Sud. Per via della sua particolare disposizione lavora con ogni tipo di swell tranne che quelle provenienti da N e NO.

5okm's from Cagliari is one of the best areas on Sardinia with various good quality waves.

A 50 kms dela Sardaigne se trouve une des meilleures zones de surf en Sardaigne avec quelques vagues de qualité variable.

IL PONTILE

A fianco di un pontile rompono onde sinistre alte fino a 3m, tendenti a tubare in partenza: lavora al meglio con swell da NE, E e SE.

A tubey left wave that can hold good size. Needs a NE swell.

De très longues droites avec une mer agitée vers l'ouest.

IL MORTO

Oltre il piccolo promontorio del PONTILE offre le sue condizioni migliori con grosse mareggiate da O. Onde destre sino a 3m molto lunghe, tubanti in diverse sezioni.

Very long rights with heavy seas from the west.

Peut marcher quand c'est trop petit à Il Morto.

L'ISOLOTTO

Ottimo spot quando al pontile le onde sono piccole. Lavora con le stesse condizioni del MORTO ma qui le onde sono sinistre e raggiungono i 2m.

Can have waves when Il Morto is small.

De très longues droites et un bon shore-break épais.

PIPELINE

Oltre l'isolotto la spiaggia di PIPELINE viene surfata prevalentemente con swell provenienti da O. Il picco più al largo forma onde destre dai 2 ai 2.5m molto lunghe. Il picco più a riva offre onde meno lunghe ma più ripide sia destre che sinistre che possono raggiungere i 2m.

Very long rights and also a good steep shore-break.

Tres longues droites et aussi un bon gros shore-break.

6. Cagliari (Poetto)

E' lo spot migliore della lunga (6km) spiaggia Cagliaritana. Lavora con swell da E, SE e S; le onde raramente superano i due metri. Ideale per i meno esperti lo spot genera onde lunghe e non troppo potenti. L'estensione dello spot è tale da non creare problemi di affollamento. Fondale sabbioso.

One of the best spots on the Island. Long and mellow waves Ideal for beginners

Un des meilleurs spots de l'île. Des vagues longues et molles idéales pour débuter.

7. Marina Romea

E' probabilmente lo spot in cui si formano le onde più consistenti dell'alto Adriatico. Lo spot si trova alla foce del fiume Lamone a Nord dell'abitato di Marina Romea. I due moli che prolungano la foce del fiume hanno provveduto a generare due secche di sabbia a Sud ed a Nord della foce, su cui rompono onde sino a 2m.

The most consistent waves of the northern Adriatic. The mouth of the river has created sandbanks giving waves up to 2m. Best in S swell.

Les vagues les plus consistantes du nord de l"Adriatique. L'embouchure de la rivière a créé des bancs avec de bonnes vagues jusqu'à 2m. Meilleur par houle de sud.

8. Porto Corsini (Diga Nord)

Lo spot si trova nel centro del paese di Porto Corsini, dove sbuca il porto di Ravenna. Su fondale sabbioso rompe un'onda destra alta sino a 2m tendente a riformarsi, che in condizioni di forte swell da SE la si può surfare (con un longboard) per circa trecento metri! Lavora anche con swell da E. Qualità dell'acqua mediocre. Spot affollato.

Popular spot in the centre of town. At the port of Ravenna a sandbar forms a right which can be long, especially on a longboard.

Un spot bien connu au centre de la ville. Dans le port de Ravenna, un banc de sable forme une droite qui peut être longue, surtout en longboard. L'eau est médiocre.

9. Marina di Ravenna

Spot speculare a Porto Corsini; lo si raggiunge prendendo il ferry boat che collega Porto Corsini a Marina di Ravenna e proseguendo verso S lungo la costa per circa 1Km. A fianco del lungo molo (2.8 Km) del porto di Ravenna si è generata una secca di sabbia che con Swell da E e N\E genera onde sinistre tendenti a riformarsi. Raramente lavora anche con swell da S. Qualità dell'acqua mediocre. Spot affollato.

Good spot for contemplation. Needs a NE or E swell.

Bon spot pour le paysage. Par houle de nord-est à est.

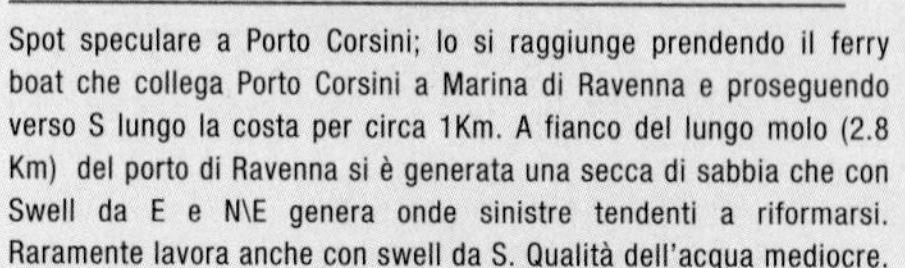

10. Lido Adriano (Gorilla).

Lo spot si trova all'estremo Sud della località di Lido Adriano, in prossimità della foce dei Fiumi Uniti. Lavora con piccole swell fino ad 1 metro da NE, E e SE. Fondale sabbioso. Qualità dell'acqua cattiva. Spot poco frequentato.

Affected by small swells from the NE-SE.

S'agite par petite houle de nord-est à sud-est.

11. Milano Marittima (Canalino).

Lo spot è situato nel centro dell'abitato di Milano Marittima alla foce di un piccolo canale di scolo delle acque piovane. I due corti moli costruiti a lato della foce del canale, hanno generato una secca sul lato Sud che con piccole swell da NE, E e SE genera onde di mediocre qualità sino ad 1 metro. Qualità dell'acqua discreta. Poco affollato.

Two small piers at the mouth of the canal create a shallow which picks up surf from the NE-SE.

Deux petites jetées à la sortie du canal créent un haut-fond qui prend la houle de nord-est à sud-est.

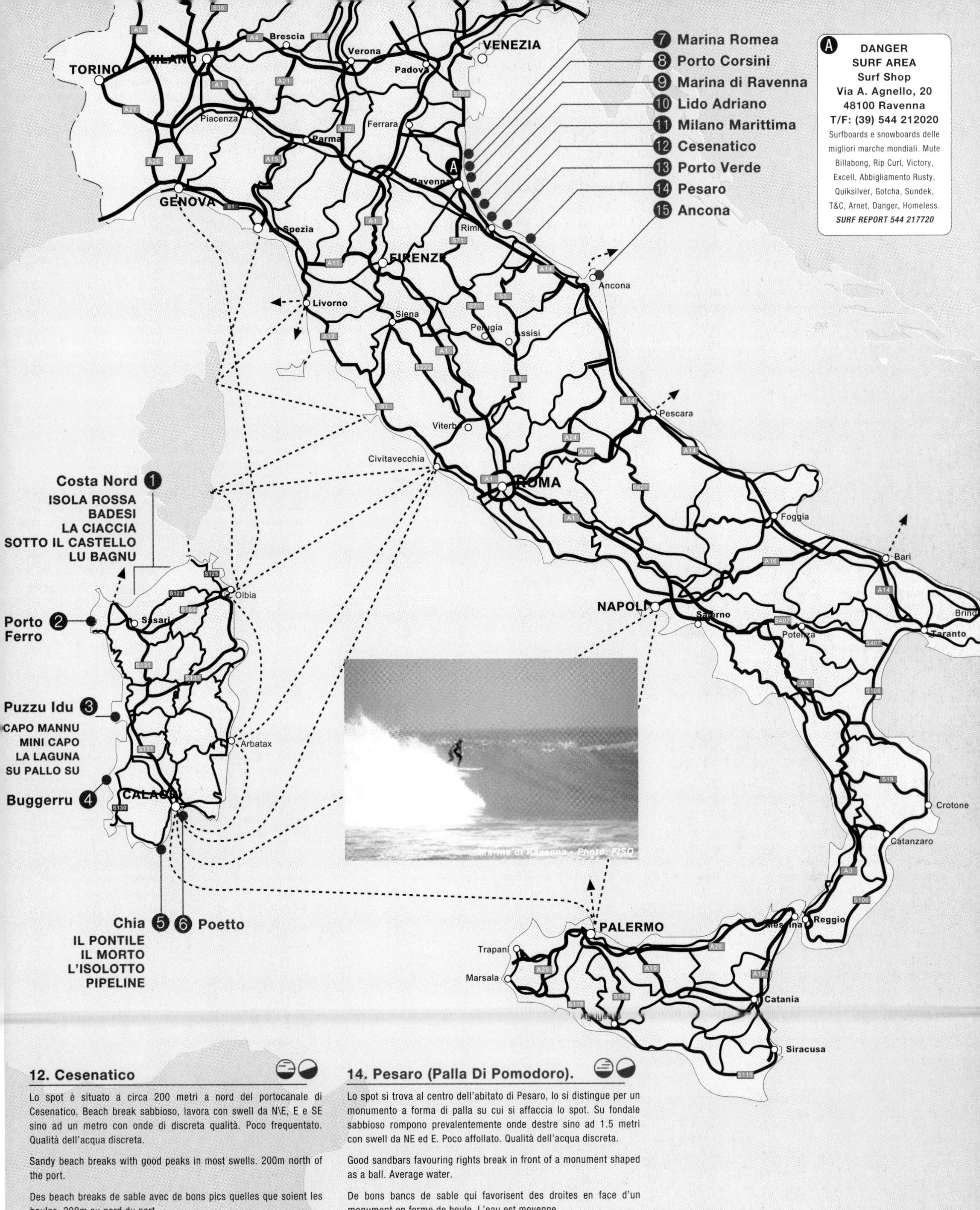

12. Cesenatico

Lo spot è situato a circa 200 metri a nord del portocanale di Cesenatico. Beach break sabbioso, lavora con swell da N\E, E e SE sino ad un metro con onde di discreta qualità. Poco frequentato. Qualità dell'acqua discreta.

Sandy beach breaks with good peaks in most swells. 200m north of the port.

Des beach breaks de sable avec de bons pics quelles que soient les houles. 200m au nord du port.

13. Porto Verde

Lo spot è situato nella località di Porto Verde a circa 10Km a Sud di Rimini. Unico spot con fondale di sassi della riviera Romagnola, si trova 200 metri a Sud della piccolissima imboccatura del porticciolo di Porto Verde. Lavora con swell da N\E ed E anche di grosse dimensioni e vento on shore. Onde prevalentemente destre sino a due metri. Qualità dell'acqua mediocre.

The only rock/reef in the area giving good rights on a NE or E swell. Average water quality. Located 200m south of the port.

Le seul reef dans le coin qui donne de bonnes droites par houle de nord-est et est. Situé à 200m au sud du port.

14. Pesaro (Palla Di Pomodoro).

Lo spot si trova al centro dell'abitato di Pesaro, lo si distingue per un monumento a forma di palla su cui si affaccia lo spot. Su fondale sabbioso rompono prevalentemente onde destre sino ad 1.5 metri con swell da NE ed E. Poco affollato. Qualità dell'acqua discreta.

Good sandbars favouring rights break in front of a monument shaped as a ball. Average water.

De bons bancs de sable qui favorisent des droites en face d'un monument en forme de boule. L'eau est moyenne.

15. Ancona (La Trave).

Lo spot è situato a circa 3Km a sud della città di Ancona. Lavora con swell da NE, E e SE. Su fondale roccioso rompono onde sino a due metri con grosse swell da SE. Qualità dell'acqua buona. Poco affollato.

3km's south of Ancona. Good water and wave quality and picks up most swells.

3kms au sud d' Ancona. Eau et vague de ùqualité qui chope la plupart des houles.

Southern Italy

Rodi Garganico, Peschici, Vieste, Barletta, Bari, Monopoli, Otranto Gallipoli, Lido di Metaponta, Lido di Policoro, Capo, Spulico and Pizzo Calabrohave.

Sicilia

Mazzara Del Vallo (various spots), Tre Fontane, Triscina, Elora, Siracusa, Cefalu, Terrasini, Capo D'Orlando and Pozzallo

Lazio, Toscana & Liguria

FISO

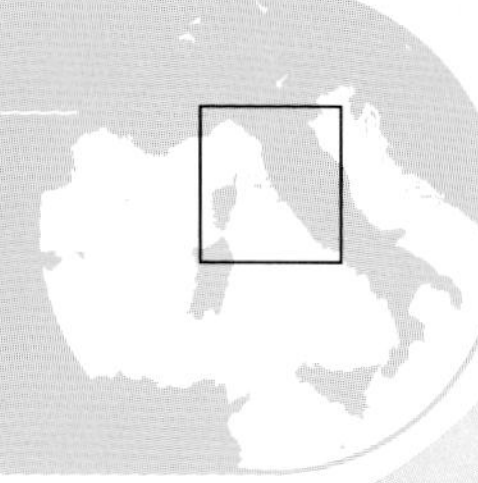

1. Varazze

Altro gioiello del Mediterraneo è l'onda che con swell da S e SE frange sulla secca artificiale di Varazze. Caratterizzato dalla ottima qualità dell'acqua e dall'affollamento questo spot offre una destra tubante che in rare condizioni può superare i 3m! Il fondale di roccia tagliente è da temere quando si incappa in un wipe out.

Another jewel in the Med breaks over artificial reef. Heavy, hollow and crowded. Wipe-outs can lead to a confrontation with the jagged rock. Works on small swells and has good water quality.

Un autre joyau des spots de la Mediterranée sur un reef artificiel. Carton, creux et peuplé. Prenez une gamelle et vous irez tâter les formations rocheuses déchiquetées. Marche par petit swell. L'eau est propre.

Vazarre - Photo: Luca Garibaldi

2. Levanto

Circa a 20km a nord di La Spezia, troviamo Levanto un piccolo paesino situato in una baia in cui entra una delle più grandi onde sinistre del Nord Italia. Lavora eccellentemente con swell da SO e sul picco centrale si formano sinistre tubanti alte sino a 3m che rompono su fondale sabbioso.

Situated in the bay breaks one of Italy's biggest lefts. A SW swell will give the best waves.

Située dans la baie, cette gauche est une des plus grosses du pays. Une houle de S-O donnera les meilleures vagues.

3. Lerici

Nel piccolo paese tipicamente ligure, frange sia una destra che una sinistra di buona qualità. Anche con forti venti da SO o con mareggiate attive LERICI funziona. Non molto frequentato presenta una buona qualità dell'acqua.

A typically small Ligurian town, often with good uncrowded waves. Can handle heavy seas and SW winds. Good water quality.

Une petite ville typique de Ligurie avec de bonnes vagues régulières sans la foule. Peut tenir des mers démontées avec des vents de SO.

4. Forte dei Marmi (Pontile)

A destra ed a sinistra dell'unico pontile della località vi sono due secche che generano distintamente una destra ed una sinistra. A causa delle correnti le secche subiscono radicali modificazioni che incidono sul funzionamento dello spot.

Good sandbars but strong currents consistently alter wave characteristics. Located about 15km's north of Viareggio with mediocre water quality.

De bons bancs de sable mais des courants infernaux qui changent constamment les caractéristiques de la vague. Situé à 15 kms au nord de Viarregio avec une qualité de l'eau qui est médiocre.

Dario Gerbella, Pontile - Photo: FISO

5. Viareggio

TITO DEL MOLO

Il lato nord del porto di Viareggio protegge un'area di spiaggia che in condizioni di mareggiate da SO genera una sinistra lunga ma poco potente.

The north side of the port has long and powerful waves with a strong SW swell. Very crowded when it works.

L'extrémité nord du port peut avoir des vagues longues et puissantes par forte houle de sud-ouest. La Chine quand ça marche.

PIAZZA MAZZINI

Circa 500m più a Nord di Tito del Molo si trova lo spot di PIAZZA MAZZINI, dove grazie alla dragatura del porto di Viareggio si è formata una secca su cui rompe una bellissima sinistra che in condizioni ottimali (scaduta da SO) raggiunge tranquillamente i 2m.

A shallow created by the dredging of the port has provided Viareggio with one of Italy's best waves. Consistent and very crowded.

Un haut-fond créé par le draguage du port est maintenant une des meilleures vagues d'Italie. Consistant et bondé.

6. Livorno (Il Sale)

Insieme a Varazze (Liguria) è uno degli spots più impegnativi della costa Ovest Italiana. L'onda del Sale è abbastanza corta ma sviluppa una potenza rilevante. Sono surfabili sia la destra che la sinistra che si generano dallo stesso picco dal take off difficoltoso. Non è difficile intubarsi appena in piedi. Lo spot è molto affollato dai bravi surfisti locali che indubbiamente sanno sfruttare al meglio le caratteristiche di queste onde. Il basso fondale roccioso è pericoloso.

One of the best spots in Italy. A powerful, tubey peak breaks in shallow water and is dominated by a hot local crew. Needs a good swell.

Un des meilleurs spots. Un pic puissant et tubulaire casse dans peu d'eau, dominé par une bande de locaux un peu survoltée. Marche avec un swell correct.

7. Lillatro

Lo spot offre 4 picchi di cui 3 su fondale roccioso. L'onda è qualitativamente molto buona anche se è non molto lunga. La qualità dell'acqua non eccelle soprattutto per la vicinanza di una fabbrica di detersivi che però stranamente regala all'acqua un colore azzurro chiaro decisamente fotogenico.

4 peaks giving short but good waves. Water is bad due to a detergent factory which nonetheless gives a photogenic blue quality to the water.

4 pics qui donnent de bonnes vagues mais courtes. L'eau est détestable à cause d'une usine de détergents qui donne à l'eau néanmoins une belle couleur bleue très photogénique.

8. Sta Marinella

PORTO

E' decisamente uno tra i migliori spots in questo tratto di costa ed offre onde pulite specie con swell da S\O. Essendo praticabile anche in condizioni di mareggiata attiva è molto affollato.

One of the best spots in the area, good with a SW swell. Can handle good size but water quality is bad due to the port.

Une bonne vague qui casse dans peu d'eau meilleure par vents de nord-ouest.

Ferrari, Levanto - Photo: FISO

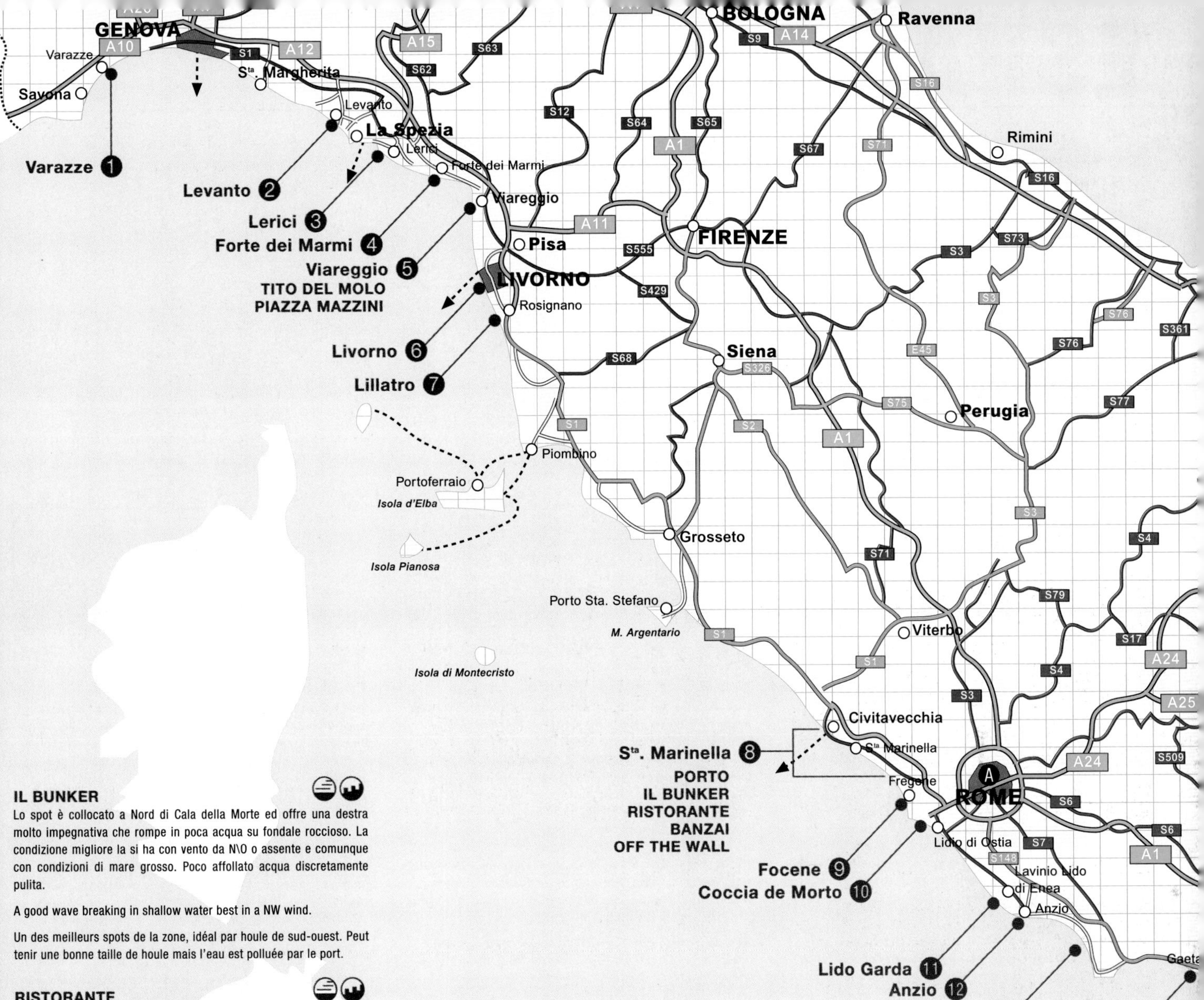

IL BUNKER

Lo spot è collocato a Nord di Cala della Morte ed offre una destra molto impegnativa che rompe in poca acqua su fondale roccioso. La condizione migliore la si ha con vento da N\O o assente e comunque con condizioni di mare grosso. Poco affollato acqua discretamente pulita.

A good wave breaking in shallow water best in a NW wind.

Un des meilleurs spots de la zone, idéal par houle de sud-ouest. Peut tenir une bonne taille de houle mais l'eau est polluée par le port.

RISTORANTE

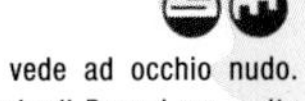

E' a circa 200m più a Nord di Banzai, si vede ad occhio nudo. Produce una destra più piccola rispetto all'onda di Banzai ma molto veloce.

Picks up a bit less swell than Banzai but has good fast waves. Not always crowded.

Chope un peu moins de swell que Banzai mais les vagues y sont plus rapides. Pas forcément la foule.

BANZAI

E' lo spot principe della costa laziale, decisamente più impegnativo degli altri a causa del fondale roccioso e dell'affollamento. Quando funziona è lo spot più frequentato dai migliori surfisti laziali, quindi poco consigliato ai principianti. Le onde, sia destre che sinistre a seconda della mareggiata, sono molto lunghe e potenti, ben surfabili sino a 3 metri. Lo spot è esposto a tutte le mareggiate, praticabile anche con vento forte. La qualità dell'acqua è buona. La massiccia presenza di ricci marini sul fondale impone l'uso dei calzari.

Called "The Prince of the Lazio coast" Banzai is powerful and gets very crowded with some of Italy's best surfers. Good water quality.

Appelé " le Prince du Lazio", Banzai est puissant et est rippé par certains des meilleurs surfers italiens.

OFF THE WALL

A 300 metri a Sud di Banzai si trova questo spot roccioso, che lavora quando Banzai non funziona. Presenta un buon picco anche se l'onda si rivela molto corta.Qualità dell'acqua buona.

Can work well when Banzai is flat. A good peak but very short waves.

Peut bien marcher quand y'a rien à Banzai. Un bon pic mais les vagues sont ultra-courtes.

9. Focene

E' la spiaggia più a Nord di Fiumicino ed è la più frequentata quando il mare non è molto grosso. Lo spot viene surfato durante le scadute e comunque con onde non superiori a 1.5m.

The most crowded spot in a small swell.

Le spot le plus peuplé par petite houle.

10. Coccia de Morto

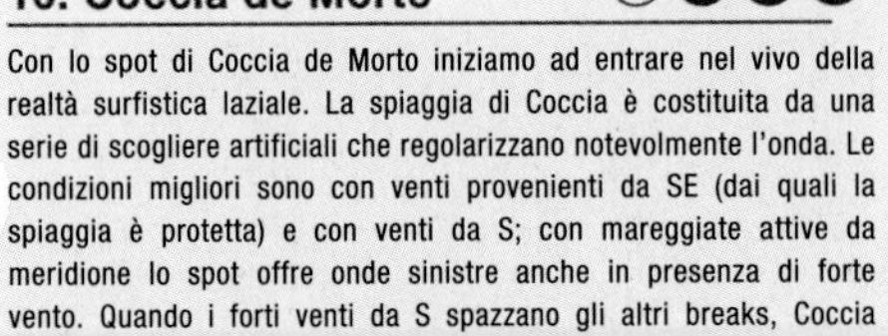

Con lo spot di Coccia de Morto iniziamo ad entrare nel vivo della realtà surfistica laziale. La spiaggia di Coccia è costituita da una serie di scogliere artificiali che regolarizzano notevolmente l'onda. Le condizioni migliori sono con venti provenienti da SE (dai quali la spiaggia è protetta) e con venti da S; con mareggiate attive de meridione lo spot offre onde sinistre discreta anche in presenza di forte vento. Quando i forti venti da S spazzano gli altri breaks, Coccia lavora con onde che possono arrivare sino 3m.

Very crowded waves of good consistency break over artificial reefs. Best swell is from the SE. Water is bad due to the port.

Des vagues bondées bien consistantes qui cassent sur un reef artificiel. La meilleure houle vient du sud-est. Un port à côté donc l'eau est moins que moyenne.

11. Lido Garda

Questo spot si trova poco più a Nord della cittadina di Anzio ed è il più conosciuto della serie di beach break che sono distribuiti lungo la costa sabbiosa che arriva sino ad Ostia.

The most popular beach break in the area north of Anzio. Water quality can be bad.

Le beach break le plus fréquenté au nord d'Anzio. Pollution.

12. Porto de Anzio

Lo spot offre delle buone condizioni per il surf, specialmente con mareggiate da SO che in inverno battono frequentemente la costa producendo onde che possono raggiungere anche i 3 metri.

Consistent spot that holds big surf, best with a SW swell. Water quality can be bad.

Spot consistant qui tient le gros surf, meilleur par houle de sud-ouest. Pollution.

13. Carrubo

Spot a Sud del promontorio del Circeo e quindi protetto dai venti provenienti da settentrione. Su un fondale di sabbia e roccia rompono onde alte fino a 2 metri. La qualità dell'acqua è ottima.

Protected from N winds by the Circeo headland. Good spot with clean water and no crowds.

Protégé des vents de nord par la péninsule de Circeo. Bon spot avec une eau limpide et pas de monde.

14. Sta Agostino

E' un ottimo spot specialmente con i venti da SE. Il fondale è sabbioso e produce onde sinistre discreta potenza e rapidità. E' spesso affollato anche da surfisti romani.

Good spot especially with winds from the SE. Waves have power and speed.

Bon spot surtout par vents de sud-est. Les vagues sont puissantes et rapides.

PIKE SURF SHOP & FACTORY
Via Giulio Quirino Giglioli, 5
00124 Roma
Tel:06 5652092
Fax:06 5652081

ESPAÑA

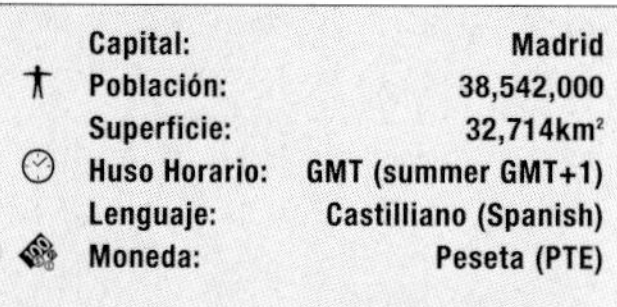

Capital:	**Madrid**
Población:	**38,542,000**
Superficie:	**32,714km²**
Huso Horario:	**GMT (summer GMT+1)**
Lenguaje:	**Castilliano (Spanish)**
Moneda:	**Peseta (PTE)**

Photo: Tim Rainger, LP

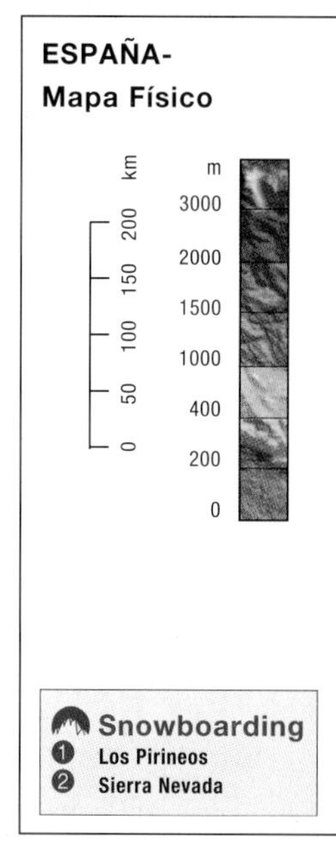

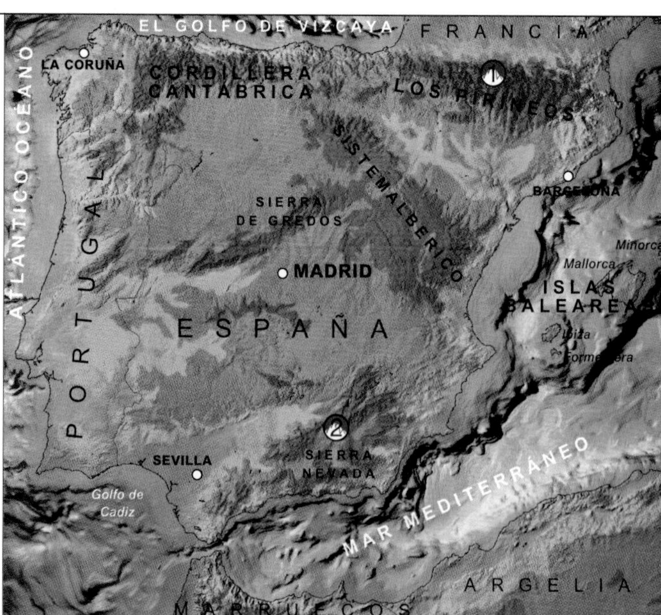

ESPAÑA

Los españoles de ahora son una gente de carácter latino, extrovertido, que disfruta de las conversaciones animadas, de las fiestas y de los estereotipos tradicionales: Julio Iglesias, el Papa, el flamenco y los toros. Durante siete siglos tras la caida del Imperio Romano casi toda la Península estuvo bajo el dominio musulmán. Hasta que los cristianos del norte terminaron la Reconquista en tiempos de los Reyes Católicos, que así mismo creyeron el alocado plan de Colón de navegar a las Indias por el oeste y afortunadamente para sus arcas se toparon con las riquezas de las civilizaciones inca y azteca. Desde esos comienzos los españoles que vivían en las zonas costeras, se aproximaban a esperar la llegada de los galeones colmados de tesoros, confiando en que no hubieran sido capturados por los piratas ingleses o portugueses.

La España de los Habsburgo dominó la Europa de los siglos XVI y XVII ... fuertemente católica fue víctima y promotora de innumerables guerras y conspiraciones, para sumirse en un oscuro letargo los siglos posteriores. La Guerra Civil devolvió la atención internacional sobre España, llegando combatientes antifascistas procedentes de todo el mundo, sin embargo el fascismo versión española del General Franco se impuso, en parte ayudado por Hitler. Favor que afortunadamente Franco no devolvió, evitando así la participación española en la Segunda Guerra Mundial. Muerto el dictador en 1975, se instauró una Monarquía democrática que entró en la Comunidad Europea en 1986 y donde desde 1982 hay un Gobierno socialista.

La Tierra Existe una enorme diversidad regional. Básicamente es una Meseta cruzada por varias cadenas montañosas y varios ríos, destacando el accidentado perfil montañoso del Norte con los Pirineos y la Cordillera Cantábrica.

SPAIN

The Spanish people today are a flamboyant, latin people given greatly to lively conversation and parties, Julio Iglesias, The Pope, flamenco and bulls, but for 700 years after the fall of Rome, nearly all Spain was Islamic, until re conquered by Christian people from the Cantabric region. The Catholic crown became the inspiration behind the reconquista at home and the conquistadores, who carved out an empire in the New World. Spain had been the only court to back Columbus' crazy plan to sail west to India, and fortunately for the coffers of the Spanish treasury, the Aztec and Inca civilisations lay in the way. From the beginning the Spanish were a beach orientated race, watching frantically for treasure ships on the horizon, hoping they hadn't been captured by English or Portuguese pirates.

Habsburg Spain of the 16 and 17C dominated European events...stridently catholic, she was both the victim and propagator of countless wars and conspiracies. She sank into relative obscurity for a few centuries, until the outbreak of the Civil war when liberals world wide arrived to fight the Fascists led by General Franco. Franco triumphed, thanks to some timely help by Hitler, but managed to avoid Hitler's fate by refusing to return the favour in WW2. After Franco's death in 1975 the monarchy was restored and today Spain has a democratically elected, socialist Govt, which joined the E.C. in 1986.

The Land in each region is diverse and often at odds with other places lying at the same latitudes. It consists mainly of a broad central plateau sloping to the S & E, crossed by various mountains and rivers.

ESPAGNE

Les espagnols sont aujourd'hui un peuple latin flamboyant qui s'adonnent aux conversations animées et aux fêtes, à Julio Iglesias, au Pape au flamenco et aux taureaux. 700 ans après la chute de Rome, pratiquement toute l'Espagne était musulmane, avant d'être reconquise par les chrétiens de la région cantabrique. Le catholicisme devint l'inspiration avant la reconquête intérieure et les conquistadors qui construirent un empire dans le Nouveau Monde. L'Espagne fut la seule à financer les projets fumeux de Chistophe Colomb de naviguer à l'ouest vers les Indes et heureusement pour les coffres du Trésor, les civilisations aztèques, mayas et incas se trouvaient sur le chemin. Depuis le début, les Espagnols furent une peuplade orientée vers la plage, regardant impatiemment les galions à l'horizon, en espérant qu'ils n'aient pas été capturés par les pirates anglais ou portugais.

Les Habsbourg du XVI et XVII siècle dominèrent les évènements en Europe d'une façon strictement catholique, en étant la victime et en propageant d'innombrables guerres et conspirations. L'Espagne commença alors à sombrer dans l'oubli pendant quelques siècles, avant que la Guerre Civile n'éclate quand les libéraux du monde entier arrivèrent pour attaquer les fascites conduits par le General Franco. Franco triompha, grâce à l'aide judicieuse d'Hitler, tout en évitant son destin en refusant de lui renvoyer la balle pendant le deuxième guerre mondiale. Après la mort de Franco en 1975, la monarchie fut restaurée et de nos jours, l'Espagne a un gouvernement démocratiquement élu, qui intégra la CEE en 1986.

Le paysage sont essentiellement de larges plaines relativement élevées en en pente vers le sud-est, interrompues par quelques montagnes et des rivières.

Aeroports

Bilbao:	**(94) 424 4300**
Santander:	**(942) 251 007**
Santiago:	**(981) 597 400**
Sevilla:	**(95) 451 6111**

Ferries

Santander (Brittany F.):	**(942) 214 500**
Bilbao (P&O):	**(94) 423 4477**

Trenes

Madrid:	**(091) 323 2121**
Santander:	**(942) 280202**
La Coruña:	**(981) 230 304**
Vigo:	**(986) 431 114**
Bilbao:	**(94) 423 8623**

Vuelos

Es posible volar a España desde cualquier aeropuerto europeo. Bilbao es un destino habitual y bastante económico para aquellos que van a surfear en el Cantábrico, y a Málaga suele haber vuelos baratísimos en invierno, que es cuando hay más olas en Andalucía. Iberia aplica estrictamente el tratamiento de las tablas como sobrepeso, lo que significa que tienes que pagar unas 12,000 pts. En Bilbao son especialmente severos, mientras que en otros sitios puedes intentar pasar sin cargo. En todo caso, informate en tu agencia de viajes.

Ferries

Es uno de los modos más relajantes de viajar a España desde el Reino Unido. Puedes optar entre Plymouth-Santander (30 horas Brittany Ferries) y Portsmouth-Bilbao (36 horas P&O Ferries) ambos trayectos son cubiertos dos veces a la semana, y aún siendo bastante caros te permiten acceder directamente a la mejor zona surfera y con tu propio coche. Desde el sur de España puedes acceder Marruecos y Canarias, y aunque tengas que atravesar la península por carretera, disponer de vehículo en ambos sitios supone una ventaja importante.

Flying

Possible from any airport in Europe and can be reasonable. Bilbao is the most popular and often cheapest destination if you plan to surf Spains northern coasts. Malaga can also be ridiculously cheap to fly to, especially in winter when the Andalucian spots work. Be warned of one thing...Iberian airways have a strict charge for surfboards and at £70, its not cheap (and impossible to get out of). Bilbao is renowned for it and it supposedly applies on all Iberian airways flights. Check before making a reservation with your travel agent.

Ferries

One of the most relaxing ways of getting to Spain from Britain is by ferry. Brittany ferries operates a twice weekly service from Plymouth to Santander. It can be quite expensive and takes 24hrs, but drops you in surf-central, in your own car. South Spain can be your springboard to either Morocco or the Canaries by ferry, and though it's a long drive from the north, the advantages of having your own car or van in both destinations are great.

L'avion

Possible de n'importe quel aéroport en Europe à des prix raisonnables. Bilbao est l'accés le plus fréquent et le moins cher si vous comptez surfez la côte nord. Malaga peut être aussi ridiculement bon marché surtout en hiver quand les spots andalous fonctionnent. Sachez quand même qu' Iberia surtaxent les planches à plus de 500 FF et il est trés difficile de ne pas payer. Bilbao est bien connu pour ça et cela s'applique pratiquement sur tous les vols avec Iberia. A vérifier auprés de votre agent de voyage au moment de réserver votre billet.

Ferries

Un des façons les moins stressantes d'aller en Espagne depuis l'Angleterre. Brittany ferries et P&O desservent deux fois par semaine la ligne Plymouth-Santander (30 heures) et Portsmouth à Bilbao (36 heures). C'est assez cher mais ça vous laisse au milieu des spots, avec votre propre voiture. Le sud de l'Espagne peut être un bon tremplin pour le Maroc ou les Canaries par ferry et bien que ce soit un long trajet depuis le nord, l'avantage de disposer de son véhicule pour les deux destinations est déterminant.

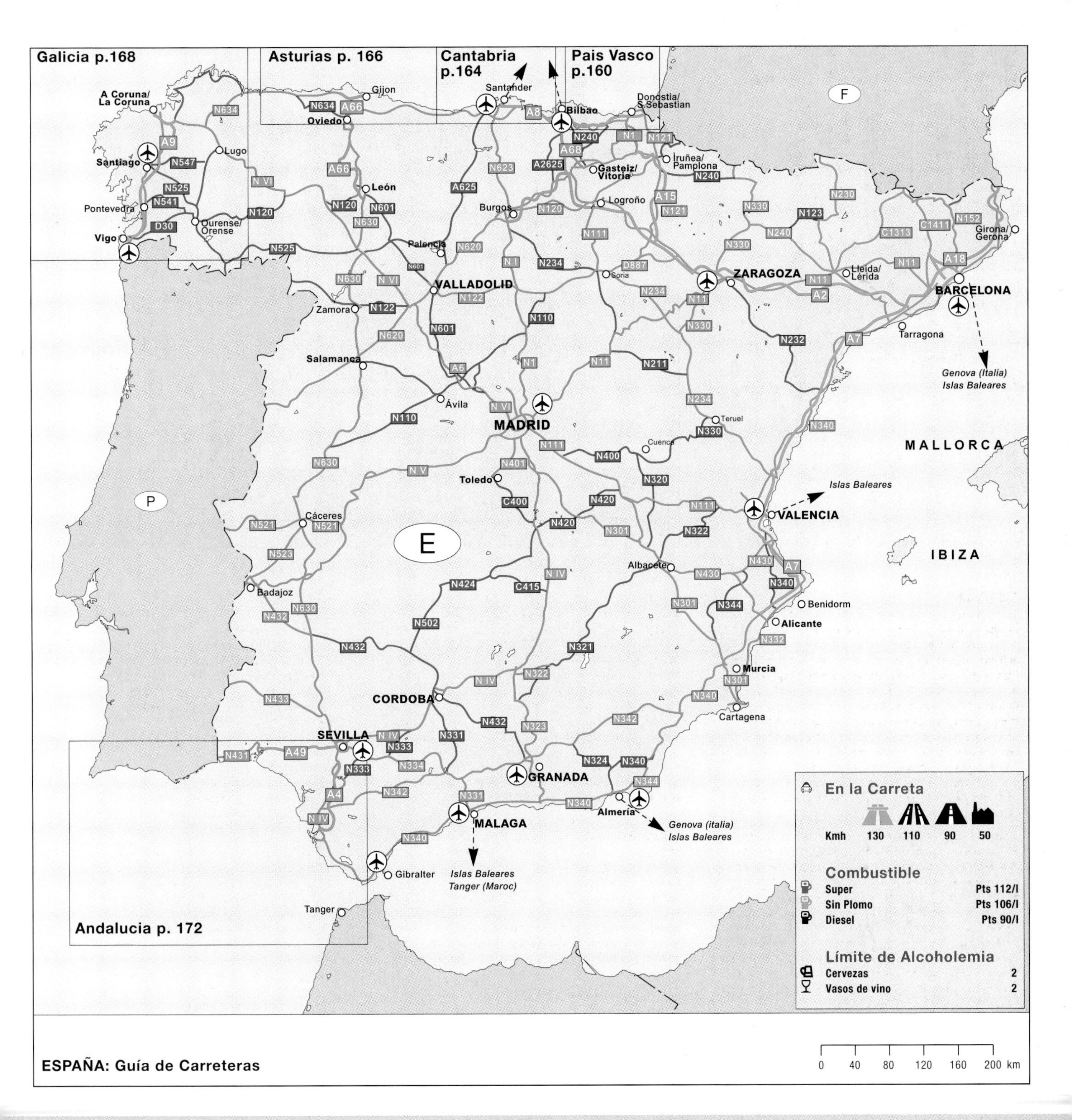

Por Carretera

Las carreteras españolas han experimentado una mejora impresionante en los últimos años, sin embargo en el norte vías de sólo un carril atraviesan zonas montañosas haciendo que los viajes se prolonguen por encima de lo esperado, sobre todo en verano. Armate de paciencia y disfuta el paisaje, pues el gran número de camiones que circula por estas zonas ententece? mucho el tráfico. En algunos sitios puedes coger una autopista de peaje como alternativa. La mayoria de los permisos de conducción son aceptados, además necesitas la tarjeta verde de seguros. Como sucede en toda Europa el riesgo de que te roben los objetos del coche es bastante elevado, si no tomas precauciones y evitas dejar cosas de valor a la vista. En Euskadi las señales y letreros son bilingües, pero en muchos casos el término en castellano está tachado, lo que puede llevarte a confusión. Ten el mapa de carreteras abierto en todo momento.

Driving

Spains roads have improved tremendously over the last few years, however Northern Spain is mountainous with windy single lane roads making journey times often a lot longer than expected, especially in summer. Take your time to enjoy the spectacular scenery and remain patient with the convoys of trucks that use these roads day and night, or take the autoroute. Most driving licenses are recognised, but you must have a green card from your insurers and a bail bond or extra legal cover on your travel policy. Car security is a nightmare in Spain as it is in much of Europe. Never leave posessions visible in a locked car where possible. Around the Pais Vasco (Euskadi), many road signs are in Euskadi and Spanish, with the Spanish crossed out on many. Can be confusing. Keep your road atlas open at all times!

La route

Les routes espagnoles se sont incroyablement améliorées sur les dernières années, cependant, le nord est montagneux avec des petites routes sinueuses rendant les trajets parfois beaucoup plus longs que prévus, surtout en été. Prenez votre temps pour apprécier le paysage grandiose plutôt que de s'impatienter derrière les convois de camions qui sillonent ces routes jour et nuit, ou prenez l'autoroute. La plupart des permis sont reconnus mais il faut vérifier que son assurance couvre aussi l'Espagne. La sécurité des voitures peut être difficile comme dans le reste de l'Europe. Si possible, ne jamais laisser d'affaires visibles même dans une voiture fermée à clé. Au Pays Basque et en Galice, beaucoup de panneaux sont bilingues avec l'espagnol barré; attention à pas vous planter. Restez les yeux rivés sur l'atlas routier.

Teléfonos

España	07 +
España	34 +
INT. Telefonista:	099 Europa
NAT.Telefonista	118
Emergência	088
Police	091

Coste de la Vida

Restaurante *	800-2500 pts
Hotel	2000-5000 pts
Camping	500pts
Caña	125 pts
Café	100 pts

Mundaka - *Photo: Eric Chauché*

Mundaka - *Photo: Jakue Andikoetxea*

Photo: Jakue Andikoetxea

el surf y el clima

A principios de los sesenta el surf llegó a la Península procedente de Biarritz, comenzando en Cantabria y Asturias para extenderse rápidamente al País Vasco. En las islas Canarias, fue introducido por surfers australianos y estadounidenses. A comienzos de los setenta, sitios como Somo, Sopelana, Bakio y Zarauz eran las Mecas del surf hispano, destacando pioneros como los Fiochi, Merodio, Dourdil, Susaeta, Beraza, Escauriaza....y tantos otros. A finales de los setenta el País Vasco concentraba el mayor número de practicantes y una incipiente industria surfera.

Al comienzo de los ochenta, comenzó la expansión a otras zonas como Galicia y la costa gaditana. Para 1987 ya existían varias tiendas de surf; marcas de ropa, trajes y accesorios estaban disponibles y apareció la primera revista nacional especializada en surf: Tres 60. Desde entonces hasta ahora, el mercado se disparó y el número de tiendas y de practicantes se ha multiplicado. La buena calidad de algunas olas del norte hace que esta sea la zona más visitada. La mayoría pasa por Mundaka siguiendo la ruta del Cantábrico hacia Portugal. Actualmente se practica incluso en el Mediterráneo, en Málaga, Valencia, Cataluña... Las mareas afectan significativamente a la mayoría de los spots, siendo pocos los que mantienen condiciones óptimas en todo punto de marea. La mayoría de los bancos facilitan gratuitamente tablas de mareas, que resultan fundamentales y deben conseguirse desde el comienzo del viaje si quieres aprovecharlo al máximo.

El Norte de España es la zona más húmeda, fría y ventosa del país. Las Cordilleras del Norte provocan la descarga de las precipitaciones procedentes de los frentes Atlánticos y separan esta zona del resto del país. Igualmente es la zona más expuesta a las marejadas. Con todo ello ha escapado al destino de convertirse en un área turística como la Costa del Sol y la Costa Brava. Galicia se proyecta dentro del Atlántico y pese a estar en la misma latitud que Marsella tiene un clima muy húmedo, más similar al de Bretaña o Cornualles que al del Sur de Francia. Tanto las regiones del sur como las de la desértica meseta central son regiones secas que además están padeciendo una fuerte sequía.

Euskal Hjerriko Surf Federation

Mikel Troittino (Euskadi)
Araba Kalea 20, 20800 Zarautz (Gipuzkoa), Spain
Tel: (020) 420 50 96 Fax: 44 159 299

Mitxel Verdes (European Committee)
Correo, 7, 48005 Bilbo, Spain
Tel: 44159 299 Fax: 44159 299

Surfing came to the Iberian Peninsula from Biarritz at the beginning of the 60's and almost spontaneously spread into Cantabria and Asturias, after moving rapidly through the País Vasco (Euskadi), arriving in the Canaries courtesy of travelling Australian and North American surfers. By the mid 70's Zarautz (Guipúzkoa), Bakio and Sopelana (Bizkaia) were considered to be surfing 'Mecca's' and surfers like Raúl Dordil, Estanis Escauriaza, Jon Susaeta and Gonzalo Gandarias stood out.

By the beginning of the 80's, surfing had expanded to Galicia and although in small numbers, even down to the coasts around Cádiz and Tarifa. By 1987 various surf shops, clothing brands, wetsuits, boards and accessories were readily available and Tres 60 emerged as the first specialised Spanish surf magazine. From then on, the market rocketed and the numbers of surfers and surf shops multiplied. Due to the good quality of some of the waves in the north, these coasts are the most frequently visited by travelling surfers. The majority head for the legendary Mundaka, then move along the N.Coast towards Portugal, though today surfing is even practised in the Mediterranean, in the provinces of Málaga, Valencia and Cataluña. Tides affect all of Spain's breaks, with few peaks remaining surfable for long, and tide-tables are provided free at most banks. These are vital and should be sought out at the beginning of any surf trip here

North Spain is the coldest, wettest and windiest part of the country. Weather systems moving in from the Atlantic shed their moisture on the coast and the Picos de Europa which separate the N from the rest of the country. The N.Coast is also the most exposed to swell, consequently it has escaped the fate of places like the Costa del Sol and the Costa Brava. Galicia projects far into the Atlantic and lies at the same latitude as Marseilles, yet is much wetter, with a climate more similar to Cornwall or Brittany than southern France. The S.E. is excessively dry, as is the bleak central tableland.

Le surf arriva sur la Péninsule Ibérique depuis Biarritz au début des années 60 et se propagea presque immédiatement vers la Cantabrie et les Asturies, après avoir rapidement traversé le Pays Basque (Euskadi), en arrivant aux Canaries grâce aux voyageurs australiens et nord américains. Au début des années 70, Somo (Cantabrie), Zarautz (Guipuzkoa), Bakio et Sopelana (Bizkaia) étaient considérés comme la Mecque des surfers comme Fiochi, Merodio, Dourdil, Escauriaza, Susaeta, Braza et plein d'autres qui pourraient aussi être considérés comme des pionniers. A la fin des années 70, le population des surfers commença à se développer et une industrie naissante apparut, surtout en Euzkadi.

Au début des années 80, le surf s'était étendu en Galice et bien qu'en petits nombres, même sur les côtes autour de Cadiz et Tarifa. En 1987, divers surf-shops, des marques de vêtements, de combinaisons, de planches et d'accessoires etaient déjà disponibles et TRES60 se lança comme le premier magazine de surf spécialisé sur le surf. A partir de là, le marché explosa et le nombre des surfers et de surf shops se multiplièrent. Compte tenu de la bonne qualité des vagues dans le nord, ces côtes sont fréquemment visitées par des surfers itinérants. La plupart s'aiguille surla vague légendaire de Mundaka, puis voyage sur la côte nord vers le Portugal. Aujourd'hui, ça surfe même en Mediterranée, dans les provinces de Malaga, de Valence et de Catalogne. Les marées concernent tous les spots espagnols avec certains d'entre eux qui restent surfables longtemps. Ces tables de marées sont disponibles gratuitement dans la plupart des banques. Elles sont vitales et doivent être récupérées au début de chaque surf-trip par ici.

Le nord de l'Espagne est la partie la plus froide, la plus humide et la plus étrange du pays. Les perturbations qui viennent de l'Atlantique perdent leur humidité sur la côte et les Picos de Europa qui séparent le nord de l'Espagne du reste du pays. Cette côte nord est aussi la plus exposée aux houles, en conséquence, elle a échappé au destin tragique comme la Costa del Sol ou la Costa Brava. La Galice se projette loin dans l'Atlantique en étant à la même latitude que Marseille mais elle est beaucoup plus humide, avec un climat plus semblable au Cornwall et à la Bretagne qu'au sud de la France. Le sud est excessivement sec tout comme le plateau central ouvert à tous vents.

SUNNY GARCIA

Punta Galea - *Photo: Jakue Andikoetxea*

El PaÌs Vasco (Euskadi) está constituido por tres provincias: Gipuzkoa y Bizkaia en la costa, y Alava en el interior. La orografía montaÒosa provoca que las carreteras discurran llenas de curvas por el verde paisaje de los valles. Sus gentes son de un carácter único e independiente y poseen un idioma propio de orÌgenes desconocidos, hablado principalmente en las zonas rurales, pero escasamente en la aglomeración urbana del Gran Bilbao, que concentra la mayoría de la población. Las fiestas de San Fermín en Pamplona (a comienzos de Julio) marcan el comienzo de la temporada festiva veraniega que se extiende hasta Septiembre por todas las poblaciones con inimitables fiestas callejeras, y, en algunos casos, corridas de toros.

Muchos spots est·n enmarcados en paisajes de gran belleza. El placer de surfear en ese entorno y la calidad de los picos ha supuesto un fuerte aumento de practicantes, sobre todo a finales de los ochenta, que unidos a los extranjeros que frecuentan algunos spots, han terminado por saturarlos. Por esta razón, se han omitido unos pocos spots para preservarlos como están, pero si eres un poco inquieto puedes encontrarlos, dado que verdaderos secret-spots apenas hay.

The Pais Vasco (Euskadi) province is made up of three smaller states of Gipuzkoa and Bizkaia covering the coast and Alava inland. The landscape is extremely mountainous and incredibly green with highways winding in and out of the valleys. Small villages and several big cities house a population of independently-minded and unique people, who have their own language - Euskera, the origins of which remain a mystery. For much of the year the area is relatively tranquil, but from the time of The Running of the Bulls, in Pamplona (Irunea) mid July, the parties begin, with each town having its own major weekend, with street parties and corridas, finishing in early September.

Surf spots along the coast are set amongst some spectacular country. The pleasures of surfing in such places, plus the excellent quality of many of its breaks has led many young Basque people to take up surfing, and combined with the numbers of drifting foreigners, many of the spots are getting quite full. Some of these breaks have been omitted at the request of local people due to the large numbers of surfers who end up in this area. If one uses initiative, there are some killer reefs and points to find.

La province du Pays Basque (Euskadi) est constituée de trois états avec le Gipuzkoa et la Bizkaia sur la côte et l'Alava à l'intérieur des terres. Le paysage y est extrêmement montagneux et incroyablemnt vert avec des autoroutes qui serpentent entre les vallées. De petits villages et quelques grandes villes abritent une population de gens uniques et indépendants, avec leur propre langue (l'Euskara), dont les origines restent un mystère. L'essentiel de l'année, l'endroit est paisible, mais à partir des fêtes de Pampelune début Juillet avec les taureaux dans la rue, la période des fêtes commence avec des célébrations et des corridas dans les villages surtout en fin de semaine, jusqu'à la fin du mois de Septembre.

Les spots de surf le long de la côte se situent dans un environnement spectaculaire. Le plaisir de surfer ces endroits ajouté à l'excellente qualité de pas mal de breaks a motivé bon nombre de jeunes basques à commencer à surfer. Combiné au nombre de surfers de passage, cela signifie un certain encombrement sur les meilleurs spots. Certains de ses spots ont été sciemment omis par respect pour les locaux qui connaissent l'importance des flux de surfers étrangers qui atterrissent là. Avec un peu de courage et de patience, il y a de super reefs et pointbreaks à découvrir.

Photo: Jakue Andikoetxea

"Sus gentes son de un carácter único e independiente y poseen un idioma propio de orÌgenes desconocidos..."

pais vasco

Meñakoz - *Photo: Jakue Andikoetxea*

Pais Vasco

Javier Amezaga
Roberto Nuño

1. La Arena

Tiene varios picos de baja calidad que rompen mejor en marea alta. Junto a la playa hay una refinería de petróleo y el agua está bastante contaminada. Hay parking en la playa, camping y bastantes surfistas locales. El ambiente es bueno.

Various poor quality peaks best at high tide. Close by there is a petrol refinery and the water is very polluted. Parking at the beach, camping and quite a few local surfers. The atmosphere is good.

Des pics pas terribles meilleurs à marée haute. A proximité, une raffinerie de pétrole, imaginez donc la qualité de l'eau. Parking sur la plage, camping et quelques locaux. Endroit sympa malgré tout.

2. Playa de Ereaga

La playa más popular en Algorta, es en el mismo centro. Necesita bastante mar - está protegida - rompe frecuentemente en invierno. En marea alta tiene un pico de izquierda muy fuerte que rompe junto al muelle y en baja, en la parte oriental de la playa, rompe la derecha de 'Yefris'. Muy contaminado.

This popular beach is located in the centre of Algorta. It's quite protected so it needs a decent swell but works regularly in winter. A powerful left breaks at high tide next to the jetty and on the eastern side a right called 'Yefris' breaks at low tide. Very polluted.

Cette plage plus fréquentée est situer au centre d'Algorta. Assez protégé, donc il faut un bon swell, genre tempête en hiver. On trouve une gauche sévère prés de la jetée alors que du côté est, c'est "Jeffries", une droite qui peut casser à marée basse.

3. Punta Galea

A unos dos kilómetros en dirección a Sopelana está el acantilado de Punta Galea, que es el cabo oriental de la Bahía de Bilbao (Abra). En la base del acantilado rompe una derecha muy larga y perfecta que aguanta todo el tamaño que venga. Rompe muy cerca del acantilado por lo que a partir de los tres metros es casi suicida. El acceso es muy malo, hay que bajar andando por un camino que está semiderruido o en barco.

Long, perfect right point which can handle any size. It breaks very close to the cliffs so anything above 3mtrs is virtually suicide. Access is difficult, you have to walk down a dodgy dirt road, or take a boat.

Une droite longue et parfaite qui tient toutes les houles. Ca casse tout prés des cailloux et aprés 3 mètres, il faut être kamikaze. Trés difficile de sortir de l'eau et d'accéder au spot: sentier casse-gueule ou bateau...

4. Sopelana

Es el area más prolífica del País Vasco. En apenas cuatro kilómetros de costa hay una docena de picos que reciben el mar de frente. En dirección Oeste-Este, primero tenemos la Playa Salvaje, con un pico de arena (Batidora) y otro de roca a la derecha de la playa (La Triangular). Este último es muy regular y puede aguantar hasta cuatro metros. La Playa de Sopelana tiene dos zonas delimitadas: Larrabasterra y Peña Txuri. En ambas rompen varios picos de arena de buena calidad. Aguanta hasta dos metros. En verano hay mucha gente surfeando y el agua está algo más sucia, aunque aceptable. Siguiendo hay una pequeña cala de roca llamada El Sitio donde rompe una ola en marea baja, preferentemente de izquierda, a partir del metro y medio y hasta los dos y medio.

4km of coast with dozens of peaks which pick up all swell. From west to east, there is Playa Salvaje (Batidora and La Triangular). The latter is consistent and can hold a 4mtr swell. The Playa de Sopelana has 2 distinctive areas: Larrabasterra and Peña Txuri both offering good quality peaks up to 2mtrs. Summer means crowds and pollution in the most populated surf area in Spain. Further on, there's a rocky cove called El Sitio where a good low tide left breaks up to 2.5mtrs.

4 kms de côtes avec une douzaine de pics qui chopent tous le swell. D'est en ouest, on trouve Playa Salvaje (Batidora et la Triangular, celui -ci pouvant tenir jusqu'à 4 m). La plage de Sopelana a 2 zones distinctes: Larrabastera et Peña Txuri qui donnent de bons pics jusqu'à 2 mètres. C'est la concentration de surfers la plus élevée en Espagne. Ensuite, on trouve El Sitio dans une crique qui peut casser à maére basse jusqu'à 2,5 m.

5. Meñakoz

Una de las derechas más grandes y potentes de Europa. La ola no es muy larga: sólo tiene la bajada y una sección tubera sobre dos puntas de roca (Los Calvos), pero rompe con especial violencia y aguanta olas de más de seis metros. Es muy peligrosa. El acceso es un camino de tierra. El último kilómetro se hace andando.

One of the biggest and most powerful rights in Europe, not very long, but it breaks with special violence and can hold waves up to 6mtrs! Naturally it is very dangerous. Access is by a dirt road with the last km done on foot.

Une des plus grosses et puissantes droites d'Europe, pas trés long mais qui casse avec une violence rare jusqu'à 6 mètres! Un gros rochers au milieu, qui en a fait flipper plus d'un. L'accés est délicat par un chemin de terre puis un sentier d'1 km.

6. Bakio

Playa con buenos picos orilleros que recibe el mar de frente por lo que hay olas con asiduidad. Se puede aparcar junta a la playa. Densa población de surfistas locales. La calidad del agua es aceptable. En verano está más contaminada.

Good quality consistent peaks get very crowded with a big local crew. Park next to the beach. The water quality varies from pretty rough to o.k.

Plage avec de bons pics et plein de locaux à respecter; On se gare prés de la plage. Quand tout va bien, l'eau est correcte.

Bakio - Photo: Jakue Andikoetxea

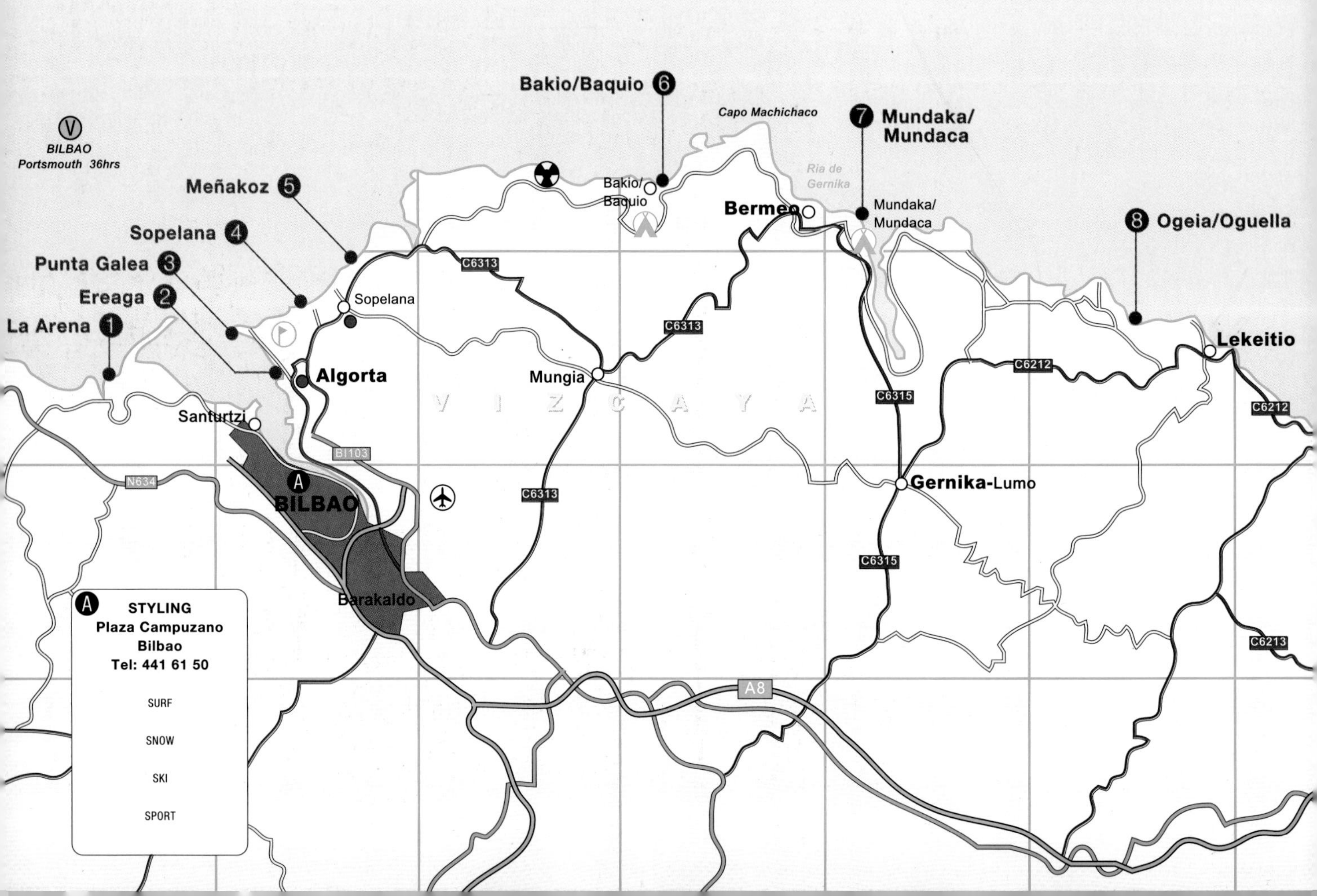

Meñakoz - *Photo: Jakue Andikoetxea*

7. Mundaka/Mundaca

Poco queda por decir sobre esta ola, la izquierda más larga y hueca de Europa que rompe sobre una sedimentación de arena que se asienta en la amplia desembocadura de la ría de Gernika. Esta ría es zona de protección del medio ambiente, por lo que el agua y el entorno se mantiene limpio. Rompe en marea baja y aguanta hasta cuatro metros. Los mejores tubos de Europa. Al otro lado de la ría se sitúan las playas de Laida y Laga, donde se pueden encontrar olas cuando no rompe Mundaka.

There's little left to be said about this wave. The longest and hollowest left in Europe which breaks over sandbanks at the mouth of the river Gernika. It works best at low tide and holds swell up to 4mtrs. On the other side of the rivermouth are the beaches of Laida and Laga where you can find waves when Mundaka isn't breaking. The river and its estuary is a W.W.F. reserve, so the water and the surroundings are kept clean.

Plus tellement de secrets à dévoiler . La gauche la plus longue et la plus creuse en Europe qui casse sur un banc de sable formé par la Gernika . Marche mieux à marée basse montante jusqu'à 4 mètres. De l'autre côté, on trouve les plages de Laïda et Laga où ça surfe quand Mundaka est flat (souvent). La rivière et son estuaire est au patrimoine écologique de l'UNESCO, c'est donc un monument de propreté et de limpidité. Evitez les jours de pointes, c'est chaud.

8. Ogeia/Oguella

Ola larga, de calidad y hueca que necesita mucho mar. Existe un proyecto para crear una playa artificial que haría desaparecer la ola y, por supuesto, un colectivo de surfistas que se opone al mismo.

Good quality long, hollow waves break on a big swell. Unfortunately there are plans to create an artificial beach which would make the waves disappear, and naturally there are a group of local surfers opposing this.

De bonnes gauches longues qui cassent par gros swell. Malheureusement, on y veut y construire une plage artificielle qui feraient disparaître les vagues. Encore des protestations. A l'est d'Ispaster.

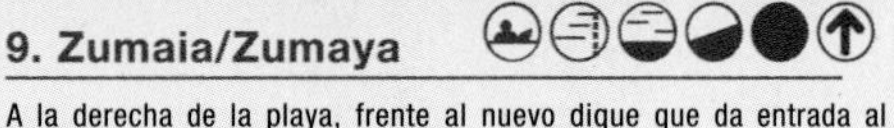

9. Zumaia/Zumaya

A la derecha de la playa, frente al nuevo dique que da entrada al puerto, hay una derecha que aguanta mucho tamaño.

In front of the new jetty that forms the entrance to the port, there's a right which can hold a big swell.

En face de la nouvelle jetée qui ferme le port, y'a une droite qui tient le gros.

10. Orrua

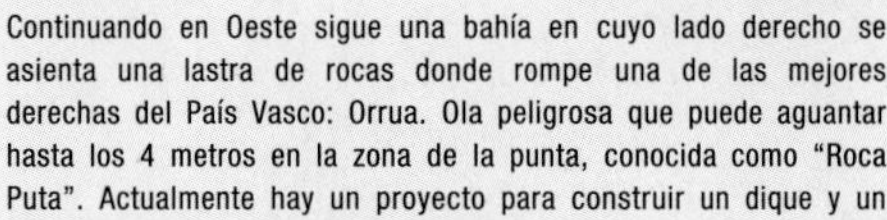

Continuando en Oeste sigue una bahía en cuyo lado derecho se asienta una lastra de rocas donde rompe una de las mejores derechas del País Vasco: Orrua. Ola peligrosa que puede aguantar hasta los 4 metros en la zona de la punta, conocida como "Roca Puta". Actualmente hay un proyecto para construir un dique y un colectivo de surfistas que se opone al proyecto.

Some of the best rights in the Pais Vasco. A dangerous wave breaking over rocks locally known as 'Roca Puta'(Whore Rock) that can hold a 4m swell. Currently there's a project to build another breakwater and a group of surfers are opposing this. Good Luck!

Orrua, alias Roca Puta, une des meilleures droites du Pays Basque, qui casse dangeuresement sur des cailloux qui se surfe jusqu'à 4m. Une construction de jetée en projet à laquelle les surfers s'opposent.

Orrua - *Photo: Jakue Andikoetxea*

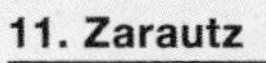

11. Zarautz

Playa amplia orientada al norte. La playa más popular de Gipuzkoa donde se celebra un campeonato del circuito ASP. Variedad de picos que rompen en todas las mareas, mejor en la alta. Las luces de las calles y los bares iluminan la playa y se puede hacer surf por la noche. En el lado Este de la playa desemboca un río contaminado.

The most popular beach town in Gipuzkoa and occasional ASP venue, has a variety of peaks all better at high tide. The lights of the streets and bars illuminate the beach allowing one to surf at night. Heavily polluted spot.

La plage la plus célèbre du Gipuzkoa site de compétitions internationales avec des pics meilleurs à marée haute; Les loupiotes des rues et des bars permettent de surfer la nuit. L'eau est gerbique.

12. Orio

Ola orillera sobre fondo de arena que rompe en una pequeña playa situada junto a la desembocadura de la ría Orio. A veces, cuando está grande, en marea baja rompe un pico en la desembocadura de la ría. Agua aceptablemente limpia. Se ve desde la autopista.

A little beach situated next to the river Orio. When it's big a peak may break into the rivermouth at low tide. Visible from the motorway.

Une petite plage située à côté de l'Orio. Marche parfois à marée basse quand c'est gros. Visible depuis l'autoroute.

13. Concha/Ondarreta

Rompe cuando Gros está pasado. Fondo de arena, olas orilleras de derecha en La Concha y de izquierda en Ondarreta. La playa está muy cuidada.

Breaks when Gros is closing out. Sand bottom righthand shore break waves in La Concha and lefthanders in Ondarreta. The beach is well maintained.

Quand ça ferme à Gros, venez checker ici pour y trouver peut-être des droites de sable à la Concha et des gauches à Ondaretta. La plage est bien tenue.

14. Playa de Gros

La playa más surfera de San Sebastián. Ola orillera sobre fondo de arena. En la parte izquierda ya no hay olas debido al espigón constuido en 1994. Agua contaminada en verano debido a la proximidad del río.

The most popular spot in San Sebastian with shorebreak waves over a sand bottom. On the left there are no longer any waves due to the jetty built in 1994. The water is heavily polluted due to the proximity to the river.

La plage la plus surfée de San Sebastian avec des vagues de shore-break sur fond de sable. Sur la gauche, il n'y a plus de vagues à cause de la jetée construite en 94. L'eau est carrément polluée par la rivière toute proche.

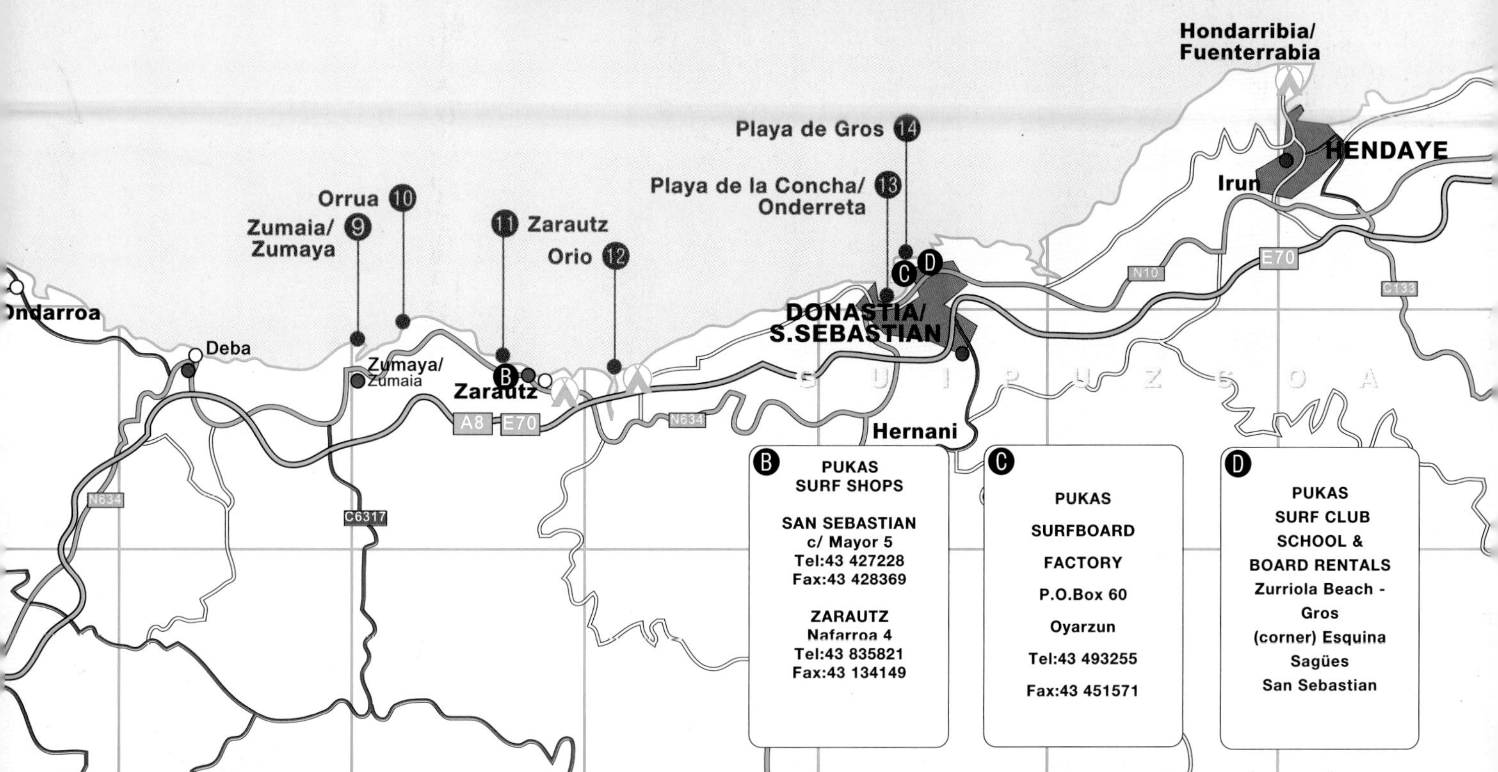

"El accidentado perfil litoral proporciona numerosos spots escondidos y calas protegidas, que se mantienen solitarias siempre que estén fuera de las aglomeraciones urbanas."

Photo: *Jakue Andikoetxea*

cantabria

Tapia - *Photo: Javier Amezaga*

El Brusco - *Photo: Jakue Andikoetxea*

Rodiles - *Photo: Javier Amezaga*

& asturias

Cantabria y Asturias comparten aproximadamente 1000 kilómetros de abrupta costa, litoral desde donde se vislumbra la Cordillera Cantábrica en la que destacan los impresionantes "Picos de Europa". Las marejadas de Norte a Oeste entran consistentes y poderosas, y toda la zona es frecuentada por surferos locales, pero sin alcanzar la masificación del País Vasco, donde las sugerentes fotos de Mundaka y de Meñakoz publicadas en las revistas surferas internacionales, han atraído un sinnúmero de visitantes. El accidentado perfil litoral proporciona numerosos spots escondidos y calas protegidas, que se mantienen solitarias siempre que estén fuera de las aglomeraciones urbanas. "Utiliza la información de esta guía siguiendo el auténtico espíritu surfero. Esperamos que el descubrimiento de nuevos picos no suponga su deterioro y abuso, en vez de su protección y disfrute, nuestra verdadera misión". **Diego Méndez.**

Cantabria and Asturias share a rugged coastline of approximately 1000 km's, backed by the impressive 'Picos de Europa'. North and west swells are consistent and powerful and the whole stretch is popular with local surfers but has escaped the masses that get lured to the Pais Vasco by the many stunning photo's of Mundaka and Meñakoz which fill the international surf mags. The coastlines indented nature means protected coves and hidden spots are numerous and outside of the built up areas, uncrowded. "Use the information in this guide in the true spirit of surfing. We hope that the discovery of new breaks won't mean they become exploited and polluted; rather enjoy and protect them - a mission for us all". **Diego Méndez**

La Cantabrie et les Asturies partagent une côte découpée d'environ 1000 kms, supportée par les impressionants "Picos de Europa". Les houles d'ouest et de nord sont consistantes et puissantes et toute cette portion est bien connue des locaux en échappant aux masses qui convergent vers le Pays Basque attirés par les photos hallucinantes de Mundaka et Meñakoz qui circulent dans les magazines à l'étranger. La côte découpée signifiequ'il y a des criques protégées avec de nombreux spots secrets et peu de monde en dehors des zones urbaines. "Utilisez cette information dans ce guide dans le plus pur esprit du surf. Nous espérons que la découverte de nouveaux spots n'entrainera pas de surexploitation ou de pollutions; profitez-en plutôt et protégez-les: une mission pour chacun d'entre nous." **Diego Méndez**

Campelo - Photo: Javier Amezaga

"Probablemente puedas surfear sólo escuchando el océano embravecido, dejando tus huellas junto a las de los pescadores que observan impasibles tus maniobras."

El perfil accidentado de la costa gallega hace que, sean cuáles sean las condiciones del viento y la dirección de la marejada, puedas encontrar olas en algún lugar. Todo el litoral gallego está expuesto al oleaje, pero es el Noroeste la zona de mayor consistencia. Probablemente puedas surfear sólo escuchando el océano embravecido, dejando tus huellas junto a las de los pescadores que observan impasibles tus maniobras. En esta tierra mágica donde las nieblas cubren los valles, los habitantes continuan contado historias sobre la "Santa Compaña", la procesión de los muertos, mientras el viento aúlla. Una tierra de verdes colinas, donde se funden armónicamente la belleza del océano con la de los bosques.

La historia del surf comienza aquí como en tantos otros lugares... La impresión inicial de un gigantesco y maravilloso Malibú supuso un amor a primera vista, un comienzo de éxtasis. Las primeras olas se surfearon en 1969 en Vigo y en 1970 en La Coruña. Mientras en otros países, la generación actual se interesa por los orígenes: los primeros surfers, las primeras tablas, etc... aquí estamos en una fase prehistórica.

The coast has a tortuous outline and you can always find waves somewhere, regardless of wind and swell direction. All of Galicia gets surf, but the N is the most consistent. You will probably be alone with the ocean's roar, your footsteps alongside those of fishermen who observe your manoeuvres with impassive gestures. It's a magic land where the mists creep down the valleys and the inhabitants still tell tales of 'Santa Compaña' (the procession of the Ghosts) while the wind howls. A land of sweet green hills with a forested cloak gently merging with the ocean's incredible beauty.

The sport's beginnings here were like so many other places...the initial glimpse of a big, beautiful Malibu was love at first sight, ecstasy from the outset. the first waves were ridden in Vigo (1969) and La Coruña (1970). In other countries, today's generation is curious about beginnings; the first surfers, the first surfboards etc...Here we are still in the 'prehistoric' phase.

Le profil accidenté de la côte galicienne fait qu'on peut toujours trouver des vagues quelque part, quelque soit la direction du vent et de la houle. Toute la Galice chope du surf mais la côte nord est plus consistante. Vous serez probablement seul avec le grondement de l'océan, empruntant les pas des pêcheurs qui scrutent les évolutions des surfers en attendant le poisson. C'est une terre magique où les brumes descendent les vallées, où les habitants racontent encore les histoires de Santa Compaña (la procession des fantômes) pendant que les vents hurlent. Une terre de collines délicieusement vertes avec un manteau de forêts qui se fondent merveilleusement dans l'océan.

Les débuts du surf ici ressemblent à partout ailleurs... La vue initiale d'un Malibu majesteux avec une belle taille de vagues fut le coup de foudre, l'extase du départ. Les premières vagues furent surfées à Vigo (1969) et à la Corogne (1970). Dans d'autres pays, la génération d'aujourd'hui est curieuse de ces débuts: les premiers surfers, les premières planches... Nous en sommes encore ici dans cette phase "préhistorique".

galicia

Carlos Bremón

Pantín - Photo: Jakue Andikoetxea

Clyd Martin, Pantín - Photo: Jakue Andikoetxea

Cantabria

Roberto Nuño

1. Playa del Meron

En la zona este del rio hay un buen banco de arena. Generalmente la izquierda es mejor con una larga pared que puede convertirse en tubo, especialmente en marea baja, con un canal de fuertes corrientes a la izquierda del pico. La playa del Meron suele estar bastante concurrida por muchos surfers que van a pasar el fin de semana en sus tiendas a la derecha de la playa. Tambien hay una desembocadura de rio pero solo rompe con fuerte swell.

On the eastern side of the river is a very good sandbank. The left is generally better, being a longer faster ride that can tube, especially at low tide, with an energy-saving channel to the left of the peak. Playa de Meron gets quite busy with a lot of surfers staying for the weekend in a campsite right next to the beach. There's also a rivermouth wave but it only breaks in a big swell.

Du côté est de la rivière se trouve un bon banc de sable. La gauche est en général meilleure étant plus rapide avec de sections à tubes surtout à marée basse avec un channel remonte-vagues à gauche du pic. Meron s'agite pas mal le week-end sur un camping directement sur la plage. Aussi une vague de rivière qui ne casse qua quand c'est gros.

2. Playa de Oyambre

Lo mejor de la playa de Jerra es que da cara al sureste y pese a esta razón atrae mucho swell y es una ideal alternativa a San Vicente. A lo contrario de San Vicente no hay tanta gente. En Oyambre atraves del rio entra mas swell. La calidad del agua es excelente.

The big plus for Playa de la Jerra is that it faces SE and still picks up a lot of swell making it an ideal alternative to San Vicente. However, unlike San Vicente it doesn't get the crowds. In Oyambre, towards the river, quite a bit more swell gets in. Water quality is excellent.

Le gros avantage, c'est que ç'est exposé SE et que ça chope quand même de la houle: bonne alternative à San Vicente sauf que peu de surfers viennent ici. A Oyambre, vers la rivière, y'a un petit peu plus de houle. L'eau est impeccable.

3. Los Locos

Una de las mejores rompientes de playa de España. Cógelo si puedes con un swell de 6 pies y sabrás por qué. Cuando el swell llega a 4 pies el pico de la derecha del ese de la playa rompe en las rocas con grandes huecos y olas rápidas. Suele haber mucha gente y es la unica playa que esta bien situada para los swells de verano ya que los vientos suelen ser del noreste. En marea alta la playa queda cubierta y solo rompen olas con fuerte swell. La calidad del agua tiende a mejorar muchísimo.

One of Spains' best beach breaks! Catch it on a clean 6ft swell and you'll see why. When the swell reaches 4ft, sometimes a righthand sand point east of the beach breaks off the rocks giving hollow, fast waves. Naturally it gets crowded and it's the only beach in summer that is well situated for the dominating winds that come from the NE. At high tide the beach gets covered and waves will only break in a big swell. Water quality tends to be pretty good.

Un des meilleurs beach-breaks d'Espagne: chopez 2 mètres propres et vous verrez pourquoi. A 1,5m, une droite creuse et rapide à l'est de la baie. A l'évidence, y'a foule surtout si c'est la seule plage qui marche, la seule bien située par vents de NE. Ne marche à marée haute que par gros swell. Plutôt propre.

4. Playa de Concha

Esta protegida de los vientos por una montaña. La mejor ola rompe en marea media. El agua esta contaminada con todo tipo de residuos industriales. En marea baja se forma un banco de arena en la desembocadura del rio de San Martín, pero para surfearlas se necesita un equipo anticontaminante.

A large headland offers good protection against winds, without blocking out all the swell. Best at mid tide. The water gets badly polluted with all sorts of industrial residues. At low tide a sand bar is formed in the rivermouth of San Martín, but surfers need to go in with anticontamination equipment.

Une tête rocheuse protège des vents sans trop filtrer la houle. Mieux à mi-marée. Du monde et une eau agrémentée de déchets industriels. A marée basse, un banc s'expose à la sortie de la San Martin: pour ceux que la reconstitution d'une marée noire intéresse...

5. Liencres Area

A través de toda la costa de Liencres rompen un buen número de picos con derechas e izquierdas, algunos de arena y otros de roca. Esta área da cara al oeste y noroeste por lo tanto, atrae mucho swell con muchos picos rompiendo durante todas las mareas. Junto con la playa de Los Locos este es el mejor y más grande de todo Cantabria. Esta larga playa está serparada en la zona este por varias secciones de rocas. En marea alta se pueden encontrar los mejores picos y con mas gente. En la zona oeste siempre está más grande y funciona de marea baja a media con vientos del sur. La calidad del agua es buena.

The coast around Liencres offers a number of good right and left, sand and rock reef breaks. The area faces W to NW and consequently picks up a lot of swell, with different peaks breaking throughout the tides. Along with Los Locos, this is the biggest and most consistent spot in Cantabria. The long beach is separated in the eastern area into various sections by rocks. At high tide, here you'll find the best and most crowded peaks. The western area is always bigger and works from low to mid tide with S winds. Water quality is good.

La côte offre ici une belle palette de droites et de gauches, sur fond de sable et rochers. La zone regarde de l'ouest au nord-ouest et chope un max de houle à toutes les marées. Avec Los Locos, c'est le plus consistent de toute la Cantabrie. Cette longue plage est scindée dans sa partie ouest par des rochers. A marée haute, vous y trouverez les meilleurs pics avec du monde dessus. Y'a plus de taille sur l'ouest, idéal aux marées plus basses avec des vents de sud. L'eau est propre.

Liencres - *Photo: Jakue Andikoetxea*

6. Playa del Sardinero

Con fuerte swell y vientos fuertes del sur y suroeste el Sardinero puede ser un spot importante que comprobar. Con otras condiciones es una miseria. Otra buena idea puede ser hacer un corto viaje a las rompientes del este y del oeste de Santander. En verano está prohibido surfear y es muy difícil encontrar un sitio donde poner la toalla.

In a big swell, with strong S or SW winds, Sardinero can be a worthwhile spot to check. Otherwise it's very missable. A far better idea is to make the short trip to the breaks east or west of Santander. In summer it's forbidden to surf and it is difficult to even find a place to lay down a towel.

Par grosse houle, avec forts vents de S/S-O, Sardinero peut soulever un petit quelque chose mais attention aux déceptions. Allez plutôt voir ailleurs, surf interdit l'été où les grande serviettes ne trouvent pas toujours de la place sur le sable. C'est là que le surf a commencé en Espagne.

7. Playa de Somo

Por la proximidad a Santander y el ferry que sale cada 20 minutos esta es la playa con más multitud de todo Cantabria. A pesar de esto las olas son buenas, los locales son flexibles y en el agua raramente hay incidentes. Durante el invierno es una playa tranquila.

Because of its proximity to Santander, with a ferry over the river every 20 mins, this beach gets the most crowded in all of Cantabria. Nevertheless, the waves are good, the locals are tolerant and incidents in the water are rare. In winter it's much calmer.

Des vagues régulières et des paquets de surfers de Santander qui débarquent aussi par le ferry (toutes les 20 mn). Ca se passe bien à en croire les locaux, surtout en hiver. Quand c'est gros, regardez vers l'île: non, vous ne rêvez pas...

Photo: Jakue Andikoetxea

8. Playa de Langre

Protegida de los vientos del oeste y del noroeste por los acantilados. Un caminillo a lo largo del acantilado te lleva hasta el centro de la playa. Es un sitio bonito para hacer surf donde la izquierda rompe en el centro de la playa, preferiblemente de marea baja a media. Rompe hasta 6 pies. Con una excelente calidad del agua.

Protected against W and NW winds by sheer cliffs, a path down the cliffs leads to the centre of the beach. The setting for a surf here is impressive. A good left breaks at the centre of the beach and it's best from low to mid tide up to 6ft. Good water quality.

Des falaises escarpées protègent des vents de O/N-O, avec un sentier qui descend vers le milieu de la plage. Cadre imposant avec une bonne gauche au centre jusqu'à 2 mètres de marée basse à mi-marée. Eau limpide.

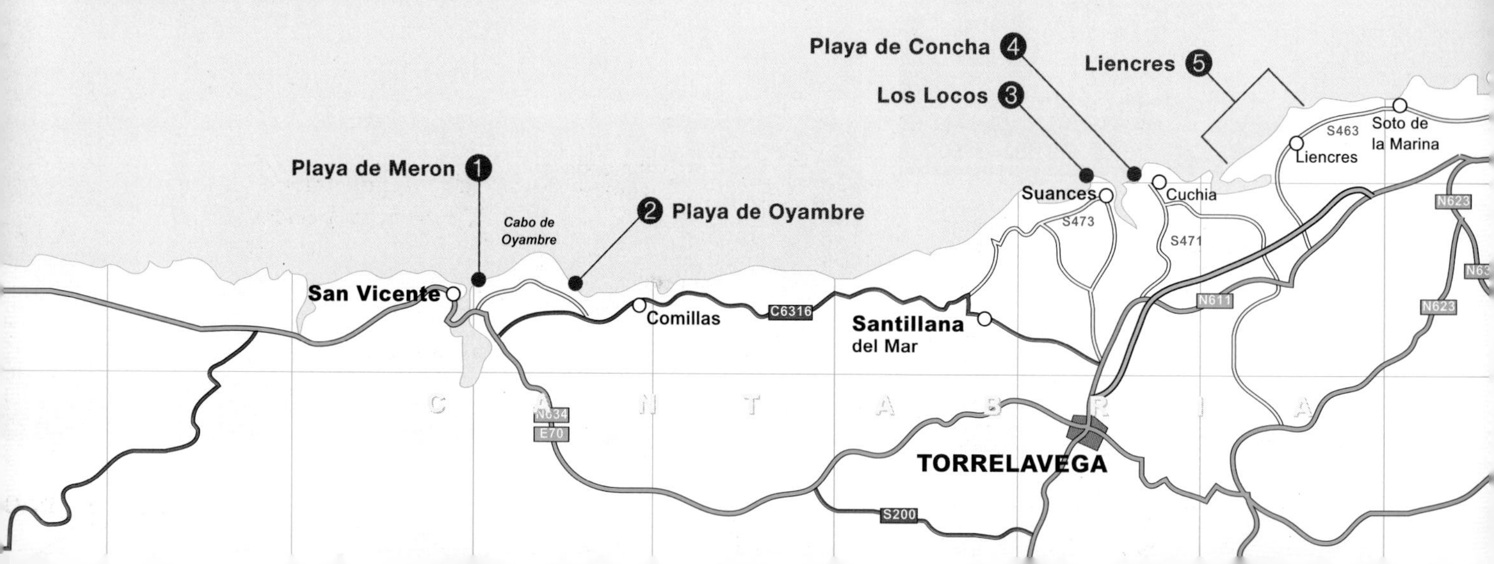

9. Galizano

En el pequeño pueblo de Galizano, puedes encontrar tres rompientes cercanas: dos calas y un point. Las olas son consistentes y no hay gente, pero hay pocos días de calidad. Aguanta el viento Nordeste.

In the tiny village of Galizano you can find three different breaks, two small coves with a point between them. The are always waves but quality days are few. Usually uncrowded. Can hold a NE wind.

On peut trouver trois spots près du petit village de Galizano: deux criques et un "point". Les vagues y sont consistantes et sans monde mais ça ne casse pas souvent bien. Tient les vents de NO.

Galizano - *Photo: Jakue Andikoetxea*

10. Playa de Ajo

La playa de Ajo y la cercana cala de Antuerta proporcionan picos potentes y de calidad. Los fondos cambian mucho, pero siempre hay olas. En verano es muy frecuentada.

Ajo beach and the nearby cove of Antuerta provide good, powerful peaks. The sandbanks shift alot, but there are always waves. Gets crowded in summer.

Une petite station qui bouge en été avec des vagues assez consistantes. De marée basse à mi-marée consistentes. De marée basse à mi-marée. Checker la crique d'Antverta à côté.

11. Playa del Ris

La mejor ola es el pico que se forma en marea alta abriendo de izquierda y de derecha. Es una ola divertida y bastante frecuentada. Esta situada en el turístico pueblo de Noja.

The best wave is a peak that breaks left and right at high tide. It's a fun wave that tends to get crowded. Located in the tourist village of Noja.

La meilleure vague est un pic droite-gauche qui se forme à marée haute. C'est une vague amusante et assez fréquentée. Situé à Noja.

El Brusco - *Photo: Jakue Andikoetxea*

12. El Brusco

Excelente rompiente de playa con picos tuberos y buena pared. Desde el aparcamiento, puede parecer que las olas son pequeñas ya que dista 400 metros del pico. Alcanza 3 metros, estando perfecto con dos metros.

Excellent beachbreak with tubey peaks and perfect walls. From the parking area (400m away) the waves always look much smaller than they are. Works up to 10ft, perfect at 6-8.

Un excellent beachbreak avec des pics tubulaires et de bons murs. Depuis le parking, on a l'impression que les vagues sont petites mais vous êtes à 400m du pic. Peut atteindre 3m, idéal à 2m.

13. Playa de Berria

Esta playa depende de los bancos de arena, normalmente en marea alta las olas son bastante buenas en el centro, mientras que en marea baja suelen ser mejores en los extremos .

Although the sandbanks shift a lot, normally at high tide the central area goes off, while at low tide it's the ends of the beach that work.

Bien que les bancs bougent beaucoup, normalement la partie centrale envoie le pâté à marée haute tandis qu'à marée basse, ça marche mieux aus extrémités.

14. Playa de Laredo

Un buen pico a probar con fuerte swell del norte. Mayoritariamente un spot de invierno donde los picos salen en la mitad de la playa. Los vientos del oeste y del noroeste le pegan bien. Merece la pena echar un vistazo a otras rompientes situadas en la misma bahía.

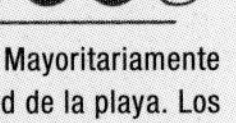

A good place to check out in a big N swell. Mainly a winter spot with the best peaks usually around the centre of the beach. Howling winds from the W and NW are no problem. Other breaks in the bay are worth a check.

Un endroit à checker quand la houle rentre épaisse de nord, surtout en hiver avec les meilleurs pics souvent au milieu de la plage. Pas de problèmes pour les grands vents de N-O/O. Il y a aussi d' autres spots dans la baie.

15. Playa de Oriñon

Esta más protegida de los fuertes vientos que la playa de Arenillas y necesita fuerte marejada para que rompa su excelente izquierda de marea baja.

More protected against strong winds than Arenillas. An excellent left which needs a big swell.

Plus protégé des vents qu'Arenillas mais nécessite un plus gros swell. Une super gauche dans un cadre dantesque.

16. Playa de Arenillas

Una ola suave pero divertida que puede aguantar vientos suaves del noroeste. Cercana a las rocas hay una corriente (útil para surfers experimentados pero peligroso para los principiantes) esto ayuda a llegar facilmente al pico.

A weak but fun wave that can handle a light NW wind. Close to the rocks there's a current (useful for experienced surfers, dangerous for beginners) that helps you get out the back.

Une vague molle qui supporte de légers vents de NO. Prés des rochers, il y a un courant quipeut vous aider à passer au fond, si tenté que vous sachiez vous en sortir.

Oriñon - *Photo: Jakue Andikoetxea*

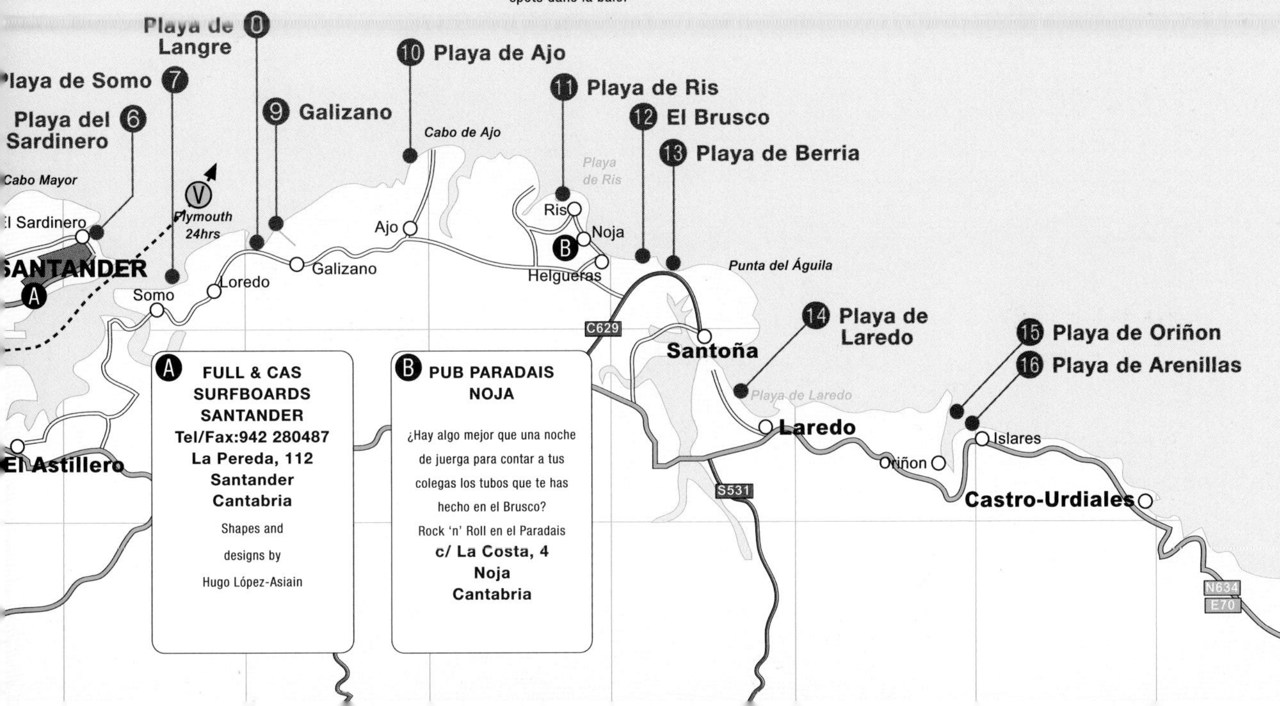

Asturias

Diego Méndez -
Picante Surf Shop

1. Playa de Peñarronda

Elige esta playa o la de Tapia ya que cuando las condiciones son buenas para una no lo son para la otra y viceversa.

Choose between here and Tapia because when the conditions are right for one, they're not for the other, and vice versa.

Comparez avec Tapia, normalement y'a toujours un spot qui marche sur les deux.

2. Tapia

Este pequeño pueblo pesquero tiene una pequeña y excelente playa que produce buenas olas. Este es uno de lso primeros sitios de Asturias en donde se empezó a hacer surf y todavía queda un pequeño grupo activo que surfea. Hay dos spots: un pico de playa que produce derechas e izquierdas y un pico de roca en la zona O de la bahía. En el pico del reef rompe una izquierda y cuando mejor esta es de 4-8ft y en marea media. El agua esta limpia.

This lovely fishing village has an excellent small beach with some good waves. It's here that some of the first surfing took place in Asturias and there's still a small but active surfing population. There are 2 spots: a beach giving rights and lefts and a rock reef on the western side of the bay. The reef breaks as a left and is best from 4-8ft at mid tide. The water is clean.

Ce charmant village de pêcheurs possède une super plage avec de bonnes vagues qui accueille parfois une épreuve EPSA. Un des berceaux du surf en Asturies et il reste une petite population de surfers cool. 2 spots: le beach-break correct et une gauche de reef à l'ouest de la baie de 1,5m à 2,5m à mi-marée. Pas de problème avec l'eau.

Tapia - *Photo: Jakue Andikoetxea*

Salinas - *Photo: Jakue Andikoetxea*

3. Navia

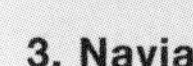

En medio de la playa una barra de arena produce excelentes derechas e izquierdas que pueden aguantar buen swell. En la parte derecha un pico llamado "El Moro" produce buenas derechas y funciona con todas las mareas. Muy contaminado.

A sandbar gives excellent rights and lefts in the middle of the beach. Can hold a good swell. To the east a point named 'El Moro' produces a good right that works on all tides. Badly polluted water.

Au milieu de la plage, un bon banc de sable avec de super gauches et droites qui ne saturent pas toujours quand c'est gros. Sur la droite, y'a un Point "El Moro" qui est une droite respectable qui marche à toutes les marées. Méga-pollué.

4. Playa de Frejulfe

Un pequeño pueblo que se encuentra en plena naturaleza con olas potentes y huecas donde no hay mucha gente. Desafortunadamente esta afectada por la contaminación de Navia. Hay intenciones de convertir este sitio en una reserva natural, ya veremos lo que pasa.

A little village set amongst wild surroundings with powerful and hollow waves and no crowds. Unfortunately it's badly affected by pollution from Navia. There are plans to make it a nature reserve so we'll see what happens.

Un petit village dans un environnement sauvage avec des vagues creuses et puissantes, sans monde. Le hic vient de Navia qui pollue à fond. Un projet est dans l'air pour en faire une réserve naturelle, à suivre...

5. Playa de Otur

Una playa tranquila con una rompiente protegida donde la mejor época es en primavera y otoño.

A quiet, sheltered beach break best in spring and autumn.

Un beach-break peinard, abrité plutôt en mi-saison.

6. Playon de Bayas

Una playa larga consistente y con poca gente que produce buenas olas hasta 6 pies. El agua esta bastante limpia.

A long, uncrowded and consistent beach which can have good waves up to 6ft. The water is pretty clean.

Une longue plage consistante sans monde qui marche bien jusqu'à 2m. L'eau y est propre.

7. Salinas y Espartal

Una playa muy popular con una buena atmosfera. En la parte derecha en Espartal hay una buena rompiente que está formada por un banco que forma una poderosa derecha con buenos huecos en marea baja. En marea alta se forman buenos picos de izquierdas y el mejor viento es del NE. A lo largo de la playa en dirección Salinas hay un montón de picos con muy buena calidad de olas. Al ser la playa tan larga recoge todo tipo de vientos y swells, dependiendo de las condiciones, siempre hay algo para elegir. Atrae todos los swells pero se llena de gente ya que esta cerca de las playas populares. El agua esta muy contaminada.

Popular beach with a good atmosphere. To the right, in Espartal, there's a breakwater which forms a good sandbank. Powerful rights with hollow sections break at low tide, while at high tide left peaks form. Best winds are from the SE. Towards Salinas, there's an abundance of peaks with good quality waves. The beach here, because it's so long, picks up all types of wind and swell, so depending on the conditions, there is always something to choose from. Though it holds a lot of swell it gets crowded as being close to very populated areas. Polluted water.

Plage trés courue avec une bonne ambiance. Du côté droit, à Espartal, y'a une jetée qui favorise la formation de droites puissantes avec des sections creuses à marée basse, alors qu'à marée haute c'est plutôt une gauche. Mieux par vents de NE. En poussant vers Salinas, une bonne moisson de pics est à attendre. La forme et la taille de la plage permettent presque toutes les conditions de vent et de houle. Ca tient bien la taille mais vu la proximité des zones urbaines, ça se bouscule parfois et l'eau est pas terrible.

8. Playa de Xago

Una buena playa para el verano ya que es una playa muy abierta y funciona con poco swell. Se llena de gente ya que está cerca de los núcleos surfistas de Aviles y Salinas.

A good beach for the summer season, because it's exposed and works in very small swells. It gets crowded since it's close to the nucleus of surfers in Aviles and Salinas.

Une plage destinée aux sessions d'été parce que trés exposée. Marche avec trés peu de houle, pas mal de monde car proche des noyaux de surfers d'Aviles et Salinas.

9. Verdicio

Un buen spot con buenos huecos cuando hay buenas condiciones. La pequeña playa de la ciudad es muy tranquila.

Attractive spot with hollow waves in the right conditions. The small beach town is very quiet.

Spot attrayant avec de bonnes vagues creuses dans les bonnes conditions. Le petit village est vraiment tranquille.

10. Gijón

PLAYA DE SAN LORENZO

La playa con más gente ya que se encuentra cerca de la ciudad. En marea baja en la parte derecha pueden rompre buenas derechas sobre un banco de arena y rocas.

This is the most crowded spot around since it's in the city. At low tide there can be good rights over a sand and rock bottom.

La plage la plus peuplée puisqu'en plein centre ville. A marée basse, sur la droite, on peut trouver de bonnes droites sur fond de sable et rochers.

EL MONGOL

Una buena opción con fuerte swell, ya que rompe una larga y potente ola. Solo hay gente cuando esta pequeño. Cuidado con las rocas.

A good option in a big swell, giving long and powerful waves. Only gets crowded when it's small. Beware of rocks.

L'option gros swell: vague longue et puissante. Moins de monde quand c'est gros. Attention aux cailloux!

PEÑARRUBIA

Al este de Gijón se encuentra esta playa de piedras redondas y arena que aguanta grandes swells. Es fácil aparcar cerca de las 3 playas.

On the eastern outskirts of Gijón you'll find a boulder and sand beach that holds a big swell. There's easy parking by all 3 beaches.

Banlieue est donc pour cette plage de sable et gros cailloux. Tient le gros. Parking facile sur les 3 accés.

11. Playa de España

Ya que esta cerca de Gijón suele haber mucha gente pero es una bonita playa con buenas olas sobre media marea.

Since it's close to Gijón it gets crowded but it's a pretty beach with some good waves best around mid tide.

Comme c'est prés de Gijon, y'a foule sur cette plage sympa avec des bonnes vagues vers la mi-marée.

Rodiles - *Photo: Jakue Andikoetxea*

12. Rodiles

Una ola en la desembocadura del rio Villaviciosa. Al oeste de la playa hay un banco de arena donde rompen izquierdas perfectas. En marea alta al O de la playa hay algunos buenos picos, donde la derecha suele ser mejor. Es la playa más famosa de Asturias por lo cual hay que tener en cuenta el localismo. Este sitio es un paraiso y con condiciones perfectas puede ser alucinante, buen camping, bares, etc...Rodiles esta considerado como reserva natural por el principado de Asturias con aguas limpias.

A wave at the mouth of the river Villaviciosa. To the west of the beach a sandbank gives some perfect lefts. At high tide on the eastern side of the beach, there are further good peaks, with the rights usually better. It's the most famous spot in Asturias but due to this, there is a "Localism" factor to contend with. The place is a paradise and when conditions are perfect it can be hallucinogenic! Good camping, bars etc. Rodiles is considered a natural reserve by the principality of Asturias and the water is clean.

Par bonne houle, une super gauche tubulaire d'abord à la sortie de la Villaviciosa, à l'ouest de la plage: plus la marée est basse, mieux c'est. A marée haute de l'autre côté, on trouve un beach break correct avec plutôt des droites. C'est LE SPOT des asturies donc vous ne serez pas seul, les locaux sont chauds. Trois campings, des bars, une réserve naturelle, une eau limpide: un petit paradis, quoi!

13. Playa de Vega

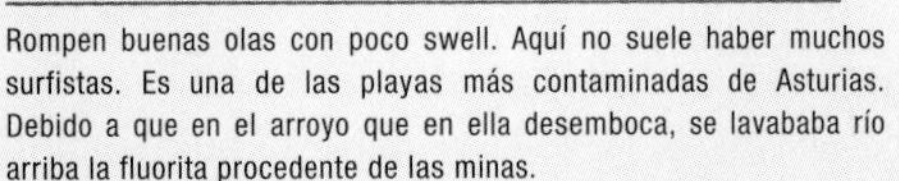

Rompen buenas olas con poco swell. Aquí no suele haber muchos surfistas. Es una de las playas más contaminadas de Asturias. Debido a que en el arroyo que en ella desemboca, se lavababa río arriba la fluorita procedente de las minas.

Good waves in a small swell. Not many surfers here. One of the most polluted beaches on the Asturian coast, due to the little creek that flows into it which is used to wash fluorite from the mines upstream. Bad news!

Bonnes vagues par petit swell avec de rares surfers. Une des plages les plus polluées des Asturies, à cause de la petite crique qui s'y jette. L'eau est en contact avec du fluor qui descend des mines en amont. Gargl!

14. Ribadesella

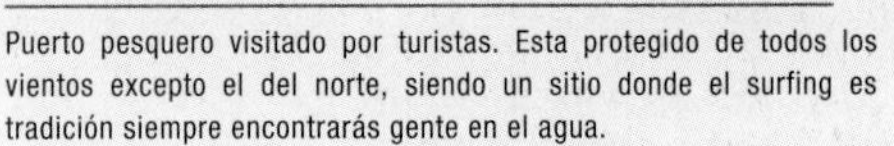

Puerto pesquero visitado por turistas. Esta protegido de todos los vientos excepto el del norte, siendo un sitio donde el surfing es tradición siempre encontrarás gente en el agua.

A fishing village, popular with tourists. It's sheltered from all winds except those coming from the North and has a surfing tradition so you'll always find people in the water.

Petit village de pêcheurs bien touristique. A l'abri de tous les vents sauf ceux de nord, toujours quelques surfers ici.

15. Playa de San Antolin

Un spot con muy poca gente que aguanta fuerte swell. Las olas se ven facilmente.

Uncrowded spot that holds a big swell. Easy views of the waves.

Spot peu fréquenté qui tient le gros. Vues rapides sur les vagues.

San Antolin - *Photo: Jakue Andikoetxea*

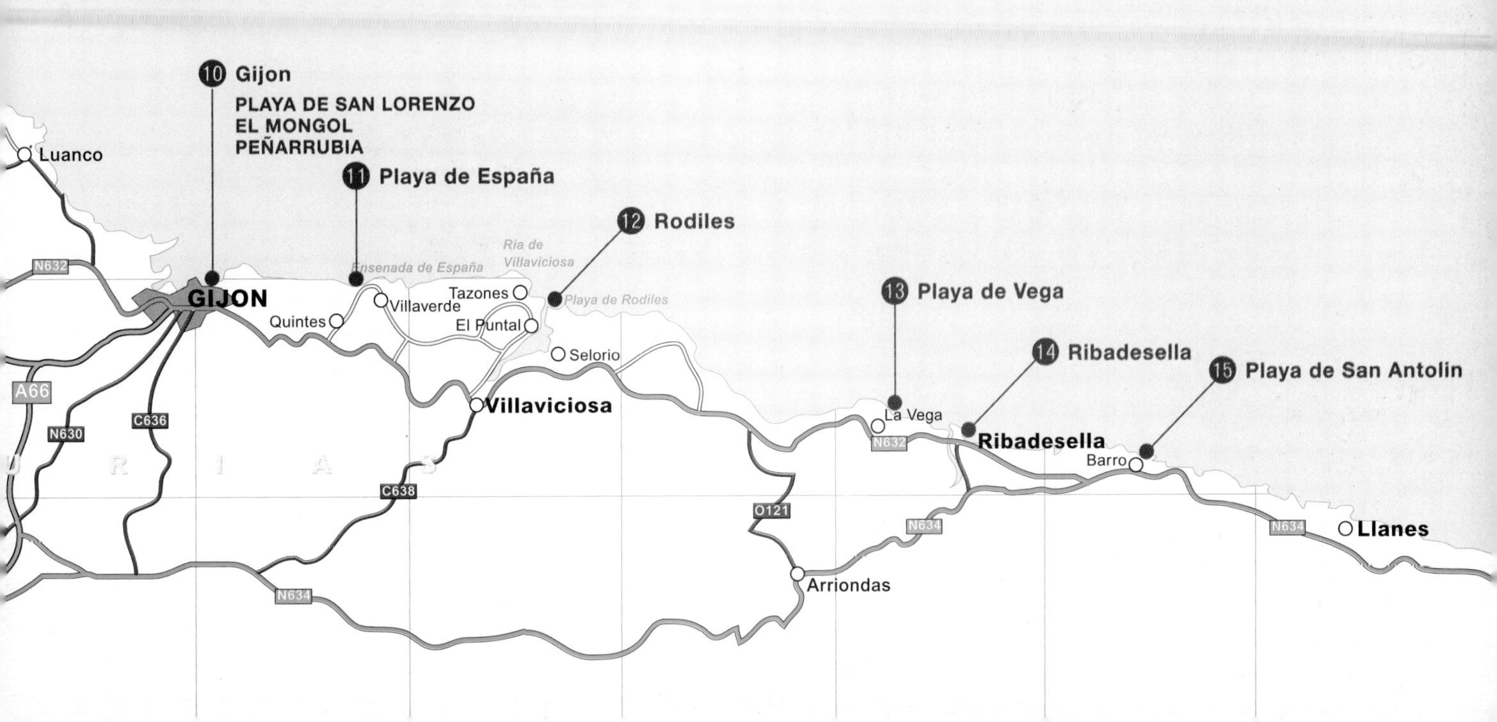

Galicia

1. Patos

Patos tiene una excelente rompiente de rocas. A la izquierda un pico de roca forma excelentes derechas y buenas izquierdas. En medio de la playa rompe una buena derecha encima de las rocas. En el extremo derecho de la playa aparece otra buena derecha que rompe sobre una hilera de rocas. Los dos primeros picos sólo son surfeados sin peligro en marea alta y el tercer pico rompe mejor en media marea. Todas estas olas rompen sólo con fuerte swell del NO y necesita vientos del S al O. En la izquierda de la playa el agua está contaminada.

Patos has some excellent rock reefs. On the left, a rock point gives excellent rights and good lefts. In the centre of the beach another good right breaks over rock. At the extreme right of the beach, a third good right breaks over another rocky ledge. The first two spots are only safely surfed at high tide and the third break is best at mid tide. All waves only break in a big NW swell and need winds from the S to W. The water is often polluted to the left of the bay.

Patos possède une kyrielle de super reefs. A gauche, une pointe rocheuse envoie d'excellentes droites et gauches. Au centre de la plage, une bonne droite sur fond rocheux. Complètement à droite, une 3° droite casse correctement sur une corniche caillouteuse. Les deux premiers spots ne sont inoffensifs qu'à marée haute, le troisième est idéal à mi-marée. Toutes ces vagues ne marchent que par gros NO avec des vents de sud ou d'ouest. A gauche, ça peut être pollué.

2. Playa de Lanzada 

Una bonita bahía más popular para los windsurfistas que produce olas con fuerte marejada.

Beautiful bay, more popular with windsurfers, only produces waves on big swells.

Superbe baie, trés populaire parmi les windsurfers, qui ne marche quand ça cartonne au large.

3. Playa de Ladeira 

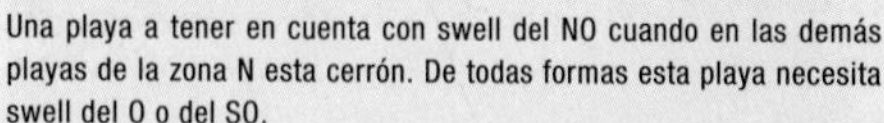

Una playa a tener en cuenta con swell del NO cuando en las demás playas de la zona N esta cerrón. De todas formas esta playa necesita swell del O o del SO.

Head here when big NW swells are closing out the beaches on the north shore of this peninsula. Otherwise, this beach needs a W or SW swell.

Venez ici quand un bon swell de NO fait fermer les plages sur la partie nord de la péninsule. Sinon, il faut un swell normal d'ouest ou de sud-ouest.

4. Playa de Rio Sieira  

Una rompiente consistente situada en algun sitio remoto de Galicia. Aquí no existe la multitud y la calidad del agua es tan buena como la mejor que puedas encontrar en cualquier otro sitio de la costa Atlántica de Europa.

A fairly consistent break situated in some of Galicia's more remote and finest countryside. Crowds here are non-existent and the water quality is as good as you'll find anywhere on Europe's Atlantic coast.

Un spot relativement consistant situé dans la campagne, une des plus reculées de Galice. Envoyez-nous une carte si vous surfez à plus de 20.

5. Playas de Louro/Lariño 

Cuando mejor funcionan estas playas es con swell del O o SO y empiezan a cerrar a partir del medio metro. Louro es la más surfeada y los dos picos se ven desde la carretera.

These beaches work best on a W or SW swell and are only really surfable up to about 5ft. Louro is generally the most surfed of the two which can both be seen from the road.

Ces plages marchent idéalement par houle d'ouest ou de sud-ouest et sont seulement surfables jusqu' à 1,5m. Louro est le plus surfé des deux, tous les deux sont visibles depuis la route.

6. Playa de Traba 

Con un swell claro del NO se pueden encontrar olas tuberas. Se llega al pico a traves de unas pistas de polvo y arena. La calidad del agua es excelente.

With a good clean NW swell one can find tubey surf here. There are a number of dirt tracks leading to the beach. Water quality is excellent.

Avec une houle décente et propre de NO, on peut trouver des tubes ici. On trouve bon nombre de chemins de terre qui vont jusqu'à la plage.

7. Malpica   

Se coge en media marea hasta 6 pies. Hay muy poca gente aunque en verano puedes encontrar visitantes debido a que la calidad del agua y las olas son estupendas.

Best at mid tide up to 6ft. Few crowds appear here, although in summer one may find travellers due to the good quality of the waves and the pleasant surroundings. The water quality is good.

Mieux à mi-marée jusqu'à deux mètres. C'est rare de voir la foule ici bien qu'on trouve des voyageurs en été attirés par les vagues sympas et le décor grandiose.

8. Playa de Razo  

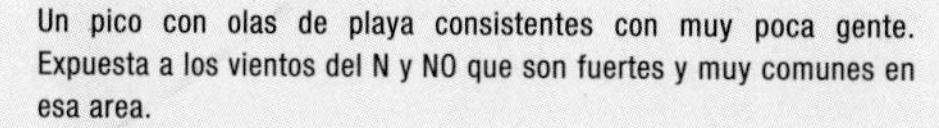

Un pico con olas de playa consistentes con muy poca gente. Expuesta a los vientos del N y NO que son fuertes y muy comunes en esa area.

Consistent beach waves with no crowds. Exposed to N and NW winds which are common and often strong.

Vagues de beach break consistantes sans monde. Exposée aux vents de N/N-O qui sont réguliers et souvent forts.

Playa de Razo - *Photo: Javier Amezaga*

9. Caión (Cayon)  

Una pequeña playa muy abierta a las marejadas del Atlántico. Rompe mejor de marea media a alta. La calidad del agua es buena.

A small beach which is relentlessly pounded by Atlantic swells, best from mid to high tide. The water quality is good.

Une petite plage qui est sans cesse battue par le houles de l'Atlantique, mieux de mi-amrée à marée haute. La qualité de l'eau est bonne.

10. Barrañan   

Una larga playa que atrae la mayoría de los swells. Cuidado con las rocas que hay a lo largo de la playa.

A long beach picking up most swells. Watch out for rocks inconveniently placed along the beach.

Une longue plage qui chope la plupart des houles. Attention aux rochers au large de la plage.

11. Sabón 

Uno de los picos a tener en cuenta por los surfers gallegos, pese a que tiene unas aguas muy contaminadas, sólo se recomienda hacer surf aquí cuando no se pueden coger olas en ningun otro sitio. Sabón puede producir olas surfeables cuando todos los demás spots están plato.

Highly regarded beach which has rideable waves when everywhere else is flat. However, the water quality is generally very bad so only surf here if it's going off.

Hautement considérée par les surfers Galiciens mais à cause de la pollution du polygone industriel, on ne vous conseille de venir surfer ici que si il n'y a rien de mieux ailleurs. Malheureusement, c'est souvent le cas parce que cette plage reçoit trés bien la houle.

12. Riazor/Orzan    

Un par de mediocres rompientes: la izquierda en mitad de la playa cuando mejor rompe es de medio a dos metros en marea baja, y el pico del reef nos da una derecha en marea media. Al estar en la ciudad ambos picos se llenan de gente y la calidad del agua es bastante pobre.

A couple of mediocre breaks; a left in the middle of the beach works best from 2-6ft at low tide, and a rock reef gives a right at mid tide. Being town breaks, both get crowded and water quality is usually very poor.

Deux breaks médiocres: une gauche au milieu de la plage qui marche mieux de 50 cms à 2ms à marée basse et un reef qui envoie une droite à mi-marée. Comme c'est en ville, attendez vous à trouver sur ces 2 spots du monde et une eau dégueu.

13. Doniños   

Olas consistentes y tuberas, su mejor momento es de marea baja a media. Hay dos accesos al pico, una por el N y otra por el S, es mejor la zona N. Uno de los spots más populares de Galicia.

Consistent tubey waves best surfed from low to mid tide. Two access points - north and south, with the north end nearly always the best. One of Galicia's most popular spots.

Vagues consistentes et tubulaires meilleures de marée basse à mi-marée . Deux accés, dont celui du nord est presque toujours le meilleur. Un des spots les plus connus en Galice.

Ferrol - *Photo: Javier Amezaga*

14. Playa de San Jorge 

Al final de la zona sur de esta bahía protegida es el lugar adecuado a elegir cuando Doniños está pasado de viento S. De marea baja a media pueden salir buenas izquierdas sobre un fondo de arena y con un canal cercano a las rocas. El resto de la bahía tambien puede tener buenas olas(sobre todo el final de la zona N) con fuerte swell, para cuando Doniños y la izquierda estén cerrando.

The southern end of this sweeping bay is the place to head for when Doniños is blown out by S winds. From low to mid tide there can be an excellent left breaking over a sand bottom with a useful channel near the rocks. The rest of the bay can also have good waves (especially the northern end) on big swells, when Doniños and the left are closing out.

L'extrémité sud de cette baie profonde est l'endoit où il faut aller quand Doninõs est gavée de vents de sud. De marée basse à mi-marée, il peut y avoir une super gauche qui casse sur du sable avec un chenal prés des rochers. Le reste de la baie peut aussi avoir de bonnes vagues (surtout au nord) par grosse houle, quand Doniños sature et que la gauche ferme.

15. Campelo  

Uno de los mejores spots de Galicia y sin duda uno de los más bonitos con un excelente surf, que en verano se puede llenar de gente. La calidad del agua es excelente.

One of Galicia's best spots, and undoubtedly one of its most beautiful, with excellent surf which can get crowded in summer. The water quality is excellent.

Un des meilleurs spot de Galice et sans doute un des plus beaux, avec des vagues remarquables qui peuvent saturer en été.

Sabón - *Photo: Javier Amezaga*

16. Valdoviño (Frouxeira)

Un buen spot a tener en cuenta cuando en las demás playas no hay olas. Frouxeira es una playa de 2 km en curva. La mejor forma de llegar a los points es por el N.

A good spot to check when surrounding beaches are flat. Frouxeira is a 2km curving beach. Three access points, easier from the north.

Un bon spot à checker quand tout le reste est plat . Frouxeira est une plage en croissant de 2 kms. 3 accés principaux, plus facile au nord.

17. Pantín

Pantin recibe mucho swell y tiene una de las mejores olas de playa de toda Galicia. Un canal a la derecha de la playa a través de las rocas te llevan al mejor pico. Las buenas olas hacen que este sitio sea elegido para la realización de competiciones y también que reciba la visita de otros surfers. La calidad del agua es excelente.

Pantín picks up a lot of swell and has some of the best beach waves in Galicia. A channel to the right of the beach through the rocks, will take you out to the best peaks. Good waves make it a popular competition venue and also popular with local and visiting surfers. Water quality is excellent.

Pantin reçoit trés bien la houle avec certaines des meilleures vagues de sable de Galice. Un chenal à droite de la plage vous amènera à travers les rochers vers les meilleurs pics. La qualité des vagues en fait un carrefour pour les compétiteurs et les voyageurs. L'eau est nickel.

18. Area de Foz

En este area hay muy buenas playas. Playa de Barreiros, Playa de Rapadoira y la Playa de Peizas. Tienen buen acceso y funcionan con poco swell. Un buen spot para el verano con buenos bares, restaurantes y campings (a pesar de que los picos se llenan de gente). La calidad del agua varía.

A number of good beaches. Playa de Barreiros, Playa de Rapadoira and Playa de Peizas are all within easy access and work on small swells. A lively spot in summer with good bars, restaurants and camp grounds (therefore the peaks get crowded). Water quality is variable.

Toute une série de beach-breaks. Les plages de Barreiros, de Rapadoira sont d'accés facile et marchent aussi par petite houle; si ça grossit allez vers l'ouest à la plage de Peizas. Un endroit animé en été avec des bars, des restaurants et des campings (où les vagues récupèrent la foule). L'eau est variable.

Foz - Photo: Javier Amezaga

19. Playa Reinante

Playa Reinante y las playas hacia el O producen muchos picos con muy poca gente. Una carretera a lo largo de la costa da buenas vistas al océano.

Playa Reinante and the beaches to the west produce many uncrowded peaks. A coast road provides good views of the ocean.

Playa Reinante et les plages à l'ouest ont plein de pics vierges. De bonnes vues sur l'océan depuis la route côtière.

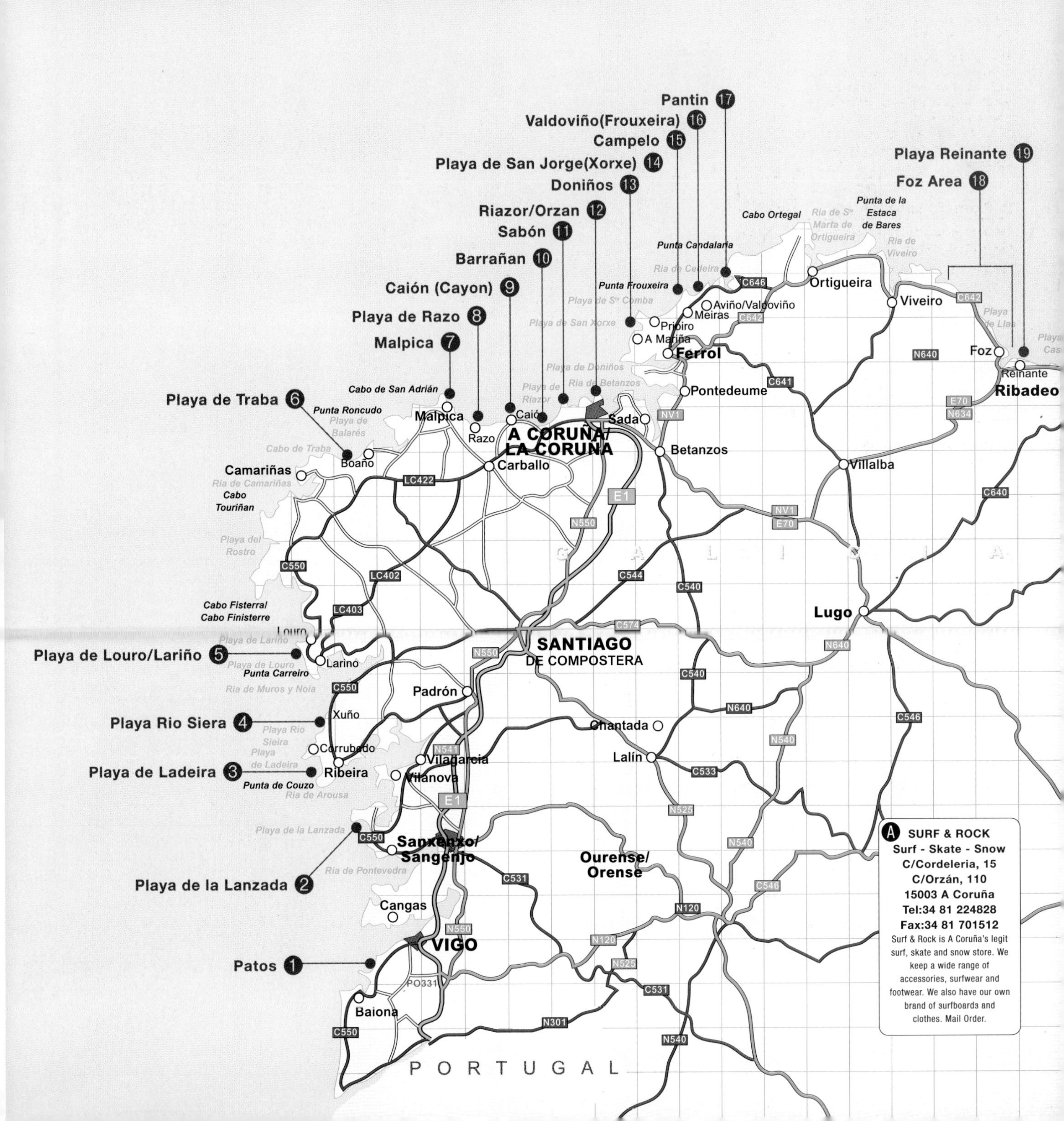

15' monster Pipeline
20' Easter Reef
or carving at the Newcastle Pro,
"Surfing is Tony Ray's life"
HEADWORX
Australia

andalucia

Photo: *Javier Amezaga*

"La zona comprendida entre la ciudad de Cádiz y Tarifa es la más apta para el surf en el sur de España."

La zona comprendida entre la ciudad de Cádiz y Tarifa es la más apta para el surf en el sur de España y la que más y mejores surf spots ofrece. Por lo general es una costa muy ventosa, con predominio del viento de Levante (Este) que con frecuencia sopla con excesiva fuerza. El otro viento dominante, el Poniente (Oeste) no es tan fuerte y trae las marejadas, pero pega on-shore y revuelve el mar. El mejor viento es el Norte que suele soplar en los meses invernales y el terral suave de la mañana.

The area between Cádiz and Tarifa has the best surf in the south of Spain. Swell comes from lows, especially those low in the Atlantic. In general it's a windy coast with predominant E winds which blow frequently and with force. The other dominant wind, from the West, is not as strong and it brings swells, but it's onshore. The best winds are from the North which blow in the winter months and the soft land winds in the morning.

La zone comprise entre la ville de Cadiz et Tarifa est la plus appropriée dans le sud de l'Espagne pour le surf,en offrant les meilleurs spots et les plus nombreux. En général, c'est une côte trés ventée, dominée par le Levant (Est) qui souffle fréquemment trés violemment. L'autre vent dominant, le Ponant (ouest) est moins fort et entraîne les houles, mais ça fait de l'on-shore et il agite la mer. Le meilleur vent est celui de nord qui souffle d'habitude dans les mois d'hiver ou le léger vent de terre du matin.

Photo: *Jakue Andikoetxea*

Photo: *Jakue Andikoetxea*

P O R T U G A L

Andalucia

Javier Amezaga
Tres 60

1. Cádiz

La ciudad de Cádiz se extiende a lo largo de una extensa península, a un lado de la cual está la bahía de Cádiz (sin olas) y al otro una larga playa que da al Atlántico y que tiene olas. Hacia la mitad de la avenida principal está la playa de Santa María del Mar, entre dos diques. Es la playa más surfeada de Cádiz, se puede coger con cualquier tamaño (es difícil que haya más de metro y medio), en marea baja y media. Con alta, las olas rebotan. La playa a la altura de la entrada de la ciudad recibe el nombre de La Cortadura. Totalmente abierta, rompe con más fuerza en marea alta. La misma playa de Cádiz se prolonga hasta la ciudad de San Fernando, donde está la playa de Camposoto, de las mismas características que la de Cortadura.

The city of Cádiz is built along an extensive peninsula. On one side is the Bay of Cádiz (with no waves) and on the other a long beach facing the Atlantic (which does have waves). About half way down the main avenue is Santa María del Mar, between two dikes. It is the most surfed beach in Cádiz, though it's rarely bigger than 1.5 m. It's best at low and mid tide...with high tide the waves rebound. The part of the beach at the entrance of the city is called La Cortadura. Totally open, the waves break with more strength at high tide. The beach of Cádiz extends to the city of San Fernando, where the beach of Camposoto has the same characteristics of La Cortadura.

La ville de Cadiz s'étend au large d'une méga-péninsule, à côté duquel on trouve la baie de Cadiz (pas de vagues) et de l'autre, une plage étendue qui donne sur l'Atlantique, des vagues donc. Vers le milieu de l'avenue principale, on trouve la plage de Santa Maria del Mar, entre deux digues. C'est la plage la plus surfée de Cadix, elle peut être bonne avec n'importe quelle taille (difficile si plus d'un mètre et demi) par marée basse ou moyenne. A marée haute, y'a du back-wash. La plage à l'entrée de la ville s'appelle la Cortadura. Complètement exposées, les vagues y cassent avec plus de puissance à marée haute. La plage s'étend jusque à San Fernando, où la plage de Camposoto présente les mêmes caractéristiques.

2. Chiclana

Es la siguiente localidad después de San Fernando en dirección a Tarifa.Tiene olas en la playa de La Barrosa, también de arena y similares características a las anteriores. Tiene una ola que a veces rompe con buen tubo, pero necesita una marejada muy fuerte. Por lo general rompen olas pequeñas.

The next location after San Fernando in the direction of Tarifa. It has waves on the beach of La Barrosa, which is also sandy and has similar characteristics to those previously mentioned. Sometimes breaks with a good tube, but it needs a very strong swell. Generally smaller than elsewhere.

C'est le prochain village aprés San Fernando. Vagues sur la plage de Barrosa, plage de sable et idem à a précédente. Y'a une vague qui casse parfois avec un tube mais il faut que ça rentre vraiment. Engénéral, c'est petit.

3. Cabo Roche

Unos pocos kilómetros antes de llegar a Conil, en la carretera, hay una entrada que pone "Urbanización Roche". A un kilómetro y medio de este punto está el Cabo Roche, con una larga playa que llega hasta Chiclana. Cabo Roche es el punto de la costa de Cádiz que más mar recibe. Casi siempre hay alguna ola. Se puede coger en todas las mareas y es una ola de estilo orillera, fuerte y hueca, sobre fondo de arena.

A few kilometres before reaching Conil, on the road, there is an entrance that says "Urbanización Roche". A kilometre and a half from here is the Cabo Roche, with a long beach which stretches to Chiclana. Cabo Roche is the point on the coast of Cádiz which receives the most swell and there is almost always some wave there. A strong and hollow shore break over a sand bottom.

Quelques kilomètres avant Conil, sur la route, y'a une entrée marquée "Urbanizacion Roche". A un kilomètre et demi de cette pointe, on trouve le Cabo Roche, avec une grande plage qui va jusqu'a Chiclana. Cabo Roche est le point de la côte le plus agité. On trouve presque tout le temps une vague. On peut surfer à toutes les marées ce shore-break puissant.

4. Conil

El pueblo de Conil es el epicentro surfero de la costa. La playa de Conil es inmensa y se extiende desde el Cabo Roche hasta el Cabo Trafalgar. Una playa de especial belleza. Si hay olas de más de un metro, se puede surfear en el mismo Conil, pero el mejor spot de esta playa está en El Palmar.

The village of Conil is the surfing epicenter on this coast. The beach is immense and of special beauty and extends from Cabo Roche to Cabo Trafalgar. If swell is bigger than 1m, one can surf in Conil itself, but the best spot is El Palmar.

Conil est l'épicentre du surf sur cette côte. La plage est immense, d'une beauté extrême, en s'étendant du Cabo Roche au Cap Trafalgar. Si les vagues font plus d'un mètre, on peut surfer Conil même mais le meilleur spot c'est Palmar.

5. El Palmar

A dos kilómetros de Conil, en la prolongación de la misma playa. Es la mejor playa de Cádiz para hacer surf. Desde medio metro ya tiene fuerza y puede aguantar hasta dos metros y medio. Rompe en todas las mareas sobre fondo de arena. Suele haber varios picos que rompen con tubo a partir de un metro y con salida para ambos lados. Olas rápidas, potentes, orilleras y de recorrido aceptable. Es un spot de alta calidad.

The best surfing beach of the Cádiz area is two kilometres from Conil. From even half a meter the waves already have strength and it can hold up to 2.5m. Fast shorebreak waves, powerful and with acceptable length. A high quality spot.

La meilleure plage de Cadix est à 2kms de Conil. A partir de presqu'un mètre, les vagues ont toujours de la puissance et tiennent jusqu'à 2,5m. Des vagues de shore-break rapides, puissantes et longues. Spot à noter dans les carnets.

6. Caños De Meca

Junto al Cabo de Trafalgar. Una lastra de roca plana levanta un pico estable. Rompe con marea baja y está bastante protegido del viento Poniente. Es una izquierda aunque a veces también da salida de derechas de peor calidad. En marea baja rompe con muy poco fondo y es cuando la ola tiene calidad, con pared, hueca y largo recorrido. Spot clásico de arrecife. Rompe a partir de medio metro, cuando en El Palmar hay por lo menos un metro.

A bed of flat rock forms a stable peak next to Cabo de Trafalgar. It breaks at low tide, protected from W winds. It's a left, although sometimes it also has rights of poor quality. At low tide it breaks with little depth and it is then that the wave has quality, walling up hollow and long. Classic reef spot. It breaks when El Palmar is at least 3ft.

A côté du cap de Trafalgar. Une langue de rocher plat soulève un pic stable. Marche à marée basse et c'est plutôt bien protégé du Ponant. C'est une gauche bien que ça puisse être une droite moyenne. A marée basse, y'a pas d'eau et c'est là que c'est bon avec du surf sur des murs creux et longs. Spot de reef typique. Casse à partir de 50 cms, quand y'a au moins un mètre à El Palmar.

Caños de Meca - *Photo: Jakue Andikoetxea*

Photo: *Javier Amezaga*

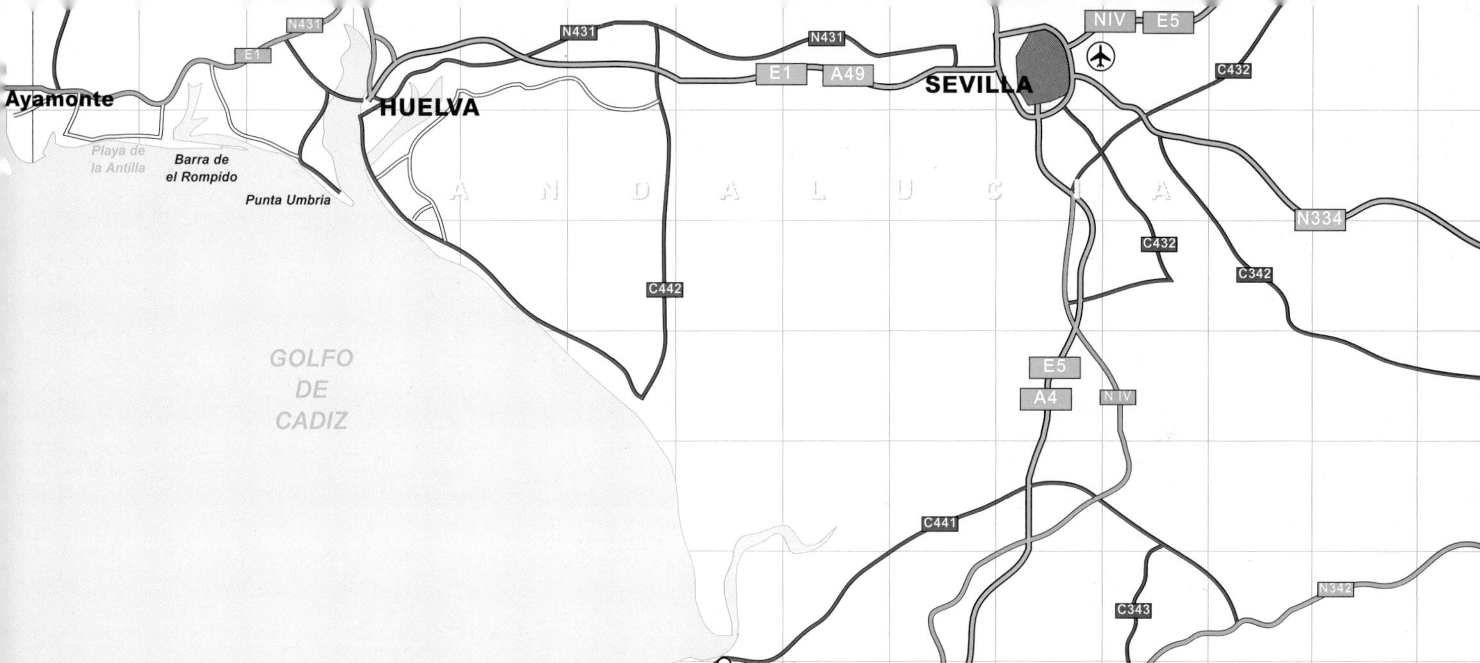

7. Barbate

A la salida de Barbate, en dirección a Zahara, hay una salida de ría que forma una lengua de arena como la de Mundaka pero en miniatura. Da una izquierda larga y juguetona que se puede surfear en todas las mareas. No necesita mucho mar (medio metro es suficiente) pero es peligrosa debido a que los pescadores colocan anzuelos en el fondo.

The river mouth forms a tongue of sand like at Mundaka but in miniature. It gives a long and playful lefthander which one can surf at all tides. It doesn't need a lot of swell (half a metre is sufficient) but it is somewhat dangerous because fishermen put hooks in the bottom of the sea bed.

A la sortie de Barbate, vers Zahara, y'a une sortie de rivère qui forme une langue de sable comme Mundaka mais miniature. Ca donne une trés longue gauche amusante à toutes les marées. Pas besoin de beaucoup de mer, 50 cms à peine. Danger à cause des pêcheurs qui mettent des hameçons au fond de l'eau.

Barbate - *Photo: Jakue Andikoetxea*

8. Zahara De Los Atunes

Entre Barbate y Zahara hay olas a lo largo de toda la costa en playas de arena, pero no se pueden surfear porque es zona militar. Sin embargo al llegar a Zahara sí se puede entrar. Hay varios picos, los mejores a la salida del pueblo en dirección sur. Fondo de arena y olas orilleras.

Between Barbate and Zahara there are waves all along the coast on sandy beaches but they can't be surfed because it's a military zone. However on reaching Zahara one can. Various peaks, the best of which are at the exit of the village going south. Sandy bottoms and shorebreaks.

Entre Barbate et Zahara, des vagues cassent le long de la côte sur du sable, mais on ne peut pas surfer parce que c'est une zone militaire. Pourtant, en entrant par Zahara, ça marche. Plusieurs pics dont les meilleurs sont à la sortie du village vers le sud. Shore-break.

9. Bolonia

Playa de 4 km que puede estar bien cuando en Tarifa sopla Levante fuerte. Es una pequeña y preciosa bahía rodeada de bosque y de dunas, en la que se encuentran las ruinas de un poblado romano.

4km beach which is good when Tarifa is blowing strong E. The small bay surrounded by wood and sandy dunes is very beautiful. There are ruins of an ancient Roman village.

4kms de plages qui marche quand Tarifa est surventée d'est. La petite baie entourée de bois et de dunes est superbe. A voir: es ruines d'un ancient village romain.

10. Los Lances

Extensa playa que llega hasta Tarifa. Hay olas, sobre todo cuanto más cerca de Tarifa, mejor. Olas orilleras sobre fondo de arena, pero no recibe mucho mar y generalmente está muy batida por el viento. Especialmente indicada para windsurfers. Pero en los escasos días que no hay viento, pueden salir buenas olas. A lo largo de la carretera hay varios campings y por lo menos una veintena de hoteles.

Extensive beach which stretches to Tarifa. There are waves, and as you get closer to Tarifa they get better, but it doesn't receive much swell and is generally battered by the wind (good for windsurfers). Along the road there are camp sites and about twenty hotels.

Plage immense qui s'étend jusqu'à Tarifa. Plus on s'approche de Tarifa, plus y'a des vagues. Shore-break qui ne reçoit que peu la houle et généralement trop venté. Surtout pour les windsurfers, mais les jours sans vents peuvent offrir des supers vagues. Le long de la route, on trouve quelques campings et au moins une vingtaine d'hôtels.

Los Lances - *Photo: Jakue Andikoetxea*

PORTUGAL

Capital:	Lisboa
População:	10,525,000
Superfície:	91,630km²
Fuso Horário:	GMT (verão GMT+1)
Language:	Português
Divisa:	Escudo (PTE)

Photo: Peter Cade

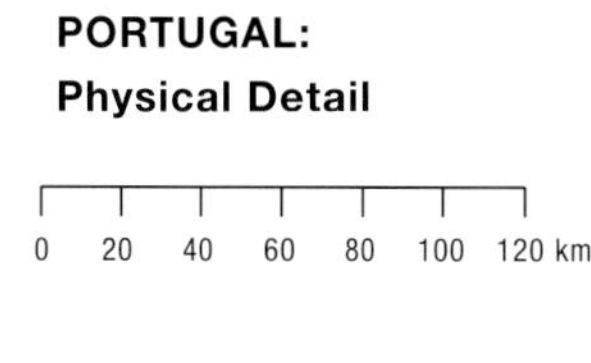

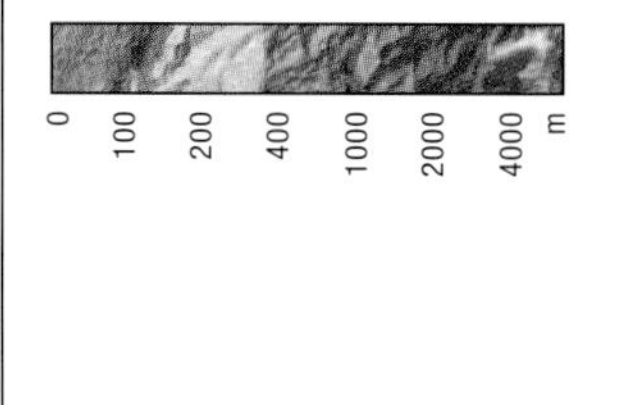

Photos: Phil Holden

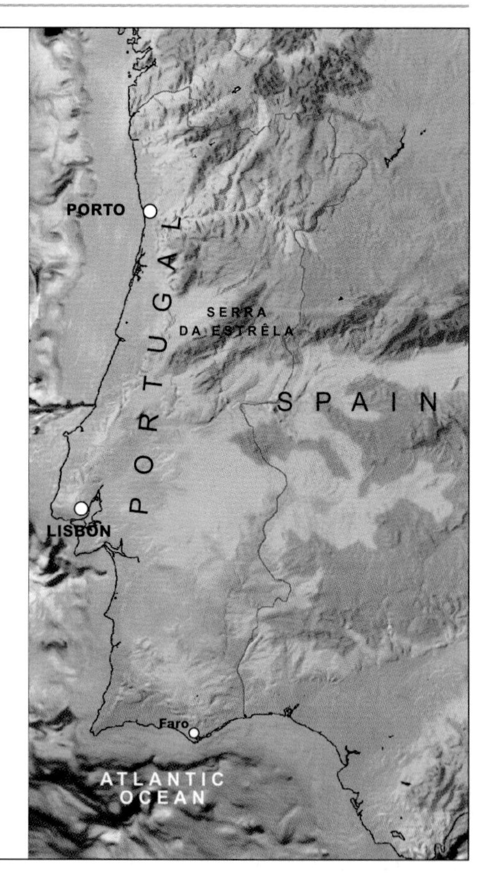

PORTUGAL

Portugal retem influlências Mouras, vizigodas, romanas, francesas e espanholas dos diferentes periudos na história em que esteve dominado por estes povos, deixando marcas genéticas, arquiteturais e físicas até hoje.

Um país que viveu uma época de grande riqueza e poder intimamente ligado ao mar "Atlântico", época essa que começou depois do principe Infante D. Henrique "O navegador" chamar a atenção do trono e da igreja para as "descobertas" e ter fundado a escola de navegaçãoem em Sagres (considerado na altura ser o fim do mundo). A Madeira e os Açores foram descobertos em 1419 e 1427 respectivamente e na altura da morte do Infante D.Herrique 1460 as ilhas de Cabo Verde e a costa leste Africana até a serra Leone já tinhão sido exploradas. Em 1487 Bartolomeu Dias, navegou até a ponta sul do continente Africano dandolhe o nome de Cabo da Boa Esperança, na esperança das boas descobertas que viriam. Vasco da Gama outro grande navegador Português abriu depois de dez anos no processo a rota maritima para India à volta do continente Africano, trazendo na sua primeira viajem um carregamento de pimenta de valor equivalente ao custo de 60 viajens iguias. Portugal ficou rapidamente a Monarquia mais rica da Europa.

Em 1914, Espanha e Portugal dividiram o Mundo (conhecido e por descobrir) ao meio, com uma linha imaginária a 370 leguas Leste das Ilhas de Cabo verde, no famoso tratado de Tordesilhas. Nos 30 anos que se seguirão a riquesa e poder de Portugal chegaram ao seu Zenit, até que uma combinação de factores sociais e políticos trouxeram um rápido declinio a Dinastia Aviz. A tristesa e o desânimo contribuiram para a formação da palavra "Saudade", gerada pela inclinação melancólica do povo português desde então.

A vida política desde então tem sido muito tomultuada. Em Abril de 1974 uma revulução sem mortes resultou no fim de meio seculo de fascismo, dando independência as colónias portuguesas. A economia portuguesa tem crescido muito desde 1975 e em 1992 deu-se o fim do processo de integração na Comunidade Europeia.

Portugal ocupa a parte situada mais a Leste do continente Europeu tendo o Oceano Atlântico a face, revelando uma influência primordial nesta terra de dislumbrantes variedades. Enquanto que no interior o visual é montanhoso e muito verde, a medida que nos dirigimos para o sul o solo torna-se mais arido e seco. A costa é vasta e deslumbrante, com muitas praias, reefs, fundos de rocha e pontões.

PORTUGAL

Portugal retains the influence of successive conquests by the Moors, Visigoths, Romans, French and the Spanish, all of whom left some genetic, architectural and social impression.

The countries fortunes have been firmly linked to the ebb and flow of the Atlantic since Prince Henry the Navigator focused the Church's attention and finances seaward, founding a school of navigation at Sagres (then considered world's end). Madeira and The Azores were discovered in 1419 and 1427 respectively, and by Henry's death in 1460 the Cap Verde Islands and the W.Coast of Africa to Sierra Leone had been explored. In 1487 Bartolemeu Dias navigated the southern tip of Africa and named it Cabo da Boa Esperanca (Cape of Good Hope) in the hope of good things to come. Within10 years Vasco de Gamma had opened up trade routes with India, and the cargo of pepper he bought back on his first trip was enough to pay its expenses 60 times over. Portugal very quickly became the richest monarchy in Europe.

In 1494 Spain and Portugal divided the world between themselves along an imaginary line 370 leagues W of the `Cap Verde Islands and for the next thirty years Portuguese wealth and power were at their zenith, until a combination of social and political factors bought a rapid end to the Dynasty of the House of Avis. The sadness of its demise reputably contributed to the term Saudade, which gives a name to the melancholic inclination of many Portuguese.

Political life since then has been tumultuous. On April 25th 1974, a bloodless coup ended half a century of near fascist rule, giving independence to all former colonies. Since 1975 there has been a period of growth and consolidation including full membership of the E.C. in1992.

Portugal, along with Ireland, occupies Europe's most westerly seaboard and the Atlantic ocean exerts a primary influence over this land of stunning variety. While the northern interior is mountainous, lush and green, it becomes progressively more arid the further south you go. The coastline is vast and wonderful with many fine stretches of beach and some world class reefs, points and jetties.

PORTUGAL

Le Portugal conserve la trace d'influences successives par les conquêtes des Moors, des Visigoths, des Romans, des Français et des Espagnols, qui ont donc laissé une partie de leurs gènes, de leur architecture ou de leur société.

La destinée du pays a toujours été liée aux allées et venues par l'Atlantique depuis qu'Henry le Navigateur a concentré l'attention et les finances de l'Eglise, en fondant une école de navigation à Sagres, alors considérée comme le bout du monde. Madère et les Açores furent respectivement découvertes en 1419 et en 1427; à la mort d'Henry les îles du Cap Vert avaient été explorées en 1460 jusqu'aux fins fond de l'Afrique de l'ouest (Sierra Leone). En 1487, Barolomeu Dias navigua jusqu'au sud de l'Afrique et le nomma le Cap de Bonne Esperance, en espoir de ce qui allait se passer. En 10 ans, Vasco de Gama avait ouvert les routes commerciales vers l'Inde. Le cargo de Poivre qu'il avait ramené de son premier voyage fut suffisant pour rembourser 60 fois ses frais. Le Portugal devient rapidement la monarchie la plus riche d'Europe.

En 1494, L'Espagne et le Portugal se partagaient le monde le long d'une ligne imaginaire 370 miles à l'ouest des îles du Cap Vert et pour les 30 années à venir, la richesse et la puissance furent au sommet, jusqu'à ce qu'une combinaison de facteurs sociaux et politiques amenèrent une fin rapide à la dynastie de la Maison d'Avis. La tristesse de cette déroute contribua à forger l'esprit du Saudade; qui évoque le tempérament souvent mélancolique de nombreux portugais.

La vie politique depuis lors a été tumultueuse. Le 25 Avril 1974, un coup d'Etat sans effusion de sang mis fin à un demi-siècle de quasi-fascisme, donnant son indépendance aux anciennes colonies. Depuis 1975, on a observé une période de croissance dont l'intégration dans la CEE en 1992 en est la preuve.

Le Portugal, comme l'Irlande, occupe la place la plus orientale de l'Europe et l'Atlantique y exerce une influence majeure sur ces terres d'une diversité hallucinante. Alors que le nord intérieur est montagneux, exubérant et vert, ça devient plus aride au fur et à mesure que l(on avance vers le sud. La côte est longue, entrecoupées de plages de sable fin, de reefs de classe mondiale, de "points" et de jetées.

Aeroporto

Lisboa:	(01) 80 20 60
	(01) 72 11 01
Porto:	(02) 948 2141
Faro:	(089) 80 02 10

Comboios

Lisboa:	(01) 888 4025
Porto:	(02) 56 41 41
Figuero da Foz:	(033) 284 83
Faro:	(089) 82 26 53

Autocarros

Lisboa:	(01) 54 58 63
Porto:	(02) 200 6954
Faro:	(089) 80 33 25
Figuero da Foz:	(033) 230 95

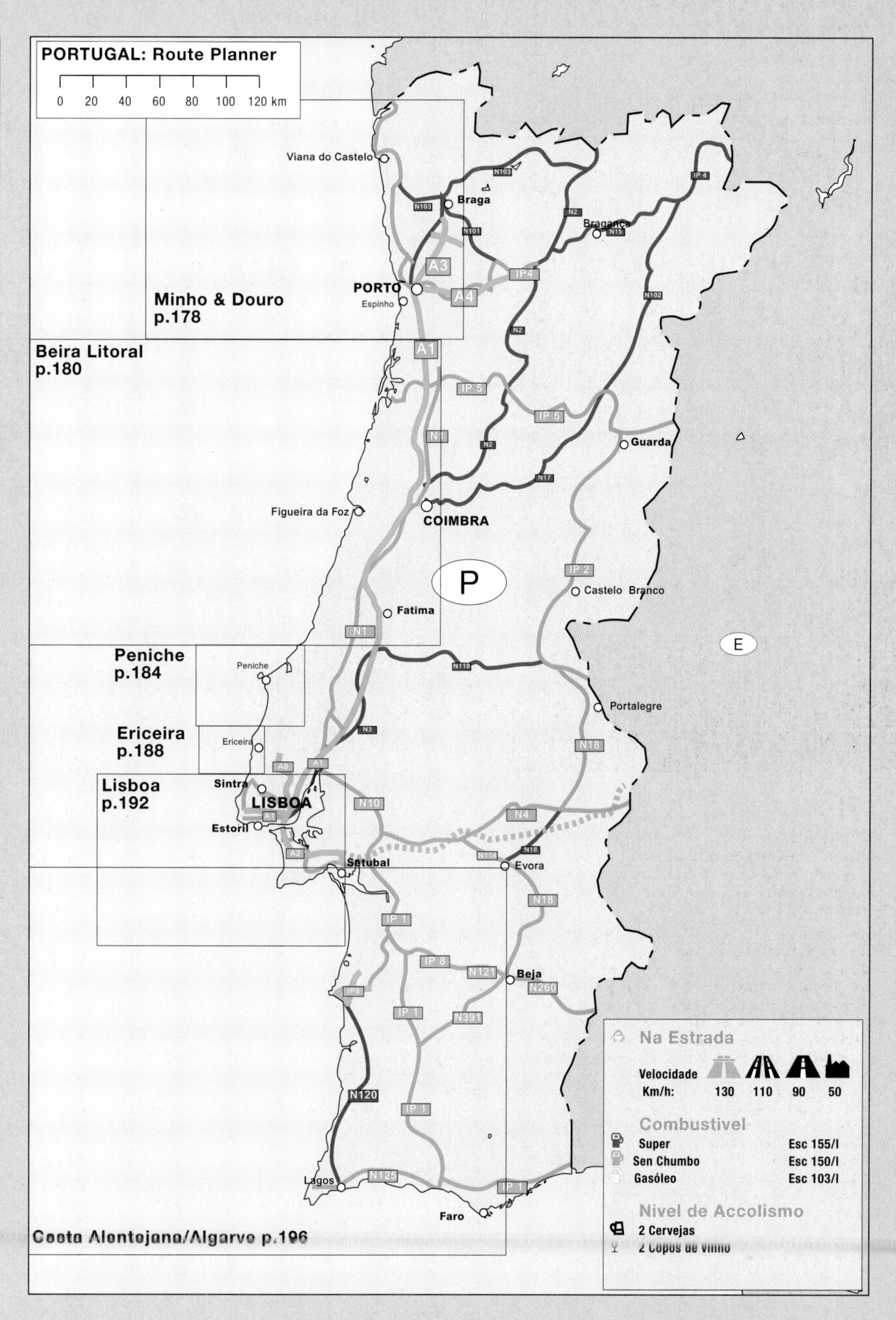

Avião

Na Europa a maior parte dos vôos baratos para Portugal são vôos "charter" para Faro, Lisboa e Porto, sendo normalmente os de Faro os mais baratos de todos.

Comboios e Autocarros

Sã operados por companhias estatais e são bastante bons, para o caso de viajar por terra. Supabus e Eurolines operam serviços bisemanais a partir de Londres e as outras cidades europeias oferecem tambem opções de comboio e autocarro.

Planes

Most of the cheapest flights within Europe to Portugal are charter flights to Faro, Lisboa and O Porto, with the Faro option usually the cheapest.

Trains and Busses

Trains as well as busses within Portugal are state run and quite good, especially if you have to do an overland route, for any reason. Supabus and Eurolines operate twice weekly services from London and all other European cities would offer train and bus options.

L'avion

La plupart des vols bon marché depuis l'Europe sont des vols charters vers Lisbonne, Porto et Faro ce dernier choix étant souvent l'option la moins chère.

Trains et bus

Les trains comme les bus sont gérés par l'état et sont assez efficaces, surtout si vous avez à faire un parcours terrestre, quelle que soit la raison; Supabus et Eurolines font la liaison deux fo s par semaine depuis Londres et toutes les autres villes d'Europe offrent des connections terrestres et ferroviaires.

Junta de Turismo

O Porto:	(02)312740
Figuera Da Foz:	(033) 22610
Peniche:	(062) 789571
Ericeira:	(061) 63122
Lisboa:	[illegible]
Faro:	(089) 803604

Automovel

Do Norte a rota tradicional para Portugal é via San Sebastian, Burgos, Valladolid e Salamanca até Coimbra. A rota por Madrid é mais longa e mais lenta. Uma vez em Portugal as estradas são radicais e as taxas de mortalidade nas estradas são das mais atlas da Europa. Lisboa na hora de ponta é uma experiencia inesquecivel, capaz de arrasar os nervos dos mais estoicos condutores. Mantenha-se sempre calmo. Aluguer de automovel custa cerca de 100 Libras por semana.

Driving

The traditional route into Portugal from north is via San Sebastien, Burgos, Valladolid and Salamanca to Coimbra. The road through Madrid to Lisboa is longer and slower. Once in Portugal, the roads are radical, and the road mortality rates are amongst the highest in Europe. Lisbon at rush hour is an unforgettable experience, capable of fraying the nerves of the steeliest drivers. So are many others. Remain calm at all times. Rental cars cost around £100 per week.

La route

La route habituelle pour aller au Portugal passe par San Sébastien, Burgos, Valladolid, Salamanca et Coimbra. L'itinéraire par Madrid jusqu'à Lisbonne est plus long et plus lent. Une fois au Portugal, les routes sont dangereuses et la mortalité est une des plus élevées d'Europe. Lisbonne aux heures de pointe est une expérience inoubliable, capable de destabiliser les automobilistes les plus endurcis, comme le sont la plupart sur ces routes. Restez calmes tout le temps. Les locations de voiture coûtent environ 800 FF par semaine.

Telefone

Portugal	00 +
Portugal	351 +
INT. Telefonista- Europa	099
INT. Telefonista- Mundo	098
NAC. Telefonista	118
Emergência	11

Custo de Vida

Restaurantes *	Esc 1500
Quartos	Esc 1500-2500
Pensaé	Esc 2500-5000
Hotel **	Esc 5000-10,000
Camping	Esc 1000
Cerveja	Esc 1505

ENVIRONMENT

Surf PORTUGAL

Coxos - Photo Pedro Jorge

World Travel

Interviews

Music

Championships

Poster inside

Nick Uricho

O Tempo

Nós adaptmaos uma expressão na Ericeira uns anos atrás que diz " A chuva de Espanha cai principalmente em Portugal" e apesar disso o tempo não é tão mau, podendo ter um inverno chuvoso especialmente no Norte. O sul tem um clima mediterraneo que raramente fica frio. O oceano no entanto está sempre mais frio que França no Verão, dado a complexidade de ventos Norte-Atlânticos, sendo as botas úteis, não só para o frio mas tambem par evitar as rochas e ouriços abundantes nesta zona. A maioria das ondas vem das baixas pressões Norte-Atlânticas, apesar de Portugal receber com frequência swells de Sul e Leste.Para informações sobre o tempo: O jornal Diário de Notícias tem óptima informação com exelentes fotografias de satélites e mapas. Na televisão, o cana 1 tem a previsão da noite, que incluem mapas e fotografias de satélite tambem.

O Surf

Eu viajei para Portugal pela primeira vez em 1978 sem intensão de lá surfar. Eu desconhecia a qualidade e quantidade de ondas neste lindo e mesterioso país. Levou-me apenas dois diais para mudar os meus planos, tendo visto Carcavelos com tubos perfeitos. Fatos e pranchas não existiam a venda em Portugal nessa altura então fui forçado a ir para França, onde comprei uma prancha e fato em segunda mão. No regresso eu fiquei dois meses a surfar Carcavelos perfeito.

Foi no Outono de 1978 e haia na altura talvez 200 surfistas em Portugal inteiro, eles devem lembra-se, pois foi um ano clássico e muitos outros tem havido desde então. Foi uma altura mágica como imagino que tenha sido em todos os lugares nessa altura. O público em geral ficava espantado por ver alguns malucos remarem para o outside em dias de 8-10 pés. Era uma actarção que levava algumas pessas a ficarem horas a ver-nos.

Como no resto do mundo, quando o surf começa, ele explode assemelhando-se a um tumor em crescimento exponêncial, Nos dezoito anos que tenho cá estado, a população surfistica cresceu para umas dezenas de milhares, em parte pela exposição das revista e alguns campeonatos ASP e EPSA. Mas isso faz parte de evolução do Surf, apereceram shapers para satisfazer a procura e com a troca de informação com shaper internacionais e surfistas profissionais, os shapers e surfistas locais tem evoluido a par com o resto do mundo.

Quando viajando por um lugar uma pessoa tem de tratar as pessoas com gostaria de ser tratado. As pessoa em Portugal são na generalidade muito amigaveis e merecem respeito. Aluguem quartos ou casas com respeito, para que mais possam vir e serem respeitados no futuro. Ninguem gostade chatices dentro d'água. Lembrem-se sempre que vocês vem para aqui para se divertirem e não para fazerem inimigos.

The Weather

We adapted an expression in Ericeira a few years back. It goes..."The rain in Spain falls mainly on Portugal", and although it's not bad by British standards, it can be quite wet, especially in the north. The south experiences a Mediterranean/ African climate which rarely gets cold. The ocean however remains cooler than France in summer due to the complexities of North Atlantic currents and booties are valuable year round (the water can be cold enough to numb the feet and sharp rocks and urchins abound), be warned. Most waves come from N.Atlantic low pressure systems, though West and South swells are common.

Weather Information: Diario de Noticias is a daily newspaper with excellent satellite pics and weather charts. On television, Channel One has the best evening predictions, including maps and satellite pictures.

The Surf

I first travelled to Portugal in 1978 with no intention of surfing. I was ignorant of the quality and quantity of waves in this strange and beautiful country. It took me roughly two days to change my gameplan, having seen perfect barrels at Carcavelos. Surfboards and wetsuits were unavaliable at that time so I was forced to head to France, where I bought a second-hand board and wetsuit. Upon return I spent two months surfing perfect Carcavelos. It was fall of '78 and there were maybe two hundred surfers in Portugal. They will remember it was a classic year and there have been many more since then. It was a magic time as I guess it must have been everywhere in surfings early days. The general public were amazed by the madmen paddling out in 8-10 ft waves. It was a crowd pleaser and people would stand for hours watching.

Like the rest of the world, wherever surfing starts, it explodes with an almost cancerous growth. Portugal is no exception and in the thirteen years I've been here, the population has grown into the tens of housands, due to magazine exposure and a number of A.S.P. and E.P.S.A. competititions. But thats all part of the evolution of surfing. Boardbuilders have grown to meet the demand and with input from travelling shapers, professional surfers and killer waves, local surfers and surfboards have evolved on par with the rest of the world.

When travelling anywhere one must treat others as one would like to be treated. People here are very friendly and helpful in general and you should treat them and their property (rented house or room) with respect so you and other surfers will be welcome in the future. Nobody likes a wave hog or bad manners in the water. Remember at all times...you are here to surf and have a good time, not to make enemies!

Le Climat

Nous avons adapté une expression à Ericeira il y quelques années qui est celle-ci: " la pluie en Espagne tombe principalement au Portugal" et bien que ce ne soit pas aussi terrible que cela, on peut avoir un temps pluvieux surtout au nord . Le sud possède un climat méditerranéen qui est rarement froid. Pourtant, l'océan reste plus froid en été qu'en France par exemple dû aux remontées de courants froids .Attention, les botillons peuvent servir tout le temps à cause de l'eau, des rochers coupants et des oursins. La plupart des vagues viennent des dépressions de l'Atlantique nord, même si des houles d'ouest et de sud ne sont pas rares.

Météorologie: le Diario de Noticias est un quotidien avec d'excellentes cartes isobariques et des prévisions de houle. A la télé, Channel One a les meilleures prévisions le soir, avec des animations satellite et des cartes marines.

Le Surf

Je suis allé au Portugal pour la première fois en 1978 sans intention de surfer. Je ne connaissais pas du tout la qualité et la quantité de vagues dans ce pays magnifique et étrange. Il me fallut à peu prés deux jours pour changer mes plans aprés avoir vu des tubes parfaits à Carcavelos. Impossible de mettre la main sur une planche ou une combinaison à ce moment-là, je dus aller en France pour acheter du matos d'occasion. Au retour, je passai deux mois à surfer Carcavelos parfait, c'était l'automne 78 et il y avait peut-être 200 surfers au Portugal. Tous s'en souviendront comme d'une année épique bien qu'il y en ait eu bien d'autres depuis. Cette époque était magique comme elle dût l'être partout aux premières heures du surf. Les gens étaient interloqués en voyant ces fous ramer vers des vagues de prés de 3m, ils adoraient çà et regardaient pendant des heures.

Comme partout ailleurs, où le surf a commencé, ça s'est répandu avec une croissance quasi-cancéreuse. Depuis 17 ans que je suis là, les surfers se sont multipliés par dizaines de mille, avec les magazines et les compétitions ASP et EPSA, mais cela fait partie du progrés, j'imagine. Les shapers eux-aussi sont apparus pour répondre à la demande et grâce aux shapers étrangers, aux pros et aux vagues d'enfer, les locaux et les planches ont évolué aussi radicalement qu'ailleurs.

Comme tout autre voyage, on doit traiter autrui comme on aimerait être traiter. Les gens d'ici sont généralement trés amicaux et hospitaliers, il faut donc les considérer ainsi que leurs biens (maisons et chambres)afin que vous ou d'autres surfers soient toujours les bienvenus. Personne n'apprécie un taxeur de vagues dans l'eau. Rappelez-vous toujours que vous êtes là pour faire du surf et vous amuser: pas vous faire des ennemis.

Minho & Douro

Photo: João Barbosa

Surf está muito desenvolvido nesta área, embora não haja tanto crowd como no Sul. A costa é especialmente boa para windsurf de ondas, dado os percistentes ventos vindos predominantemente de Norte e Leste. No entanto a Ragião tem potencial para muitas descobertas. O Porto sendo a capital industrial do país, e tambem a área mais populada, pelo que o crowd está todo concentrado aqui. Alguns bons surfistas com os Irmõas Ribas que listam-se entre os primeiros surfistas de Portugal ou o Zé Skate, que durante algum tempo dividiu os titulos dos campeonatos nacionais com o Dapim.

Surfing is strong here but numbers in the water are generally much fewer than further south. The coast is especially good for wave jumping, with winds coming predominantly from the N.W., though the whole region holds potential for significant further discovery. Porto is the industrial capital of Portugal and the most crowded region in the north. Some well known names come from this town, like the Ribas brothers, who were among the first to have surfed in Portugal, and Zé Skate who divided national contest honours with Dapim (Portugals most famous surfer) for a long time.

Le surf est bien développé bien qu'on y trouve moins de surfers que dans le sud. La côte est surtout adaptée au saut de vagues avec des vents dominants de NO. La région reste encore à explorer. Porto est la capitale industrielle du pays et la région du nord la plus peuplée. Certains des meilleurs surfers en viennent comme les frères Ribas, parmi les premier surfers au Portugal, et Zé Skate qui partagea pendant les honneurs des compétitions nationales avec Dapim, le surfer portugais le plus célèbre.

1. Moledo

Um forte meio arruinado guarda uma bancada de areia muito longa na saída do Rio Minho, que divide Espanha de Portugal. Uma boa onda que oferece boas condicções para o surf e wind-surf.

A half-ruined fort guards the rivermouth from a long spit. The river is the border line between Portugal and Spain. A good beach break offers fun conditions for surfing and wave-sailing.

Un vieux fort à moitié en ruine protège la rivière d'une grande langue de sable. Cette rivière est la frontière entre le Portugal et l'Espagne. Un bon beach-break offre des conditions sympas pour le surf et le windsurf.

2. Vila Praia de Âncora

Uma onda longa na saída de um rio. Dependendo dos fundos de areia, pode ser uma das melhores ondas da zona. A água não é muito limpa e o crowd é uma constante.

A long river mouth, which can be one of the best spots in the area depending on the sand bar. The water is a little polluted and crowds are a constant factor.

Une vague longue à la sortie d'une rivière, qui peut être une des meilleures vagues du coin. L'eau est un peu polluée et du monde à l'eau en permanence.

3. Afife

Uma das mais consistentes ondas de Viana do Castelo. Há uma série de picos multiplos que, dependendo dos fundos, podem aguentar grandes swells. No verão quase nunca fica flat, e a água é muito pura.

The most consistent wave in Viana do Castelo. It's a multiple peak beach which handles big swell. In the summer it's almost never flat and the water is pure.

La vague la plus consistante de Viana do Castelo, une plage avec plusieurs pics qui tient bien le gros. Même en été, il y a toujours quelque chose et l'eau est propre.

4. Viana do Castelo

Praia de areia que aguenta ondas de 2-10 pés nos dois lados do rio. Lugar principal para a prática de "fun-board" no norte. Uma bonita cidade com óptimos restaurantes. Um ferry pode nos levar para o Cabedelo.

Beach break, holds surf from 2-10ft on both sides of the rivermouth. Focal point for northen fun-boarders. Lively town with great restaurants. A ferry from here takes you to Cabedelo.

Beach break qui marche de 50cms à 3m des deux côtés de la rivière. Lieu principal pour la pratique du Fun-board en été. Une ville animée avec de bons restos, prenez le ferry pour aller à Cabadelo.

5. Esposende

Outro pedaço de praia, virado a oeste, dividido por um rio mais ou menos grande.

Another strech of west facing beach, broken by a moderate sized river.

Encore une étendue de plage exposée ouest, partagée par une rivière plus ou moins grande.

6. Aguçadoura

É uma praia muito bonita, com uma grande extensão de areia e muitos picos consistentes. Não aguenta muito swell sem fechar. Em dias pequenos noutros lugares, aqui estará sempre maior.

A long sandy beach, with consistent peaks. On small days one can always find bigger waves here then elsewhere.

Une plage longue avec des pics consistants. Quand c'est petit ailleurs, c'est souvent plus gros ici.

7. Póvoa do Varzim

Uma esquerda que sai de rochas e areia misturadas. As rochas são afiadas, fazendo das marés mais cheias apostas mais cautelosas. É preciso um bom swell para ficar bom.

Lefthander off the rock and sand bars on the beach. The rocks are sharp making mid to high tide a safer bet. Needs a good sized swell to work.

Une gauche sur fond de rochers mélangés avec du sable. Gaffe aux cailloux qui sont plutôt tranchants, mieux vaut éviter les marées basses. Il faut un bon swell pour que ça marche.

8. Vila do Conde

Praia de areia a sul da Póvoa de Varzim. Muito consistente e normalmente um bom lugar para a prática de wind Surf.

Beach break south of Póvoa do Varzim. Very consistent breaks and normally good spot for wave sailing also.

Plage de sable au sud de Povoa. Des breaks trés consistents, souvent favorables au windsurf aussi.

9. Azurára

Funciona com as mesmas condições de Vila do Conde. Praia muito boa para Body Board, dado os seus quebra-cocos na areia. Normalmente, não costuma estar muito crowd e a água é muito boa.

Works with similar conditions to Vila do Conde. Good beach for body-boarding due to the heavy shore break. Its not usually crowded and the water is very good.

Mêmes conditions que Vila do Conde. Un shore-break carton parfait pour le bodyboard. Pas forcément du monde et une eau impeccable.

10. Leça

O pico mais consistente do Porto, costuma ter sempre ondas mesmo no verão. Tem umas rochas mas as ondas normalmente são longe delas. Há um grande pontão do Porto de Leça que gera bons fundos no inverno. A água não é muito boa.

The most consistent spot in the Porto area, rarely gets flat, even in the summer and the harbour helps form good sand bars in the winter. The water quality is however, bad.

Le pic le plus régulier de Porto, où ça surfe toujours même en été. Le port aves ses digues de cailloux favorise de bons bancs de sable en hiver. L'eau est plutôt gerbique.

Espinho - Photo: João Valente

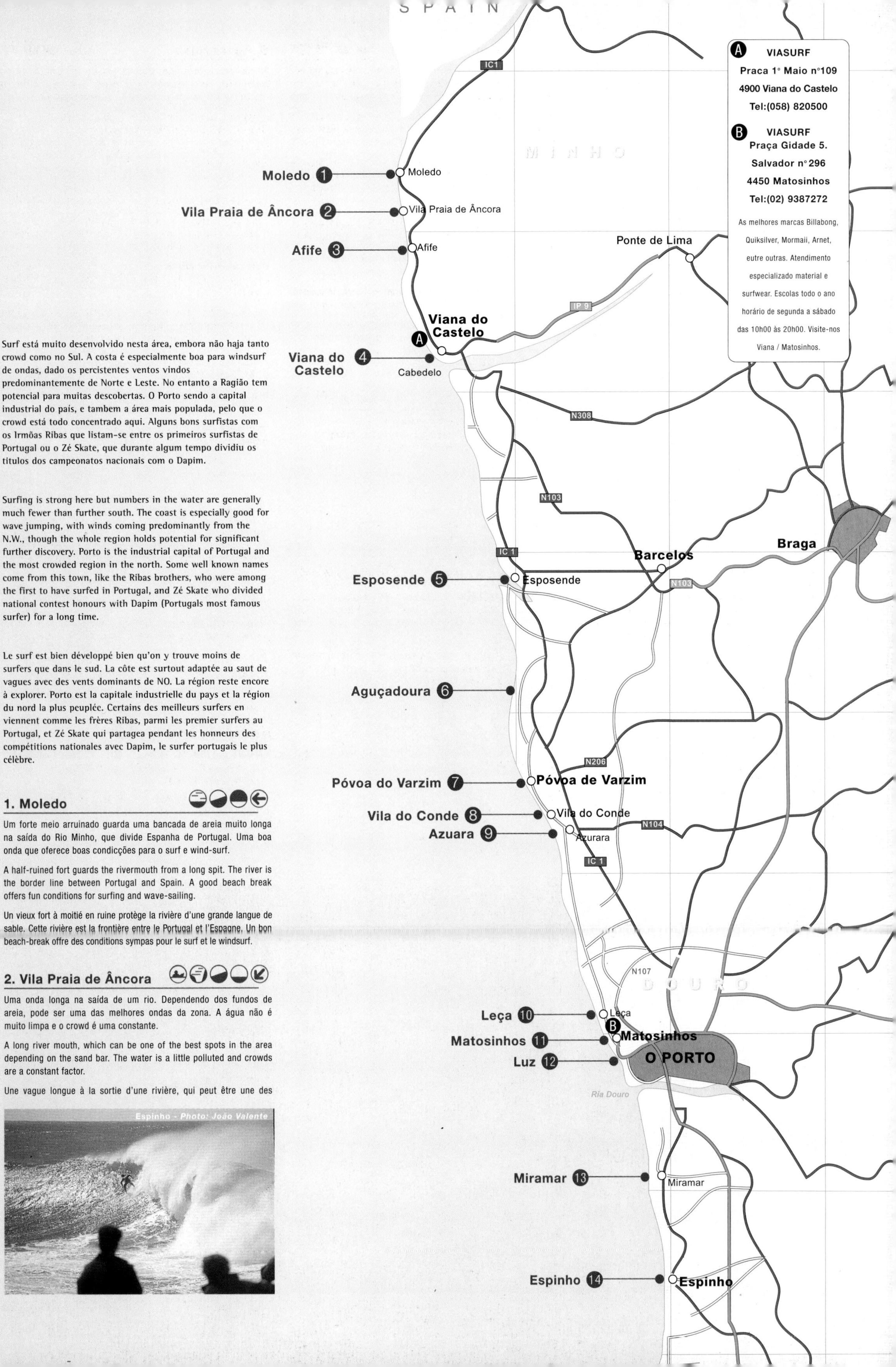

Surf está muito desenvolvido nesta área, embora não haja tanto crowd como no Sul. A costa é especialmente boa para windsurf de ondas, dado os persistentes ventos vindos predominantemente de Norte e Leste. No entanto a Ragião tem potencial para muitas descobertas. O Porto sendo a capital industrial do país, e tambem a área mais populada, pelo que o crowd está todo concentrado aqui. Alguns bons surfistas com os Irmõas Ribas que listam-se entre os primeiros surfistas de Portugal ou o Zé Skate, que durante algum tempo dividiu os titulos dos campeonatos nacionais com o Dapim.

Surfing is strong here but numbers in the water are generally much fewer than further south. The coast is especially good for wave jumping, with winds coming predominantly from the N.W., though the whole region holds potential for significant further discovery. Porto is the industrial capital of Portugal and the most crowded region in the north. Some well known names come from this town, like the Ribas brothers, who were among the first to have surfed in Portugal, and Zé Skate who divided national contest honours with Dapim (Portugals most famous surfer) for a long time.

Le surf est bien développé bien qu'on y trouve moins de surfers que dans le sud. La côte est surtout adaptée au saut de vagues avec des vents dominants de NO. La région reste encore à explorer. Porto est la capitale industrielle du pays et la région du nord la plus peuplée. Certains des meilleurs surfers en viennent comme les frères Ribas, parmi les premier surfers au Portugal, et Zé Skate qui partagea pendant les honneurs des compétitions nationales avec Dapim, le surfer portugais le plus célèbre.

1. Moledo

Um forte meio arruinado guarda uma bancada de areia muito longa na saída do Rio Minho, que divide Espanha de Portugal. Uma boa onda que oferece boas condicções para o surf e wind-surf.

A half-ruined fort guards the rivermouth from a long spit. The river is the border line between Portugal and Spain. A good beach break offers fun conditions for surfing and wave-sailing.

Un vieux fort à moitié en ruine protège la rivière d'une grande langue de sable. Cette rivière est la frontière entre le Portugal et l'Espagne. Un bon beach-break offre des conditions sympas pour le surf et le windsurf.

2. Vila Praia de Âncora

Uma onda longa na saída de um rio. Dependendo dos fundos de areia, pode ser uma das melhores ondas da zona. A água não é muito limpa e o crowd é uma constante.

A long river mouth, which can be one of the best spots in the area depending on the sand bar. The water is a little polluted and crowds are a constant factor.

Une vague longue à la sortie d'une rivière, qui peut être une des

Espinho - Photo: João Valente

Beira Litoral

Esta área é melhor descrita como semi-explorada. Pontões, ondas em saidas de rios, picos de pedras em sitios esquisitos e kilometros de praias quase vasias extendem-se por esta costa. Nazaré tem ganho a fama de ter as maiores ondas do País, dado na costa haver uma racha muito funda em forma de dedo que aponta directamente para a praia da Nazaré.

Não há muitos surfistas conhecidos desta zona, sendo o "Tomaz da Figheira" o mais famoso, principalmete pela sua pericia em ondas grandes. A sua terra natal Figueira da Foz possue uma das mais compridas ondas do país, podendo extender-se por dezenas de metros em dias bons buarcos

This area could best be described as semi explored. Jetties, rivermouths and the odd well placed rock break the miles of almost empty beaches which stretch north. Nazare has gained fame for big waves due to a finger of deep water pointing straight at the town. Joao Valeñte has described Nazare as the most underrated spot in the country. Figueira da Foz has also gained a become known amongst keen European travellers and 'Tomaz da Figueira"is the most well known local, especially for his abilties in big waves. His town is home to Buarcos, one of the longest waves in Portugal.

Cette zone reste encore à moitié explorée. Jetées, sorties de rivières et des rochers bien placés de temps en temps interrompent des kilomètres de plages désertes qui s'étendent jusqu'au nord. Nazaré s'est fait connaître comme un spot de gros grâce à un doigt d'eau profonde qui se dirige vers la ville. João Valente le considère comme le spot le plus sous-estimé du pays. Figueira da Foz est bien connue aussi de surfers européens avec de Tomaz de Figueira, le plus local des locaux surtout dans les grosses vagues. On y trouve Buarcos, une des plus longues vagues du Portugal.

1. Furadouro

Esta onda é em cima de uma bancada de areia com rochas. Não aguenta muitos swells, mas com 5 pés é muito boa e tem secções tubulares. Normalmente, não há crowd e a água é muito limpa. Bom Hotel se for preciso alojamento.

Breaks over a sand and rocky bottom. It dosen't hold big swells but up to 6ft you'll find quite a good wave, with cover up sections. Normaly there aren't any crowds. There is a very good hotel in the area.

Casse sur fond de sable et de cailloux. Ca tient pas le gros mais jusqu'à 2m, vous devriez avoir une vague agréable avec des sections à tubes. Normalement, y'a pas grand monde et un bon hôtel tout prés.

2. Praia da Barra

Hoje em dia, só funciona com grandes swells. Tem uma onda para os dois lados. Empreendimentos de veraneio estragaram esta onda...

Breaks both directions, now only on big swells. Beach development killed this spot...

Ne marche plus aujourd'hui que par gros swell, de part et d'autre de la jetée. Les constructions ont défiguré cette vague, encore une ...

3. Costa Nova

Pontões formão boas ondas a sul da saída do rio Vouga. Aqui estão algumas das melhores ondas deste bocado da costa. Quando está grande, há uma remada grande até ao "out side" por isso, esperar e observar uma correnteza que puxe para fora pode valer a pena antes de entrar na água.

Good jetties south of the River Vouga produce some of the best waves along this stretch of coast. When it's big the paddle out can be arduous, so finding a rip to go out on can be well worth while.

De bonnes jetées au sud de Vouga ont permis la formation de bons bancs de sable, parmi les meilleurs du coin. Quand c'est gros, passer la barre n'a rien d'évident alors essayez de repérer un chenal qui vous aidera à ramer.

4. Praia de Mira

Típica praia urbana, com ondas muito consistentes ao longo de extensas dunas de areia, Normalmente não há crowd.

Typical beach town and consistent beach waves set amongst extensive dunes. Generally uncrowded.

Plage de ville typique avec des vagues supra-consistentes derrière des dune qui n'en finissent plus. Rarement peuplé .

Buarcos - Photo: Dan Hutton

Figueira da Foz - Photo: Dan Hutton

5. Buarcos

Uma longa direita sobre um fundo de areia e rochas a mistura, mesmo em frente au Hotel Tamagueira. Esta onda aguenta grandes swells e não costuma haver problemas de crowd fora da época alta (verão).

Very long right over rocky bottom and also sand bars in front of Hotel Tamagueira. The beach holds good sized swells and has no crowd problems outside high season (summer).

Une trés longue droite sur fond de sable et rochers, en face de l'hôtel Tamagueira. Cette vague tient presque toute les tailles et n'est pas souvent prise d'assaut sauf en été. Courants.

6. Cabedelo

No lado sul do Rio Mondego, um famigerado pier corre para dentro do mar por uns 500 metros. Uma longa e perfeita direita quebra sobre um fundo de areia com bons tubos. Uma corrente muito útil passa ao lado do pier. Normalmente há algum crowd mas, as ondas são mais que suficientes para todos.

On the south side of the River Mondego, a tarmac pier runs to the sea for about 1/2 Km. A long classic right breaks on the sandbanks with thick lips and grinding barrels. A useful rip runs alongside the pier. Usually it is crowded but there are more than enough waves for everyone.

Au sud de la Montego, une jetée goudronnée va en mer sur 500 mètres. Une droite classique et longue avec une lèvre épaisse et des tubes déments. Un courant utile le long de la jetée. Toujours un peu de monde mais souvent une vague pour chacun.

7. São Pedro de Muel

Raramente surfada, esta onda de fundo de rochas, quebra a Oeste da Marinha Grande. Há um hotel da juventude mesmo por cima do mar que funciona de 1 de Maio até 30 de Setembro.

Rarely surfed sand & rock bottom spot breaks west of Marinha Grande. A seasonal Youth Hostel open from May 1-Sept 30 sits right on the sea.

Rarement surfée, cette vague casse sur fond de sable et rochers, à l'ouest de Marinha Grande. Une auberge de jeunesse sur le sable de Mai à Septembre.

8. Nazaré

O "Surf Report" chama-lhe a onda do "big surf" Português. 6-22 pés... e fundo de areia ... Certamente uma área de praia que aguenta grandes ondas. Uma área muito funda em forma de dedo aponta para Nazaré e constantes swells atingem a praia com muita força. Condicções muito radicais e "provavelmente a onda mais substimada de Portugal". Joao Valente

The Surf Report calls it: "Portugal's big wave spot... 6-22 ft ... sand bottom. Certainly a strech of coast which holds large waves. A long finger of deep ocean points to Nazare and consequently swells hit the beaches from extremely deep water. Very radical conditions.

Le Surf Report la décrit ainsi "Le spot du gros du Portugal de 2m à 6-7m sur fond de sable". Une plage qui tient les méga-houles donc avec une fosse au large faisant un doigt qui pointe Nazaré et qui concentre la puissance de la houle. Des conditions extrêmes et la vague la plus sous-estimée selon Joao Valente de Surf Portugal.

Nazaré - Photo: João Barbosa

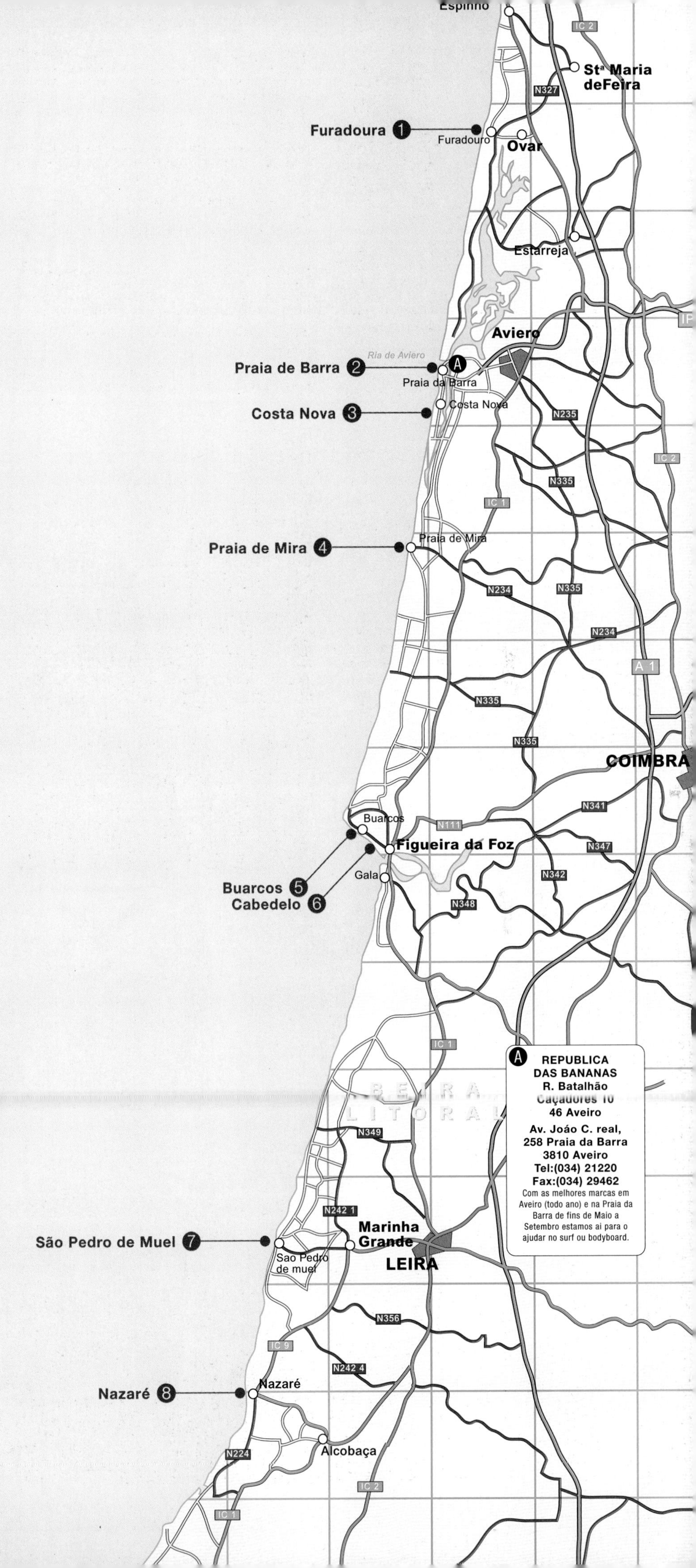

BYRON
surfboards

BYRON®
surfboards

peniche

Peniche é um dos portos pesqueiros mais activos em Portugal, até o seculo XII, esta área era uma ilha. Hoje em dia a ilha, está ligada ao continente por um aterramento artificial. A fortaleza do seculo XII foi uma das mais notórias prisões portuguesas, sendo hoje em dia apenas um monumento contra o fascismo.

A cidade tem sido um ponto de grande atracção surfistica, devido a grande variedade de picos que funcionão com quase todos os ventos dentro de uma raio de 15Km. Swells pequenos de Norte que quase não quebram na Ericeira, geram boas ondas nas praias Norte de Peniche. Swells de Sul e ventos de Norte fazem a famosa onda de Supertubos começar a quebrar algumas pranchas.

A Norte de Peniche o crowd diminui substancialmete. As áreas ao redor de Peniche são basicamete pequeneas vilas com um óptimo vibrações amigaveis.

Peniche is one of Portugals' busiest fishing ports and was an island until the 12C, now joined to the mainland by a narrow causeway. Its 12C "Fortaleza" was one of Portugals' most notorious jails, now an impressive monument against fascism.

The town has been a magnet for surfers for at least a decade due to the large variety of spots working in different conditions within a 10 mile radius. North swells which hardly register around Ericeira can be breaking on the beaches north, and in south swells or north winds Supers turns on with board snapping power. From Peniche north the crowds thin substantially.

The surrounding areas are small and the vibe is friendly, though things can get a bit hassly in the water at the main breaks and foriegners might need a bit of patience with drop-ins...we strongly suggest you use it.

Peniche est un des ports les plus animés du Portugal. C'était une île jusqu'au XII° siècle, maintenant reliée au continent par une étroite bande de terres. Sa forteresse du XII° était l'une des prisons les plus célèbres, reconvertie aujourd'hui en un monument impressionnant contre le fascisme.

La ville agit comme un aimant à surfers depuis une dizaine d'années, grâce à la grande variété de spots qui marchent avec des conditions différentes dans un rayon de 15 kms. Les swells de nord qui ne donnent presque rien sur Ericeira peuvent bien casser sur les breaks du nord. Par houle de sud et vents de nord, 'Supers' devient une machine à casser des planches. Au Nord, la foule se réduit considérablement. Les villages environnant sont de petite taille et l'atmosphère y est relax.

"...swells de Sul e ventos de Norte fazem Supertubos começar a quebrar algumas pranchas..."

Andre Pedrosa - *Photo: João Valente*

Photo: Eric Chauché

Supertubos - *Photo: João Valente*

A esquerda, Consolação - *Photo: João Valente*

Peniche

1. Praia da Foz do Arelho

A praia vai desde Peniche até Foz do Arelho sem interrupções. É uma boa praia com boas ondas na saída do rio.

The beach runs from Peniche to Foz in a pretty uninterupted stretch northwards. Good beach and rivermouth waves.

Cette plage qui va de Peniche à Foz est sans interruption. Bonnes vagues à l'embouchure.

2. Ferrel

Pode-se ver a praia do Baleal, e quando está pequeno, num dia com swell de SW, pode ser o maior lugar para se surfar. Há uma trilha que corre ao longo de toda a praia, é dificil de encontrar esta trilha, masa procura pode valer apena.

You can see the beach from Baleal and in a small N swell when everywhere else is crap and the wind SW, Ferral can be head high and pumping. A track runs along the length of the beach - finding it can be tricky but worthwhile.

Visible depuis Baleal; quand c'est petit pourri par vents de S-O à Baleal, Ferral peut être mieux que surprenant. Des pistes sillonnent le long de la côte, pas faciles à s'orienter mais ça vaut la galère.

Ferral - *Photo: Tim Rainger, LP*

3. Lagide

Boas esquerdas, quebrando sobre um reef infectado de ouriços. Muito raso e perigoso na maré baixa. O parque em frente desta onda costuma estar cheio de carrinhas estrangeiras.

High quality left breaking over an urchin infested reef. Dangerously shallow at low tide. Loads of campervans hang out in the car park.

Une belle gauche sur un reef infesté d'oursins, d'où certains risques à marée basse. Pas mal de vans sur le parking en face en général .

Lagide - *Photo: Matin Jakobssen*

4. Praia do Baleal

Esta praia é enorme com um formato de meia lua. Protegida do vento funciona melhor quando há mais swell. ou quando o resto das praias estão com ventos"side Off".

Protected scallop-shaped beach just north of Peniche works best in large swells or when the rest of the coast is cross shore.

Plage en croissant de lune juste au nord de Peniche qui marche bien par grosse houle quand les vents sur les autres plages sont cross-shore.

5. Molho Leste

Onda protegida, com bons picos quando a nortada está forte, e todos os outros picos estão maus. É facil para estacionar o carro.

Protected spot with good right peaks when north winds are blowing everywhere else to shit. Easy parking.

Spot protégé par les digues avec, à l'abri des vents de nord, avec de bonnes droites rapides. Parking à proximité.

6. Supertubos

O nome fala por si. Uma fábrica de peixe dá um cheiro característico a esta zona, e apesar das ondas perfeitas, o crowd pode estragar a surfada. Supertubos funciona com S swell.

The name speaks for itself. The nearby fish factory lends flavour to the experience and although the lefts are wicked, crowds can mar the enjoyment. Supertubes is a S swell break.

Tout est dans le nom. L'usine de poisson à côté balance une odeur pestilentielle. Par houle de sud, les gauches peuvent y être démentes mais attention au monde.

Supertubos - *Photo: Tim McKenna*

7. Consolação

Uma direita sobre um fundo de rochas, que costuma sér bastante cheia. Normalmente mais pequeno que Supertubos, e no entanto um bom pico e a água é exelente.

Righthander over a rocky bottom, often fat, with a hollower left on the N side of the point. Less swell gets in here than at Supertubes, but it's a very pretty spot with excellent water quality.

Une droite, souvent épaisse, sur fond de rochers. D'habitude plus petit qu'à Supertubos mais le décor est grandiose et l'eau impeccable. décor est grandiose et l'eau impeccable.

8. Praia da Areia Branca

Boa praia com ondas na saida de um rio.

Good beach break and rivermouth waves.

Bon beach break et une sortie de rivière .

9. Santa Cruz

É uma óptima praia, trabalha com as mesmas condições de vento que a Ericeira, é e bastante popular como praia de Wind Surf tambem, especialmente no verão.

Particularly good beach works in similar conditions to the Ericeira breaks and is also a popular wave-sailing venue, especially in summer.

Une plage vraiment bonne avec les mêmes conditions que les spots d'Ericeira. Trés prise des windsurfers surtout en été.

Molho Leste - *Photo: Phil Holden*

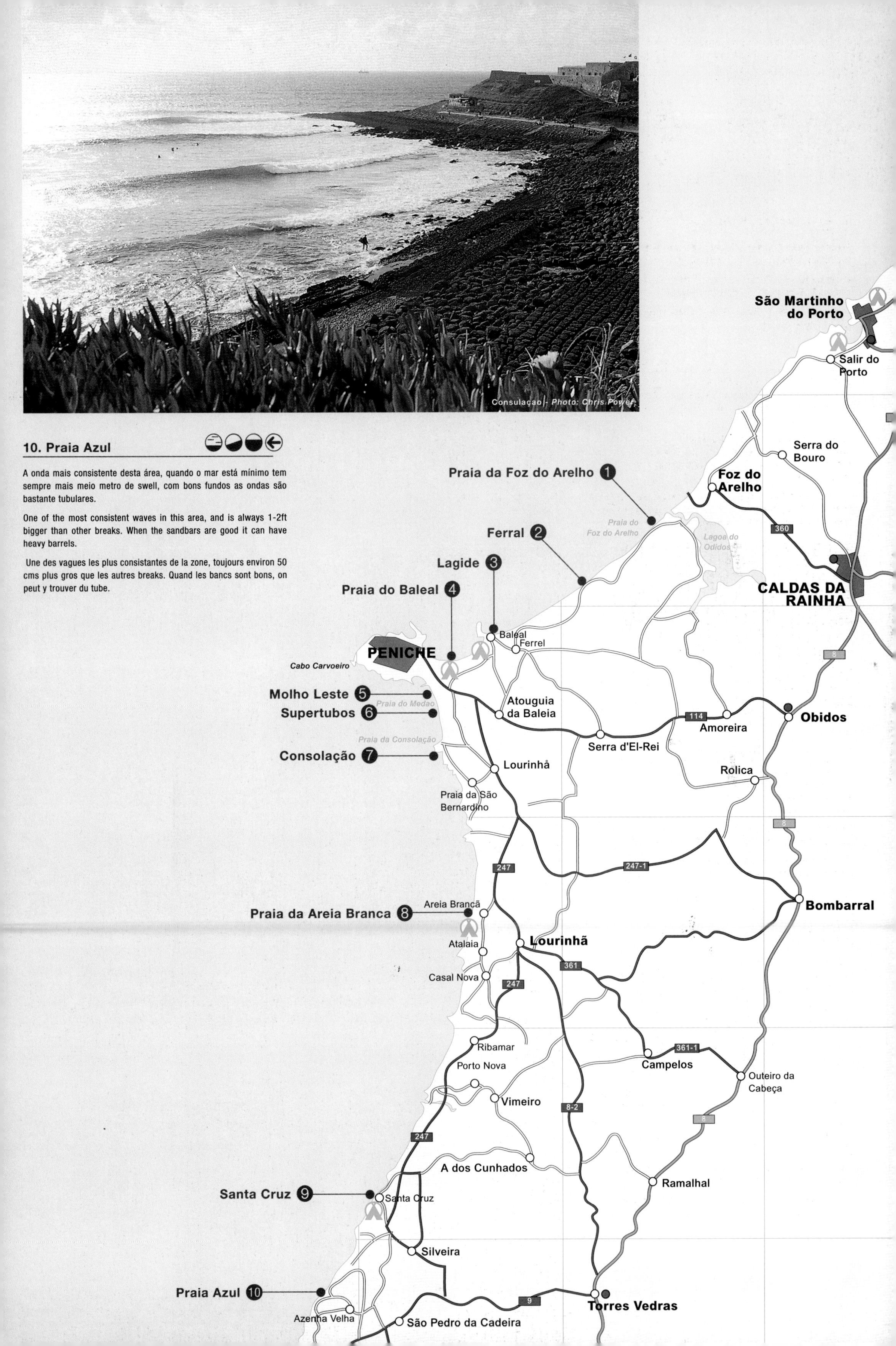

Consulaçao - Photo: Chris Power

10. Praia Azul

A onda mais consistente desta área, quando o mar está mínimo tem sempre mais meio metro de swell, com bons fundos as ondas são bastante tubulares.

One of the most consistent waves in this area, and is always 1-2ft bigger than other breaks. When the sandbars are good it can have heavy barrels.

Une des vagues les plus consistantes de la zone, toujours environ 50 cms plus gros que les autres breaks. Quand les bancs sont bons, on peut y trouver du tube.

Semente
SURFBOARDS SURFWEAR
Miguel Fortes Photo: Alex Oliveira

Semente
SURFBOARDS SURFWEAR
RABO DA RAPOSA, RIBAMAR, 2640 PORTUGAL
TEL 061 63552 / 061 864448 FAX 061 864630

Tadeu Pereira, Pedra Branca - *Photo: João Valente*

ericeira

Nick Uricho

"...Há picos cobrindo cerca de 20 Km de estrada nesta área, ou 11 Km de mar. Nesta área Incluem-se alguns dos melhores fundos de corais e picos de rocha na Europa..."

Ericeira é a meca do surf português. À uns 15 anos atras, erá apenas uma pequena vila de pescadores, e as 'surftrips' para aqui eram raras e exitantes. Quartos e comida eram quase de graça e os arredores da vila tinham pequenas povoações com casas branquinhas e todo o ambiente do campo. As praias eram limpas e não havia parques de campismo nem crowd na água. Apesar de ter mudado muito desde então, o ambiente de vila pescatoria contiua muito presente.

Há picos cobrindo cerca de 20 Km de estrada nesta área, ou 11 Km de mar. Nesta área Incluem-se alguns dos melhores fundos de corais e picos de rocha da Europa. Alem de surfista eu sou um avido mergulhador e tenho pesquisado os fundos exaustivamente. Ventos Offshore para todos os picos são do quadrante est.

Ericeira was and is the Mecca of Portugeuse surfing. In the early days it was a small fishing village and trips here were rare and really exciting. Rooms and food were dirt cheap and surrounding towns beautiful with white washed houses and a country vibe to everything. Beaches were unspoilt, carparks non-existent and crowds never a problem. Although It has changed since, its character remains essentially the same.

The spots cover about 20 km by road and 11km by water. They include some of the best reefs, points and beach breaks in Europe. As well as a keen surfer, I'm an avid diver and have researched the bottom conditions pretty thoroughly. Offshore winds for all spots come from the East.

Ericeira était et est encore la Mecque du surf Portugais. Au début, c'était un petit village de pêcheurs avec peu de voyageurs. Les piaules et la bouffe étaient ridiculement pas chers, les villages environnant étaient superbes avec des maisons en murs blanchis et on trouvait une ambiance campagnarde partout. Les plages étaient vierges, les parkings inexistants et il n'y avait jamais la foule. Bien que ça ait changé aujourd'hui, ces caractéristiques restent globalement valables.

Les spots couvrent environ 20 kms par la route et 11 par la mer. Ils incluent certains des meilleurs reefs, 'points' et beach-breaks d'Europe. Surfer motivé mais aussi plongeur passionné, j'ai fouillé srupuleusement les fonds marins. Les vents off-shore pour tous les spots sont dans le quart Est.

Praia Norte - *Photo: Phil Holden*

Entertenimento alternativo na praia - *Photo: Mark Stevenson*

Ericeira

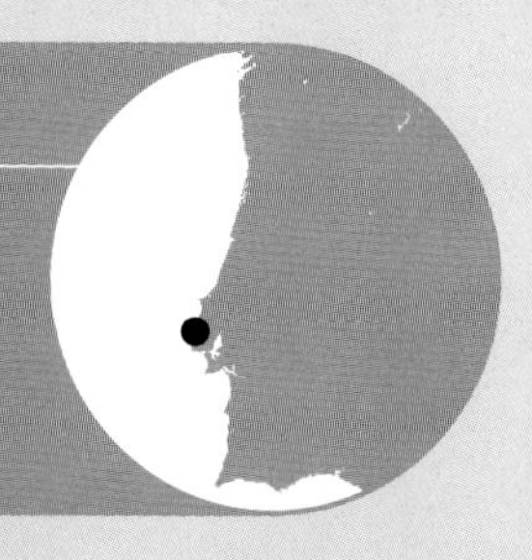

Nick Urrichio - *Semente*

Shane Herring, Reef - *Photo: Zé Pirrayt*

1. São Lourenço

A versão Portuguesa de Sunset aguenta swells gigantes, se vierem da direcção certa. Quando está grande, é importante ter atenção para ocasionais swells de oeste. Esta onda tem um drop tipo elevador, e uma rápida e oca secção no inside. N e NW swell são os melhores, e pode aguentar um pouco de vento sul.

The Portuguese version of Sunset can hold giant surf if the swell direction is correct. Keep an eye out for sneaker sets from the west when it's big. Elevetor drops and very fast hollow sections. N and NW swell is the best, will hold a little south wind.

La version portugaise de Sunset qui peut tenir des méga-houles si la direction est adéquate, à savoir N/N-O. Quand c'est gros, faites gaffe aux séries surprise qui viennent de l'ouest. Un take-off dans le vide et des sections rapides et creuses. Tient un peu le vent de sud.

São Lourenço - *Photo: João Valente*

2. Coxos

Melhor com swell de N-NW e meia maré, mas também pode ser surfado com maré alta. É uma pequena baía comparada com outros picos, por isso, quando está grande, há muitas correntes. A remada para o out side é forte e leva-se muito na cabeça.

Legendary right point, best with N-NW swells on mid to low tide, but can be surfed right through high. It's a small bay, so when it's big, currents can be heavy. Lots of paddling and clean-ups. Unforgiving, powerful and humbling on big days.

Droite légendaire, par houle de N/N-O de marée basse à mi-marée, qui peut être surfée jusqu'à la marée haute mais attention à la sortie. C'est une petite baie c'est pourquoi ça brasse terrible quand ç'est gros: puissant, impardonnable et force le respect dans ce cas.

3. Crazy Left

É uma onda tubular ao lado sul da baía dos Coxos. Em dias de S-SW swell, ondas buraco, rápidas e fortes quebram sobre uma bancada de pedra. A melhor altura é na maré cheia.

A tubey wave on the south side of Coxos bay. On S-SW days, hollow, fast and powerful waves break over rocky bottom. High tide better.

Une vague tubulaire au sud de la baie de Coxos. Par houle de S/S-O, c'est creux, rapide et puissant avec un fond craignos. Meilleur à marée haute.

Dapin, Crazy Left - *Photo: João Valente*

4. Pontinha

Remando ou andando para norte de Ribeira D'ilhas, está esta onda. Quebra com swells de N-NW ficando perfeita mas, quando o swell roda um pouco para W começa a fechar. O fundo é achatado cheio de ouriços. 3-12 ft.

Paddle or walk north from Ribeira D'ilhas. On N-NW swells the wave can be perfect, but closes when direction becomes too westerly. Flat, urchin-infested reef bottom. 3-12 ft.

A distance de rame ou de marche depuis Ribeira. Par houle de N/N-O, ça peut être parfait mais ferme dès que c'est trop ouest. Fond plat et infesté d'oursins, de 1 à 4 mètres.

5. Ribeira D'ilhas

Onda versatil com variados picos. Funciona com quase todos os swells mas, é melhor com W-NW . Quando está boa é uma das mais longas ondas da área. É também um dos mais consistentes picos do verão. 2-12ft.

A versatile bay with various peaks. Will work on most swells but best on W-NW. When good, one of the longest waves in the area. One of the most consistent spots in the summer holds 2-12ft.

Une baie changeante avec divers pics. Trés consistant et meilleur par N/N-O. Quand c'est bon, une des droites les plus longues qui tient jusqu'à 4 mètres. Du monde à l'eau.

6. Reef

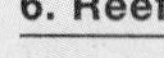

Com um fundo muito raso con apenas 3 pés, quebra ao lado de uma zona de profundidade con 20 pés para a direita. Quando está bom é uma onda mágica mas, não há ninguém que ao surfar muito esta onda não acabe com umas feridas do Reef.

It's 20 ft deep to the right side of the peak and 3ft where you are dropping in, geting shallower on the inside. When it's on it's pure magic but no one surfs it a lot without paying the fiddler. 3-16 ft.

Y'a 6 mètres de fond à droite du pic et 1 mètre au take-off, avec encore moins de fond à l'inside. Quand c'est clean, c'est magique mais quiconque surfe ici souvent paye un tribu un jour ou l'autre. De 1 à 5 mètres.

7. Backdoor

Normalmente, é um pico de verão e trabalha com N-NW swells. Tem umas secções buraco e é um pouco assustador na maré vazia.

Usually a summer time break, works best with N-NW swells. Holds some very hollow sections. Sketchy on low tide.

Généralement, un spot d'été qui marche par N/N-O avec des sections ultra-creuses. Casse-gueule à marée basse.

8. Pedra Branca

Funciona melhor com swells de S-SW, e aguenta grandes swells quando estes vêm da direcção certa. É mais um fundo de rocha com grandes buracos. O swell vem de águas profundas, e forma picos com muita velocidade e força na plataforma (Suicídio na maré vazia). Em dias bons, parece Pipeline. 3-10ft.

Extremely hollow left reef break located in front of the camping and caravan park North of Ericeira. Works best on S-SW swells, holding large surf if the direction is perfect. The bottom is a rock platform with big holes. The swell comes out of deep water, so peaks with speed and power. (suicide at low tide) It's got a pipe-ish look on good days. 3-10ft.

Mieux par houle de S/S-O, qui tient le gros si la direction est optimale. Le fond est une plateforme avec des cavernes. La houle arrive en eau profonde donc vitesse et puissance au programme, suicidaire à marée basse avec un look pipelinesque quand c'est parfait, de 1 à 3 mètres.

Almir Salazar, Pedra Branca - *Photo: Thierry Organoff*

9. Praia do Norte

Funciona com todas as direcções de swell mas, é conhecida pelas suas longas direitas de swells de N. O Pico fica muito seco na maré vazia. 3-12ft.

Will work with all swell directions, but best known for the the long rights from the N. The point is very dry on low tide. 3-12ft.

Marche avec toutes les houles, mais plus réputé pour les droites par houle de nord. Peu d'eau sur la zone de take-off à marée basse. De 1 à 4 mètres.

10. Praia do Peixe

Precisa de um swell sólido de preferência de SW . Pode ficar muito poluída no verão principalmente por causa do esgoto sem tratamento.

Needs a solid swell. Can get very polluted in the summer months because of a raw sewage outlet.

Spot de repli par tempête. Trés pollué en été à cause des égoûts.

Praia do Peixe - *Photo: Mark Stevenson*

11. Furnas

Só trabalha com um grande swell de N-NW. É a última hipótese quando tudo na Ericeira está gigante e impossível, e quando não há vontade de guiar para muito longe.

Only works with big N-NW swell. It's the last chance when everything thing else in Ericeira is huge and you don't feel like driving.

Marche uniquement par grosse houle de N/N-O, dernier recours quand tout ferme et que vous ne vous sentez pas prêt à tailler la route.

12. Foz do Lizandro

Uma onda à saída de um rio que se forma quando o fundo está correcto. Melhor com S-SW swells. Tem um backwash forte na maré cheia. Aguenta um considerável tamanho de onda. 3-10ft.

A classic rivermouth wave when the fickle sand bars settle correctly. Best on a S-W swell, with a strong backwash on high tide. Can hold some size and deal out some power. 3-10ft.

Une bonne sortie de rivière si les bancs capricieux se forment correctement. Mieux par houle de S-O, avec un méchant back-wash à marée haute. Peut tenir la taille et envoyer le pâté. De 1 à 3 m.

13. São Julião

Funciona com quase todas as direcções de swell dependendo do fundo. É um pico de ondas pequenas que se desmancha facilmente. 2-6ft.

Works on most swell directions and tides depending on sand flow. This is a small 2-6ft spot that maxes-out easily.

Marche par toutes les directions de houle et marées selon les courants. Beach break de 50cms à 2 mètres qui sature facilement.

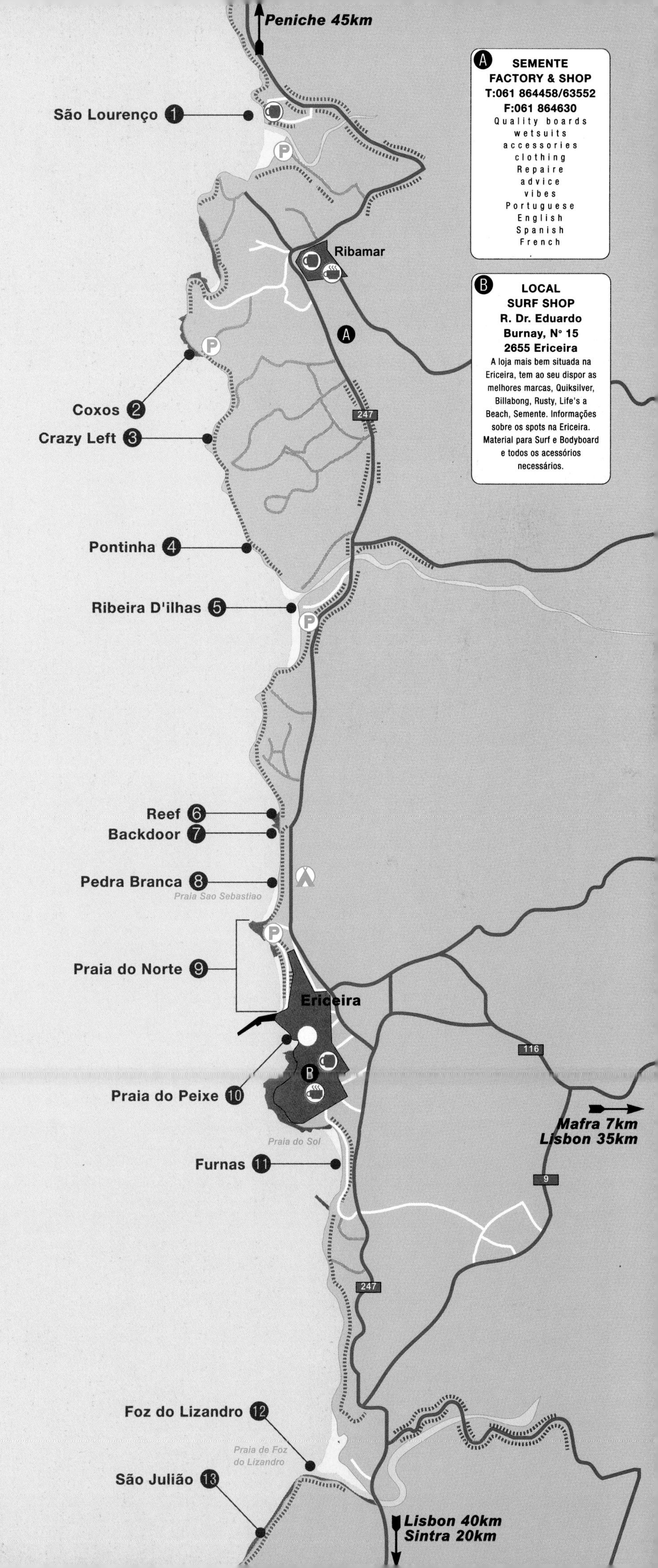

"...sendo
uma onda
urbana,
costuma
estar muito
crowd..."

Pescando no Monte Estoril - *Photo: Phil Holden*

lisboa

Lisboa está entre 7 montanhas e o rio Tejo. As origens estão rodeadas de mistério, mas o seu nome vem do Finicano 'Allis Ubbo' ou 'porto bonito'. Apesar de ter sido quase toda destruida no terremoto de 1755, a cidade e os variados palácios reais de Sintra dão visões Históricas "de tirar a respiração". Os swells de Norte e Leste fazem quebrar ondas consistentes nas praias viradas à Leste. No inverno, os picos da Linha do Estoril são palco de surf explosivo que caracterizam a zona urbanistica e a evolução do esporte neste país. Foi sem dúvida nesta costa que o surf Português nasceu e é aqui que uma grande parte da industia surfistica está sediada, perto das rotas internacionas, do mercado e das ondas.

Lisbon lies on 7 low hills at the mouth of the river Tajus. Her origins are shrouded in mystery, but her name comes from the Phoenican "Allis Ubbo" or "delightful port", and though the old town was raised in a massive earthquake in 1755, the city and the various royal palaces at Sintra provide a breathtaking glimpse into history. North and West swells break consistently on the west facing beaches. In big West and South swells, the Estoril line becomes the scene of frantic activity for Lisbons' bustling surf community. It was along this coast that wave sports began and it is here that much of the surf industry can be found, close to international travel routes, markets and good waves.

Lisbonne se trouve sur 7 collines à l'embouchure du Tage. Ses origines sont voilées de mystère mais son nom vient du Phénicien "Allis Ubbo" ou "Port Délicieux" et bien que la vieille ville ait été soulevée pendant le tremblement de terre de 1755, la ville et les palaces royaux de Sintra offrent des vues plongeantes dans l'histoire à en perdre haleine. Les trois côtes fonctionnent. Les houles de nord et d'ouest cassent de façon consistante sur les plages de Guincho, Praia Grande et Costa da Caparica. Par grosse houle de N-O ou de sud, les "points" et les reefs de la ligne d'Estoril deviennent le théâtre d'une activité surf débordante de la communauté trépidante des surfers locaux. C'est sans conteste le long de cette côte que les sports de vagues sont nés et c'est donc ici qu'on peut trouver la majorité de l'industrie du surf, proche des grands axes de communication, des marchés et des bonnes plages.

Bolina - *Photo: João Valente*

Lisbon

Gonçalo Bonneville, Santo Amaro - *Photo: L.M.Frazão*

1. Praia Grande/Pequena

As mais consistentes praias de Lisboa, conhecida pelas suas ondas poderosas, e por ser um dos poucos lugares que não entra "Nortada". A praia Pequena e a zona norte da praia grande, funciona com as mesmas condições, mas costuma estar menos crowd. A água das mais limpas de Lisboa.

The most consistent spot in the Lisbon area, and one of few places protected from summer north winds. Powerful waves with an infamous shorebreak. Praia Pequena is the northern continuation of the same beach with similar characteristics but less crowds. Water is some of the cleanest in the Lisbon area.

Le spot le plus consistent autour de Lisbonne, qui plus est, protégé des vents de nord en été. Vagues puissantes avec un shore-break carton. Praia Pequena est juste au nord avec quelques rochers en plus et du monde en moins. L'eau la plus clean du coin aussi.

2. Praia do Guincho

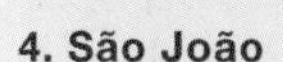

Guincho é a mais popular praia de windsurf de Portugal. Nortadas constantes no verão geram condições perfeitas para o Wind Surf. Durante todo o ano o Guincho costuma ter sempre bom surf.

Photos of huge surf published in Surfer Magazine in September 1967 first made the waiting world aware of Portugal's surf potential. Guincho is Portugal's most popular wave sailing location with strong summer NW winds providing classic sailing conditions. Strong swells do the same for the surf conditions.

Des photos publiées dans SURFER en Septembre 1967 d'énormes paquets à Guincho ont donné au monde l'image du potentiel de surf au Portugal. C'est d'abord un spot de windsurf en été avec de forts vents de NO. Souvent du bon surf aussi avec des gauches qui tiennent la taille.

Guincho - *Photo: Phil Holden*

3. Monte Estoril

É uma onda cheia, mas aguenta swell's com tamanho. Tem canal quando o mar está grande. O acesso, é parcando o carro em Cascais ou na Poça e andando até lá. Pouco crowd normalmente.

It's a fat wave, but it handles big swells (with a nice channel on big days), since the point is far out to sea. The bigger it is, the further out it will break. The only access is by parking in São João or Cascais, and walking for 5 minutes. It's usually uncrowded. Water quality is improving, but not clean yet.

Une vague épaisse qui tient le gros avec un chenal idéal quand c'est gros, assez loin du bord. Plus gros c'est, plus ça pète loin. L'accés se fait par le parking de São João ou Cascais, en marchant 5 minutes. Pas trop de monde en général.

Monte Estoril - ***Photo: João Valente***

4. São João

BOLINA

Uma das melhores ondas da linha, é intensa e curta tendo nos melhores dias um bom tubo e terminando em cima das rochas. Não é aconselhavel para iniciantes. Costuma ter crowd. A água é suja, tendo um esgoto mesmo em frente.

One of the best spots on the "Linha do Estoril"; an intense and hollow wave which ends over the rocks, so not recommended for beginners. Usually it's crowded, respect for the locals is essential. Water quality is bad due to a sewage pipe in front of the point.

Un des meilleurs spots de la "ligne Estoril (train)", une vague creuse et intense qui termine sur la caillasse; par forcément pour débutants. Bien pris d'assaut par les locaux, méfiance! Une sortie d'égoût en face du spot.

POÇA

É uma onda normal. Berço de muitos dos melhores surfistas Portugueses, tal como Goncalo Bonne Ville, Pirujinho e Paulo do Bairro. Normalmente está crowd. A água está a melhorar mas ainda está suja.

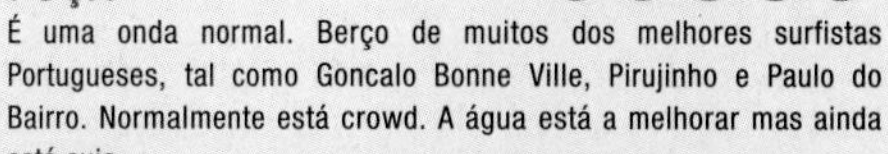

It's an average wave, a little fat, though you can get a cover up at the take off. Some of the best Portuguese surfers began their careers here, including Joao Bonne Ville, Pirujinho, Paulo do Bairro and Gatinho. It's usually crowded; the water quality is improving.

Une vague moyenne, un peu épaisse malgré une section à tube au départ. Souvent peuplé et jardin de pas mal de champions.

AZARUJINHA

Uma das melhores ondas pequenas da linha. Começa num fundo de rocha terminando depois na areia. A água é poluida mas está melhorando.

This is probably one of the best small waves on the Estoril line and very protected from onshore winds. The take off is over a rock bottom, but ends on sand. Water quality poor but improving.

Un des meilleurs paris quand c'est petit, trés protégé des vents on-shore. Le take-off se fait sur du rocher et termine sur du sable. L'eau n'est pas terrible.

5. São Pedro

BICO

Onda comprida, um pouco cheia com uma ou duas secções buraco. Customa parecer melhor no estacionamento do que realmente é. Normalmente está meior do que no resto da linha, dado o pico estar mais exposto. Custuma estar crowd. A qualidade d'água não é má, e está melhorando.

A very long wave, a bit fat with one or two hollower sections. Usually looks better from the parking lot than what it is, but waves are usually bigger here than elsewhere nearby because the point is more exposed to swell. Normally it's crowded, but on good days there are plenty of waves for everyone. The water quality is not bad, and improving.

Une droite trés longue, un peu épaisse avec une ou deux sections creuses. Parait généralement depuis le parking mieux qu'elle n'est en réalité mais ça prend mieux la houle que partout ailleurs. Souvent du monde mais quand ça marche, ça débite!

BAFUREIRA

Está ao lado do Bico e funciona com o mesmo swell. Sendo mais curta, compensa por estar menos crowd normalmente. A qualidade d'água é normal.

It's right beside Bico and handles the same kind of swell. It's a little shorter, but usually much less crowded. A good option for very crowded days. The water quality is average.

Juste à côté de Bico avec la même exposition à la houle à quelque chose prés. Un petit peu plus court mais moins fréquenté: une bonne option donc quand c'est la Chine à côté.

6. Parede

Talvez a onda mais rara de funcionar com todo o seu potencial. Já foi comparada a J-Bay por Picuruta Salazar. É muito rapida e normalmente os locais só surfam uma ou duas secções. A água tem uma qualidade aceitavel e está melhorando.

Maybe the rarest wave in Portugal to break to it's full potential. It's been compared to J-Bay when it does (very fast). Normally the locals just surf one or two sections of it. The water quality is not bad and a new development may improve it.

Rare, trés rare pour que ça casse à 100%: parfois comparé à la Jeffreys' Bay, droite trés rapide donc. Normalement, les locaux surfent une ou deux sections.

7. Carcavelos

Um dos primeiros picos a ser surfado em portugal. Quando está com grande swells de NW, as esquerdas predominão. Sendo uma onda urbana, costuma estar muito crowd. Problemas do esgoto que costumavam ser terriveís, tem sido ultimamente controlados, com o novo emissário.

One of the first Portuguese surf breaks to be ridden. In strong NW swell, lefts predominate. Being a central-city break, it's usually crowded. Sewage problems which have tended to be terrible in the past are in the process of improvement as a new sewage pipe will take waste further out to sea.

Un des premiers spots du Portugal. Par bon swell de NO, les gauches prédominent. Etant un spot urbain, y'a toujours foule. Les problèmes d'écoulement des eaux usées sont résolus, en jetant tout plus au large.

Carcavelos - *Photo: João Valente*

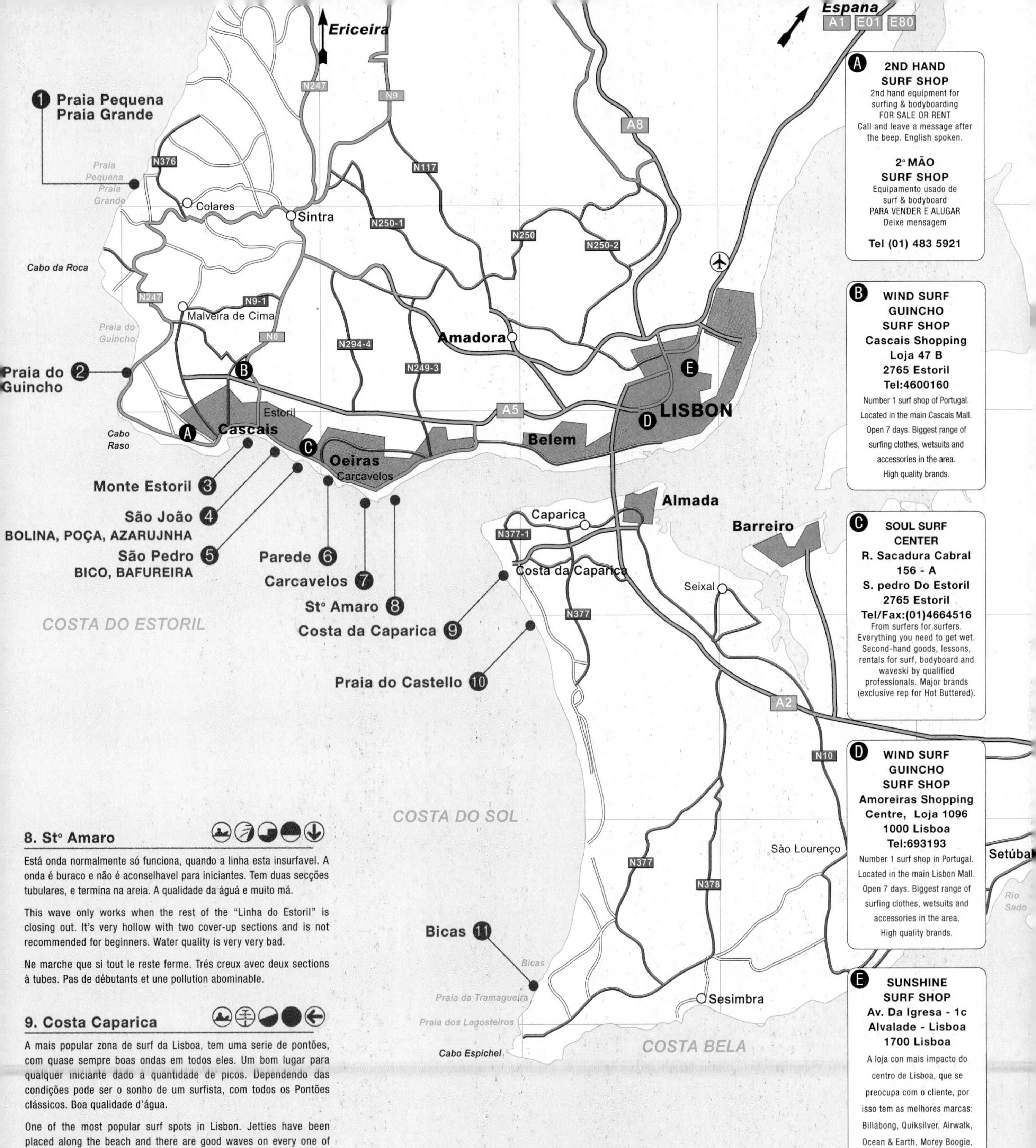

A — 2ND HAND SURF SHOP
2nd hand equipment for surfing & bodyboarding
FOR SALE OR RENT
Call and leave a message after the beep. English spoken.

2° MÃO SURF SHOP
Equipamento usado de surf & bodyboard
PARA VENDER E ALUGAR
Deixe mensagem

Tel (01) 483 5921

B — WIND SURF GUINCHO SURF SHOP
Cascais Shopping
Loja 47 B
2765 Estoril
Tel:4600160
Number 1 surf shop of Portugal. Located in the main Cascais Mall. Open 7 days. Biggest range of surfing clothes, wetsuits and accessories in the area. High quality brands.

C — SOUL SURF CENTER
R. Sacadura Cabral 156 - A
S. pedro Do Estoril
2765 Estoril
Tel/Fax:(01)4664516
From surfers for surfers. Everything you need to get wet. Second-hand goods, lessons, rentals for surf, bodyboard and waveski by qualified professionals. Major brands (exclusive rep for Hot Buttered).

D — WIND SURF GUINCHO SURF SHOP
Amoreiras Shopping Centre, Loja 1096
1000 Lisboa
Tel:693193
Number 1 surf shop in Portugal. Located in the main Lisbon Mall. Open 7 days. Biggest range of surfing clothes, wetsuits and accessories in the area. High quality brands.

E — SUNSHINE SURF SHOP
Av. Da Igresa - 1c
Alvalade - Lisboa
1700 Lisboa
A loja con mais impacto do centro de Lisboa, que se preocupa com o cliente, por isso tem as melhores marcas: Billabong, Quiksilver, Airwalk, Ocean & Earth, Morey Boogie, O'Neill, roupas e acessórios.

8. St° Amaro

Está onda normalmente só funciona, quando a linha esta insurfavel. A onda é buraco e não é aconselhavel para iniciantes. Tem duas secções tubulares, e termina na areia. A qualidade da águá e muito má.

This wave only works when the rest of the "Linha do Estoril" is closing out. It's very hollow with two cover-up sections and is not recommended for beginners. Water quality is very very bad.

Ne marche que si tout le reste ferme. Trés creux avec deux sections à tubes. Pas de débutants et une pollution abominable.

9. Costa Caparica

A mais popular zona de surf da Lisboa, tem uma serie de pontões, com quase sempre boas ondas em todos eles. Um bom lugar para qualquer iniciante dado a quantidade de picos. Dependendo das condições pode ser o sonho de um surfista, com todos os Pontões clássicos. Boa qualidade d'água.

One of the most popular surf spots in Lisbon. Jetties have been placed along the beach and there are good waves on every one of them. A good place for beginners, not only for the quantity of peaks, but because the waves are mellow. When it's good, Costa da Caparica can be a dream. The water quality is also good.

Le plus long beach-break de Lisbonne. Les jetées sur la plage créent de bons bancs de sable. Un endroit idéal pour débutants non seulement pour le nombre de pics mais pour la mollesse des vagues. Cela dit, ça peut être fantastique. L'eau y est propre.

Costa Caparica - *Photo: Luis Quinta*

10. Praia do Castello

Cosuma estar pouco crowd. A praia tem criado bons bancos de areia que geram ondas clássicas. Dependendo de como está o banco de areia, pode ser uma esquerda ou uma direita bem definida, mas normal são picos múltiplos. A qualidade da água e das melhores que se pode encontrar na zona de Lisboa, muito transparente.

Depending on the sand bar, it can be a righthander or a left, but normaly it's multiple peaks of a consistently high quality. The water is some of the cleanest in the Lisbon area, and crowds are minimal.

Selon les bancs, c'est droite ou gauche mais y'a souvent pas mal de pics de trés bonne qualité. L'eau est parmi les plus pures de Lisbonne et la foule est minime.

11. Bicas

Esta onda é rara, só costuma dar bem, poucas vezes no ano. É uma esquerda perfeita e aguenta grandes swells, tendo tambem umas secções tubulares. A qualidade da água é exelente.

Only breaks a couple of times a year but it's a perfect lefthander which handles substantial amounts of swell. The water quality is excellent.

Quelques fois par an seulement pour cette gauche magique qui attend patiemment les gros swells pour s'activer. Tubes.

Photo: João Valente

sul

O sul de Portugal permanece um dos inigmas Europeus. Vários picos clássicos tem sido encontrados e existem rumores de muitos mais. Kilometros de praias com vários picos e reefs para o sul de Portugal mantem o espirito de aventura bem vivo em Portugal. A costa Leste é sem dúvida a mais consistente desta área, mas a costa entre Sagres até Faro quando recebe swells tem ondas clássicas. O clima é dos melhores Europeus, sendo ideal para acampamento. A água é a mais limpa que se pode encontrar, cristalina e mais quente que no resto de Portugal. Faro é o lugar de chegada mais barato para turistas quando estes compram as suas passagens fora de Portugal.

South Portugal remains one of Europes' enigmas. Various good peaks have been found and many more are rumoured. Miles of empty beaches with a conglomeration of unfound points and reefs way down south keep the feeling of adventure strong here. The W facing Atlantic coast is undoubtedly the most consistent, but the Algarve, between Sagres and Faro definately gets waves. The climate is one of Europes' most favourable making camping an enjoyable experience, and if you avoid the tourist traps, the water is remarkably clean. Faro is the cheapest place to fly to in Portugal and car rentals are easy to arrange.

Le sud du Portugal reste encore une énigme pour beaucoup, certains pics ont été trouvés, d'autres sont uniquement soupçonnés. Des kilomètres de plages et de spots secrets y conservent ici un goût d'aventure. La côte Atlantique exposée ouest est certainement la plus consistente et l'Algarve, entre Sagres et Faro, reçoit aussi des vagues. Le climat est un des plus favorables d'Europe, ce qui rend le camping vraiment agréable et si vous évitez les pièges à touristes, l'eau est remarquablement propre. Faro est la destination aérienne la moins chère du Portugal avec des locations de voitures faciles à trouver.

"...kilometros de praias com vários picos e reefs para o sul de Portugal mantem o espirito de aventura bem vivo em Portugal..."

Photo: Thierry Organoff

Bubas, Arrifana - Photo: João Valente

Costa Alentejana/ Algarve

1. Cabo de Sines

Esta onda está localisada em frente ao famoso complexo de Sines. Tem um pontão que costuma formar bons fundos de areia. Dependendo dos fundos as ondas são óptimas. Normalmente não há muito crowd.

This spot is located in front of the infamous Sines industrial plant. The wave starts on a jetty and depending on the sand bars, it can be quite good. Usually uncrowded.

Ce spot se situe en face de l'infâme complexe industriel. La vague part d'une jetée et en fonction des bancs, peut être sympathique. Pas de monde normalement.

2. São Torpes

É uma praia que funciona com as mesmas condições de Sines, normal mente tambem não costuma ter muito crowd e a água e bastante limpa.

Pretty average wave works in the same conditions as Sines, normally uncrowded. The water is pretty good.

Une vague correcte qui marche dans les mêmes conditions que Sines. L'eau y est de bonne qualité.

3. Porto Corvo

Esta onda fica entre a Ilha do Pessegueiro e a costa e, pode aguentar dias de grande swell. É uma esquerda poderosa, tem umas secções tubulares depedendo da maré.

The wave breaks between an Island (Pesseguiro) and the shore. It can hold big swell and depending on the tide, it has little cover up sections.

La vague casse entre l'île de Pessiguiro et le rivage. Peut tenir la houle et à la bonne marée, il y a des petites sections à tubes.

4. Malhão

A mais popular praia de Vila Nova costuma ser muito consistente, estando poucas vezes totalmente flat. A onda varía com os fundos de areia mas, normalmente, tem uma boa formação. A água e cristalina.

The most famous spot in the "Vila Nova" area, rarely gets flat. The quality of the wave depends on the sand bar, but it's consistently good, and the water is crystal clear.

Le spot la plus couru de la zone de Vila Nova qui peut être ultra-consistant, étant rarement flat. La qualité de la vague est variable mais souvent bien formée et l'eau est cristalline.

5. Cogumelo

É um pico perfeito, que começa ao lado de uma rocha apelidada de cogumelo e depois rola perfeita sobre um fundo de rochas até o inside aonde se encontra um porto. Normalmente precisa de um swell maior para quebrar boa. água é cristalina.

It's a perfect wave beginning beside a big rock called "Cogumelo", and rolling all the way to the inside over a rocky bottom. Normally it needs a bigger swell to work well, and the water is of good quality.

Un pic parfait, qui démarre prés d'un rocher "le Cogumelo" et déroulant jusqu'à l'inside sur un fond rocher. Par houle de bonne taille pour être classique. Rien à dire sur l'eau.

6. Praia de Odeceixe

É uma boa praia de areia. As ondas depedem do fundo de areia mas, como esta praia é protegida do vento, costuma ser uma boa opção em dias de muito vento.

A good beach break and when everywhere nearby is suffering from strong winds, the protection offered by the cliffs here make it a good choice. Located a few km's down a windy, hazardous road.

Un bon beach break, protégé des vents par les falaises quand les spots alentours sont gavés de vents.

7. Carriagem

Esta onda funciona com o mesmo tipo de swell que Odeceixe, embora não seja tão protegida. A formação das ondas é razoavel e a água é muito limpa.

Works in the same conditions as Odeceixe, though not so protected from the winds. The wave is O.K. and the water very clean.

Mêmes conditions qu'Odeceixe, bien que moins abrité. La vague est correcte et l'eau est propre.

8. Monte Clérigo

Uma praia muito bonita com fundo de areia e picos multiplos. Aguenta swells grandes e a formação das ondas depende dos fundos.

A very nice beach which can hold big swells, but the quality of the wave depends on the sand bar, which varies.

Une superbe plage qui tient bien les grosses houles mais la qualité de la vague dépend des bancs de sable, qui bougent beaucoup.

9. Arrifana

Esta onda é a mais versatil do sul. Se o mar estiver grande, tem uma direita poderosa que ocasionalmente passa por cima de duas rochas no inside. Se estiver pequeno, tem no meio da praia um pico perfeito para os dois lados com bons tubinhos.

The most versatile spot in the South of Portugal. On big days, there is a huge right breaking off the north of the bay, that occasionally runs over two big rocks on the inside. On small days there's a peaky wave in the middle of the beach with nice little tubes.

Le spot le plus versatile du sud du Portugal. Quand c'est gros, une méga-droite casse au nord de la baie, qui passe de temps en temps sur deux gros rochers qui émergent. Quand c'est plus petit, on trouve une gauche courte au milieu de la baie avec des tubes sympas.

Arrifana - *Photo: Thierry Organoff*

10. Carrapateira

Uma boa onda, abrigada do vento, e normalmente com pouco crowd. Os fundos variam muito mas quando está fica tão perfeito quanto uma onda pode ser.

It's a nice spot, sheltered from heavy winds and normally uncrowded. The sand bars determine the wave quality, but when they are good, this place can be perfect.

Un spot agréable, abrité des vents forts et souvent sans monde. Les bancs de sable déterminent la qualité de la vague et ça peut être fantastique.

11. Beliche

Esta onda precisa de um grande swell de N ou um swell normal de sul para faze-la quebrar. Normalmente está sempre crowd. A onda tem um pico triangular perfeito com um tubo certo em quase todas as ondas.

It's a hollow wave that needs either a good size N swell, or an average S swell to make it work. It's usually very crowded because it's a perfect peak, with tube sections on most waves.

Une vague creuse qui demande un bon swell de nord ou un swell de sud pour marcher. Souvent beaucoup de monde parce que les pics sont parfaits avec des sections à tubes sur la plupart des vagues.

12. Tonel

Esta onda é muito parecida com o Beliche mas, como está mais protegida, costuma ter menos swell. Tem uma Pousada da Juventude logo, acomodações não são problema (especialmente no inverno).

Works with the same conditions as Beliche. There is a Youth hostel overlooking the Point, so accommodation isn't a problem especially in the winter.

Marche avec les mêmes conditions que Belixe, mais plus exposé et donc plus de houle. Il y a une auberge de jeunesse qui surplombe la baie, donc pas de problème de logement surtout en hiver.

13. Mareta

É uma onda perfeita para os dois lados quando quebra mas é preciso um grande swell para ela funcionar. Normalmente, é uma boa opção quando o Tunel está "close out".

A perfect peak, but it takes a big swell to make it break. It's usually a good option when Tunel is closing out.

Un pic parfait mais il faut que ça rentre énorme pour activer les bancs, il faut que Tunel sature à max.

14. Zavial

Esta onda funciona com o mesmo tipo de condições que a Mareta. A onda é bastante longa com uma secção tubular. A água é muito limpa.

Zavial breaks in the same conditions as Mareta. It's a long righthander, and has a cover up section. The water is of good quality.

Zavial casse dans les mêmes conditions que Mareta. Une longue droite avec des sections à tubes. L'eau y est super propre.

Zé dos Caes, Zavial - *Photo: Thiery Organoff*

15. Praia da Rocha

Esta foi a primeira que nos vem a cabeça quando pensamos no Algarve, e é o pico mais perto de Faro. Famosa pelos seus tubos normalmente quebra para a esquerda. Dado a situação da praia costuma estar muito crowd nos dias bons.

This was the first known Algarve break and is the closest spot to Faro. Famous for its barrels, which normally break left. Due to the location of the spot it can get very crowded on good days.

C'était le premier break connu du Portugal car le plus proche de Faro. Célèbre pour ses tubes qui cassent normalement en gauche. Attention au peuple!

Praia da Rocha - *Photo: Thiery Organoff*

Carrapateira - *Photo: João Valente*

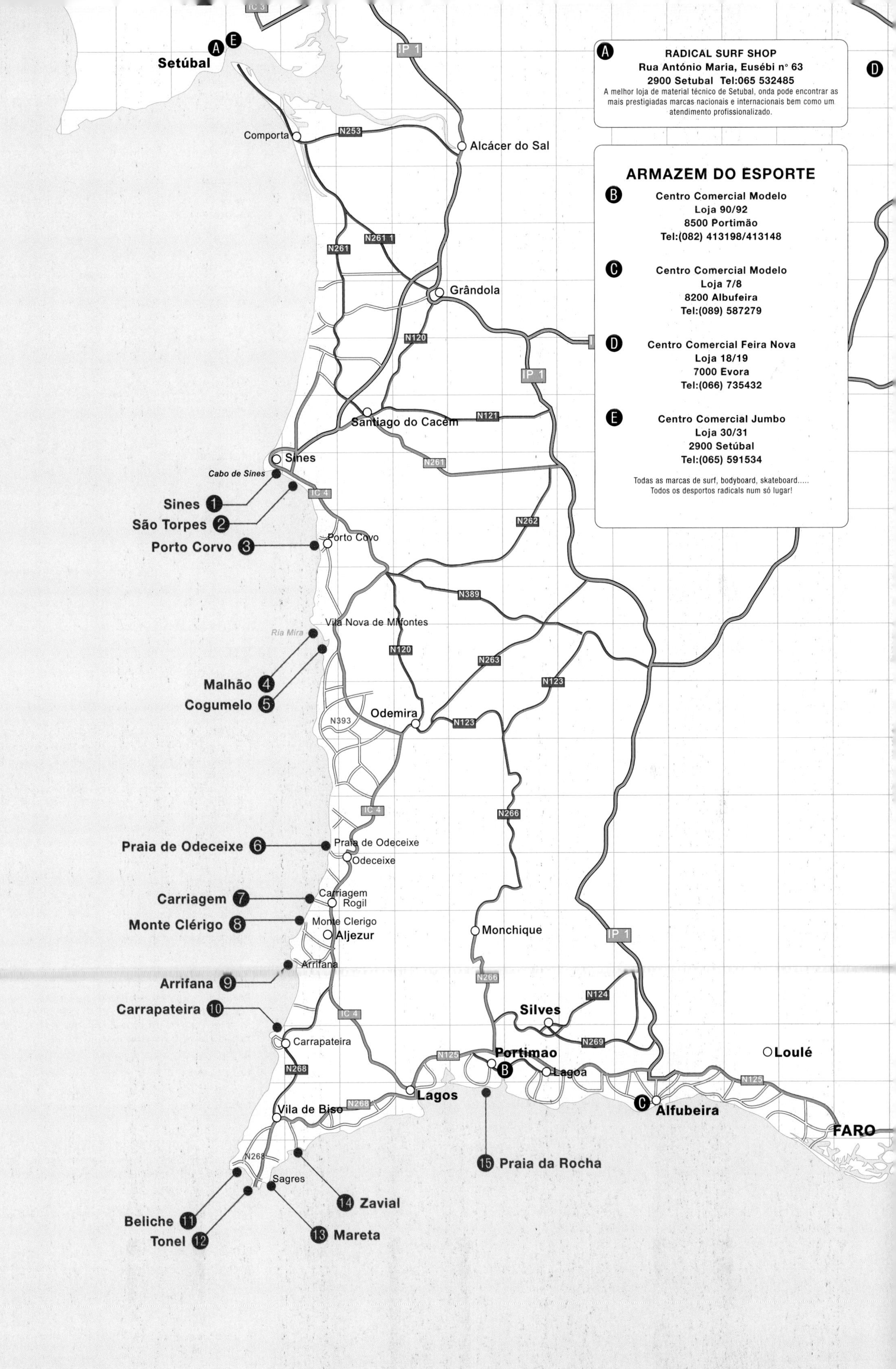

RADICAL SURF SHOP
Rua António Maria, Eusébi nº 63
2900 Setubal Tel:065 532485
A melhor loja de material técnico de Setubal, onda pode encontrar as mais prestigiadas marcas nacionais e internacionais bem como um atendimento profissionalizado.
ARMAZEM DO ESPORTE
Centro Comercial Modelo
Loja 90/92
8500 Portimão
Tel:(082) 413198/413148
Centro Comercial Modelo
Loja 7/8
8200 Albufeira
Tel:(089) 587279
Centro Comercial Feira Nova
Loja 18/19
7000 Evora
Tel:(066) 735432
Centro Comercial Jumbo
Loja 30/31
2900 Setúbal
Tel:(065) 591534
Todas as marcas de surf, bodyboard, skateboard.....
Todos os desportos radicais num só lugar!
Setúbal
IC 3
IP 1
Comporta
N253
Alcácer do Sal
N261
N261 1
Grândola
N120
IP 1
Santiago do Cacém
N121
Sines
Cabo de Sines
N261
IC 4
Sines 1
São Torpes 2
Porto Corvo 3
Porto Covo
N262
N389
Vila Nova de Milfontes
Ria Mira
N120
N263
N123
Malhão 4
Cogumelo 5
Odemira
N393
N123
IC 4
N266
Praia de Odeceixe 6
Praia de Odeceixe
Odeceixe
Carriagem 7
Carriagem
Rogil
Monte Clérigo 8
Monte Clerigo
Aljezur
Monchique
IP 1
Arrifana
Arrifana 9
N266
Carrapateira 10
IC 4
Silves
N124
N269
Carrapateira
Portimao
N125
Lagoa
Loulé
N268
Lagos
Vila de Biso
N268
Alfubeira
N125
FARO
N268
Sagres
Praia da Rocha 15
Zavial 14
Beliche 11
Tonel 12
Mareta 13

MAROC المغرب

Capitale:	**Rabat**
Population:	**25,061,000**
Superficie:	**710,895km²**
Fuseau Horaire:	**GMT +1(summer GMT+2)**
Langue:	**Arabic, French, Spanish, Berber**
Monnaie:	**Moroccan Dirham (MAD)**

Snowboarding
Fevrier - Avril

1. **Haut Atlas: Oukaïmeden**
2. **Midi Atlas: Mischliffen**
3. **Anti Atlas: Bou Iblane**

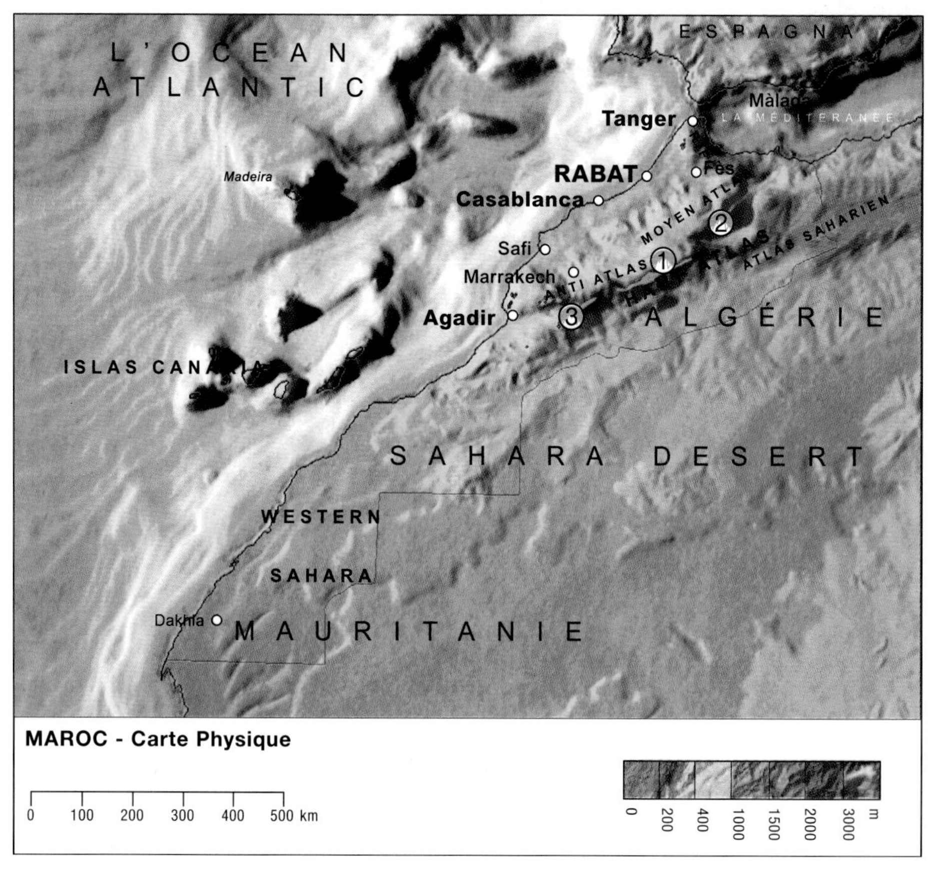

MAROC

De tradition Musulmane profonde, le Maroc est une fusion curieuse et colorée des cultures européennes et arabe (berbère), avec une histoire fascinante pleine de romance. Bien qu'état modéré, le code social des musulmans doit être respecté surtout en public bien que les habitudes vestimentaires à la plage soient plus relax. Le français est la langue européenne la plus parlée et la langue officielle du gouvernement. Considérant la gentillesse des gens, la beauté de la côte et des montagnes et les autres ressources naturelles, on comprend aisément que tout européen qui se respecte doit passer un jour par là.

MAROC

Islamic and deeply traditional, Morocco is a curious and colourful fusion of European and Arab (Berber) culture, with little evidence of militant fundamentalism. Though moderate, Muslim social codes should be adhered to, especially in public places, though dress codes are usually a lot more relaxed at the beach. French is the main European language spoken and the language of government and officialdom. Consider the kindness of the people, the beauty of the coasts and mountains and its other natural resources and you'll understand that any well travelled European surfer has to trip here.

MARRUECOS

Marruecos es un país Islámico de arraigadas tradiciones, cuya fascinante historia está cargada de romanticismo y en el que se produce una curiosa y colorista fusión entre la cultura árabe-bereber y la europea. Al tratarse de un país musulmán, aunque sea moderado, hay que respetar y adaptarse a sus costumbres y tradiciones, sobre todo en los lugares públicos. Pero en la playa estos usos sociales son menos estrictos. El idioma europeo más hablado es el francés, que es la lengua empleada por el Gobierno y la Administración. Teniendo en consideración la amabilidad de sus gentes, la belleza de sus costas, de sus montañas y de sus otros recursos naturales, es fácil entender que se trata de un destino obligatorio para los surfers viajeros de toda Europa.

Visas

Tous les membres de la CEE (sauf les ressortissants du Benelux), les Américains, les Australiens et les Néo-Zélandais n'ont pas besoin de visa au-dessus de 90 jours. Si vous êtes israëliens ou Sud-Africains, on eput vous refuser l'accés.

L'avion

En général, les surfers volent jusqu'à Tanger, Agadir ou Casablanca. Le sprix depuis la Grande-Bretagne sont raisonnables. Depuis le continent, conduire ou prendre le train peut revenir moins cher.

Ferry

Le trajet le plus fréquent et le meilleur marché pour les véhicules se fait entre Algeciras et Ceuta, une enclave espagnole mais pour les piétons, la liaiosn avec Tanger prend moins de temps et subit moins d'aléas.

Locations de voiture

facilement disponible, l'option la moins chère et la plus répandue est la Renault 4. C'est toujours mieux d'organiser la location avec les billets d'avion parce que plus facile et moins cher.

Les articles de luxe

Tout ce qui a de la valeur qui est introduit au Maroc est enregistré et déclaré sur votre passeport (appareil photo, planche...). Il faut les ramener avec vous ou il faudra payer 100% de taxes. Si vous vous faites faucher, il vous faut une lettre de la police. Une planche cassée doit être ramenée, si vous vendez une planche neuve, demandez à récupérer une rougne (ils ne vérifient pas).

Visas

U.K. and Europeans (except Dutch, Belgium and Luxembourg), U.S.A., Aus and N.Z. do not require a visa for stays of up to 90 days. If you have an Israeli or Sth African stamp in your passport, you may be refused entry.

Flying

Nearly all surfers will fly to either Tangier, Agadir or Casablanca. Prices from the UK are reasonable but from France, Spain or Portugal, driving or catching a train could work out cheaper.

Ferries

The most popular, frequent and cheapest route for vehicles is Algeciras to Ceuta (a Spanish enclave), but for pedestrians the route to Tangier is much less time and aggravation.

Car Hire

Car hire is widely available, the cheapest and most widespread option being the Renault 4. It is often a good idea to organise car hire when booking a flight, as this can work out better.

Bonded consumer items

Anything of value you take into Morocco will be recorded and declared on your passport (surfboards etc...)You must leave with these items or you will be charged 100% duty. If your belongings are stolen, you will need a letter from the police. Broken surfboards must be brought back to the border.

Visados

Los Europeos, estadounidenses, australianos y neozelandeses no necesitan visados para estancias inferiores a 90 días. Si tienes un visado israelí o sudafricano en tu pasaporte, pueden denegarte la entrada en el país.

Vuelos

Habitualmente los surfers vuelan a Tánger, Agadir o Casablanca. Los precios de los vuelos desde Gran Bretaña son aceptables, pero desde el resto de Europa suele resultar más barato conducir o tomar un tren.

Ferries

The most popular, frequent and cheapest route for vehicles is Algeciras to Ceuta (a Spanish enclave), but for pedestrians the route to Tangier is much less time and aggravation.

Alquiler de vehículos

Es fácil encontrar coches de alquiler. La opción más barata y popular es el Renault 4. Una buena idea es contratar el vehículo de alquiler junto con el vuelo.

Artículos de Consumo

Declaración de artículos de consumo. Aquellos productos de valor que introduzcas en el país (cámaras, tablas...) deben ser declarados y registrados en tu pasaporte. Si al salir no llevas contigo alguno de estos artículos, te cargarán un arancel del 100%. En caso de que te hayan robado necesitas un justificante de la denuncia ante la policía. Para evitar problemas lleva hasta la frontera tus tablas incluso si has partido alguna.

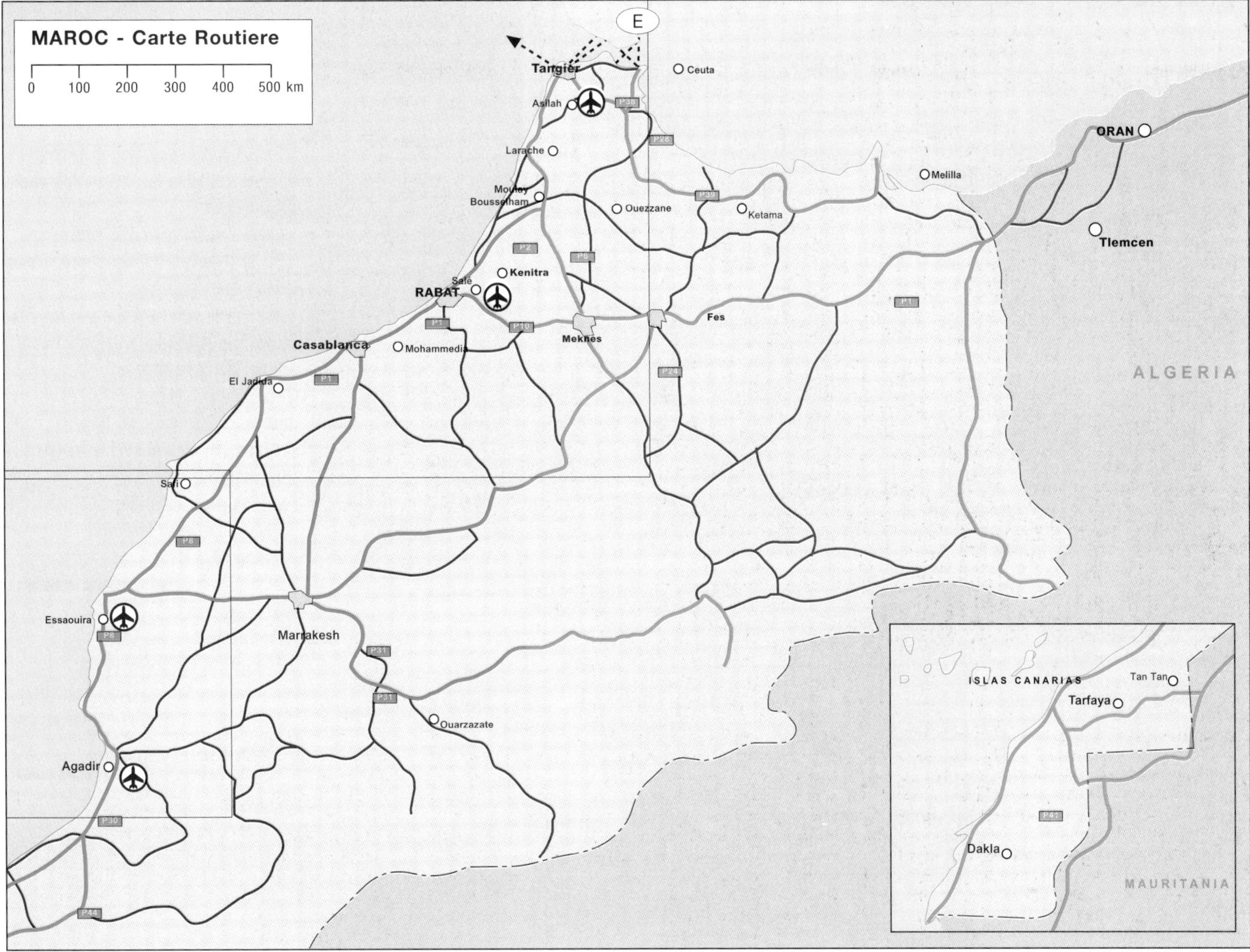

Voyager

Plutôt facile. Si vous êtes venus en voiture depuis l'Europe, vous trouverez un bon réseau routier surtout sur le littoral. Quoiqu'il arrive, les garagistes sont bon marché et rapides à la réparation. Le réseau de bus est vraiment bon marché et souvent plaisant, malgré la patience exigée et les courbatures sur les fesses. Une option pour le voyageur courageux sans trop de tunes.

Drogue

Bien que le pays soit réputé pour fumer du bon haschich pas cher, attention aux flics et aux informateurs qui sont actifs surtout dans les zones de production de le Rif, en faisant des barrages routiers et des fouilles à tout moment. Plus d'un voyageur prudent s'est déjà fait prendre.

Les prix

Comme dans la plupart de pays du Tiers-Monde, le marchandage est une pratique courante. Un taxi peut demander 500 dirhams alors que d'autres ont payé 200 ou 300 dirhams. Soyez toujours amicaux, souriez tout le temps, en vous faites pas emmerder et ne soyez pas pressé.

Le logement

Tout est possible du camping sauvage et des chambres de base aux forfaits dans les hôtels luxueux. Une chambre pas chère sur la côte coûte environ 30 dirhams la nuit. A vous de choisir selon votre budget.

Driving

Getting around Morocco is pretty easy. If you've driven down from Europe you'll be greeted with a good road system (especially along the coast) and Moroccan mechanics can be cheap and fast in the event of a breakdown. The bus network is also very cheap and often fun, though patience required, and a guaranteed sore butt, make it an option for the more hardy or budget traveller.

Drugs

Though Morocco has a reputation for being a great place to smoke good cheap hash, the police and informers are active, and especially in the Rif Mts (the Hash producing area), random roadblocks and search points have taken out many an otherwise careful traveller. Be warned.

The Price system

Like in most poorer countries in the world, bartering is standard practice. A taxi driver might ask for 500dh when other people are paying 200-300dh. Always be friendly, always smile, don't get hassled and don't be in a hurry.

Accommodation:

All options are available from free camping and basic rooms to package accommodation and high class hotels. A cheap room at the coast could cost 30dh (£2.50) per night. Choose depending on budget!

Moverse por Marruecos

Es muy sencillo. Tan fácil como seguir la carretera de la costa, si has conducido desde Europa. En caso de avería mecánica, los talleres marroquíes pueden ser rápidos y económicos. Para los viajeros duros y de bajo presupuesto está el autobús que, además de barato suele ser divertido, siempre que dispongas de mucha paciencia y de un culo resistente.

Drogas

La reputación del hashis marroquí por su calidad y bajo coste, no debe ocultar los riesgos de algún chivatazo o de ser detenido por la policía apostada en controles de carretera, especialmente en las zonas productoras de los Montes Rif.

Sistema de precios

Como en la mayoría de los países pobres el regateo es la práctica habitual. Un taxista te puede pedir el doble que el anterior por el mismo recorrido. No tengas prisa, sonríe, muéstrate amable y no entres en discusiones.

Alojamiento

Puedes elegir cualquier opción desde la acampada libre, pasando por cuartos o apartamentos de alquiler hasta hoteles de lujo. Por 30 dinares, unas 500 pts, puedes alquilar una habitación en la zona costera. Elige en función de tu presupuesto.

Telephone

Maroc	**00+**
Maroc	**212 +**
P Police	**19**
Medical	**15**
Tangier	**09**
Casablanca	**02**
Rabat	**07**
Marrakesh	**04**
Agadir	**08**
Essaouira	**04**
Sidi Ifni	**08**

Cost of Living

Restaurant *	**25-40 dh**
Medinas	**25-40 dh**
Hotel *	**100-400 dh**
Camping	**5-10 dh**

Aeroports

CASABLANCA-	
Royal Air Maroc:	**31 11 57**
Air France:	**29 30 30**
British Airways:	**30 76 07**
AGADIR-	
Royal Air Maroc:	**84 08 08**
Menara tours:	**93 52 11**

Association Cap Surf
159 Bd. Yacoub El Mansour Appt. 10, 3me Etage
Tél: 98 41 14 Fax: 98 15 01

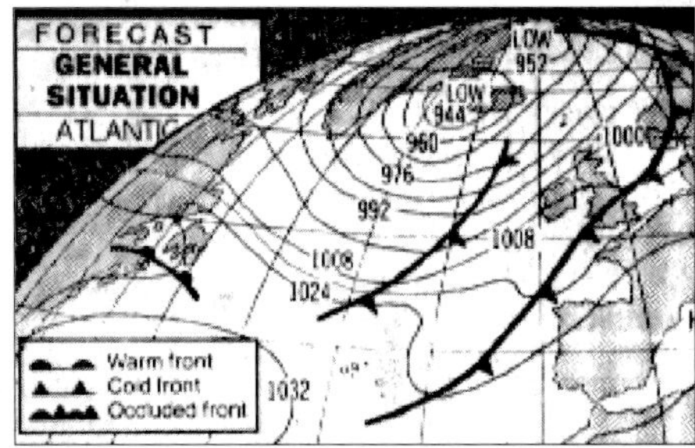

le surf et la climate

On pourrait défendre le fait que le Maroc devrait faire partie du "Guide Stormrider en Afrique" mais les vacances de surf ne correspondent pas forcément avec les divisions politiques. D'abord, en étant un mélange entre les cultures arabes et français et particulièrement visité par les européens, le Maroc a été adopté comme une destination européenne à part entière. Ensuite, le pays reçoit les mêmes houles que les autres pays d'Europe de l'ouest, avec un littoral atlantique qui ressemble au sud du Portugal.

De par son climat chaud, son réservoir de droites vierges sans requins, ni coraux, ni été ni maladies, c'est une alternative idéale à l'hiver en Europe si l'on pas de temps ou d'argent (ou les deux). Ca reçoit les mêmes houles que le reste de l'Atlantique de l'ouest. Les tripotées de droites et de bons beach breaks l'ont rendu un must pour les trippers depuis presque 20 ans.

L'hiver a toujours été la saison typique pour les voyageurs. Les dépressions régulières qui circulent sur l'Atlantique nord envoient toute la houle mais de par sa position méridionale, le Maroc évite les températures froides et les fronts qui balayent l'Europe. Des vagues puissantes et propres se lèvent régulièrement avec une eau et un air à la bonne température. Le surf au printemps ou à l'automne est comparable sauf qu'il fait plus chaud et qu'il y a moins de monde à l'eau. L'été, comme partout en Europe, c'est souvent le calme plat avec des températures torrides. Dans les zones montagneuses ou désertiques au sud, on cuit pendant la journée alors que ça se rafraîchit drôlement la nuit. Equipez-vous en conséquence.

One might argue that Morocco should be part of a "Stormrider Guide: Africa" but surfing holidays do not always coincide neatly with political divisions. Firstly, being a blend of Arabic and French culture, and intensely visited by Europeans, it has been adopted as full European destination. Secondly, the country receives the same swells as western Europe.

Considering its warm climate, it's untapped stash of uncrowded rights with no sharks, no coral, no winter and no disease, it is a perfect winter escape for Europeans short of either time or money. Moroccos' myriad right points and glorious beach breaks have been popular with surf travellers for nearly two decades.

Winter time has always been the most popular season. Consistant Low Pressure systems circling the North Atlantic provide all the swell, but being so far south, Morocco misses out on the cold weather and frontal systems that blow over Europe. Clean, solid surf is a regular occurrence, and the air and water temperatures perfect. The surf in Spring and autumn is similar but the air is hotter and it's less crowded. Summer, like elsewhere in Europe, can see long flat spells and soaring temperatures. The mountainous interior and desert south, whilst baking during during the day, cool significantly at night. Go prepared.

Más de uno pensará qué pinta Marruecos en una guía surfera de Europa, pero se puede argumentar que los viajes surferos no han de coincidir necesariamente con las divisiones políticas. Desde esta óptica, se puede afirmar que Marruecos es un destino habitual y tradicional del surfer europeo, donde se da una mezcla de cultura árabe y francesa y a donde acuden gran cantidad de turistas procedentes de Europa. Además, su litoral recibe exactamente las mismas marejadas que el resto de la costa Atlántica-Oeste de Europa, siendo populares sus incontables points de derechas y gloriosas rompientes de playa entre los surfers europeos durante dos décadas.

El invierno es tradicionalmente la estación más popular. Profundas borrascas del Atlántico Norte envían las olas, pero al estar tan al sur, Marruecos se libra de los frentes que atraviesan toda Europa dejando un tiempo frío y desapacible. Marejadas sólidas y ordenadas con temperaturas agradables, tanto en tierra como en el agua, son algo habitual. En Primavera y Otoño las condiciones son similares, aunque hace m·s calor y hay menos gente en el agua. El verano, al igual que el del resto de Europa, trae los días sin olas y las temperaturas agobiantes. Si vas a las montañas del interior o al desierto vete muy preparado, si no te puedes asfixiar durante el día y pasar frío a las noches.

le nord

Presque tous ceux qui viennent au Maroc foncent droit vers le sud autour des vagues connues d'Agadir, en oubliant une des zones avec des vagues de qualité , les plus consistantes de l'hémisphère nord. Avec 1000 kms de côtes exposées directement nord ouest, situées suffisamment au sud pour éviter les venst et le froid en prenant les mêmes houles qu'aux Canaries, ça paraît incroyable que cette partie ait été ignorée si longtemps. Les villes cosmopollites de Rabat, de Casablanca et deTanger abritent une population en pleine croissance de jeunes surfers qui ont tout de suite compris ce qui se passait du côté de l'océan. L'association Cap Surf et uncertain nombre de surf shops de Casa ont rendu le surf plus accessible en organisant des compétitions (comme un EPSA à Jack Beach) en envoyant une équipe nationale aux championnats du monde amateurs au Brésil en 1994. La zone de Tanger au nord à Rabat comprend surtout des beach breaks tandis que de Rabat à Casa et Safi, lea côte est plus découpée avec une plus grande variété de vagues. En ayant une vue septentrionnale, ça peut faire un bon mètre ici alors que c'est le lac au sud.

Nearly all visitors to Morocco head south to the famous waves around Agadir, missing out on some of the most consistent, quality surfing areas in the northern hemisphere. With 1000 km's of coastline facing directly into the northwest Atlantic, situated far enough south to escape the winds and cold, yet picking up the same swells as the Canaries, it seems incredible that it has been ignored for so long. The cosmopolitan cities of Rabat, Casablanca and Tanger house growing populations of keen young surfers who have not taken long to realise what's going on around them. The Association Cap Surf and a number of surf shops in Casablanca are making surfing more accessible, organising contests (like the EPSA event held at Jack Beach), and getting the Maroc team to the World Amateur Championships in Brazil, 1994. The area from Tanger in the north to Rabat is predominantly beach breaks and from Rabat, past Casablanca to Safi, the coast gets more rugged and a much greater variety of waves can be found. Having a more northerly aspect, it can be head high here when down south is flat.

Prácticamente todo los que van a surfear a Marruecos se dirigen a las famosas olas de la zona de Agadir, perdiéndose una de las mejores y más consistentes zonas surferas del hemisferio norte. Son 1000 km's de litoral abierto al Atlántico, situados suficientemente al sur para escapar de los frentes fríos y a la vez recibir las mismas marejadas que Canarias por lo que parece increíble entender porque ha permanecido tanto tiempo ignorada. Las cosmopolitas ciudades de Rabat, Casablanca y Tánger albergan un creciente número de jóvenes surfers que son conscientes de las buenas olas que poseen. La Asociación Cap Surf y unas cuantas tiendas de surf de Casablanca están acercando el surf a la gente, organizando campeonatos como el EPSA celebrado en Jack Beach y llevando al equipo marroquí al Campeonato del Mundo Amateur celebrado en 1994 en Brasil. En el area que va de Tanger a Rabat abundan las olas de playa, mientras que Rabat a Safi la costa es más accidentada y por lo tanto existe una mayor variedad de rompientes. La orientación de este costa hace que en ocasiones puedas surfear metro y medio cuando en el sur está plato

Photos: Mark Stevenson

Photo: Eric Chauché

Photo: Eric Chauché

Photo: Eric Chauché

"...une des zones avec des vagues de qualité , les plus consistantes de l'hémisphère nord..."

Le Nord

Association Cap Surf

Photo: Mark Stevenson

1. Oualidia

Une baie abritée idéale pour les débutants. La preuve, c'est un surf-camp organisé avec toutes les installations, surtout en tente. Un petit paradis pour apprendre à surfer.

A sheltered bay ideal for beginners since it's a well organised surf-camp with all kind of facilities. Something of a paradise for starting surfing.

En una bahía protegida se encuentra este paraíso ideal para principiantes, puesto que existe un surf-camp bien organizado y con toda clase de comodidades.

2. Sidi Bouzid Plage

Un shore-break avec un point-break en droite.

A shore-break and another right point break.

Una orillera y un point de derechas.

3. El Jadida-Plage

Une droite sous-estimée près de la jetée, à checker absolument quand c'est gros et par vents de sud. Un beach break à proximité. En face d'un hôtel de luxe.

Underrated right by the jetty, best checked in a big swell with south winds. A beach break as well. Facing a fancy hotel.

Ola infravalorada. Rompe junto al rompeolas con fuerte marejada y vientos del sur. También hay una ola de playa. En frente de un hotel de lujo.

4. Azemmour-Plage

Une plage de sable tranquille avec quelques vagues par houle moyenne. Meilleur au descendant jusqu'à marée basse.

Quiet sandy beach getting some waves in a medium swell. Best on the outgoing to low tide.

Tranquila playa arenosa que recibe olas con una marejada mediana. Mejor con la marea bajando.

5. Jack Beach

3 minutes au sud de Dar Bouazza, ce spot prend bien la houle. Un bon beach break de mi-marée à marée haute. Site idéal pour les compétitions pour sa consistance.

Just 3min south of Dar-Bouazza and gathering a lot of swell: a good beach break from mid-to-high tide. Contest site since it's consistent.

A tres minutos al sur de Dar Bouazza, se encuentra esta rompiente de playa que recibe mucho mar y por ello ha sido lugar de celebración de campeonatos. De media a alta.

Jack Beach - *Photo: Association Cap Surf*

6. Dar Bouazza

Une gauche réputée qui s'enroule autour d'un cap, meilleur à marée basse. C'est une vague longue si vous démarrez à l'"Inter", le pic au large qui connecte parfois avec le pointbreak. Attention à la Bobine, une chaudière d'un bateau qui a coulé, en fin de vague. Des rochers à éviter aussi et surtout une concentration d'oursins phénoménale qui vous feront certainement penser à avoir des chaussons à semelle dure ainsi qu'une pince à épiler. Beaucoup de monde à l'évidence.

A famous left wrapping around a point with no long walls but good cut-back sections. A long wave if you take-off at "L'Inter" (the outside section that sometimes connects with the point). Best at low tide. Beware of a ship boiler called " La Bobine" when surfing the final section. Sharp rocks and urchins, so hard-sole booties are an idea. Crowds for sure.

Una famosa izquierda que se enrosca a lo largo de una punta de roca. Es una ola larga si la coges en su sección exterior L'Inter, que a veces conecta con la sección interior en donde hay que tener cuidado con la caldera sumergida de un barco hundido ("La Bobine"). Los escarpines no están de más ya que el fondo es afilado y está repleto de erizos. Mejor en marea baja. Multitud asegurada.

7. Casablanca

La capitale économique du Maroc a des plages consistantes comme Monica, Mohammedia, Zeneta ou Paloma qui marchent toute l'année. Toutes ces plages sont gavées de courants quand c'est gros.

Morocco's financial capital has consistent beaches which include Monica Plage, Zeneta Plage, Mohammedia Plage y Paloma Plage They work all year and have currents when big.

En la capital económica de Marruecos hay playas que funcionan a lo largo de todo el año como Monica Plage, Zeneta Plage, Mohammedia Plage y Paloma Plage. Cuando está grande en todas ellas aparecen corrientes fuertes.

8. Pont Blondin

Ainsi nommé aprés qu'un soldat combattit ici pendant le débarquement américain de la deuxième guerre mondiale. Quelques bons jours avec pas mal de locaux.

Named after a soldier who fought here during the American debarkment. Some good days with a concentration of friendly locals.

El nombre procede de un soldado americano que luchó aquí durante el desembarco de la II Guerra Mundial. Hay dìas buenos en los que se suele llenar de locales.

9. Sablette-Plage

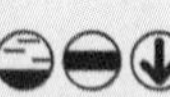

Une bonne gauche, meilleure entre 1 et 2 mètres par houle et vent de nord.

A good point breaking left, best between 4-8' with a N swell and N winds. Disputed peaks even on the beach.

Un buen point de izquierdas. Su punto óptimo con olas de uno a dos metros, mar del norte y viento de la misma dirección.

10. Bouznika Plage

Une anse sympa abritée des alizés, avec de bonnes droites avec une houle moyenne à grosse. Attention aux courants et aux oursins. Meilleur par vents de N/N-E à marée basse.

A nice cove sheltered from trade winds, producing good rights that need a medium to big swell. Currents when big and urchins to avoid. Best with N-NE winds at low tide.

Una preciosa cala abrigada de los alisios con una buena derecha si hay bastante mar. Presta atención a las corrientes y a los erizos. Mejor con marea baja y vientos del Norte-Nordeste.

11. Oued Cherrat

Spot de sable et de rochers qui résiste les vents d'ouest, fréquenté toute l'année surtout par les bodyboards. Attention aux rochers quand vous ramez.

Reef and beach break, very popular all year long which handles W winds. Beware the reefs when going out. Lots of bodyboarders.

Arrecife y playa. Frecuentado todo el año, sobre todo por corcheros. Soporta el viento oeste. Cuidado con las rocas al entrar.

12. Skhirat-Plage

Un point-break de gauches le long d'une jetée, de préférence au montant de marée basse à mi-marée. Marche par petite houle. Allez sur la plage si le point-break est trop encombré.

The Point is a left breaking alongside the jetty, best at incoming mid-to-low tide. Goes off in a small swell (up to 6'). Try the Beach Break if The Point gets too crowded.

Un point de izquierdas paralelo al espigón, mejor subiendo de baja a media. Funciona con poco mar. Si hay demasiada gente en el point, puedes probar suerte en la playa.

13. Rabat-Salé

Profitez des curiosités de la capitale et de son ambiance magique. N'oubliez pas ses vagues non plus, proches de la jetée encore une fois. Pas moins de 4 gauches (plongeoir, Cascade, Kbair & Bergama) et 4 droites (La pointe, Doura, Brema,shore-break de Salé). Il faut que ca rentre gros.

Enjoy the scenery of the capital and its magic atmosphere. Don't miss the waves close to the jetty as well...no less than 4 lefts (Plongeoir, Cascade, Kbair & Bergama) and 4 rights (La pointe Doura, Brema, shore break de Salé). Needs a big swell.

Disfruta de la atmósfera mágica de la capital. Pero no te pierdas las olas del malecón...nada menos que cuatro izquierdas (Plongeir, Cascade, Kbair y Bergama) y cuatro derechas (La Pointe Doura, Brema y la orillera de Salé). Necesita bastante mar.

Karim Chaibal, Salé-Rabat - *Photo: Association Cap Surf*

14. Plage des Nations

Souvent un beach break trop rapide. Plutôt consistant.

Often a fast beach break. Quite consistent.

Ola de playa consistente y rápida.

15. Mehdiya Plage

Le berceau du surf au Maroc puisque les soldats de la base américaine y ont commencé à surfer dans les années 50. Une droite qui casse à partir d'une jetée rocheuse par grosse houle.

Find the rock groin then wait for a big swell. There should be a right breaking off it. Mid-to-high tide usually better. The cradle of surfing in Morocco due to the USmilitary base nearby.

Es la cuna del surf en Marruecos debido a la existencia de una base militar estadounidense, algunos de cuyos residentes comenzaron a surfear aquí en los años cincuenta. Es una derecha que rompe junto al espigón.

Mehdiya Plage - Photo: Miles Masterson

16. Mouslay Bousselham

Plage correcte qui marche mieux de mi-marée à marée haute. Un joli lagon difficile à atteindre sans un 4x4.

O.K. beach that works best from mid-to-high tide. A nice lagoon, but hard to reach without a 4x4.

Una ola de playa aceptable, mejor de media marea a alta. Hay una preciosa laguna, pero es difícil llegar sin un 4x4.

17. Plage Loukos

7kms au nord de Larache. Une gauche le long de la jetée à mi-marée. Off-shore pratiquement tout le temps.

The Plage de Loukos, 7kms north of Larache, has a left alongside the jetty at mid-tide. Off-shore nearly all the time.

Situada 7 kms. al norte de Larache, aquí rompe una izquierda en marea media junto al rompeolas. El viento predominante sopla de tierra.

18. Briech

Une plage consistente qui reçoit un festival de musique en été.

A consistent beach called Briech. Mid-to-high tide. Famous music festival in summer.

Una playa consistente que en verano alberga un famoso festival musical.

19. Tanger

Pas forcément la première zone de surf mais vaut le coup d'oeil pour le pittoresque et la culture. Un carrefour depuis la nuit des temps de toutes sortes de contrebandiers, réinventé par les écrivains de la Beat generation. Manque cruellement de consistance mais on y trouve de super reefs et de belles plages comme la plage Sol, qui marche quand c'est petit ou Aroussa Bahe au Cap Spartel, une droite sur du reef et du sable. Attention aux rochers au pic.

Not the primo surf zone but worth a visit for its beauty and culture. Historically the cross-roads for many types of smuggler, reinvented by the writers of the beat generation. Lacks consistency but there are brilliant reefs and beaches like Plage Sol that works in small swell, or Aroussa Bahe 12 kms W at Cape Spartel (facing the Ba Kacem Café), a right over reef and sand. Beware of the rock at the peak.

No es una zona importante por sus olas, pero si por su atractivo cultural y natural. Los escritores de la generación beat le dieron un significado especial. No es un lugar de surf consistente, pero sus playas como Plage Sol, que funciona con poco mar, o arrecifes como Aroussa Bahe en el Cabo Espartel (en frente del Café Ba Kacem), una derecha sobre roca y arena (cuidado con la roca que hay en el pico) pueden tener días brillantes.

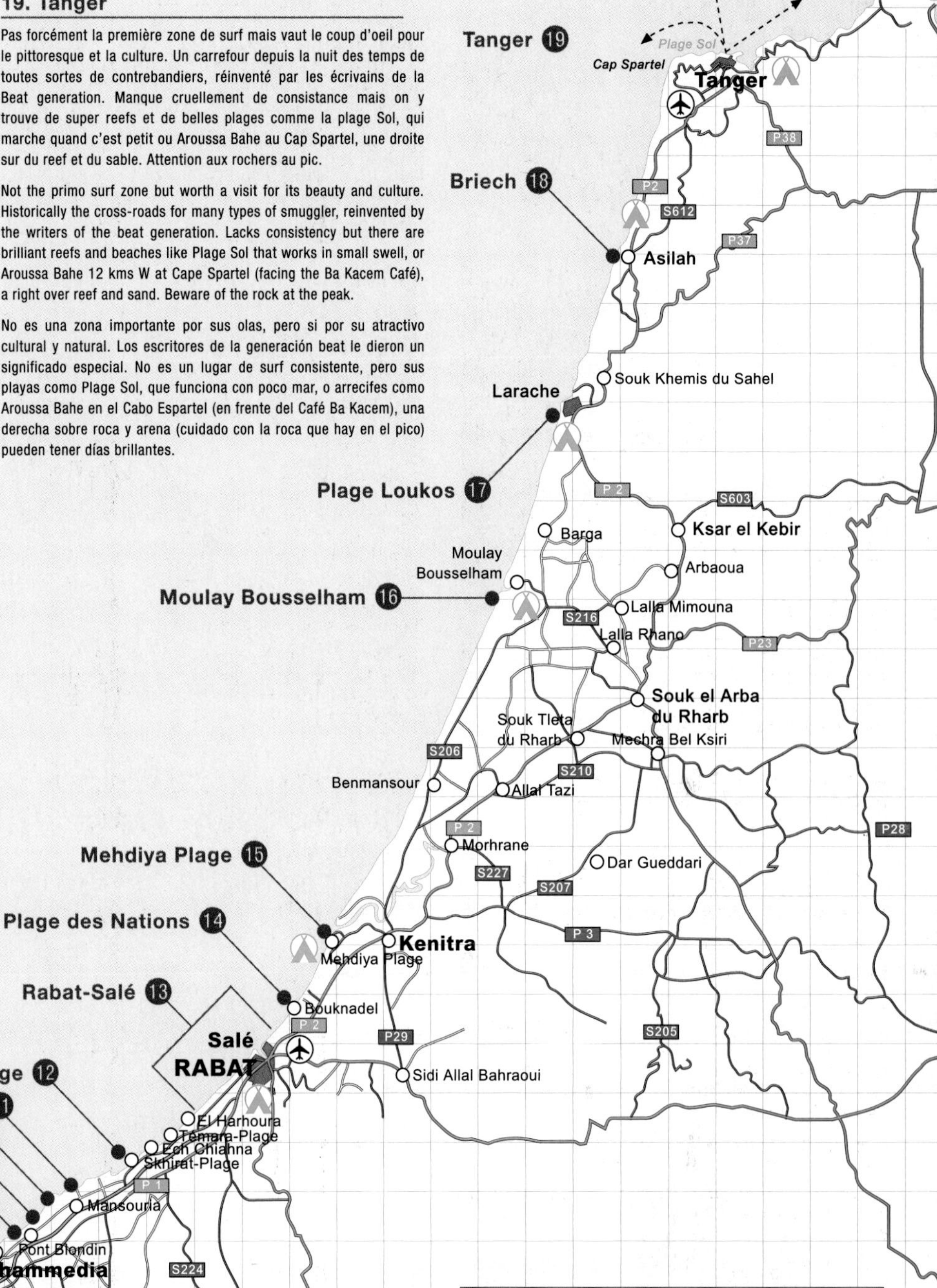

La plupart des très bons spots au Maroc se trouvent à et autour de Tarhazoute, à approximativement 30 mns au nord-ouest d'Agadir. Les vols pour le Sud marocain atterrissent à l'aéroport d'Agadir. A l'aéroport, vous pouvez trouver un taxi sans problémes (environ 150 dirams soit 100 francs). Les vans arriveront du nord après Cap Rhir et s'installeront le plus souvent à un endroit surplombant Anchor Point et Mystery Point, et si vous ne détériorez pas le site, il n'y aura aucun probléme (mise à part la très peu officielle taxe locale de parking). Si vous souhaitez éviter le camping sauvage, il y a un camping à l'entrée sud de Tarhazoute. Des maisons sont à louer pour pas cher, souvent avec des vues sur mer impressionnantes, avec l'électricité mais sans l'eau courante. L'eau est rare en raison de la proximité du Sahara; ainsi le lavage se fait avec des seaux, ou au Hammam (cela ressemble aux bains turcs).

Many of thre best spots in Morocco can be found in and around Tarhazoute, approx 30 mins NW of Agadir. Flights to the south of Morocco arrive at Agadir international airport. From the airport you can take a taxi to Agadir and continue to the coast by bus, or taxi all the way (approx150 diram / £12.50). Campervans will arrive from the North past Cap Rhir and usually park on the point overlooking Anchor and Mystery Points, and if you keep a clean site, there will be no problem (apart from the unofficial local parking "tax"). If you want to camp legally, there's a camp site on the south entrance to Tarhazoute. Houses can also be rented cheaply, often with amazing sea views, and will have electricity but no running water. Water is scarce due to proximity to the Sahara so washing is done with buckets, or at a Hammam (like a Turkish bath).

En los alrededores de Tarhazoute (30 minutos al Noroeste de Agadir) se concentran bastantes de los mejores spots marroquíes. Los vuelos dirigidos al sur de Marruecos aterrizan en el Aeropuerto de Agadir. Desde el aeropuerto puedes tomar un taxi a Agadir y desde allí seguir en autobús o hacer todo el recorrido en taxi (unos 150 dinares / 2500 pts). Las autocaravanas que bajan del Norrte pasando el Cabo Rhir suelen aparcar en un lugar desde donde se divisan los points de Anchor y Mistery. Si mantienes limpio el lugar, no tendrás problemas al margen de la itasa extraoficialí de aparcamiento. Si quieres hacer acampada legal, tienes un camping en el acceso sur a Tarhazoute. También puedes alquilar casitas bastante baratas, a menudo con vistas del mar fabulosas, con electricidad pero sin agua corriente. El agua es un bien escaso debido a la proximidad del Sahara. Por eso, se lava en palanganas o en un Hamman (parecido a un baño turco).

le sud

Martijn Drenth

Chameau - *Photo: Eric Chauche*

Souk - *Photo: Marc Feniès*

Pointe d'Immousane - *Photo: Marc Féniès*

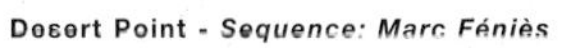

Desert Point - ***Sequence: Marc Féniès***

Le Sud

Associaton Cap Surf
Matt Moon
Martijn Drenth

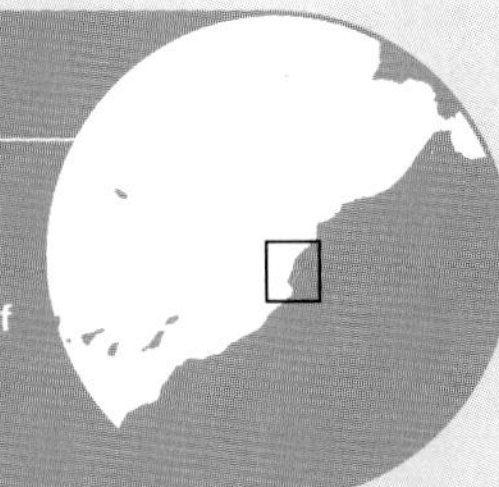

1. Safi

Une autre droite de reef 2kms au nord de Safi nommé Racelafaa. Par grosse houle, c'est une des meilleures vagues du pays.

Another right reef 2kms north of Safi named Racelafaa. Needs a big swell to be one of the best waves in the country.

Unos dos kilómetros al norte de Safi rompe esta derecha de arrecife llamada Racelafaa, que con una marejada potente se convierte en una de las mejores olas del país.

2. Pointe d'Immesouane

Bonnes vagues rarement surfées.

Good waves but rarely surfed.

Buenas olas poco surfeadas.

Pnte d'Immesouane - *Photo: Association Cap Surf*

3. Tamri-plage

Bon beach break à environ 4 kms du village. Passez à marée basse par petite houle et vents off-shore.

Good beach break about 4 kms from the village. Check at low tide with a small swell and off-shore winds.

En marea baja, con poco mar y viento terral encontrar·s buenas olas en esta playa situada a 4 kms. del pueblo.

4. La Bouilloire

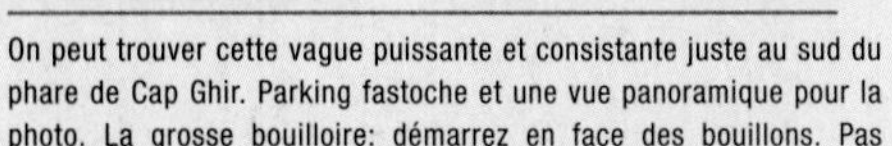

On peut trouver cette vague puissante et consistante juste au sud du phare de Cap Ghir. Parking fastoche et une vue panoramique pour la photo. La grosse bouilloire: démarrez en face des bouillons. Pas facile d'entrer et de sortir de l'eau, surtout à cause des oursins.

This consistent and powerful wave can be found just Sth of the lighthouse of Cap Ghir. Easy parking and good overview. Big Boilers: take off in front of the boil. Tricky getting in and out of the water. Urchins.

Al sur del faro de Cap Rhir se encuentra esta consistente y potente ola. El aparcamiento es fácil y las vistas excelentes. El acceso a la ola es complicado. Erizos.

Boilers - *Photo: Chris Power*

Desert Point - *Photo: Mark Fénies*

5. Killer Point

Ainsi nommé parce que des orques épaulards se promènent de temps en temps(!). La vague démarre en face d'un gros rocher, puis on arrive à l'inside qui est la meilleure partie. Se surfe jusqu'à très gros. Abrité des vents de nord. Attention aux cavernes en face des vagues. Le chemin peut être glissant.

So named after the Killer whales that can sometimes be found cruising around here.The wave starts in front of a big rock and is best on the inside and holds big time swells. Sheltered from N wind. Beware the caves that face the waves. Slippery walking track.

Las orcas (ballenas asesinas) que a veces pasan por las inmediaciones han servido para poner nombre a esta ola que comienza a romper frente a una roca. Aguanta grandes marejadas y est· protegida del viento norte. La mejor secciÛn es la final, pero atento a las cuevas que hay frente a la ola. El camino de acceso es resbaladizo.

Killer Point - *Photo: Chris Power*

6. La Source

Sur l'inside de Mystery Point. Seulement quand c'est petit. De l'eau douce jaillit de rochers sur la plage où on peut se rincer et la combard par la même occasion. Meilleur à marée montante par houle moyenne.

On the inside of Mystery Point. Small days only. Fresh water bubbles up from onshore rock formations where you can rinse your face and wetsuit. Best at incoming tide on a medium swell.

En los dÌas de poco mar en la sección interior de Mistery Point y con la marea subiendo se puede coger esta ola. En la orilla hay manantiales de agua dulce, perfectos para aclarar el traje y darse un remojón.

7. Mystery Point

Une vague qui suce à max avec une zone de take-off restreinte. Mieux avec une houle de taille moyenne. Les routards squattent là au-dessus de la falaise, en camping sauvage jusqu'à récemment. Les locaux ont commencé à venir demander 5 dirhams pour chaque nuit. Il vaut mieux être en nombre parce que la police ne viendra pas vous aider si elle sait que vous êtes là.

Very sucky wave with small take off area best with a medium size swell. Travelling surfers camp here on the cliffs, free until recently. Locals have started coming around in the morning asking for 5Dh per night. Safety is numbers here as the Police won't help you if they know you are staying here.

Ola muy chupona, necesita una marejada de tamaño medio. El pico es muy definido. Suele haber surfers acampados en los acantilados. Hasta ahora la acampada era libre, pero los lugareños han empezado a pedir 5 dinares por noche. Por motivos de seguridad es mejor pagar, porque si te roban la policÌa no te va a atender por hacer acampada libre.

8. Pointe des Ancres

La vague la plus célèbre du Maroc qui nécessite un gros swell pour marcher. Même si y'a pas mal de monde, l'ambiance n'est pas trop tendue à l'eau. Ramez depuis la plage au nord (long mais sûr) quand c'est petit ou jetez-vous de l'avancée rocheuse mais attention au timing avec les séries. Au retour, revenez par la plage ou surfez le plus loin possible jusqu'à la plage au sud. A marée haute, ça peut être difficile de monter sur les rochers, y'a déjà eu des planches de cassées entre les rochers.

Morocco's most famous wave needs a big swell to break and while it gets crowded, the atmosphere remains pretty friendly. Paddle out either from the beach to the N (a long but safe paddle) on small days, or jump off the point (good timing is crucial). Coming in, either paddle back to the beach N, or surf down the point and paddle to the small beach to the S. High tide can be very difficult coming in over the rocks (many boards have snapped between rocks).

Es la ola más famosa de Marruecos, necesita fuerte marejada. Suele saturarse de gente, pero la atmósfera es amigable. El acceso se realiza desde la playa situada al norte (una remada larga pero segura) en los días pequeños o desde la punta de rocas (es crucial elegir el momento apropiado para saltar). Para salir se puede volver por la misma playa o por otra pequeñita situada al final de la ola. En marea alta la salida es dificultosa, se suelen romper muchas tablas sobre las rocas.

Pointe des Ancres - *Photo: Chris Power*

9. Hash Point

Au nord de Tarhazoute. La vérité est que les surfers qui fument trop ont la flemme d'aller jusqu'à Anchor, d'où le nom!

Nth beach in the village of Tarhazoute. So named for the surfers who smoke too much and can't be bothered to walk to Anchors.

En el pueblo de Tarhazoute está esta playa orientada al norte que recibe su nombre de los surfers que han fumado demasiado para molestarse en ir hasta Anchor.

10. Panorama's

Une vague ronde et rapide qui casse en face du bar/ restaurant Panorama à Tarhazoute.

Fast and round wave breaking in front of Panorama's bar/restaurant in the village of Tarhazoute.

En frente del Bar-Restaurante Panorama del pueblo de Tarazhoute rompe esta rapida y cóncava ola.

11. Banana Beach 

Plage à l'embouchure de la rivière à sec à Tamrhakht. Une vague amusante de 1m à 1,5m. Ferme à marée basse et par grosse houle.

Beach on the mouth of a dried-up river at the village of Tamrhakht. Fun wave between 4-6 ft. Closes out at low tide and bigger swells.

En la boca de un río seco en el pueblo de Tamrhakht rompe esta divertida ola. Cierra en marea baja y a partir del metro y medio.

12. Le Rocher du Diable 

Une gauche tubulaire qu'il faut checker, à 2kms au sud de Banana beach.

A tuby left worth checking, 2km Sth of Banana beach.

Izquierda tubera situada 2 kms. al sur de Banana.

13. Tifnite 

Une portion de plage sans aménagements juste au sud d'Agadir.

Undeveloped stretch of beach just Sth of Agadir.

Extensión de playa salvaje al sur de Agadir.

14. Oued Massa 

Un beach break à Sidi-Rbat dans une réserve naturelle, à checker quand c'est petit et que le vent souffle du sud. Un endroit idéaPl pour mater les oiseaux aussi.

Beach break in Sidi-Rbat and natural reserve, to be checked with a small swell and S wind. Hot spot for bird watching.

Rompiente de playa en la reserva natural de Sidi-Rbat donde podrás avistar innumerables especies de aves. Lo mejor días de poco mar y viento sur.

15. Sidi Moussa d'Aglou 

Un autre beach break sympa avec de bonnes vagues par petit swell. Attention aux filets de pêcheurs quand vous sortez ou entrez dans l'eau.

Another gentle beach with good waves in a small swell. Beware nets while getting in and out.

Buena playa para días pequeños. Vigila las redes de los pescadores al entrar y salir del agua.

La Désert Sud

La côte marocaine s'étend encore, complètement vierge, sur presque 2000kms jusqu'à la frontière avec l'ex-Sahara Occidental. Vous serez en plein désert alors équiipez-vous en conséquence. Passez sur des spots comme Mirleft-plage (une droite par houle moyenne), Sidi-Ifni (des breaks sur des jetées près du port), Tarfaya (une épave sur la plage), Laayoun (abrité des vents de nord), Ad Dakhla et Lagouira.

The Moroccan coast still extends almost unexplored for nearly 2,000 kms to the border with Occidental Sahara. You're going to hit the desert so be prepared for it! Check spots like Mirleft-Plage (a medium swell right), Sidi-Ifni (jetties & harbour breaks), Tarfaya (shipwrecks on beach), Laayoun (sheltered from N winds), Ad Dakhla

La costa marroquí se prolonga casi 2000 kms. hasta la frontera con el Sahara Occidental. Vete muy bien preparado si piensas meterte en el desierto. Algunos spots a visitar son: Mirleft-Plage (derecha con marejada media), Sidi-Ifni (olas en espigones y malecones), Tarfaya (barcos hundidos en la playa), Laayoun (protegido del viento norte), Ad Dakhla y Lagouira.

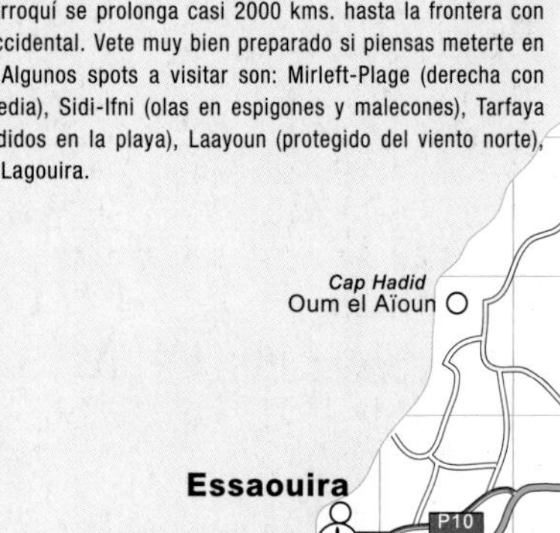

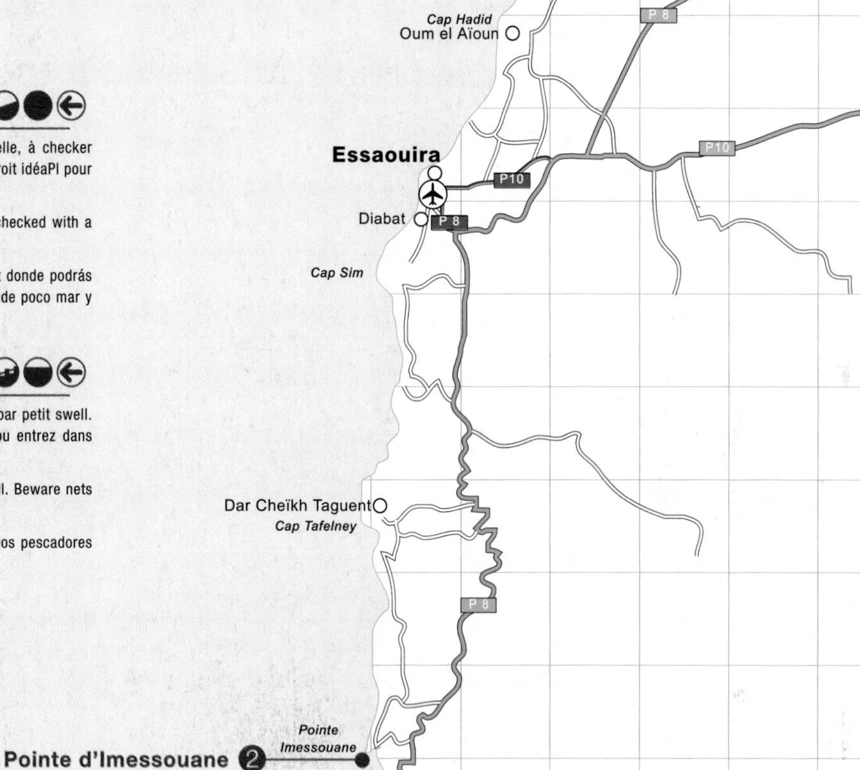

Tarhazoute

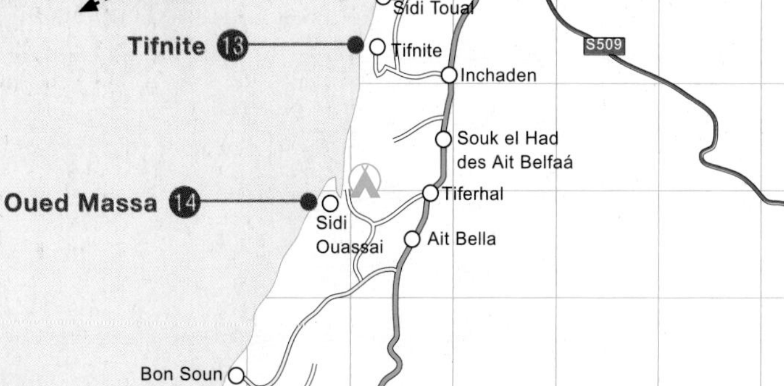

Capital:	
Lanzarote:	Arrecife
Fuerteventura:	Puerto del Rosario
Gran Canaria:	Las Palmas de G.C.
Tenerife:	Santa Cruz de Tenerife
Población:	1,690,000
Lanzarote:	40,000
Fuerteventura:	20,000
Gran Canaria:	520,000
Tenerife:	607,000
Superficie:	7,770km²
Huso Horario:	GMT (summer GMT+1)
Lenguaje:	Castilliano (Spanish)
Moneda:	Peseta (PTE)

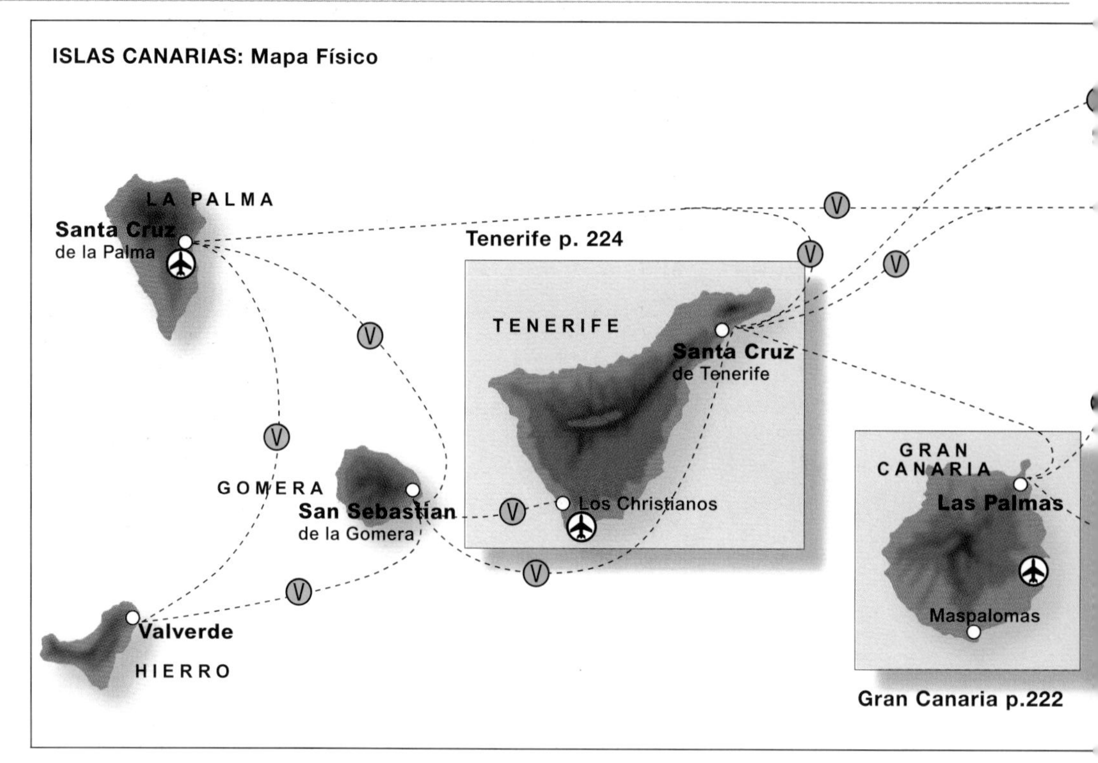

Photo: Phil Holden

ISLAS CANARIAS

El archipeligo volcánico de las Canarias está formado por siete islas principales, situadas a una latitud de 28°N. Su clima templado y atemperado por el Océano Atlántico les ha dado el nobre de Islas Afortunadas. Sus primeros habitantes fueron los aborígenes Guanches. Existe controversia sobre el modo en que pudieron llegar a las islas. La teoría más aceptada es que eran descendientes de los bereberes del NE de Africa. La historia nos ha legado poco de los Guanches debido a la rapiña del proceso colonizador. En los siglos XIII y XIV marinos portugueses, franceses, genoveses y mallorquines arribaron a las islas, siendo al principio bien recibidos, pero en 1402 las cosas se torcieron y tras un siglo de sangrientos combates los Guanches prácticamente habían desaparecido y los españoles habían colonizado las islas. Posteriormente las islas fueron una etapa esencial en los viajes entre Europa y América. Colón arribó a Gran Canaria en el viaje del Descubrimiento de América en 1492. Este tráfico marítimo sufrió los ataques de los piratas ingleses, holandeses y musulmanes. En 1797 Lord Nelson desafió la soberania española pero fue derrotado, perdió un brazo y a 226 de sus hombres.

Desde entonces los principales invasores han sido los turistas ingleses, alemanes, escandinavos, franceses y españoles, que llegan a las islas aprovechando las atractivas ofertas turisticas, sobre todo en invierno cuando el frío aprieta en el Norte de Europa. Esta búsqueda del sol y la playa ha provocado la construcción de ciudades como Playa del Inglés y Playa de las Américas, destinos accesibles a cualquier bolsillo.

THE CANARY ISLANDS

The Canaries are a volcanic chain of 7 main islands, lying at a latitude of 28 N. They have been called the "fortunate islands" due to the mild, consistent climate, influenced most by the Atlantic Ocean.

The earliest inhabitants of these islands are believed to be the aboriginal Guanches but how they got there is open to debate. The most popular theory is that they were descended from the Berbers of North West Africa. History has left us little of the Guanches due to the ravages of the colonisation process. In the 13th and 14th century Portuguese, French, Genoese and Majorcan navigators visited the islands and at first were welcomed. Things began to change in 1402 and after about a hundred years of bloody warring, the Guanches were virtually wiped out. The Spanish had colonised the islands.

Over the years the Canaries established themselves as a major staging post between Europe and the Americas. Columbus sailed from Gran Canaria on his voyage of discovery to America in 1492. Cargo and passengers were plagued by pirates from many countries, including the English, the Dutch and the Moors. In 1797 Lord Nelson challenged the Spanish sovereignty but was defeated, lost an arm, and 226 of his men were killed.

Since then, tourists have been the major invading force. English, German, Scandinavian, French and Spanish people flock to the islands on various package deals, especially in winter when the more northerly European countries get cold. They come for the sun, sea and surf with purpose built towns such as Playa del Inglés or Playa Las Americas offering package deals to hell.

LES ILES CANARIES

Les Canaries sont une chaîne volcanique de 7 îles principalement à la latitude de 28 Nord. On les a appelé les 'îles chanceuses' pour leur climat doux et ensoleillé, surtout influencé par l'océan atlantique.

Les premiers habitants des îles sont supposés être les Guanches aborigènes sans qu'on sache trop comment ils sont arrivés. La théorie la plus courante est qu'ils descendaient des Berbères d'Afrique du Nord. L'histoire ne nous a pas laissés grand chose des Guanches à cause des ravages de la colonisation. Aux XIII et XIV siècles, les navigateurs portugais, les français, génois ou ceux des Baléares visitèrent les îles et furent les bienvenus au début mais les choses commencèrent à changer en 1402 et après des siècles de guerres sanglantes, les Guanches furent carrément éliminés. Les Espagnols avaient alors colonisé l'île.

Ils s'affirmèrent assez rapidement comme un point de passage obligé entre l'Europe et les Amériques.D'ailleurs, Colomb partit de Gran Canaria lors de son voyage pour découvrir l'Amérique en 1492. Plein de navires marchands et de passagers furent attaqués par des pirates de toutes nationalités comme les Anglais, les Hollandais et les Maures. En 1797, Lord Nelson défia la souveraineté espagnole mais ce fut un échec puisqu'il perdit un bras et 226 de ses hommes.

Depuis lors, les touristes ont été les principaux envahisseurs. Angles, Allemands, Scandinaves, Français et Espagnols partent en force sur ces îles sur différents types de forfaits, surtout en hiver quand les pays les plus au nord de l'Europe deviennent polaires. Ils viennent pour le soleil, la mer et les stations balnéaires construites à cet effet comme Playa del Ingles ou Playa Las Americas qui offrent différents forfaits pour l'enfer.

Vuelos

Hay vuelos que parten de un montón de ciudades europeas hacia los aereopuertos internacionales de Gran Canaria, Tenerife, Lanzarote y Fuerteventura. Via Londres suele ser la mejor ruta y especialmente barata si estás preparado para volar en cuaiquier momento.

Alquiler de Coches

Apenas existe transporte público por lo que es casi obligatorio alquilar un vehiculo. Los precios varían mucho, son negociables y suelen ser más baratos en las ciudades que en los aeropuertos. Tienen bacas disponibles pero no siempre pulpos. Son válidos los permisos de conducir europeos, sin embargo otros requieren de una licencia internacional.

Ferries

La compania Transmed cubre en 39h el trayecto Cádiz-Canarias . Existen servicios uniendo las islas principales, tanto para vehículos como para viajeros.

Flights

Flights leave from a number of European cities bound for the Canaries. There are international airports on Gran Canaria, Tenerife, Lanzarote and Fuerteventura. The cheapest way to get there is unquestionably via London and prices can be ludicrously cheap if you're prepared to travel with little warning (see London, Pg?).

Ferries

The Canaries are serviced by a 'Transmed' car/passenger ferry that leaves Spain from Cádiz and takes approximately 39 hours. They also operate inter-island vehicle and passenger ferries and jetfoils between all the main islands.

Car Rental

Renting a car is just about obligatory but prices can vary considerably. Europeans might find their national drivers license okay, others are advised that an international license is required.

Les vols

Les liaisons aériennes existent avec la plupart des capitales européennes. Les aéroports internationaux sont sur Gran Canaria, Tenerife, Lanzarote et Fuerteventura. Le moins cher d'y aller est évidemment de Londres avec des prix dérisoires si vous êtes prêts à voyager en stand by.

Les Ferries

les Canaries sont desservis par le "Transmed", un bateau qui transporte passagers et voitures depuis Cadiz en Espagne. le trajet dure environ 39 heures. Les ferries et jetfoils opérent aussi et entre les îles principales.

Location de Voitures

Les transports en commun sont pratiquement inexistants aussi est-il quasi-obligatoire de louer une voiture mais les prix varient considérablement. Les barres sur le toit sont disponibles de temps en temps mais n'hésitez pas à prendre une paire de soft-racks. Les européens peuvent se servir de leurs permis de conduire.

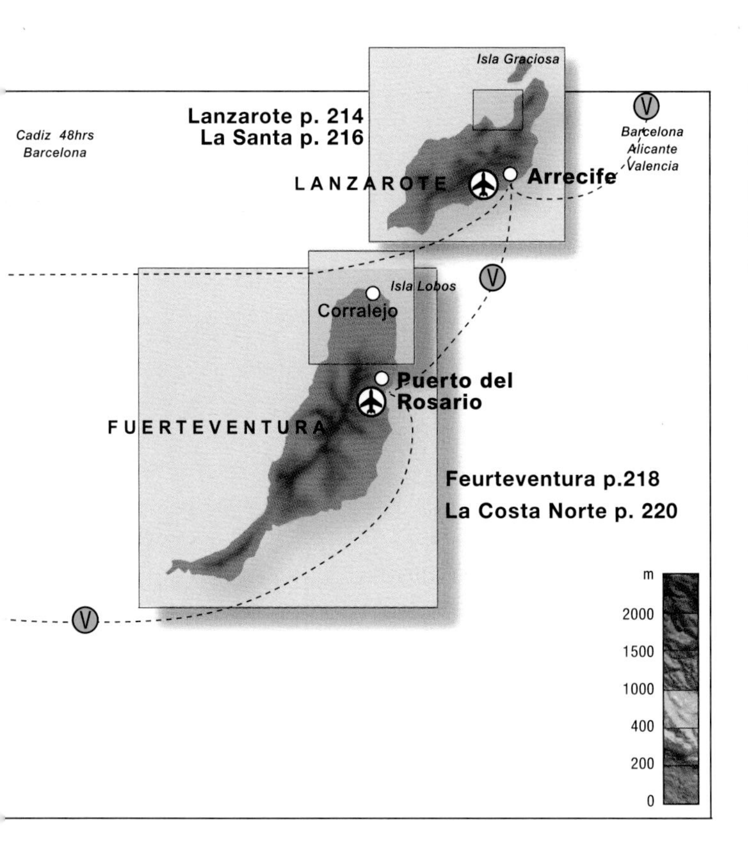

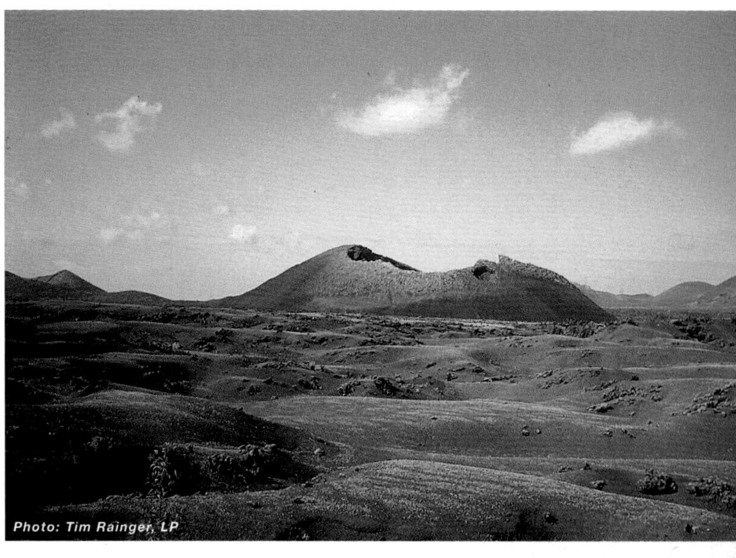

Photo: Tim Rainger, LP

Photo: Tim Rainger LP

Photo: Xavier Gonzales

Las tempreturas oscilan entre 18°C y 24°C en invierno y entre 24°C y 32°C en verano. Las precipitaciones son escasas, especialmente en Lanzarote y Fuerteventura. Los vientos predominantes soplan del NE al NO. Ocasionalmente entra el Sirocco, que sopla del Este procedente de Africa trayendo arena del desierto del Sahara en suspensión. A la mayoria de los turistas les desagrada el Sirocco, sin embargo a los surfers les encanta ya que sopla terral en las olas del oeste de las islas. El viento constante mantiene el ambiente fresco incluso en los dias más calurosos, por lo que especialmente si estás en el agua el fuerte sol pasa inadvertido. Protégete con crema.

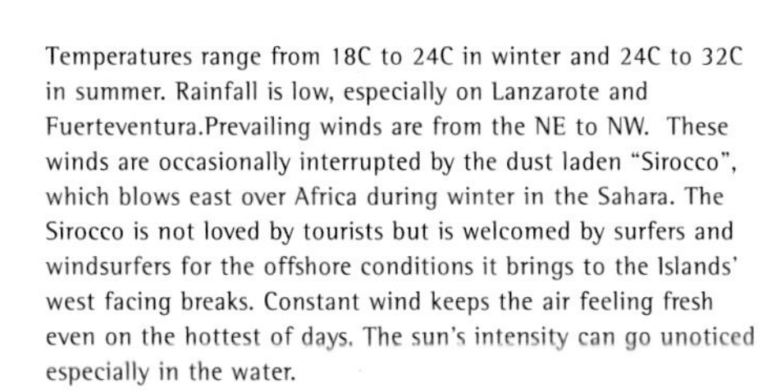

Temperatures range from 18C to 24C in winter and 24C to 32C in summer. Rainfall is low, especially on Lanzarote and Fuerteventura.Prevailing winds are from the NE to NW. These winds are occasionally interrupted by the dust laden "Sirocco", which blows east over Africa during winter in the Sahara. The Sirocco is not loved by tourists but is welcomed by surfers and windsurfers for the offshore conditions it brings to the Islands' west facing breaks. Constant wind keeps the air feeling fresh even on the hottest of days. The sun's intensity can go unoticed especially in the water.

Les températures y varient en hiver de 18 à 24 degrés en été et de 24 à 32 degrés en été. Peu de pluie, surtout sur Lanzarote et Fuerteventura. Les vents dominants viennent du NE ou NO. Ces vents sont interrompus de temps en temps par le Sirocco chargé de poussières, qui souffle à l'est depuis le Sahara africain en hiver. Les touristes ne l'apprécient guère contrairement aux surfers et windsurfers qui ont des conditions off-shore idéales sur les spots exposés ouest. Le vent constant conserve une certaine fraîcheur même les jours les plus chauds. L'intensité solaire peut être insoupçonnée, surtout dans l'eau.

Despiazamientos

Pese a que los vuelos y el alojamiento pueden ser baratos, vivir es caro. El camping es el modo más económico, pero no está muy desarrollado ni es muy aconsejable. Puedes encontrar multitud de alojamientos, pero a menudo los mejores precios se encuentran contratando todo un paquete. Los ailmentos típicos son similares a los del resto de España como la paella, las tapas y el marisco que no es especialmente barato pero si de buena calidad. Un buen seguro de viaje puede evitarte muchos problemas en el caso de accidente tanto en carretera como en el agua. Los acuerdos sanitarios vigentes con España son también aplicables en Canarias.

Travelling Around

Despite cheap air fares and the cheap accommodation, food can be expensive. Camping is probably the cheapest way to stay, though this is not encouraged by the authorities and can have unpleasant endings. Self-catering accommodation is freely available and is often most competitive as part of a package deal. Local foods include traditional Spanish standards, paella, tapas of various kinds, and especially sea food which unfortunately is not exceptionally cheap, but undoubtedly good.

Spain's health agreements with other nations are applicable. Naturally comprehensive health/travel insurance will save many headaches in the event of any serious injury in the surf or on the roads.

Se Promener

Malgré les vols et les logements bon marché, la vie peut être chère. Le camping est sans doute la façon la moins chère de loger, bien que peu encouragé par les autorités et attention à ce que ça ne finisse pas mal. Les logements avec cuisine sont faciles à trouver et sont souvent plus compétitifs quand réservés dans un forfait. La cuisine locale se compose des grands classiques de la cuisine espagnole (Paella, Tapas de toutes sortes) et surtout de produits de la mer, d'une qualité irréprochable, qui ne sont malheureusement pas donnés.

Les accords sanitaires de l'Espagne avec les autres pays sont valables. Bien sûr, une assurance complète pour Santé et Voyages vous évitera bein des ennuis si vous avez un problème en surfant ou sur la route.

Teléfonos

España	07+
Lanz, Feurte, Gran Can.	+34 28
Tenerife, Gom, Hierro, La P.	+34 22
NAT.Telefonista	003
Emergência	088
Police	091

Coste de la Vida

Restaurante *	800-2500 pts
Hotel	2000-5000 pts
Caña	125 pts
Café	100 pts

El Quemao - *Photo: Alex Williams*

Cotillo, Fuerteventura - *Photo: Peter Cade*

El Conquistador - *Photo: Jakue Andikoetxea*

El Confital - *Photo: Jakue Andikoetxea*

el surf

Muchos surfers se refieren a las Canarias como el Hawaii del Atlántico. En esta capitulo se describe con detalle cuatro de las islas: Lanzarote y Fuerteventura son mejores destinos que Tenerife y Gran Canaria, pese a que en todos las islas hay olas de gran calidad.

Los mejores recuerdos de los surfaris a Canarias son las imágenes de olas huecas romplendo sobre arrecifes de lava con un poder sólo comparable al de algunas de las olas más fuertes del planeta. Otro aspecto atractivo son los dias calurosos y soleados en los que puedes surfear a pelo o en traje corto. El invierno suele ser la mejor estación con marejadas consistentes y buen tiempo. Muchos surfers y windsurfers pasan aquí temporadas de dos a tres meses para regresar en primavera a sus hogares. Las temperaturas del agua oscilan poco durante el año, entre los 18C del invierno y los 22C del verano. Se puede pasar todo el año en traje corto, sin embargo en invierno predominan los integrales.

La masificación de los spots ha sido un problema tradicional, que en Gran Canaria y Tenerife se ha traducido en un fortísimo localismo, es difícil entender como se ha llegado a un punto tan exacerbado, incluyendo robos y agresiones que suponen el lado más feo y contraproducente del surf. Una de las razones de esta situación es la falta de respeto hacia los locales por parte de los visitantes. Es necesario un cambio de actitudes por ambas partes para poder disfrutar del surf en un entomo amigable y no agresivo. En Lanzarote la situación no es tan mala aunque cada vez hay más gente, lo cierto es que no hay demasiados locales y los spots son bastante abundantes. Fuerteventura es un destino emergente y poco poblado, donde aún no hay problemas. Sin duda quedan rompientes por surfear en todos las islas.

The Hawaii of the Atlantic is the term most used by surfers when talking about the Canary Islands. In this chapter there is detailed information on 4 of the islands. Lanzarote and Fuerteventura are unquestionably better surf destinations than Tenerife and Gran Canaria, but all the islands are popular and they all receive good waves.

Memories of surf trips to the Canaries will conjure up images of gnarly, uneven, lava reefs, hollow waves and a power comparable to just about anywhere in the world. Hot sunny days surfing in board shorts or a short wetsuit are also enticing aspects of Canarian surf. Winter is always the best season and consistent swells and good weather come at an affordable price. Many surfers and windsurfers hole up here for 2 or 3 months of the year before heading back home for spring surf. Water temperatures vary little throughout the year, remaining at a respectable 18C in winter and 22C in summer. A short suit will keep you comfortable much of the year although most people surf in a steamer in winter.

Crowds will always be a talking point here. On Gran Canaria and Tenerife the problems have led to a heavy "locals only" attitude, which although partially understandable, should never have come to the point where it is now. Rip-offs and aggro are an ugly, unnecessary side of surfing, detrimental to the activity in every way. Some of the reasons for this are the vast numbers of surf hungry foreigners who have not shown enough respect to the locals for whom these breaks are home. A change from both sides is the only hope of being able to go to these places as friends rather than enemies. Lanzarote is not as bad, although crowding is quickly getting worse but less locals and more breaks ease the situation. Fuerteventura is the newest and least populated island in the Canaries. There are definitely still breaks that go unridden on all the islands.

Le Hawaï de l'Atlantique est l'expression la plus utilisée par les surfers pour qualifier les Canaries. Dans ce chapître, l'information est donnée pour 4 îles. Lanzarote et Fuerteventura sont indiscutablement les meilleures destinations pour surfer que Tenerife et Gran Canaria bien que toutes ces îles soient connues et reçoivent de bonnes vagues.

Les souvenirs de surf trips aux Canaries évoquent des images de reefs de lave, méchants et irréguliers avec des vagues creuses dont la puissance est comparable à ce qu'on peut trouver dans le monde entier. Surfer en short ou avec un petite combinaison avec du soleil est un des aspects alléchants de la destination. L'hiver est toujours la meilleure saison où houles consistantes et climat agréable sont à un prix très abordable. Pas mal de surfers et de windsurfers se calent ici 2 à 3 mois de l'année avant de revenir pour le printemps. La température de l'eau varie très peu tout au long de l'année, oscillant autour de 18 C en hiver et 22 C en été. Un springsuit sera suffisant la plupart du temps bien que plein de surfers surfent en intégrale pendant l'hiver.

La foule sera toujours un sujet brûlant. Sur Gran Canaria et Tenerife, les problèmes ont mené à des réactions de localisme qu'on peut comprendre en partie mais qui ne devraient jamais atteindre le niveau de certaines violences maintenant. Les vols et l'aggressivité sont la face la plus condamnable du surf, qui détériorent l'activité à tous les niveaux. Une des raisons de cela est le nombre impressionnant de surfers étrangers avides qui n'ont pas manifesté suffisamment de respect à l'égard des locaux pour qui ces spots sont chez eux. Un changement des deux côtés est le seul espoir pour que chacun puisse voyager en ami et non pas en ennemi. La situation à Lanzarote est moins flagrante parce qu'il y a moins de locaux et plus de spots, même si la foule se développe rapidement. Fuerteventura apparaît maintenant comme le nouveau territoire d'exploration en étant l'île la moins peuplée des Canaries. Il y a encore des spots insurfés sur toutes ces îles.

ISLAS DE CANARIAS

Lanzarote

Pedro - *La Santa Surf*

Esta sorprendente unión de fuego y agua en la zona situada más al E del archipiélago canario parece la superficie lunar. La erosión apenas ha tenido tiempo para trabajar en la superficie y solo unos pocos líquenes sobreviven sobre la fría lava.

En la última década ha sido uno de los sitios más calurosos de Europa donde encontrar olas potentes y consistentes. Las mejores olas de la isla se encuentran en el N con dos costas llenas de picos de reef que nos ofrecen un buen surf si acompañan las condiciones. Los swells del N al O producen olas en la zona O de la isla. El swell del N pega en la costa E. El swell del S (el más común durante el verano) puede producir buenas olas por toda la costa S y E aunque durante el invierno es el swell del N y del O el que da a Lanzarote su buena reputación entre surfistas de todo el mundo.

Sin duda alguna los mejores spots son poco profundos y sobre arrecife de lava. Ha sido surfeada hasta 15 pies y esto ocurre frecuentemente. Es común el uso de tablas largas, así como que éstas se partan por el poder de las olas . La mayoría de los surfers extranjeros son ingleses, australianos, americanos, escandinavos y alemanes. Hay un montón de surfistas locales entre los que se puede incluir a un gran grupo de bodyboarders. Es entendible el fuerte espíritu de localismo, pero no llega a ser tan fuerte como en otras islas.

This astonishing union of fire and water is the easternmost in the Canarian archipelago and looks, to all intents and purposes, like the surface of the moon. Erosion has hardly had time to work on the landscape and only a few lichens survive on the barely cold lava.

For at least a decade it has been one of the hottest spots in Europe to find powerful, consistent surf. The best waves on the island are found in the north with both coasts hosting classic reefs offering good surf in an array of conditions. Swells from the N to W produce waves on the W coast and islands. N swells strike the E coast. S swells (most common in summer), can produce good waves around the S and E coasts, although it is the winter N and W swells that have built Lanzarote's reputation amongst the surfing community world-wide.

Virtually without exception, the best spots are shallow, lava reefs. Surf of up to 15ft has been ridden and this occurs with some frequency. Big boards are common, as are broken boards. The majority of foreign surfers are English, with a complement of Kiwis, Australians, Americans, Scandinavians and Germans. There is a strong local surfing population which includes a high proportion of bodyboarders, who keep largely to themselves. Whilst the spirit of localism is understandably strong here, it hasn't yet led to the behaviour seen on other Islands.

Cet étonnant mélange de feu et d'eau est l'île la plus à l'est de l'archipel canarien et ressemble virtuellement à la surface de la lune. L'erosion n'a pratiquement pas eu de temps pour faire son boulot sur le paysage et seulement quelques lichens arrivent à survivre sur cette lave à peine froide.

Pendant au moins dix ans, ça a été un des endroits les plus convoités d'Europe pour trouver des vagues puissantes et consistantes. Les meilleures vagues de l'île se trouvent au nord dont les deux côtes abritent de super reefs donnant de bonnes conditions dans pas mal de conditions. Les houles de nord et d'ouest donnent des vagues sur la côte ouest et sur les îles. Les houles de nord atteignent la côte est. Les houles de sud, surtout en été, peuvent donner de bonnes vagues sur les côtes Est et Sud, bien que ce soit les swells hivernaux de nord et d'ouest qui ont construit la réputation de Lanzarote dans la communauté du surf dans le monde.

Presque sans exception, les meilleurs spots sont sur de la lave avec peu d'eau. On peut surfer jusqu'à 5 mètres et ça arrive plus souvent qu'on ne pense. On y voit souvent des grandes planches, de même que des planches cassées. La majorité des étrangers sont anglais aidés par les néo-zélandais, les australiens, les américains, les Scandinaves et les allemands. Parmi les locaux qui sont nombreux, on trouve de plus en plus de bodyboarders, qui restent vraiment entre eux. Alors que l'esprit de localisme est naturellement fort ici, ça n'a pas mené au comportement qu'on a pu observer sur les autres îles.

1. Playa de Janubio

El pico mas conocido en el S de la costa O, con 1 km de arena negra en frente de las salinas. Las olas rompen en la playa o en los reefs del extremo N de la bahía.

The southern most known surf location on the west coast, 1km of black sand beach in front of the salt flats. Waves break on the beach and on reefs at the northern end of the bay.

Le spot référencé le plus au sud de la côte ouest, 1 km de plage de sable noir en face de marais salants. Les vagues cassent sur la plage et sur du reef au nord de la baie.

2. El Golfo

El reef de afuera del Golfo puede producir derechas tuberas. Es menos surfeado que los otros picos de la isla. El pico es visible desde el pueblo.

The outside reefs at El Golfo can produce tubey rights. They are surfed less frequently than the other breaks on the island. Visible from town.

Les reefs au large d'El Golfo peuvent donner des droites tubulaires. Ils sont surfé moins fréquemment que les autres breaks de l'île. Visible depuis la ville.

El Golfo - *Photo: Peter Cade*

3. Playa de la Cantería

1500 metros abajo del acantilado del Mirador del Rio se encuentra una buena rompiente de reef expuesta al swell del N. Está muy protegida de los vientos del S y del O. El sitio es espectacular, el gran acantilado se une al océano en un paisaje de inusual belleza. Cuando mejor funciona es en marea alta.

1500' below the cliffs of Mirador del Rio, there's a good left reef break, exposed to N swell. It recieves maximum protection from winds from the S or W. The location is breathtaking - the cliffs loom straight out of the ocean, dwarfing everything else. Works best at high tide.

1500 mètres au-dessous des falaises du Mirador del Rio, il y a une bonne gauche de reef, exposée aux swells de nord. Elle reçoit une protection maximale des vents de sud ou d'ouest. L'endroit est à couper le souffle-les falaises surgissent droitde l'océan, minimisant tout le reste. Meilleur à marée haute.

4. Jameos del Agua

Está situada en el NE. Una hilera de rocas deja una izquierda. Funciona con swell del N y vientos del SO al NO. El swell del S suele pegar en verano acompañado del viento del N. Hay posibilidad de que conecten dos picos o que cierren, dependiendo de las condiciones. Esta situado al N del parking de Jameos del Agua.

The northernmost in a string of lefthand reefs and points. They work in a N swell with a wind from SW to NW. S swells break here in summer, with accompanying N trade winds. The two peaks can either connect or close out depending on conditions. The outside reef is a favourite amongst wave-jumpers. Located north of the car park at Jameos del Agua.

Le plus au nord d'une tripotée de gauches de reefs et de "points". Elles cassent par houle de nord avce un vent de SO à NO. Les houles de sud cassent ici en été, accompagnés par les alizés de nord. Les deux pics peuvent ou connecter ou fermer selon les conditions. le reef outside est un must pour les sauteurs de vagues en windsurf. Situé au nord du parking à Jameos del Agua.

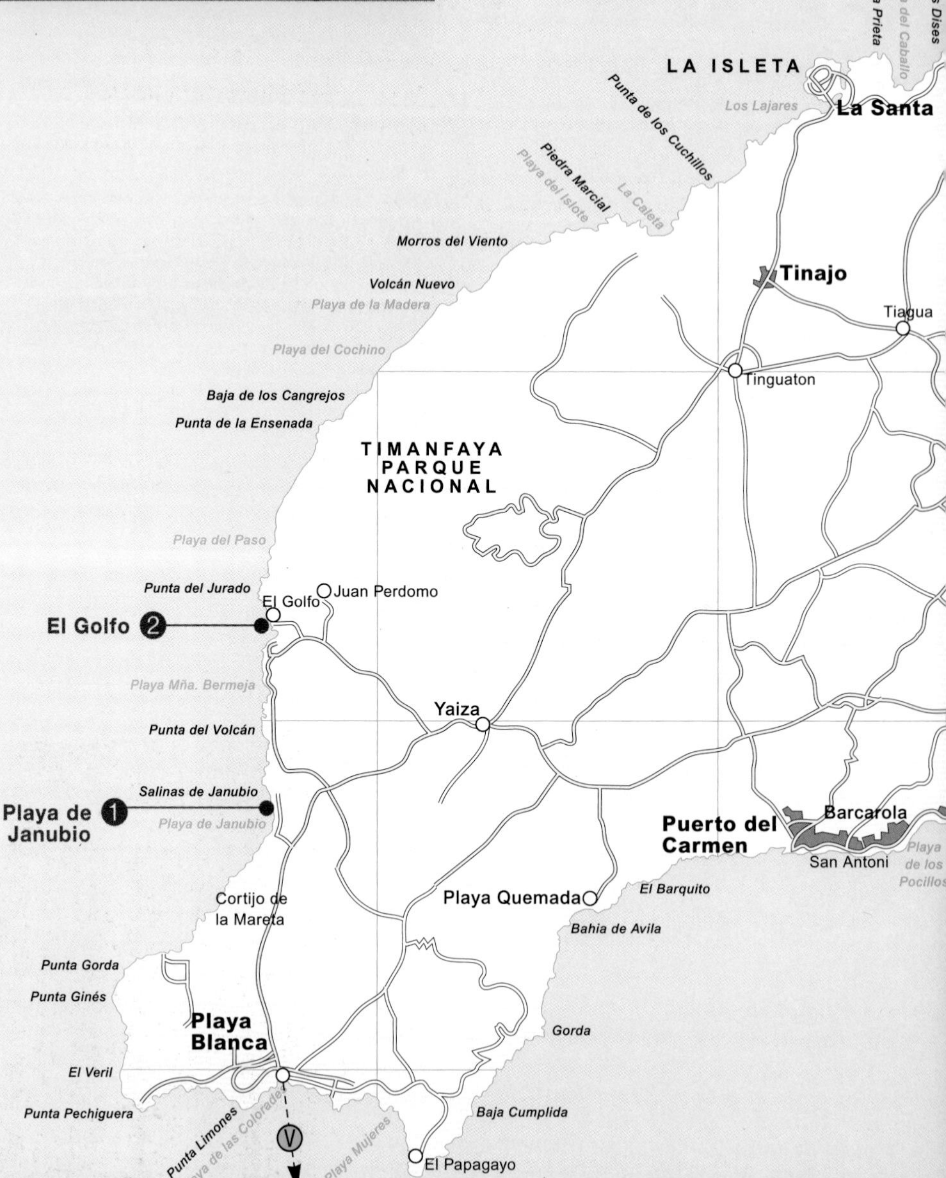

Jameos del Agua - Photo: The Gill

5. Punta Usaje

Es un pico de izquierdas poco profundo situado a medio km de Jameos del Agua, rompe junto a la orilla. Solo funciona con fuerte swell del N, la mejor marea es de media a alta. Una pista de tierra te lleva al pico desde el parking de Jameos del Agua.

A shallow left point, 1/2km south of Jameos del Agua, breaking close to the shore. It works only on a big N swell, best from mid to high tide. A dirt track leads to the break from the car park at Jameos del Agua.

Une gauche avec peu de fond, 500m au sud de Jameos del Agua, qui casse prés du bord. Ca casse seulement par grosse houle de nord, de préférence de mi-marée à marée haute. Un chemin terreux mène au spot depuis le parking de Jameos.

6. Punta de Mujeres

Rompe derecha e izquierda, justo al sur del pueblo y funciona con swell del N y del S. Cuando mejor funciona es con viento del O o NO y marea alta.

Right and left reef break, just south of the village, which works in N and S swells. Faces ESE, best in a W or NW wind at high tide.

Un spot de droites et de gauches, juste au sud du village, qui casse par houle de nord et sud. Exposé est/sud-est, mieux par vent d'ouest/nord-ouest à marée haute.

Punta Mujeres - Photo: WPR

7. Arrieta

El pico se encuentra en unas rocas junto al pueblo de Arrieta donde sale una ola que nunca cambia, poco profunda, chupona y peligrosa.

A few reefs facing ESE at the town of Arrieta, all are invariably sucky, very shallow and very dangerous.

Une poignée de reefs exposés est/sud-est sur Arrieta, qui suce tous invariablement, avec peu d'eau et un réel danger.

8. Playa de la Garita

En la parte S del pueblo de Arrieta se encuentra una pequeña playa con un pico de rocas en la izquierda. Sale una buena derecha e izquierda dando una buena ola para los principiantes y puede estar muy bueno en marea baja. Las olas rompen bajo un viejo embarcadero junto a la playa.

At the south edge of Arrieta there is a small beach with a rocky left point. Lefts and rights provide a good beginners break which can get very good. best at low tide. Waves are under threat due to the construction of a pier and beach front/promenade area.

Dans la partie sud d'Arrieta se trouve une petite plage avec une gauche de reef. Aussi des pics faciles pour les débutants qui peuvent être nets. De préférence à marée basse. Les vagues y sont menacées à cause de la construction d'une jetée sur le front de mer.

Isla Graciosa

La isla de la Graciosa cubre un área de 42 km cuadrados con una población de unas 800 personas que son pescadores y que están promocionando el turismo para ganarse la vida. A lo largo de toda la costa se encuentran playas de arenas desiertas y muchos picos de reef poco surfeados salvo por los más aventureros. El pueblo principal es Caleta del Sebo donde llega el ferry desde Orzola.

Graciosa covers an area of 42km, populated by about 800 people who rely on fishing and increasingly, tourism, for their livelihood. The coastline has many deserted white sandy beaches and around these beaches unridden reefs await the adventurous. The main town is Caleta del Sabo where the ferry arrives from Orzola.

Graciosa couvre une zone de 42 kms, avec environ 800 habitants qui vivent de la pêche et de plus en plus du tourisme. Le littoral a pas mal de plages de sable blanc vierges truffés de reefs insurfés qui appellent à l'aventure. La ville principale est Caleta del Sabo où le ferry arrive d'Orzola.

Costa Este - Photo: The Gill

La Santa

Pedro - *La Santa Surf*

Morro Negro - *Photo: Alex Williams*

Este tramo de costa va desde el pueblo de la Santa hasta la punta N de la playa de Famara. Esta catalogado como una de las mejores zonas de olas de Europa. Recoge los swells del N y O y ofrece numerosas rompientes orientadas a diferentes direcciones. Hay una buena playa para los principiantes, con buenos reefs accesibles para surfear todavía no descubiertos.

Se puede encontrar alojamiento en Famara y con suerte en la Santa (ver anuncio) o sino tambien en el complejo deportivo (donde hay un supermercado). Mucha gente hace camping junto a Morro Negro en una explanada que da a la rompiente. Tambien en San Juan. Anda con cuidado por que suele haber problemas, vigila bien tus cosas.

La Santa to the northern tip of Playa Famara, must rate as one of the best wave locations in Europe. It picks up all N and W swells and offers a variety of breaks facing in numerous directions. There is a good beach for beginners, a number of accessible reefs combined with the strong smell of undiscovered surf.

One can find accommodation at La Santa, Famara and also at the sports complex. Pedro from La Santa Surf can organise most options and if you want to camp (which is becoming a problem with the police) it's best to consult with him first. There is a supermarket in the village.

La partie côtière qui va du village de la Santa à l'extrémité nord de la plage de Famara peut se targuer d'être une des meilleures zones de surf en Europe. Elle prend toutes les houles de nord à ouest en offrant une variété de spots exposés différemment. On trouve une bonne plage pour les débutants, bon nombre de reefs facilement accessibles qui flairent bon le surf inexploré.

On peut se loger sur Famara, peut-être sur La Santa ou sur le complexe sportif avec un supermarché aussi. Plein de trippers campent tout prés de Morro Negro sur un terrain nivelé surplombant le break. On peut crécher aussi à San Juan. La sécurité, cependant, est un poblème. Sachez-le.

Spencer Hargraves, El Quemao - *Photo: Mike Searle*

1. El Quemao

Rompe una corta y chupona izquierda cerca de la orilla frente al pueblo de la Santa. El mejor swell es el del O al NO acompañado de vientos del S al E. El pico se ve desde muchos sitios del pueblo. Se encuentra junto al puerto.

A short sucky left breaking close to the shore in front of the village of La Santa. Optimum swell is from the W to NW with accompanying S to E winds. The break is visible from many vantage points in town. From the village of La Santa, walk to the harbour.

Une gauche courte qui suce cassant prés de la Santa. Le swell idéal vient d'O/NO avec des vents de sud et d'est. Le spot est visible de pas mal de points saillants dans le village. Depuis le village, marchez jusqu'au port.

El Quemao - *Photo: Alex Williams*

2. La Santa Left

Aqui rompe un potente pico sobre las rocas en marea baja, pero el agua las cubre, es excelente; rápido, chupón y consistente. Recoge todos los swells y amenudo suele ser la única rompiente que funciona en toda la isla cuando el viento es de componente N y en toda la costa O esta pegando onshore. La derecha que es mas corta siempre es surfeada. El pico se ve desde la carretera general.

A thick lipped beast breaks over exposed rock at low tide, but as the water covers it, the reef turns on the goods; fast, sucky and consistent. It collects all swell and is often the only break working on the island when the wind is in the N quarter and the other W coast spots are onshore. A right which is always shorter, is often ridden. The break is visible from the main road.

Un gros barrel avec une lèvre épaisse qui casse sur des caillasses qui émergent à marée basse. Quand la marée recouvre le reef, ça envoie encore le pâté. Rapide, ultra-creux et consistant. Récupère toutes les houles en étant souvent le seul spot qui marche sur l'île quand le vent vient du nord et que les autres spots de la côte ouest sont on-shore. Une droite qui est toujours plus courte et donc rarement surfée. Parfaitement matable depuis la route.

3. Morro Negro

Rompe una seria derecha sobre reef al final del S de "La Isleta". Este reef puede aguantar fuerte swell y ha sido surfeada hasta 15 pies. Generalmente rompen 3 secciones independientes pero en dias buenos pueden conectar dando una larga y potente ola. No tan conocido por sus tubos como en otros picos de la isla, es uno de los spots que mas gente atrae en toda la isla, cuando mejor funciona es con swell del N al NO. Entrar y salir puede ser dificil, algunos locales saltan directamente, otros se contentan con remar desde dentro.

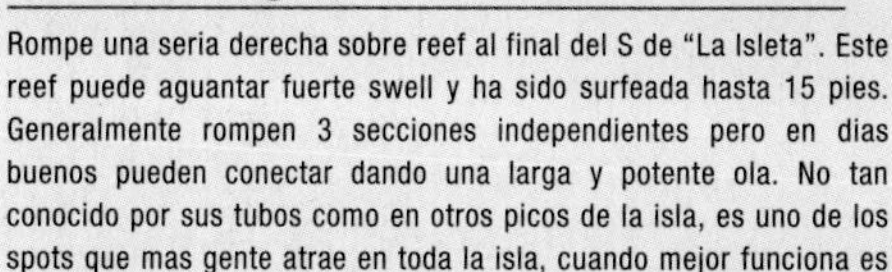

A serious right reef breaking on the S end of 'La Isleta'. The reef can hold big swells and has been ridden up to 15ft. It generally has three sections which work independently, though on a good day all can connect up, giving long, powerful rides. Not as renowned for its tubes as other breaks on the island, nonetheless it is one of the biggest draw cards in the islands, at its best when the swell is N to NW. Getting in and out can be a difficult exercise, some of the locals jump off the end of the point straight out the back, others are content to paddle around to the break from the inside.

Une droite qui fait pas rire casse au sud de la "Isleta".Le reef peut tenir jusqu'à gros puisqu'a été surfé jusqu'à 5m. Souvent 3 sections qui marchent indépendamment bien que sur les bons jours, elles peuvent connecter et donner des vagues longues et puissantes. Pas aussi réputé pour ses tubes que les voisines mais considérée comme un des atouts de l'île, de préférence quand la houle vient de N/NO. Se mettre à l'eau et sortir peut être un exercice difficile, certains locaux se jettent à l'eau du bout de la pointe direct au line-up, d'autres se contentent de ramer depuis l'inside.

4. Boca del Abajo

Una izquierda que chupa y luego se deshace en una profunda bahía. La ola es excelente hasta 10 pies y cuando el swell es fuerte es relativamente facil salir remando.

A left which sucks off the sea bottom and breaks into a calm, deeper bay. The wave is excellent to 10ft, and even when the swell is big, the paddle out remains relatively easy.

Une gauche qui aspire depuis le fond et qui casse dans une baie calme, plus profonde. La vague est géniale jusqu'à 3m et même quand c'est gros, la rame reste relativement facile.

5. Caleta de Cabelo

Una izquierda situada al O de la bahía, que rompe sobre un fondo poco profundo. Cuando mejor funciona es con swell del N o del NE en marea alta.

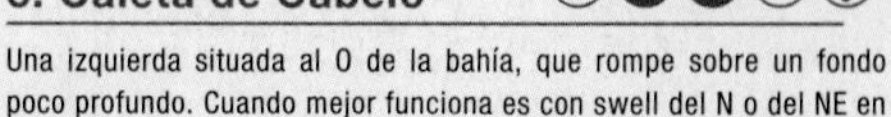

A left located on the W side of the bay, breaking in shallow water. It's best on a N or NW swell at high tide.

Une gauche située à l'ouest de la baie, qui casse à fleur d'eau. Meilleur par houle de nord à nord-ouest à marée haute.

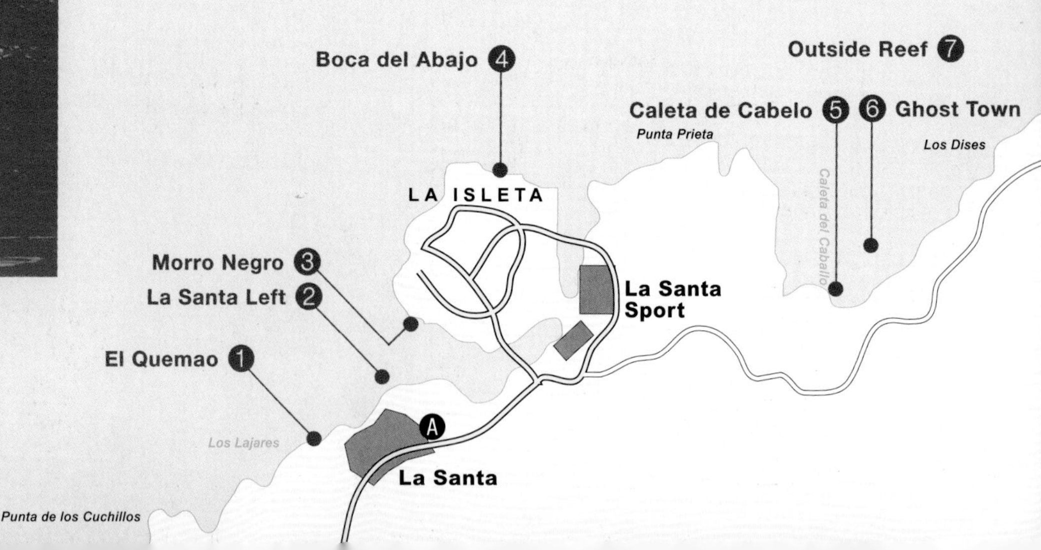

San Juan - Photo: Alex Williams

6. Ghost Town

Un espectacular pico rompe en la bahía a la derecha del pueblo de Caballo cuando las demas rompientes esta mas grande de dos metros. Tiene reputación como una de las rompientes con olas de mayor tamaño de todo Canarias.

A spectacular peak breaks in the bay to the right of the town of Caballo when other breaks are 2mtrs+. Has a reputation as one of the Canaries foremost big wave breaks.

Un pic ahurrissant qui casse dans la baie à droite de la ville de Caballo quand les autres spots font plus de 2m. Considéré comme un des spots de gros proéminents des Canaries.

7. Outside Reef

Una potente ola rompe a 500 metros hacia el mar con fuerte swell del N cuando esta mas grande de 4 metros. No consta de que haya sido surfeada y existe muy poca información sobre este pico. Puede que sea la ola mas grande de todo Canarias, puede ser un mito.

A bombora breaks 500mtrs out to sea when the swell is max N, from 4m and up. We've no confirmed accounts of anyone surfing it - very little in the way of real information exists. It could be the big wave of the Canaries, it could be a myth.

Un reef à 500 mètres au large quand la houle vient trés au nord, à partir de 4m. On a aucune confirmation de savoir qui a surfé là, pas grand monde à vrai dire. Ca pourrait être le Waïmea des Canaries comme une hallu complète.

8. San Juan

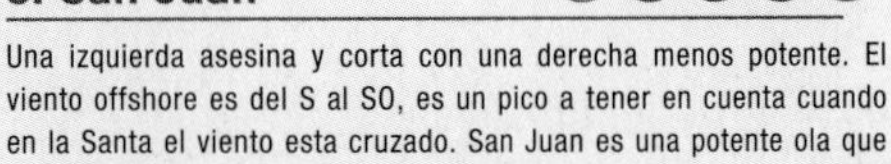

Una izquierda asesina y corta con una derecha menos potente. El viento offshore es del S al SO, es un pico a tener en cuenta cuando en la Santa el viento esta cruzado. San Juan es una potente ola que puede atraer swell cuando en los demas sitios esta muy pequeño para surfear.

A killer left and a shorter, less consistent right. Offshores are S to SW - a valuable backstop when La Santa is cross shore. San Juan is a powerful wave which can have swell when other breaks are too small to surf.

Une gauche de folie et une droite plus courte et moins régulière. L'off-shore est au S/SO- une alternative intéressante quand la Santa est cross-shore. San Juan ne manque pas de puissance quand les autres spots sont trop petits pour surfer.

9. La Caleta de Famara

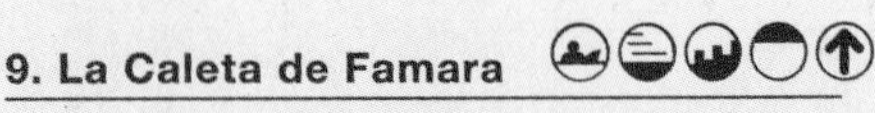

Otro pico de rocas que produce buenas izquierdas y el mejortamaño es de 1 a 3 metros. Se sale remando frente al pico. Mejor en marea alta.

Another shallow reef produces more dredgy lefts best surfed between 1 and 3m. Paddle out from the breakwater. Best at high tide.

Un autre reef craignos qui envoie encore des gauches assassines, plus surfables entre 1 et 3m. Ramez depuis la jetée. Meilleur à marée haute.

10. Playa de Famara

Excelentes olas de playa con poca gente. Generalmente el N esta mas grande pero para llegar alli hay que conducir atraves de unas pistas de tierra atravesando una pequeña montaña (esta protegido de los vientos del NO) antes de descender hacia la costa. Uno de los mejores spots para surfear especialmente con condiciones de Sirocco.

Excellent beach waves, without intense crowd scenes. Generally the N is bigger, but to get there you have to drive up the side of the mountain range (which shelters it from the NE winds), before descending to the coast. One of Lanzarote's best wavesailing spots, especially in Sirocco conditions.

Super beach break sans les tensions de la Chine. Généralement, le nord est plus gros mais pour y aller, il faut rouler en haut du flanc de la montagne (qui abrite le spot des vents de NE) avant de redescendre sur la côte. Un des meilleurs spots de windsurf, surtout avec le Sirocco.

11. Las Bajas

Situado al N de la bahía es una rompiente de roca que rompe a 200metros del SO de la roca llamada las Bajas. Hay una larga remada. El pico es visible desde la carretera N de la playa. Es una ola peligrosa no apta para principiantes.

Located at the N end of the bay is a reef which breaks 200m to the south west of rocks called Las Bajas. It's a long paddle out to sea, but obviously worth it if conditions are right. The break is visible from the road north of the beach. It's a dangerous wave, not for beginners. Sharky spot, rarely, if ever surfed.

Situé au nord de la baie, ce reef qui déroule environ 200m au sud ouest de ces rochers appelés Las Bajas. Il faut aller loin au large mais ca vaut le coup de rame quand les conditions sont bonnes. On peut mater depuis la route au nord de la plage. C'est dangereux, débutants s'abstenir.

Playa Famara - Photo: W.P.R.

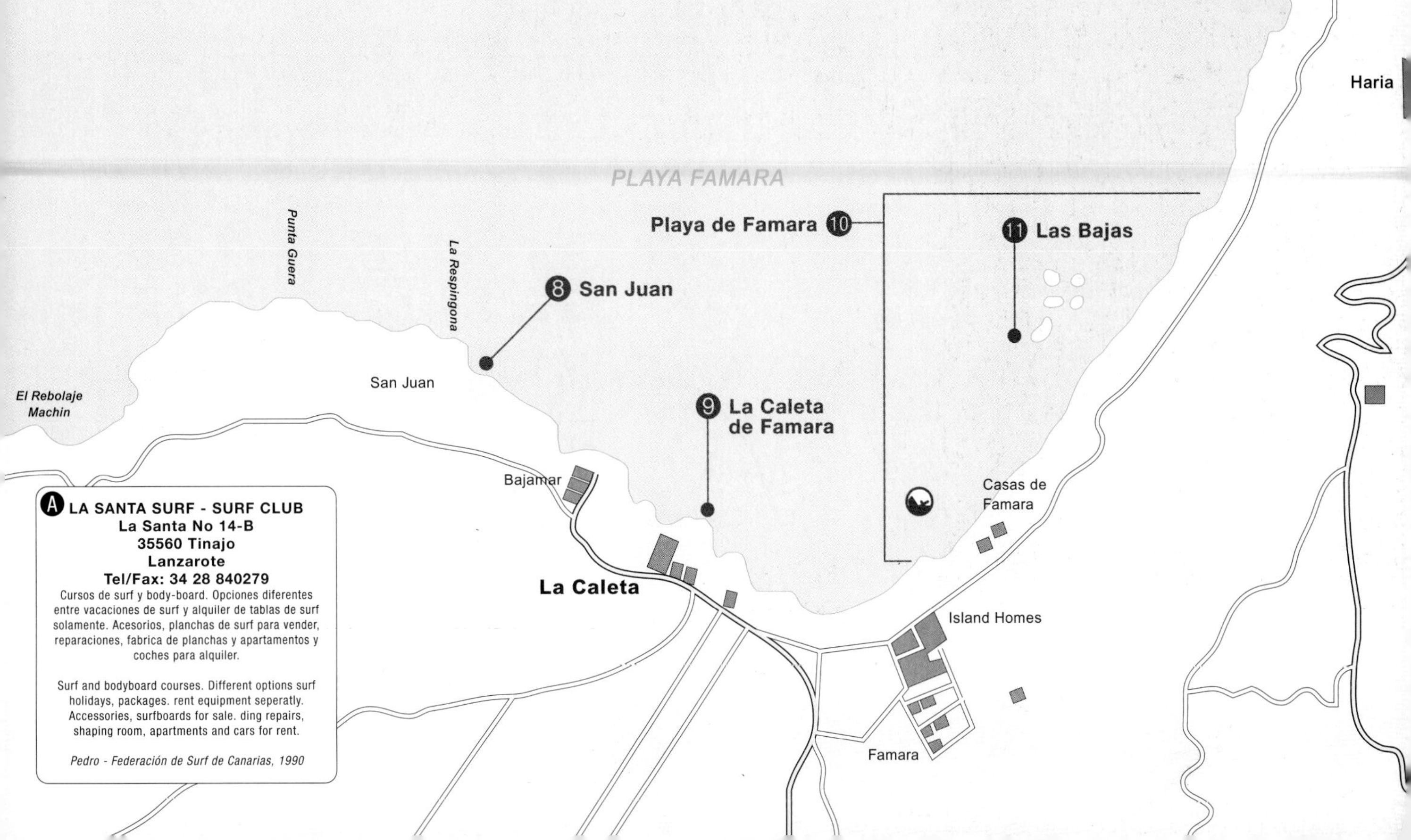

A LA SANTA SURF - SURF CLUB
La Santa No 14-B
35560 Tinajo
Lanzarote
Tel/Fax: 34 28 840279

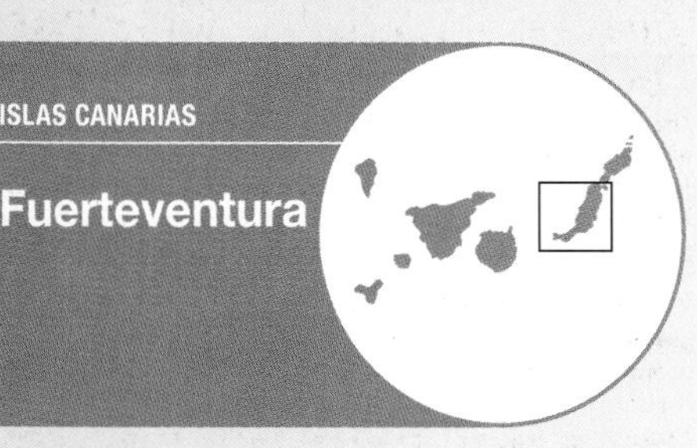

Fuerteventura

Fuerteventura es la segunda isla más grande de las Islas Canarias, situada solamente a 90 km de la costa Africana. Es conocida como "Isla de la Soledad" y tiene mas kilómetros de playas de arena que las otras islas Canarias. Muchas partes de la isla están desiertas y está considerada como uno de los mejores sitios de Europa para hacer surf heavy y con poca gente. La costa N y O y la Isla de Lobos son las principales zonas de surf, ya que la costa E y SE son mejores para el windsurf o el baño.

La costa O recibe potentes marejadas pero el acceso es muy dificultoso. Entre Cotillo y Punta del Tigre se pueden encontrar miles de reefs y playas de arena a lo largo de la costa que están totalmente expuestos a las olas del Atlántico, ya que es un sitio muy desolado en medio de una naturaleza desolada y un mar embravecido, donde se encuentran unos pocos pueblos pesqueros. A lo largo de la costa hay muy pocas carreteras e incluso los 4X4 suelen tener dificultades.

La península de Jandia recibe los swells y es un espléndido sitio con un gran potencial de olas sin descubrir en el sur de la isla. Las playas de arena que corren a lo largo de la zona E son preciosas cuando están vacías, con un agua azul turquesa y donde la multitud no es común. En estos spots las mejores olas rompen a bastantes kilómetros de la zona turística. Sotavento es el sitio con más actividad y puede ser un buen sitio base.

Fuerteventura is the second largest island in the Canary group located only 90km from the coast of Africa. It is commonly known as "Isla de Soledad" and has more sandy beaches than the other islands. Many remain deserted thus it rates as one of the best places in Europe to surf heavy, uncrowded waves. The N and W coasts and Lobos Island are the main areas, with the E and S shores offering better windsurfing and swimming conditions.

The west coast receives masses of swell but access is extremely restricted. Between Cotillo and Punta del Tigre, miles of reefs and sandy beaches form a coastline that has little protection from Atlantic waves. Because of its desolate nature and wild seas, only a few fishing villages punctuate its length. Roads to the coast are few and even 4wd vehicles experience difficulties.

The Jandia Peninsula also picks up swell and there is still tremendous undiscovered potential in the south of the island. The sandy beaches which line its eastern shores are beautiful if a little empty, but the water is turquoise blue and crowds are not commonplace around most of the surf spots - the best waves break miles from most tourist activity. Sotavento is the most popular activity centre and can be a good place to base yourself.

Fuerteventura est la deuxième plus grande île des Canaries en superficie, à seulement 90 kms de l'Afrique. On l'appelle souvent 'l'île de la solitude" avec plus de plages sablonneuses que toutes les autres îles. Beaucoup restent désertes c'est pourquoi c'est une des meilleures destinations d'Europe pour surfer des vagues qui cartonnent sans la foule. Les côtes nord et ouest et l'île de Lobos sont les zones principales, sachnat que les côtes sud et est sont plus propices au windsurf ou à la baignade.

la côte ouest reçoit énormément de swell mais son accés est extrêmement limité. Entre Cotillo et Punta del Tigre, des kilomètres de reefs et de plages forment un littoral trés peu protégé des vagues de l'Atlantique. A cause de la désolation ambiante et ses eaux agitées, peu de villages de pêcheurs jalonnent cette côte. Les routes y sont rares et même les 4x4 ont du mal à passer.

La peninsule de Jandia est aussi bien exposée aux houles et il existe encore un potentiel incroyable au sud de l'île. Les plages de sable qui bordent le rivage oriental sont superbes mais un peu vides; l'eau y est bleu turquoise et c'est carrément rare d'être trop nombreux autour des spots. Les meilleures vagues cassent à des kilomètres de toute activité touristique. Sotavento en est un peu le centre; c'est un camp de base assez pratique.

1. Punta del Tigre

El swell viene rápido de aguas profundas formando una rompiente veloz y poderosa sobre un reef de lava poco profundo. Pocas veces surfeada por lo remoto del lugar, pero un buen sitio a tener en cuenta con swell del sur.

Swell comes out of deep water fast and break with speed and power over a shallow lava reef. Rarely surfed due to its remoteness, but worth a look if there's a south swell running.

La houle arrive en eau profonde et forme une vague rapide et puissante sur un reef de lave à fleur d'eau. rarement surfé à cause de son isolement, amis vaut le coup d'oeil quand ça rentre.

2. Playa de Pared

Una playa de arena negra que recoge mucho swell. En esta playa puede romper desde medio hasta 3 metros. En la zona S de Fuerteventura es muy difícil encontrar surfers ya que está muy poco explorado pero tiene un potencial de olas inmenso. Las corrientes son mayores en esta parte de la costa, por lo que debes tener especial precaución. Aparca cerca de la playa.

Black sand beach that picks up loads of swell which breaks on any tide from 1-10ft. Surfers and wave-jumpers are a much rarer sight in southern Fuerteventura and this area is little explored but potential is immense. Rips are strong along this part of the coast so take extra care. Parking near the beach.

Une plage de sable noir trés bien exposée avec des vagues à n'imorte quelle marée de 30 cms à 3m. Les surfers et windsurfers se sont plutôt rares au sud de l'île et cette zone peu explorée a un potentiel phénoménal. Les courants le long de cette route sont forts, méfiance! Se garer prés de la plage.

Sud Oeste - Photo: The Gill

Photo: Peter Cade

Playa de los Muertos
Punta de la Nao
Punta del Viento
Punta del Canal
Playa de Garcey
Risco Blanco
Cueva de Lobos
Playa de Anamay
Punta Anamay
Punta de las Goteras
Chilegua
Playa Negras
Playa de Ugan
Playa de las Hermosas
Punta de Guadalupe
Playa de la Pared
Playa de la Pared 2
Playa del Viejo Rey
Punta de Burraco
Los Roquetes
Agua Tres Piedras
Playa de Barlovento de Jandia
Matas Blancas
Costa Calma
Esmeralda
Jandia
Punta de los Molinillos
Playa de Matas Blancas
Punta Paloma
Playa de Puerto Rico
Punta de Barlovento
Caleta de la Madera
Roque del Moro
Punta Pesebre
Punta Cotillo
Punta del Tigre
Punta de Jandia
Playa de Sotavento de Jandia
El Esquinzo
Boca del Esquinzo
4 Sotavento
Morro del Jable
Stella Canaris
Playa Jandia
Playa de las Pilas
Playa de Juan Gómez
Punta del Viento
Punta del Tigre 1

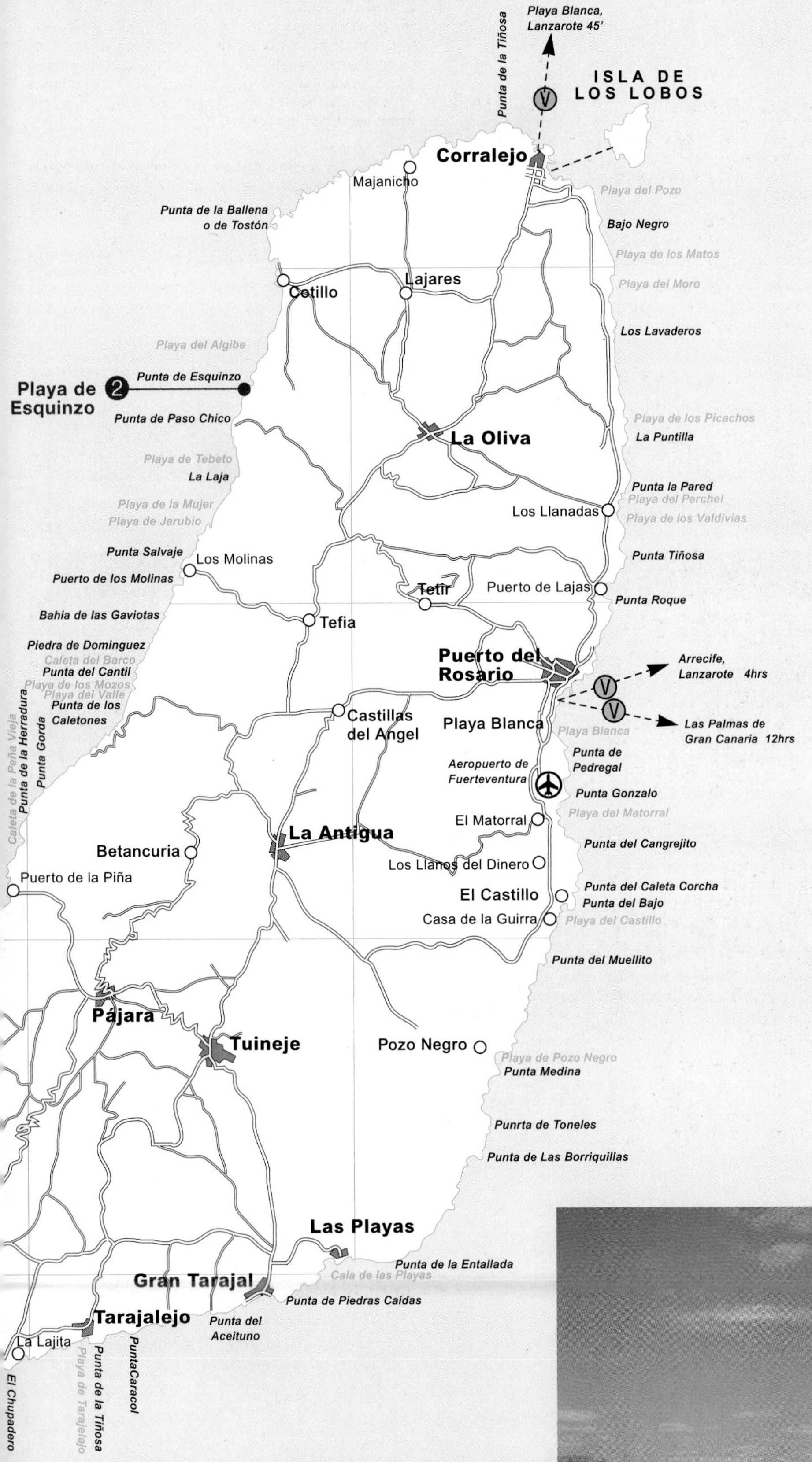

3. Playa de Esquinzo

Hard to find and consequently crowd free. It receives a lot of swell and works best at high tide. Esquinzo is signposted off the main road north of La Oliva. From there the road leads through the desert following an unmarked road with many unmarked turn-offs. If you don't end up here, then you could well end up somewhere better. Good luck!

Hard to find and consequently crowd free. It receives a lot of swell and works best at high tide. Esquinzo is signposted off the main road north of La Oliva. From there the road leads through the desert following an unmarked road with many unmarked turn-offs. If you don't end up here, then you could well end up somewhere better. Good luck!

Hard to find and consequently crowd free. It receives a lot of swell and works best at high tide. Esquinzo is signposted off the main road north of La Oliva. From there the road leads through the desert following an unmarked road with many unmarked turn-offs. If you don't end up here, then you could well end up somewhere better. Good luck!

The Gorge - *Photo:Peter Cade*

4. Sotavento

Una de las playas más famosas de todo el mundo para practicar windsurf con vientos por encima de fuerza 5 una media de 23 a 25 días al mes. Ten precaución con los fuertes vientos offshore a no ser que quieras viajar a Sudamérica. En mareas fuertes (con luna nueva y llena) se forma una laguna frente al hotel, perfecta para la navegación de velocidad, salvo por el excesivo número de windsurfers atraidos a este lugar. Muchos funeros se quedan en Las Dunas para evitar trasladarse muy lejos con el equipo.

One of the world's most famous windsurfing beaches, with wind above force 5 on average 23-25 days a month! Beware of strong offshore winds unless you're planning a trip to South America. On big tides (new and full moon) a lagoon is created by the hotel that's perfect for speed-sailing, except for the crowds that such a good spot attracts. Many sailors launch at Las Dunas to avoid having to carry equipment far.

Une des plages de windsurf les plus connues dans le monde, avec des vents de force 5 en moyenne de 23 à 25 jours par mois. Attention aux venst off-shore à décorner les boeufs à moins que vous ne vouliez aller en Amerique du sud. Pendant les grandes marées (pleine et nouvelle lunes), un lagon se forme prés de l'hotel, ce qui est parfait pour faire de la vitesse, sauf que tout le monde est attiré par ce spot. Pas mal de voileux démarrent depuis Las Dunas pour éviter de porter le matos jusque là.

Playa del Jandia - *Photo: Peter Cade*

Costa Norte - *Photo: Tim Rainger, LP*

La Costa Norte

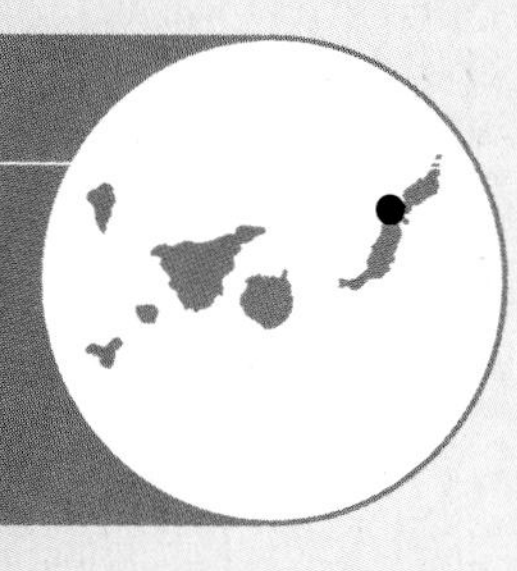

Acceso a la costa Norte es fácil; un camino corre para 20kms al lado de arrecifes volcánicos que recogen todo el swell del N. Corralejo es donde la mayoría de surfistas se alojan y hay buenos bares, restaurantes, cafeteras y supermercados asi que es un sitio donde es fácil cuidarse pero a la vez no es muy barato.

Access to the N coast is easy; a track runs for 20kms alongside volcanic reefs which pick up all N swell. Corralejo is where most surfers stay and there are good bars, restaurants, supermarkets, patisseries and cafés. It's an easy place to look after yourself, though once again not extremely cheap.

L'acces sur la cote nord est facile. On trouve un chemin qui mene aux reefs volcaniques sur 20kms, qui chopent tous les swells de nord. Corralejo est la village ou la plupart des surfers se logent, on y trouve de bons bars, des restaurants, des supermarches, des patisseries et des cafes. Il est facile de se debrouiller seul, meme si ça n'est pas toujours bon marché.

1. Cotillo (South Beach)

En el extremo sur de este pueblo polvoriento de estilo mejicano se encuentra una extensa playa de arena. El asentamiento de esta playa presenta un reborde que hace que la ola salga siempre en mismo sitio independiente de la marea. Es famoso para el Wave-jumping y se halla protegido de los vientos del norte.

At the southern end of this dusty, Mexican style village is a long sandy beach. The sea bed has a distinctive ledge which causes the waves to jack up in virtually the same place whatever the tide state or swell size. It's a popular wave-jumping spot and the northern end receives protection from N winds.

A l'extrémité est de ce village poussiéreux, style Mexique, commence une longue vague de sable. Le littoral a un angle particulier qui font lever les vagues presque au même endroit quelles que soient la marée ou la houle. Encore un spot de prédilection pour windsurfers, du côté nord, c'est protégé des vents de nord.

Mike Raven, Cotillo - *Photo: Alex Williams*

2. Spew Pits

Este reef se llena cuando en la costa N está pequeño. Con el Siroco los vientos soplarán del E durante mucho tiempo, y es Offshore. Se encuentra al norte del puerto de Cotillo.

A reef that has its name for a reason! A popular spot that gets busy when the North shore is small. If the Sirocco is on, then winds will often blow easterly for long periods of time, and that's offshore! North of the harbour in Cotillo.

Un reef qui n'a pas volé son nom (le pic qui crache)! Un pic connu qui devient encombré quand c'est petit sur la côte nord. Si le Sirocco souffle alors les vents d'est seront réguliers, ça signifie off-shore! Au nord du port c'est Cotillo.

The Bubble - *Photo: Peter Cade*

3. Heirro

En la misma bahía al oeste de Yarro. Derechas de buena calidad pero la gente no suele llegar hasta aquí por la carretera. Las condiciones óptimas se dan aquí con swell del N y NO y viento del sur.

In the same bay west of Yarro. More good quality rights, but the crowds often don't travel this far along the track. Optimum conditions here are a N or NW swell of any size (it can hold a swell) and a wind from down south.

Dans la même baie que Yarro. Encore des bonnes droites mais les gens ont tendance à ne pas aller aussi loin sur le chemin. Des conditions optima ici par n'importe quelle houle de N/NO (tient la taille) et un vent de sud.

4. Yarro

No tan tubera como la derecha, pero es una buena ola con paredes ideales para maniobras. Recoge mucho swell dando olas divertidas hasta cuando está pequeño. Se llena de gente.

Not as tubey as the right, but it's still an excellent wave with good walls for manoeuvers. Picks up a lot of swell giving fun rides even when it's small. It can also get crowded.

Pas aussi tubulaire que la droite mais c'est également une vague top avec des bons murs pour les manoeuvres. Chope pas mal de houle et même quand c'est petit ça vaut le coup. Du monde aussi.

5. The Bubble

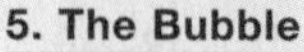

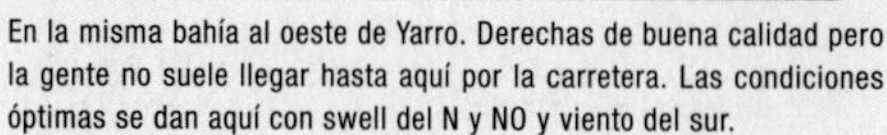

Una de las mejores y más consistentes olas de la costa norte rompe en un reef en la franja este de la bahía. Sale una derecha con tubos excepcionales en el típico reef volcánico. Lo más habitual y seguro es de media marea a alta. La ola se suele llenar de gente pero la calidad compensa la cantidad. Para salir rema por las rocas al oeste de la bahía. Se encuentra a 1 Km al oeste de Majanicho. Se han hecho pequeños refugios circulares detrás de una furgoneta vieja abandonada.

One of the most consistent waves on the north shore breaks on the reef at the eastern fringe of the bay. A right of exceptional quality tubes mercilessly on a typically sharp and shallow volcanic reef. Mid to high tide is safer and more popular. Can get crowded. Located about 1km west of Majanicho. Small circular shelters have been set up beyond a wrecked VW Kombi.

Une des vagues les plus consistantes de la côte nord casse sur du récif sur la limite orientale de la baie. Une droite dont les tubes sont d'une qualité exceptionnelle en cassant sans pitié sur de la lave coupante. Mieux vaut éviter la marée basse. Il peut y avoir pas mal de monde. Environ 1km à l'ouest de Majanicho. Des petits abris ont été construits sous une carcasse de van VW.

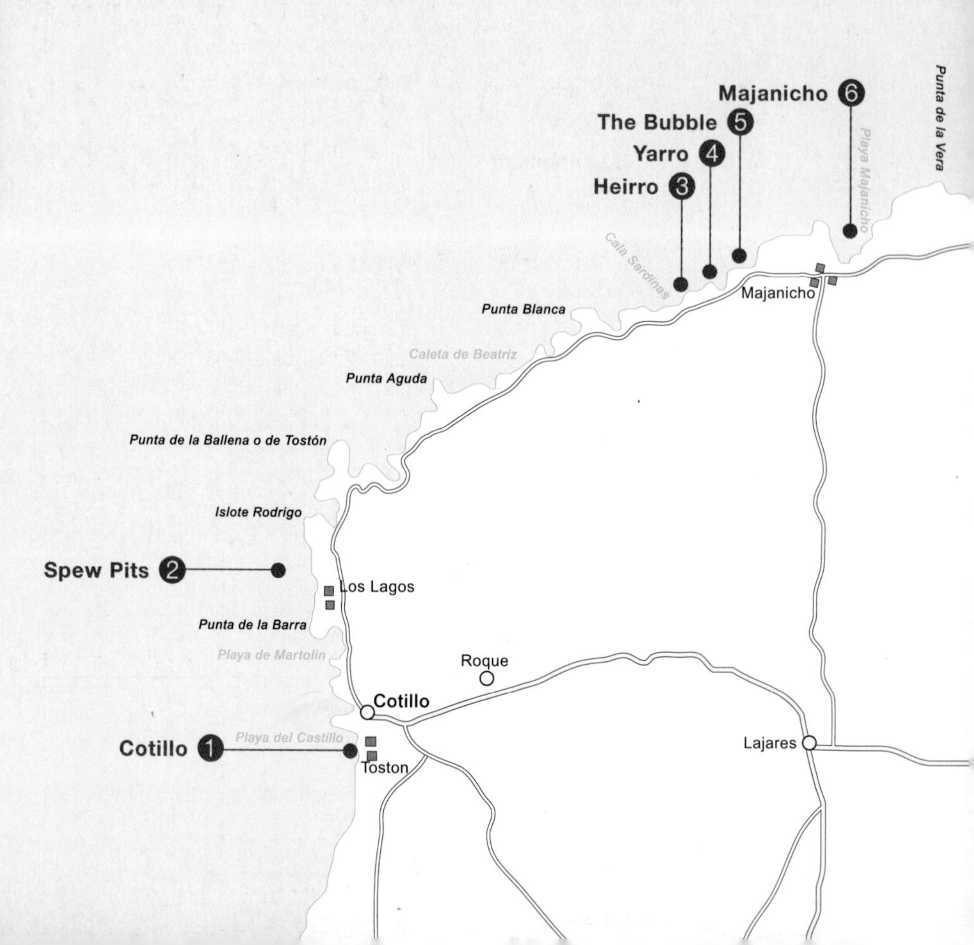

6. Majanicho

A medio camino de la estropeada carretera del norte se encuentra este destartalado pueblo pesquero. La bahía en la que se asienta produce buenas olas de derecha. Puede coger buen tamaño, y hay que tener cuidado en las caídas.

About halfway along the car battering N track lies a ramshackle fishing village. The bay on which the village has been built around can provide right reef/point waves. They remain surfable up to a good size, but even if it isn't big, watch out! It can be a dangerous place to wipe out.

A peu prés à mi-chemin de la route défoncée qui va vers le nord se trouve un petit village de pêche délabré. La baie sur laquelle le village a été construit peut avoir des droites de "point" sur du reef. Ca tient une taille respectable mais quand c'est gros, ATTENTION, c'est pas l'endroit idéal pour tomber..

Majanicho - *Photo: Alex Williams*

7. Mechihonas

Recoge más swell que el resto de spots de Fuerteventura. Las derechas no son muy fuertes y las izquierdas rompen en aguas más profundas. Es un sitio popular ya que los picos cambian y la gente queda desperdigada por la zona.

Picks up more swell than most of Fuerteventura's spots. The waves here are peaky rights and lefts that break in relatively deep water (for Fuerteventura). A popular spot but because the peaks shift, the crowds get spread around the point.

Chope plus de houle que la plupart des spots de Fuerteventura. Les vagues ici sont des droites-gauches en pic qui cassent dans pas mal d'eau (tout est relatif). Un spot convoité mais comme lepic est changeant, la foule s'étale autour du "point".

8. Suicides

Se trata de un reef de aguas poco profundas en el que no se surfea mucho. El nombre le viene de que los errores se pagan muy caros. Se encuentra a 1 Km al O de Generosa.

A good but seldom surfed reef breaking in shallow water. Suicides implies correctly - mistakes can be painful! There is no indicator as to the location of the break. It is about 1km west of Generosa.

Un reef rarement surfé qui casse dans peu d'eau. Suicides signifie en clair que chaque erreur peut être douloureuse. Il n'y a aucun panneau pour indiquer le spot. Environ 1km à l'ouest de Generosa.

9. Generosa

Es otro reef de izquierda tubera que se encuentra a 1 Km de Shooting Gallery. Las olas son muy buenas y no se llena tanto de gente. A un Km de Shooting Gallery hay un ligero desvío hacia la derecha. A no ser que el swell sea muy grande la ola no será visible.

Another hollow left. The waves can be good here and it doesn't get as crowded as many of the other breaks. About 1km after Shooting Gallery is a slight run off to the right. The wave will not be visible unless the swell is huge.

Une autre gauche creuse. Les vagues peuvent être bonnes ici et y'a moins de monde que sur les autres spots. A peu prés 1km de Shooting Gallery, un sentier descend sur la droite. La vague sera invisible à moins que ce soit énorme.

10. Shooting Gallery

Reef de izquierdas orientado hacia el NE. En marea baja cubre poco, saliendo una ola tubera y rápida. Al subir la marea es más fácil. Es conocido y muy frecuentado por corcheros y funeros. Con un buen swell también sale una derecha. Se encuentra cerca de una pequeña central térmica.

A left reef facing NE. Low tide at Shooting Gallery is hollow, shallow and fast. The higher the tide gets, the easier it gets. A popular wave jumping and boogie boarding spot which can get crowded.

Une gauche de reef exposée nord-est. La marée basse y est creuse, sans profondeur et rapide. Plus la marée est haute, plus ça devient facile. Plein de windsurfers et de bodyboards pour gâcher la vague.

Shooting Gallery - *Photo: Alex Williams*

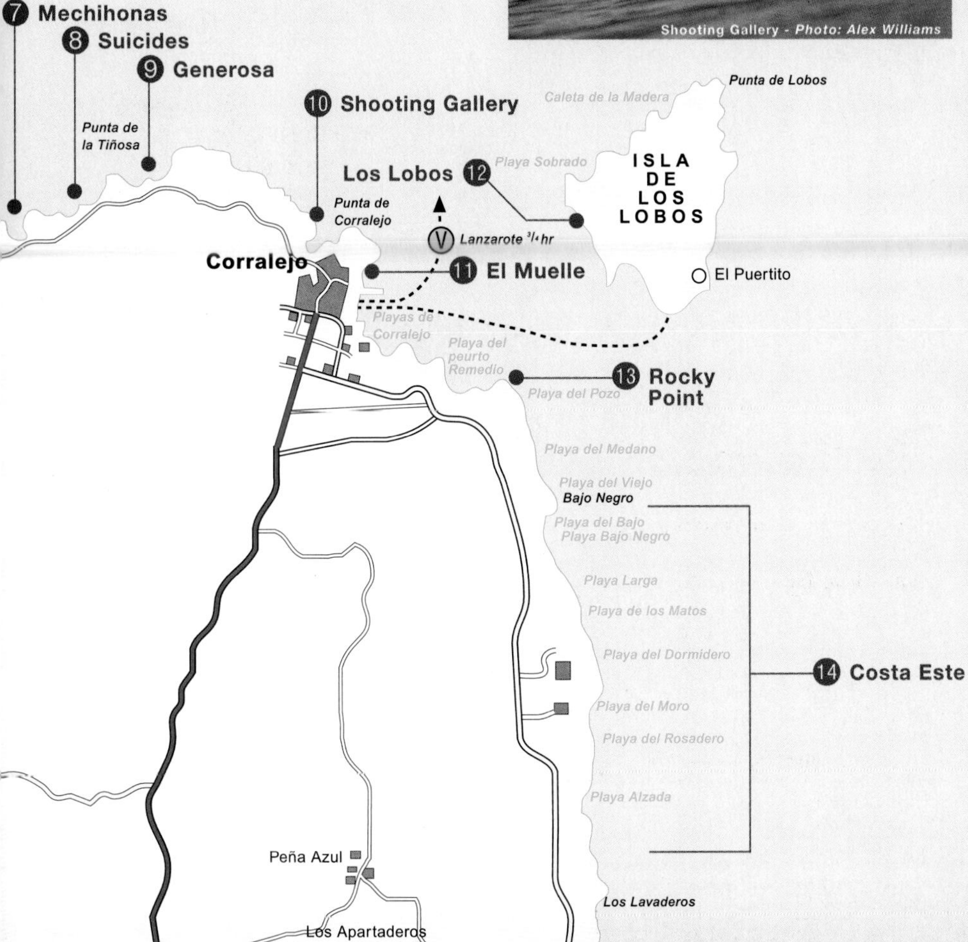

11. El Muelle

Detrás de la pared del puerto en Corralejo, hay una izquierda muy conocida. Aquí han aprendido a surfear muchos locales por su proximidad a Corralejo. Preferible con marea baja. Respeta a los locales.

Behind the harbour wall in Corralejo, a deservedly popular left. Many of the locals learnt to surf at this break due to its proximity to Corralejo. Low tide is preferred. Give the grommies their space!

Derrière le mur à Corralejo, une gauche convoitée qui le mérite. Plein de locaux ont commencé à surfer sur ce break parce que c'est proche de Corralejo. Mieux à marée basse.

Corralejo - *Photo: Alex Williams*

12. Los Lobos

Es una pequeña isla volcánica (6,5 Km cuadrados). Su nombre le viene de los lobos marinos que se alimentaban en estas aguas ricas en pesca. Con swell del N o NO y vientos del S o E, pueden salir olas de hasta 400m con paredes limpias y tubos perfectos. Con los swells más grandes se puede ver la ola desde Fuerteventura.

Los Lobos is a small volcanic island (6.5 sq km) named after the seals (lobos marinas) who used to feed in the fish-rich waters that surround it. With a N or NW swell and S or E winds, it can provide 400 metre rides with fast walling sections and clean tubes. On a big swell the wave can clearly be seen from Fuerteventura as it powers its way around the island.

Los Lobos est une petite île volcanique (6,5 km2) ainsi nommée quand les phoques (loups de mer) se nourrissaient dans les eaux poissonneuses qui l'entourent. Avec une houle de N/NO et des vents de sud et d'est, on peut trouver une vague de 400m avec de bons murs et des tubes sympas. Qaund ça rentre gros, la vague est clairement visible de Fuerteventura pendant qu'elle tourne avec puissnace autour de l'île.

Lobos - *Photo: Phil Holden*

13. Rocky Point

Es uno de los sitios más conocidos de Fuerteventura, lo mejor de marea media a alta. Cuando las olas de más al norte empiezan a cerrar, Rocky Point comienza a llenarse de gente, tanto de surfistas como de funeros.

One of Fuerteventura's most popular spots. When the breaks further north start closing out, then Rocky Point starts to suffer from crowding, from both surfers and wave-jumpers.

Un des spots les plus fréquentés de Fuerteventura. Quand les spots plus au nord commencent à fermer alors Rcoky Point commence à saturer de surfers et windsurfers à la fois.

14. Costa Este

Las enormes dunas de arena que se extienden al sur de Corralejo son reserva natural y la costa se ha convertido en una popular área windsurfera. Normalmente el mar está en calma y para poder surfear hacen falta grandes swells del N o S.

The extensive sand dunes that run south of Corralejo are a nature reserve and the coast has become a popular windsurfing centre. Normally the seas are calm here so surfing is only possible on a big N or S swell. Many facilities.

Les méga-dunes de sable qui s'étendent au sud de Corralejo sont des réserves naturelles alors que la côte s'est convertie en parc à windsurfers. Normalement, la mer y est calme c'est pourquoi on ne surfe que par giga-houle de nord ou par houle de sud. Plein de services à disposition.

Gran Canaria

Miguel Ortega -
Orca Surf Shop

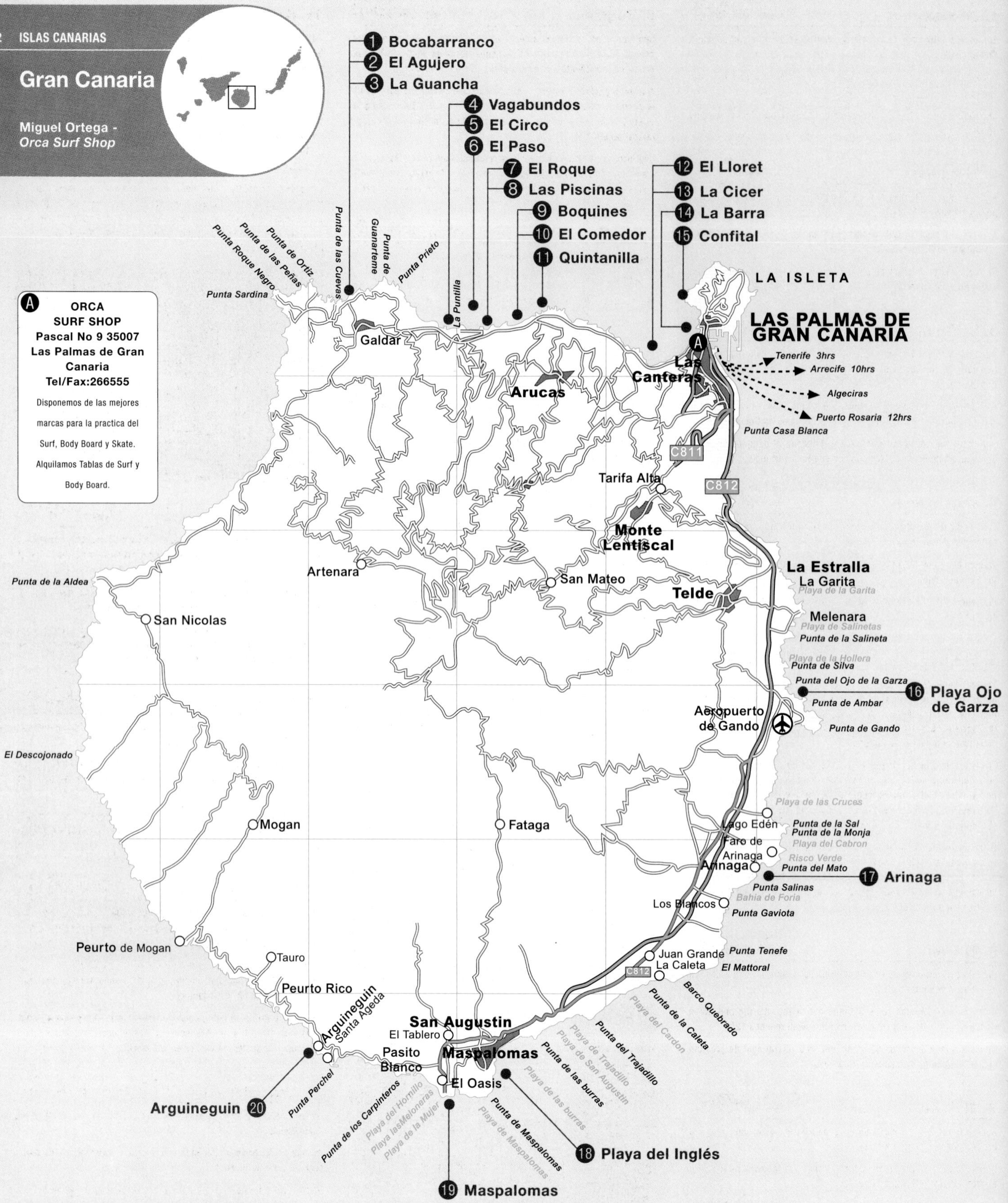

1. Bocabarranco
2. El Agujero
3. La Guancha
4. Vagabundos
5. El Circo
6. El Paso
7. El Roque
8. Las Piscinas
9. Boquines
10. El Comedor
11. Quintanilla
12. El Lloret
13. La Cicer
14. La Barra
15. Confital
16. Playa Ojo de Garza
17. Arinaga
18. Playa del Inglés
19. Maspalomas
20. Arguineguin

A ORCA SURF SHOP
Pascal No 9 35007
Las Palmas de Gran Canaria
Tel/Fax:266555
Disponemos de las mejores marcas para la practica del Surf, Body Board y Skate.
Alquilamos Tablas de Surf y Body Board.

LAS PALMAS DE GRAN CANARIA

Tenerife 3hrs
Arrecife 10hrs
Algeciras
Puerto Rosaria 12hrs

El perfil redondeado de la Isla de Gran Canaria ofrece una variada costa en la que las olas están presentes bajo una diversidad de condiciones. La Costa Norte es la que más oleaje recibe y es la zona surfera más popular de la isla. Todas las tiendas de surf de la isla están ubicadas en Las Palmas donde, asimismo, reside la mayoría de los surfers. Gran Canaria al igual que Tenerife y a diferencia de Fuerteventura y de Lanzarote, no es una isla muy favorable para el surfista viajero, debido a la mayor masificación y al localismo. Por esta razón, es realmente difícil disfrutar de las mejores olas de la isla, situadas en la poblada Costa Norte. Sin embargo, la Costa Oeste recibe marejadas épicas y alberga spots poco frecuentados no marcados en el mapa, pero fáciles de hallar. Si vas a Gran Canaria puedes encontrar muy buenas olas en estos lugares, que son los que el surfer viajero debe buscar para disfrutar con plenitud del surf que la isla ofrece.

Gran Canaria's roughly circular shape offers a choice of coasts, with surf under different conditions. The North Coast picks up the most swell and is easily the most popular area on the island. All the surf shops on Gran Canaria lie in Las Palmas as do the majority of surfers. Gran Canaria, like Tenerife, is not as favourable for travelling surfers as Lanzarote or Fuerteventura due to heavier crowds and localism problems. The best waves on the island are harder to enjoy due to these factor. The North Coast is the most populated, but the W coast must recieve epic swell. Good waves can definitely be had on Gran Canaria if you do end up here and there are some uncrowded surf spots not marked on the map which are easy enough to find. These are the places that a travelling surfer must seek out if he or she is to fully enjoy Gran Canaria's surf.

La forme quasi-circulaire de Gran Canaria permet un choix de côtes avec du surf dans des conditions différentes. La côte nord qui chope le plus de houle est la zone la plus connue pour surfer. Tous les surf shops de l'île sont sur Las Palmas tout comme la plupart des surfers. Gran Canaria, comme Tenerife, n'est pas aussi adéquat pour les surfers étrangers que Lanzarote ou Fuerteventura à cause du monde et des problèmes de localisme. A cause de ça, il est difficile d'apprécier les meilleures vagues de l'île situées sur la côte nord. Sans aucun doute, la côte orientale reçoit super bien la houle avec de spots peu fréquentés qui ne sont pas marqués sur la carte. Si vous allez sur Gran Canaria, vous pourrez y trouver de bons spots, qui sont ceux que le tripper recherche pour profiter pleinement des vagues qu'offre l'île.

1. Bocabarranco

En marea alta tiene su mejor punto este consistente spot. Contaminado.

A consistent spot best at high tide. The water gets polluted with sewage.

Un spot consistant meilleur à marée haute mais pollué par les égoûts.

2. El Agujero

A 300 metros de Bocabarranco. Es un pico corto y hueco frecuentado por los locales de Galdar.

A short and hollow peak popular with locals from Galdar. Located 300mtrs from Bocabarranco.

Un pic creux et puissant qu'apprécient les locaux de Galdar. Juste à 300m de Bocabarranca.

3. La Guancha

Derecha rompiendo en mar abierto. Corta, tubera y peligrosa al estar rodeada de acantilados. Se accede del mismo modo que a Bocabarranco.

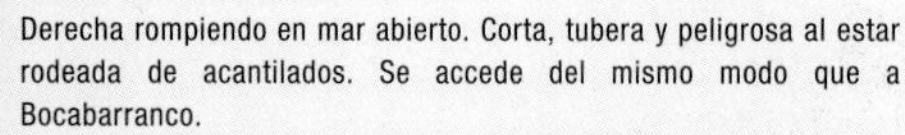

A righthander breaking into open sea, short tubey and dangerous since it's surrounded by cliffs. Access is the same as Bocabarranco.

Une droite qui casse au large: courte, tubulaire et dangereuse parce qu'entourée de falaises. Même accés que Bocabarranco.

4. Vagabundo

Varios picos en fondo de arena. Funciona todo el año, pero especialmente en verano.

Various sand bottom peaks. It works all year round, but especially in the summer months.

Plusieurs pics de beach-break qui marchent toute l'année mais surtout en été.

5. El Circo

Puedes encontrar dos olas. La primera un pico con salida a ambos lados, que rompe hueco y rápido en marea alta. En marea baja funciona una izquierda más larga pero no tan hueca. El cercano restaurante "Los Pescaditos" contamina con sus residuos. Se ha detectado la presencia de tiburones.

There are two breaks here; the first is a right and left peak with a very quick and hollow take-off that breaks at high tide. A lefthander that's not as hollow but is longer works at low tide. Located behind the restaurant "Los Pescaditos". Contaminated from restaurant garbage. Be warned of the presence of sharks.

Deux spots ici. Le premier est un pic avec un take-off des deux côtés, creux et rapide à marée haute. A marée basse, y'a une gauche moins creuse mais plus longue. Située derrrière le resto "Los Pescaditos" dont les déchets polluent le spot. Sachez qu'il y a des squales qui patrouillent.

6. El Paso

Una ola excelente situada a 300 metros mar adentro. Es la única ola surfeable con cuatro metros.

A great break situated some 300mtrs out to sea. It's the only wave on the island that can be surfed when the swell reaches 12ft.

Un super break à environ 300m en mer, le seul vrai spot de gros qui se surfe même au dessus de 3-4 mètres.

7. El Roque

Rompe frente a una roca grande. La bajada es r·pida, pero luego la ola se ralentiza. Funciona en verano.

Breaks in front of a big rock with a fast take off, followed by a slower section. Works in the summer months.

Casse en face d'un gros rocher avec un take-off rapide, suivi d'une section plus lente. Marche pendant les mois d'été.

Las Piscinas

Se llega del mismo modo que al Roque. Es una derecha larga y tubera.

Long tubing right. Access is the same as el Roque.

Une droite longue et tubulaire. L'accés est le même que pour "el Roque"

9. Boquines

Una amplia bahía con arrecifes a ambos extremos. En su parte Este hay una derecha larga de marea media. En la parte Oeste hay una ola corta pero divertida debido a la radicalidad de la bajada.

A wide bay with rocky reef breaks at both ends. On the eastern end is a righthander, giving long rides, best at mid tide. The wave on the western side of the bay may be shorter but can be fun due to the radical take-off.

Une large baie avec des breaks de reef aux deux extrémités. A l'est, c'est une droite plutôt longue meilleure à mi-marée. La vague à l'ouest est plus courte mais plus tecnhique avec un take-off radical.

10. El Comedor

Ola poderosa frecuentada por los locales de San Andrés.

A powerful wave popular with locals from San Andrés.

Une vague puissante bien connue des locaux de San Andres.

11. Quintanilla

Si funciona puedes encontrar olas perfectas de largo recorrido. Situada junto a la discoteca "Quintanilla"

Can have perfect long rides when on. Located near the dance hall "Quintanilla".

Peut avoir un déferlement parfait quand ça marche. Situé à côté de la boîte "Quintanilla".

12. El Lloret (La Lloreta)

Buenas olas que no soportan el viento cruzado. Pese a ser muy frecuentado, el ambiente en el agua es bastante bueno.

Good waves but can't handle side. Gets crowded but the atmosphere here is reasonably friendly.

C'est bon sauf si ça souffle side-shore. Du monde mais l'ambiance reste relativement amicale.

13. La Barra

Una de las más famosas zonas bugueras de toda Europa, se divide en 3 áreas. Los Muellitos en la parte Oeste de la playa, junto al rompeolas. Aquí las olas son rápidas y tuberas cayendo en fondo de roca. El Bufo en la mitad de la playa ofrece buenas olas rompiendo sobre arena. En el Piti Point el fondo es de arena y rocas, y las olas son más largas que en el Bufo, aunque con menor fuerza. Situada en la parte O de la playa de las Canteras.

One of Europe's most popular boogie boarders' break with three named areas. Los Muellitos lies at the W end of the beach, next to the breakwater and has a rock bottom with fast and tubey waves. El Bufo is the area in the middle of the beach with good sand bottom waves. El Piti Point has a sand and rock bottom with Longer waves than El Bufo (but they break with less power). Located on the west side of Playa Las Canteras.

Un des vagues d'Europe les plus célèbres pour le bodyboard qui comprend trois pics. Los Muellitos qui se trouve à l'ouest de la baie, prés de la digue casse sur du caillou avec de bons tubes. Ensuite, El Bufo, au milieu de la baie est un bon beach-break de sable. Enfin, El Piti Point sur fond mixte est une plus longue vague qu'El Bufo mais casse moins puissamment. Situé à l'ouest de la Playa de Canteras.

La Cicer - Photo: Simon McComb

14. La Barra

Precioso escenario el que configuran la playa de arena dorada y la laguna color turquesa que forma el arrecife situado a 500 metros de la orilla. No es un sitio para olas grandes. Es muy popular entre los corcheros.

Excellent set-up with a fine golden sand beach, a turquoise lagoon and a lava reef handily positioned 500 metres from shore. Not a big wave venue, and especially popular with boogie boarders.

Superbe endroit avec une plage dorée de sable fin, un lagon turquoise et un reef de lave idéalement placé à 500m du bord. Pas vraiment un spot de grosses vagues et bien apprécié des boogies.

15. Confital

Es un lugar famoso por sus excelentes olas y por su localismo duro. El arrecife proporciona una derecha que es considerada una de las mejores olas de Canarias. La bajada es fuerte y chupona, y el tubo muy limpio. Se coge mejor en marea alta. No dejes el coche sin vigilancia.

Confital is famous for two things: great waves and heavy localism. The main attraction is a right reef considered one of the best waves in the Canaries. A sucky take-off is followed by some clean barrels, best caught at full tide. Do not leave a vehicle here unattended.

On connaît Confital pour deus choses:une super vague et un localisme gravissime. Le sujet de discorde est cette droite de reef qui est des meilleures vagues des Canaries. Un take-off qui suce est suivi par des tubes secs, meilleurs à marée haute. Ne pas laissez sa caisse sans surveillance.

Confital - Photo: Jakue Andikoetxea

16. Playa Ojo de Garza

Sólo funciona con grandes mares del N. No es un sitio demasiado bueno, pero al estar junto al aeropuerto permite ver si hay olas al llegar a la isla.

Only works on big N swells. Not a great place. Waves break just by the airport so if you fly in you can get a swell check here.

Ne marche que par grosse houle de nord. Pas un endroit transcendant mais les vagues cassent tout prés de l'aéroport ce qui est pratique à checker quand on arrive par avion.

17. Arinaga

Ola corta, hueca y muy rápida. El habitual viento terral hace que sea la ola más apreciada de la Costa Este.

A very fast wave which is both hollow and short. The fact that it's often offshore here makes it the most esteemed wave on the East coast.

Une vague trés rapide qui est à la fois creuse et courte. La fait qu'il y ait souvent off-shore ici la rend le spot le plus apprécié de la côte est.

18. Playa del Inglés

Una ciudad de bloques amontonados construidos para el turismo. No es habitual que lleguen marejadas limpias, pero es frecuente que haya olas de viento divertidas para los funeros.

Another breeze block city built purposefully for the tourist industry. Clean swells are rare but onshore choppy waves are common and these can be fun for wave-jumpers.

Une autre barrière de béton pour touristes. Les houles propres y sont rares car on y trouve plus souvent des mioses immondes, plus propices pour sauter les vagues en windsurf.

19. Maspalomas

Diversos picos a ambos lados del faro, uno de los spots más populares del S.

Various peaks break either side of the lighthouse. One of the most popular spots in the south.

Divers pics qui cassent des deux côtés du phare. Un de spots les plus populaires dans le sud.

20. Arguineguin

Una de las pocas zonas verdes que quedan en el Suroeste de Gran Canaria está amenazada por las decisiones de los lÌderes polÌticos. Es una ola divertida que fue muy popular entre los surferos freaks de los aÒos setenta. Los anocheceres de este lugar son preciosos.

One of the few green areas left in the SW of Gran Canaria is in danger due to decisions by political leaders. It's a fun wave that was very popular amongst the "Surfer Freaks" during the 70's. Sunsets are beautiful here.

Une des quelques zones vertes au sud-ouest de Gran Canaria qui est malheureusement menacée par des décisions politiques. Une vague sympa qui était souvent surfé par les "Surfer Freaks" dans les années 70. N'y manquez pas les couchers de soleil.

Tenerife

A.D.E.S.

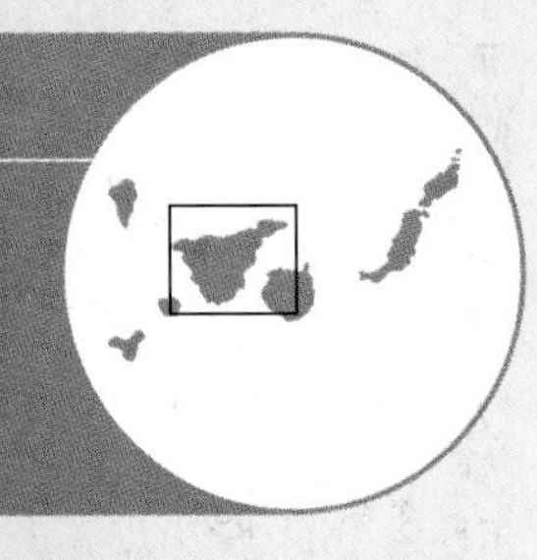

A.D.E.S necesita ayuda

La información sobre Tenerife la ha facilitado la Asociación para la Defensa del Surf (ADES). El desarrollo turístico de la isla ha puesto en peligro muchas de las rompientes. Playas artificiales y diques son los principales riesgos, y algunas olas se han perdido definitivamente.

Hay un nuevo proyecto de construcción de playa artificial, en la zona NO de la isla de Tenerife; situado en el pueblo de La Caleta de Interian (Garachico). El problema es que el proyecto contemplado destruye 3 olas importantes y con ello desaparece el surf de esa zona. A.D.E.S. a dado unas consideraciones sobre ese proyecto de regeneración de esta la playa. A la vez, ha ofrecido una propuesta alternativa a dicho proyecto pero, por ahora está todo ahi. Pero, sighe la destrucción de la naturaleza. ¿Como parar la especulación? Es un reto que tiene la isla.

Hay dos áreas surferas principales: el Suroeste, de playa de las Américas a los Gigantes (25 Kms. al norte); y el norte hasta la playa de los Troches. Son zonas bien comunicadas y muy urbanizadas. Playa de las Américas es un triste ejemplo de una mala concepción del turismo, mientras que la belleza del norte de la isla es incomparable.

A.D.E.S. needs help....Please contact us

Information for this chapter has been provide by La Asociación para la Defensa del Surf (ADES). The developments forced on this island by the encroaching tourist trade threatens many of the best surf breaks. Artificial beach formation and jetty developments are the biggest problems with several locations already irreparably altered.

There is a new building project to create an artificial beach in the NW area of the island, at a village called 'La Caleta de Interian' (Garachico). The problem is that the proposed project will destroy 3 important waves and in doing so will leave the area void of any surf at all. A.D.E.S. has considered this proposed regeneration of the beach and we have offered an alternative proposal to the project - and that is how things stand at the moment. But the destruction of the natural enviroment continues elsewhere. How can we stop this speculation? It is a common goal for the island to work towards.

There are two main areas to find waves here - firstly on the south west coast from Playa de las Américas to los Gigantes approximately 25kms to the north, and secondly along the north coast up to Playa de los Troches. Main roads service these areas and they are also the scene of intense urbanisation. Playa de las Américas is one of the ugliest examples of the tourist fungus mutating, and although the northern coast of Tenerife is uniquely beautiful it is also the most heavily populated region in the group.

L'ADES a besoin d'aide.

C'est la Asociacion para la Defensa del Surf (ADES) qui nous a fourni les informations pour ce chapitre. Le développement touristique menace la plupart des meilleurs spots. La construction de plages artificielles et de jetées sont les plus gros points noirs avec plusieurs lieux déjà irrémédiablement endommagés.

Un nouveau projet de construction vient de voir le jour dans le but de créer une plage artificielle au NO de l'île de Tenerife, dans le village de Caleta de Interain (Garachico). Le problème est que le projet proposé va détruire 3 vagues majeures de ce spot en laissant l'endroit sans aucunes vagues surfables. A.D.E.S a analysé la proposition de fabriquer une plage à Caleta de Interain. L'association a même offert une alternative au projet. On en est là pour l'instant. Cependant, la destruction de l'environnement naturel continue ailleurs. Comment pouvons nous arrêter cette spéculation? C'est un but commun pour tous les habitants de l'île d'aller en avant.

Il existe deux zones principales où l'on peut trouver des vagues ici. D'une part sur la côte sud-ouest de Playa de las Américas jusqu'à los Gigantes environ 25kms au nord; et d'autre part le long de la côte nord jusqu'à Playa de los Troches. Des routes nationales desservent ces zones qui sont, par ailleurs, largement urbanisées. Playa de las Américas est un des exemples les plus moches d'une mutation à vocation touristique, et bien que la côte nord de Tenerife soit d'une beauté unique, c'est également la plus fortement peuplée de la région.

1. El Confital

La izquierda más tubera de la isla. Necesita mares del Sur, aguantando un par de metros. Mejor en verano y primavera.

Most tubey left on Tenerife. Needs a S-SE-SW swell and will break up to 2m. Best in spring and summer.

La gauche la plus tubulaire de Tenerife. Exige une houle de sud/sud-est/sud-ouest et fonctionnera jusqu'à 2m. Les meilleures périodes sont le printemps et l'été.

2. Las Galletas

Lo mejor es la izquierda, aunque un espigón ha reducido su recorrido. Funciona con mar del Sur hasta los dos metros. Mejor en marea baja.

The left is the better ride atthough its length has been shortened considerably due to the construction of a pier. Needs a S-SE-SW swell and is best at low tide up to 2m.

La gauche est la meilleure, bien qu' elle soit bien moins longue depuis qu'on y a construit une digue. A besoin d'une houle de sud/sud-est/sud-ouest et est meilleure à marée basse jusqu'à 2m.

3. La Fitenia - The Desert

Es una de las mejores olas del sur de la isla y va a desaparecer. Da derechas e izquierdas, siendo mejores las primeras. Mares del Sur hasta tres metros.

One of the best waves in south Tenerife will disappear due to construction! Left and right with the right being a better ride. S-SE-SW swell with waves up to 3m.

Une des meilleures vagues du sud de Tenerife qui va disparaître en raison d'un programme de construction! Une gauche et une droite avec une préférence pour la droite. Nécessite un swell sud/sud-est/sud-ouest avec des vagues jusqu'à 3m.

4. El Conquistador

Olas tranquilas frente al Hotel Conquistador. Mejor las izquierdas.

Mellow waves in front of the Hotel Conquistador. Lefts are better.

Vagues tranquilles devant l'hotel Conquistador. Les gauches sont meilleures.

5. La Derecha del Cartel

 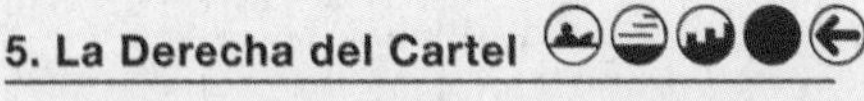

Excelente derecha amenazada. Rompe todo el año menos en verano, con mar del O-NO. Alcanza tres metros. Frente al Hotel Conquistador.

Threatened wave! Excellent right with NW-W swell breaking mainly in autumn, winter and spring up to 3m. Located in front of the Hotel Conquistador. Best at mid tide.

Vague menacée! Excellente droite avec un swell de nord-ouest/ouest, marchant essentiellement en automne, hiver et printemps jusqu'à 3m. Située devant l'hotel Conquistador.

6. La Izquierda/Spanish Left

Sin duda la mejor y más famosa ola tinerfeña. Se encuentra amenazada. Es una izquierda larga y tubera que atrae a muchos extranjeros. Mar del O-NO. Visible desde el paseo de las Américas.

Threatened wave! Undoubtedly the best and most famous wave of Tenerife. Long tubey left with a NW-W swell up to 3m. Many foreigners come to surf this wave...you can see it in front of the main drag at Las Américas.

Vague menacée! Certainement la plus belle et la plus célèbre vague de Tenerife. Une longue gauche qui tube avec une houle de nord-ouest/ouest jusqu'à 3m. Beaucoup d'étrangers viennent surfer cette vague... vous pouvez la voir devant le ponton principal de Las Américas.

La Izquierda - Photo: Jakue Andikoetxea

7. Punta Blanca - K16

Ola amenazada al igual que los spots más cercanos. Poderosa izquierda, corta, intensa y vertical. Marejada del NO hasta tres metros. Es popular entre los visitantes.

Threatened wave! Left, short and intense due to steepness and power of wave. NW swell up to 3m. A popular break with foreigners. Other waves in the vicinity are also threatened.

Vague menacée! Une gauche, courte et intense en raison de la pente et de la puissance de la vague. Une houle de nord-ouest jusqu'à 3 m. Pas mal d'étrangers sur ce spot fréquenté. Les autres vagues des environs sont également menacées.

K16 - Photo: Peter Cade

8. La Caleta

Ambas olas están en peligro. Son olas potentes y peligrosas que alcanzan los tres metros y funcionan todo el año. Mar del N y NO.

A right and left both threatened by construction! N-NW swell up to 3m with waves all year round. Both waves are somewhat hazardous.

La gauche et la droite sont toutes deux menacées par une construction! Un swell de nord/nord-ouest jusqu'à 3m avec des vagues toute l'année. Les deux vagues sont quelque peu dangereuses.

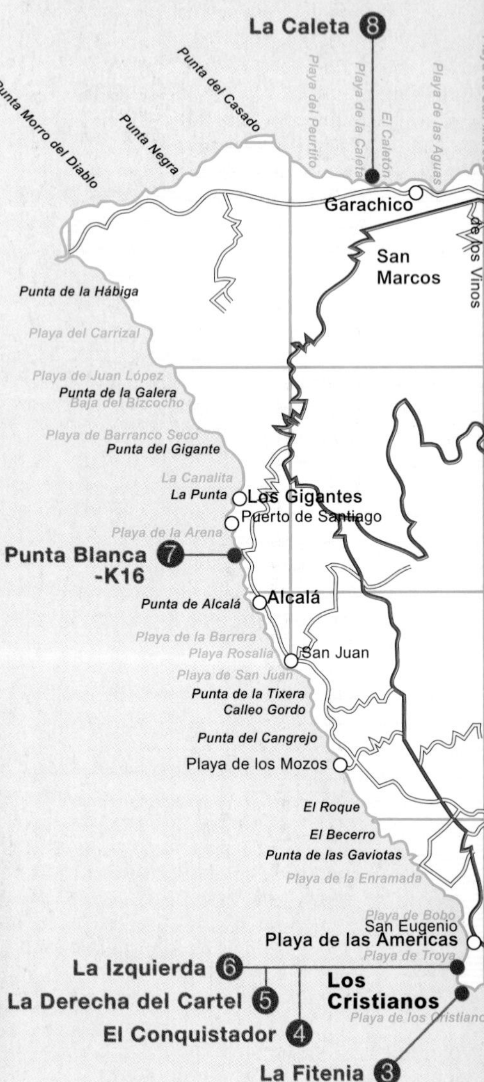

9. Playa del Sorocco

Powerful sand and rock bottom waves in a N swell up to 3m. Popular break with waves all year round.

Powerful sand and rock bottom waves in a N swell up to 3m. Popular break with waves all year round.

Rompiente sobre arena y rocas. Aguanta tres metros con mar del Norte. Es bastanta frecuentada ya que funciona todo el año.

10. El Charco

Amenazada por la construcción de piscinas. Es una izquierda grande (hasta 4m) y de largo recorrido. Funciona mejor en otoño e invierno con marejadas del NO. Una ola para surfers con experiencia.

Threatened by construction of swimming pools! A big long left for experienced surfers. NW swell up to 4m. Best in autumn and winter.

Menacée par la construction de piscines! Une grosse gauche et longue réservée aux bons surfeurs. Une houle de nord-ouest jusqu'à 4m. Meilleures saisons: automne et hiver.

11. Fuera de la Bajeta

Excelente y larga derecha, también amenazada. Ola de invierno con mares del N-NO. Aguanta tamaño.

Threatened wave! A very good long righthander. Needs a N-NW swell and holds good size. Best in winter.

Vague menacée! Une très bonne droite et longue. A besoin d'un swell de nord/nord-ouest et tient bien la houle. Meilleure en hiver.

12. Los Dos Hermanos

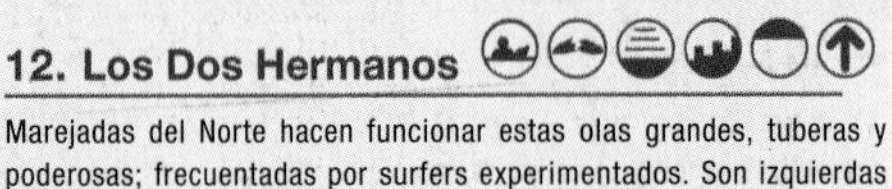

Marejadas del Norte hacen funcionar estas olas grandes, tuberas y poderosas; frecuentadas por surfers experimentados. Son izquierdas y derechas que llegan a los cuatro metros rompiendo en el marco de una bahía impresionante.

Powerful right and lefts in spectacular bay Big, tubey and popular with more experienced surfers. N-NE-NW swell up to 4m. Best in

Droite et gauches puissantes à l'intérieur d'une baie impressionnante. Gros, tubulaire et fréquenté avec pas mal de bons surfeurs. Swell de nord/nord-est/nord-ouest jusqu'à 4m. Meilleur en hiver.

Los Dos Hermanos - *Photo: Tim Rain*

Playa del Socorro 9, PUERTO DE LA CRUZ, Punta Brava, La Romántica, San Juan de la Rambla, La Orotava, Tabaiba, Santa María del Mar, Las Arenitas, Candelaria, El Socorro, Puerto de Güimar, El Tablado, Fondeadero de Fasnia, Poris de Abona, San Miguel de Tajao, El Médano, Aeropuerto Reina Sofia (INT.), El Abrigo, El Palm-Mar, Costa del Silencio, Las Galletas, El Confital 1, Las Galletas 2, MT. TEIDE 3715M, Teleférica Cable Car Telepherique

13. Almáciga

Derecha que funciona todo el año. Ideal para principiantes.

Righthander, good for beginners, works on any swell all year round.

Cette droite, bonne pour les débutants, marche avec n'importe quel swell tout au long de l'année.

14. Igueste de San Andrés

Buena izquierda, larga y tubera con mucho brazo. Mares del Nordeste al Sureste; todas las mareas, aunque mejor en alta. Rompe sobre arena y rocas planas. Suele estar mejor en invierno. Alcanza dos metros y medio.

Good long tubey left with long walls. NE-N-SE swell on all tides though best at high. Breaks over smooth rocks and sand. Best in winter up to 2.5m.

Bonne gauche tubulaire et longue formant de longs murs. Bien que meilleure à marée haute, elle marche avec n'importe quelle marée par swell de nord-est/nord/sud-est. Elle pète sur des rochers lisses et du sable. Meilleure en hiver jusqu'à 2.5 m.

LA NATURALEZA HACE LAS OLAS NOSOTROS VAMOS A SALVARLAS UNETE AHORA

46 Threatened Waves of Tenerife!

Tenerife Tour; Candelaria; Pal-Mar; La Izquierda del Cristianmar; El Conquistador; Derecha del Cartel "Billboards"; El Bunquer; La Ballena; Izquierda de Tenerife "Spanish Left"; Punta Blanca "K-16"; La del Medio; La del Chalet; La Concha; La Izquierda del Pueblo; La Izquierda de la Caleta; El Charcón; Baja del Diablo; Baja del Bizcochado; Pico de Fuera; El Charco; Fuera la Baja Nueva; Baja Nueva; El Desague; La Derecha de Candelaria; El Roquete; Fuera del Roquete; El Lastradero; La Baja Chica; La Cueva de Mejia; La Bajeta; Por Allá de la Bajeta; Fuera de la Bajeta.

AÇORES

	Population:	**+/-241,000**
	Area:	**2,344 km²**
	Time:	**GMT -1 (verão GMT)**
	Language:	**Português**
	Currency:	**1$(Escudo)=100 centavos (PTE)**

Photo: Alex Williams

Photo: Alex Williams

Intodução

Uma cadeia massiva de vulcanos sub-aquáticos estendem-se ao longo do Atlântico, desde ???Iceland??? até quase à Antartida. O arquipelo dos Açores são os picos mais altos dessa cadeia no meio do Atlântico.

õve ilhas principais constituem o arquipelo que se situa a 11200 kilometros a Leste de Lisboa, no meio do oceano. Tal como à Madeira (outra ilha mais a norte no Atlântico), a maior parte da costa submerge radicalmente no mar.

O que começou como uma idéia meio louca para nós, transformou-se numa viagem, tal como se passou com o primeiro homem que cá veio.

As ilhas foram descobertas e descritas em mapas por um jovem navegador Árabe chamado Sherif Mohand Adersi, o qual fez uma serie de viagens extraordinárias em 1220. Sozinho no vasto mar desconhecido ele velejou para leste na direção do sol poente, empurrando as fronteiras desconhecidas do mundo, motivado pela sua sede de curiosidade. Redescorbertas por navegadores Portugueses em 1427, os Açores tornou-se a principal base portuguesa para o comércio entre as Américas, India e Portugal durante os seculos seguintes sendo hoje parte integrante do território Portugues, com a denominaçao de região autónoma.

Introduction

A massive sub-sea Volcanic chain runs the entire length of the Atlantic, from Iceland almost to Antarctica. The Azores archipelago represents the highest peaks of the mid- Atlantic ridge. Nine main islands make up the group which lie some 700 miles west of Lisbon, in mid- ocean. Like on Madeira, Portugal's other Nth Atlantic islands, much of the land subsides steeply into the sea.

What started out as a wild idea for us, grew to become a journey, as it had been for the first man here. The islands were discovered and eventually mapped for the first time by a young Arab navigator named Sherif Mohamed al Adresi, who made a series of extraordinary Atlantic voyages by 1220. Alone in a vast sea of nothingness, he sailed west into the setting sun, pushing the boundaries of the known world motivated by a thirst for knowledge. Others followed and in 1427 the Portuguese rediscovered and claimed the islands and since then they have been Portugals main staging post for cross-Atlantic travel. Some stayed and some sailed on. Today a rich and unique culture remains.

Intro

Une importante chaîne de montagnes sous-marines court sur toute la longueur de l'Atlantique, de l'Islande pratiquement jusqu'à l'Atlantique. L'archipel des Açores représente les sommets de cette crête au milieu de l'Atlantique. Neuf îles composent ce groupe qui se situe à environ 1000 kms à l'ouest de Lisbonne, en plein océan. Comme à Madère,d'autre îles du Portugal dans l'Atlantique Nord, l'essentiel des terres surgit brusquément de l'océan.

Ce qui a commencé comme une idée étrange pour nous, s'est transformé en voyage, comme ça l'a été pour le premier homme ici. Les îles furent découvertes et finalement cartographiées par un jeune navigateur arabe, Sherif Mohamed Al Adresi, qui fit toute une série d'expéditions aventureuses en 1220. Seul dans le vaste océan, il se dirigea à l'ouest vers le soleil couchant, repoussant les limites du monde connu, motivé par la soif de savoir. D'autres suivirent sa route et en 1427, les Portugais redécouvrirent et revendiquèrent ces îles et depuis lors, elles ont été le relai principal des Portugais pour les transatlantiques. Certains s'y établirent, d'autres continuèrent leurs routes. Aujourd'hui, une culture unique reste vivante.

With thanks for generous assistance:
ICEP (Portuguese Tourist Office)
22-25a Sackville St,
London, W1X 1DE
Tel: 0171 494 1441
Fax: 0171 494 1868

Na Estrada

Velocidade Km/h:	80	60	40

Combustivel

Super	**Esc 150/l**
Sen Chumbo	**Esc 150/l**
Gasóleo	**Esc 77/l**

Viajando

Todos os Voôs partem de Lisboa e o preço de uma viagem de ida e volata é mais ou menos 38.000$00 esc. As viagens entre ilhas podem ser feitas ou por Aviões ou por barco. Há aviões todos os dias entre todas as ilhas o ano inteiro, mas barcos que são mais baratos, tem um horario mais restrito no inverno (quando nós precisamos mais deles), e estão sempre sujeitos a cancelações devido ao mau tempo. A chatice é que as pranchas são um grande problema para os pequenos espaços de carga dos aviões inter ilhas especialmente no inverno. Os aviões são o principal canal de comunicação para a economia das ilhas e dado a necessidade das populações locais para transportar coisas no inverno, as pranchas são colocadas no fim da lista de coisas a transportar, por serem dispensaveis. Isto quer dizer que o transporte das prachas no próprio dia está sujeito a um factor sorte.

Uma vez nas ilhas, carro é essencial, e os alugueres não são baratos. Como não existem quartos e pensões para se alugar as acomodações estão restritas a hoteis, acampamentos ou conhecimentos. Não certemente um destino barato para turistas de fora de Portugal, não existem infraestroturas em grande escala para turismo e não parece que seja para ai que o turismo desta zona se inclinará. As juntas de turismo são muito eficientes, nós recomedamos a consulata destas quando planearem a vossa viagem.

Travelling Around

All flights depart from Lisbon and the price of a return ticket is about £160.00 at the time of writing. Inter-island travel is either by ferry or plane. Flights run daily to-and-fro between the islands all year round, but the ferries, which are cheaper, run a reduced timetable during the winter (when you need them most), with occasional cancellations due to bad weather. The snag is that surfboards present difficulties for the small cargo holds on the planes, especially in winter. The airline is the transport and communications mainstay of the economy and due to local needs, boards are considered dispensable and are packed last on the plane. This can mean they don't get on for a few days. You might be lucky and you might not too!

Once on the islands, a car is a must and rentals aren't cheap. With few dormidas and pensiones, accommodation is limited but reasonably priced. It is not a bucket shop destination with facilities on a large scale, nor will it ever be. The tourist boards are all extremely efficient and helpful, we suggest you use them.

Voyager

Tous les départs se font de Lisbonne avec des prix aller-retour autour de 1500 FF au moment où on écrit ces lignes. Les transfers inter-îles se font par bateau ou par avion. Les vols sont quasi-quotidiens entre les îles toute l'année contrairement aux ferries, meilleur marché, qui naviguent moins souvent en hiver quand c'est le plus utile avec des annulations fréquentes quand la mer est trop grosse. Le hic est que les planches sont parfois difficiles à transporter dans les petits avions, surtout en hiver. L'avion est le moyen de transport le plus utilisé pour tous usages, les planches ne sont donc pas considérées comme indispensable et sont donc embarquées en dernier. Cela veut dire en clair qu'elles partiront dès qu'il y aura de la place: c'est un peu la loterie !

Une fois sur l'île, la voiture est indispensable et les locations ne sont pas données. Pas de pensions ni de chambres d'hôtes, le logement est limité aux hôtels, ou alors au camping ou il faut vous faire inviter. C'est tout sauf une destination de masses avec des aménagements à grande échelle et ça ne le sera jamais. Les offices de tourisme sont extrémement aimables et compétents, n'hésitez surtout pas à faire appel à leurs services.

Photo: Tim Rainger, LP

ILHA GRACIOSA

Santa Cruz da Graciosa

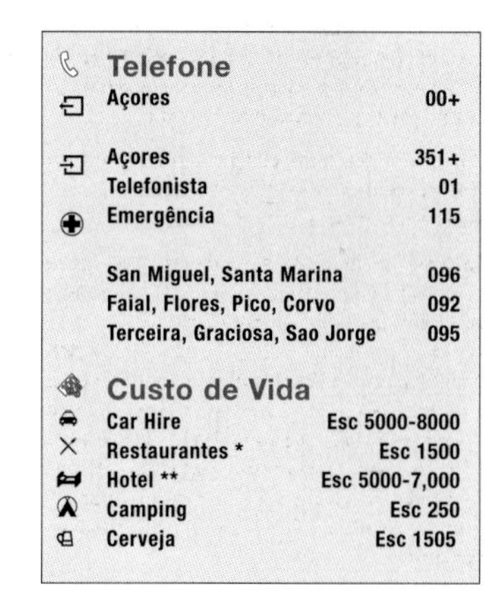

Telefone

Açores	00+
Açores	351+
Telefonista	01
Emergência	115
San Miguel, Santa Marina	096
Faial, Flores, Pico, Corvo	092
Terceira, Graciosa, Sao Jorge	095

Custo de Vida

Car Hire	Esc 5000-8000
Restaurantes *	Esc 1500
Hotel **	Esc 5000-7,000
Camping	Esc 250
Cerveja	Esc 1505

Junta de Turismo

SAO MIGUEL
A Infante D.Henrique, 9500 Ponta Delgada,
Tel: 25743 Fax: 22211

FAIAL
Rua Vasco de Gama, 9900 Horta, Faial
Tel: 22237

TERCEIRA
Rua Carreira dos Cavalos, 47A
9700 Angra do Herismo
Tel: 23393 Fax: 27661

PICO
Aparthotel Caravelos, 99500 Madalana
Tel: 92500

SANTA MARINA
Posto do Turismo Aeroporto
9580 Vila do Porto Tel: 86355

ILHA DE SÃO MIGUEL

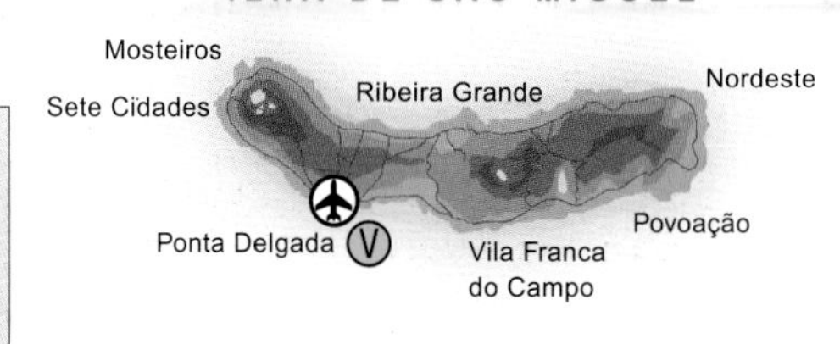

ILHA DE SANTA MARIA

Photo: Alex Williams

Photo: Alex Williams

O Surf

As ilhas recebem swells abundantes e há descrições de as primeiras surfadas terem sido nos anos 60 em pranchas feitas em casa, no entanto pouco ou nehum contaco foi feito com surfistas extrangeiros até os anos 70, quando um grupo de militares da base americana aperceberam-se do potêncial ao seu redor. A fama se espalhou mas ainda não muito. Como todas as direções vão dar a Lisboa, os surfistas portuguese são os mais assiduos visitantes, apesar de ter vindo a crescer o número de aventureiros Neozelandeses, australinaos e americanos e europeus que já surfaram este gupo de ilhas intensas e verdes. O surf vem de todas as direções, apesar de terem normalmente uma duração curta devido a proximidade do arquipelo ao sistema de baixas pressões. Sistemas frontais regularmente trazem swells, ao contrário das Canárias que estão a 4800 km mais para Sul. Chuva é uma constante todo o ano.

The Surf

They receive abundant swell and home made boards were reportedly being ridden by the early sixties, however little contact was made with foreign surfers until the seventies, when a group of US Air Force personnel got wise to the potential surrounding them. The word has spread but not that far yet. As all roads lead to Lisbon, Portuguese surfers are the most common visitors, though growing numbers of adventurous Kiwis, Aussies, Americans and other European nationals have ridden waves on this dramatic and verdant island group. Surf comes from the N, NW, W, and S, though it is often of short duration due to the islands' proximity to the weather systems which bring the swell. Frontal systems regularly accompany the waves, unlike on The Canaries which lie 2-300 miles further south. Rain is a daily occurrence year round.

Le Surf

L'archipel reçoit beaucoup de houle. Les planches fabriquées localement furent surfées en premier au début des années 60, bien que peu de contacts furent pris avec des surfers étrangers jusqu'aux années 70, quand un groupe de soldats américains se rendit compte du potentiel environnant. Le bruit s'est répandu mais sans faire de raffût. Comme toutes les routes passent par Lisbonne, les surfers portugais sont les visiteurs les plus fréquents, bien qu'un nombre croissant d'aventuriers d'origines différentes viennent tâter les vagues de l'archipel. La houle vient du nord, nord-ouest, ouest et sud, elle est souvent de courte durée vu la proximité des îles aux dépressions qui génèrent la houle. Il est fréquent que les fronts accompagnent les vagues, contrairement aux Canaries qui se positionnent 4 à 600 kms au sud. Il pleut presque tous les jours toute l'année.

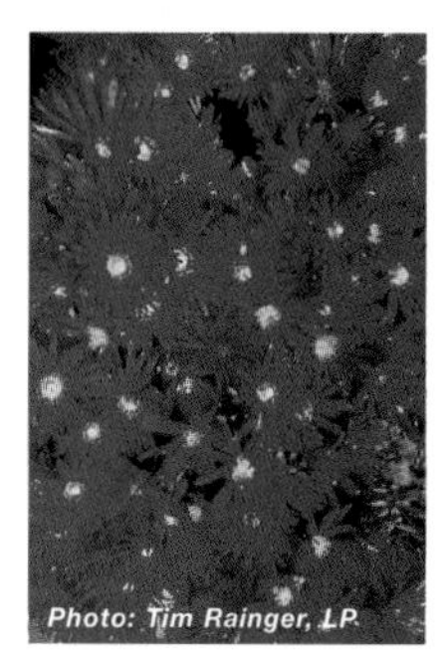

Photo: Tim Rainger, LP.

Photo: Alex Williams

METEOROLOGIA

28 DE ABRIL DE 1995

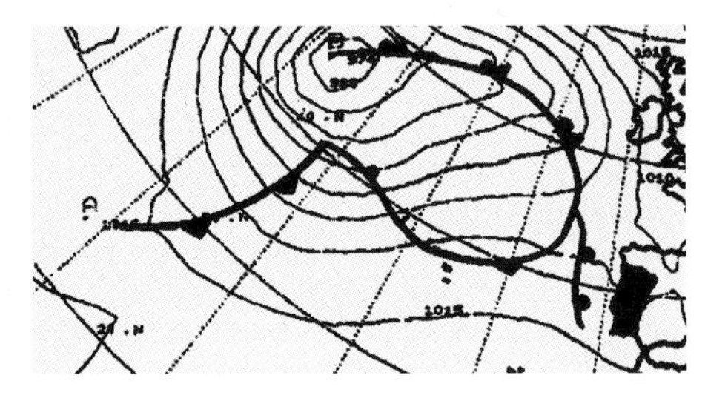

O Tempo

Climatéricamente, os Açores são influenciados por uma alta pressão situada no meio do Atlântico, contibuindo para ventos predominantemente de de Norte e de Leste. A temperatura, tal como nas Canárias é moderada dado a presença envolvente do Atlântico, e varia entre 13 e 25 graus no verão. A àgua é fria no inverno, morna no verão e cheia de exótica fauna marinha incluindo alguns dos maiores tubarões brancos e polvos do planeta.

The Weather

Climatically, the islands are influenced by the "Azores mid-Atlantic high", a consistent area of high pressure centred in this region, contributing to the prevailing N and W winds. Air temperatures, as on the Canaries are moderated by the Atlantic's surrounding presence and vary between 55F in winter and 75F in summer. The water is cool in winter, warm in summer, and filled with weird marine life, including some of the planets largest species of shark and squid.

Le Climat

Climatiquement, ces îles sont influencées par l'anticyclone des Açores, une zone de hautes pressions centrée donc autour de l'archipel. Les vents dominants sont donc de nord et d'ouest. Les températures comme aux Canaries sont modérées par l'Atlantique en variant de 12°c en hiver à 22°c en été. L'eau est fraîche en hiver, chaude en été, remplie d'une faune aquatique inquiétante, comprenant certaines des plus grosses espèces de requins et de pieuvres.

Photo: Alex Williams

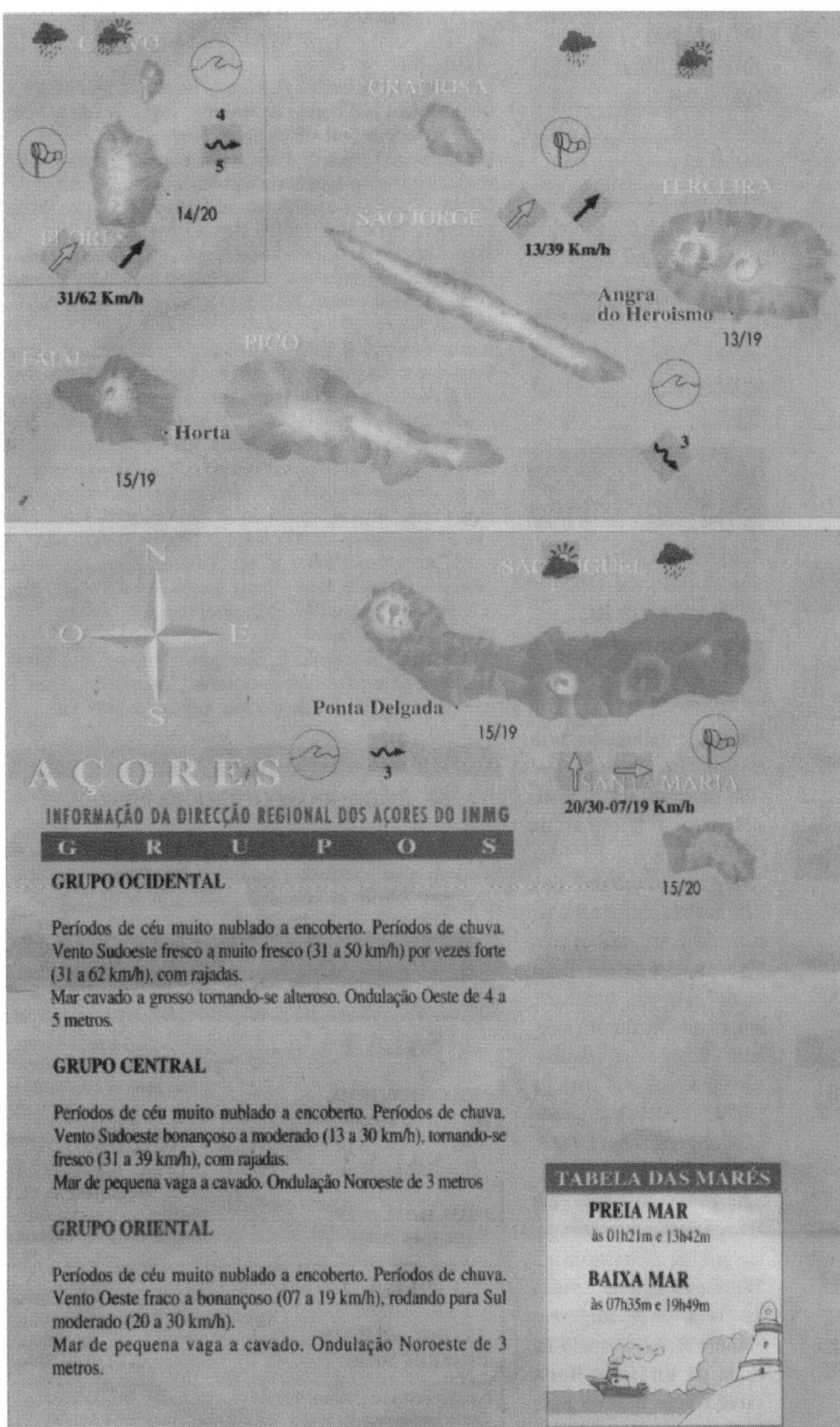
FLORES
4
5
14/20
31/62 Km/h
GRACIOSA
SÃO JORGE
13/39 Km/h
TERCEIRA
Angra do Heroismo
13/19
FAIAL
PICO
Horta
15/19
3
N
O
E
S
SÃO MIGUEL
Ponta Delgada
15/19
AÇORES
3
SANTA MARIA
20/30-07/19 Km/h
15/20
INFORMAÇÃO DA DIRECÇÃO REGIONAL DOS AÇORES DO INMG
GRUPOS
GRUPO OCIDENTAL
Períodos de céu muito nublado a encoberto. Períodos de chuva. Vento Sudoeste fresco a muito fresco (31 a 50 km/h) por vezes forte (31 a 62 km/h), com rajadas.
Mar cavado a grosso tornando-se alteroso. Ondulação Oeste de 4 a 5 metros.
GRUPO CENTRAL
Períodos de céu muito nublado a encoberto. Períodos de chuva. Vento Sudoeste bonançoso a moderado (13 a 30 km/h), tornando-se fresco (31 a 39 km/h), com rajadas.
Mar de pequena vaga a cavado. Ondulação Noroeste de 3 metros
GRUPO ORIENTAL
Períodos de céu muito nublado a encoberto. Períodos de chuva. Vento Oeste fraco a bonançoso (07 a 19 km/h), rodando para Sul moderado (20 a 30 km/h).
Mar de pequena vaga a cavado. Ondulação Noroeste de 3 metros.
TABELA DAS MARÉS
PREIA MAR
às 01h21m e 13h42m
BAIXA MAR
às 07h35m e 19h49m

LEGENDA

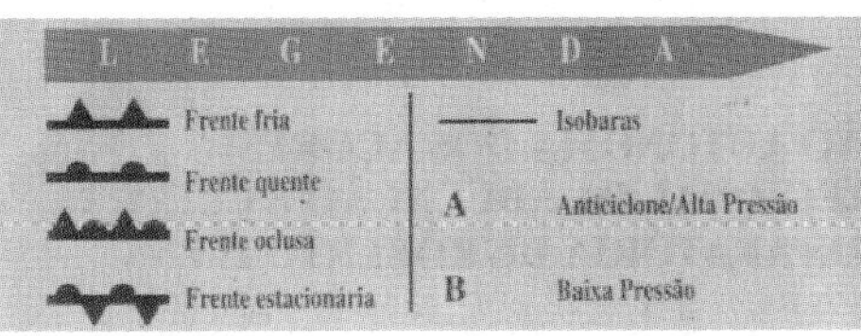

Frente fria
Frente quente
Frente oclusa
Frente estacionária

Isobaras
A Anticiclone/Alta Pressão
B Baixa Pressão

Céu limpo
Céu pouco nublados
Céu com periodos de muito nublado
Céu encoberto

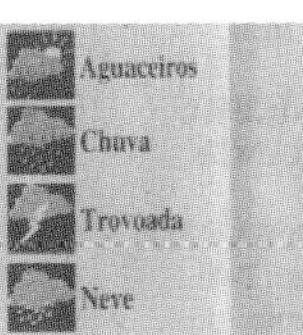

Aguaceiros
Chuva
Trovoada
Neve

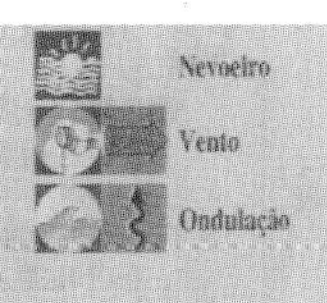

Nevoeiro
Vento
Ondulação

SITUAÇÃO OBSERVADA ONTEM

FLORES	20 • 14	Muito Nublado
HORTA	19 • 15	Muito Nublado
ANGRA	19 • 13	Nublina
P. DELGADA	19 • 15	Nublina
STª. MARIA	20 • 15	Nublina

Photo: Tim Rainger, LP

Photo: Tim Rainger, LP

Photo: Tim Rainger, LP

Photo: Alex Williams

Photo: Tim Rainger, LP

Photo: Alex Williams

Photo: Alex Williams

Photo: Alex Williams

Photo: Alex Williams

Photo: Alex Williams

Photo: Tim Rainger, LP

Photo: Alex Williams

Photo: Tim Rainger, LP

Photo: Alex Williams

Photo: Alex Williams

Photo: Alex Williams

Photo: Tim Rainger, LP

Photo: Tim Rainger, LP

Faial

Dubbed the Azure isle because of its magnificent hydrangeas of every shade of blue. Horta, the capital boasts a swashbuckling history of naval battles and political struggle. A couple of good reefs.

Surnommée l'île azuréenne pour ses magnifiques hortensias maculés de bleu. Horta, la capitale peut se vanter d'une histoire rebondissante de batailles navales et de luttes politiques. Quelques bons reefs.

Corvo

A ilha mais a leste do arquipelogo, não tem aeroporto, e embora haja dscições de ondas nesta ilha, nós não temos informações que confirmem esse facto.

The most westerly island is unserviced by the airline, and though reputed to have some waves, we've no firm info.

L'île la plus à l'ouest de toutes n'est pas desservie par l'aérien et bien qu'on la soupçonne d'avoir des vagues, aucune info n'est confirmée.

Flores

Como o nome indica, é uma ilha gloriosa que costumava ser uma base de misseis Franceses até 1993. Há pouca informação sobre o surf lá.

As the name implies, a glorious island that used to also be a French missile base (until 1993). Little information exists on surf spots, though one or two no doubt exist.

comme son nom l'indique, c'est une île pleine de fleurs qui a abrité une base militaire de lancement jusqu'en 1993. Peu de renseignements sur les spots de surf.

Pico

Pouco populada, mas cheia de cultura, O Pico é montanha mais alta de Portugal, tendo neve no seu topo no inverno. Alguns surf spots, mas mais uma vez eles estão um pouco separados.

Lightly populated but full of culture, Pico is Portugal's highest mountain and snow capped in winter. A few spots once again, some distance apart.

Faiblement peuplé mais plein de culture, Pico est la plus haute montagne du Portugal, recouvert de neige en hiver. Quelques spots parsemés.

São Jorge:

Longa, fina e incrivelmete ingrime, São Jorge está muito pouco populada com uma longa história de terremotos e cataclismos. Alguns picos, um tem acesso de carro. Há muito poucas acomodações, o que torna a ilha um pouco "hardcore", com desinos do tipo "leve tudo que possa precisar". Chuva e ventos fortes avalanches de terra dificultam o caminho.

Long, thin and incredibly steep, Sao Jorge is a sparsely populated island with a history of earthquakes & cataclysm. Only a couple of spots, one accessible by road. Very few accommodation options make it a strictly hard-core, "walk in with all you need" destination. Rain, strong winds and huge landslides.

Long, étroit et incroyablement abrupt, São Jorge est inégalement peuplé avec un passé de tremblements de terre et autres cataclysmes plutôt lourd. Seulement quelques spots, seulement accessibles par la route. Très peu d'hébergements seulement pour les purs et durs qui sont prêts marcher avec tout le nécessaire de survie. Pluies, vents forts et glissements de terrain.

Photo: Alex Williams

Photo: Alex Williams

Graciosa

Esta ilha graciosa é um calma visão rural, com campo dividido em vários quadradinhos, montanhas suaves cheias de arvores e pequenas plantações viniculas. Uma pequena ilha com um ou dois spots.

The graceful Isle is a quiet rural haven with chequered fields, gently sloping wooded hills and small vineyards. A small island with one or two spots.

L'île pleine de grâce est un havre de pays avec des champs murés, des collines douces et boisées avec de petits vignobles. Une petite île avec un ou deux spots.

Terceira

A mais populosa, históricamente rica e cosmopolita ilha do arquipelogo. A bela capital Angra do Heroismo (monumento mundial) é uma cidade contuida no maior forte do empério Poruguês, actualmente equipado com equipamento moderno. Existem três ou quatro spots, bem separados um dos outos.

The most densely populated, historically rich and cosmopolitan of the group. The beautiful capital, Angra de Herismo is a "world heritage" town built on the site of the largest fort in the old Portuguese empire, now equipped with all modern facilities. Three or four surf spots, a long way apart.

L'île la plus peuplée, chargée d'histoire et la plus cosmopolitaine du groupe. La capitale, Angra do Heroismo est classée au patrimoiñne mondial, elle est construite sur les restes d'un fort d'un ancien empire portugais, maintenant équipée de tous les services. Trois ou quatre spots éparpillés.

São Miguel

A maior ilha, abriga tambem a maior cidade do arquipelogo Ponta Delgada. Tem alguns bons reefs e picos de rochas alem de ter a maior quantidade de praias do arquipelogo. Outras atracções incluem a vida noturna e as Furnas. Existem já bastantes locais nesta ilha.

The biggest island also houses the biggest town, Ponta Delgada. Some good reefs and points, also the biggest and best beaches on the chain. Other attractions include night-life and the thermal hot pools at Furnas. Quite a few locals.

La plus grande des îles a aussi la plus grande des villes: Ponta Delgada. Quelques bons reefs et des pointbreaks, avec les plages les plus importantes, les meilleures de l'archipel. Une vie nocturne un peu animée et des souces d'eau chaude à Furnas. Quelques locaux.

Santa Maria

A primeira ilha a ter sido povoada, sendo localisada na ponta mais a Sudeste do arquipelogo, foi povoada por um punhado de portugueses oiundos do algarve. Vila do Porto, a capital da ilha é a mais velha cidade dos Açores.

The earliest settled and most S and E of the islands was inhabited by a handful of pioneers and their families from the Algarve. Vila do Porto, the islands capital is the oldest town on the Azores.

La première conquise, la plus au sud-est des autres îles, qui fût habitée par une poignée de pionniers avec leur famille depuis l'Algarve. Vila do Porto, la capitale de l'île est la plus vieille des Açores.

Photo: Alex Williams

surf dynamics

All Photos: Alex Williams

Dinâmica Do Surf

Cada ilha tem um limitado número de spots, dado o relvo da costa. Apenas São Miguel tem boas praias com surf (depois da Praia da Vitoria na ilha Terceira ter sido destruido pelo desmensurado porto que foi construido). Os reefs remanecentes são sem dúvida razos e perigosos. Acesso para muitas das melhores ondas é dificil e perigoso dado os constantes desprendimentos de terra causados pelas constantes chuvas e ingremes encostas. Pranchas partidas e raspões em reefs são práticas comuns. Assim como águas vivas.

Existem surfistas nesta ilhas e eles são um bando de criativos individualistas, que apreciam muito o que têm e trabalham duramente para proteger, das forças destrutivas herdadas do crescimento do seculo XX e das influências negativas e deterioradas da hetica surfistica internacional.

Eles discutiram, assuntos que rodeiam o as viagen de surf nos dias de hoje de uma maneira inteligente e razoavel e formaram um veiculo para divulgar as aspirações desse grupo em relação as viagens que tenham com destino os Açores. Este grupo existem numa foma livre e solta e incluie todos os habitantes de uma destas ilhas. Eles estão bem organizados e quando nós chegamos ao Arquipelogo eles nos esperavam e tinham sido convidados para o fazer.

Nós não demos nomes a alguns dos spots que encontramos em respeito aos locais. O ponto de vista deles ficou bem claro: Primeiro os swells tem uma duração curta. Segundo não existem muitos picos em cada ilha. Terceiro já existem muitos surfistas nas ilhas esperando pelo surf, o qual na sua maioria esta bem exposto, pelo que se fores para lá com "mente aberta" e uma atitude humilde , serás provavelmente bem recebido. Se queres surfar as melhores ondas da ilha, vais precisar da ajuda dos locais. Se fores humilde vão te dar as dicas se não não te dizem nada. É simples!! É impossivel chegar-se a ilhas com pranchas sem ser notado, pois há poucos caminhos e estes foram todos descobertos pelos surfistas ou seus familiares. Uma vez nas ilhas, não poderás escapar as consequências do teu comportamento. É altura para seres "cool". Não sujes. Não "mijes" em público". Não "guies à abrir". Não maltrates os locais e fazendeiros. Não "dropines". Seja simpático. Respeite o ambiente familiar. Nós tivemos uma ópima viagem, e tu tambem podes ter!

Surf Dynamics

Each island has a limited number of surf spots due to the steep landscape. With few quality beach breaks (after the glorious Praia Vittoria on Terciera was destroyed by an oversized port construction), the remaining reefs are without exception shallow and dangerous. Access to many of the best waves is difficult and perilous due to constant landslides caused by frequent rain and steep terrain. Snapped boards and reef rubbings are very common. So are jelly fish.

There are surfers here and they are an individualistic and creative bunch, who fully appreciate what they have, and who work hard to protect it, both from the destructive forces inherent in 20th Century growth, and the negative influences of a deteriorating international surf ethic.

They have discussed the issues which surround modern surf travel amongst themselves in a reasonable way and formed a vehicle for realising their aspirations for the future of wave riding on these islands. Their society exists in a loose format and includes all the inhabitants of one particular island. They were well organised when they met us, as they had been invited to do.

We have not named the few spots we found out of respect to their wishes. They made their points very clearly. Firstly the surf is often of short duration. Second there are only a few breaks on each island. Thirdly there are already enough surfers on each island ready and waiting to surf most of what is on offer. So...if you come here with an open mind and relaxed attitude, you will probably be welcome. If you want to get the best surf, you'll need their help. If you're humble you'll get it. If not, you won't. Simple. It's impossible to arrive with surfboards unnoticed, as there are few ways in and all are manned by some surfers or their families. Once here, you cannot escape the consequences of your behaviour. Time to be cool. No trash. No pissing in public. No badass driving. No aggravation to the local surfers and farmers. No drop-ins. Be friendly. Respect the family vibe. We had an incredible trip, so could you.

Ambiances

Chaque île a un nombre limité de spots à cause des nombreuses falaises. San Miguel est la seule île à posséder un bon beach brea (après que la glorieuse Praia Vitoria sur Terceira fut détruite par la construction d'un port démesuré) . Les reefs sont sans exception à fleur d'eau et dangereux. L'accès aux meilleures vagues est difficile voire périlleuse à cause des glissements de terrain provoqués par des pluies incessantes et la déclivité des terrains. Les planches cassées et les chocs sur le reef sont fréquents, tout comme les méduses.

Il y a des surfers là qui forment un groupe individualiste et créatif, qui apprécient pleinement ce qu'ils ont et font le maximum pour le protéger, à la fois des forces imhérentes du progrès du XX siècle et des influences négatives de la démocratisation du surf dans le monde.

Ils ont réfléchi raisonnablement aux problèmes qui entourent les voyages des surfers récemment. Ils ont donc formé une association pour concrétiser leurs désirs quant au futur de la glisse aquatique sur ces îles. Leur groupement est informel et inclut les habitants d'une île en particulier. Ils étaient bien organisés quand on les a rencontrés.

Nous n'avons pas nommé les quelques spots trouvés par respect de leurs désirs. Ils se sont fait comprendre très clairement. Primo, la houle est souvent de courte durée. Segundo, on trouve peu de spots sur ces îles. Tercio, y'a déjà suffisamment de surfers sur chaque île pour surfer l'essentiel de ce qui reste à surfer. Donc, si vous venez ici avec l'esprit ouvert et une attitude cool, vous serez probablement le bienvenu. Si vous vous trouver les meilleures conditions, vous aurez certainement besoin de leur aide. Avec un peu d'humilité et de patience, vous trouverez ce que vous cherchez. Il est impossible d'arriver avec des planches incognito parce qu'il n'y a pas 36 entrées et qu'il y a toujours un surfer qui y traînent ou quelqu'un de la famille. Une fois sur place, on ne peut échapper aux conséquences de ses actes: soyez cool, pas de déchets par terre, pas de miction en public, pas de conduite de chauffards. N. agacez pas non plus les locaux ou les fermiers. Pas de taxe au take-off. Soyez amical et respecñtez les mentalités locales. Nous avons eu un trip incroyable, pourquoi pas vous?

SURFERS AGAINST SEWAGE

"All sewage is treated before discharge." so said the Prime Minister of Britain, Margaret Thatcher, in 1989 on a national television programme. At the that very moment some 400 million gallons of untreated sewage was being discharged around the coast of Britain every single day.

Throughout Europe there was a similar situation. A large part of the population was literally shitting on the beaches. The coastal waters were being used as a huge septic tank and toxic dump. Governments were seemingly quite happy to let people bathe and surf in a soup of their own excrement. The effect on wildlife is also devastating. Whilst fish stocks plummet an people get ill the Governments still want more discussions.

This blatant disregard for the marine environment is something that every surfer, windsurfer and recreational water user must stand up and fight. The health of the planet depends on the health of the oceans. As people who take a great deal of pleasure from the sea it is largely up to you to stand up for the rights (and lefts) of the seas. We, at the SAS and Surfrider Foundations can do a lot, but without your direct input and commitment we cannot achieve all that is needed.

Many beaches are tested throughout the summer period but testing stops at the end of the Bathing Season. Many surf/windsurf breaks are not tested at all as they are not designated bathing waters. Some sewage treatment works are then switched off at the end of the bathing season as according to Governments people are not using the sea.

The tests are inadequate as they are for organisms that die off rapidly in saltwater whereas human pathogens such as Hepatitis A can survive for months under similar conditions. The standards must be tightened in order to protect health.

"Toutes les eaux usées sont traitées avant d'être évacuées", ainsi s'exprimait à la télévision, Margaret Thatcher, Premier Ministre anglais, en 1989. En ce moment même, quelque 1818 millions de litres d'eaux usées non traitées sont déversées le long des côtes anglaises chaque jour! Partout en Europe, on a retrouvé ces problèmes. Une grande partie de la population "chie" littéralement sur les plages. Les eaux côtières firent office de fosse sceptique géante et de décharge publique très dangereuse. Les différents gouvernements donnèrent l'impression d'être presque contents de laisser se baigner les surfeurs et les gens dans une "bassine" remplie de leurs propres déjections. Les effets sur la nature sont également dévastateurs. Pendant que les réserves de poissons dégringolent et qu'on rend les gens malades, les gouvernements se perdent en conjectures.

Cette indifférence flagrante en ce qui concerne l'environnement maritime est une chose à laquelle tout surfeur, tout windsurfeur, tout bodysurfeur et tout nageur occasionnel ou non doit s'opposer et pour laquelle il doit se battre. La santé de la planète est intimement liée à celle des océans. Faisant partie de ceux pour qui la mer est un plaisir, vous devez être le défenseur des droits (et droites!) des mers. Nous, à SAS et à Surfrider Foundation, nous pouvons faire beaucoup, mais sans votre énergie et votre concours, nous ne pouvons réaliser tout ce qui est nécessaire.

Beaucoup de plages subissent des contrôles tout au long de la période estivale mais les relevés s'arrêtent à la fin de la saison touristique. Beaucoup de vagues de surf et windsurf ne sont pas contrôlées du tout étant donné qu'elles ne sont pas considérées comme des zones de baignade à part entière. De plus des centres de traitement ferment à la fin de la saison des baignades puisque, selon les gouvernements, les gens n' "utilisent" plus la mer.

Les tests sont inadaptés étant donné qu'ils sont faits pour détecter des organismes qui meurent rapidement dans l'eau salée. Or les agents pathogènes tels que ceux de l'hépatite A, qui peuvent résister pendant des mois dans ces mêmes conditions, ne sont pas pris en compte. Les normes doivent être ajustées afin que notre santé soit réellement préservée.

"Todas las aguas residuales son tratadas antes de ser vertidas" dijo la Primera Ministro Margaret Thatcher en 1989 en un programa de la televisión inglesa. En ese mismo momento unos 400 millones de galones de vertidos no tratados eran desaguados diariamente en las costas del Reino Unido.

En Europa la situación era similar. Se podría afirmar que la mayoría de la población estaba defecando en las playas. Las aguas costeras estaban siendo usadas como pozo séptico y para vertidos tóxicos. los Gobiernos no estaban preocupados por dejar baÒarse a la población entre sus propios excrementos. Además el efecto sobre la vida marina estaba siendo devastador. Los bancos de peces se reducían y había personas enfermando... y los Gobiernos querían seguir debatiendo.

Esta falta de respeto hacia la ecología marina, debe ser motivo para que cada surfer, windsurfer o simple bañista se oponga a esta situación. La salud del planeta depende de la de sus océanos. Tratándonos de individuos que disfrutamos en el mar y del mar, somos los más indicados para encabezar esta lucha pÚr los derechos de los mares. Desde la SAS y desde la Surfrider Foundation se está tratando de hacer muchas cosas, pero sin tu ayuda y compromiso serán insuficientes.

Muchas playas sólo se analizan en verano que es la temporada de baño y en invierno?... Además muchos spots no playeros no se analizan al no ser calificados como lugares de baño. Muchos tratamientos del agua cesan al finalizar el verano, porque para las Autoridades en el resto del año no hay gente metida en el agua.

Los análisis son poco adecuados, ya que se miden microorganismos que mueren rápidamente en el medio marino, mientras que hay patógenos como la Hepatitis A que pueden sobrevivir meses en esas condiciones. Hay que afinar más los niveles permitidos de cara a la protección de la salud pública.

Capbreton, France: *Photo - Surfrider Foundation*

Some Horrible Facts

The UK dumps 300 million gallons of sewage every single day. In addition there are 2 million tonnes of toxic waste discharged every year.

More than a million tonnes of nitrogen flows down the Rhine every year.

3.9 tonnes of Mercury are discharged into the North Sea from the Rhine every year.

4 areas off the British coast have been used to dump a total of 145,000 tonnes of chemical weapons including nerve gas, arsenic bombs and phosgene gas.

More than 500 million tonnes of raw sewage are discharged into the Mediterranean every year.

Levels of hazardous chemicals found in samples of whale blubber taken from 4 whales found dead on the Belgian coast were so high that the whale carcasses themselves classified as toxic waste.

Constatations Alarmantes

Le Royaume-Uni déverse quelque 1350 millions de litres d'eaux usées chaque jour. En plus on se débarasse chaque année de 2 millions de tonnes de déchets toxiques.

Chaque année, plus d'un million de tonnes d'azote descendent du Rhin.

Chaque année, 3,9 tonnes de mercure quittent le Rhin pour rejoindre la Mer Du Nord.

Quatre zones au large de la côte anglaise servent de dépotoir pour 145000 tonnes d'armes chimiques, y compris les gaz neuroplégiques, les bombes à l'arsenic et les gaz au phosgéne.

Chaque année, plus de 500 millions de tonnes de déchets sont évacués tels quels dans la Méditerrannée.

Les concentrations en produits chimiques trouvées sur des échantillons de blancs de baleine prélevés sur 4 baleines récupérées mortes sur la côte belge étaient si élevées que les carcasses elles-mêmes ont été considérées comme déchets toxiques.

Algunas Cifras Terribles

En el Reino Unido se vierten diariamente 300 millones de galones de aguas residuales al mar. Además anualmente son arrojadas dos millones de toneladas de vertidos tóxicos.

Desde el Rin llegan anualmente al Mar del Norte m·s de un millón de toneladas de nitrógeno y 3,9 de mercurio.

Cuatro zonas distintas de la costa británica han sido utilizadas para deshacerse de 145.000 toneladas de armas químicas, incluyendo gas nervioso, bombas de arsénico y fosgeno.

El Mediterráneo recibe anualmente 500 millones de toneladas de residuos sin tratar.

Los niveles de sustancias químicas nocivas presentes en 4 ejemplares de ballena encontrados en las costas belgas, eran tan elevados que los propios despojos del animal llegaban al nivel de vertido tóxico.

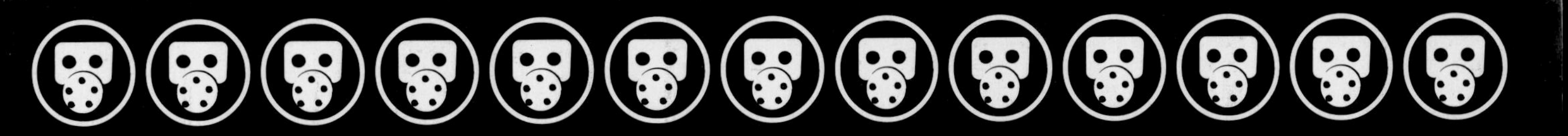

The Laws

There are a number of laws that require Governments to clean up the coast:

The EC Bathing Water Directive 76/160/EEC - Now under revision in order to tighten the standards. Applies to designated Bathing Waters only.

The EC Urban Waste Water Treatment Directive 91/271/EEC - Requires a level of treatment to all sewage discharges of population over 10,000 by the year 2001 and 2,000-10,000 populations by the year 2006.

The laws of Personal Injury and Nuisance, Trespass, The Environmental Protection Act 1990 - check the statute book for your respective country. These are laws applying to individual countries.

In 1994 SAS took representatives from the surfing, windsurfing and boogie boarding world for a meet with the President of the European Parliament in Strassbourg. This was to push for tighter standards and to apply pressure on Governments to comply with the Directives. The EC Bathing Water Directive is now under revision and will be updated with tighter standards that are far more health related.

One thing we made very clear to the European Parliament and European Commission in Brussels, was that the wetsuit had completely changed the way we use the seas. The numbers of people spending time in the water has increased hugely, throughout far longer periods of the year and for far greater lengths of time per session. The more time spent in the water the more fun! Unless it's polluted, in which case the more time spent in the water the greater the risk of an infection!

We Have The Technology

One of the great things about the sewage debate is that there is an achievable end point. Good sewage treatment is available at often a cheaper cost than building long sea outfalls which simply pump the problem out of sight out of mind. Preliminary, primary and secondary treatment followed by ultra violet light disinfection produces excellent results. The island of Jersey applies this technology and in 1995 won the British Airways Tourism for Tomorrow Awards for the scheme. This will give them a significant advantage in their marketing for the tourist industry.

Microfiltration is another brilliant way of treating sewage but the cost of such plants is very high.

We have found that the above set of figures proves our case very strongly. (Faecal coliforms are naturally occurring bacteria of the gut and are present in all sewage. They are easily measured and used as an indicator of the presence of sewage).

This was presented to the House of Lords Select Committee in July 1994 and SAS said: "That it would therefore be preferable to bathe in Jersey's outfall pipe than on a Government passed beach." In August 1994 SAS were invited to do just that.

It is for this reason that SAS feel that "end of pipe" standards are the real way forward. Everything else will be down to the vagaries of the testing regime, weather, tides and wave conditions.

Les Lois

Il existe un certain nombre de lois qui obligent les gouvernements à débarasser la côte de ses pollutions.

La directive 76/160/EEC sur les eaux de baignade au sein de la Communauté - actuellement en révision afin d'abaisser les seuils - ne s'appliquent qu'aux eaux dites de baignade.

La directive 91/271/EEC sur le traitement des eaux usées au sein de la Communauté exige un certain degré de traitement pour toute évacuation d'eaux usées pour des zones d'habitation de plus de 10000 habitants d'ici l'an 2001 et pour des zones de 2000 à 10000 habitants d'ici l'an 2006.

Les lois concernant les notions de blessure et de nuisance, d'introduction illicite, de protection de l'environnement sont entrées en vigueur en 1990. Vous pouvez vérifier les statuts de votre pays. Car il y a des lois qui ne s'appliquent qu'à un pays en particulier. La directive sur les eaux de baignade de la Communauté est actuellement en révision et sera réactualisée avec des seuils d'acceptation plus sévères qui seront nettement plus liés à la notion de santé.

Une chose que nous avons expliquée très clairement au Parlement Européen et à la Comission Européenne de Bruxelles, est que l'utilisation de la combinaison a complètement bouleversé notre façon d'"utiliser" la mer. Le nombre de personnes passant du temps à l'eau a énormément augmenté; et ils sont à l'eau de plus en plus longtemps et tout au long de l'année. On voudrait croire que plus on passe de temps à l'eau, mieux c'est! Mais voilà, il y a la pollution. Ainsi, plus on reste longtemps à l'eau, plus on augmente le risque d'infection!

Nous Possédons La Technologie

L'un des points clés du débat sur le problème des eaux usées, est qu'on peut y mettre un terme. De bons traitements des eaux sont opérationnels à un prix plus avantageux que les conduites géantes, qui ne font que porter le problème hors de notre champ de vision. Un traitement préliminaire, puis un premier puis un second suivi d'une désinfection aux UV donnent d'excellents résultats. L'île de Jersey applique cette technologie et en 1995 ce projet a reçu le prix du concours"un tourisme pour demain" proposé par British Airways. Cela donnera à cette technique un avantage certain au niveau marketing auprès de l'industrie touristique.

La microfiltration est une autre façon de traiter les eaux usées mais le coût d'une telle centrale est très élevé.

Quelques chiffres parlent d'eux-mêmes. Les coliformes - provenant des matières fécales- sont des bactéries des intestins et sont présents dans tous les types d'eaux usées. Ils sont facilement décelables et sont utilisés comme détecteurs d'eaux usées.

Ce fut présenté au Comité de sélection de la Chambre des Lords en juillet 1994 et SAS avait dit"Il appparait ainsi préférable de se baigner à la sortie d'une conduite à Jersey que de se baigner sur une plage "autorisée" par le gouvernement".

C'est pourquoi SAS pense que l'on se dirige vers la fin des normes "à l'ancienne". On sera alors plus préoccupé par les caprices d'un régime, du temps, des marées et des conditions de vagues.

Legislacion

Existen unas cuantas normas legales que exigen a los Gobiernos tener limpias sus costas:La Directiva Comunitaria sobre aguas de baño (76/160/EEC). Se está revisando a fin de endurecer más los requisitos. Se aplica únicamente en aquellas aguas calificadas como de baño.La Directiva Comunitaria sobre tratamiento de aguas de deshecho urbanas (91/271/EEC). Establece los niveles de tratamiento de los desagües en poblaciones con más de 10.000 habitantes (obligatorios para el 2001) y en poblaciones de entre 2.000 y 10.000 residentes (obligatorios para el 2006).Las leyes de daños personales, responsabilidad civil, y la Ley de Protección Medioambiental de 1990. Estas leyes son de carácter nacional, infórmate sobre las de aplicación en el tuyo.

En 1994 SAS llevó a representantes del mundo del surf, windsurf y boogie a una reuniÛn con el Presidente del Parlamento Europeo en Estrasburgo. El propósito era endurecer la normativa y presionar a los Gobiernos para que cumplan las Directivas.

Como se ha mencionado, está en revisión la Directiva de aguas de baño desde unos criterios de mayor preocupación por la salud pública.

Un punto b·sico que se subrayó ante el Parlamento y la Comisión Europea es la transformación radical que ha supuesto el traje de neopreno en la relación entre el hombre y el medio acuático. La gente que pasa largas sesiones en el agua durante todas las estaciones del año, se ha multiplicado enormemente y con ella la posibilidad de contraer infecciones. Permanecer mucho tiempo en el agua resulta divertido, pero también supone un riesgo para la salud.

Disponemos de La Technologia

El aspecto más positivo de esta controversia sobre las aguas resiuales es la existencia de un objetivo claro y alcanzable. Un buen tratamiento de los vertidos puede hacerse a menor coste que la construcción de emisarios submarinos que sólo sirven para poner la mierda fuera del alcance de la vista. Ojos que no ven... Un tratamiento en tres etapas: preliminar, primaria y secundaria, seguido de desinfección con rayos ultravioleta, proporciona excelentes resultados. En la isla de Jersey se aplica esta tecnología y por ello ha ganado en 1995 el Premio Turismo del Mañana, que concede British Airways. Esta es una buena ventaja competitiva para el marketing turisticode la isla. La microfiltraciÛn es otro tratamiento eficaz, pero de coste muy elevado.

La siguiente tabla proporciona unas cifras muy significativas de lo dicho anteriormente: (los coliformes fecales son bacterias intestinales presentes en las aguas residuales, son de fácil medición por lo que se utilizan para saber el nivel de residuos presentes en el agua).

Estos datos se presentaron ante una Comisión de la House of Lords en Julio de 1994 y SAS dijo: "De aquí se deduce que es mejor bañarse en un desagüe de Jersey que en una playa calificada apta por el Gobierno".

En Agosto de ese año la SAS fue invitada a hacer lo que había afirmado.SAS piensa que cualquier recogida de muestras debe hacerse en las salidas de desagüe, porque de otro modo, la variabilidad de las condiciones tiempo, mareas, olas... puede alterar los resultados.

Ultra Violet Treatment - Jersey

Treatment Type	Coliforms per 100ml
Raw/screening	10,000,000
Primary	1,000,000
Secondary	100,000
Tertiary (ultra violetdisinfection- Jersey)	35
Government passed beaches	anything less than 2,000

Traitement type	Coliformes par 100 ml
Niveau au test de dépistage	10,000,000
Premier	1,000,000
Second	100,000
Troisième (désinfection aux UV- Jersey)	35
"acceptée" par le gouvernement	moins de 2000

Tipo de tratamiento	Coliformes por 100 ml.
Bruto/Filtrado	10.000.000
Primario	1.000.000
Secundario	100.000
Terciario(desinfecciÛn UVA-Jersey)	35
Playas aptas según el Gobierno	menos de 2.000

Photo: Chris Hines of Surfers Against Sewage sticks his head up Jersey's outfall pipe.Chris Hines of Surfers Against Sewage sticks his head up Jersey's outfall pipe.

Photo: Glen Rankin

The Future

The future is yours, as individuals intimately involved with the oceans we are all in a prime position to monitor the marine environment and to tell the world what is happening. It's time to give something back, it's time to lock into a new wave of politics. The politics of the planet.

In order to achieve these goals we need to lobby as a number of member states. We need strong groups in all countries throughout Europe and we need them to be supported and active.

There are a lot of people out there who say: "I can't do anything, it's not up to me etc." But we'd better all believe it: We can do something and it is up to us.

"GET ON BOARD - YOU ARE RESPONSIBLE FOR THE FUTURE!" DO IT NOW! THERE WILL BE NO EXCUSES LATER!"

Le Futur

Le futur est ce que vous en ferez; et il existe une interdépendance entre l'homme et l'océan. Nous sommes tous concernés au premier chef et devons être à l'écoute de ce milieu qui est le nôtre. Il est temps de lui rendre la pareille, d'arrêter de nouvelles mesures sur le plan politique pour élaborer un véritable plan de sauvetage de la planète.

Afin d'atteindre ces objectifs, nous avons besoin de mouvements d'opinion ainsi qu'un certain nombre de politiques. Nous avons besoin de la mobilisation de groupes forts dans tous les pays d'Europe pour qu'ils nous soutiennent et nous encouragent.Il y a beaucoup de gens qui disent "je ne peux rien faire, ce n'est pas de mon ressort..." Alors que notre leitmotiv devrait être "nous pouvons faire quelque chose et cela dépend de nous".

"À L'ABORDAGE, NOUS SOMMES RESPONSABLES DU FUTUR!" FAISONS LE MAINTENANT! NOUS N'AURONT PAS D'EXCUSES PLUS TARD!"

El Futuro

El futuro está en nuestras manos, desde el momento en que al estar en contacto con el medio marino somos los más indicados para alertar al resto de la gente sobre lo que está ocurriendo. Es el momento de darse cuenta que a la polİtica tradicional hay que sustituirla por una polİtica del planeta.

Para conseguir esto, debemos funcionar como un lobby de cara a la Comunidad, y para ello se requieren organizaciones nacionales potentes y activas. Muchos decimos "No se puede hacer nada, no va conmigo..."pero es mejor hacer algo, ya que depende de nosotros, somos responsables del futuro. Mejor cuanto antes, luego no valdrán las excusas.

"PERO ES MEJOR HACER ALGO, YA QUE DEPENDE DE NOSOTROS, SOMOS RESPONSABLES DEL FUTURO. MEJOR CUANTO ANTES, LUEGO NO VALDRÁN LAS EXCUSAS!"

Azorean Purity-*Photo: Alex Williams*

"Think of a future with no pollution just clean, crisp waves..."

"Pensons à un avenir sans pollution avec juste des vagues "proprement appétissantes".

"Piensa en un futuro no contaminado, sólo olas limpias y cristalinas..."

What You Can Do!

Join Surfers Against Sewage, Surfrider Foundation or whatever campaigns running in your country.

If you see a pollution incident report it to the council, the Government monitoring body (NRA in the UK) and to SAS or the equivalent.

If you get ill DO VISIT YOUR DOCTOR.

Then contact your organisation and ask for a medical form and return it. This data will be fed directly to the European Commission on the Environment.

Tell others and encourage them to get involved.

Think about panty liners, condoms, cotton buds, detergents, oil or anything else that you may flush down the loo.

Que Pouvons Nous Faire?

Rejoindre Surfers Against Sewage, Surfrider Foundation ou tout autre mouvement existant dans votre pays.

Si vous êtes témoin d'un accident dû à la pollution, adressez vous à votre mairie, aux instances gouvernementales (NRA au Royaume-Uni) et à SAS ou son équivalent.

Si vous vous sentez mal, il faut absolument VOIR VOTRE MÉDECIN.

Puis contactez votre association et demandez un formulaire avant de le renvoyer dûment rempli. Les informations iront directement à la Commission Européenne pour l'Environnement.

En parler aux autres et faire en sorte qu'ils se sentent impliqués.

Ne jetez pas dans les toilettes serviettes hygiéniques, préservatifs, cotons-tiges, détergents et autres déchets !

¿Que Podemos Hacer?

Apúntate a Surfers Against Sewage, la Surfrider Foundation o a cualquier organización o campaña que se desarrolle en tu país.

Si detectas un vertido, denúncialo a las autoridades (Ayuntamiento, responsables sanitarios) o a organizaciones ecologistas.

Si enfermas por la contaminación, vete al médico. Pero, luego acude con tu parte médico a alguna de las organizaciones citadas. Esta informaciÓn se registra y pasa directamente al banco de datos de la Comisión Europea de Medio Ambiente.

Promociona entre tus allegados la necesidad de cambiar de actitud y pasar a la acción.

Piensa a dónde van a parar los detergentes, aceites, pantys, condones, bolas de algodón, etc. cada vez que tiras de la cadena.

Surfers Against Sewage

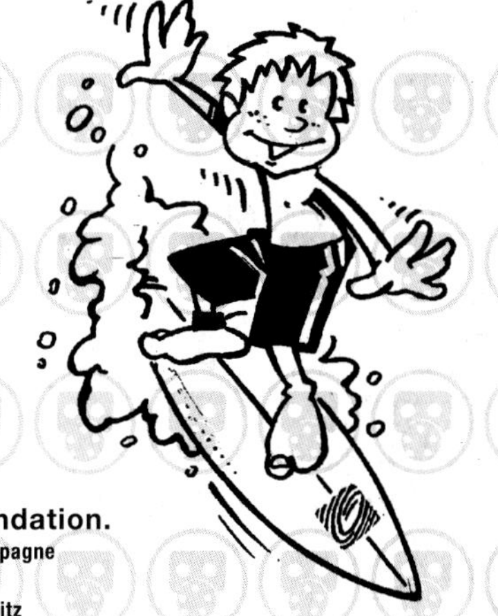

Surfers Against Sewage Ltd.
Registered in England N/2920815
Registered Office, The Old Counthouse
Warehouse, Wheal Kitty, St
Agnes. Cornwall, TR5 ORE
Tel: 0872 55 3001
Fax: 0872 55 2615

Surfrider Foundation.
79 Bis Rue D'Espagne
Villa Sion
64200 Biarritz
Tel: (33) 59 23 54 99

A national campaign for clean and safe seas and beaches

In order to establish a basic file on people who have experienced health problems potentially caused by bathing or immersion in Sewage contaminated waters we would like you to fill out this simple form.

These files and their contents will not be published without the permission of the person involved. We may use a summary of cases, but would not use names without permission .We may approach you if we feel your case would be useful in the furthering of our campaign.

Une campagne nationale pourdes plages et des mers propres et sûres.

Dans le but d'établir un simple fichier des gens qui ont eu des problèmes de santé liés d'une façon probable à un bain de mer ou quelconque immersion dans des eaux contaminées par les égoûts, on aimerait que vous remplissiez cette fiche toute simple.

Cette fiche et leurs données ne seront pas publiées sans l'autorisation de la personne concernée. On utilisera certains cas mais on ne donnera pas de nom sans votre accord.On vous contactera peut-être si on trouve votre cas utile pour la suite de cette campagne.

Una campaña para playas y mares limpias y seguras.

Dentro de la campaña por la limpieza de mares y playas y con el propósito de conocer los problemas de salud causados por la contaminación de las aguas, se ha establecido un banco de datos al que puedes contribuir cumplimentando el formulario adjunto.

Esta información es archivada y utilizada únicamente de un modo agregado y resumido, no se usan datos individuales si no es con autorización expresa del interesando. En el supuesto de que tu caso fuese significativo nos pondriamos en contacto contigo.

Name/Nom/Nombre ______________________

Address/Adresse/Apellidos ______________________

Tel: ____________

Details of health problem ______________________
Descriptions des problèmes de santé ______________________
Detalles del problema de salud ______________________

Did you visit a doctor?
Avez-vous été voir un médecin? ✔ X
¿Has acudido al médico?

Do medical records exist?
Y-a t-il un dossier médical? ✔ X
¿Ha sido registrado el caso en tu historial médico?

When did you go in the polluted water? ______________________
Quand êtes-vous allé dans cette eau polluée? ______________________
¿Cuándo se ha originado el problema? ______________________

Where did you go in the water? ______________________
Où était-ce? ______________________
¿Dónde se ha originado el problema? ______________________

Did you lose work due to health problems?
Avez-vous perdu votre travail à cause de ces problèmes? ✔ X
¿Te ha supuesto la enfermedad no acudir al trabajo?

Are you unemployed or claiming benefit of any type?
Etes-vous au chômage et cherchez-vous à obtenir des compensations finacièrer? ✔ X
¿Estás desempleado o solicitando alguna ayuda?

Thank you for your time
Merci pour votre temps
Gracias por la atención prestada

INDEX

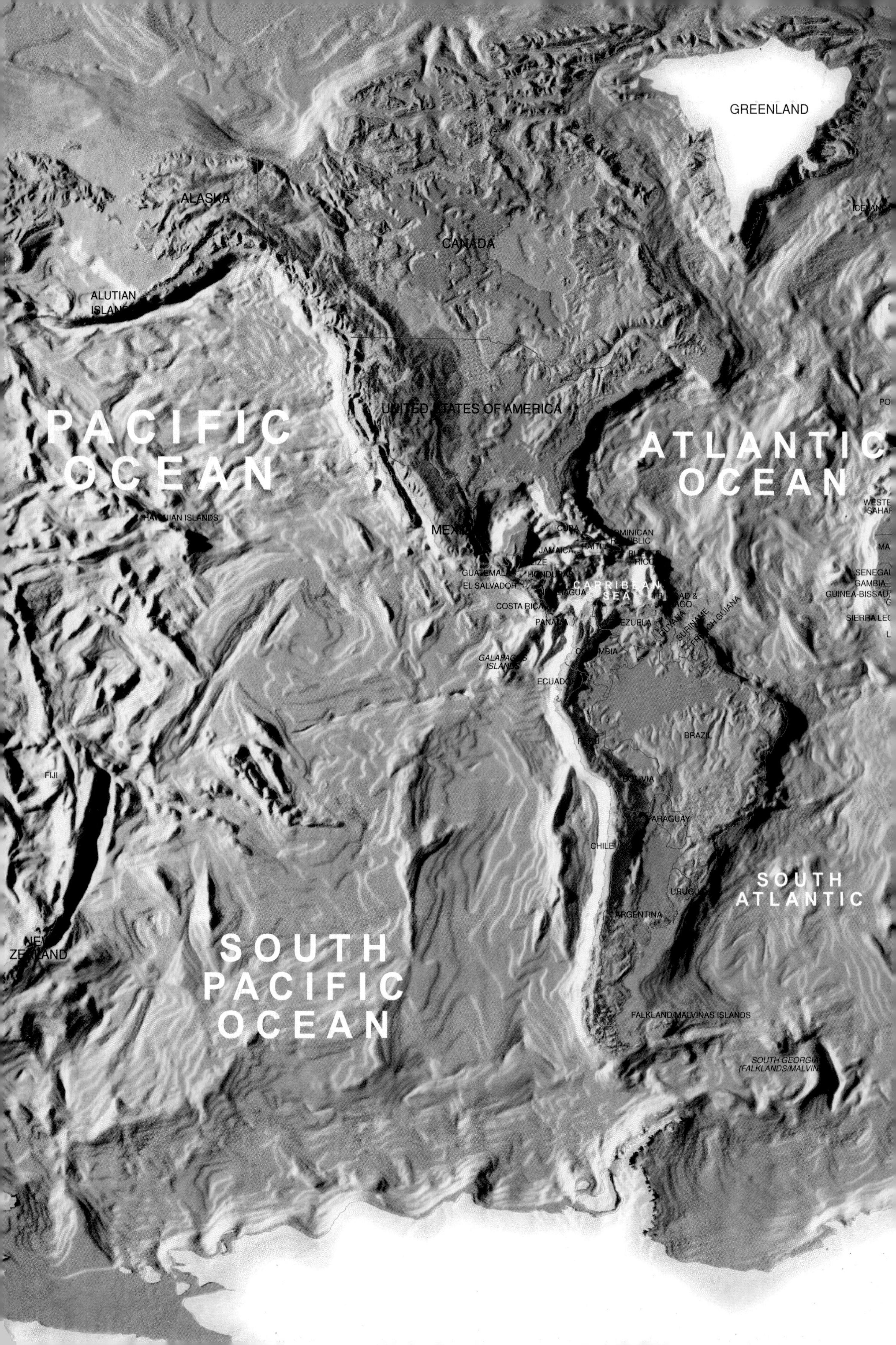

GREENLAND
ALASKA
CANADA
ALUTIAN
PACIFIC OCEAN
UNITED STATES OF AMERICA
ATLANTIC OCEAN
DOMINICAN REPUBLIC
JAMAICA
HAITI
GUATEMALA
HONDURAS
EL SALVADOR
CARRIBEAN SEA
COSTA RICA
GUYANA
SURINAME
FRENCH GUIANA
ECUADOR
BRAZIL
PERU
BOLIVIA
PARAGUAY
CHILE
ARGENTINA
SOUTH ATLANTIC
FIJI
SOUTH PACIFIC OCEAN
FALKLAND/MALVINAS ISLANDS
SENEGAL
GAMBIA
GUINEA-BISSAU